Environmental Enforcement Networks

NEW HORIZONS IN ENVIRONMENTAL AND ENERGY LAW

Series Editors: Kurt Deketelaere, *Professor of Law, University of Leuven, Belgium and University of Dundee, Scotland* and Zen Makuch, *Reader in Law, Barrister, Imperial College, London, UK*

Environmental law – including the pressing considerations of energy law and climate change – is an increasingly important area of legal research and practice. Given the growing interdependence of global society and the significant steps being made towards environmental protection and energy efficiency, there are few people untouched by environmental and energy lawmaking processes.

At the same time, environmental and energy law is at a crossroads. The command and control methodology that evolved in the 1960s and 1970s for air, land and water protection may have reached the limit of its environmental protection achievements. New life needs to be injected into our environmental protection regimes – perhaps through the concept of sustainability in its environmental, economic and social forms. The same goes for energy policy and law, where liberalization, environmental protection and security of supply are at the centre of attention. This important series seeks to press forward the boundaries of environmental and energy law through innovative research into environmental and energy law, doctrine and case law. Adopting a wide interpretation of environmental and energy law, it includes contributions from both leading and emerging international scholars.

Titles in the series include:

Energy for the 21st Century
Opportunities and Challenges for Liquefied Natural Gas (LNG)
Susan L. Sakmar

Emissions Trading Design
A Critical Overview
Stefan E. Weishaar

EU Environmental Legislation
Legal Perspectives on Regulatory Strategies
Edited by Marjan Peeters and Rosa Uylenburg

Polar Oceans Governance in an Era of Environmental Change
Edited by Tim Stephens and David L. VanderZwaag

The Fragmentation of Global Climate Governance
Consequences and Management of Regime Interactions
Harro van Asselt

Renewable Energy Law in the EU
Legal Perspectives on Bottom-up Approaches
Edited by Marjan Peeters and Thomas Schomerus

Environmental Enforcement Networks
Concepts, Implementation and Effectiveness
Edited by Michael Faure, Peter De Smedt and An Stas

Environmental Enforcement Networks

Concepts, Implementation and Effectiveness

Edited by

Michael Faure

Professor, Maastricht University, Maastricht and Erasmus School of Law, Rotterdam, the Netherlands; Chairman of the Flemish High Council of Environmental Enforcement (VHRM), Brussels, Belgium

Peter De Smedt

Attorney at Law, LDR, Ghent, Belgium

An Stas

Permanent Secretary, Flemish High Council of Environmental Enforcement (VHRM), Brussels, Belgium

NEW HORIZONS IN ENVIRONMENTAL AND ENERGY LAW

EE Edward Elgar PUBLISHING

Cheltenham, UK • Northampton, MA, USA

Published by
Edward Elgar Publishing Limited
The Lypiatts
15 Lansdown Road
Cheltenham
Glos GL50 2JA
UK

Edward Elgar Publishing, Inc.
William Pratt House
9 Dewey Court
Northampton
Massachusetts 01060
USA

A catalogue record for this book
is available from the British Library

Library of Congress Control Number: 2014954947

This book is available electronically in the Elgaronline
Law subject collection
DOI 10.4337/9781783477401

MIX
Paper from responsible sources
FSC® C013056

ISBN 978 1 78347 739 5 (cased)
ISBN 978 1 78347 740 1 (eBook)

Typeset by Servis Filmsetting Ltd, Stockport, Cheshire
Printed and bound in Great Britain by T.J. International Ltd, Padstow

Contents

Figures

Tables

Contributors

Miroslav Angelov, Official, Directorate-General Environment of the European Commission, Belgium.

Bernadette Araba Adjei, Principal Legal Officer, Legal and Monitoring Department of the Water Resources Commission, Ghana.

Gunnar Baldwin, Jr, Consultant, INECE Secretariat, International Network for Environmental Compliance and Enforcement, USA.

Kay Bergamini, Chief, Enforcement Division, Superintendence of the Environment, Government of Chile, Chile.

Susan Elizabeth Bromm, Director, Office of Federal Activities and US Co-chair of the CEC Enforcement Working Group, Office of Enforcement and Compliance Assurance, US Environmental Protection Agency, USA.

Liam Cashman, Official, Directorate-General Environment of the European Commission, Belgium.

Tony Circelli, CEO, South Australian Environment Protection Authority; Vice Chair, Australasian Environmental Law Enforcement and Regulators neTwork (AELERT), Australia.

Martin de Bree, Rotterdam School of Management, Erasmus University, the Netherlands; Managing Director Next Step Management BV, the Netherlands.

Han de Haas, Researcher, Erasmus University, Rotterdam School of Management, Erasmus University, the Netherlands.

Peter De Smedt, Attorney at Law, LDR, Belgium.

Michael Faure, Chairman of the Flemish High Council of Environmental Enforcement, Belgium.

William Fawcett, EPA Network Secretary (2011–2014); European Environment Agency, Denmark.

Danielle Fest Grabiel, Law Fellow, Institute for Governance & Sustainable Development, USA.

Campbell Gemmell, Professor of Environmental Regulation and Policy, University of Glasgow, UK; Consulting Partner, Canopus Scotland, UK. CEO, South Australian Environment Protection Authority to May 2014 and member of the Australasian Environmental Law Enforcement and Regulators neTwork (AELERT), Australia.

Jo Gerardu, a co-founder of the International Network for Environmental Compliance and Enforcement, USA, and consultant to the INECE Secretariat, USA.

Frans Geysels, Chief Superintendent, Head of the Environmental Crime Service, Belgian Federal Judicial Police, Belgium.

Robert George Heiss, Director, International Compliance Assurance Division, Office of Enforcement and Compliance Assurance, US Environmental Protection Agency, USA.

Esther Janssen, Managing Director, Culture-Inc., the Netherlands.

Emmanuel B. Kasimbazi, Associate Professor, the School of Law, Makerere University, Kampala, Uganda; legal consultant and advocate of the High Court of Uganda, Uganda.

Meredith Koparova, Program Manager, INECE Secretariat/Earthspace, International Network for Environmental Compliance and Enforcement, USA.

Deborah Kopsick, Environmental Protection Specialist and US Environmental Protection Agency Lead on Commission for Environmental Cooperation Enforcement Working Group, International Compliance Assurance Division, Office of Federal Activities, US Environmental Protection Agency, USA.

Luc Lavrysen, Judge in the Belgian Constitutional Court, Belgium; President of the European Union Forum of Judges for the Environment, Belgium.

James Lehane, Assistant Director (Investigations), Australian Pesticides and Veterinary Medicines Authority, Australia.

Xinyuan Lu, Director, Subcommittee of Environmental Enforcement of the Chinese Society for Environmental Sciences, China.

Eugène Lubieniecki, independent environmental contractor, following 30 years with the US Environmental Protection Agency Civil and Criminal Enforcement and Compliance Program, USA.

Kenneth Markowitz, Managing Director of the INECE Secretariat, International Network for Environmental Compliance and Enforcement, USA.

Paul Meerman, Regional Environmental Protection Agency Midden– and West–Brabant (OMWB), the Netherlands.

Larsey Mensah, Director, Legal Department, Environmental Protection Agency, Ghana.

Juan Carlos Monckeberg, Superintendent, Superintendence of the Environment, Government of Chile, Chile.

Gerphas Opondo, Regional Coordinator, East African Network for Environmental Compliance and Enforcement, Kenya.

LeRoy Paddock, Associate Dean for Environmental Law Studies at The George Washington University, USA.

Cristian Pérez, Biodiversity & International Relations Officer, Enforcement Division, Superintendence of the Environment, Government of Chile, Chile.

Grant Pink, Adjunct Research Fellow, School of Law, University of New England, Australia; Director, Regulatory Capability and Performance Section, Australian Government's Department of the Environment, Australia.

Hu Qin, Senior Project Manager, Environmental Defense Fund China Program, China.

Henk Ruessink, Coordinating Special International Advisor, Human Environment and Transport Inspectorate, the Netherlands.

Zerrin Savaşan, Assistant Professor, Faculty of Economics and Adminstrative Sciences, Department of International Relations, Selçuk University, Turkey.

An Stas, Permanent Secretary of the Flemish High Council of Environmental Enforcement, Belgium.

Grazia Maria Vagliasindi, Researcher of Criminal Law at the University of Catania, Department of Law, Italy.

Edward van Asch, PhD candidate at the University of Sheffield, UK.

Jun Yang, Program Assistant, Environmental Defense Fund China Program, China.

Durwood Zaelke, Director, Institute for Governance and Sustainable Development, USA.

Abbreviations

ACPO	Association of Chief Police Officers (United Kingdom)
AECEN	Asian Environmental Compliance and Enforcement Network
AELERT	Australasian Environmental Law Enforcement and Regulators neTwork
AIC	Arondissemental Information Crosspoint (Belgium)
ARPAs	Agenzie Regionali per la Protezione dell'Ambiente
Basel Convention	the Basel Convention on the Control of Transboundary Movements of Hazardous Wastes and their Disposal
BAT	Best Available Technology
BR	Better Regulation
CAFE	Clean Air For Europe
CCS	Carbon Capture and Storage
CEC	Commission for Environmental Cooperation
CEMS	Continuous Emission Monitoring System
CEO	Chief Executive Officer
CITES	Convention on International Trade in Endangered Species of Wild Fauna and Flora
CLAPV	Center for Legal Assistance to Pollution Victims (China)
CM	Compliance Mechanisms
COMIFAC	Conference of Ministers in Charge of Forests of Central Africa
CoPs	Communities of Practice
CSES	Chinese Society for Environmental Sciences
CUPL	China University of Political Science and Law
DAH	Highway Police (Belgium)
DIA	Direzione Investigativa Antimaffia (Italy)
DOJ	Department of Justice (US)
EA	Environment Agency
EANECE	East African Network for Environmental Compliance and Enforcement
EAP	Environment Action Programme (Europe)

ECHA	European Chemicals Agency
ECEN	Environmental Compliance and Enforcement Network (Ghana)
ECENA	Environmental Compliance and Enforcement Network for Accession
ECOS	Environmental Council of States (US)
EEA	European Environment Agency
EEAs	Environmental Enforcement Agencies
EENs	Environmental Enforcement Networks
EFFACE	European Union Action to Fight Environmental Crime
EIA	environmental impact assessment
ENCA	European Network of Heads of Nature Conservation Agencies
ENFORCE	Environmental Network for Optimizing Regulatory Compliance on Illegal Traffic
ENPE	European Network of Prosecutors for the Environment (EU)
EPA	Environment Protection Agency
EPANet	European Network of the Heads of Environment Protection Agencies
EPP	Environmental Public Prosecutor (Belgium)
ERAs	environmental regulatory agencies
EU	European Union
EUFJE	European Union Forum of Judges for the Environment
FHCE	Flemish High Council of Environmental Enforcement
FJP	Federal Judicial Police (Belgium)
FLETC	Federal Law Enforcement Training Center (US)
FYP	Five Year Plan (China)
GDP	gross domestic product
GHGs	greenhouse gases
GMOs	genetically modified organisms
GNEP	Global Network for Environmental Prosecutors
ICCWC	International Consortium on Combating Wildlife Crime
ICEF	International Court of the Environment Foundation
ICT	information and communication technology
I-EPA	Irish Environment Protection Agency
IGs	interest groups
IMPEL	European Union Network for the Implementation and Enforcement of Environmental Law
IMPEL TFS	European Union Network for Implementation and

	Enforcement of Environmental Law Transfrontier Shipments of Waste Programme
INECE	International Network for Environmental Compliance and Enforcement
Inspire	Infrastructure for Spatial Information in the European Community
IPE	Institute of Public and Environment Affairs (China)
ISPRA	Istituto Superiore per la Protezione e la Ricerca Ambientale (formerly called Agenzia per la protezione dell'Ambiente e del Territorio, APAT)
IUCN	International Union for Conservation of Nature
KE	Knowledge Exchange
KLEEPA	Knowledge, Legislation, Education, Economic, Planning, Advice
LATF	Lusaka Agreement Task Force
MEA	Multilateral environmental agreements
MEEA	Midwest Environmental Enforcement Association
MEN	Maghreb Enforcement Network
MEP	Ministry of Environmental Protection (China)
MOU	Memorandum of Understanding
NAFTA	North American Free Trade Agreement
NCEA	the Netherlands Commission for Environmental Assessment
NCIS	Naval Criminal Investigative Service (US)
NEC	National Emissions Ceilings
NECEMA	Regional Planning Committee of the Network for Environmental Compliance and Enforcement in the Maghreb
NEEP	Northeast Environmental Enforcement Project (US)
NEIC	National Enforcement Investigation Center (US)
NEM	Network Evaluation Matrix
NEPB	National Environmental Protection Bureau (China)
NEPM	National Environmental Protection Measures
NESTs	National Environmental Security Task Forces
NGO	Non-Governmental Organisation
NHEEPA	Network of Heads of European Environment Protection Agencies (known by EEA as EPANet)
NIEA	Northern Ireland Environmental Agency
NIECE	Network for Ireland's Environmental Compliance and Enforcement
NSCLNR	National Security Committee on Lands and Natural Resources

NWOG	National Waste Operations Group (AELERT)
OBPR	Office of Best Practice Regulation
OECD	Organisation for Economic Co-operation and Development
OJ	Official Journal
PAW	Partnership for Action against Wildlife Crime (UK)
Port	Port of Huntington
Port Project	the Port of Huntington Project
PPP	Public Prosecutors Project
R@IN	Regional Association Information Network (US)
Ra.C.I.S	Raggruppamento Carabinieri Investigazioni Scientifiche (Carabinieri Scientific Investigations Group)
RCRA	Resource Conservation and Recovery Act (US)
Reach	Registration, Evaluation, Authorization and Restriction of Chemicals
REC	Regional Environmental Centre (Turkey)
Redia	Red de inspección ambiental
REN	Regional Enforcement Network
REPIN	Regulatory Environmental Programme Implementation Network
RMCEI	Recommended Minimum Criteria for Environmental Inspections (EU Member States)
RP	research participant
SA	South Australia
SAR	special administrative region
SCEW	Standing Council on Environment and Water
SEE	Subcommittee of Environmental Enforcement (China)
SEEN	Southern Environmental Enforcement Network (US)
SEP	Supplemental Enforcement Projects (US)
SEPA	Scottish Environment Protection Agency
SEPA	State Environmental Protection Agency (China)
SESN	Seaport Environmental Security Network
SMEs	Small and Medium Sized Enterprises
SoE	State of the Environment
SPC	Railway Police (Belgium)
SPN	Maritime Police (Belgium)
SWOT	strengths, weaknesses, opportunities and threats
T&D	Training and Development
TFEU	Treaty on the Functioning of the European Union
TFS	Transfrontier Shipment of Waste

UBA	The German Federal Environment Agency
UN	United Nations
UNCED	United Nations Conference on Environment and Development
UNE	University of New England
UNECE	United Nations Economic Commission for Europe
UNEP	United Nations Environment Programme
UNEP-ROAP	United Nations Environment Programme Regional Office for Asia and the Pacific
UNODC	United Nations Office of Drugs and Crime
US	United States
US EPA	United States Environmental Protection Agency
USCG	United States Coast Guard
USEPA	United States Environmental Protection Agency
VHRM	Vlaamse Hoge Raad voor de Milieuhandhaving (Flemish High Council of Environmental Enforcement)
Vic EPA	Victoria Environmental Protection Agency (Australia)
VROM	the Netherlands' Ministry of Housing, Spatial Planning and Environment
WANECE	West African Network for Environmental Compliance and Enforcement
WCO	World Customs Organization
WEEE	Waste Electrical and Electronic Equipment
WFD	Water Framework Directive
WSP	Western States Project (US)
WSSD	World Summit on Sustainable Development
WWF	World Wild Fund for Nature

Introduction

Michael Faure, Peter De Smedt and An Stas

1. REASONS FOR THIS BOOK

This book is the result of an international conference that has been organized on 13–14 November 2013 in Brussels by the Flemish High Council of Environmental Enforcement under the auspices of the International Network for Environmental Compliance and Enforcement (INECE). The main goal of the conference and hence of this resulting volume was to address the phenomenon of networking with respect to the enforcement of environmental law in a more systemic and academic manner. There has been for a long time in many countries experience with a large variety of different networks in the area of environmental enforcement. The reasons for the creation of those networks are usually relatively straightforward: given limited assets of enforcement agencies, there is a lot to be gained by joining forces and by sharing information via networking. The bottom line is hence that networking can increase the effectiveness of environmental enforcement and therefore equally contribute to the quality of the environment.

The problem is, however, that although in some legal systems (mostly in Europe and in the US) a lot of experience with networking in the area of environmental enforcement exists, this is less so in other, mostly developing, legal systems. Moreover, environmental enforcement networks can be of totally different characters. In some cases, there are transboundary (often also regional) networks; in other cases, networks have a rather vertical character within one country and yet in other situations there are topic specific networks, e.g. focusing on problems with transboundary waste.

Although, academic literature is focusing more and more on environmental enforcement networks,[1] the topic is to a large extent understudied by academics. Perhaps wrongly so, the conditions under which

[1] See more particularly the seminal work of Grant Pink, 'Environmental Enforcement Networks: a Qualitative Analysis' (2010), http://ssrn.com/abstract=1803179.

environmental enforcement networking could be successful has by many perhaps too much been considered as a practical or at best policy relevant issue. As this volume will make clear, it is also possible to approach environmental enforcement networks in a more systematic, say even academic, manner. Environmental enforcement networking can in that sense be considered as one of the many forms of 'smart' enforcement. Given the already mentioned problem of limited budgets of enforcement agencies (and in times of crisis they may even be reducing), networking can be seen as a potentially cost-effective mechanism of environmental enforcement.

Less is known, however, on the precise conditions under which particular environmental enforcement networks may be less or more effective or, in other words, what could be considered 'best practices' as far as environmental enforcement networking is concerned.

Since, in fact, no academic book exists on environmental enforcement networks which attempt to provide an integrated analysis of this phenomenon, there were important reasons for this volume. This book has in fact many objectives. The most modest objective is at the same time an important one: simply providing information to all interested readers on the phenomenon of environmental enforcement networking, thus providing insights in what type of environmental enforcement networks have emerged at the world-wide level. Already this simple presentation of various models of effective networking, including transboundary, regional and thematic networks, can already provide valuable information. It sheds light on where apparently at a practical level there is a demand for those environmental enforcement networks. Moreover, an attempt will also be made, following the model developed earlier by Grant Pink and James Lehane,[2] to categorize the various types of environmental enforcement networks according to their specific goals and quality of the collaboration. In addition, this book will also enlighten the potential advantages of networks and will hence explain how potential benefits can be generated by joining efforts as far as enforcement activities are concerned. Finally, the most ambitious task of this book is undoubtedly to also provide criteria for 'best practices' as far as environmental enforcement networking is concerned. The various chapters in this book will, to the extent possible, try to explain why particular cases of networking have been particularly successful. This can thus provide an important element of learning for

---

[2] G. Pink and J. Lehane, 'Environmental Enforcement Networks: Development of a Network Evaluation Matrix' in International Network for Environmental Compliance and Enforcement, INECE 9th International Conference on Environmental Compliance and Enforcement, Conference Proceedings, 20–24 June 2011, Whistler, British Columbia, Canada (Washington, 2011).

others who may wish to set up environmental enforcement networks as well as contributing to the effectiveness of their enforcement efforts.

The book therefore aims at contributing to the academic literature on the effectiveness of environmental enforcement and at the same time also wishes to add to the policy debate by indicating criteria under which this type of environmental enforcement networking may prove to be effective.

2. METHODOLOGY

For the complex objectives that this book has set itself, a variety of different methodologies will be followed.

2.1 Multi-disciplinarity

It may be clear that even though environmental enforcement may be at the core of environmental law, the question of the effectiveness of environmental enforcement networks can surely not be addressed by lawyers alone. Hence, the reader will notice that within this book, there are undoubtedly many contributions by lawyers, but many contributions by others as well. For example in order to know what may inhibit an effective networking, one also needs to look into cultural elements which may constitute impediments for such a networking (as Chapter 3 does); moreover, in addition to a legal, also an economic approach is necessary, for example to examine under what conditions self-regulation could also be considered as an effective instrument of environmental enforcement (Chapter 10). Finally, much of the practical information on the functioning of networking is often available with experts from totally different backgrounds such as, for example, officers from the European Commission (Chapter 18) or police officers with many years of experience in networks aiming at remedying transboundary shipment of waste (Chapter 25).

2.2 Legal Interdisciplinary

Moreover, within the legal domain, a variety of legal disciplines are also used. Insights into the effectiveness of environmental enforcement networks obviously require knowledge of environmental law. However, enforcement is very closely related to criminal law and criminal procedure. Moreover, procedural law and the art of judging also play an important role in the effectiveness of environmental enforcement. As a result, even in the chapters with a stronger legal focus, a legal interdisciplinary approach is followed.

This interdisciplinary approach is also related to the fact that not only a theoretical approach to networking is followed. It may be clear that one will learn most about the effectiveness of environmental enforcement networks by examining how particular networks are functioning and have functioned in the past. Therefore, many of the chapters in Parts III and IV, which address the practical functioning of networking, often provide an empirical approach by examining how particular networks have functioned and developed in practice.

2.3 Comparative Approach

Finally, it may be clear that many of the networks that are discussed and described in this book are not confined to the boundaries of one country. Many networks are regional and cross-borders of particular legal systems. Moreover, some networks even have global ambitions, like the International Network on Environmental Compliance and Enforcement (INECE) itself.[3] As a result of the strong focus on the benefits of networks of a transboundary nature, many of the chapters also follow a comparative approach.

3. FRAMEWORK AND PARTNERS

The conference that was at the basis of the current book was organized by the Flemish High Council of Environmental Enforcement (VHRM). This Flemish High Council of Environmental Enforcement[4] was created in 2009 and since its creation has been active in the international area of environmental enforcement. The VHRM is a member of the European Union Network for the Implementation and Enforcement of Environmental Law (IMPEL) and is involved in the activities of the International Network for Environmental Compliance and Enforcement (INECE). As an international network on environmental compliance and enforcement, INECE has always initiated research into the effectiveness of various enforcement models. It was one of the topics of a seminar preceding the last international conference organized by INECE in Whistler (Canada) in June 2012.[5]

The Flemish High Council of Environmental Enforcement has always been very interested in the question of how enforcement cooperation can

---

3 See further on INECE: www.inece.org.

4 www.vhrm.be.

5 See the proceedings: http://inece.org/conference/9/confproceedings/.

be effectively organized between different partners in the enforcement chain. Therefore, the VHRM decided to contribute to executing the INECE agenda of improving collaboration between the partners in the environmental enforcement chain, and that is why the VHRM decided to organize its 2013 annual conference on the topic of environmental enforcement networks: concepts, implementation and effectiveness.

The main partners behind the conference, which constitute the basis of the current volume, were hence this VHRM (of the Flemish Region) and INECE.

4. TOPICS

In order to attain the objectives for this book mentioned above, contributors were invited to provide insights on a variety of topics related to the quality of environmental enforcement networking. Hence, participants were invited to contribute *inter alia* on:

- Benchmarks and criteria for optimal transboundary environmental enforcement networks;
- Possibilities of networks between various inspection authorities, both national and transboundary;
- Networking between administrative (inspection authorities, administrative sanctioning) and criminal enforcement and sanctioning authorities (public prosecutor's office), both national and transboundary;
- Thematic networks;
- National, regional and transboundary case studies discussing any of the above; and
- Theoretical concepts underpinning practical network cooperation.

5. STRUCTURE OF THIS BOOK

At a conference in November 2013, almost 40 papers were presented. An editorial process took place as a result of which 26 papers were selected to be included in this volume. Those papers were submitted to an editorial process resulting in the current 26 chapters. The organization of the book into four different parts resulted in the following structure.

Part I provides first a general theory of environmental enforcement networking. Chapter 1 by Grant Pink describes the theory, practice and potential of environmental enforcement networks; next, in Chapter 2,

Campbell Gemmell places the importance of environmental networking in the framework of the better regulation agenda. Chapter 3 by Esther Janssen uses culture theory to explain some key success factors for environmental cooperation across cultures. In Chapter 4 Zerrin Savaşan provides a comparative analysis of four different networks. Chapter 5 by Grant Pink and James Lehane describes the network evaluation matrix, showing how it is possible to assess and evaluate environmental enforcement networks.

Part II then turns to the important point of the potential benefits of networks. Therefore James Lehane in Chapter 6 provides a critical analysis of environmental enforcement networks. In Chapter 7 Grant Pink addresses the important issue of the added value of environmental enforcement networks especially in times of reducing resources and budgets. Campbell Gemmell and Tony Circelli in Chapter 8 describe the mutual relationship between environmental regulation and enforcement networks and show the importance of networks as facilitating knowledge exchange. Edward van Asch shows in Chapter 9 how, more particularly with respect to the case of wildlife crime, networking can enable global responses and a more effective coordination. In Chapter 10, Martin de Bree, Han de Haas and Paul Meerman discuss the important question of how environmental enforcement networking and supervision could function within a model of self-regulation.

Part III then describes and analyses a variety of so-called thematic networks. A first network is the Lusaka Agreement Task Force for Wildlife Crime Enforcement, discussed by Emmanuel B. Kasimbazi in Chapter 11. Eugène Lubieniecki discusses the enforcement network of the Huntington Port in the US in Chapter 12. Luc Lavrysen then presents the well-known European Union Forum of Judges for the Environment (EUFJE) in Chapter 13. Chapter 14 presents the well-known seaport initiative of INECE aiming at the prevention of illegal hazardous waste shipments.

In addition to these more thematic networks, Part IV provides an overview of a variety of rather horizontal networks. Chapter 15 by Deborah Kopsick and Susan Elizabeth Bromm presents the North American working group on Environmental Enforcement and Compliance. William Fawcett shows the advantages of informal environmental networking via the network of the Environmental Protection Agency in the EU in Chapter 16. One of the hosts of the conference preceding this volume is INECE. The working of INECE is presented by several co-authors in Chapter 17. Chapter 18 by Miroslav Angelov and Liam Cashman of the European Commission discusses the importance of environmental networking for the implementation of EU environmental law and also addresses the evolution of regulation concerning environmental inspections. Gerphas Opondo presents in Chapter 19 the case of the East African Network for Environmental Compliance and Enforcement (EANECE).

In Part V, LeRoy Paddock returns to the US in Chapter 20 by presenting the regional environmental enforcement networks there. Chapter 21 by Bernadette Araba Adjei and Larsey Mensah discuss Ghana's efforts at creating environmental enforcement networks. The specific case of Italy is discussed by Grazia Maria Vagliasindi in Chapter 22. The case of China with its many challenges in environmental law enforcement is discussed by several co-authors in Chapter 23. Environmental enforcement networking efforts in Chile are discussed in detail in Chapter 24. Frans Geysels presents the efforts concerning environmental enforcement by the Belgian police in Chapter 25. The host of the conference, the Flemish High Council of Environmental Enforcement, is presented in Chapter 26 by Michael Faure and An Stas.

The final chapter provides concluding and comparative remarks by the editors.

6. CONTRIBUTORS

The 26 chapters to this volume have been written by a large variety of different authors coming often from different backgrounds, both academia as well as practice. Grant Pink is connected to the Law School of the University of New England (UNE) and equally works for Australian Government's Department of the Environment. James Lehane works for the Australian Pesticides and Veterinary Medicines Authority. Campbell Gemmell is Professor of Environmental Regulation and Policy at the University of Glasgow. He is also Consulting Partner of the Scottish Environmental Protection Agency. Tony Circelli is CEO South Australian EPA and Vice Chair of AELERT. Esther Janssen is managing director of Culture-Inc. Zerrin Savaşan is connected to the Department of International Relations of the Selçuk University in Turkey. William Fawcett works for the European Environment Agency in Denmark. Edward van Asch is a PhD candidate at the University of Sheffield in the UK. Martin de Bree is connected to the Rotterdam School of Management of Erasmus University Rotterdam in the Netherlands; Han de Haas works for Erasmus University in the Netherlands and Paul Meerman for the Regional Environmental Protection Agency of Midden- and West-Brabant, also in the Netherlands. Emmanuel Kasimbazi is connected to the Law School of the Makerere University in Kampala (Uganda). Eugène Lubieniecki is an independent environmental contractor in the US. Luc Lavrysen is a Judge in the Belgian Constitutional Court in Brussels and President of the European Union of Judges for the Environment (EUFJE). Jo Gerardu is a co-founder of INECE and acts as a consultant to the INECE Secretariat. Durwood Zaelke is the Director of the Institute for Governance and Sustainable Development, Kenneth Markowitz is the Managing Director and Meredith Koparova is the Program Manager at the INECE Secretariat in Washington, DC (US). Gunnar Baldwin is a consultant to the INECE Secretariat. Danielle Grabiel is a law fellow at the Institute for Governance & Sustainable Development in Washington, (US) and Robert Heiss is the Director of the International Compliance Assurance Division of the US Environmental Protection Agency in Washington, DC (US). Deborah Kopsick is also with the International Compliance Assurance Division of the Environmental Protection Agency in Washington (US). Susan Bromm works for the US Environmental Protection Agency. Henk Ruessink is Coordinating Special International Advisor with the Human Environment and Transport Inspectorate. Miroslav Angelov and Liam Cashman are connected to Directorate-General Environment of the European Commission in Brussels (Belgium). Gerphas Opondo is the Regional Coordinator of the East African Network for Environmental Compliance and Enforcement (EANECE). LeRoy Paddock is connected to the George Washington University in Washington, DC (US). Bernadette Araba Adjei is the Principal Legal Officer of the Water Resources Commission of Ghana; Larsey Mensah is the Director of the legal department of the Environmental Protection Agency in Ghana. Grazia Maria Vagliasindi is connected to the University of Catania (Italy). Xinyuan Lu is connected to the Chinese Society for Environmental Sciences; Hu Qin is with the Environmental Defense Fund China Program and Jun Yang also works for the Environmental Defense Fund China Program. Both institutions are in Beijing (China). Juan Carlos Monckeberg, Kay Bergamini and Cristian Pérez are all with the Superintendence of the Environment of the government of Chile in Santiago. Frans Geysels is with the Environmental Crime Service of the Belgian Federal Judicial Police in Brussels (Belgium). Michael Faure and An Stas are with the Flemish High Council of Environmental Enforcement (VHRM) in Brussels (Belgium).

This wide variety of contributors shows not only totally different backgrounds (a collection of many disciplines, but also academics, practitioners and policy makers), the contributors also represent many of the main existing (like INECE) or emerging (as in Chile) networks. This wide variety of authors therefore guarantees that insights from many disciplines in different parts of the world are brought together in this volume.

7. ACKNOWLEDGEMENTS

As editors of this volume, we owe thanks to many who made this volume and, especially, the conference proceedings possible. We obviously owe thanks to the presenters at the conference and those who were subsequently willing to undertake the drafting of the various chapters and going through the intensive editorial and review process to which we submitted them. The entire conference was prepared by an informal organizing committee that met several times to select papers and organize the conference programme. In addition to the editors of this volume, also Henk Ruessink gave us invaluable help. The same was true for Jo Gerardu who, from INECE and jointly with our partners from the Netherlands, provided us with help on many fronts, for example by distributing the initial call for papers to the impressive INECE network.

The conference and the following book would not have been possible without the help of various authorities in the Flemish Region. We first of all would like to thank Mrs Joke Schauvliege, who at the time of the organization of the conference was the Flemish minister of Environment, Nature and Culture.[6] We do realize that, especially in a political climate where one often tends to focus on the immediate benefits for the primary voters (in the Flemish Region) it is very courageous for someone with political responsibility to encourage the Flemish High Council of Environmental Enforcement to develop and participate in international networks. 'Our' minister Joke Schauvliege has always recognized the importance of networking and internationalization for the quality of inspection and enforcement in the Flemish Region and we very much appreciate her support. We equally owe thanks to Mr Jean-Pierre Heirman, secretary-general of the department of the Environment for his support of the work of the Flemish High Council of Environmental Enforcement.

Moreover, incredible work has been done in the preparation of the conference and afterwards during the editorial process especially by Laïla Macharis. We are truly grateful since we realize that without her help, this volume would simply not have existed.

Finally, we owe thanks to our publisher Edward Elgar for guiding us in a very pleasant and agreeable way through the entire editorial process and making sure that a book with fine contents also receives the cover, format and layout that such contents deserve.

---

[6] At the time of editing this volume (June 2014), we are still in a period where a new Flemish government has to be formed, as a result of which it is still unknown who might be the next Flemish Minister for the Environment.

PART I

General theory

1. Environmental enforcement networks: theory, practice and potential

Grant Pink*

1. INTRODUCTION

Individuals, such as Professor Dr Michael Faure of the Flemish High Council of Environmental Enforcement (VHRM), Ken Markowitz of the International Network for Environmental Compliance and Enforcement (INECE) and John Merritt of the Australasian Environmental Law Enforcement and Regulators neTwork (AELERT), have for many years now been stressing the importance of the role performed by environmental enforcement networks (hereafter EENs or networks).

These individuals and others[1] frequently detail the issues and challenges

---

* Adjunct Research Fellow, School of Law, University of New England (UNE), Armidale, NSW, 2351, Australia (gpink2@une.edu.au); Director, Regulatory Capability and Performance Section, Australian Government's Department of the Environment, GPO Box 787, Canberra, ACT, 2600 (grant.pink@environment.gov.au); PhD Candidate, School of Behavioural, Cognitive and Social Sciences, UNE (gpink2@myune.edu.au). Any views or opinions expressed in this chapter are those of the author and not those of the University of New England, the Australian Government, or the Department of the Environment.

This chapter is adapted from a keynote address delivered on 13 November 2013 during the *Environmental Enforcement Networks: Concepts, Implementation and Effectiveness* conference in Brussels, Belgium. The author acknowledges and thanks Dr Matthew Marshall and Ms An Stas for their advice and assistance in recasting the address into a chapter.

[1] O'Leary, G and Lynott, DJ, 'The Effective Use of an Environmental Enforcement Network in Ireland' in INECE, 9th International Conference on Environmental Compliance and Enforcement: 24 June 2011, Whistler, British Columbia, Canada: Proceedings, INECE: Washington, 2011; Nicholson, M, 'Networking in Europe: How Networking and Cooperation have Helped Respond to Environmental Compliance and Enforcement Challenges in Impel Member Countries' in INECE, 9th International Conference on Environmental Compliance and Enforcement: 24 June 2011, Whistler, British Columbia, Canada: Proceedings,

that draw participants together in various environmental enforcement networks (EENs or networks) activities including meetings, workshops and conferences. An element of each of these activities contributes towards participants gaining a more complete understanding of how EENs operate and function. Through a greater understanding of EENs, participants are better placed to leverage additional or enhanced benefits from EENs.

Anecdotally speaking, for over a decade now, what has become evident is that various professionals are drawn to or are called to environmental regulation and enforcement, such that it appears it is often more of a vocation than just a job. The professionals who attend various fora associated with EENs include people who could work in any number of government agencies, or non-governmental organisations (NGOs) across a number of important issues, or be involved in capacity building across those issues. Instead they choose, often quite deliberately, to invest their efforts and make their contribution to environmental protection by taking roles associated with regulation and enforcement.

The various fora reinforce the critical role EENs play in providing and building capacity for environmental regulatory agencies around the world. References in this chapter to the critical role played by EENs include: when they *operate* individually, bilaterally or multilaterally, and when they *function* at the sub-national, national, regional and international level.

1.1 Acknowledgments and Additional Context

It is broadly accepted that mainstream environmental protection agencies have existed for more than 40 years[2] and that the first EENs have now been operating for more than 20 years.[3] Therefore, it is common for

---

INECE: Washington, 2011; Pink, G and Lehane, J, 'Environmental Enforcement Networks: Development of a Network Evaluation Matrix' in INECE, 9th International Conference on Environmental Compliance and Enforcement: 24 June 2011, Whistler, British Columbia, Canada: Proceedings, INECE: Washington, 2011; Stas, A, 'The Flemish High Council of Environmental Enforcement – A Coordinated Environmental Enforcement Policy' in INECE, 9th International Conference on Environmental Compliance and Enforcement: 24 June 2011, Whistler, British Columbia, Canada: Proceedings, INECE: Washington, 2011.

[2] For example; the Swedish Environmental Protection Agency, United States Environment Protection Agency and the Victorian Environment Protection Agency were established in 1967, 1970 and 1971 respectively.

[3] Most notably INECE (the International Network for Environmental Compliance and Enforcement) established in 1990 at the international level and IMPEL (the European Union Network for the Implementation and Enforcement of Environmental Law) established in 1992 at a regional level.

participants at the various fora to include EEN founders: these are the *elders* of the field.

These *elders* between them comprise an immense body of knowledge and experience as they:

- Were foundational members and key players in the bilateral partnership between the Dutch and the US which led to the launch of the International Network for Environmental Compliance and Enforcement (INECE) over 20 years ago and they remain actively involved to this day;
- Have similarly launched, or injected fresh ideas and energy into subnational (provincial), national and regional EENs;
- Have had experiences as officeholders and advocates for EENs in and across numerous countries; and
- On a daily basis intersect and interact with EENs.

Therefore, one of the key messages associated with engagement at the various EENs fora is to enable and encourage participants to draw upon this body of experience and knowledge. Not to do so is not only an opportunity missed – but wasted. At the same time, in terms of skills, knowledge and experience, EENs need to embrace fresh thinking and different perspectives, such as those emerging from more recently established networks.[4]

Taking a forward-looking approach enables all participants, regardless of whether it is their twentieth year in networks or it happens to be their first, to make a valuable contribution by adding their fresh perspectives as well as by testing and challenging other participants in terms of the current practices of EENs.

1.2 Phases of Network Involvement and Corresponding Benefits

EENs and managers alike should remain aware of the fact that participants, much like EENs and organisations themselves, are at various stages of professional maturity and competence. Furthermore, these different stages are graduated in such a way that as participants' awareness increases, so too does their ability to access and realise benefits (at an individual and agency level).

---

4 Like the Jordan Network of Environmental Compliance and Enforcement (JNECE) launched in July 2013, the West African Network for Environmental Compliance and Enforcement (WANECE) launched in September 2013 and the East African Network for Environmental Compliance and Enforcement (EANECE) launched in May 2010.

Generally, the stages of maturity divide into the following loose categories:

Phase 1 – '*exposed but sub-conscious*': In this phase it is not uncommon for participants to be vaguely aware of EENs and start attending network events. Despite this, their understanding of EENs remains extremely limited and lessons learned are not being captured.

Phase 2 – '*increasingly aware but not involved*': In this phase participants consciously attend network events but don't actively participate, they don't necessarily return lessons back to their home agency and their understanding of EENs is developing but remains basic.

Phase 3 – '*aware and involved*': In this phase participants begin to actively engage and perform a liaison or conduit type role between the network and their home agency. Often lessons learned are informally returned to the home agency and greater alignment between the activities of the home agency and network are identified. Participants now possess a sound working knowledge of EENs.

Phase 4 – '*acutely aware and deeply involved*': In this phase participants assume a key role in the EEN (e.g. project leader, member of the secretariat or board) and often become involved in the activities of a sister or overlapping network. The participant's home agency recognises engagement with EENs as a core activity and often incorporates the EEN role into the job description of the individual concerned. This phase sees extensive (sometime seamless) alignment between the activities of the home agency and the EEN. The participant's knowledge of EENs is comprehensive, which is necessary as their role often involves an aspect of high level advocacy for and on behalf of the EEN.

Phase 5 – '*researching networks*': This phase sees participants researching EENs, as a social construct, in an effort to make them more effective for the individuals, agencies and institutions who subscribe to them. Phase 4 and 5 can often occur concurrently.

2. THE THEORY OF NETWORKS

2.1 Research

In terms of the theory of networks there are three types of contributors: *academic*, *practitioner* and *pracademic*:

- Academic research is produced in academic and research institutions such as universities and think-tanks;
- Practitioner research refers to that conducted by those involved in the operational and practically oriented project work of networks; and
- Pracademic research is an academic contribution informed by the researcher's professional experience.

2.2 What Are Networks? What Is Networking?

There are some assumptions and misconceptions that can be associated with networks and networking. The two terms are used frequently and in such a way that they can become intertwined or be used interchangeably.

The three most common *hits* returned when conducting standard research into networks relate to 'business networking', 'social networking' and 'computer networks' (e.g. information and communication technology (ICT) systems).

Business networking can attract a stigma. It is often associated with shaking hands, exchanging business cards and is seen as involving a level of self-promotion. Simply put, it is an interaction about businesses. Business people, or commercial entities, are trying to make connections with people in an attempt to offer them a product or service, and enter into a commercial relationship with them.

Social networking has become increasingly pervasive in society. It involves making connections with people who are family, friends, colleagues and associates and then, in turn, connecting with their family, friends, colleagues and associates.

Computer (or data) networks allow computers to exchange data. There are some interesting comparisons, for illustrative purposes, between computer networks and EENs. In terms of:

- Servers: these take the form of EEN boards;
- Network nodes: these reflect the roles performed by clusters and project teams within EENs;
- Network links: these are akin to country/agency focal points and members; and
- Network engineers: these are the EEN secretariat.

This overview on networks and networking, from a broader context, provides a sense of what it is participants do when they *network* as a network. Equally it provides an insight into what it is others think participants might be doing when they *network* within a network.

It is clear that not all networking is the same and not all networking (even at the same event) will be considered the same by all participants. As such – to challenge the collective thinking – the question 'Are networks really networks?' can be asked.

2.3 Networks, Communities of Practice or Hybrid: and Does it Really Matter?

To start the consideration it is worth noting that within professions, across workplaces and even at a national level when people meet to consider problems and develop solutions one of the terms in use is 'Communities of Practice' (CoPs).

Jean Lave and Etienne Wenger's book *Situated Learning: Legitimate Peripheral Participation* (1991) involved an analysis of five case studies of traditional apprenticeship systems. In it they observed how in each case a whole community served as a living curriculum for the newcomer. They called these communities 'communities of practice'.[5]

Wenger, McDermott and Snyder's book *Cultivating Communities of Practice: A Guide to Managing Knowledge* (2002) explains why communities of practice are a 'key to managing knowledge' and 'provides practical advice on the art of cultivating communities and on creating an organizational context to support communities'.[6] CoPs like EENs are not static – they need ongoing maintenance.

Wenger, McDermott and Snyder's work '. . . creatively responds to two important issues that face all organisations: how to cultivate human imagination, and how to organise knowledge that is capable of tackling messy problems in the world without boundaries'.[7] To a large extent that is precisely what EENs are attempting to do.

Environmental offences and crimes neither recognise nor respect borders whether they are sub-national, national or regional. Environmental regulation and enforcement is becoming an increasingly globalised issue. As such, gaining a greater appreciation of the techniques and approaches used by CoPs, is something worth considering, given that 'CoPs are groups of people who share a concern, a set of problems, or a passion

---

[5] Wenger has written comprehensively on Communities of Practice and related matters. For more information on these writings (articles and books) including summaries see http://wenger-trayner.com/etienne/books/

[6] Ibid.

[7] Wenger, E, McDermott, RA and Snyder, W, *Cultivating Communities of Practice: A Guide to Managing Knowledge*, Boston USA: Harvard Business School Publishing, 2002, back cover.

about a topic, and who deepen their knowledge and expertise in this area by interacting on an ongoing basis'.[8]

2.4 Communities of Practice

Lave and Wenger[9] suggest that CoPs require three components, and those components are domain, community and practice. Considering each in turn:

- **Domain**
  'A CoP has an identity defined by a shared domain of interest (e.g. radiologists . . . history teachers . . . football fans, etc.); it's not just a network of people or club of friends. Membership implies a commitment to the domain.'[10]
- **Community**
  'A necessary component is that members of a specific domain interact and engage in shared activities, help each other, and share information with each other.'[11]
  'They build relationships that enable them to learn from each other. In this way, merely sharing the same job does not necessitate a CoP. A static website . . . is not a community of practice.'[12]
  'There needs to be people who interact and learn together in order for a CoP to be formed. Note that members do not necessarily work together daily, however [but would sometimes meet informally and that] these kinds of interactions were essential to making them a CoP.'[13]
- **Practice**
  'A CoP is not just people who have an interest in something (e.g. sports or agriculture practices). The third requirement for a CoP is that the members are *practitioners*.'[14]
  '. . . interaction needs to be developed over time. A conversation with . . . an expert on a subject matter that interests you does not

---

[8] Ibid., p.4.
[9] Lave, J and Wenger, E, *Communities of Practice: Learning, Meaning, and Identity*, Cambridge: Cambridge University Press, 1998.
[10] See Learning-Theories, n.d., at http://www.learning-theories.com/communities-of-practice-lave-and-wenger.html
[11] Ibid.
[12] Ibid.
[13] Ibid.
[14] Ibid.

in itself make a CoP. Informal conversations held by people of the same profession . . . help people share and develop a set of cases and stories that can become a shared repertoire for their practice, whether they realize it or not'.[15]

Together, these aspects precisely describe the essence of EENs.

2.5 Types of Networks

EENs actually share characteristics with the three types of networks that Slaughter identifies: information networks, enforcement networks and harmonisation networks.[16]

- **Information networks**
  'The glue of any transgovernmental network is the exchange of information and ideas. Put a group of environmental regulators, central bankers, or utilities commissioners in a room and they will begin talking about different techniques of regulation, commiserating about common problems, and brainstorming new approaches'.[17]
- **Enforcement networks**
  '[This] type of network focuses primarily on enhancing cooperation among national regulators to enforce existing national laws and rules. As the subjects they regulate – from criminals to corporations – move across borders, they must expand their regulatory reach by initiating contact with their foreign counterparts.'[18]
  'At a very concrete level, enforcement cooperation is exactly the sharing of information and the collaborative development of specific enforcement strategies in individual cases. The next step is cooperating in strategic priority setting and targeting . . .'[19]

It is worth noting that capacity building is common to most enforcement networks. This, however, is quite often not based on altruism – instead '[i]t results from a recognition that a global regulatory system based on transgovernmental networks is only as strong as its weakest link'.[20]

---

[15] Ibid.

[16] See Slaughter, A M, *A New World Order*, New Jersey: Princeton University Press, 2004, pp. 52–61 for a comprehensive overview of the three types of networks.

[17] Ibid., p. 52.

[18] Ibid., p. 55.

[19] Ibid, pp. 56–57.

[20] Ibid, p. 57.

- **Harmonisation networks**
  '. . . regulators may work together to harmonise regulatory standards, such as product-safety standards, with the overt aim of achieving efficiency'.[21]

A tangible example of this, across the European Union, driven by the European Union Network for the Implementation and Enforcement of Environmental Law (IMPEL), is the Recommended Minimum Criteria for Environmental Inspections (RMCEI) which is an attempt to achieve operational standardisation in spite of legislation and political differences.[22]

As Slaughter states, overall the three types of network contain parallel processes and points of convergence:

> '[These] three types of networks have overlapping functions – harmonisation and enforcement networks also exchange information and offer assistance; information networks can also make common policy for their members under certain circumstances'.[23]

While EENs have these component parts, it is the focus and priority afforded information, enforcement and harmonisation that varies. Focus and priority can also vary significantly within a particular EEN, between clusters[24] or even between projects within a cluster.

2.6 Primary Actors in Networks

EENs tend to be made up of: governmental regulators, international governmental organisations, non-governmental organisations, consultants and, increasingly, academic and research institutions. In limited contexts, EENs can involve industry peak bodies and the regulated community.

---

21 Ibid, p. 59.

22 For more detailed information on the RMCEI see IMPEL (http://impel.eu/), n.d.; Liebregts, T M and Kramers, R, 'Doing the Rights Things: A Step-by-step Guidance for Planning of Environmental Inspections' in INECE, 8th International Conference on Environmental Compliance and Enforcement: 5–11 April 2008, Cape Town, South Africa: Proceedings (London: Cameron May Ltd, 2008).

23 Slaughter, A M, *A New World Order*, Princeton, NJ: Princeton University Press, 2004, p. 52.

24 In some networks clusters are known by other names such as working groups or sub-committees. These various bodies often propose, develop, conduct, review and monitor projects undertaken under the auspice of the network. For more information on clusters see http://impel.eu/about/clusters/ (IMPEL) and https://aelert.net/cluster-working-groups/ (AELERT).

2.7 Three Levels of Networks

Slaughter considers that there are three 'levels' of network activity, which are networks comprised of:

- Executive officials that develop within established international organisations;
- Officials that develop under agreements negotiated by heads of state; and
- National regulators that develop outside any formal framework.[25]

Slaughter suggests that the last group, the networks of national regulators, has attracted the most attention over the past decade.[26] Adding that what characterises this level of network is that they '. . . arise spontaneously from a need to work together to address common problems; in some cases members interact sufficiently autonomously to require the institutionalization of their activities'.[27]

2.8 What Constitutes an Environmental Enforcement Network?

In terms of EENs, as perhaps particularly understood by participants at EEN fora, Andrew Farmer's (2007) work is both informative and accurate. In his book, *Handbook of Environmental Protection and Enforcement: Principles and Practice*, he sets aside a chapter on networking,[28] thoroughly covering the issue.

Farmer describes the structure and function of six more formally established networks of varying ages. Specifically he details the development, growth, activities, management and general functioning of the following networks:

- INECE;
- IMPEL;
- Commission for Environmental Cooperation (CEC);
- Asian Environmental Compliance and Enforcement Network (AECEN);

---

[25] Ibid., p. 45.
[26] Ibid.
[27] Ibid.
[28] See Chapter 9 – 'Networking' in Farmer, A, *Handbook of Environmental Protection and Enforcement: Principles and Practice*, London: Earthscan, 2007, pp. 249–262.

- Regulatory Environmental Programme Implementation Network (REPIN); and
- Maghreb Enforcement Network (MEN).

Farmer's work will be considered in greater detail in the next section, 'Networks in Practice', but at this juncture it is worth noting that while the mission statements of networks contain information about their respective focus and goals, the literature has established that there are a number of functions which appear common to EENs. These include:

- Building relationships and strengthening capacity across jurisdictions;
- Sharing of information and experiences;
- Raising awareness and improving environmental compliance and enforcement efforts; and
- Developing consistent and standardised practices and procedures to support implementation of environmental enforcement.[29]

Additional variety in the role and focus of EENs can be seen in the numerous works of INECE, which is reflected in the information that it has developed, collated and maintained over a 25-year period.[30]

3. NETWORKS IN PRACTICE

3.1 Overview of Research

In 2010 the author conducted research into EENs. As 'action research' it was research that related to a real-world problem or issue and sought a real-world practical solution.[31]

---

[29] As an example, refer to the purpose and mission statements of the following networks: AELERT http://www.aelert.net; INECE http://www.inece.org; and the Network for Ireland's Environmental Compliance and Enforcement (NIECE) http://www.epa.ie/enforcement/network/#.UwAlzVVWFIo

[30] The INECE website contains a vast amount of information across a myriad of issues relating to compliance and enforcement of environmental law. It also details the history, theory and practice of environmental enforcement networks themselves. Most notably from a research perspective it contains the proceedings from the nine conferences (1990, 1992, 1994, 1996, 1998, 2002, 2005, 2008 and 2011) held thus far.

[31] For more on action research see O'Leary, Z, *The Essential Guide to Doing Research*, London: Sage, 2007, p. 139 and Robson, C, *Real World Research*, 2nd edn, Malden, MA: Blackwell Publishing, 2002.

3.1.1 Research questions

In terms of the research, the study sought to answer two questions:

- Was there utility in environmental enforcement networks?; and
- If utility was established, how can environmental enforcement agencies maximise the benefit they derive from their involvement with environmental enforcement networks?

3.1.2 Research participants

Importantly, to give the research practical application, all of the research participants surveyed in the course of the study had:

- Direct environmental compliance and enforcement responsibilities within a national or provincial, environmental enforcement agency; and
- They also had formal roles within one or more of the networks studied.

The research participants were well placed to provide information relevant to the research questions as collectively they have contributed, participated in and gained experience from seven countries, eight agencies, 14 networks (covering those that are sub-national, national, regional and global) and have had associations with networks that have been established for between six and 25 years. It is also worth noting that they have had approximately from ten to forty years of experience in government service, and have had experience as an office holder in a network ranging from three to 22 years.[32]

3.2 Research Data

The research data, whether in questionnaire or interview format, focused on collecting information across four broad areas namely: *Involvement, Value, Effectiveness* and *Support* for networks.

3.2.1 Questionnaire

The questionnaire consisted of nine questions which were specifically designed to elicit information relating to:

---

[32] See Pink, G, 'Environmental Enforcement Networks: A Qualitative Analysis', 2010, http://ssrn.com/abstract=1803179 (accessed on 14 April 2011), pp. 15–16.

- The number of networks that a particular agency was actively associated with (Q1);
- An assessment of return for effort expended (Q2);
- The main benefits and challenges encountered through an agency's association with various networks (Q3 & 4);
- How information from the network is made available to agency staff and their level of understanding of the network (Q5, 6 & 8); and
- The level of support provided by an agency to networks (Q7 & 9).

3.2.2 Interview

The interview consisted of six questions which were specifically designed to elicit more detailed and comprehensive information than that which was obtained from the questionnaire. The interview questions sought specific examples and descriptions of:

- The benefits of networks (Q1);
- The challenges of networks (Q2);
- The strategies employed by agencies to derive enhanced benefits from networks (Q1);
- The strategies employed by networks to provide greater benefits to members (Q4); and
- General advice that might be of use to those considering involvement in networks (Q5 & 6).

3.3 Analysis

The questionnaire and interview data were initially subjected to iterative thematic analysis to determine the dominant and common themes.[33]

The results were subjected to an analysis of strengths, weaknesses, opportunities, and threats (SWOT).[34] The outcomes of the SWOT analysis were then assessed and shaped into the policy options and recommendations for agencies considering involvement with networks.

---

[33] Ibid., p. 18.

[34] For more on SWOT analysis and its application see Heldon, CE, 'Exploratory Analysis Tools' in J Ratcliffe (ed.), *Strategic Thinking in Criminal Intelligence*, 2nd edn, Sydney: The Federation Press, 2009, 124–146 and Prunckun, H, *Handbook of Scientific Methods of Inquiry for Intelligence Analysis*, Lanham: Scarecrow, 2010, pp. 136–137.

3.4 Findings

3.4.1 Overview

The objective of this research was to arrive at a set of policy options that could be considered by decision makers within agencies as part of assessing how their agency might obtain greater benefits from network association.

Table 1.1 shows the themes that emerged from an examination of each of the SWOT factors. The findings were consistent with those of Farmer, who notes that EENs differ in terms of formality, spanning the range of informal, semi-formal and formal.[35] Equally, the research confirmed, through participant testimony, that '. . . [e]nforcement networks typically spring up due to the inability of government officials in one country to enforce that country's laws'.[36] The research also corroborated the comments of Achim Steiner, the Executive Director of the United Nations Environment Programme (UNEP) who believes that '. . . cooperation occurs only when diverse national interests converge, participating officers have been able to step outside narrow national boundaries, [and] understand each other's issues . . .'.[37]

3.4.2 The study

The study established that there is utility in networks across the countries and networks studied. It also identified a range of strategies and activities that could be used by environmental enforcement agencies to assist them in maximising the benefits they derive from their network engagement.

The literature (*academic, practitioner* and *pracademic* alike) noted a proliferation of networks since the 1990s. It also reinforced the key role played by institutions such as INECE globally, as well as regional EENs (with IMPEL and AELERT providing an example from each hemisphere).

The study, as action research, focused particular attention on how agencies might best utilise networks to assist them in achieving improved environmental enforcement outcomes. Moreover it determined that EENs:

---

[35] See Farmer, A, *Handbook of Environmental Protection and Enforcement: Principles and Practice*, London: Earthscan, 2007, pp. 249–262.

[36] Slaughter, A-M, *A New World Order*, New Jersey: Princeton University Press, 2004, p. 19.

[37] Steiner, A, Foreword in *Networking Counts: Combating Illegal Trade in Ozone Depleting Substances*, Paris: United Nations Environment Programme, 2007, p. 2.

Table 1.1 SWOT analytical matrix – environmental enforcement networks

	Analysis of Strengths, Weaknesses, Opportunities and Threats	
	Supportive	Detrimental
Internal (to networks)	*Strengths* • Enhanced contacts • Operational benefits • Accessing better practices	*Weaknesses* • Lack of active participation • Lack of resources • Criticality of network secretariats • Project completion rates
External (to networks)	*Opportunities* • Representation • Reporting • Benefits • Communication • Events • Knowledge management	*Threats* • Inability to sustain internal capacity • Loss of key staff • Inadequate information distribution

- require a strong ongoing secretariat;
- require ongoing commitment and leadership (which frequently falls to an energised few);
- are reliant upon *ad hoc* resources from disparate sources (which tend to involve a disproportionate resource burden on some members);
- lack enforceable governance arrangements; and
- involve a transitory (and at times non-representative) membership drawn from a variety of government and non-government organisations (often with vastly competing interests).[38]

The research produced 12 suggestions or recommendations as to how agencies might derive additional or increased benefit from EENs. Because these recommendations relate to potential benefits, as they resulted from the practical research, they will be covered in section 4, 'Potential of Networks'.

3.4.3 Maximising benefits of network engagement: four broad areas – involvement, value, effectiveness and support

As stated previously, the recommendations relate to the four broad areas of *involvement, value, effectiveness* and *support* (IVES):[39]

---

[38] Pink, G., 'Environmental Enforcement Networks: A Qualitative Analysis', 2010, http://ssrn.com/abstract=1803179 (accessed on 14 April 2011), p. 8.

[39] Ibid., p. 802.

- *Involvement* – Why do agencies and people become involved in networks?
- *Value* – What is the value that agencies hope to get out of their network interaction – and to some extent how is this value perceived and how is the value measured?
- *Effectiveness* – How effectively do agencies consider the networks are operating and where they would like them to operate more effectively?
- *Support* – What is the support that networks require to be in a position to be able to support network members?

4. POTENTIAL OF NETWORKS

4.1 Actual and Potential Benefits

Anderson suggests that '[if] a network structure is viewed as providing opportunity, then a key research question involves better understanding the characteristics that affect actors' abilities to realize this opportunity'.[40]

Whereas Adler and Kwon consider 'it is important to differentiate between the *potential* opportunities that social networks provide and *realised* opportunities'.[41]

In highlighting that there are potential and realised benefits (or value) in networks, Farmer concluded his chapter on networks with a checklist for environmental enforcement agencies (EEAs). His checklist was for agencies that are already participating in networks. It suggests how EEAs can maximise their benefit from such association. It also provides a prompt for those EEAs who are contemplating participating in networks. The checklist, asked:

1. Has the environmental enforcement authority a designated person responsible for coordination with the network?
2. Is it responsible for part-funding of network activities and, if so, is this fully incorporated in relevant financial planning?
3. Are effective mechanisms in place to identify staff members who might most effectively participate in relevant network activities?

---

[40] Anderson, M H, 'Social Networks and the Cognitive Motivation to Realize Network Opportunities: A Study of Managers' Information Gathering Behaviors', in *Journal of Organizational Behavior*, 2008, vol. 29, 51–78, p. 54.

[41] Ibid., citing Adler and Kwon, 2002.

4. Are effective mechanisms in place to disseminate the results of network activities to those in the environmental enforcement authority who would benefit?[42]

4.2 Maximising and Leveraging Benefits

The purpose of the author's previous research was to arrive at a set of policy options that could be considered by decision makers within environmental regulatory agencies, as part of assessing how their agency might be able to obtain greater benefits from network association. The results of the study suggest there are strategies and activities that agencies can utilise in an effort to gain greater benefit from their association with networks.

4.3 Strategies for Increasing Benefits – Considering a Value Cycle

It is important that any strategy directed towards increasing benefits recognises that benefits, especially in terms of value, occur within a cycle and/or in phases.

Wenger, Trayner and de Laat suggest that there are five phases to a value cycle. These phases are:

- Immediate value: activities and interactions;
- Potential value: knowledge capital;
- Applied value: changes in practice;
- Realised value: performance improvement; and
- Reframing value: redefining success.[43]

4.3.1 Immediate value: activities and interactions

'This is the most basic cycle of value creation. It considers networking/community activities and interactions as having value in and of themselves'.[44] This is a common occurrence in the meetings, workshops and conferences convened by EENs – participants come together to share, compare and improve – it is how EENs operate. Network members benefit

---

[42] Farmer, A, *Handbook of Environmental Protection and Enforcement: Principles and Practice*, London: Earthscan, 2007, p. 262.

[43] Wenger, E, Trayner, B and de Laat, M, 'Promoting and Assessing Value Creation in Communities and Networks: A Conceptual Framework', Ruud de Moor Centrum, Open Universiteit, Rapport 18, 2011, http://www.open.ou.nl/rslmlt/Wenger_Trayner_DeLaat_Value_creation.pdf, pp. 19–21.

[44] Ibid., p. 19.

from sharing perspectives and finding similarities and commonalities of experience.[45]

4.3.2 Potential value: knowledge capital

It is important to realise (especially for those participants new to networks and for sponsoring agencies or funders) that not all the value produced by a community of practice or a network is immediately realised. Instead, like any relationship, 'activities and interactions can produce "knowledge capital" whose value lies in its potential to be realized later'.[46] What is interesting about potential value is 'that this potential can be useful even if it is never realized'.[47] For instance, one can learn from others what to do in a certain set of circumstances based upon that other party's experience. So even if that occurrence never eventuates there is potential value in the sense that 'it is useful and reassuring to have that knowledge just in case'.[48]

4.3.3 Applied value: changes in practice

Following on, 'knowledge capital' is a potential value, which may or may not be put into use. Whereby:

> Adapting and applying knowledge capital in different contexts can lead to changes or innovations in actions, practice, tools, approaches, or organizational systems. Looking at applied value means identifying the ways practice has changed in the process of leveraging knowledge capital.[49]

4.3.4 Realised value: performance improvement

Equally, 'new practices or tools are not enough, even when applied'.[50]

> It is therefore [critically] important not to simply assume that improved performance is the case when people change their practice, but to reflect on what effects the application of knowledge capital is having on the achievement of what matters to stakeholders, including members who apply a new practice.[51]

---

45 Pink, G, 'Environmental Enforcement Networks: A Qualitative Analysis', 2010, http://ssrn.com/abstract=1803179 (accessed on 14 April 2011).

46 Wenger, E, Trayner, B and de Laat, M, 'Promoting and Assessing Value Creation in Communities and Networks: A Conceptual Framework', Ruud de Moor Centrum, Open Universiteit, Rapport 18, 2011, http://www.open.ou.nl/rslmlt/Wenger_Trayner_DeLaat_Value_creation.pdf, p. 19.

47 Ibid.

48 Ibid.

49 Ibid., pp. 20–21.

50 Ibid., p. 21.

51 Ibid.

4.3.5 Reframing value: redefining success

This is the last cycle of value creation and it 'is achieved when social learning causes a reconsideration of the learning imperatives and the criteria by which success is defined'.[52] 'This can include reframing strategies, goals, as well as values. It can also include proposing new metrics for performance that reflect the new definition of success'.[53]

5. CONCLUDING THOUGHTS AND REMARKS

Around twenty years ago when networks were starting up, there may have been a speculative aspect to engagement with them and the corresponding value expected from them. It is suspected that the thinking at the time would have been something like: *bringing like-minded people together, who share common or similar challenges and attempting to capture and leverage the learnings and benefits, surely can only help*. Most likely the thinking was without further or more complex consideration or agenda than that mentioned.

However, as time has passed, budgets have become tighter and key performance indicators more pervasive and prominent. As a result, there has been, and continues to be, a greater focus on the 'value proposition' for an agency's association with and involvement in networks.[54]

In answer, networks provide individuals, teams and agencies with access to an array of environmental compliance and enforcement expertise. Access to expertise such as this is particularly valued by practitioners and network office holders alike. Both these groups hope networks continue, especially when resources are reducing and are subject to closer examination.[55]

Networks seem able to provide unique utility in the particular field of environmental compliance and enforcement. Networks have the ability to coalesce environmental compliance and enforcement expertise. This enables agencies to engage in bilateral or multilateral projects and initiatives. This multiplication factor enables agencies to be involved in and

52 Ibid.

53 Ibid.

54 See Chapter 7 'Environmental Enforcement Networks: Their "Value Proposition" During Times of Reducing Resources and Budgets' from Grant Pink in *Part II Benefits of Networks*.

55 Pink, G, 'Assessing the Utility of Environmental Enforcement Networks: Maximising Benefits to Members' in INECE, 9th International Conference on Environmental Compliance and Enforcement: 24 June 2011, Whistler, British Columbia, Canada: Proceedings, INECE: Washington, 2011, pp. 802–803.

benefit from projects and initiatives, which had it not been for the network most likely would not have come to fruition.[56]

The need to engage with networks and the benefits of this engagement in accessing the multiplication factor mentioned above is widely supported. For example, Achim Steiner, Executive Director, UNEP, states:

> At UNEP, we believe global problems need global partnerships . . . [E]nforcement networking is one small example of the benefit of such cooperation.[57]

Professor Malcolm Sparrow of the Harvard Business School, states:

> If practitioners bite off too much, chances are they will choke. Bite off too little, and nobody will much care. Obviously an agency can take bigger bites than an individual or a department; and a consortium of institutions can presumably take even bigger bites without being overwhelmed.[58]

Professor Campbell Gemmell and Tony Circelli, CEO and Deputy CEO respectively of the South Australian Environment Protection Authority, in drawing upon their experiences with a number of EENs in Europe and Australasia, highlight and reflect upon the parallels and intersections of the *journeys* that environmental regulators take – and how it is we must learn from one another.[59]

Ken Markowitz, Managing Director of the INECE Secretariat, refers to the importance of 'networks that *do*, not networks that *are*'. This sentiment is consistent with the viewpoint expressed by Farmer, who suggests that 'networking for its own sake (a "talking shop") has little value'.[60]

Overall, this desire to maximise the value of environmental enforcement networks will lead to the achievement of progress and improvement in the

---

[56] Pink, G, 'Environmental Enforcement Networks: A Qualitative Analysis', 2010, http://ssrn.com/abstract=1803179 (accessed on 14 April 2011), pp. 62–63.

[57] Steiner, A, Foreword in *Networking Counts: Combating Illegal Trade in Ozone Depleting Substances*, Paris: United Nations Environment Programme, 2007, p. 2.

[58] Sparrow, MK, *The Character of Harms: Operational Challenges in Control*, New York: Cambridge University Press, 2008, p. 84.

[59] See Chapter 8 from 'Part II Benefits of Networks' in this volume, 'Environmental Regulation and Enforcement Networks Operating in Tandem: a Very Effective Vehicle for Driving Efficiencies and Facilitating Knowledge Exchange and Transfer'.

[60] Farmer, A, *Handbook of Environmental Protection and Enforcement: Principles and Practice*, London: Earthscan, 2007, p. 261.

fields of environmental regulation and protection. It is also recognition of the fact that we are all in this together.

BIBLIOGRAPHY

Adler, PS and Kwon, SW, 'Social Capital: Prospects for a New Concept', *Academy of Management Review* (2002), vol. 27, 17–40.

Anderson, MH, 'Social Networks and the Cognitive Motivation to Realize Network Opportunities: a Study of Managers' Information Gathering Behaviors', *Journal of Organizational Behavior* (2008), vol. 29, 51–78.

Bricknell, S, 'Environmental Crime in Australia', *AIC Reports: Research and Public Policy Series 109* (Canberra: Australian Institute of Criminology 2010).

Clifford, M and Edwards, T, *Environmental Crime* (2nd edn, Burlington MA: Jones & Bartlett Learning 2012).

Elliott, L, 'Combating Transnational Environmental Crime: "Joined Up" Thinking About Transnational Networks', in K Kangaspunta and IH Marshall (eds), *Eco-Crime and Justice: Essays on Environmental Crime* (Turin: UNICRI 2009), 55–77.

European Union Implementation and Enforcement of Environmental Law (IMPEL) website 'Cluster i: Improving Implementation of EU Environmental Law (Permitting, Inspection, Enforcement and Smarter Regulation)', http://impel.eu/cluster-i/ (n.d.) (accessed 21 February 2014).

Farmer, A, *Handbook of Environmental Protection and Enforcement: Principles and Practice* (London: Earthscan 2007).

Gemmell, JC (Campbell) and Circelli, T, 'Environmental Regulation and Enforcement Networks Operating in Tandem: a Very Effective Vehicle for Driving Efficiencies and Facilitating Knowledge Exchange and Transfer', Conference Paper. *Environmental Enforcement Networks: Concepts, Implementation and Effectiveness* (Brussels: Flemish High Council on Environmental Enforcement 2013).

Heldon, CE, 'Exploratory Analysis Tools' in J Ratcliffe (ed.), *Strategic Thinking in Criminal Intelligence* (2nd edn, Sydney: The Federation Press 2009), 124–146.

International Criminal Policing Organisation (INTERPOL), *Environmental Crime Programme; Strategic Plan 2011–2013* (Lyon: INTERPOL 2011), http://www.interpol.int/content/download/12670/87152/version/3/file/StrategicPlan2011–2013.pdf (accessed 15 October 2013).

International Network for Environmental Compliance and Enforcement (INECE), *Principles of Environmental Compliance and Enforcement Handbook, April 2009* (INECE 2009).

International Network for Environmental Compliance and Enforcement (INECE), 'Manual for Creating and Sustaining Regional Environmental Compliance and Enforcement Networks' (2012), http://inece.org/resource/network_manual/ (accessed 5 June 2012).

Lave, J and Wenger, E, *Situated Learning: Legitimate Peripheral Participation* (Cambridge: Cambridge University Press 1991).

Lave, J and Wenger, E, *Communities of Practice: Learning, Meaning, and Identity* (Cambridge: Cambridge University Press 1998).

Learning-Theories: http://www.learning-theories.com/communities-of-practice-lave-and-wenger.html (n.d.) (accessed 21 February 2014).

Lehane, J and Pink, G, 'Evolution of a Regional Environmental Enforcement Network: The Australasian Environmental Law Enforcement and Regulators neTwork (AELERT)' in INECE, *9th International Conference on Environmental Compliance and Enforcement: 24 June 2011, Whistler, British Columbia, Canada: Proceedings* (Washington: INECE 2011).

Liebregts, TM and Kramers, R, 'Doing the Rights Things: A Step-by-Step Guidance for Planning of Environmental Inspections' in INECE, *8th International Conference on Environmental Compliance and Enforcement: 5–11 April 2008, Cape Town, South Africa: Proceedings* (London: Cameron May Ltd 2008).

Mays, N and Pope, C, 'Rigour and Qualitative Research', *British Medical Journal* (1995) vol. 311, 109–112.

Miles, MB and Huberman, AM, *Qualitative Data Analysis: An Expanded Source Book* (2nd edn, Thousand Oaks, CA: Sage Publications 1994).

Nicholson, M, 'Networking in Europe: How Networking and Cooperation have Helped Respond to Environmental Compliance and Enforcement Challenges in Impel Member Countries' in *INECE, 9th International Conference on Environmental Compliance and Enforcement: 24 June 2011, Whistler, British Columbia, Canada: Proceedings* (Washington: INECE 2011).

O'Leary, G and Lynott, DJ, 'The Effective Use of an Environmental Enforcement Network in Ireland' in International Network for Environmental Compliance and Enforcement in *INECE, 9th International Conference on Environmental Compliance and Enforcement: 24 June 2011, Whistler, British Columbia, Canada: Proceedings* (Washington: INECE 2011).

O'Leary, Z, *The Essential Guide to Doing Research* (London: Sage 2007).

Organisation for Economic Co-operation and Development (OECD), *Funding Environmental Compliance Assurance: Lessons Learned from International Experience* (Paris: OECD 2005).

Pink, G, 'Assessing the Utility of Environmental Enforcement Networks: Maximising Benefits to Members' in *INECE, 9th International Conference on Environmental Compliance and Enforcement: 24 June 2011, Whistler, British Columbia, Canada: Proceedings* (Washington: INECE 2011).

Pink, G, *Environmental Enforcement Networks: A Qualitative Analysis* (2010), http://ssrn.com/abstract=1803179 (accessed on 14 April 2011).

Pink, G, 'Environmental Enforcement Networks: Their "Value Proposition" During Times of Reducing Resources and Budgets', Conference Paper. *Environmental Enforcement Networks: Concepts, Implementation and Effectiveness* (Brussels: Flemish High Council on Environmental Enforcement 2013).

Pink, G and Lehane, J, 'Environmental Enforcement Networks: Development of a Network Evaluation Matrix' in *INECE, 9th International Conference on Environmental Compliance and Enforcement: 24 June 2011, Whistler, British Columbia, Canada: Proceedings* (Washington: INECE 2011).

Pink, G and Lehane, J, 'Evaluation and Assessing Environmental Enforcement Networks: Through Use of the Network Evaluation Matrix', Conference Paper. *Environmental Enforcement Networks: Concepts, Implementation and Effectiveness* (Brussels: Flemish High Council on Environmental Enforcement 2013).

Prunckun, H, *Handbook of Scientific Methods of Inquiry for Intelligence Analysis* (Lanham: Scarecrow 2010).
Robson, C, *Real World Research* (2nd edn, Malden, MA: Blackwell Publishing 2002).
Slaughter, A-M, *A New World Order* (New Jersey: Princeton University Press 2004).
Spapens, T, 'Cross-border Police Cooperation in Tackling Environmental Crime' in *INECE, 9th International Conference on Environmental Compliance and Enforcement: 24 June 2011, Whistler, British Columbia, Canada: Proceedings* (Washington: INECE 2011).
Sparrow, MK, *The Character of Harms: Operational Challenges in Control* (New York: Cambridge University Press 2008).
Stas, A, 'The Flemish High Council of Environmental Enforcement – A Coordinated Environmental Enforcement Policy' in *INECE, 9th International Conference on Environmental Compliance and Enforcement: 24 June 2011, Whistler, British Columbia, Canada: Proceedings* (Washington: INECE 2011).
Steiner, A, Foreword in *Networking Counts: Combating Illegal Trade in Ozone Depleting Substances* (Paris: United Nations Environment Programme 2007), 2.
United Nations Office on Drugs and Crime (UNODC), *The Globalization of Crime: A Transnational Organized Crime Threat Assessment* (Vienna: UNODC 2010).
Wenger, E, website: http://wenger-trayner.com/etienne/books (n.d.) (accessed 21 February 2014).
Wenger, E, McDermott, RA, and Snyder, W, *Cultivating Communities of Practice: A Guide to Managing Knowledge* (Boston USA: Harvard Business School Publishing 2002).
Wenger, E, Trayner, B and de Laat, M, *Promoting and Assessing Value Creation in Communities and Networks: A Conceptual Framework* (Ruud de Moor Centrum, Open Universiteit, Rapport 18 2011), http://www.open.ou.nl/rslmlt/Wenger_Trayner_DeLaat_Value_creation.pdf
White, R, *Crimes Against Nature: Environmental Criminology and Ecological Justice* (Devon: Willan Publishing 2008).
White, R, (ed.) *Environmental Crime: A Reader* (Devon: Willan Publishing 2009).
White, R, 'Environmental Law Enforcement: The Importance of Global Networks and Collaborative Practices', *Australasian Policing: A Journal of Professional Practice and Research* (2011) vol. 3, no 1, 16–22.
White, R, 'NGO Engagement in Environmental Law Enforcement: Critical Reflections', *Australasian Policing: A Journal of Professional Practice and Research* (2012) vol. 4, no 1, 7–11.
Wijbenga, B, Ruessink, H, De Wit, A, and Kapitein, P, 'Environmental Policing in the 21st Century – Background, Organisation and Experience in the Netherlands' in *INECE, 8th International Conference on Environmental Compliance and Enforcement: 5–11 April 2008, Cape Town, South Africa: Proceedings* (London: Cameron May Ltd 2008).
World Customs Organization (WCO), *The Green Customs Initiative – Customs Protecting the Environment* (n.d.), http://www.greencustoms.org/background/ (accessed on 8 October 2013).

Zaelke, D, Kaniaru, D, and Kružíková, E, (eds) *Making Law Work: Environmental Compliance & Sustainable Development, Volume 1* (London: Cameron May Ltd 2005a).
Zaelke, D, Kaniaru, D, and Kružíková, E, (eds) *Making Law Work: Environmental Compliance & Sustainable Development, Volume 2* (London: Cameron May Ltd 2005b).

2. Better regulation, enforcement and networking: co-dependency for the global environment

Campbell Gemmell[1]

1. INTRODUCTION

The development, exchange and deployment of best practice environmental regulation lies at the centre of environmental networks and is a core mission area for most, if not all Environment(al) Protection Agencies (EPAs).

Environmental regulation and enforcement today deploys an extensive toolkit in pursuit of an effective protective craft.[2, 3] The toolkit and craftsmanship required to use it relate to the 'tools of government'.[4] In practical terms, this is about effective and skilful training and experience in assessing environmental problems, ensuring the scientific assessments underpinning regulation are sound, managing the harm potentially arising from environmental pressures, licensing the facility or operator or operation appropriately to limit releases to atmosphere, waters, land and waste or recovery facilities, and managing compliance and regulatory relationships thereafter in an effective and efficient manner.[5]

This paper seeks to set the context for a discussion on the value of networks, locating that in the experience of regulators and regulatory bodies, specifically this author's experience in Scotland and the European Union (EU) over a number of years, as well as more recent experience

---

[1] Professor JC Gemmell, Professor of Environmental Regulation and Policy, University of Glasgow and Consulting Partner, Canopus Scotland.

[2] MK Sparrow, *The Regulatory Craft: Controlling Risks, Solving Problems, and Managing Compliance*, 2000.

[3] MK Sparrow, *The Character of Harms: Operational Challenges in Control*, 2008.

[4] A Freiberg, *The Tools of Regulation*, 2010.

[5] JC Gemmell and EM Scott, 'Environmental regulation, sustainability and risk', *Sustainability*.

in Australia, and in particular in South Australia. It also draws heavily on material and an approach set out in Gemmell and Scott,[6] considering environmental regulation, sustainability and risk, and introduces the nine facets of 'better' environmental regulation. The experience in scope includes 'war stories' and comparisons from Scotland, the EU and Australia and hence environment protection and regulatory compliance and enforcement in theory and practice, building on issues across jurisdictions. It also asks the questions: What makes for 'good'? What leads to success or failure? What are the critical factors? What matters? What is the role of the 'authorising environment'?[7, 8] and What drives best knowledge exchange?

A final piece of context for this chapter is provided when recollecting the major developments and trends in environment protection over the last 160 years or so and particularly focusing on the great progress achieved in the last 40 years. This progress started with basic sewer system needs and public health (e.g. the drinking water challenges of cholera and diphtheria), progressing through reticulated sewer and water delivery systems and on to end-of-pipe pollution solutions for air and water, further through to smoke management and other air quality initiatives, local government and private sector waste management collection and processing technologies, the management of chemicals including pesticides, veterinary medicines, endocrine disruptors, diffuse pollution initiatives and through a whole succession, in Europe in particular, of directives and regulations designed to reduce environmental harms. Australia's National Environment Protection Measures (NEPM) have sought to achieve similar objectives for the states and territories but given the federal model in place, largely on a voluntary and only partially effective basis.

1.1 Timeline: Pre-2000

Key legislative and state of (often water) environment drivers were assembled into packages of interventions, associated with and allocated to the newly established EPAs from the late 1960s, with Sweden, the USA and the state of Victoria leading the way. A whole series of new EPAs followed through the 1980s and 1990s, given an additional boost by the focus on

---

[6] Ibid.

[7] J Benington and MH Moore, *Public value: theory and practice*, 2011.

[8] MH Moore, *Creating Public Value: Strategic Management in Government*, 1995.

managing environmental damage and seeing this in a development and sustainability context following the first Rio Conference[9] in 1992.

So, from the late 19th and early 20th centuries' smogs and new sewer systems and on to Carson[10] and then Rio, one can broadly map the sweep of environment protection coming of age, largely using the law and pollution control technology and engineering underpinned by the core sciences of, initially chemistry and biology, with extension into ecology and hydrology. Once major sources were tackled, the focus moved on to diffuse pollution, with particular emphasis required on data gathering, monitoring, assessment and detective work on sources and impacts and more subtle interventions with relevant stakeholders, for example farmers.

The 1970s–1990s were characterized by a growing focus on understanding cause and linkages, identifying new pressures and chemicals in use, seeking greater responsibility and living within our environmental or resource limits, leading to the precautionary principle and the notion of the 'polluter pays', but much was focused on 'end of pipe'. Led largely by the emerging focus on outcomes from the US EPA, the core brown environmental media: air, water, land, waste, radioactivity became work areas clearly defined, with their own toolkits and sometimes forming departments or units within EPAs, with the risk of creating technical and operational silos. From the early 1990s and boosted into the turn of the millennium by systems thinking and lifecycle analyses, 'green' environment links, waste and resources planning, embedded energy, industrial symbiosis, etc. emerged and in some places took hold. At the same time, environmental justice, land use planning system issues, economic instruments and policies to promote and tools to analyse and utilize sustainability and risk management grew in significance.

1.2 Post-2000

The burden of legislation applying to businesses as well as requiring administration and delivery by EPAs reached a pivotal point in the early 2000s and regulatory agency and business feedback loops became significant. This period of political and stakeholder challenge coincided with the arrival of the Global Financial Crisis as the focus was moving on to energy, climate change, environmental and clean technologies and

9 United Nations Conference on Environment and Development (UNCED), Rio de Janeiro, 3–14 June 1992.

10 Rachel Carson was the author of *Silent Spring* (1962) which challenged the practices of farmers, agricultural scientists and the government, and called for a change in the way humankind viewed the natural world.

green growth in a constrained and underperforming economic context. In parallel, in teams with theoretical focus and those policy specialists looking at the emerging work of 'better regulation', the work of Professor Malcolm Sparrow was coming to light, with his books of 2000 and 2008,[11] his Harvard and overseas courses, and the notion, approach and analytical toolkit of 'The Harms Agenda' reaching practitioners.

There developed a greater sense of what was going on in other jurisdictions and in other disciplinary areas including in government policy work as the concepts of cost benefit, evaluation and ultimately contestability emerged. Economic valuation of benefits but also of ecosystems and their deliverable services had become more common, and because of the challenges of delivering development projects through the land use planning systems, in grouped, economic policy and programme terms, strategic environmental assessment has built upon the project-level impact statements and assessments in use for over 30 years. Often highly debatable and contentious in detail, these approaches have provided very useful frameworks for discussion of benefits, costs and impacts and raised the debate at least.

Another trend seems relevant: that of the need for integration. Framework directives in Europe in the 1990s began the process of herding many smaller directives with very specific goals into a larger more general context. Whilst water was very successfully assembled and waste had at least two faltering attempts, air seemed even more sensitive politically and elusive, with *Clean Air for Europe* (CAFE)[12] never quite achieving the scope, scale, ambition and buy-in that the others have. But it was about more than just tidying the acquis.

The *Integrated Pollution Prevention and Control Directive* was an attempt, largely successful, to combine small and large industry regulatory effort to integrate media and ensure that industrial emissions could be seen as a whole. Involving landfill sites as well as oil recyclers, etc., showed the wide scope of the directive and it connected in issues of chemicals,

---

[11] *The Regulatory Craft: Controlling Risks, Solving Problems, and Managing Compliance* (2000) and *The Character of Harms: Operational Challenges in Control* (2008).

[12] CAFE or Clean Air for Europe was a Programme of the European Union which was the policy framework for the period 2001–2005. It was launched in March 2001, and aimed to develop a long-term, strategic and integrated policy to protect against the significant effects of air pollution on human health and environment. CAFE generated Air Quality Directives and a National Emission Ceilings (NEC) Directive and was succeeded in 2006 by the Thematic Strategy on Air Pollution for the period 2006–2010.

combustion and prior focus on best available techniques and technology to deliver cleaner, lower energy using industrial processes as well as managing abatement better.

Further still, under budget pressures and with an increasing legacy of damage as well as an increasing volume of laws to police, a focus emerged on coping, identifying the important and solving problems (i.e. not just working down a list of regulatory 'to do' items). There was also, as staffing and teams had to be cut, an appreciation that skills developed in one media team could be applied elsewhere, and succession planning often had not been done and hence expertise was leaving and not being replaced. Resource sharing, skills exchange, the approach taken to engaging with licensed bodies and operational and strategic partners all gained greater significance and focus.

But throughout the history of environmental protection there also appear to have been the swings of the pendulum, from being too close to industry and captured by their priorities and lobbying, all the way to campaigning zeal in championing impacted community interests and achieving reform, and thus the polarity of development versus environment has never been far away. One person's level playing field or proportionality is to another's, 'letting them away with it' or failing to recognize local needs or the poor behaviour of a regulated party. Risk is often in the eye of the beholder and this is never easy. All the more reason then for sharing experience.

1.3 Towards Real Networking

Provision of technical assistance between and among EPAs and governments in aid as well as professional and technical exchange areas have been ongoing since the 1970s but necessity has driven more and more of us to seek out, through personal referrals, conferences, the occasional paper, etc., those who might be able to assist. Larger EPAs and those with a naturally outward looking leadership or disposition, as well as where governments have supported this approach, have been most able to do this. The US EPA, the Environment Agency (EA) and Scottish Environment Protection Agency (SEPA) are good longer-term examples. The German Federal Environment Agency (UBA), various Dutch agencies and the Swedish EPA have also generously and habitually assisted others. Although information- rather than regulation-focused and skilled, the European Environment Agency (EEA) has also contributed very strongly here, often with direct and very useful EU Commission engagement.

Now more than ever, as regulators focus on living within their means, or more precisely the means they can afford, there appears to be serious value in, need for and benefits from the knowledge exchange embedded in environmental regulation and enforcement networks.

2. WHAT IS BETTER REGULATION?

Better regulation always begs the question 'better than what?' but generally it is well understood that regulators have sought or been driven to make things better: to improve regulatory practice over time, reflecting environmental, financial, government, industry, scientific and technology as well as administrative developments. It is also clear that a key dimension of 'better' can often be around costs and effort required. Hence 'simpler' and notions of greater relevance, efficiency and effectiveness are relevant as well as lesser 'burden'.

'Environmental regulation is a fundamental means of securing sustainable development. Regulations should have a focus on real environmental outcomes, including the state of the environment and the hazards focusing on tackling harms and risks'.[13]

2.1 Better Regulation, the UK and Ireland, and the EU

Since 1997, the four main bodies (EA, SEPA, the Irish Environmental Protection Agency (I-EPA) and, in more recent years, the Environment Agency of Northern Ireland (NIEA))[14] in the brown environment in the UK and Ireland have come together regularly at officer and at chief executive and director levels, and this has proved to be a very powerful mechanism for implementation planning, policy development, general sharing, reassurance, bench marking, collaboration in project delivery, etc., despite separate jurisdictions, legal frameworks and tools, etc. Physical proximity as well as the fact that all four bodies often deal with the same licensed operators and issues in the broader market place have served as strong binding agents as well as constructive, collaborative relationships at staff and senior management levels.

Members from the EA, I-EPA, SEPA and NIEA have also been

---

[13] JC Gemmell and EM Scott, 'Environmental regulation, sustainability and risk', *Sustainability*.

[14] Northern Ireland Environmental Agency, formerly the Environment and Heritage Service. Also, Wales has been represented through EA hitherto. Welsh external interests may be handled in future through a separate Welsh Assembly Government based entity model.

prominent participants in the EU networks 'European Union Network for the Implementation and Enforcement of Environmental Law' (IMPEL) and 'Network of Heads of European Environment Protection Agencies' (NHEEPA) (known by EEA as EPANet) and this has further extended the value of the more local networking by tapping into and ultimately being centrally involved in shaping the agendas and benefits of these larger trans-European networks as well of course as ensuring input to the EU institutions (Commission, Parliament and EEA) on compliance, enforcement and policy implementation issues. The NHEEPA Better Regulation Interest Group played a significant role in sharing key regulatory performance information and developing policy stances in areas of common interest across a range of EPAs in Europe and consolidating these for their benefit as well as to enable meaningful input to and discussion with the Commission. This led to a number of formal 'statements' (e.g. Prague, Oslo, see section 3.3) being produced (see also Gemmell and Scott,[15] EEA[16]/EPANet[17]).

2.2 Better Regulation = ?

Generally, it is clear that 'better' can mean a number of different things, subject to who uses the term. Commonly it is short-hand for proportionate, risk-based and essentially simpler, and thus, probably 'less'. To be 'better', the regulator would expect and be expected to have and demonstrate an understanding of the issues that matter to those involved and impacted. It would possess a good toolkit to address these and good performance data. There would be less of a 'burden' on the regulated. They and the regulations would cause less political 'grief', impose lower costs, but generally would also be seen not to be encouraging lower standards or performance and would still be improving compliance performance. Overall, however, a dimension of 'better' would be a good reputational 'tone' while improving outcomes in the environment as well as for society and the economy. Whilst potentially somewhat utopian, this might be the better policy goal.

Particularly in the context of the post-2001 world, with, in Europe, the Water Framework Directive in place as well as the policy packages around the Commission and Council's Gothenburg and Lisbon statements,

---

15 JC Gemmell and EM Scott, 'Environmental regulation, sustainability and risk', *Sustainability*.

16 http://www.eea.europa.eu/

17 http://epanet.ew.eea.europa.eu/

with the developing 6th Environment Action Programme (EAP), with new technologies, with the Integrated Pollution Prevention and Control Directive and both the strengthening of technically detailed BAT documentation and the integration of aspects of waste and air regulation into a larger but tighter industry-related framework, and then the financial crisis and economic imperatives coming into sharper focus, legal issues as well as genuine demonstration of willingness to reduce burdens and listen to industry, etc. had additional energy and facets.

Better data were and are needed to demonstrate an understanding of the issues that matter, hence both State of the Environment (SoE) reporting and compliance information needed upgrading and to be 'in use'. Better ways of doing a regulatory job were and are needed, refining a good toolkit to address these and not just licences, some of which in the EU Water Framework Directive and Integrated Pollution Prevention and Control Directive context needed reform to prevent them becoming too massive and detailed, intervening hugely in the running of businesses, properly the concern of owners and operators, rather than focusing on setting and monitoring key outcomes.

Also 'how do we know what's happening?' – what information does the regulator have and need, what are good compliance/performance data. Broad elements can be understood: less 'burden' on the regulated – fewer political complaints; lower costs – for the operator or developer and for the regulator too, to keep licence fees down and strike a balance with declining government budgets and increasing staff unit costs; quantitatively fewer incidents and improving compliance performance.

Harder to answer and demonstrate are: the mythical beast of the level playing field – given different staff, activities, records and reputations of companies and how they work in a market place, etc.; good reputational 'tone' – with the community, with investors or the company board, ministers, fellow tax or health and safety regulators etc. – this could be good in parts but which bit of the tone matters most?; and *quis custodet custodes*? – is the objectivity or independence of and trust in the regulator solid? How do we know? This last point may lie behind the Commission's ongoing concern to have an über-regulator, in some aspects, to be clear that the state regulators are doing their jobs objectively well, genuinely securing compliance with EU law and delivering policy objectives. In the end it has to be clear that a compelling story based on sound data should be told concerning the aforementioned improving outcomes in the environment, society and the economy.

2.3 Better Regulation and Harms

Tension between the burden on regulators of implementing the acquis of legislation and the desire to focus on delivering project activity that tackles state of the environment pressures and impacts or Sparrovian 'harms' have also come to the fore in the last five years or so, or at least been named as such. Sparrow has helped to re-energize regulators, giving them once more some professional confidence and self-respect, and helped them to focus on effective problem solving (see South Australia EPA).[18] This could be expressed, variably defiantly, as 'Regulation is good!', and of course good regulation is even better!

Sparrow[19] highlighted 'the regulator's dilemma' about the tensions and balances to be faced, often around economic development versus environment, which is still prevalent in some jurisdictions. However, regulators and policy reviewers appear to see clear and continuing evidence that unfettered market forces generally leave us with problems. It seems tautologous that unvalued or undervalued resources are just that. Many regulators believe that environment and society have been treated as, but are not, externalities, considering that regulation mediates and should mediate the space between the real physical world and the market.

In most economic development and tourism functions in government, for example, there appears a general recognition that a poor quality environment is an impediment to development, to investment and to a successful, competitive economy. Contrarily, the construction phase, again if poorly regulated, can be such that development itself may undermine competitive advantage, even if just for a time. However, both realizations may not be sufficient to prevent ongoing damaging exploitation and under-investment in protection.

In social and economic policy terms, the frame of reference for the environment and the seriousness attached to environmental factors seems to be complex and interrelated. How environmental and sustainability harms and risks are handled will impact on the effectiveness of, and authorizing environment for, the environmental regulator and the priority given to the technical issue. If sustainability is seen as the small, almost elusive area of overlap of the Venn circles of environment, economy and society, rather than the more all-encompassing 'fried egg' diagram of

---

18 South Australian Environment Protection Authority (SA EPA), *Becoming a Harms-Based Regulator – Developing a Problem-Solving Culture*, 2013.

19 MK Sparrow, *The Regulatory Craft: Controlling Risks, Solving Problems, and Managing Compliance*, 2000.

the Deming-perceived interconnected system (whereby, in ranked terms and concentric circles, the economy is a construct within society, in turn located within the physical reality of the environment, with many interconnections running between levels), different priorities and perceptions emerge.

The complexity of the reality here and the interplay of different elements rather than a false choice or dichotomy of development versus environment, highlights that regulation of the environment is perhaps 'more art than science'?[20, 21] It may be more politics even than art. But regulation involves the notion of regulatory craftsmanship: application of the 'tools of government' and more; training and experience in environmental problems identification; robust scientific assessments; practices for managing the potential harms; appropriate licensing of operators, facilities and operations; subsequent managing of compliance and regulatory relationships. Diplomacy may figure too and have just as much significance as engineering, law or science.

3. WHAT IS IN SCOPE FOR BETTER REGULATION AND NECESSARY ENFORCEMENT THEN IN THE SCOTTISH, EU, SOUTH AUSTRALIAN AND AUSTRALASIAN EXPERIENCE?

Legal frameworks and key tools are well advanced around very common standard elements, captured generally by the acronym KLEEPA – **knowledge** (scientific principles and analytical approaches, SoE reporting, various assessments of state and condition assembled from sample and trend data and prioritized licensed releases, etc.), **legislation** and legal tools, **education** and information provision to improve operator performance, **economic** instruments (packaging, emissions trading, etc.), land use **planning** system inputs to control development, and **advice** – to ministers, parliaments, etc. This is further detailed in Gemmell and Scott.[22]

---

[20] MK Sparrow, *The Regulatory Craft: Controlling Risks, Solving Problems, and Managing Compliance*, 2000.

[21] MK Sparrow, *The Character of Harms: Operational Challenges in Control*, 2008.

[22] JC Gemmell and EM Scott, 'Environmental regulation, sustainability and risk', *Sustainability*.

3.1 Better Regulation and Capturing and Sharing Case Studies – Networking Value

Experience suggests that in both policy and practice terms, local 'war stories' or case studies, can be very instructive and help regulators share experience and develop common ground at staff and leadership levels as well as honing case handling, analytical and strategy development skills (Sparrow 2000, 2008). Given the number of EPAs now in existence and regional and international collaborations, environmental regulators and enforcement networks are now a significant community of knowledge and interest. We can all learn therefore from case studies. Most recently, and relevant here, Giles[23] sets out the next generation compliance model that the US EPA is developing.

Additionally, the emerging focus on harms[24, 25, 26] has helped remove some of the tension around legal compliance, resources and the polarity of 'polluter pays' versus environment as a development drag and on to dealing with current real problems.

Gemmell and Circelli[27] outlined a set of benefits of networking as also similarly set out in Pink and Lehane.[28] They also highlighted the two central blended elements for success in delivering the wide-ranging benefits that effective networking, focusing on real problems and ensuring the best tools for the job are deployed, can bring. First, authority based upon politically savvy and experienced senior organizational leaders in the regulatory sphere coming together (motivated to identify and solve complex problems and challenges, through sharing expertise and experience developed from delivering and influencing policy and focused on its practical implementation); and secondly, the practical technical and operational regulatory practice knowledge and expertise of a 'doing' organization.

---

[23] C Giles, 'Next generation compliance', *The Environmental Forum*, 2013.

[24] MK Sparrow, *The Character of Harms: Operational Challenges in Control*, 2008.

[25] South Australian Environment Protection Authority (SA EPA), *Becoming a Harms-Based Regulator – Developing a Problem-Solving Culture*, 2013.

[26] JC Gemmell and EM Scott, 'Environmental regulation, sustainability and risk', 2013.

[27] JC Gemmell and T Circelli, *Environmental Regulation and Enforcement Networks Operating in Tandem: a Very Effective Vehicle for Driving Efficiencies and Facilitating Knowledge Exchange and Transfer*, International Conference on Environmental Enforcement Networks, Brussels, 13–14 Nov 2013, VHRM/INECE.

[28] G Pink and J Lehane, *Evaluating and Assessing Environmental Enforcement Networks: Through Use of the Network Evaluation Matrix*, 2013.

3.2 Better Regulation and Australia

Gemmell and Circelli[29] give a number of examples of good practice experience developed within the Australasian Environmental Law, Enforcement and Regulators neTwork (AELERT)[30] and also of value to share with others outside Australia.

On the AELERT website, John Merritt, CEO of the Victoria State EPA (Vic EPA) and Chair of AELERT declared:

> The problems faced by environmental regulators are not original or isolated to any one territory, region or country. These shared problems require persistence, perseverance and collaboration to find solutions . . . We must look to and learn from the experiences of our peers locally, nationally and internationally and be prepared to try something new. This combination of passion, persistence, collaboration and willingness to try something new is what unites us as AELERT members.

3.3 Better Regulation and NHEEPA

NHEEPA, established over the period 2001–2003 by interactions between the Chair of the Scottish EPA, EU Commission Directorate General, Executive Director of the EEA and a range of other EPA figures, met in first full plenary in November 2003. Since the inaugural meeting in Copenhagen, the network has met in plenary twice per annum and has established a thriving suite of interest groups.

NHEEPA (known by EEA as EPANet) is an informal, standalone, self-sustaining, largely *in camera* network for 'heads' of agencies, differentiating it from IMPEL, where technical or policy leads come together to look

---

[29] JC Gemmell and T Circelli, *Environmental Regulation and Enforcement Networks Operating in Tandem: a Very Effective Vehicle for Driving Efficiencies and Facilitating Knowledge Exchange and Transfer*, International Conference on Environmental Enforcement Networks, Brussels, 13–14 November 2013, VHRM/INECE.

[30] AELERT was established in 2004. Membership by the end of 2013 was over 150, from various sectors and from all nine Australian jurisdictions and New Zealand, including all EPAs and most state and territory departments and related bodies leading on the environment, including the Federal environment department. There are also a variety of members interested and active in regulation of mining, primary industries, worker health and safety, etc. http://www.scotland.gov.uk/Topics/Business-Industry/support/better-regulation/regulatory-review-group; https://www.wbginvestmentclimate.org/uploads/BetterBusinessRegulationDenmark.pdf; https://www.gov.uk/government/groups/better-regulation-executive

at the substance of implementation issues, under the co-ordinating and co-funded aegis of the EU Commission. As indicated earlier, NHEEPA has provided from time to time strategic and practical perspectives, producing short reports, for example:

- *Prague Statement on Good Environmental Regulation and Competitiveness* (November 2005);
- *Helsinki Statement on Barriers to Good Environmental Regulation* (January 2007); and
- *Oslo Statement on Improving the Effectiveness of EU Environmental Regulation – A Future Vision* (April 2008).

NHEEPA has provided input to the EU2020 Strategy: advice on various implementation issues, alongside IMPEL; policy inputs on better regulation, carbon capture and storage (CCS) etc., and was actively involved in the review of the 6th EAP and framing of the 7th EAP. In essence it has been a resource for the EU's institutions and has helped forge from a position of experience and knowledge, common goals, shared vision . . . and insight.

NHEEPA arranges its work on specific topics through various interest groups (IGs). Examples of current (2013) working IGs include: better regulation, CCS, climate change adaptation, sustainable use of natural resources, genetically modified organisms (GMOs), international cooperation, green economy and noise. Groups are intended to be 'task-and-finish'. Some IGs have completed their work, for example agriculture, environment and health, and performance and evaluation.

3.4 Where Does Networking Contribute – Regulatory Domain Comparisons

It is clear that most EPAs and the two networks principally featured in this paper have much in common, namely robust enforcement and the need for better compliance performance generally – tackling illegal dumping; improving waste management and soil and waste resource value recovery; site soil and groundwater contamination; managing water resources (be it a matter of scarcity or excess, quality and allocation to users are important and contentious); urban air quality; environmental protection and land use planning and development processes; harmonization; natural resource management, interactions and integration; staffing and financial resources – quantum and quality; distance to market or local scale of market.

How regulators face up to various challenges is part of how to stay in business and continue to make a difference in the real world, that is, the search to achieve the outcomes. It also takes us back to the notion of public value raised earlier and Bennington and Moore's[31] focus on the issue of 'authorizing environment' as a key part of an assessment of public value.

4. THE BENEFITS OF BETTER REGULATION IN PRACTICE

Consolidating the elements identified above, better regulation has emerged, in various tailored forms and with a panoply of tools in the broad KLEEPA set (see section 3).

4.1 Improving Operational Effectiveness – Better Regulation

Targeting specific tools to a clearly understood and segmented regulatory operating environment works best in the framework of the regulatory spectrum.[32] One can understand when speaking of the two ends of the spectrum, criminal and champion, that there is a need to police wilful bad behaviour or repeated failure and punish those who deliberately break the law, *pour encourager les autres*, while educating and enabling the willing, recognizing and learning from and with good operators and those who excel and go 'beyond compliance'.

The key action words are also clear and lead to tool selection, information needs, staff skills, etc., thus making it clearer for the regulator to develop and deploy 'Reward, Recognise, Enable, Inform, Enforce'. When combined with an outcome rather than an activity focus, a different approach can also be taken to action within the spectrum. The regulator will focus on outcomes and the difference made as opposed to the number of inspections carried out and samples taken. The operations of the regulator need to be supported by simpler and slicker systems. Action is driven by robust risk assessment. Law enforcers use detailed audits for higher risk sites and use automated and online interactions for low risk sites. The operator is seen in an industry or sector context, often working with trade representative bodies to co-produce performance improvement and share industry knowledge, developing a wider community of interest, with far better engagement. But the philosophy simplifies to

31 J Benington and MH Moore, *Public Value: Theory and Practice*, 2011.

32 JC Gemmell and EM Scott, 'Environmental regulation, sustainability and risk', 2013.

'advice and support for the willing, swift, firm and effective enforcement for the unwilling'.

It is also clear that the industry must be better understood as regulators, both their process realities and their financial and competitive ones. An enforcing entity must stand in their shoes, not on their toes. To achieve this, and to help with the need to recognize the view that the regulatory burden may be or at least seem excessive, there have been a number of attempts to find, understand and quantify the burden. Notable among these efforts (all web-accessible) have been:

- Regulatory Review Group[33] (Scotland) – various, largely annual reports;
- 'Burden Hunters'[34] (Denmark);
- Better Regulation Executive[35] (UK Whitehall) – red tape reduction/challenge reports; and
- OECD Reports.[36]

And when the spend identified is assessed in Gross Domestic Product or turnover terms it has appeared modest. It is hard for the regulator to take on board the issues wholly when it seems rare that one can find 'burden' arguments robustly justified.

Additionally, the notion of 'customer' is easy to take seriously for those who consistently operate at the champion end of the spectrum. It is much harder to take the same view of convicted criminals and repeat offenders. Nonetheless it is necessary to gain end-user perspectives and consider how closely these fit with the concepts of the delivery of obligations and the securing of public interest prosecutions, where it is often unarguable that society needs to see behaviour change and better outcomes.

Also, 'smart' regulation, and the language of deregulation must be resisted if they mean business or economic perspectives are the principal drivers for regulation that remains, at the expense of the underpinning and interconnected values of natural capital and ecosystem services . . . or failing to protect the community and the 'small voices'.

Finally here, in the Australian context, there is at present a drive for

---

[33] http://www.scotland.gov.uk/Topics/Business-Industry/support/better-regulation/regulatory-review-group

[34] https://www.wbginvestmentclimate.org/uploads/BetterBusinessRegulationDenmark.pdf

[35] https://www.gov.uk/government/groups/better-regulation-executive

[36] JC Gemmell and EM Scott, 'Environmental regulation, sustainability and risk', 2013.

'productivity' and deregulation – seemingly a way of minimizing the protections afforded vulnerable environments and communities – and often a distraction from well-thought-out simplification and de-cluttering that might otherwise reduce the necessary burden, by removing duplication and needless complexity and process steps. The Fyfe White Paper (unpublished) and emerging work by both the Office of Best Practice Regulation and AELERT are instructive here as is some of the work of the South Australia Advanced Manufacturing Council and the seminal 'Manufacturing Works'. There is clearly more to do.

4.2 Australia and Europe

From rather different origins and in very different socio-political structures, there are several similarities or at least similar key issues to be confronted. The fundamentals appear comparable – *being* an EPA, the choices around securing good governance, the powers allowed and the challenges of building a robust funding model. Much of that appears to apply in North America too. Whilst many European agencies and the US EPA are funded largely from the public purse, most of Australia has strayed well off the track, on the funding issue at least, as public benefit funding seems to have been removed almost totally.

There are questions to be asked about the size of the task – the necessary scale of an organization to discharge the statutory duties or the will of the government of the day, including staffing and funding levels.

Does government or society want a trusted advisor and reporter on the state of the environment, both locally and the 'big picture'? Is the EPA resourced and empowered to achieve this?

Is a standalone organization wanted that has an element of arm's length independence in its regulatory and compliance assessment and enforcement functions? In the EU there are many models. Often licensing and enforcement aspects are more localized than the national regulator's strategic focus. EA and SEPA are both unique in covering the full range of duties. In Australia, the governance model of South Australia is being mirrored to a greater or lesser extent in New South Wales and Victoria.

In terms of customer focus for the regulated sectors versus community engagement or citizen access to information or scientific input, there is much diversity and rhetoric does not always match reality or resources. It also connects with tough questions of 'What is the public good?' and 'What is public value?', and hence who should pay, especially if the honest answer is to a significant degree the taxpayer; but governments do not wish to make it so.

Equally, if the balance of funding should follow the logic of the polluter pays and bring balance to the oft times claim of 'toothless tiger', what is the place, and who sets the level, of licence fees, failure management costs, penalties – criminal and civil – public costs and impacts, remediation, and even restorative justice?

Finally, lifting our sights to the bigger picture – where do sustainable development goals, growth in Gross Domestic Product versus acceptable levels of environmental exploitation and damage, ecosystem services, energy and transport policy interfaces and climate change all fit?

These are all tough issues to answer but all affect the regulator's operating environment and may determine the effectiveness and tractability of better regulation goals. They may also all be areas in which networking can provide the one organization with a bigger, better informed world view from a fellow practitioner.

4.3 Global Best Regulatory Practice, Benchmarking and Collaboration

It may well be that the issues covered in section 4.2 resonate with emerging EPAs and networks in Africa, Asia and Latin America. Interestingly, embryonic networking is emerging, as opposed to agency level bilateral knowledge exchange, in China. The need is enormous, in all media seemingly, and China has the potential, from a terrible base, to leapfrog the learning of Europe, the US and Australia, where challenge and remedy took up to 200 years to connect. Wang[37] sets out some of the near catastrophic challenges faced but the potential for valuable collaboration and deep knowledge exchange appears enormous too.

The review conducted by Gemmell and Scott[38] sought to identify the whole suite of issues that make for an effective EPA delivering a better regulation model. The framework proposed had nine facets (legal, cultural, informational, technological, societal and political):

1. An acquis or codex of environmental law, to provide the framework for protection against harms;
2. A regulatory methodology (and spirit) rooted in longer-term values;
3. First-class policy-relevant scientific data, intelligence and advice to underpin, assess and review;

---

[37] AL Wang, 'The search for sustainable legitimacy: environmental law and bureaucracy in China', *Harvard Environmental Law Review*, 2013.

[38] JC Gemmell and EM Scott, 'Environmental regulation, sustainability and risk', 2013.

4. A supply of talented environment-aware analysts, environment state reporters, students and researchers with the education, skills and experience to integrate environmental information and understanding with other disciplines and issues. This is, even where partly in place, vulnerable to media, political, economic and academic policy pressures;
5. Technological innovation and quick and effective application and transfer of better lower-resource-using materials and processes. This is wholly possible at modest cost;
6. An interested, educated, responsible and balanced media with the patience and creativity to help communicate sometimes difficult subjects. This appears a particular challenge;
7. An interested, educated and responsible populace, willing to be engaged and both robust processes and willing regulators to enable this. This may challenge political power and conventional wisdom;
8. Moral framework – the ethical dimension, especially recognition by the individual, industry and society that safeguards the environment, intergenerational equity and sustainability matters; and
9. The wider societal leadership needed and robust engagement with all key stakeholders.

And so now, a tenth is suggested: access to, membership of and effective use of appropriate regulatory networks.

Gemmell and Circelli[39] set out a range of project activities and overall benefits produced by working collaboratively in a network environment, and the attributes and maturity of networks have been very fully set out by Pink,[40, 41] Lehane and Pink,[42] and Pink and Lehane,[43] among others.

---

[39] JC Gemmell and T Circelli, *Environmental Regulation and Enforcement Networks Operating in Tandem: A Very Effective Vehicle for Driving Efficiencies and Facilitating Knowledge Exchange and Transfer*, International Conference on Environmental Enforcement Networks, Brussels, 13–14 November 2013, VHRM/INECE.

[40] G Pink, 'Assessing the utility of environmental enforcement networks: Maximising benefits to members', Proceedings of the 9th International Conference on Environmental Compliance and Enforcement, 20–24 June 2011.

[41] G Pink, *Environmental Enforcement Networks: Theory, Practice and Potential*, 2013.

[42] J Lehane and G Pink, 'Evolution of a regional environmental enforcement network: The Australasian Environmental Law Enforcement and Regulators neTwork (AELERT)', Proceedings of the 9th International Conference on Environmental Compliance and Enforcement, 20–24 June 2011.

[43] G Pink and J Lehane, *Evaluating and Assessing Environmental Enforcement Networks: Through Use of the Network Evaluation Matrix*, 2013.

Several aspects of the context for network-level better regulation and knowledge exchange have been covered in this paper. Briefly returning to sections 3.3 and 3.4, it is worth considering in the current more politicized and more financially constrained environment that there is a useful distinction to be drawn between network types. There is the potential for global, regional, thematic etc. focus, but there is also technical versus leadership differentiation.

4.4 Networks for Policy Implementation and Impact Versus Networks for Officer Knowledge Exchange and Collaboration on and Development of Technical Issues

The development of the NHEEPA in 2001–2003, leading to its launch in 2004 was quickly identified by its members as well as by the EU Commission as a vehicle not so much for technical co-operation and shared assessment, peer review and support to formal EU process such as Best Available Techniques Reference documents (BREF) preparation and review, etc. as per IMPEL, as for establishing and tapping into the leadership and most senior management shared views on the problems or successes of implementation of EU policy and directives, largely outside the more inevitably politicized environment of member states' official views. Members could air judgements and experience and establish common ground, potentially of great mutual and EU-institution-wide value as well as explore desirable new work and collaborative initiatives that might enhance implementation impact, compliance success and desirable legislative reform. It also provided a relatively 'safe space' simply for personal and collective learning and reflection on the challenges of leadership and of policy for EPA chief executives (CEs). Some of the value and contribution of this network is captured in EPANet/EEA.[44]

A similar dimension has developed in Australia over the role of departmental CEs and heads coming together in the federal context of the Council of Australian Governments in Canberra, essentially advising and supporting ministers versus the strategic and operational knowledge exchanges needed for day-to-day and year-to-year delivery work across the jurisdictions on the ground. Indeed the space is gradually emerging where AELERT or the new group of Heads of EPAs, rather than the Council of Australian Governments/Standing Council on Environment and Water/ Senior Officials Committee environment may be more productive for

[44] EPANet/EEA, *The EPA Network – Sharing Experiences Across Europe*, 2013.

policy implementation dialogue outside the more politicized atmosphere of the Standing Council on Environment and Water.

5. CONCLUSIONS

This chapter seeks to describe how environmental protection and its compliance and enforcement components have come to be as they are now and connect this to a vision of a future where EPAs have reached a higher level of operational impact. That greater impact would be based on realizing the benefits of regulatory and enforcement networks, built on knowledge sharing whereby enforcement agencies are working effectively together, not individually, in isolation or ignorance. They will have built their individual and collective capacity through knowledge exchange, with many opportunities realized through bilateral and multi-partner collaboration. This will lead to more robust policing, crime reduction and other beneficial impacts. The goal should be to use networks to achieve excellence that benefits our community of interest and the environment at large. Some further details on the specific value of networks from Australia are set out in Gemmell and Circelli (Chapter 8, this volume), and other chapters in this book will focus more specifically on the contributions made by the EU and other networks.

This chapter, however, endorses the value of networks generally in the author's experience and places this in the context of the various facets of good and better regulation. What is clear, given the expanding family of EPAs worldwide and the range and significance of their work and the skills and experience of their staff, is that someone or some organization is on the same journey, maybe even on the same path, maybe ahead, behind or beside each of us on our own journey, but almost certainly able and willing to help or learn. For the future of better regulation, that is an invaluable asset.

ACKNOWLEDGEMENTS

Thanks are due to Tony Circelli, Grant Pink and Avril Gold especially and also colleagues across the networks from Scotland and the NHEEPA family to South Australia and Australasia overall.

My bona fides are based on an initial academic background: degrees from University of Aberdeen in Geography BSc (Hons) and Glaciology PhD. I have 28 years' post-doctoral involvement in environment and development policy areas with a focus on implementation. I have been awarded a Professorship in Environment Regulation and Policy, University of Glasgow and an Adjunct Professorship at the Centre for Environmental Risk and Remediation, University of South Australia. I was CEO of the Scottish EPA (2003–12) and CEO of the South Australia EPA (2012–14).

BIBLIOGRAPHY

J Benington and MH Moore, *Public Value: Theory and Practice* (Palgrave Macmillan 2011).

R Carson, *Silent Spring* (Houghton Mifflin 1962).

EPANet/EEA, *The EPA Network – Sharing Experiences Across Europe* (2013), http://epanet.ew.eea.europa.eu/fol249409/epa-brochure-final-web.pdf/download (accessed 14 February 2014).

A Freiberg, *The Tools of Regulation* (Federation Press NSW 2010).

JC Gemmell and T Circelli, *Environmental Regulation and Enforcement Networks Operating in Tandem: A Very Effective Vehicle for Driving Efficiencies and Facilitating Knowledge Exchange and Transfer* (International Conference on Environmental Enforcement Networks Brussels 13–14 Nov 2013 VHRM/INECE).

JC Gemmell and EM Scott, 'Guest editorial' (2012) *Risk Management* 14(1) doi:10.1057/rm.2011.20.

JC Gemmell and EM Scott, 'Environmental regulation, sustainability and risk' (2013) *Sustainability Accounting, Management and Policy Journal* 4(2), 120–144.

C Giles, 'Next generation compliance' (2013) *The Environmental Forum* 30(5), 22–26.

INECE, *Performance Management Guidance for Compliance and Enforcement Practitioners* (Draft 2nd edition 2008).

INECE, 'Enforcement cooperation: strengthening environmental governance' (2011) Proceedings of the 9th International Conference, Whistler, Canada.

J Lehane and G Pink, 'Evolution of a regional environmental enforcement network: The Australasian Environmental Law Enforcement and Regulators neTwork (AELERT)', Proceedings of the 9th International Conference on Environmental Compliance and Enforcement, 20–24 June 2011. International Network for Environmental Compliance and Enforcement (INECE), British Columbia, Canada. http://inece.org/conference/9/papers/Lehane-Pink_AELERT_Australia_Final.pdf (accessed 24 February 2014).

MH Moore, *Creating Public Value: Strategic Management in Government* (Harvard University Press 1995).

NHEEPA, *The Contribution of Good Environmental Regulation to Competitiveness aka 'The Prague Statement'* (2005).

G Pink, 'Assessing the utility of environmental enforcement networks: Maximising benefits to members', Proceedings of the 9th International Conference on Environmental Compliance and Enforcement, 20–24 June 2011. International Network for Environmental Compliance and Enforcement (INECE), British Columbia, Canada, http://inece.org/conference/9/papers/Pink_EENs_Australia_Final.pdf (accessed 14 February 2014).

G Pink, *Environmental Enforcement Networks: Theory, Practice and Potential* (2013).

G Pink and J Lehane, *Evaluating and Assessing Environmental Enforcement Networks: Through Use of the Network Evaluation Matrix* (2013).
South Australian Environment Protection Authority (SA EPA), *Becoming a Harms-Based Regulator – Developing a Problem-Solving Culture* (2013), http://www.epa.sa.gov.au/xstd_files/Licensing/Report/change_harms.pdf (accessed 24 February 2014).
MK Sparrow, *The Regulatory Craft: Controlling Risks, Solving Problems, and Managing Compliance* (The Brookings Institution 2000).
MK Sparrow, *The Character of Harms: Operational Challenges in Control* (Cambridge University Press 2008).
AL Wang, 'The search for sustainable legitimacy: environmental law and bureaucracy in China' (2013) *Harvard Environmental Law Review* 37, 365–440.

3. Connecting cultures: towards sustainable networking: key success factors for environmental cooperation across cultures

Esther Janssen*

1. WHAT IS CULTURE?

Culture is a set of shared and enduring meaning, values, and beliefs that characterize national, ethnic, or other groups and orient their behaviour (Mulholland 1991).[1] Culture is the way in which a group of people solves problems and reconciles dilemmas (Trompenaars 1998).[2] There are several ways to describe culture, but in all definitions it relates to how people think and act and it distinguishes one group of people from another. Culture can also be viewed as the DNA of a certain group of people and as such can't be changed very easily.

1.1 Cultural Layers

Any individual is culturally 'programmed' since birth about his or her basic beliefs and values.[3] Our families and communities teach us about what is right or wrong, good or bad, how to think, speak and behave. In addition, religious backgrounds, ethnic roots, gender, education, social class, etc. influence our mental programming. Assessing and understanding culture, therefore, is complex and we have to be cautious about simple stereotyping. Still, for reasons of identification and comparison we define a group of people or a culture based on their *shared* beliefs, value systems and

* Managing Director Culture-Inc. www.culture-inc.com; ejanssen@culture-inc.com

[1] J. Mulholland, *The Language of Negotiation*, London (1991).

[2] F. Trompenaars, *Riding the Waves of Culture*, New York (1998), 6.

[3] G. Hofstede, *Cultures & Organizations*, London (1991), 4.

behaviours. Most people have images and thoughts about other cultures, whether it's about the British, Italians, Americans, Arabs or Chinese. And in most countries people love to make jokes about their neighbouring countries, if they are not fighting with them. Perceiving cultures is most of all in the eye of the beholder. For example, Belgian people may identify themselves as primarily Flemish or Walloon. But within Europe, they will mostly be regarded as Belgian, and in the eyes of most Chinese they will be regarded as Europeans or just Westerners.

1.2 Why Does Culture Matter?

The world is getting smaller and our interactions have increased drastically over the last decades, physically as well as virtually. People travel around the world to meet and conduct business with each other as never before. Our communication skills to connect with each other smoothly and to be successful in our collaborations have become key competencies. Simultaneously, the world faces challenges that can only be overcome on a global level. This requires an even more intensive collaboration between countries in the near future.

2. CULTURES AROUND THE WORLD (THE LEWIS MODEL)

In building stronger environmental enforcement networks, regional and global, it may be useful to compare various countries and get a feel for their cultural similarities and potential differences. Richard D. Lewis has classified three main cultural categories:[4]

- *Linear-actives* – those who plan, schedule, organize, pursue action chains, do one thing at a time. Germans and Swiss are in this group;
- *Multi-actives* – those lively, loquacious peoples who do many things at once, planning their priorities not according to a time schedule but to the relative thrill or importance that each appointment brings with it. Italians, Latin Americans and Arabs are members of this group; and
- *Reactives* – those cultures that prioritize courtesy and respect, listening quietly and calmly to their interlocutors and reacting carefully to the other side's proposals. Chinese, Japanese and Finns are in this group.

---

[4] R. Lewis, *When Cultures Collide*, Boston (1996), 'Preface', xviii–xix.

2.1 Communicating Styles

Linear-actives focus their communication on sharing content, multi-actives focus on the relationship and on sharing feelings, reactives prefer harmonious interactions. One could also say, linear-actives like written communication, multi-actives verbal communication and debate, and reactives prefer a more silent and non-verbal approach. For example, when sending an email to an Arab or African colleague it is advisable to follow-up with a phone call since people perceive written communication as impersonal and thus less urgent. Written communication in these cultures should, however, indulge in formal, polite and personal phrases. Americans and Australians on the other hand prefer quick short messages that focus on the key message only.

In communicating with each other we all interpret words and signals according to our own cultural mind-sets. Some people may appreciate direct speech as an expression of honesty where others conceive such communication as being upfront and impolite. Our communication is thus filtered by our value systems and communication styles.

E.T. Hall[5] distinguishes between high-context and low-context cultures. The latter focus on conveying the message as straight as possible, whereas high-context cultures need much more information in order to be able to interpret the message correctly. For example, to high-context cultures it is important to know why you were running late and what happened on the way to the meeting as opposed to just saying or perhaps apologizing if you were late. The extra load of information is a burden to people from low-context cultures who get confused about the relevance of all these sidesteps and/or may get impatient because they want to proceed.

2.2 The Language Barrier

In addition, we have to overcome the language barrier, especially when people have to communicate in a non-native language. The English word 'interesting' can be interpreted in very different ways. Some people take it literally and will elaborate some more about the subject matter, whereas an English person may have meant to say 'I don't think it is interesting at all, forget about it'. In international conversations it is recommended to check how the message is actually understood.

---

[5] E.T. Hall, *Beyond Culture*, New York (1976).

The world is becoming more flat as we communicate more and more in virtual networks. In virtual communication the message is not being supported by non-verbal signals. Instead, we have to rely on words only, thereby raising the language barrier. Next to the potential misunderstandings as a result of differences in communication styles as described above, the actual message itself may get lost in translation. Many non-native English speakers translate from their mother tongue and in doing so they may introduce expressions that are not even known in English. Some resort to the use of Google translate or similar applications to translate texts in another language. These tools enable us to perhaps communicate in each other's languages more easily but the message is almost literally out of our hands since we are not able to check what is actually being conveyed. Translation tools, therefore, should be used with care and always backed up by a short introduction explaining the purpose of the message.

3. CROSS-CULTURAL CHALLENGES IN ENVIRONMENTAL ENFORCEMENT COOPERATION

In finding international solutions for global challenges such as environmental protection we need to recognize and reconcile locally developed policies and actions that are embedded in the local cultural context. Several cultural dimensions may impact the way that countries address environmental protection and their collaboration in this area. In particular, I would like to address four dimensions that feature in many cross-cultural theories[6] and that are relevant to environmental enforcement practices:

- The amount of control people believe they can exert on their environment;
- The universal versus flexible nature of rules and their implementation;
- The way people develop relationships and build trust; and
- The way people manage time in relation to achieving goals.

---

[6] F. Trompenaars, *Riding the Waves of Culture*, New York (1998), 141–156.

3.1 Internal or External Control

Do we control our environment or are we controlled by it? In my country of origin, the Netherlands, people share the basic belief that we can control our living environment and that we all have an individual responsibility to take good care and intervene whenever we think it's necessary. This is how we conquered the land from the raging seas in the past and to this day. We take this attitude of feeling responsible and a proactive stance with us in our daily affairs.

Such thinking is beyond belief in most Asian or reactive cultures, where people genuinely feel that they are at the hands of the Gods, fate or the universe, and that as a result one's power to intervene in situations that are not one's own are almost non-existent. The notion of bearing any individual responsibility for the outcome of processes seems ludicrous to most Asians. To them, control is synonymous with putting his or her best effort into something and accepting any outcome as a result. From a reactive perspective the world is holistic and everything is related. An environmental disaster will affect nature and humans as a whole. This notion could actually serve as a compelling argument for cross-border collaboration. But even so, it may be helpful to be aware that there exist fundamental different beliefs about the ability to control the environment or climate change as such.

3.2 Universal or Flexible Rules

What is more important: rules or relationships? Linear-active cultures adhere to the notion that the rule of law is applicable to everybody equally at all times. Exceptions merely reflect the universal character of rules. If the situation calls for it, additional or new rules will be developed. In contrast, many multi-active and reactive cultures feel that rules should be applied according to the specific circumstances and taking personal matters into account. Exceptions are more easily accepted because rules are seen more as guiding principles than as fixed instructions.

Environmental policies and regulations are implemented by the responsible national enforcement bodies. Differences exist between countries and even between organizations as to how these regulations are being interpreted and enforced in daily practice. Even the notion itself of creating a level playing field may give rise to different cultural perspectives on universal or flexible rules and on the concept of fairness.

3.3 Low Trust or High Trust

Do we trust others instantly or do we build trust over time? In cross-cultural theory,[7] we can distinguish between low-trust and high-trust cultures. Most linear-active cultures tend to start with a fairly high level of trust when they first meet other people. Subsequently, this trust level can be broken down by not adhering to agreements on deadlines, promises, results, quality, and so on.

Vice versa, in low-trust cultures people tend to not trust anybody outside of their inner family circle. Building trustworthy relations in these cultures takes a lot of time. Reactives, and to a somewhat lesser degree multi-actives, first need to know the character of the person and his/her networks before getting down to business.

In international conferences linear-actives value the content of the meeting and presentations, they appreciate written papers and joint declarations. Multi-actives and reactives will attach greater importance to who is at the meeting and in spending time with them over the coffee breaks and dinners. Their appreciation of an event would at least include good hospitality, the venue and fine catering.

3.4 Time and Planning

Are your actions future, present or past oriented? Linear-actives are very much focused on achieving goals in the (mid-term) future. They want to keep moving to the next level in the shortest and most efficient way possible. For multi-active cultures this almost rigid process is hard to handle. Here, agendas (if used at all) are determined by daily affairs and relationships that call upon one's attention. Priority is given to the network. So if you want to be first on the list, be important! Then there are cultures to which past experiences and interactions determine today's events. Those events give meaning to what is happening today and give directions for next steps. Time is very much subjective, so agreeing on a date is merely an intention to deliver, not a guarantee.

In discussing and planning an international enforcement agenda, it is recommended to take into account these different notions of time when discussing visions for the future, cooperation and action plans.

---

[7] F. Fukuyama, *Trust: The Social Virtues and the Creation of Prosperity*, London (1995), 23–33.

4. ORGANIZATIONAL AND PROFESSIONAL CULTURES

Organizations are formed by and through people. As such they are living organisms that develop preferred ways of working, decision-making processes, communication patterns and a unique identity that employees can identify with. Each organization has developed a distinct DNA pattern resulting from its own history and heroes. There are several dimensions that can vary greatly between organizations.[8] Amongst other factors, we can distinguish between:

- People versus result centrality; is the organization driven by the needs of its employees or by the desired business/policy results?
- Internal drive versus external responsiveness; is the organization primarily focused on influencing and controlling the outside world (inside-out) or is it mostly responding to the environment and the needs of its clients/stakeholders (outside-in)?
- Short-term versus long-term orientation; to what extent does the organization focus on short-term gains for itself (quick wins) or on long-term benefits for all stakeholders.
- Hierarchical versus egalitarian; is the organization managed along strong hierarchical lines (top-down) or do employees share responsibility in the decision-making process (bottom-up)?
- Individual versus group orientation; to what extent do employees primarily work as individuals or as part of a group/team?

There exist 'dominant' organizational types in various cultures and countries, but probably more defining is the sector or industry in which the organization operates.

Legal enforcement bodies are in the business of implementing and enforcing laws and regulations; enforcement officers are confronted with the practical implications of non-compliance. As a result they will have developed a different mind-set and perspective than policy makers, politicians, commercial companies and NGOs working in the same sector. The views and interests of these stakeholders may diverge at times but they all reflect part of environmental enforcement realities that need to be taken into account. In trying to collaborate with other organizations it is helpful to understand the dynamics within these organizations and to define appropriate responses toward its representatives. In realizing international

---

[8] F. Trompenaars, *Riding the Waves of Culture*, New York (1998), 157–181.

enforcement networks it is equally helpful to look for the cultural values and methods that are typical for organizations that are responsible for environmental enforcement. Such a shared professional culture transcends national cultures and can serve as a binding force.

5. CONCLUSION: RECONCILING CULTURES

How can we develop stable and smooth international networks when there are still differences in the way environmental policies are being construed and enforced? I would like to suggest a three-tiered approach.

First, we need to avoid the pitfall of stressing one's own cultural preference as the most effective one for all. What is effective varies from one cultural context to another. The fact that enforcement professionals bring forward their own distinct methods and practices basically puts more options on the table that could benefit everybody. In sharing best practices, enforcement professionals can continue to improve their operations and thus contribute to the overall outcome. Instead of choosing between universal or flexible rules, one may opt for a combined approach, agreeing on the outcome but allowing for multiple enforcement degrees or practices.

Secondly, we can benefit from a common professional culture that circumvents our sometimes-differing national cultures. Shared experiences and working methods greatly enhance collaboration. Enforcement professionals around the world have similar tasks (implementation of enforcement policies) and they have developed similar operations. They have developed their own methodology and speech that every enforcer can understand and identify with. As such, environmental enforcement networks help to create a shared or third culture that allows the participants to collaborate more effectively. In any cross-cultural setting it is having an overall ambition or common goal that brings people together.

Finally, cross-cultural competence relates to the ability to Respect, Recognize and Reconcile different cultures. In creating a more lasting or sustainable environmental enforcement collaboration all parties need to adapt their communication and management styles, taking into account the dominant culture of the project/situation at hand.

BIBLIOGRAPHY

F. Fukuyama: *Trust: The Social Virtues and the Creation of Prosperity*. Hamish Hamilton, London (1995).

E.T. Hall: *Beyond Culture*. Anchor Press, New York (1976).
E.T. Hall & M.T. Hall: *Understanding Cultural Differences*. Intercultural Press, Yarmouth, ME (1990).
G. Hofstede: *Cultures & Organizations*. McGraw-Hill, London (1991).
R. Lewis: *When Cultures Collide*. Nicholas Brealey Publishing, Boston, MA (1996).
J. Mulholland: *The Language of Negotiation*. Routledge, London (1991).
F. Trompenaars: *Riding the Waves of Culture*. McGraw-Hill, New York (1998).

4. The role of networks in ensuring compliance and strengthening coordination: a comparative analysis on INECE, ECENA, RENA and REC Turkey

Zerrin Savaşan*

1. INTRODUCTION: COMPLIANCE, COMPLIANCE MECHANISMS, PARTNERSHIP NETWORKS

The compliance issue has turned out to be one of the major concerns for global environmental governance (GEG) in both international environmental law (IEL) and international environmental politics (IEP) in recent decades.

To illustrate, the need to strengthen *compliance* has been precisely stressed in Agenda 21 (chapter 8, para. 21; chapter 39, para. 9)[1] as a response to effective governance of environmental problems. *Agenda 21* is currently a soft-law document, it has no binding effect in international law. However, when the efforts to create an all-encompassing UN Treaty – the Draft International Covenant on Environment and Development which contains provisions for reporting, compliance mechanisms and dispute-settlement mechanisms (Articles 67, 68, 69) – are taken into account, its soft-law recommendations become more important. This is particularly because this draft Covenant aims not only to consolidate existing legal principles related to the environment and development, but also to convert Agenda 21's soft-law recommendations into legally binding hard international law.[2]

* Department of International Relations/Selçuk University, Konya/Turkey, email: szerrin@selcuk.edu.tr.

[1] Agenda 21, http://www.unep.org/documents.multilingual/default.asp?DocumentID=52&ArticleID=56&l=en (accessed 13 May 2011).

[2] International Union for Conservation of Nature and Natural Resources (IUCN) Environmental Law Programme, 'Draft International Covenant on

The United Nations Environment Programme (UNEP) Special Session of the Governing Council (GC) held in 2000 also recognizes the central significance of compliance, enforcement and liability besides capacity building. UNEP, particularly with the adoption of the Programme for the Development and Periodic Review of Environmental Law for the First Decade of the 21st Century (Montevideo III Programme) in 2001, starts to take the compliance issue as a core concern, stressing the ineffectiveness of environmental law (Decision 21/23).[3] In 2002, it adopted Guidelines on Compliance with and Enforcement of Multilateral Environmental Agreements (MEAs), of which Chapter I addresses specifically compliance with MEAs.[4]

In the same year, in the World Summit on Sustainable Development (WSSD), the need to promote compliance and so the establishment and operation of mechanisms that can improve and maintain compliance emerged as a core theme of GEG.

Very recently, in the Rio+20 UN Conference, held in Rio de Janeiro, Brazil, from 20 to 22 June 2012, the compliance issue is not specifically emphasized, most probably due to the fact that the Conference's particular focus was on establishing the concept of the green economy and building an institutional framework for materializing sustainable development goals. However, through the Conference's non-binding document, *The Future We Want*, it is also reaffirmed that, 'the means of implementation identified in Agenda 21, the Programme for the Further Implementation of Agenda 21, the Johannesburg Plan of Implementation . . . are indispensable for achieving the full and effective translation of sustainable development commitments into tangible sustainable development outcomes'.[5]

Environment and Development' (Environmental Policy and Law Paper No. 31 Rev. 3. 4th edn, 2010), http://www.uncsd2012.org/content/documents/IUCN%20Intl%20Covenant%20on%20Env%20and%20Dev%20EPLP-031-rev3.pdf.2010 (accessed 28 January 2012).

[3] United Nations Environment Programme Governing Council 'Decision 21/23 The Programme for the Development and Periodic Review of Environmental Law for the First Decade of the Twenty-first Century' (2001), http://www.unep.org/hazardoussubstances/Portals/9/Lead_Cadmium/docs/GC_mandates/GC_21_6_English.pdf (accessed 8 May 2011).

[4] United Nations Environment Programme Governing Council, 'Decision 21/23 The Programme for the Development and Periodic Review of Environmental Law for the First Decade of the Twenty-first Century' (2001), http://www.unep.org/gc/gc21/ (accessed 7 November 2014).

[5] Rio+20 Report, Report of the United Nations Conference on Sustainable Development (2012), A/CONF.216/16, 48, http://www.uncsd2012.org/content/documents/814UNCSD%20REPORT%20final%20revs.pdf (accessed 18 February 2013).

Overall, through these developments, it has been realized that it is not sufficient to adopt legally binding commitments on environmental issues for success in coping with environmental problems, the adoption of environmental agreements is only the beginning of the process. It is necessary to provide full compliance to ensure effectiveness of both these agreements and of environmental governance, due to the fact that, '[c]ompliance remains an important objective not only because it often correlates with better levels of environmental protection, but also because it improves environmental governance by maintaining the credibility of environmental regimes . . .'.[6]

In fact, for an effective global governance, beside other areas of concern, it is also necessary to ensure the actors' compliance with the agreements that they have participated in. If all the actors adhere to their agreement commitments, even if the problem cannot be solved completely, this forms an important step towards incrementally better compliance, better governance and ultimately better sustainable development.

This awareness of the significance of compliance among the IEP and IEL scholars has led to serious debates, and the discussion has begun over which are the best ways to enable the states to meet the environmental agreements' obligations, and thus enable them to comply with the commitments under these agreements. Thus, the gradually increased attention which is being given to the issue of compliance has generated new mechanisms called 'compliance mechanisms' in the field of environmental protection, which supplement the available means under the rules of international law. Though the number of these that have already been developed is not so high, and most of them are in the process of being developed, they are expected to strengthen compliance and then to strengthen environmental governance – or at least to play a significant role. However, they have also some weaknesses which can undermine their effectiveness.[7]

One of their weaknesses is their inability to create a system in which many CMs of different MEAs can interact more efficiently and effectively in realizing compliance as an ultimate goal. In order to overcome this weakness, there are several suggestions on improving the coordination, for example:

---

[6] Tim Stephens, *International Courts and Environmental Protection* (2009), pp. 63–64.

[7] See Zerrin Savaşan, *Compliance Mechanisms under Multilateral Environmental Agreements: A Comparative Analysis of Compliance Mechanisms under Montreal and Kyoto Protocols* (unpublished PhD thesis, METU, Ankara 2013), pp. 208–239 for the details on the weaknesses of the CMs.

- Developing a sort of general code for CMs;[8]
- Entrusting a single body with addressing compliance issues;[9]
- Clustering the issue of MEAs;[10]
- Creating a permanent location for a number of COPs or co-locating MEA secretariats;[11] and
- Arranging regular meetings of representatives from different mechanisms.

Besides these suggestions, transgovernmental partnership networks (PNs) can also have an important potential to produce and to strengthen the informal or formal ways of cooperation and coordination between the parties to mechanisms. In fact, as Raustiala (2002) also states, many theories of compliance also imply a positive role for networks in promoting compliance.[12]

---

[8] Astrid Epiney, 'The Role of NGOs in the Process of Ensuring Compliance with MEAs', in Ulrich Beyerlin, Peter-Tobias Stoll and Rüdiger Wolfrum (eds), *Ensuring Compliance with Multilateral Environmental Agreements: A Dialogue between Practitioners and Academia* (2006), pp. 273–300.

[9] Ulrich Beyerlin, Peter-Tobias Stoll and Rüdiger Wolfrum, 'Conclusions from MEA Compliance', in Ulrich Beyerlin, Peter-Tobias Stoll and Rüdiger Wolfrum (eds), *Ensuring Compliance with Multilateral Environmental Agreements: Academic Analysis and Views from Practice* (2006), pp. 359–369; Markus Ehrmann, 'Procedures of Compliance Control in International Environmental Treaties' (2002); Cesare Pitea, 'Multiplication and Overlap of Non-Compliance Procedures and Mechanisms: Towards Better Coordination?', in Tullio Treves, Attila Tanzi, Laura Pineschi, Cesare Pitea, Chiara Ragni and Francesca Romanin Jacur (eds), *Non-Compliance Procedures and Mechanisms and the Effectiveness of International Environmental Agreements* (2009).

[10] On the issue of clustering, the Second Consultative Meeting of MEAs on IEG agreed that, clustering of MEAs for promoting collaboration and coordination should be carried out at the sectoral level (e.g. the biodiversity-related conventions, the land conventions, the chemicals and hazardous wastes conventions, the atmosphere conventions and the regional seas conventions and related agreements), the functional level (e.g. trade-related MEAs, conventions with prior-informed consent procedures and conventions with customs procedures) and the regional level (e.g. capacity-building, enforcement and compliance, etc.); UNEP (2006). See also Sebastian Oberthür, *Clustering of Multilateral Environmental Agreements: Potentials and Limitations. International Environmental Agreements: Politics, Law and Economics* (Kluwer Academic 2002), pp. 317–340 for the details on clustering.

[11] Sebastian Oberthür, *Clustering of Multilateral Environmental Agreements: Potentials and Limitations. International Environmental Agreements: Politics, Law and Economics* (2002), pp. 317–340.

[12] Kal Raustiala, 'The Architecture of International Cooperation: Transgovernmental Networks and the Future of International Law' (2002)

In this respect, this chapter aims to question whether partnership networks (or partnership coalitions) can play a role in ensuring the parties' compliance with their commitments under multilateral environmental agreements and in strengthening coordination between different compliance mechanisms.

While making its analysis, it rests on a comparative analysis of four case studies, INECE, ECENA, RENA and REC Turkey, and on interviews made with the experts working for these networks to learn about their practical experiences. These four networks are chosen as case studies, because they represent different levels: global, regional and local/national. So, they can provide basic and comparative information concerning global, regional and national networks.

The interviews carried out with the experts working for these networks consist of mainly two parts: general questions on the structure of the network and specific questions on environmental compliance and enforcement. The questions were posed to uncover the experts' practical experiences, observations, descriptions and recommendations on:

- Their expectations from the networking on compliance and enforcement issues;
- The networks' advantages or disadvantages/problems to be coped with;
- Which network plays a more crucial role in ensuring compliance;
- The relationship between the networks and NGOs;
- The coordination provided between different networks on environmental compliance and enforcement issues and between staff working for different activities;
- The relationship (direct or indirect) with the compliance mechanisms (CMs) under multilateral environmental agreements (MEAs) within the network;
- The coordination to be provided between the CMs and networks; and
- Transparency in network activities.

In the chapter, firstly, some brief information is given on the concepts of compliance, compliance mechanisms and partnership networks. Then, why and how they have been developed is scrutinized. Thirdly, their

---

Virginia Journal of International Law, p. 83, http://www2.law.ucla.edu/raustiala/publications/Architecture%20of%20International%20Cooperation.pdf (accessed 10 May 2010).

activities in ensuring compliance and also strengthening coordination are particularly focused on. A comparative analysis is made on the case studies to find out the fields that they have been successful in and where they have failed. Furthermore, based on a comprehensive assessment of their major weaknesses the chapter investigates in two areas, ensuring compliance and strengthening coordination, discovering what can be learned from their weaknesses to yield the desired results for enhancing compliance and how they can be overcome. Finally, based on its findings, the chapter makes a concluding assessment of the analysis.

2. CONCEPTUAL FRAMEWORK

For the purposes of this part of the study focusing on compliance, CMs and PNs, three key concepts should be clarified at the outset: compliance, CM under MEAs, and PNs.

In fact, in order to facilitate the discussion on the role of PNs in ensuring the parties' compliance with their commitments under multilateral environmental agreements and in strengthening coordination between all stakeholders and also between different compliance mechanisms, it is substantially necessary to clarify what these concepts mean in the context of this study and what should be understood from them.

2.1 Compliance

In order to avoid conceptual confusion, the concept of compliance should be distinguished from the related concepts of enforcement, implementation and effectiveness. In contrast to the concept of enforcement, it does not always require an enforcer or the use of force to comply, as it can occur without such compulsion. It also 'goes beyond implementation',[13] due to the fact that implementation is 'neither a necessary nor a sufficient'[14] concept for explaining compliance. Indeed, it is not necessary because compliance can occur automatically if practice in the national system is the same as the international commitments without any need

---

[13] Abram Chayes, Antonia H. Chayes and Ronald Mitchell, 'Managing Compliance: A Comparative Perspective', in Edith Brown Weiss and Harold Karan Jacobson (eds), *Engaging Countries: Strengthening Compliance with International Environmental Accords* (1998), p. 39.

[14] Kal Raustiala and Anne-Marie Slaughter, 'International Law, International Relations and Compliance', in Walter Carlsnaes, Thomas Risse and Beth A Simmons (eds), *The Handbook of International Relations* (2002), p. 539.

for a new regulation in the national system. It is not sufficient because implementation does not always produce meeting the requirements and being compliant with the obligations. Finally, in the concept of effectiveness, rather than the conformity of behaviour to rules, the outcome of this conformity is taken into account. That is, for a rule to be effective, it should lead to prescribed behaviours or outcomes; there should be a causal linkage between a legal rule and behaviour. Therefore, compliance can be 'neither necessary nor sufficient'[15] for explaining effectiveness.

In the existing literature, the concept of compliance is generally defined as the behaviour of an actor in conformity with legal rules. These rules can be about procedural requirements like the adoption of necessary secondary regulations, the establishment of related institutions, agencies, or the reporting and monitoring on the compliance, and substantive requirements which are intended to achieve the goals of the legal rules in question, as in controlling the activity, stopping it, changing the application standards of it, etc. So, the concept of compliance includes two main dimensions: procedural and substantive,[16] but, in evaluating compliance, it is useful to distinguish these two dimensions, but also compliance with the spirit of the agreement.[17] In fact, it can also be defined as 'upholding the

---

[15] Ronald Mitchell, 'Compliance Theory: An Overview', in Jacob Werksman, James Cameron and Peter Roderick (eds), *Improving Compliance with International Environmental Law* (1996), p. 25. Kal Raustiala and Anne-Marie Slaughter, 'International Law, International Relations and Compliance', in Walter Carlsnaes, Thomas Risse and Beth A Simmons (eds), *The Handbook of International Relations* (Sage 2002), p. 539.

[16] Helmut Breitmeier, Oran R. Young and Michael Zürn, *Analyzing International Environmental Regimes: From Case Study to Database* (2006); Pamela S. Chasek, David Leonard Downie and Janet Welsh Brown, *Global Environmental Politics* (2006); T.E. Crossen, 'The Kyoto Protocol Compliance Regime: Origins, Outcomes and the Amendment Dilemma', *Official Journal of the Resource Management Law Association of New Zealand Inc.* (2004); Teall Crossen, 'Multilateral Environmental Agreements and the Compliance Continuum' (2003) The Berkeley Electronic Press Legal Series, p. 36 https://www.ippc.int/sites/default/files/documents/1182330508307_Compliance_and_theory_MEAs.pdf; Harold Karan Jacobson and Edith Brown Weiss, 'Assessing the Record and Designing Strategies to Engage Countries', in Edith Brown Weiss and Harold Karan Jacobson (eds), *Engaging Countries: Strengthening Compliance with International Environmental Accords* (1998), 511–554; Jimin Zhao, 'Implementing International Environmental Treaties in Developing Countries: China's Compliance with the Montreal Protocol' (2005).

[17] Edith Brown Weiss, 'Understanding Compliance with International Environmental Agreements: The Baker's Dozen Myths' (1999) *University of Richmond Law Review*, http://heinonline.org/HOL/Page?handle=hein.journals/urich32&div=65&g_sent=1&collection=journals (accessed 7 May 2010); Edith

spirit' of the agreement.[18] Yet, when the concept of compliance has been extended to upholding the spirit of the agreement, it becomes extremely difficult to make an 'empirical analysis'.[19]

In the context of this study, the main concern is compliance mechanisms created by different MEAs. So, the focus will be primarily on whether the states' (parties to the related MEA) behaviour conforms to the agreement-based requirements (procedural-substantive), because of MEAs' compliance mechanisms, rather than conforming to the broader categories of other non-explicit rules, like principle and norms and upholding the spirit of the treaty. Thus, according to this definition, non-compliance occurs when the states' behaviour departs from the related MEAs' requirements.

2.2 Compliance Mechanism under Multilateral Environmental Agreements (MEAs)[20]

According to the UNEP's definition,[21] CMs created under MEAs are designed to encourage compliance by their four components and so have to be identified under these four main headings. These are:

- *Gathering information reviewing national performance of MEAs*: involves mechanisms for reviewing and assessing the performance of the parties in order to identify compliance problems beforehand;

Brown Weiss and Harold Karan Jacobson 'Strengthening Compliance with International Environmental Accords', in Paul F. Diehl (ed.), *The Politics of Global Governance, International Organizations in an Interdependent World* (2001).

[18] Adil Najam, Mihaela Papa and Nadaa Taiyab, *Global Environmental Governance: A Reform Agenda* (2006), p. 46.

[19] Teall Crossen, 'Multilateral Environmental Agreements and the Compliance Continuum' (2003), The Berkeley Electronic Press Legal Series, 36; Ronald Mitchell, 'Compliance Theory: An Overview' in Jacob Werksman, James Cameron and Peter Roderick (eds), *Improving Compliance with International Environmental Law* (1996).

[20] See for details on CMs under MEAs, Zerrin Savaşan, *Compliance Mechanisms under Multilateral Environmental Agreements: A Comparative Analysis of Compliance Mechanisms under Montreal and Kyoto Protocols* (unpublished PhD thesis, METU, Ankara, 2013); Tullio Treves, Attila Tanzi, Laura Pineschi, Cesare Pitea, Chiara Ragni and Francesca Romanin Jacur (eds), *Non-Compliance Procedures and Mechanisms and the Effectiveness of International Environmental Agreements* (Asser 2009).

[21] UNEP, *Comparative Analysis of Compliance Mechanisms under Selected Multilateral Environmental Agreements* (2007), http://www.unep.org/publications/contents/pub_details_search.asp?ID=3926 (accessed 8 May 2011).

- *Institutionalized multilateral non-compliance procedures (NCPs)*: involves institutional structure (ComplCom/ImplCom), powers and functions and procedural phases/guarantees;
- *Multilateral non-compliance response measures*: involves appropriate responses (positive and negative) to non-compliance to produce and maintain a sufficient level of compliance acceptable by the parties; and
- *Dispute settlement procedures (DSPs)*: involves traditional means of settling disputes (diplomatic and judicial means).

It should be noted that some NCPs, in setting up provisions relating to two components of this definition (information-gathering, response measures), can already involve these two components in themselves, so the concept of the CM can be employed to substitute NCPs as well. On the other hand, UNEP's definition as stated above, in line with the recent tendency defining the CM as 'an extension of the defining characteristics of a non-compliance procedure',[22] rather than merely mentioning the non-compliance procedures as a component of the mechanism, also identifies two other components (information-gathering, response measures) explicitly and separately as components of the mechanism. In addition to them, the DSPs are also counted as one of the components of a CM under the MEAs together with NCPs, response measures and gathering information. In this study, DSPs are excluded, because they are 'external' mechanisms relying on third parties, while the others are 'internal' mechanisms which are 'controlled by the parties to the MEA themselves'.[23]

In brief, the CMs have been evolved under MEAs in three steps, involving particularly three aims together: reporting-monitoring-verification, preventing non-compliance; an institutional/procedural structure/assessment on the compliance status within this structure, facilitating compliance; response measures.

In this sense, this identification involves three types of mechanisms of ensuring compliance all together, in itself establishing a *sui generis* structure for a CM. That is, the CMs include in themselves both confrontational means (like withdrawal of privileges of membership or trade restrictions) and non-confrontational means (like compliance assistance, capacity building), and also some procedural

---

[22] Kal Raustiala, *Reporting and Review Institutions in 10 Selected Multilateral Environmental Agreements* (2001), 14.

[23] Gunther Handl, 'Compliance Control Mechanisms and International Environmental Obligations' (1997), p. 32.

safeguards which are not defined in the scope of confrontational or non-confrontational means.

The CMs under MEAs generally operate through the Committees (ImplCom/ComplCom) created under the NCPs and the following institutions established under MEAs, which can also be called 'autonomous institutional arrangements':[24] a conference or meeting of the parties (COP/MOP), a secretariat and one or more subsidiary-advisory bodies (technical or scientific bodies), and a financial mechanism. In addition to them, a compliance body (ComplCom/ImplCom) created under the NCPs of the relevant MEAs is also raised as an important part of the CMs under MEAs.

2.3 Partnership Networks

There can be numerous usages of the terms network and partnership, and all these different usages can result in a complex structure which makes it difficult to know what should be understood when these terms are used.

When the term network is taken as a broad term, the UN can also be defined as a network of governments.[25] However, more specifically, it should be defined as 'a form of cooperation involving governments or government officials (also NGOs and [the] business community in some cases) that operates without a formal treaty or international institution'.[26] So, it can be argued that, networks create 'loosely-structured, peer-to-peer ties developed through frequent interaction rather than formal negotiation',[27] 'involv[ing]specialized domestic officials *directly* interacting with each other, often with minimal supervision by foreign ministers'.[28] Networks can be created for a variety of reasons and can embody a variety of structures.[29] They can be both formal and informal associations and they can be created at different levels ranging from global to regional and local. They

---

[24] Robin R. Churchill and Geir Ulfstein, 'Autonomous Institutional Arrangements in Multilateral Environmental Agreements: A Little Noticed Phenomenon in International Law' (2000).

[25] Durwood Zaelke, Donald Kaniaru and Eva Kružíková (eds), *Making Law Work: Environmental Compliance & Sustainable Development* (Cameron May 2005), p. 383.

[26] Ibid.

[27] Kal Raustiala, 'The Architecture of International Cooperation: Transgovernmental Networks and the Future of International Law' (2002) *Virginia Journal of International Law*, p. 5.

[28] Ibid.

[29] For the details on the literature of the environmental enforcement networks, see Grant William Pink, 'Environmental Enforcement Networks: A Qualitative Analysis' (2010), pp. 5–10.

are dynamic both because of their evolution over time and relationships with their peers. This dynamic feature can provide them with different processes of operating: networking, coordination, cooperation and collaboration (partnership and collaboration can be used interchangeably).[30]

Therefore, it becomes here necessary also to clarify the conceptualization/classification of the relationships including networking, coordination, cooperation and collaboration (it is possible to explain this continuum of relationships with different classifications, for example, some explain this continuum of relationships in five groups: coexistence, contracting, networking, cooperation, partnership).[31] The continuum demonstrates that the nature of the relationship depends on the needs, purposes and the willingness of the partners, so they do not always involve 'formal joined up arrangements'[32] and 'the extent to which goals, power, resources, risks, successes and accountabilities are shared across the continuum varies'.[33]

Himmelman (2001)[34] also describes coalition (which can be used interchangeably for network) 'as an organization of organizations working together for a common purpose'[35] and mentions this classification of networking, coordinating, cooperating and collaborating as four basic strategies which the organizations can use within the coalition.

In Himmelman's (2001)[36] taxonomy:

- Networking is defined as a strategy for organizations in their initial stages for sharing information with partner groups, which does not require a formal agreement across partner groups and so much time, trust or sharing of resources;
- Coordinating involves not only information sharing, but also changing activities for mutual benefits. So, it requires more time and trust than networking;
- Cooperating, in addition to sharing information and changing activities, also requires sharing resources, so, more time-trust and turf than the two strategies mentioned above; and

---

30 State Government of Victoria (2007), http://unpan1.un.org/intradoc/groups/public/documents/apcity/unpan031822.pdf (accessed 12 March 2013).

31 State Government of Victoria, Department of Education (n.d.), http://www.education.vic.gov.au/Documents/school/principals/community/relationshipcontinuum.pdf (accessed 12 March 2013).

32 State Government of Victoria (2007).

33 Ibid.

34 Arthur T. Himmelman, 'On Coalitions and the Transformation of Power Relations: Collaborative Betterment and Collaborative Empowerment' (2001).

35 Ibid.

36 Ibid.

- Collaborating, additionally to the tasks of the previously mentioned strategies, also requires a willingness to enhance the capacity of another, and the highest levels of time-trust and turf.[37] It can thus have a degree of formality and contractual obligations. Not all relationships move to a collaboration/partnership.[38]

Due to the fact that partnership networks render flexibility for working cooperatively to the states and prevent strict formality of traditional international organizations, generally, in all fields of world politics, it can be argued that 'networks, not treaties and international organizations, will be the primary vehicle for international cooperation in the future'.[39] Particularly in the field of environmental issues, networks are essential due to the cross-border nature of the majority of the environment-related issues. So, they can be explained as 'the blueprint for the international architecture of the 21st century', as Slaughter (1997) does.[40] In fact, particularly in the field of compliance, transgovernmental networks, 'involving the component institutions of states – such as legislators, regulators, and enforcement and compliance officials – interacting directly with their peers around the world',[41] play crucial roles in advancing compliance and enforcement of environmental obligations through promoting cooperation among government officials, international institutions and private actors, and fostering the political will to prevent transboundary environmental problems and to respond to them.

3. DEVELOPMENT OF PARTNERSHIP NETWORKS: INECE, ECENA, RENA AND REC

3.1 Reasons behind the Development of Partnership Networks

The instruments relied on to protect and enhance the environment have so far reflected the dominant position of sovereign states in both the development and implementation of environmental law and politics. However, in

---

[37] Ibid.

[38] State Government of Victoria, Department of Education.

[39] Kal Raustiala, 'The Architecture of International Cooperation: Transgovernmental Networks and the Future of International Law' (2002) *Virginia Journal of International Law*, p. 11.

[40] Anne-Marie Slaughter, 'The Real New World Order' (1997).

[41] Durwood Zaelke, Donald Kaniaru and Eva Kružíková (eds), *Making Law Work: Environmental Compliance & Sustainable Development* (2005), p. 383.

recent decades, the international system based on sovereign states and the concept of sovereignty has altered in many aspects. Particularly, in IEL, the concept of state sovereignty involving two notions, *territorial integrity* and *sovereignty*, in itself, cannot be revoked absolutely.

In addition, because environmental law has distinct characteristics compared to fields of international law,[42] it has addressed not only local and national but also global problems. And, if the issues at stake are of a common or even global nature, environmental problems can concern a great number of actors, not only all states, but a great number of other related actors. This is particularly because IEL does not reflect only the interests and concerns of states, but also the common concerns and interests of the whole world community. This results in the interdependence between states which necessities cooperation between them for addressing collective environmental concerns, and allows the application of special treatment for developing and least-developed states through the principle of common but differentiated responsibilities.[43] That is, although it is generally accepted that the responsibility for global environmental problems such as global warming and ozone depletion belong more to the industrialized countries rather than developing countries, the cooperation of all countries (even if they have different responsibilities) in the world is essential to lead to effective solutions for these problems. This cooperation is to a large extent provided by MEA-based regimes today.[44] The main roles are granted to the states in these regimes as well. Indeed, even if IEL and also IEP has been to a large extent shaped and improved through a process of inter-state negotiation, that is, 'inter-State cooperation',[45] non-state actors and also sub-state actors have also played significant roles in that process.[46] Furthermore, in line with the fact that

---

[42] Daniel Bodansky, Jutta Brunnée and Ellen Hey (eds), *The Oxford Handbook of International Environmental Law* (2007); David Hunter, James Salzman and Durwood Zaelke, *International Environmental Law and Policy* (2002); W. Lang 'From Environmental Protection to Sustainable Development: Challenges for International Law', in W. Lang (ed.), *Sustainable Development and International Law* (1995).

[43] Daniel Bodansky, Jutta Brunnée and Ellen Hey (eds), *The Oxford Handbook of International Environmental Law* (2007); David Hunter, James Salzman and Durwood Zaelke, *International Environmental Law and Policy* (2002).

[44] Daniel Bodansky, Jutta Brunnée and Ellen Hey (eds), *The Oxford Handbook of International Environmental Law* (2007).

[45] David Hunter, James Salzman and Durwood Zaelke, *International Environmental Law and Policy* (2002), p. 446.

[46] Daniel Bodansky, Jutta Brunnée and Ellen Hey (eds), *The Oxford Handbook of International Environmental Law* (2007); David Hunter, James Salzman and

'many international environmental problems have significant impacts that are difficult to reverse',[47] preventative approaches, and so 'preventative dispute avoidance',[48] instead of 'ex-post evaluation'[49] after the breach or damage has occurred, have become more important and more favoured in principle in IEL. In fact, in contrast to the traditional means that concentrate on dispute settling, prevention 'focuses on the management of environmental problems leading to disputes'.[50]

The nature of the MEAs has been also another preparatory reason for the creation of the CMs within MEAs. MEAs are often related to common environmental issues producing global benefits or costs for the whole world community rather than individual interests or costs for any one state. Indeed, non-compliance with an MEA can often damage the interests of the whole world community, rather than those of any one state. So, a non-compliant act of the state cannot always be linked smoothly with the injury of another state. Within MEAs it is indeed difficult, even impossible, to have recourse to 'the traditional paradigm of bilateralism',[51] and thus to establish the 'causal link' between the injured state or states and the non-compliant act of another state.[52] So, MEAs do not involve reciprocal obligations as different from bilateral agreements.

In recent decades, the limitations inherent in the traditional means of settling disputes and ensuring compliance, such as the Law of Treaties, state responsibility and DSPs, have also begun to be questioned further and found steadily more ill-equipped. All discussion on these limitations has raised the need for the creation of new mechanisms with features making CMs more attractive and applying for them preferable. In fact,

Durwood Zaelke, *International Environmental Law and Policy* (2002).

[47] David Hunter, James Salzman and Durwood Zaelke, *International Environmental Law and Policy* (2002), p. 457.

[48] C. Potzold, 'Multilateral Environmental Agreements: Contributions to Global Environmental Governance: Are Non-Compliance Mechanisms a Viable Alternative to the More Traditional Forms of International Dispute Settlement for the Resolution of Global Environmental Problems?' Society for Environmental Law and Economics, UBC Conference Paper (2009), p. 4.

[49] Tim Enderlin, 'Alpine Convention: A Different Compliance Mechanism' (2003), p. 155.

[50] Cesare Romano, 'International Dispute Settlement', in Daniel Bodansky, Jutta Brunnée and Ellen Hey (eds), *The Oxford Handbook of International Environmental Law* (2007), p. 1038.

[51] Gunther Handl, 'Compliance Control Mechanisms and International Environmental Obligations' (1997), p. 34.

[52] Xueman Wang and Glenn Wiser, 'The Implementation and Compliance Regimes under the Climate Change Convention and its Kyoto Protocol' (2002), p. 182.

the insufficiency of traditional means and dissatisfaction with them has increasingly motivated the emergence and continuing growth of new mechanisms to address environmental concerns in the management of relations between the contracting parties of the MEAs and in the settlement of the present (and also probable) environmental problems between them.[53]

Overall, it is possible to speak about two types of reasons providing the development of compliance mechanisms: preparatory reasons (involving the change in the international system and the concept of sovereignty, features of IEL and MEAs) and triggering reasons (involving the limitations of traditional means and the features making CMs more attractive and preferable).

Besides the three factors counted generally for explaining the rise of networks, technological innovation, the rise of the regulatory state, and globalization (economic interdependence),[54] these reasons can also be applied for explaining the factors behind the emergence of the PNs.

3.2 The Development of INECE, ECENA, RENA AND REC

3.2.1 International Network for Environmental Compliance and Enforcement (INECE)

INECE came into being as a result of the Organisation for Economic Cooperation and Development (OECD)'s three national case studies (using the United States, the Netherlands and the United Kingdom) on the effectiveness of compliance monitoring and enforcement of environmental policies. The study showed the necessity of engagement in the promotion of compliance with environmental laws or policies, and the environmental

[53] Ulrich Beyerlin, Peter-Tobias Stoll and Rüdiger Wolfrum, 'Conclusions from MEA Compliance', in Ulrich Beyerlin, Peter-Tobias Stoll and Rüdiger Wolfrum (eds), *Ensuring Compliance with Multilateral Environmental Agreements: Academic Analysis and Views from Practice* (2006); Robin R. Churchill and Geir Ulfstein, 'Autonomous Institutional Arrangements in Multilateral Environmental Agreements: A Little Noticed Phenomenon in International Law' (2000); Attila Tanzi and Cesare Pitea, 'Non-Compliance Mechanisms: Lessons Learned and the Way Forward', in Tullio Treves, Attila Tanzi, Laura Pineschi, Cesare Pitea, Chiara Ragni and Francesca Romanin Jacur (eds), *Non-Compliance Procedures and Mechanisms and the Effectiveness of International Environmental Agreements* (2009); Xueman Wang and Glenn Wiser, 'The Implementation and Compliance Regimes under the Climate Change Convention and its Kyoto Protocol' (2002).

[54] K. Raustiala, 2002, 'The Architecture of International Cooperation: Transgovernmental Networks and the Future of International Law', *Virginia Journal of International Law*, pp. 11–17.

agencies of the Netherlands and the United States – the United State Environmental Protection Agency together with the Dutch Inspectorate for the Environment – established INECE as a global network in 1989 with a Memorandum of Understanding resulting in an exchange of experience among enforcement personnel.

Its key partners include the Netherlands' Ministry of Housing, Spatial Planning and Environment (VROM), the United States Environmental Protection Agency (USEPA), the European Commission, the United Nations Environment Programme (UNEP), World Bank Institute, European Commission, Organisation for Economic Cooperation and Development (OECD), the Environment Agency of England and Wales, Brazil's Environmental Protection Agency, Environment Canada and the Netherlands Ministry of Infrastructure and the Environment, among others.

It has a decision-making body called the Executive Committee which has primary responsibility for the implementation of its Strategic Plan and work plans, in cooperation with the Secretariat which coordinates financial and in-kind support from INECE partners and ensures the participants' communication on cooperative compliance and enforcement activities. Its Global Council provides expertise and advice on the development and implementation of its Strategic Plan. It also utilizes evaluation mechanisms including review from the Executive Committee, Global Council, project partners and outside experts for assuring its effective governance.

Due to the fact that INECE is not an organization that employs inspectors or enforcers, but is a network with more than 4,000 participants, the staff selected for working in the project activities are divided into working groups. They are selected from qualified individuals who are competent for the project through knowledge of the subject matter.

In brief, from 1989 to date, in 25 years, INECE has organized nine conferences on Environmental Compliance and Enforcement, and grown into an informal transgovernmental network with more than 4,000 practitioners including inspectors, prosecutors, regulators, parliamentarians, judges, etc. who participate in the network from over 140 countries, principally from governments, but also from NGOs, academia and institutions.[55]

3.2.2 The Environmental Compliance and Enforcement Network for Accession (ECENA)

This was established by high-level officials from the environment ministries of South Eastern Europe (SEE) in Sofia, Bulgaria, in March 2005, as

---

[55] This part was prepared on the basis of the documentation provided on the website of the INECE network: http://inece.org (accessed 18 December 2012).

an informal network of environmental authorities from EU candidate and potential candidate countries. Its main task was to ensure the compliance of its member countries with EU environmental requirements.

The members of ECENA were Albania, Bosnia and Herzegovina, Bulgaria, Croatia, Kosovo (as defined under UNSCR 1244), the former Yugoslav Republic of Macedonia, Montenegro, Serbia, Turkey and the European Commission.

The network consisted of country coordinators from all member countries, and it held a plenary meeting once a year with the participation of the country network coordinators and partner organizations (e.g. IMPEL, INECE). The plenary meeting was the main decision-taking body of the network, preparing strategic decisions and actions. The network activities were operated under a multi-annual work programme, divided into thematic clusters.

It also had a Secretariat managed by the Regional Environmental Center (REC), which provided the communication between its national network coordinators and other members of the network and managed the exchange of information from other similar compliance and enforcement networks, such as the European Union Network for the Implementation and Enforcement of Environmental Law (IMPEL), the International Network for Environmental Compliance and Enforcement (INECE); and the Regulatory Environmental Programme Implementation Network (REPIN), and from and to the European Commission, international organizations and donors. It also reviewed progress made in ECENA activities for each plenary meeting, while reviews were carried out by members of ECENA of their national key achievements in environmental regulatory compliance and enforcement.

It was assisted by the Secretariat, held by the REC until 2010, it was then managed by a consortium led by RENA, an Austrian consulting firm, Human Dynamics as its Working Group 4.[56]

3.2.3 The Regional Environmental Network for Accession (RENA)

This network was managed by the European Commission to enhance regional cooperation as complementary to existing bilateral dialogues between the European Commission and the beneficiary countries in the Western Balkans (Albania, Bosnia & Herzegovina, Croatia, FYR Macedonia, Kosovo, Montenegro, Serbia) and Turkey.

The network was conducted both at the political level through

---

[56] This part was prepared on the basis of the documentation provided on the website of the ECENA network: http://ecena.rec.org (accessed 18 December 2012).

Ministerial meetings and the working level through RENA, administered by the RENA Steering Committee.

The Steering Committee was established to approve work plans, progress final reports and working group mandates, and to implement the work programme. As well as through the RENA Steering Committee, the project activities were closely monitored and coordinated by the European Commission-DG Environment and other DGs. Its meetings were organized biannually (and more often, if needed). Its members involved a representative from the European Commission/DG Environment/Chair and the selected focal points of each beneficiary country/voting members.

Implementation of its activities, including capacity building workshops, seminars, trainings and pilot projects, was managed, coordinated and logistically supported by the RENA Secretariat and implemented through the four RENA Working Groups, which covered the priority areas that were agreed by the Environment Ministers in June 2007:

Working Group 1 – Strategic Planning and Investments;
Working Group 2 – Climate Change;
Working Group 3 – Cross Border Cooperation and Multilateral Agreements;
Working Group 4 – Environmental Compliance and Enforcement Network for Accession (ECENA).

In order to facilitate coordination during its implementation, each beneficiary country has nominated a RENA National Focal Point to be responsible for national coordination of activities and also a Coordinator for each Working Group.

All related activities produced under the ECENA network in the period March 2010–March 2013 were created by RENA, and it was completed on March 2013.[57]

3.2.4 Regional Environmental Center (REC) Turkey Country Office

The Regional Environmental Center (REC) is an independent and not-for-profit international organization established in Hungary in 1990. Besides its Central Office, it also has 17 country offices. However, it also operates in other countries which do not have offices by implementing programmes specific to the Black Sea and the Caucasus.

---

[57] This part was prepared on the basis of the documentation provided on the website of the RENA network: www.renanetwork.org (accessed 18 December 2012).

The REC Turkey Country Office (REC Turkey) is one of its country offices. It was founded in May 2004 in Ankara, and recently has continued to operate through its two offices – the Central Ankara Office and the Istanbul Project Office.

REC Turkey plays an effective role in dealing with the problems of environmental protection (regarding the fields of EU environmental legislation, sustainable development, environmental politics, biodiversity and natural conservation, climate change, renewable energy, etc.) in Turkey by providing a forum not only for the government, but also non-governmental organizations (NGOs), private sector and other environmental stakeholders (such as local authorities, academia, media, the public, etc.) and thus supporting their cooperation and collaboration.[58]

4. ENSURING COMPLIANCE-STRENGTHENING COORDINATION: THE ROLE OF PARTNERSHIP NETWORKS

Achieving the characteristics of better compliance in CMs appears undoubtedly to be based on further coordination providing coherent attitudes through good communications and dialogue between all parties. In fact, with better coordination, all of these efforts to address the problems of the mechanisms can help speed up the progress towards better compliance, as well as GEG, providing the most effective use of resources, ensuring coherence/consistency and avoiding duplication among similar bodies.

There is indeed an obvious and urgent need for strong coordination and creating synergies and interactions across the components of the same CM, but also different CMs, particularly for those within the same cluster, together with strengthened CMs.[59]

---

[58] This part was prepared on the basis of the documentation provided on the website of the network REC Turkey: www.rec.org.tr (accessed 18 December 2012).

[59] Ulrich Beyerlin, Peter-Tobias Stoll and Rüdiger Wolfrum, 'Conclusions from MEA Compliance', in Ulrich Beyerlin, Peter-Tobias Stoll and Rüdiger Wolfrum (eds), *Ensuring Compliance with Multilateral Environmental Agreements: Academic Analysis and Views from Practice* (2006); W. Bradnee Chambers, *Interlinkages and the Effectiveness of MEAs* (UN University 2008); Pamela S. Chasek, David Leonard Downie and Janet Welsh Brown, *Global Environmental Politics* (2006); Marc A. Levy, Oran R. Young and Michael Zürn, 'The Study of International Regimes' (1995); Sebastian Oberthür, The Climate Change Regime: Interactions with ICAO, IMO and the EU Burden-Sharing Agreement' in Sebastian Oberthür and Thomas Gebring (eds) *Institutional Interaction in GEG, Synergy and Conflict among International and EU Policies* (MIT 2006), pp. 53–72;

Then, in order to achieve better compliance in the short run and environmental governance through CMs in the long run, as a first step the suggestion is made to strengthen the existing informal ways of cooperation and coordination between the parties of mechanisms,[60] and, as a further step, to aim to produce formal ways of coordination leading the various compliance mechanisms regarding themselves not as isolated entities, but rather as parts of a global effort to protect the environment for the benefit of present and future generations.

So, it is essential to analyse how the partnership networks can encourage and support coordination between all stakeholders, but also between CMs and themselves, and how opportunities for coordination can be expanded.

In the light of four case studies, INECE, ECENA, RENA and REC Turkey, from now on, their activities in ensuring compliance and also strengthening coordination between compliance mechanisms are particularly focused on and a comparative analysis is made to discover their strengths and potential weaknesses in ensuring compliance and also strengthening coordination.

Sebastian Oberthür, *Clustering of Multilateral Environmental Agreements: Potentials and Limitations. International Environmental Agreements: Politics, Law and Economics* (2002); Sebastian Oberthür, 'Linkages between the Montreal and Kyoto Protocols, Enhancing Synergies between Protecting the Ozone Layer and the Global Climate' (2001); Sebastian Oberthür and Thomas Gebring, 'Conceptual Foundations of Institutional Interaction', in Sebastian Oberthür and Thomas Gebring, (eds), *Institutional Interaction in GEG, Synergy and Conflict among International and EU Policies* (2006); Cesare Pitea, 'Multiplication and Overlap of Non-Compliance Procedures and Mechanisms: Towards Better Coordination?', in Tullio Treves, Attila Tanzi, Laura Pineschi, Cesare Pitea, Chiara Ragni, Francesca Romanin Jacur (eds), *Non-Compliance Procedures and Mechanisms and the Effectiveness of International Environmental Agreements* (2009); Rüdiger Wolfrum and Nele Matz, *Conflicts in International Environmental Law* (2003).

[60] Steinar Andresen, 'Global Environmental Governance: UN Fragmentation and Co-ordination', in Olav Schram Stokke and Oystein B. Thommessen (eds), *Yearbook of International Co-operation on Environment and Development* (2001); Cesare Pitea, 'Multiplication and Overlap of Non-Compliance Procedures and Mechanisms: Towards Better Coordination?', in Tullio Treves, Attila Tanzi, Laura Pineschi, Cesare Pitea, Chiara Ragni, Francesca Romanin Jacur (eds), *Non-Compliance Procedures and Mechanisms and the Effectiveness of International Environmental Agreements* (2009); Kal Raustiala, *Reporting and Review Institutions in 10 Selected Multilateral Environmental Agreements* (2001), p. 14, http://www.unep.org/geo/GEO3/pdfs/MEA%20PM%2070%20Part%20A%20FFF.pdf (accessed 18 April 2010).

4.1 INECE[61]

4.1.1 Ensuring compliance

Strengths:

- It builds and strengthens compliance and enforcement networks at all levels of governance – national, regional and global.
- It launches regional networks including in Europe, the European Accession countries, Eastern Europe, the Caucasus and central Asia region, Australasia, Asia, East Africa, the Arab region, North Africa, North America, and Central America (CCAD).
- Regional networks can provide harmonization of the gap between global and local interests and provide a forum to communicate that compliance and enforcement are not just important for environmental protection, but also that they have economic as well as social benefits.
- Besides its regional networks, it has supported topic-specific networks on a number of issues including water pollution, wildlife trafficking, seaports security, and a prosecutors network, Themis, which is dedicated to responding to illegal logging and other environmental crimes in South Eastern European countries and the Ukraine.
- Through its website, publications, newsletters, conferences and training, and being active in hosting meetings and participating in international panels on compliance and enforcement, it shares and disseminates information on compliance and enforcement issues, and thus provides transparency in its activities as well as increasing the awareness of government stakeholders, policy makers, businesses, and the public regarding the importance of compliance with and enforcement of environmental laws for achieving environmental protection goals.
- For strengthening the capacity of all those working in the field of compliance and enforcement, it has created a great number of instruments, such as compliance and enforcement indicators and provides worldwide training in the principles of environmental compliance and enforcement, ensuring compliance with existing policies

[61] This part was prepared on the basis of the interviews with the experts working for the INECE network (consisting of mainly two parts: general questions on the structure of the network and specific questions on environmental compliance and enforcement) and the documentation provided on the website of the network: http://inece.org (accessed 18 December 2012).

and measures to reduce emissions to air; the International Network for Environmental Compliance Training Professionals; the handbook of principles of environmental compliance and enforcement, a technical support document on illegal logging, etc.

- It works with judicial bodies around the world to help promote the exchange of ideas between court systems and develop a judicial networking to empower members of the judiciary who are engaged in environmental decision making.

Weaknesses:

- Its activities are funded by international organizations; funding is tight given the economic constraints. So, at the moment, funding presents as the most important problem.

4.1.2 Strengthening coordination

Strengths:

- Cooperation can help develop the necessary tools and programmes for both preventing and resolving transboundary environmental problems. It includes all these benefits of cooperation at global level available in informal transgovernmental networks.
- This cooperation also enables enforcement and programme administration officials, policy makers, public prosecutors and the judiciary to work together.
- On the cooperation managed with intergovernmental organizations/non-governmental organizations on environmental compliance and enforcement issues, NGOs participate in the INECE network and contribute whenever possible.
- With respect to the coordination of the activities, project leaders are responsible for the results of the project together with the participating countries or organizations.
- On the coordination provided between different networks on environmental compliance and enforcement issues, with other regional, global or national networks, working together is seen as a must for networks at all levels.

Weaknesses:

- On the relationship (direct or indirect) with the CMs under MEAs within the network, INECE does not have any relationship with the compliance mechanisms.

- On the coordination that can be provided between the CMs and networks, as INECE does not have any relationship with the compliance mechanisms, it is not applicable to INECE.

4.2 ECENA[62]

4.2.1 Ensuring compliance

Strengths:

- The network activities were operated under a multi-annual work programme, divided into thematic clusters.
- It provided a bottom-up approach to the resolution of the problems.
- The network was run by multi-donor assistance, with adequate financial means.
- The staff in the REC were employed for a variety of projects and activities. In this sense, a common set of criteria did apply. For instance, good communication and coordination skills developed interpersonal skills. Specific expertise and training skills are required for the capacity-building actions, in particular for content development and training delivery.
- The Secretariat (REC) established a website for the ECENA network, which was operational until 2010. The website provided a very transparent forum for sharing the project activities and results, as well as the work and publications of the partner networks and organizations.

Weaknesses:

- As the network's means were generally soft tools, they could be ineffective in practice. However, considering that what made it successful were those soft tools, and as they had more flexibility than traditional means, this can be thought of not as a weakness but as a strength.
- If the network did not have a strong ownership in the member countries and political support, it did not achieve an adequate activity rate in the country.

---

[62] This part was prepared on the basis of the interviews with the experts working for the ECENA network (consisting of mainly two parts: general questions on the structure of the network and specific questions on environmental compliance and enforcement) and the documentation provided on the website of the network: http://ecena.rec.org (accessed 18 December 2012).

4.2.2 Strengthening coordination

Strengths:

- The Secretariat worked closely together, with weekly coordination meetings, to provide the coordination between staff working for different activities. As it was a small team (four people) it was not difficult to coordinate properly.

Weaknesses:

- Although NGOs were occasionally involved in the training activities, they were not part of the network.
- The coordination with the sister networks was done through regular communication (email, telephone) and regular meetings (cross-participation on each other's events, plenary/steering group meetings). One contact point per network could be more helpful, addressing always the same person.
- There was not any relationship (direct or indirect) with the CMs under MEAs within the network.

4.3 RENA[63]

4.3.1 Ensuring compliance

Strengths:

- It builds capacity and information/experience exchange amongst the beneficiary countries, enforcement agencies and inspecting bodies relating to the implementation of environmental *acquis*, strengthening the capacities of the beneficiary countries' administration for the upcoming stages in the EU accession process, and compliance with environmental legislation.
- It increases efficient implementation and enforcement of environmental legislation.
- It provides a forum for better understanding of the specific problems and potential solutions of implementation and enforcement of specific laws.

---

[63] This part was prepared on the basis of the interviews with the experts working for the network ECENA (consisting of mainly two parts: general questions on the structure of the network and specific questions on the environmental compliance and enforcement) and the documentation provided in the web site of the network: www.renanetwork.org (accessed 18 December 2012).

- It also creates a pool of well-trained environmental inspectors and permit writers, capable of performing their tasks of implementation and enforcement of the environmental *acquis*.
- Its activities are divided into sector specific Working Groups. Some of the activities are horizontal by their nature and as such are carefully coordinated in order to avoid overlaps and duplications. The development and implementation of activities is planned and carried out in close collaboration with the beneficiaries, in order to achieve maximum results. In order to facilitate communication and coordination during the implementation of the project, each beneficiary country has nominated a RENA National Focal Point. Apart from the nomination of Focal Points to be responsible for national coordination of activities, the beneficiary countries have also nominated a Coordinator for each Working Group.
- One of the Working Groups on the implementation of project activities is specifically on the Environmental Compliance and Enforcement Network for Accession (WG 4). That is, compliance is regarded as one of the priority areas agreed by the Environment Ministers in June 2007.
- As most of the countries share a similar language and a more or less similar organizational structure and legislative background through the network, they can reach common solutions more easily. Perhaps, because of that, beneficiary country governments have shown their incontestable willingness to participate in RENA/ECRAN.
- It finances its activities via EU funding with a fixed budget allocation. The activities are planned in line with the allocated budget, and the financial resources available are sufficient for successful implementation.
- The budget for the RENA secretariat is about 5 million euros over a period of three years. The follow-up programme ECRAN (Environment and Climate Change Regional Accession Network) will work with the same budget, but in addition 5 million euros will be added through the involvement of the resources of the Technical Assistance Information Exchange (TAIEX) programme (so 10 million).

Weaknesses:

- Different levels of know-how, experience, progress between member countries in the transposition, implementation and enforcement require differentiated approaches in the delivery of regional activities. In the RENA region, there are different levels of capacity in place in the field of developing and implementing climate and environment policies to align with the EU climate *acquis*. As regards existing and planned policies and measures, considerable efforts are needed in all RENA beneficiary countries to converge with the EU *acquis*. Even Croatia needs to continue to take steps to achieve legislative alignment and implementation of the EU environment and climate *acquis*.

- From consultations with the country coordinators and the conclusion from the Progress Reports, it seems that all RENA countries are required to significantly step up their human resources and skills capacity to implement the elements of the environment and climate *acquis* in their countries.
- There is a need to build more technical and knowledge capacity on all elements of the environment climate *acquis*. For instance, all RENA beneficiaries, except for Croatia, lack targets for reductions of greenhouse gas (GHG) emissions and lack clear strategies to implement the EU climate *acquis*. Turkey has a national climate change action plan outlining policy actions towards the reduction of GHGs, but there is no national target. In the absence of targets, any national climate change strategy will remain generic, not integrated and with sector targets at best. As a matter of priority, RENA beneficiaries are to be encouraged to start working towards a national or regional target that will form the basis for developing a roadmap towards reducing GHG emissions.
- In all countries the number of staff in the relevant line ministries and background institutions is insufficient.
- In general, environmental compliance issues should be transparent and publicly available. All findings, reports and outputs are already available on its website providing for a full transparency of implemented activities and results achieved. However, inspection reports are also to be open to the public, which is becoming a general trend, and in some cases general reports are to be made available by law.
- Language barriers, low absorption capacities of public administration and lack of funding (except EU funding) can also be regarded as other weaknesses.

4.3.2 Strengthening coordination

Strengths:

- Coordination has been established with relevant networks such as IMPEL, INTERPOL, GREENFORCE and INECE. Some of the trainings under RENA were organized in close collaboration with the listed networks. One separate activity was focused on supporting the participation of beneficiary countries' representatives at the relevant meetings, and training was organized by related networks.

- The networks that are of primary interest for enforcement in the beneficiary countries are those networks that actively work on the enforcement of the EU environment and climate *acquis*. IMPEL and GREENFORCE are the main networks that should be considered and recommended. Membership of IMPEL is now open for all beneficiary countries within the RENA programme. With IMPEL membership a more broad participation of inspectors in the various clusters of IMPEL can be supported. A new activity is proposed which considers the participation in the European Union Forum of Judges for the Environment (EUFJE). This association is open to all EU and European Free Trade Association judges. The objective of the Forum is to promote the enforcement of national, European and international environmental law by contributing to judges acquiring a better knowledge of environmental law, by exchanging judicial decisions and by sharing experience in the area of training in environmental law. Along the same lines, the newly established European Network of Prosecutors for the Environment (ENPE) can be mentioned as a network that helps practitioners to connect; to share experiences and data on environmental crime and to look at crucial issues linked to the environment. Considering enforcement in the European Union, also EUROPOL has to be mentioned as an important organization. In this respect especially the informal network to fight organized environmental crime which is facilitated by EUROPOL should be noted – ENVICRIMENET.
- Other networks which are of secondary relevance are INTERPOL and INECE because of their international perspective. The practice established under RENA will continue under ECRAN when it comes to this task. ECRAN will finance participation of up to one representative from the beneficiary country to the relevant meetings of related networks. The request for financing will be addressed to the ECRAN Secretariat who will arrange the logistics upon approval of the EC.
- The organization of up to three annual meetings of nominated ECENA WG Coordinators is included in this task. The ECRAN Secretariat will be responsible for the preparation of agendas, discussion papers and background materials for annual meetings. The annual meetings will be used to discuss the implemented and planned activities, evaluate the progress made and provide inputs as necessary.
- The qualifications sought for the staff elected to work in the project activities have been determined during the Inception Phase of the

project and are divided into education and general and specific professional experience. Specific professional experience is the part which is changed in line with the activity to be implemented by a certain expert, which should encompass extensive project management experience on multi-national projects related to the environment in new EU member states and/or SEE countries and extensive project management experience including experience in coordination of teams of experts, as well as an understanding of legal and implementation issues.

Weaknesses:

- Every country has its own system on the coordination between staff working for different activities. Yet, it is generally provided through both staff meetings and document sharing. More harmonization is required. Presently, there is an exchange of information, but unofficially, on how things work in the various countries.
- In RENA, the NGOs are invited to participate in some subject areas (e.g. for nature conservation, they are important drivers). RENA has also established cooperation with the Environment Forum which represents NGOs from the region. Members of the Environment Forum were always invited to all activities implemented under RENA. However, deeper involvement of NGOs remains necessary. NGOs also need substantial training on technical and regulatory issues in relation to the environmental *acquis*. For instance, if NGOs are not knowledgeable enough to understand the technical aspects of environmental permits, opportunities will be missed to couple economics with environmental objectives.
- The relationship with the CMs under MEAs within the network is more or less indirect, particularly through WG 3 Activities, as enforcement of the MEAs are integrated in the legislation (Aarhus, Espoo), but sometimes also directly related (CITES, PIC procedure, UNFCCC).

4.4 REC Turkey Country Office[64]

4.4.1 Ensuring compliance

Strengths:

---

[64] This part was prepared on the basis of the interviews with the experts working for the network REC Turkey (consisting of mainly two parts: general

- It works on EU environmental legislation, sustainable development, environmental politics, environmental education, biodiversity and natural conservation, climate change, renewable energy, environmental information, waste management. So it is not directly involved in the compliance issue, but indirectly it contributes to the improvement of compliance with its activities.
- It organizes trainings and seminars, publishing books and reports and establishing platforms and initiating tools.
- It prepares regulatory impact analyses (RIAs) to assist the implementation of the EU nature conservation directives in an appropriate way in terms of economic, environmental and social aspects at minimum costs, like the directive of the European Parliament and of the Council of 27 January 2003 on Waste Electrical and Electronic Equipment, or the Directive of the European Parliament and of the Council of 4 December 2000 on the Incineration of Waste.
- It involves qualified long-term personnel or short-term consultants on environmental issues.

Weaknesses:

- It does not work specifically on compliance and enforcement issues.
- REC does not seek to make a profit in its operation. REC derives its financial support from the donor organizations of the projects that it has conducted and from the EU, the World Bank, embassies and private firms. Lack of funding can be an important issue here as well.

4.4.2 Strengthening coordination

Strengths:

- It brings all related environmental stakeholders in Turkey through the related projects, and provides cooperation and coordination between them.

Weaknesses:

---

questions on the structure of the network and specific questions on environmental compliance and enforcement) and the documentation provided on the website of the network: www.rec.org.tr (accessed 18 December 2012).

- There is no relationship (direct or indirect) with the CMs under MEAs within the network, and it seems not possible to have one because it is just a country office of REC.

5. LESSONS LEARNED FROM CASE STUDIES: SUGGESTIONS FOR IMPROVEMENT

In this section, looking at the assessment of the major weaknesses of the networks undermining efforts to ensure better compliance and coordination, what can be learned from them for enhancing compliance will be examined and also the possible improvements of these weaknesses will be focused on. Therefore, on the basis of two dimensions – ensuring compliance and strengthening coordination – in a comparative analysis between case studies, firstly, the lessons learned will be highlighted, then suggestions for improving the conditions for more effective and better coordinated networks will be discussed.

The analysis shows that over the past years since the networks in question have been established, considerable efforts have been made to improve compliance and enforcement (directly or indirectly), not only in the implementation of domestic environmental laws but also in improving the effectiveness of multilateral environmental agreements. As these networks have improved compliance and enforcement, they have also ensured the potential for leading to the rule of law, good governance and sustainable development, as they also depend upon each other.

These achievements are very significant. However, the analysis also clarifies that there are still growing weaknesses/challenges within the networks which need to be overcome with respect to two dimensions: ensuring compliance and coordination. In addition, strengthening environmental compliance and enforcement still requires renewed/continuous efforts to be undertaken to promote the coordination between key actors, such as government officials, particularly inspectors, investigators and prosecutors, legislators, judiciary, the regulated community and the public, non-governmental organizations, media, the international community, including donors and international organizations, and particularly for the compliance issue, perhaps between PNs and CMs.

Here are the lessons learned from the assessment made on the major weaknesses of the networks in the study on the basis of two dimensions – ensuring compliance and strengthening coordination.

Ensuring compliance:

- *Funding*: It is provided by international organizations (for INECE) or by the EU through projects (ECENA, RENA, REC Turkey). Nevertheless, as there is no regular financial resource for expenses, it is difficult for the networks to function effectively.
  In order to increase the funding opportunities, the networks should convince the donors that investing in the activities aiming to promote compliance not only promotes compliance and contributes to the protection of the environment, but also affects the economy as well. It should be clearly stated that this provides resource efficiency which halts the degradation of ecosystems, and the loss of biodiversity is inextricably linked to human well-being, economic growth and prosperity. If this message can be adopted by donors investing in the activities, they become more willing and able to see the networks as an opportunity and not as a threat.
- *Working Area*: ECENA, RENA and the REC Turkey Country Office do not work specifically on compliance and enforcement issues. However, ECENA and RENA have a specific working group on the issue.
  More networks specifically working on the compliance issue can be established, efforts at domestic and international levels can be strengthened for this aim, and harmonized rules can be designed for these networks.
- *Others*: Language barriers, different levels of experience and progress between member countries, low absorption capacities of public administration can also be regarded as other weaknesses.
  In order to decrease the different levels (in terms of technical, financial or administrative capacity) in countries which the networks has worked with, facilitation tools (like positive discrimination for the ones which have more restricted opportunities) for assisting them can be created.

Strengthening coordination:

- *The coordination between staff in the network*: For regional networks, every country has its own system, so a more harmonized system can be considered for better working.
- *The coordination with the sister networks*: One contact point per network for providing the coordination with others can be more helpful to prevent excessive time and service consuming.
- *NGO participation*: Despite all developments regarding this issue, deeper involvement of NGOs (particularly NGOs trained in

technical and regulatory issues in relation to the environmental *acquis*) is still required.

- *The relationship with the CMs within the network*: All four networks have no direct relation to the CMs (sometimes they just have a more or less indirect relationship).
- *The coordination between the CMs and networks*: As there is no relation between them, it appears not applicable for now.

Interviews carried out with the experts working for the networks in question show that they think that it might be beneficial to have relationships with CMs, but management of these can be difficult. For regional and local networks, it is difficult as they do not have a great deal of relations regarding the MEAs and so CMs, and so almost no experience in these issues. For INECE, it is difficult because these were not tried before by the network, and so it does not have any experience here too.

It should be underlined here that, moving into the future, the transgovernmental networks on compliance networks can appear as crucial means of ensuring compliance and coordination, but it becomes necessary to formulate a more systematic approach in addressing the problem of coordination between CMs and PNs. New channels should be sought for effective compliance and coordination, and specifically cooperation and coordination between CMs and these networks, as the most lacking side of the networks is that they have no (or little) relationships with CMs. Remarkably, the networks particularly established by the aims of promoting compliance, like INECE, are to have relationships with these mechanisms, as they can seriously contribute to the effective functioning of them, specifically to their facilitation phases. Moreover, they can contribute to the coordination between different CMs, operating like a coordinator between these mechanisms, in the long term.

Here there are some suggestions on how they can work together:

- Like NGOs, they can participate in their meetings as observers, or nominated positions can be dedicated to the networks for involvement and coordination with CMs.
- Appropriate communication mechanisms to ensure all or some participants of the networks have access to all information and to all or some proceedings of the CMs.
- Reporting arrangements can be considered, and related participants of the network can report on the related issues given by the CMs.
- For the long term, particularly, INECE as the key global network on compliance issue, can undertake the task of coordinating the relations between different CMs.

6. CONCLUSION

The design of this research was based on the main research question asking whether partnership networks can play a role in ensuring the parties' compliance with their commitments under multilateral environmental agreements and in strengthening coordination between all stakeholders and also different compliance mechanisms.

The research method applied is a comparative case analysis and interviews carried out with the experts working for the networks in question to learn their practical experiences. It rested on four case studies, INECE, ECENA, RENA and the REC Turkey country office.

It firstly clarified the concepts of compliance, compliance mechanism and partnership network. Secondly, it questioned the reasons behind the development of these networks, and the processes that they have undergone. Thirdly, it made a comparative analysis based on its four case studies and discovered their strengths and weaknesses in ensuring compliance and also strengthening coordination. Fourthly, it discussed how their weaknesses can be overcome and provided some recommendations for their improvement in ensuring better compliance and coordination.

Overall, the analysis demonstrated that all these networks at different levels – local, regional, global – play crucial roles regarding environmental compliance and enforcement issues. They appear as complementing each other. Depending on their objective, they all perform their own functions. For worldwide experience sharing and comparison of systems, the global, and maybe in some parts the regional, levels can be defined as having better tools; however for in-country coordination and communication or meeting national environmental quality targets, the national networks of certain institutions can be more efficient. Nonetheless, they have some weaknesses in terms of two aspects: ensuring compliance and coordination. Therefore, it becomes necessary to formulate new ways of addressing these issues. The most lacking side of the networks appears to be their having no (or few) relationships with CMs. Particularly, INECE as a global network with the specific aim of promoting compliance should have relationships with these mechanisms, as it can both contribute to the effective functioning of them, and also to the coordination between different CMs in the long term, operating like a coordinator between these mechanisms.

BIBLIOGRAPHY

Agenda 21, available at: http://www.unep.org/documents.multilingual/default.asp?DocumentID=52&ArticleID=56&l=en

Andresen, S., 2001, 'Global Environmental Governance: UN Fragmentation and Co-ordination', in Stokke, O.S. and Thommessen, O.B. (eds), *Yearbook of International Co-operation on Environment and Development* (pp. 19–26). London: Earthscan.

Beyerlin, U., Stoll, P.T. and Wolfrum, R., 2006, 'Conclusions from MEA Compliance', in Beyerlin, U., Stoll, P.T. and Wolfrum, R. (eds), *Ensuring Compliance with Multilateral Environmental Agreements: Academic Analysis and Views from Practice* (pp. 359–369).The Netherlands: Koninklijke Brill NV.

Bodansky, D., Brunnée, J. and Hey, E., 2007, 'International Environmental Law: Mapping the Field', in Bodansky, D., Brunnée, J. and Hey, E. (eds), *The Oxford Handbook of International Environmental Law* (pp. 1–28). New York: Oxford University Press.

Breitmeier, H., Young, O.R. and Zürn, M., 2006, *Analyzing International Environmental Regimes: From Case Study to Database*. Cambridge: MIT Press.

Chasek, P.S., Downie, D.L. and Brown, J.W., 2006, *Global Environmental Politics*. Boulder, CO: Westview Press.

Chayes, A. and Chayes, A., 1995, *The New Sovereignty: Compliance with International Regulatory Agreements*. Cambridge, MA: Harvard University Press.

Chayes, A.H., Chayes, A. and Mitchell, R.B., 1995, 'Active Compliance Management in Environmental Treaties', in Lang, W. (ed.), *Sustainable Development and International Law* (pp. 75–89). London: Boston: Graham & Trotman/M. Nijhoff.

Chayes, A., Chayes, A.H. and Mitchell, R.B., 1998, 'Managing Compliance: A Comparative Perspective', in Weiss, E.B. and Jacobson, H.K. (eds), *Engaging Countries: Strengthenıng Compliance wıth International Environmental Accords* (pp. 39–62). Cambridge, MA: MIT Press.

Churchill, R.R. and Ulfstein, G., 2000, 'Autonomous Institutional Arrangements in Multilateral Environmental Agreements: A Little Noticed Phenomenon in International Law', *The American Journal of International Law*, 94(4), 623–659.

Crossen, T., 2003, 'Multilateral Environmental Agreements and the Compliance Continuum' (2003), The Berkeley Electronic Press Legal Series, p. 36. available at: https://www.ippc.int/sites/default/files/documents/1182330508307_Compliance_and_theory_MEAs.pdf

Crossen, T.E., 2004, 'The Kyoto Protocol Compliance Regime: Origins, Outcomes and the Amendment Dilemma', *Official Journal of the Resource Management Law Association of New Zealand Inc.*, I(XII), 1–6.

Decision 21/23, United Nations Environment Programme Governing Council (9 February 2001) available at: http://www.unep.org/gc/gc21/

Ehrmann, M., 2002, 'Procedures of Compliance Control in International Environmental Treaties', *Colorado Journal of International Environmental Law and Policy*, 13(2), 377–444.

Enderlin, T., 2003, 'Alpine Convention: A Different Compliance Mechanism', *Environmental Policy and Law*, 33(3–4), 155–162.

Epiney, A., 2006, 'The Role of NGOs in the Process of Ensuring Compliance with MEAs', in Beyerlin, U., Stoll, P.T. and Wolfrum, R. (eds), *Ensuring Compliance with Multilateral Environmental Agreements: A Dialogue between Practitioners and Academia* (pp. 273–300). The Netherlands: Koninklijke Brill NV.

Fisher, R., 1981, *Improving Compliance with International Law*. Charlottesville: University Press of Virginia.

Handl, G., 1997, 'Compliance Control Mechanisms and International Environmental Obligations', *Tulane Journal of International and Comparative Law*, 5, 29–51.
Himmelman, A.T., 2001, 'On Coalitions and the Transformation of Power Relations: Collaborative Betterment and Collaborative Empowerment', *American Journal of Community Psychology*, 29(2), 277–278.
Hunter, D., Salzman, J. and Zaelke, D., 2002, *International Environmental Law and Policy*. New York: Foundation Press.
International Union for Conservation of Nature and Natural Resources (IUCN) Environmental Law Programme 2010, 'Draft International Covenant on Environment and Development', Environmental Policy and Law Paper No. 31 Rev. 3. Fourth edition: Updated Text. Prepared in cooperation with the International Council of Environmental Law. Gland, Switzerland: IUCN. Available at: http://www.uncsd2012.org/content/documents/IUCN%20Intl%20Covenant%20on%20Env%20and%20Dev%20EPLP-031-rev3.pdf
Jacobson, H.K. and Weiss, E.B., 1998, 'Assessing the Record and Designing Strategies to Engage Countries', in Weiss, E.B. and Jacobson, H.K. (eds), *Engaging Countries: Strengthening Compliance with International Environmental Accords* (pp. 511–554). Cambridge, MA: MIT Press.
Lang, W., 1995, 'From Environmental Protection to Sustainable Development: Challenges for International Law', in Lang, W. (ed.), *Sustainable Development and International Law*. London and Boston: Graham & Trotman/M. Nijhoff.
Levy, M.A., Young, O.R. and Zürn, M., 1995, 'The Study of International Regimes', *EJoIR*, 1(3), 267–330.
Mitchell, R.B., 1994, 'Regime Design Matters: Intentional Oil Pollution and Treaty Compliance', *International Organization*, 48(3), 425–458.
Mitchell, R.B., 1996, 'Compliance Theory: An Overview', in Werksman, J., Cameron, J. and Roderick, P. (eds), *Improving Compliance with International Environmental Law* (pp. 3–28). London: Earthscan.
Najam, A., Papa, M. and Taiyab, N., 2006, *Global Environmental Governance: A Reform Agenda*. Available at: http://www.iisd.org/pdf/2006/geg.pdf
Oberthür, S., 2001, 'Linkages between the Montreal and Kyoto Protocols, Enhancing Synergies between Protecting the Ozone Layer and the Global Climate', *International Environmental Agreements: Politics, Law and Economics*, 1(3), 357–377.
Oberthür, S., 2002, *Clustering of Multilateral Environmental Agreements: Potentials and Limitations. International Environmental Agreements: Politics, Law and Economics*, 2, 317–340. The Netherlands: Kluwer Academic Publishers.
Oberthür, S., 2006, 'The Climate Change Regime: Interactions with ICAO, IMO and the EU Burden-Sharing Agreement', in Oberthür, S. and Gebring, T. (eds), *Institutional Interaction in GEG: Synergy and Conflict among International and EU Policies* (pp. 53–72). Cambridge, MA: MIT Press.
Oberthür, S. and Gebring, T., 2006, 'Conceptual Foundations of Institutional Interaction' in Oberthür, S. and Gebring, T. (eds), *Institutional Interaction in GEG: Synergy and Conflict among International and EU Policies* (pp. 19–52). Cambridge, MA: MIT Press.
Pink, G.W., 2010, 'Environmental Enforcement Networks: A Qualitative Analysis'. Available at: http://papers.ssrn.com/sol3/papers.cfm?abstract_id=1803179
Pitea, C., 2009, 'Multiplication and Overlap of Non-Compliance Procedures and Mechanisms: Towards Better Coordination?', in Treves, T., Tanzi, A., Pineschi,

L., Pitea, C., Ragni, C. and Jacur, F.R. (eds), *Non-Compliance Procedures and Mechanisms and the Effectiveness of International Environmental Agreements* (pp. 439–452). The Hague: T.M.C. Asser Press.

Raustiala, K., 2001, *Reporting and Review Institutions in 10 Selected Multilateral Environmental Agreements*, 14. Available at: http://www.unep.org/geo/GEO3/pdfs/MEA%20PM%2070%20Part%20A%20FFF.pdf (accessed 18 April 2010).

Raustiala, K., 2002, 'The Architecture of International Cooperation: Transgovernmental Networks and the Future of International Law', *Virginia Journal of International Law*, 43(1), 1–92. Available at: http://www2.law.ucla.edu/raustiala/publications/Architecture%20of%20International%20Cooperation.pdf (accessed 10 May 2010).

Raustiala, K. and Slaughter, A., 2002, 'International Law, International Relations and Compliance', in Carlsnaes, W., Risse, T. and Simmons, B.A. (eds), *The Handbook of International Relations* (pp. 538–558). London: Sage.

Rio+20 Report, 2012, *Report of the United Nations Conference on Sustainable Development*. Rio de Janeiro, Brazil, 20–22 June 2012. A/CONF.216/16. Available at: http://www.uncsd2012.org/content/documents/814UNCSD%20REPORT%20final%20revs.pdf

Romano, C.P.R., 2007, 'International Dispute Settlement', in Bodansky, D., Brunnée, J. and Hey, E. (eds), *The Oxford Handbook of International Environmental Law* (pp. 1036–1056). New York: Oxford University Press.

Slaughter, A., 1997, 'The Real New World Order', *Foreign Affairs*, 76(5), 183–197.

State Government of Victoria, 2007, available at: http://unpan1.un.org/intradoc/groups/public/documents/apcity/unpan031822.pdf

State Government of Victoria, Department of Education (n.d.), available at: http://www.education.vic.gov.au/Documents/school/principals/community/relationshipcontinuum.pdf

Stephens, T., 2009, *International Courts and Environmental Protection*. Cambridge and New York: Cambridge University Press.

Tanzi, A. and Pitea, C., 2009, 'Non-Compliance Mechanisms: Lessons Learned and the Way Forward', in Treves, T., Tanzi, A., Pineschi, L., Pitea, C., Ragni, C. and Jacur, F.R. (eds), *Non-Compliance Procedures and Mechanisms and the Effectiveness of International Environmental Agreements* (pp. 569–580). The Hague: T.M.C. Asser Press.

Treves, T., Tanzi, A., Pineschi, L., Pitea, C., Ragni, C. and Jacur, F.R. (eds), 2009, *Non-Compliance Procedures and Mechanisms and the Effectiveness of International Environmental Agreements*. The Hague: T.M.C. Asser Press.

UNEP, 2006, *Manual on Compliance with and Enforcement of Multilateral Environmental Agreements*. Nairobi: UNEP. Available at: http://www.unep.org/publications/contents/pub_details_search.asp?ID=3905

UNEP, 2007, *Comparative Analysis of Compliance Mechanisms under Selected Multilateral Environmental Agreements*. Nairobi: UNEP. Available at: http://www.unep.org/publications/contents/pub_details_search.asp?ID=3926

Wang, X. and Wiser, G., 2002, 'The Implementation and Compliance Regimes under the Climate Change Convention and its Kyoto Protocol', *Review of European Community and International Environmental Law*, 11(2), 181–198.

Wasserman, C.E., 1994, *The Principles of Environmental Enforcement and Beyond: Building Institutional Capacity. Third International Conference on Environmental Enforcement Proceedings*, Vol.1. Available at: http://nepis.epa.gov/Exe/ZyPDF.cgi/20005DN2.PDF?Dockey=20005DN2.PDF

Weiss, E.B., 1999, 'Understanding Compliance with International Environmental Agreements: The Baker's Dozen Myths', *University of Richmond Law Review*. Available at: http://heinonline.org/HOL/Page?handle=hein.journals/urich32&div=65&g_sent=1&collection=journals

Weiss, E.B. and Jacobson, H.K., 2001, 'Strengthening Compliance with International Environmental Accords', in Paul F. Diehl (ed.), *The Politics of Global Governance, International Organizations in an Interdependent World* (pp. 406–435). Boulder, CO: Lynne Rienner.

Wolfrum, R. and Matz, N., 2003, *Conflicts in International Environmental Law*. Berlin: Springer.

Zaelke, D., Kaniaru, D. and Kružíková, E. (eds), 2005, *Making Law Work: Environmental Compliance & Sustainable Development, Volume 2*. London: Cameron May Ltd.

Zhao, J., 2005, 'Implementing International Environmental Treaties in Developing Countries: China's Compliance with the Montreal Protocol', *Global Environmental Politics*, 5(1), 58–81.

5. Evaluating and assessing environmental enforcement networks: through use of the network evaluation matrix

Grant Pink* and James Lehane†

1. INTRODUCTION

Environmental Enforcement Networks (hereafter EENs or networks) generally have different foci in terms of commodities, sectors and regulated communities. Networks can also be quite specific in terms of the nature of their regulatory, compliance and enforcement activities, initiatives (e.g. undertaking joint inspections or collaborative projects) and responses (whether administrative, civil or criminal in nature)[1] that the EEN undertakes.

For the purposes of this chapter, the term environmental enforcement network/s (EEN/s) is used. Equally, environmental compliance and enforcement network/s could have been used as they are both used somewhat interchangeably. Irrespective, both are *networks* that direct their efforts towards ensuring that environmental laws, regulations and standards are complied with.

This chapter considers the *past*, *present* and *future* of EENs, as their role, purpose, utility and importance has been the subject of much discussion.

* Adjunct Research Fellow, School of Law, University of New England (UNE), Armidale, NSW, 2351, Australia, gpink2@une.edu.au; PhD Candidate, School of Behavioural, Cognitive and Social Sciences, UNE, gpink2@myune.edu.au

† Assistant Director (Investigations), Australian Pesticides and Veterinary Medicines Authority. C/- PO Box 6182, Kingston, ACT 2604, Australia, email: james.lehane@apvma.gov.au

[1] For more information on the various sanctions being used against environmental crime and transnational environmental crime, refer to Pink, G, 'Law Enforcement Responses to Transnational Environmental Crime: Choices, Challenges and Culture', Transnational Environmental Crime Project Working Paper 5/2013 (Canberra: Department of International Relations, Australian National University 2013).

Moreover, this discussion has increasingly resulted in the focused research of Regional EENs.[2]

This chapter commences with an overview of EENs in terms of their past and present before moving on to consider their future. Given the nature of EENs and the fact that they will largely shape their own future, the central issue of this chapter considers the research results and analysis arising from the input of the research participants who are actively engaged in Regional EENs. The chapter concludes with recommendations based upon their input.

2. BACKGROUND – ENVIRONMENTAL ENFORCEMENT NETWORKS

It is acknowledged that environmental crime is increasingly becoming inter-jurisdictional and global in nature. In response, environmental compliance and enforcement agencies ('environmental agencies') are looking for ways

---

[2] Farmer, A, *Handbook of Environmental Protection & Enforcement: Principles & Practice* (London: Earthscan 2007); Lehane, J & Pink, G, 'Evolution of a Regional Environmental Enforcement Network: The Australasian Environmental Law Enforcement and Regulators neTwork (AELERT)' in *INECE, 9th International Conference on Environmental Compliance and Enforcement, Conference Proceedings, 24 June 2011, Whistler, British Columbia, Canada* (Washington 2011). Available at http://inece.org/conference/9/proceedings/76_LehanePink.pdf; Nicholson, M, 'Networking in Europe: How Networking and Cooperation have Helped Respond to Environmental Compliance and Enforcement Challenges in IMPEL Member Countries' in *INECE, 9th International Conference on Environmental Compliance and Enforcement, Conference Proceedings, 20–24 June 2011, Whistler, British Columbia, Canada* (Washington, 2011). Available at http://inece.org/conference/9/proceedings/77_Nicholson.pdf; O'Leary, G & Lynott, DJ, 'The Effective Use of an Environmental Enforcement Network in Ireland' in *INECE, 9th International Conference on Environmental Compliance and Enforcement, Conference Proceedings, 24 June 2011, Whistler, British Columbia, Canada* (Washington, 2011). Available at http://inece.org/conference/9/proceedings/78_O'LearyLynott.pdf; Opondo, GK, 'Creating and Sustaining Regional Environmental Compliance and Enforcement Networks: Lessons from the East African Network for Environmental Compliance & Enforcement' in *INECE, 9th International Conference on Environmental Compliance and Enforcement, Conference Proceedings, 24 June 2011, Whistler, British Columbia, Canada* (Washington, 2011). Available at http://inece.org/conference/9/proceedings/79_Opondo.pdf; and Stas, A, 'The Flemish High Council of Environmental Enforcement – A Coordinated Environmental Enforcement Policy' in *INECE, 9th International Conference on Environmental Compliance and Enforcement, Conference Proceedings, 24 June 2011, Whistler, British Columbia, Canada* (Washington, 2011). Available at http://inece.org/conference/9/proceedings/82_Stas.pdf

to increase their regulatory reach.[3] One such way that agencies are doing this is through participation in environmental enforcement networks, which have proliferated since the 1990s. This proliferation has seen practitioners and agencies increasingly involving themselves and investing in networks.[4]

The mission statements of *networks* contain information about their respective focus, goals and objectives. The literature establishes that there are a number of characteristics which appear common to networks, such as:

- Building relationships and strengthening capacity across jurisdictions;
- Sharing of information and experiences;
- Raising awareness and improving environmental compliance and environment efforts; and
- Developing consistent and standardised practices and procedures to support the implementation of environmental enforcement.[5]

2.1 The Past – A Brief History of Networks

EENs have been in existence for around 25 years. During this time, EENs have been established at sub-national, national, regional and international levels. They focus on various environmental commodities and topics, including but not limited to:

- Wildlife smuggling; [6]
- Electronic waste and organised crime; [7]

---

[3] Slaughter, A-M, *A New World Order* (Princeton, NJ: Princeton University Press, 2004), p. 55.

[4] Pink, G, 'Assessing the Utility of Environmental Enforcement Networks: Maximising Benefits to Members' in *INECE, 9th International Conference on Environmental Compliance and Enforcement, Conference Proceedings, 24 June 2011, Whistler, British Columbia, Canada* (Washington, 2011), p. 797.

[5] Pink, G, 'Environmental Enforcement Networks: A Qualitative Analysis' (December 7, 2010). Available at Social Science Research Network: http://ssrn.com/abstract=1803179 (accessed 14 April 2011).

[6] Scanlon, J, 'Speech delivered to the 79th Interpol General Assembly, 8 November, Doha, Qatar' (2010), at para. 8. Available at: http://www.cites.org/eng/news/SG/2010/SG_statement_interpol_doha.shtml (accessed 22 June 2011); Association of Southeast Asian Nations Wildlife Enforcement Network (ASEAN-WEN) *Wildlife Enforcement Network: Action Update July–September 2010* (n.d). Available at: http://www.asean-wen.org/index.php?option=com_docman&task=doc_download&gid=45&Itemid=96 (accessed 18 July 2011).

[7] International Criminal Police Organization (INTERPOL) *Electronic Waste and Organised Crime: Assessing the Links: Phase II Report for the Interpol Pollution Crimes Working Group* (France: INTERPOL, 2009).

- Ozone-depleting substances; [8] and
- Capacity building.[9]

EENs have directed their efforts towards different disciplines such as policy development, operational (investigative and inspection) activities, capacity building and information sharing. A common theme running through EENs irrespective of their jurisdiction, commodity or discipline has been the need for networks to demonstrate where they add value (referred to as the *value proposition* for members).

In response to the *value proposition* issue, governing bodies and the secretariats of EENs operate with a continuous pressure to find balance, satisfying and delivering to the wide-ranging needs and expectations of members. This quite often, but not always, can involve issues associated with *Membership*, *Finances*, *Governance*, *Support* and *Deliverables.*

The Network Evaluation Matrix[10] – an assessment tool for EENs, designed by the authors in 2011 – puts forward a range of maturity levels relating to these issues. It remains up to each individual EEN to determine what form, function and activity it wants to be or pursue. Whether or not an EEN seeks to migrate between the NEM levels of maturity remains the decision of the EEN leadership team on behalf of its membership.

---

[8] United Nations Environment Programme (UNEP) *Networking Counts: Combating Illegal Trade in Ozone Depleting Substances* (Paris: UNEP 2007).

[9] Implementation and Enforcement of Environmental Law (IMPEL) *Enforcement of EU Waste Shipment Regulation: 'Learning by Doing'* (Interim Project Report, 12 October 2009) at p. iii. Available at: http://www.vrominspectie.nl/Images/Interim%20%20Report%20IMPEL%20TFS_tcm293–273297.pdf (accessed 18 January 2011); Heiss, R, Ruessink, H, Isarin, N, Koparova, M and Grabiel, D, 'International Hazardous Waste Inspection Project at Seaports: Results and Recommendations' in *INECE, 9th International Conference on Environmental Compliance and Enforcement, Conference Proceedings, 24 June 2011, Whistler, British Columbia, Canada* (Washington, 2011). Available at http://inece.org/conference/9/proceedings/25_HeissEtAl.pdf; International Network for Environmental Compliance and Enforcement – Seaport Environmental Security Network (INECE-SESN) *International Hazardous Waste Inspection Project at Seaports: Results and Recommendations* (2010). Available at: http://www.inece.org/seaport/exercise/INECE_SeaportInspectionProjectOutcomes_22dec.pdf (accessed 18 June 2011); Pink, G and Lehane, J 'Environmental Enforcement Networks: Their Role in Climate Change Enforcement' in White, R (ed.) *Climate Change from a Criminological Perspective* (New York: Springer 2012).

[10] For more information on the launch of the NEM, refer to page 9 of *INECE, 9th International Conference on Environmental Compliance and Enforcement: 24 June 2011, Whistler, British Columbia, Canada, Proceedings* (Washington: INECE 2011).

Progress (in terms of network maturity) may be unwanted, unnecessary, not achievable or not attainable due to a variety of management, political, economic or structural factors. The lens through which the NEM is viewed may influence any assessments with the interpretation of NEM criteria factors potentially resulting in assessments that are accurate to local conditions and reality. For instance, a small sub-national informal network could be found to be *Mature* to *Well Established* due to the factors within its sphere of influence. By the same token, a large regional EEN may be assessed as *Fragile* given the viewpoint of reviewers at a certain point in time.

2.2 The Present – Contemporary Pressures and Challenges for Networks

Value proposition is a ubiquitous issue which has the potential to influence most aspects of a network's operations and activities; as such it underpinned the development of the NEM.

2.2.1 Development of the Network Evaluation Matrix (NEM)

The NEM is an assessment tool to categorise the maturity levels of existing networks. The NEM is based upon:

- Five levels of network maturity: *Absent*, *Emerging*, *Fragile*, *Maturing* and *Well Established*; and
- Five core functional categories: *Membership*, *Finances*, *Governance*, *Support* and *Deliverables.*

Each of the five core functional categories is further broken down into sub-criteria, which show the relative maturity of the network within the separate core functional categories. These ratings collectively result in an overall level of EEN maturity. A summary of the NEM is depicted in Table 5.1.

The NEM is an easy to use tool based upon other organisational

Table 5.1 Summary of the Network Evaluation Matrix

	Membership	Finances	Governance	Support	Deliverables
Absent Emerging	Membership	Budget	Access	Liaison	Events
Fragile	Leadership	Contributions	Review	Support base	Outcomes
Maturing Well Established	Value	Project funding	Structures	Supporting functions	Products

capability maturity models.[11] The complete matrix, including descriptors of sub-criteria, is reproduced in Appendix 5.1. Importantly, the NEM deliberately excludes reference to specific commodities and professional streams to reduce the risk of any one area or criterion being prioritised through additional weighting.

2.2.2 Launch of the Network Evaluation Matrix

The NEM was formally launched at the Regional Networks Summit as part of the Ninth International Conference for Environmental Compliance and Enforcement in 2011. The authors tested the prototype on their regional EEN peers and reported at the time of launching.[12] As an indicator of network evolution, the NEM appeared to provide guidance on areas for improvement and use as a focusing tool.

2.2.3 Regional networks – a self-assessment opportunity

Subsequent to the 2011 Regional Networks Summit and influenced by the interest shown by participants in the NEM, the International Network for Environmental Compliance and Enforcement (INECE) developed and published an online manual, the 'Manual for Creating and Sustaining Regional Environmental Compliance and Enforcement Networks'.[13] The Manual draws heavily on the NEM's components.

2.2.4 Purpose and objectives of this research

The purpose of this research was to subject the NEM to further testing by having a random selection of six Regional EENs use the NEM to conduct a self-assessment of their network. Survey participants were asked to:

- Use the NEM to rate their network's maturity against each of the individual five core functional categories as well as overall;
- Indicate how their EENs overall rating from using the NEM compared to what their intuitive rating of their EEN was prior to using the NEM;
- Indicate whether or not the NEM was helpful in terms of the future planning for their EEN and whether or not their EEN would be prepared to be involved in a peer review process; and

---

[11] Carnegie Mellon University, *Capability Maturity Model Integration* (2011). Available at http://www.sei.cmu.edu/cmmi/ (accessed 14 March 2011).

[12] Lehane and Pink (2011).

[13] International Network for Environmental Compliance and Enforcement, *Manual for Creating and Sustaining Regional Environmental Compliance and Enforcement Networks* (2012). Online publication available at: http://inece.org/resource/network_manual/

- Provide suggestions for how the NEM might be improved and for how a peer review process might be conducted.

The objective of this research was to ensure that the Regional EENs fully considered and tested the NEM such that it is considered fit for purpose, so that it might be considered a necessary assessment tool that forms a part of a range of activities on which to base a peer review process of networks.

2.3 The Future – Where Next for Networks?

What does the future hold for networks? Will they change substantially, a moderate amount, or will they largely stay the same into the future? While it is highly likely that networks will remain in place for some time to come, their specific form, function and focus should change over time in response to shifting needs and requirements of members. This belief is based upon the following facts:

- Networks share more in common with one another than they have differences;
- Globalisation and technological advances have increased the general ease by which transnational environmental crime can be transacted;
- The public expect a coordinated response by its environmental regulators and enforcers;[14] and
- Reduced public expenditure tends to require innovative approaches, and establishing or maintaining an enforcement network may be one appropriate approach.[15]

Gerardu and Wasserman expressed the original and foundational argument in favour of EENs over 20 years ago and the sentiment expressed remains and will continue to be current in the field of effective environmental regulation. They suggested that: '[it] is not only possible but essential that nations seek to learn from each other what works and what does not work to achieve widespread compliance with environmental requirements in different settings'.[16]

---

[14] Pink (2010), p.1.

[15] See Chapter 6 in this volume.

[16] Gerardu, J and Wasserman, C (eds), 'Conference Purpose and Goals' in *International Conference on Environmental Enforcement: Conference Proceedings (Volume II, September 22–25, 1992)* (Budapest, Hungary 1992), p.9.

3. RESEARCH METHODOLOGY

3.1 Overview

A mixed method approach was used as part of an exploratory study to examine how officials engaged in or having previous experience with EENs might consider how the NEM could be improved and be developed further as part of a peer review process. The study sought to gain a more comprehensive understanding of the administrative, project, operational and policy challenges confronting Regional EENs so that practical solutions and support could be provided.

3.2 Research Participants

The research focused on the perspectives of a small sample of officials (research participants). The research participants were identified through purposive sampling.[17] The purposive approach sought to '. . . identify specific groups . . . [who] possess characteristics or live in circumstances relevant to the social phenomenon being studied'.[18] Data was collected directly from the research participants in the form of a combined short multiple-choice and short answer questionnaire.

3.3 Sample Set

Information provided by the INECE Secretariat, at the time of writing, indicated that there are approximately 20 major EENs operating around the world. As such, a random sample of six Regional EENs was made with three individuals involved in the operations of each EEN being offered the opportunity to be a research participant. This sample set was identified as being statistically valid, with the 18 research participants deemed suitable to represent the broad views across the six EENs.[19] The research participants were selected based on their involvement within the EENs, at the board, secretariat and member level, with one participant per EEN role being chosen for each level of involvement. However, in one instance, one

---

[17] Miles, MB and Huberman, AM, *Qualitative Data Analysis: An Expanded Source Book* (2nd edn, Thousand Oaks, CA: Sage Publications 1994).

[18] Mays, N and Pope, C, 'Rigour and Qualitative Research', *British Medical Journal* (1995), vol. 311, 109–112 at p. 109.

[19] Torbeck, LD 'Statistical Solutions: Square Root of (N) + 1 Sampling Plan: Is the square root of (N) + 1 a statistically valid scheme?', *Pharmaceutical Technology* (2009), vol. 33, issue 10, 128.

of the EENs provided an additional response for one of the levels (it is for this reason that the total sample set was 19).

3.4 Data Collection

Data collection involved asking the research participants 11 questions. Nine of which were multiple-choice survey questions and were quantitative in nature, and two were short answer questions that sought more qualitative information.

The responses of the research participants were de-identified by coding with a prefix. The prefix 'RB' was allocated to research participants that were either a member of the network's board or governing body; the prefix 'RS' to those who worked within the network's secretariat; and the prefix 'RM' to those that were active members of the network with sufficient experience and knowledge of the activities and operations of the network to be able to complete the survey. In addition to the prefix, a number from 1 to 19 was allocated chronologically across all respondent codes to ensure full accounting of responses.

Of the 19 surveys disseminated to research participants, 14 completed responses were received, representing a 74% response rate.

3.4.1 Survey questions

Research participants were asked to carry out a self-assessment of their EEN by using and reviewing the NEM, and answering 11 survey questions using predominantly Likert Scale responses. Likert Scale responses involve providing a series of options to statements where respondents are asked to indicate their level of agreement or disagreement. The questions are reproduced in Appendix 5.2.

3.4.2 Data collation

The data was collated into a series of Microsoft Excel spreadsheets, with one spreadsheet for each question. The responses were analysed and depicted in a variety of charts to specifically draw out the findings. In respect to the short response questions, Microsoft Word documents were created through which responses could be compared and contrasted so that keywords and themes could be identified and explored.

4. RESEARCH RESULTS

Responses against the five core functional categories obtained the following results:

Question 1 – Members

The *Maturing* rating at 64% (n = 9) was by far the most prominent rating. When combined with a *Well Established* rating at 21% (n = 3) the result was that 85% of the research participants rated their EEN at *Maturing* or higher. Only two respondents categorised their EEN as being *Fragile* in this category.

Question 2 – Finances

The *Maturing* rating at 71% (n = 10) was by far the most prominent rating. When combined with a *Well Established* rating at 14% (n = 2) the result was that 85% of the research participants rated their EEN at *Maturing* or higher. Two respondents assessed their EEN as being *Fragile* based on the *Finances* criteria.

Question 3 – Governance

The *Maturing* rating at 64% (n = 9) was by far the most prominent rating. When combined with a *Well Established* rating at 21% (n = 3) the result was that 85% of the research participants rated their EEN at *Maturing* or higher. Two respondents rated their EENs as *Fragile* in relation to *Governance*, with none reporting *Governance* as *Absent* or *Emerging*.

Question 4 – Support

The ratings for *Support* were spread across four ratings: *Emerging* (7% (n = 1)), *Fragile* (14% (n = 2)), *Maturing* (50% (n = 7)), and *Well Established* (28% (n = 4)). Collectively, 78% of the research participants rated their EEN at *Maturing* or higher.

Question 5 – Deliverables

In terms of *Deliverables*, the *Maturing* rating at 57% (n = 8) was the most prominent rating. Combined with a *Well Established* rating at 43% (n = 6), all of the research participants rated their EENs as *Maturing* or higher for *Deliverables*.

Question 6 – Overall Rating when Using the NEM

When applying the NEM as the basis for their assessment, the combined overall ratings for the EENs were: *Fragile* (14% (n = 2)), *Maturing*

(71% (n = 10)) and *Well Established* (14% (n = 2)) respectively. Based on this, 85% of the research participants rated their EEN at *Maturing* or higher.

Question 7 – Respondents' Overall Rating when Compared with their Intuitive pre-NEM Thoughts

When the research participants were asked how the NEM-based rating compared to what they intuitively thought the rating of their EEN would be, all but one thought it was at the level they expected it to be. The remaining research participant thought the rating as indicated by the NEM was lower than expected.

Question 8 – Usefulness of the NEM

None of the research participants considered that using and applying the NEM was *Of no use at all*. Thirty-six per cent (or n = 5) suggested that the NEM was *Very helpful*, and when combined with the 28% (n=4) who considered it to be *Somewhat helpful*, 62% of research participants rated the usefulness of the NEM at *Somewhat helpful* or higher. Where 21% (n = 3) found the NEM *Neither un-useful or useful*, another 14% (n = 2) only found the NEM to be *Of some use*.

Question 9 – Preparedness to be Involved in NEM Peer-review Process

The research participants universally supported this proposal. One research participant made a comment beyond the scope of the question but within this context, there was unanimous support for this proposal. Research participants indicated that they thought their EEN would (57% (n = 8)) or would be likely (36% (n = 5)) to participate in a peer review of EENs. The 'unsure/unknown' response from the research participant (7% (n = 1)) for the reasons above is considered an anomaly.

Question 10 – Sought Suggestions for Improvements to the NEM

The written responses provided by the research participants for this question were diverse. They ranged from suggesting that no changes, some changes and in one instance major changes to the NEM should be considered. The diversity of responses is evident in the following selected extracts:

> [i]t has also had an impact on how the network is viewed by the members. Some see their membership as an obligation rather than an advantage (RS14)
>
> I was impressed and do not really have any suggestions for improvement . . . (RS8)

> . . . each indicator within a functional category sometimes varied and did not always fit within the pre-determined level of maturity . . . [adding that] . . . these elements may not all progress at the same rate at the same time. (RS5)
>
> I think that the sections of membership, finance, governance and support should be consolidated into 2–3 categories as the evaluation is too heavily weighted on the administration of the network. (RB10)
>
> The maturity rating could be (made) more detailed, especially for those criteria that are not yet well established – to get a better insight into what elements need more work. (RM15)
>
> I think it is certainly a very useful instrument. The only issue is that you put always three different items to judge the maturity. (RB13)
>
> Difficult to determine maturity category for 'support' and 'deliverables' as some relevant sub-categories are in one level and others in another level. (RS11)
>
> [with] . . . self-assessment, there is the likelihood that we may apply our own prejudices (sometimes unknowingly) to determine our level of success and maturity. (RS17)

Question 11 – Sought Suggestions for How a Peer-to-peer Review of EENs Might be Progressed

Responses provided here followed on from Question 9 and even with the anomalous response, the research participants unanimously indicated that their EEN would most likely be interested in participating in a peer review of EENs. In terms of suggestions as to how such a process might be advanced, the research participants volunteered the following:

> . . . [some aspects used in] a peer review procedure for reviewing individual country performance . . . might be useful in peer review of EENs. (RB7)
>
> It may be difficult for a peer EEN to assess another EEN, e.g. on what evidence would they be able to assess all elements . . . Objective evidence would be most useful I'd suspect. Perhaps member survey would be useful for this, perhaps member survey is an indicator of maturity in itself? (RS5)
>
> Peer to peer review is probably best undertaken by a mature EEN and used to help an emerging or fragile network to address its problems. It is expected that a mature network would have relevant lessons to pass on . . . (RS2)
>
> . . . let one EEN make an assessment concerning the outcomes (papers, guidelines, events . . .) of another EEN by comparing the outcomes with their own. This also makes it a 'best practices learning' and gives the EEN new ideas on how to serve its members better. (RS14)
>
> . . . perhaps small bilateral working groups could be established to review good practices and procedures as well as what we would term as 'opportunities for development'. And 'Practically, this could be delivered at the next INECE conference'. (RS8)
>
> Shared case studies on how network activities delivered outcomes for the environment, what worked [and] what didn't. (RB10)
>
> Of course in theory it is very well possible to organise a peer review since (differently than for enforcement) one has clear benchmarks thanks to your NEM. The best method would probably be the way one organises research assessment

in academia as well: to appoint an international committee of experts under the heading of an international independent organisation (such as e.g. INECE) and ask them to evaluate different networks. It should be clear from the outset that the criteria to judge the EENs are clear. Given the existence of the NEM that should not be a problem. (RB13)

Establish EEN Review Working Group based on survey findings – progress from there. (RS11)

A pilot project for select[ed] networks might be a good beginning point. And . . . peer review will work best where the assessed is prepared to provide documented evidence to enable the assessor to make an objective judgement. (RS17)

5. ANALYSIS AND DISCUSSION

5.1 Utility of the Network Evaluation Matrix

This small, but focused, exploratory study reinforced the utility of the NEM. It did so through considered responses based on the comprehensive and diverse experience of research participants who all had key roles and/ or experience with one or more regional EEN.

Given the research participants' wealth of experience and knowledge of their respective networks, the group was well placed to provide input and make recommendations around future and more focused usage of the NEM.

5.2 Issues Arising from the Results

It is beyond the scope of this paper to investigate issues relating to definitions, for example, one respondent provided comment that indicated a different interpretation of regional (e.g. sub-regional within a nation state as opposed to the broader regional across nation states concept).

Based on the results, at this point in time, it is considered that the NEM need not be changed. The NEM is not a 'one size that fits all *perfectly*' model, rather it is a 'one size that fits all *adequately*' model – especially as part of a peer review process.

Many research participants proposed amendments to the NEM that would give it a more specific emphasis. There may be scope and benefit in adapting the NEM by developing subsets which could be commodity, sector and stakeholder specific. For example, given the interest in establishing global wildlife enforcement networks, it is conceivable that a highly specific and customised NEM may be something that administrators, practitioners and sponsors might consider a worthwhile pursuit. However, this iteration of the NEM retains its original and more general application.

5.3 Usefulness of the Process

This body of research proved useful to further test the utility and robustness of the NEM. The responses and comments of the research participants could be used to inform the basis of further work and discussions by an expert panel or similar that may be established to progress the peer review process.

5.4 Improvements and Future Application

The research participants were comfortable and satisfied that the NEM was 'fit for purpose', but noted that some improvements might be considered. Given the comments provided, these improvements range from minor and functional to the NEM's overall philosophical approach. Not all of the recommended changes fall within the specific intent and scope of what the NEM was designed and developed to do. However, these suggestions may prove useful and form the basis for the development of an additional and more specific assessment tool. There is clearly scope to modify or augment the NEM with the authors taking further advice and considering the relevant specific components.

5.5 Next Steps

The research participants made a clear and strong preference, as part of this research, for the progression of the NEM towards a peer review process being something that should be pursued with a view to being established. This approach now needs to be further tested and explored during subsequent bilateral and multilateral gatherings of EENs.

6. CONCLUSION

This chapter has provided an overview of what environmental enforcement networks (EENs) are – and briefly overviewed the circumstances in which they are established – and detailed what it is they focus their efforts on.

The research has also outlined some of the challenges that EENs face. In many ways, these challenges relate to an ongoing tension for EENs to develop products and services, while creating opportunities for members, that enable them to better and more effectively carry out their environmental compliance and enforcement obligations as regulators and enforcers.

The Network Evaluation Matrix (NEM) was used by a group of research participants to undertake a short self-assessment of their EEN.

The research identified a number of follow-up actions that require further consideration.

This research supports the recommendations of its participants and advocates for the establishment of an independent or collective expert panel/committee focused on the peer-to-peer review process. An entity such as International Network for Environmental Compliance and Enforcement (INECE) may be best placed to facilitate, if not oversee, such arrangements.

Finally, the broader use and application of the NEM, by all EENs, will allow for the focused and sustained refinement of the NEM. The establishment of peer reviews of regional EENs is an ideal precursor activity to advance the support and guidance for regional EENs. Such reviews could occur when neighbouring regional EENs come together at bilateral events or when regional EENs come together multilaterally under the auspices of a global conference focused on environmental enforcement networks.

BIBLIOGRAPHY

Association of Southeast Asian Nations Wildlife Enforcement Network (ASEAN-WEN) *Wildlife Enforcement Network: Action Update July-September 2010* (n.d.), http://www.asean-wen.org/index.php/reports-publications/file/27-asean-wen-action-update-july-september-2010 (accessed 18 July 2011).

Carnegie Mellon University, *Capability Maturity Model Integration* (2011), http://www.sei.cmu.edu/cmmi/ (accessed 14 March 2011).

Clifford, M and Edwards, T, *Environmental Crime* (2nd edn, Burlington MA: Jones & Bartlett Learning 2012).

Farmer, A, *Handbook of Environmental Protection & Enforcement: Principles & Practice* (London: Earthscan 2007).

Gerardu, J and Wasserman, C (eds), 'Conference Purpose and Goals' in *International Conference on Environmental Enforcement: Conference Proceedings (Volume II, September 22–25, 1992)* (Budapest, Hungary 1992).

Gerardu, JJA and Zaelke, D, 'The Importance of International Environmental Enforcement Networks', *Environmental Law Network International* (2005) no 2, 3–7.

Heiss, R, Ruessink, H, Isarin, N, Koparova, M and Grabiel, D, 'International Hazardous Waste Inspection Project at Seaports: Results and Recommendations' in *INECE, 9th International Conference on Environmental Compliance and Enforcement: 24 June 2011, Whistler, British Columbia, Canada: Proceedings* (INECE: Washington 2011).

Implementation and Enforcement of Environmental Law (IMPEL) *Enforcement of EU Waste Shipment Regulation: 'Learning by Doing'* (Interim Project Report, 12 October 2009), http://www.vrominspectie.nl/Images/Interim%20%20Report%20IMPEL%20TFS_tcm293-273297.pdf (accessed 18 January 2011).

International Criminal Police Organization (INTERPOL), *Electronic Waste and Organised Crime: Assessing the Links: Phase II Report for the Interpol Pollution Crimes Working Group* (France: INTERPOL 2009).

International Network for Environmental Compliance and Enforcement (INECE), *Raising Awareness, Developing Networks, Strengthening Capacity* (Brochure) (n.d.).

International Network for Environmental Compliance and Enforcement (INECE), *INECE 9th International Conference on Environmental Compliance and Enforcement, Conference Proceedings, 24 June 2011, Whistler, British Columbia, Canada* (INECE: Washington 2011).

International Network for Environmental Compliance and Enforcement – Seaport Environmental Security Network (INECE-SESN), *International Hazardous Waste Inspection Project at Seaports: Results and Recommendations* (2010), http://www.inece.org/seaport/exercise/INECE_SeaportInspectionProjectOutcomes_22dec.pdf (accessed 18 June 2011).

International Network for Environmental Compliance and Enforcement (INECE), *Manual for Creating and Sustaining Regional Environmental Compliance and Enforcement Networks* (2012). Online publication available at: http://inece.org/resource/network_manual/ (accessed on 5 June 2012).

Lehane, J, 'Towards a Critical Analysis of Environmental Enforcement Networks' in Flemish High Council on Environmental Enforcement, *Environmental Enforcement Networks: Concepts, Implementation and Effectiveness: Proceedings* (Brussels, in press 2014).

Lehane, J and Pink, G, 'Evolution of a Regional Environmental Enforcement Network: The Australasian Environmental Law Enforcement and Regulators neTwork (AELERT)' in *INECE, 9th International Conference on Environmental Compliance and Enforcement: 24 June 2011, Whistler, British Columbia, Canada: Proceedings* (INECE: Washington 2011).

Mays, N and Pope, C, 'Rigour and Qualitative Research', *British Medical Journal* (1995) vol. 311, 109–112.

Miles, MB and Huberman, AM, *Qualitative Data Analysis: An Expanded Source Book* (2nd edn, Thousand Oaks, CA: Sage Publications 1994).

Nicholson, M, 'Networking in Europe: How Networking and Cooperation have Helped Respond to Environmental Compliance and Enforcement Challenges in IMPEL Member Countries' in *INECE, 9th International Conference on Environmental Compliance and Enforcement: 24 June 2011, Whistler, British Columbia, Canada: Proceedings* (INECE: Washington 2011).

O'Leary, G and Lynott, DJ, 'The Effective Use of an Environmental Enforcement Network in Ireland' in *INECE, 9th International Conference on Environmental Compliance and Enforcement: 24 June 2011, Whistler, British Columbia, Canada: Proceedings* (INECE: Washington 2011).

Opondo, GK, 'Creating and Sustaining Regional Environmental Compliance and Enforcement Networks: Lessons from the East African Network for Environmental Compliance & Enforcement' in *INECE, 9th International Conference on Environmental Compliance and Enforcement: 24 June 2011, Whistler, British Columbia, Canada: Proceedings* (INECE: Washington 2011).

Pink, G, 'Environmental Enforcement Networks: A Qualitative Analysis' (2010), http://ssrn.com/abstract=1803179 (accessed on 14 April 2011).

Pink, G, 'Assessing the Utility of Environmental Enforcement Networks: Maximising Benefits to Members', in *INECE, 9th International Conference on*

Environmental Compliance and Enforcement: 24 June 2011, Whistler, British Columbia, Canada: Proceedings (INECE: Washington 2011), 797–804.

Pink, G, 'Law Enforcement Responses to Transnational Environmental Crime: Choices, Challenges and Culture', Transnational Environmental Crime Project Working Paper 5/2013 (Canberra: Department of International Relations, Australian National University 2013).

Pink, G and Lehane, J, 'Environmental Enforcement Networks: Development of a Network Evaluation Matrix' in *INECE, 9th International Conference on Environmental Compliance and Enforcement: 24 June 2011, Whistler, British Columbia, Canada: Proceedings* (INECE: Washington 2011), 805–821.

Pink, G and Lehane, J, 'Environmental Enforcement Networks: Their Role in Climate Change Enforcement' in White, R (ed.) *Climate Change from a Criminological Perspective* (New York: Springer 2012), 109–133.

Scanlon, J, 'Speech delivered to the 79th INTERPOL General Assembly, 8 November, Doha, Qatar' (2010), http://cites.org/eng/news/sg/2010/SG_statement_interpol_doha.php (accessed 22 June 2011).

Slaughter, A-M, *A New World Order* (Princeton, NJ: Princeton University Press 2004).

Stas, A, 'The Flemish High Council of Environmental Enforcement – A Coordinated Environmental Enforcement Policy' in *INECE, 9th International Conference on Environmental Compliance and Enforcement: 24 June 2011, Whistler, British Columbia, Canada: Proceedings* (INECE: Washington 2011).

Torbeck, LD, 'Statistical Solutions: Square Root of (N) + 1 Sampling Plan: Is the Square Root of (N) + 1 a Statistically Valid Scheme?', *Pharmaceutical Technology* (2009) vol. 33, issue 10, 128.

United Nations Environment Programme (UNEP), *Networking Counts: Combating Illegal Trade in Ozone Depleting Substances* (Paris: UNEP 2007).

White, R, *Crimes Against Nature: Environmental Criminology and Ecological Justice* (Devon: Willan Publishing 2008).

Wijbenga, B, Ruessink, H, De Wit, A, and Kapitein, P, 'Environmental Policing in the 21st Century – Background, Organisation and Experience in the Netherlands' in *INECE, 8th International Conference on Environmental Compliance and Enforcement, 5–11 April 2008, Cape Town, South Africa, Proceedings* (London: Cameron May Ltd 2008), 323–333.

Zaelke, D, Kaniaru, D, and Kružíková, E (eds), *Making Law Work: Environmental Compliance & Sustainable Development, Volume 1* (London: Cameron May Ltd 2005a).

Zaelke, D, Kaniaru, D, and Kružíková, E (eds), *Making Law Work: Environmental Compliance & Sustainable Development, Volume 2* (London: Cameron May Ltd 2005b).

APPENDIX 5.1 THE EVALUATION NETWORK

Members	Finances	Governance	Support	Deliverables
Absent Criteria				
N/A	N/A	N/A	N/A	N/A
Emerging Criteria				
Membership Typically low within networks' sphere of influence. Restricted to core member agencies or individuals operating within networks' sphere of influence.	***Budget*** Non-existent or modest to initiate/ commence the network.	***Access*** Member access to foundational and guiding documents. No open source access to networks guiding documents.	***Liaison*** Limited or no liaison with other networks.	***Events*** A few singular events for members. Limited number of members working together on specific projects.
Leadership Few individuals/ member agencies take lead role across network.	***Contributions*** Limited in-kind contributions restricted to central core member agencies or individuals.	***Review*** Informal review by foundation members.	***Support base*** Network effectiveness reliant on core members providing ad hoc coordination.	***Outcomes*** Prospective members considering potential of network. Limited functionality within network to deliver outcomes.
Value Negligible or questionable value to non-core members. Core members only	***Project funding*** Non-existent or minimal.	***Structures*** General Aims and Objectives laid down. Typically developing and fluid.	***Supporting functions*** Base level administrative tasks undertaken for network.	***Products*** Low number of publications disseminated. Publication limited to contributions of members.

active participants with few benefits realised.		No written procedures.	If not for a few key individuals, network would not continue.	
		Fragile Criteria		
Members	**Finances**	**Governance**	**Support**	**Deliverables**
Membership Generally increasing across significant actors within network sphere of influence.	***Budget*** Contributions are spasmodic and are made by small number of sources. Not sustainable.	***Access*** Central repository of information and communiqués to members. Limited open source access to networks guiding documents.	***Liaison*** Emergent and exploratory liaison with other networks undertaken. Information sought from other networks.	***Events*** Irregular events with increasing frequency. Preliminary attempts to undertake cooperative exercises.
Leadership Wider range of key individuals/member agencies taking on leadership roles across network.	***Contributions*** Few core member agencies/individuals providing in-kind support.	***Review*** Regular changing of operating rules, Constitutional documents, etc. to fit circumstances.	***Support base*** Growing level of support base. Increasing numbers of interested individuals.	***Outcomes*** Low level coordination to deliver outcomes. Members seeking benefits.
Value Tangible benefits available for active members. Most members inactive/passive and question value of network. Low level communications	***Project funding*** Very limited, if available. Sourced from lead member in project team.	***Structures*** Guiding documentation developed reactively to situations. Clear Aims and Objectives set out for network.	***Supporting functions*** Central support function to support membership and administrative tasks only.	***Products*** Infrequent publications being developed and disseminated. Range of network members contributing to publications.

APPENDIX 5.1 CONTINUED

Fragile Criteria				
Members	**Finances**	**Governance**	**Support**	**Deliverables**
disseminated to members from core members.				
Maturing Criteria				
Members	**Finances**	**Governance**	**Support**	**Deliverables**
Membership Expanded to reach critical/core number of potential members within relevant network area of operation.	***Budget*** Sufficient funding for network to continue for short to medium term (2–3 years).	***Access*** Increasing access of members to network steering/guiding documents. Open source access to limited network-produced documents.	***Liaison*** Interest by and liaison with other networks. Capacity and capability discussions to identify areas of commonality.	***Events*** Held on semi-regular basis. Delivered across network. Range of events relevant to all members. Restricted range of members working conjointly.
Leadership Critical mass of individuals/member agencies take on leadership roles. Wide range of membership not represented in leadership roles.	***Contributions*** In-kind support provided by central member agencies/ individuals.	***Review*** Third Party review of constitutional documents and guidance considered.	***Support base*** Widening support base across network sphere of influence.	***Outcomes*** Member agencies receiving identifiable benefits. Individuals professionally realise benefits.

Value	***Project funding***	***Structures***	***Supporting functions***	***Products***
Leading members displaying demonstrable benefits through active participation. Level of inactive/ passive members reducing. Increasing engagement and communication between members.	Project funding – increasing but ad hoc. Project leaders are able to source limited funding to support project.	Proactive development of guiding documentation with consultation across membership. Development of Operation and Strategic Plans to set direction of network.	Administrative tasks major part of function. Low level of coordination and project capacity.	Are of useable standard and considered as a step towards better practice across industry. Contributions from those outside of network being included.

		Well Established Criteria		
Members	**Finances**	**Governance**	**Support**	**Deliverables**
Membership	***Budget***	***Access***	***Liaison***	***Events***
Maximum or near maximum of possible members within relevant operation of network coverage.	Secured on permanent basis. Sustainable arrangements.	Open and transparent access to network steering papers across membership and support base. Foundational and guiding documents available as open source.	Level of support from other networks seen through interaction and joint activities. Good working relationships between networks.	Held regularly and well attended. Coordinated centrally for delivery across membership. Members readily work collaboratively.

APPENDIX 5.1 CONTINUED

Well Established Criteria				
Members	**Finances**	**Governance**	**Support**	**Deliverables**
Leadership	***Contributions***	***Review***	***Support base***	***Outcomes***
Large proportion of members taking leadership roles across network.	High proportion of members contributing in-kind support to projects, events and initiatives.	Governance structures reviewed and consistent with better practice. Subject to external scrutiny and review.	Strong support and contribution base from practitioner and senior management alike.	Delivering tangible benefits to members. Serve as attractor drawing new members into network. Members overtly promoting the benefits of involvement.
Value	***Project funding***	***Structures***	***Supporting functions***	***Products***
Majority of members readily realise benefits of membership attained through active participation. Open communication across members.	Projects driven by/within network are readily funded. Projects undertaken by network bring in associated funding.	Robust written governance structures in place. Membership well represented on guiding body.	Central function for coordinating network activities, project and events. Administrative tasks minor part of function.	High standard and considered better practice across industry. Subject to review and improvement process. Wide range of contributors to network publications.

APPENDIX 5.2 SURVEY QUESTIONS

What do you consider to be the maturity rating of your EEN – please select the most appropriate description and **highlight it in bold:**

Q1 *against the **Members** (yellow) core functional category?*
Absent (0) Emerging (1) Fragile (2) Maturing (3) Well Established (4)

Q2 *against the **Finances** (orange) core functional category?*
Absent (0) Emerging (1) Fragile (2) Maturing (3) Well Established (4)

Q3 *against the **Governance** (green) core functional category?*
Absent (0) Emerging (1) Fragile (2) Maturing (3) Well Established (4)

Q4 *against the **Support** (purple) core functional category?*
Absent (0) Emerging (1) Fragile (2) Maturing (3) Well Established (4)

Q5 *against the **Deliverables** (pink) core functional category?*
Absent (0) Emerging (1) Fragile (2) Maturing (3) Well Established (4)

Please now total all of the bracketed numbers appearing in <u>your bolded responses for Q1 to Q5</u>

0 = *Absent*	1–7 = *Emerging*	8–13 = *Fragile*	14–17 = *Maturing*	18–20 = *Well Established*

Q6 Using the key above what is your **Overall** *(blue) rating?*
Absent Emerging Fragile Maturing Well Established

Q7 *How does the overall rating (at question 6 above) compare to what you thought the maturity level of your EEN might have been before you were using the NEM?*

Significantly lower	Lower	What I expected	Higher	Significantly higher

APPENDIX 5.2 SURVEY QUESTIONS

Q8 *What description most accurately describes how helpful undertaking this self-assessment was in terms of informing your EEN's future planning?*

Of no use at all	Of some use	Neither un-useful or useful	Somewhat helpful	Very helpful

Q9 *Do you think your EEN would be prepared to be involved (either as an assessor or the assessed) in a peer review of your EEN by another EEN?*

No	Unlikely	Unsure/unknown	Likely	Yes

3.3.2 Short Answer Questions

Having used and applied the Network Evaluation Matrix (NEM) to your EEN – please provide a short written response **(2–5 short sentences are sufficient):**

Q10 *Do you have any suggestions for how the NEM might be improved?*

Q11 *Do you have any suggestions as to how a Peer to Peer Review of EENs by EENs might best be progressed?*

PART II

Benefits of networks

6. Towards a critical analysis of environmental enforcement networks

James Lehane*

Cooperation makes enforcers smarter and more effective.[1]

1. INTRODUCTION

This chapter presents a critical analysis of environmental enforcement networks to determine how their formation, function and operation influence or enable them to deliver their intended outcomes.

1.1 Environmental Enforcement Networks

The development and expansion of environmental enforcement networks has been well documented over the years.[2] These networks operate

* Assistant Director (Investigations), Australian Pesticides and Veterinary Medicines Authority. PO Box 6182, Kingston, Australian Capital Territory, Australia 2604. Email: james.lehane@apvma.gov.au. Former Executive Officer, Australasian Environmental Law Enforcement and Regulators neTwork (AELERT).

[1] McCabe, C, 'Panel Speech to Ninth International Conference on Environmental Compliance and Enforcement', noted in Grabiel, D and Heiss, R (2011) *Panel I: The Value of Enforcement Cooperation*, in International Network for Environmental Compliance and Enforcement, *INECE, 9th International Conference on Environmental Compliance and Enforcement, Conference Proceedings, 20–24 June 2011, Whistler, British Columbia, Canada* (Washington, 2011). Available at http://inece.org/conference/9/proceedings/09_panel1.pdf

[2] Boogers, S, 'Networking among Environmental Prosecutors (Workshop G2 Report)', in International Network for Environmental Compliance and Enforcement, *INECE, 9th International Conference on Environmental Compliance and Enforcement, Conference Proceedings, 20–24 June 2011, Whistler, British*

across the range of geographical and geopolitical boundaries, at international, regional, national and sub-national level. Previous analyses have

---

Columbia, Canada (Washington, 2011). Available at http://inece.org/conference/9/proceedings/19_TrackG.pdf; Bromm, SE, 'North America's Commission for Environmental Cooperation: One Example of a Successful Regional Network' in International Network for Environmental Compliance and Enforcement, *INECE 9th International Conference on Environmental Compliance and Enforcement, Conference Proceedings, 20–24 June 2011, Whistler, British Columbia, Canada* (Washington, 2011). Available at http://inece.org/conference/9/proceedings/74_Bromm.pdf; Derder, MR and Zyani, B, 'The Network for Environmental Compliance and Enforcement in Morocco (NECEMAR): An INECE Initiative Supported by a Strong Moroccan Political Will', in International Network for Environmental Compliance and Enforcement, *INECE, 9th International Conference on Environmental Compliance and Enforcement, Conference Proceedings, 20–24 June 2011, Whistler, British Columbia, Canada* (Washington, 2011). Available at http://inece.org/conference/9/proceedings/75_DerderZyani.pdf; Lehane, J and Pink, G, 'Evolution of a Regional Environmental Enforcement Network: The Australasian Environmental Law Enforcement and Regulators neTwork (AELERT)', in International Network for Environmental Compliance and Enforcement, *INECE, 9th International Conference on Environmental Compliance and Enforcement, Conference Proceedings, 20–24 June 2011, Whistler, British Columbia, Canada* (Washington, 2011). Available at http://inece.org/conference/9/proceedings/76_LehanePink.pdf; Nicholson, M, 'Networking in Europe: How Networking and Cooperation have Helped Respond to Environmental Compliance and Enforcement Challenges in Impel Member Countries', in International Network for Environmental Compliance and Enforcement, *INECE, 9th International Conference on Environmental Compliance and Enforcement, Conference Proceedings, 20–24 June 2011, Whistler, British Columbia, Canada* (Washington, 2011). Available at http://inece.org/conference/9/proceedings/77_Nicholson.pdf; O'Leary, G and Lynott, DJ, 'The Effective Use of an Environmental Enforcement Network in Ireland', in International Network for Environmental Compliance and Enforcement, *INECE, 9th International Conference on Environmental Compliance and Enforcement, Conference Proceedings, 20–24 June 2011, Whistler, British Columbia, Canada* (Washington, 2011). Available at http://inece.org/conference/9/proceedings/78_O'LearyLynott.pdf; Opondo, GK, 'Creating and Sustaining Regional Environmental Compliance and Enforcement Networks: Lessons from the East African Network for Environmental Compliance & Enforcement', in International Network for Environmental Compliance and Enforcement, *INECE, 9th International Conference on Environmental Compliance and Enforcement, Conference Proceedings, 20–24 June 2011, Whistler, British Columbia, Canada* (Washington, 2011). Available at http://inece.org/conference/9/proceedings/79_Opondo.pdf; Stas, A, 'The Flemish High Council of Environmental Enforcement – A Coordinated Environmental Enforcement Policy', in International Network for Environmental Compliance and Enforcement, *INECE, 9th International Conference on Environmental Compliance and Enforcement, Conference Proceedings, 20–24 June 2011, Whistler, British Columbia, Canada* (Washington, 2011). Available at http://inece.org/conference/9/proceedings/82_Stas.pdf

considered policy development and capacity building through to operational and information sharing functions.

Networks are established at certain times for a range of reasons. The form and structure they take is impacted and guided by the underlying reasons for establishing the network, how it was established and where it was established. Networks can be structured formally or informally, with or without clear governance structures; with the primary aim of their activities and membership effort relating directly to their agreed charter.

1.2 The Network Evaluation Matrix

In 2011, Pink and Lehane[3] launched the Network Evaluation Matrix (the Matrix) to identify areas where environmental enforcement networks can develop and be maintained as part of establishing and building their organisational maturity.

This Matrix was developed to analyse the approximate organisational maturity of environmental enforcement networks. Periodic review of the Matrix in the light of feedback from members of environmental enforcement networks based on their experiences is beneficial. Such review strengthens the value of the tool and provides better guidance to users in the future.

2. BACKGROUND LITERATURE

2.1 A Need for Networks?

It is widely acknowledged that combating and disrupting illegal transit networks is a difficult task.[4] With the continued rapid growth in technology and global trade, entities involved in illegal trade are seen as 'increasingly entrepreneurial' and 'fluid'.[5]

---

[3] Pink, G and Lehane, J, 'Environmental Enforcement Networks: Development of a Network Evaluation Matrix', in International Network for Environmental Compliance and Enforcement, *INECE, 9th International Conference on Environmental Compliance and Enforcement, Conference Proceedings, 20–24 June 2011, Whistler, British Columbia, Canada* (Washington, 2011). Available at http://inece.org/conference/9/proceedings/81_PinkLehane.pdf

[4] Mackenzie, S, 'Organised Crime and Common Transit Networks', *Trends and Issues in Crime and Criminal Justice*, No. 23 (July 2002). Australian Institute of Criminology, Canberra, Australia.

[5] Mackenzie (2002) op. cit., p. 3.

To counter this rising threat of global and transnational crime, law enforcement agencies are increasingly employing a 'networks to counterbalance networks'[6] approach in their attempts to deal with evolving situations confronting them. Since the first International Enforcement Workshop in 1990,[7] a theme emerged within conference proceedings of all future International Conferences on Environmental Compliance and Enforcement recognising the need for cooperation and networking within enforcement and regulatory agencies. This need does not appear to have decreased.

The regional nature of most environmental enforcement networks has an unknown level of potential to work in their favour. Cooperation between close and interdependent countries on more than one issue for mutual gain is a form of regionalism.[8] The concept of regionalism continues to be observed and documented in environmental enforcement networks and may provide a functional model for enhancing cooperation between nation states, organisations and individuals.

With the regionalism of networks providing potential for mutual gains, the increasing impact of globalisation is changing transnational trade, economic practice and reducing cultural barriers to trade, travel and information exchange.[9] The existing networks that operate globally are in a unique position to gain an oversight of global trends and should be able to assist regional enforcement networks to remain alert to emerging issues and to respond accordingly once the specific issue begins to impact within national jurisdictions.

Slaughter[10] sets out a set of potential opportunities for networks to maximise their value, through:

> 1) developing a concept of dual function for all government officials; 2) increasing the visibility and accessibility of government networks; 3) Developing more

---

[6] Slaughter, AM and Zaring, D, 'Networking Goes International: An Update' (2006) *Annual Review of the Law and Social Science* (Annu. Rev. Law Soc. Sci).

[7] United States Environmental Protection Agency and the Netherlands Ministry of Housing, Physical Planning and Environment (Organizers), *International Enforcement Workshop Proceedings* (1990).

[8] Heron, WM, 'A Critical Assessment of the Relevance of a Concept of Cooperative Security' (2000) *Australian Defence Force Journal*, No. 140 January/February 2000: 25–30, at 28.

[9] Ibid.

[10] Slaughter, AM, 'Disaggregated Sovereignty: Towards the Public Accountability of Global Government Networks', in *Government and Opposition Ltd* (2004a). Oxford: Blackwell Publishing, pp. 159–190, at p. 163. First published online, 17 March 2004, DOI: 10.1111/j.1477–7053.2004.00119.x.

> legislative networks; 4) Using government networks to mobilize a wide range of nongovernmental actors; and 5) a customized set of solutions developed by domestic polities themselves.

Kauppi and Viotti [11] suggest that by pooling resources within a network, outcomes will be enhanced at a lower cost than when members are working independently. The ancient writings of Thucydides also include non-state actors, with a call for leaders to 'imag[e] events from the perspective of other(s)'.[12]

2.2 Maximising Benefits of Networks

Some of the strongest advocates for networks and communities in recent times provide a degree of realism to the consideration of networks. Wenger, Trayner and de Laat warn us that '[t]he danger of network is noise and diffusion'.[13]

Within this *network of noise* are the many competing interests and operational needs of network members, which require a 'strong sense of direction on the part of individuals'.[14] This would necessitate a strong leadership team across the network to set its strategic direction and communicate that direction to guide those involved. Concerns about noise within a network should be countered by strong leadership, clear network structure and shared purpose, so that involved network members can make progress.

Research outside of the network focus provides guidance where teams are mixed with cooperative and competitive members, with competitive members maximising their own benefits (potentially at the cost to the team) whilst strategically releasing information to cooperative team members.[15] Stepping outside the focus on networks, there is a clear path emerging to indicate that information gained from organisational management,

---

[11] Kauppi, M and Viotti, P, *The Global Philosophers: World Politics and Western Thought* (1992). New York: Macmillan, p. 57.

[12] Ibid.

[13] Wenger, E, Trayner, B and de Laat, M, *Promoting and Assessing Value Creation in Communities and Networks: A Conceptual Framework* (2011). Ruud de Moor Centrum, Open Universiteit. Rapport 18. (available at http://wenger-trayner.com/documents/Wenger_Trayner_DeLaat_Value_creation.pdf), p. 11.

[14] Ibid.

[15] Hollingshead, AB, Wittenbaum, GM, Jacobsohn, GC and Fraidin, SN, 'Competitive Members in Cooperative Groups', *Submission to 18th Annual Conference of the International Association for Conflict Management (IACM 2005)*: Seville, Spain. Available at http://ssrn.com/abstract=732643

culture and leadership has a significant role to play in better understanding and managing networks.[16]

2.3 Critical Issues for Networks

Many legal issues add confusion to the complexity of working across jurisdictional boundaries on operational issues.[17] Network and capacity building are extremely important.[18] Using cross-boundary connections and networks makes it easier to exchange ideas, practices, procedures and training. This can be facilitated on a more informal basis without the need for strict compliance with legal process for evidentiary reasons.

Participants involved in the Regional Environmental Compliance and Enforcement Networks workshop at the 2011 International Conference for Environmental Compliance and Enforcement identified a range of challenges confronting networks.[19] These challenges align with the four core principles of networks:

1. *Involvement*: engagement of active participants within the network;
2. *Value*: ensuring the network value-adds to the memberships needs;
3. *Effectiveness*: having clear communication flows about the network and from members; and

---

[16] Lomas, J, 'The In-between World of Knowledge Brokering', *British Medical Journal (BMJ)*, 20 January 2007, Vol. 334; O'Flynn, J, 'The Cult of Collaboration in Public Policy', *The Australian Journal of Public Administration* (2009), 68(1): 112–116; Lesser, EL and Storck, J, 'Communities of Practice and Organizational Performance', *IBM Systems Journal* (2001) 40(4): 831–841; Vlaar, PWL, Van Den Bosch, FAJ and Volberda, HW, 'Coping with Problems of Understanding in Interorganizational Relationships: Using Formalization as a Means to Make Sense' (July 24, 2006). *ERIM Report Series Reference No. ERS-2006-034-STR*. Available at http://ssrn.com/abstract=920229

[17] Spapens, T, 'Cross-border Police Cooperation in Tackling Environmental Crime', in International Network for Environmental Compliance and Enforcement, *INECE, 9th International Conference on Environmental Compliance and Enforcement, Conference Proceedings, 20–24 June 2011, Whistler, British Columbia, Canada* (Washington, 2011). Available at http://inece.org/conference/9/proceedings/31_Spapens.pdf

[18] Ibid., p. 246.

[19] Lehane, J, 'Regional Environmental Compliance and Enforcement Networks (Workshop G4 report)', in International Network for Environmental Compliance and Enforcement, *INECE, 9th International Conference on Environmental Compliance and Enforcement, Conference Proceedings, 20–24 June 2011, Whistler, British Columbia, Canada* (Washington, 2011), at p. 132. Available at http://inece.org/conference/9/proceedings/19_TrackG.pdf

4. *Support*: sustainable funding and support from senior officials in member agencies.[20]

For environmental enforcement networks to develop and maintain a level of effectiveness, they 'must have adequate access to resources and information'.[21] The Network Evaluation Matrix developed by Pink and Lehane[22] provides guidance for personnel involved in managing environmental enforcement networks on potential options that may assist such a network to mature to its fullest potential.

> Network dynamics is a function of not just the social network, but a meta-matrix of networks – not the least of which are the knowledge network (who knows what), the information network (what ideas are related to what), and the assignment network (who is doing what).[23]

Underlying the whole system of network dynamics is the need to 'build trust and establish relationships among their participants that then create incentives' to progress the business of the network.[24]

Carley, Lee and Krackhardt[25] break their meta-matrix analysis of

---

[20] Pink, G, 'Environmental Enforcement Networks: A Qualitative Analysis' (December 7, 2010) (2010). Available at Social Science Research Network http://ssrn.com/abstract=1803179 (14 April 2011), pp. 54–56; Pink, G, 'Assessing the Utility of Environmental Enforcement Networks: Maximising Benefits to Members', in International Network for Environmental Compliance and Enforcement, *INECE, 9th International Conference on Environmental Compliance and Enforcement, Conference Proceedings, 20–24 June 2011, Whistler, British Columbia, Canada* (Washington, 2011), pp. 797–804; Lehane (2011) op. cit.

[21] International Network for Environmental Compliance and Enforcement (Executive Planning Committee Co-Chairs), 'Conference Outcomes: Whistler Statement. Executive Planning Committee Co-Chairs, Final Conference Statement: 9th INECE International Conference on Environmental Compliance and Enforcement', in International Network for Environmental Compliance and Enforcement, *INECE, 9th International Conference on Environmental Compliance and Enforcement, Conference Proceedings, 20–24 June 2011, Whistler, British Columbia, Canada* (Washington, 2011a). Available at http://inece.org/conference/9/proceedings/04_WhistlerStatement.pdf

[22] Pink and Lehane (2011) op. cit.

[23] Carley, KM, Lee, J-S and Krackhardt, D, 'Destabilizing Networks' (2002) *Connections* 24(3):79–92, at p. 83.

[24] Slaughter, AM, 'The Power and Legitimacy of Government Networks', in Alfred Herrhausen Society for International Dialogue, *The Partnership Principle, New Forms of Governance in the 21st Century* (2004b). London: Archetype Publications. Available at http://www.princeton.edu/~slaughtr/Articles/GovtNetworks.pdf (28 September 2013).

[25] Carley, Lee and Krackhardt (2002) op. cit.

networks into factors of Agents, Knowledge and Tasks, of which various other components such as knowledge, information or assignment (work/task) networks are taken into consideration. Specific individuals may be identified as 'network actors', who are central to the power and connectedness of a network and share information outside of the direct network resulting in increased similarities between the two networks.[26] As with most networks and organisations, the loss of individuals from within that inner core may reduce the network's performance, if only temporarily.[27]

3. METHODOLOGY

3.1 Critical Analysis

Taking the broader literature into account, networks can be summarised as being about mission, people and deliverables. Having a clearly established mission sets the direction, focus and structure of the network, with the people forming the membership and putting various strategies into place to achieve the mission through a range of deliverables. This may be the authors' simplistic view of the world; however, it aligns with the more detailed Network Evaluation Matrix and other related research.

The research that informed this chapter involved a preliminary step towards undertaking a critical analysis of environmental enforcement networks utilising a variety of analysis methods that have evolved from more traditional law enforcement intelligence analysis. Eight networks covering a geographically dispersed area were randomly chosen for consideration, and are listed in Table 6.1.

3.2 Content Analysis

To capture the raw essence of these networks, their websites were utilised to obtain specific information on the network's operations and establishment. As such, the About Us (or equivalent) webpage was captured in Portable Document Format (PDF) to preserve content as at the date of capture. Other network information such as Constitution, Terms of Reference and Strategic Plans were also captured in PDF format to preserve and store the information.

---

[26] Ibid.

[27] Ibid.

Table 6.1 List of international and regional environmental enforcement networks considered

International	INECE	International Network for Environmental Compliance and Enforcement
	ICCWC	International Consortium on Combating Wildlife Crime
Regional	AECEN	Asian Environmental Compliance and Enforcement Network
	AELERT	Australasian Environmental Law Enforcement and Regulators neTwork
	CEC	Commission for Environmental Cooperation
	EANECE	East African Network for Environmental Compliance and Enforcement
	IMPEL	European Union Network for the Implementation and Enforcement of Environmental Law
	NECEMA	Regional Planning Committee of the Network for Environmental Compliance and Enforcement in the Maghreb

Data from the captured documents was extracted by copying and processing through two online Word Cloud processing websites – Wordle[28] and Tagxedo.[29] These Word Cloud processors are open source web pages that analyse raw text and return results based on frequency of the use of words within the submitted text data. This approach is objective because it avoids interpretation bias on the part of the analyst.

Preliminary comparison undertaken between the two Word Cloud processors indicated that the Tagxedo processor provided a higher level of review and ability to save the output in a picture format instead of the limited PDF output of Wordle. Given the identified restrictions, use of the Wordle programme was discontinued during the analysis phase and the results initially obtained are not considered in this paper.

As part of utilising the Word Cloud analysis, the returned Word Cloud text was restricted to the 100 most used words within the raw text. The word rankings were screen captured and manually entered into a table to present the top ten words represented from the About Us websites. These top ten words identify the issues of highest importance and use.

[28] www.wordle.net
[29] www.tagxedo.com

4. OVERALL ANALYSIS

Analysis of the key issues of importance to environmental enforcement networks provides insight into the networks' focal points and, potentially, their modes of operation.

The networks were assessed according to:

- Their level of formality in establishment;
- What constitutes the network membership (individuals, government agencies, non-governmental organisations); and
- Stated mandates and area of operations.

These three areas were selected to identify why and how networks were established as they were deemed to be effective indicators relating to the mission, people and deliverables within any given network.

5. FINDINGS

Initial consideration of how networks were established and their level of formality indicates that there is a tendency to create informal environmental enforcement networks, as depicted in Table 6.2.

The content analysis of the *About Us* information from the selected networks subject to analysis provides guidance about their areas of focus and their geographical sphere of influence. For the two network collaborations clearly identifiable as working across the global stage, the content analysis revealed the following descriptors set out in Table 6.3.

Analysing the content from regional environmental enforcement networks identified the key descriptors in descending order from the *About Us* pages of the respective networks, as shown in Table 6.4.

In relation to the methodology used, the content analysis did not identify any areas that were not readily identifiable from reviewing the web pages of the respective networks. The content analysis provides an objective assessment of the top issues of relevance by numerical count of the words used, however, it does not prioritise them with any degree of situational awareness. As a tool, it is useful to gain an appreciation, but not for more rigorous analysis. The Tagxedo website utilised to undertake this content analysis was fit for purpose given the function it was expected to do. The Tagxedo content analysis also provided high quality images for presentation of the analysis.

Table 6.2 *Formality, membership and mandates of environmental enforcement networks*

Network	Level of formality	Member constituents	Mandates and area of operations
INECE	Informal	Individuals – by subscription to news. Regional networks – directly or by informal association.	Global network aiming to improve enforcement through better cooperation, strengthen capacities and raise awareness of the importance of environmental compliance and enforcement.[a]
ICCWC	Formal	International treaty secretariats	Global agencies agreeing to highlight the importance of fighting against wildlife crimes, working collaboratively to support national law enforcement agencies and regional enforcement networks, joint capacity building and operational support.[b]
AECEN	Informal	Government agencies	'To promote improved compliance with environmental legal requirements in Asia through regional exchange of innovative policies and practices.'[c]
AELERT	Informal	Government agencies	Across all levels of government in Australia and New Zealand, 'The objective of the network is to: • Improve operational effectiveness • Enhance regulatory compliance capacity, and • Promote consistency of approach to operational regulatory reform.'[d]
CEC	Formal	Government agencies	North American commission established by Agreement associated with a regional free trade agreement to 'facilitate collaboration and public participation to foster conservation, protection and enhancement of the North American environment.'[e]
EANECE	Informal	Government agencies	East African network to strengthen relationships between countries and government organisations, improve cooperation and information sharing, promote the development and implementation of guiding documents, and enhance the enforcement capacity of members.[f]
IMPEL	Formal	Government agencies	An 'international non-profit association of the environmental authorities' across the European Union referred to in legislation and directives concerning the implementation and enforcement of

Table 6.2 (continued)

Network	Level of formality	Member constituents	Mandates and area of operations
			environmental law through awareness raising, capacity building, peer review and information exchange.[g]
NECEMA	Informal	Government agencies	Across the Maghreb region of Northern Africa, with the aim of promoting good environmental governance by developing enforcement networks, strengthening capacity and raising awareness of the importance of environmental compliance and enforcement.[h]

Notes:

[a] International Network for Environmental Compliance and Enforcement (INECE) *About: INECE's Goals*. INECE Website. Available at www.inece.org/about (7 August 2013) (2013a).

[b] Secretary-General of the Convention on International Trade in Endangered Species of Wild Fauna and Flora (CITES) *Letter of Understanding* (2010). Available at www.cites.org/eng/news/pr/2010/ICCWC_memo.pdf (28 September 2013).

[c] Asian Environmental Compliance and Enforcement Network (AECEN) *Who We Are: About AECEN*. AECEN Website. Available at www.aecen.org/about-aecen (7 September 2013).

[d] Australasian Environmental Law Enforcement and Regulators neTwork (AELERT) *About Us*. AELERT Website. Available at https://aelert.net/about-us/ (28 August 2013).

[e] Commission for Environmental Cooperation (CEC) *About the CEC*. CEC Website. Available at www.cec.org/Page.asp?PageID=1226&SiteNodeID=310&BL_ExpandID=154 (5 September 2013).

[f] East African Network for Environmental Compliance & Enforcement (EANECE) *Overview*. EANECE Website. Available at www.eanece.org/overview.php (5 September 2013).

[g] European Union Network for the Implementation and Enforcement of Environmental Law (IMPEL) *About IMPEL*. IMPEL Website. Available at www.impel.eu/about (27 August 2013).

[h] Network for Environmental Compliance and Enforcement in the Maghreb (NECEMA), *The First Regional Planning Committee meeting of NECEMA: 20–21 February 2006* (2006). Available through the NECEMA webpages hosted by INECE http://inece.org/mena/rabat/necema_tor.pdf (28 September 2013).

Table 6.3 Top ten issues of interest by international environmental enforcement networks

INECE	ICCWC
Environmental	Wildlife
Compliance	Crimes
Enforcement	Related
Development	Violation
Implementation	General
INECE	International
Governance	Secretary
Organisations	Enforcement
Sustainable	National
International	Law

6. DISCUSSION

At the global level, the International Network for Environmental Compliance and Enforcement (INECE) 'develops, promotes, and implements practical and innovative activities to strengthen environmental compliance and enforcement at all levels of governance'.[30] Gathered under the INECE umbrella are numerous regional and topical networks;[31] some established directly by INECE, others established by other means that now work and/or participate collaboratively with INECE and other networks around the world. The breadth of networks sitting or associated with INECE may well be a contributing factor to the global network being referred to as the '*network of networks*'.[32]

Regional environmental enforcement networks were found to have a range of interests as a focus of network activities and attention. Not surprisingly, there is a degree of overlap between the stated areas of interest

[30] International Network for Environmental Compliance and Enforcement (Executive Planning Committee Co-Chairs) (2011a) op. cit.

[31] Ibid.

[32] International Network for Environmental Compliance and Enforcement (INECE), 'Summary Report: Summit of Regional Network Leadership: Creating and Sustaining Regional Environmental Compliance and Enforcement Networks', in International Network for Environmental Compliance and Enforcement, *INECE, 9th International Conference on Environmental Compliance and Enforcement, Conference Proceedings, 20–24 June 2011, Whistler, British Columbia, Canada* (Washington, 2011b). Available at http://inece.org/conference/9/proceedings/05_SummitRegionalNetworkLeadership.pdf

Table 6.4 Top ten issues of interest by regional environmental enforcement networks

AECEN	AELERT	CEC	EANECE	IMPEL	NECEMA
Environmental	Environmental	Environmental	Environmental	Environmental	Regional
Development	Sustainable	Cooperation	Enforcement	European	Environmental
AECEN	AELERT	Council	Network	Implementation	NECEMA
Asia	Advancement	Protection	Compliance	IMPEL	Networks
Members	Network	North	Countries	Enforcement	Coordinator
Enforcement	Regulators	Public	EANECE	Member	Enforcement
Agencies	Practice	Commission	African	Association	Participants
Regional	Cooperative	American	East	Network	INECE
Environment	Promotion	Environment	Regional	EU	Development
Network	Operational	Country	Implementation	Legislation	Country

to each network and partner regional enforcement networks (Table 6.4). These major threads identified by analysis indicate that networks promote themselves as being collaborative, focused on the environment and relating to enforcement. The commonality of interests may provide a baseline from which any future cross-network collaboration or partnerships could build upon.

Reviewing open source information that the networks post on their websites indicated that apart from the occasional dated news item posted on their websites, there is little, if any, information to tell interested parties how the networks were achieving their stated goals and objectives. Information such as Annual Reports or Project Tracking reports were generally (with few exceptions) lacking. Making such public documents available for external parties would improve the transparency of networks, which may assist in gaining greater public and political support for the networks' activities.

Despite not achieving ranking in the Top Ten Content items, a major theme emerging from network published documentation such as their *About Us* web pages and similar, is the enhancement and capacity building across their members. This thread holds for international networks such as INECE and the partnership established under the ICCWC. There are numerous instances of capacity-building programmes documented by these networks being delivered at various times and locations across different commodities and skill sets.

Sharing of capacity-building training material and programmes can be seen in part through an INECE hosted 'Environmental Compliance Training Resource Library'.[33] As with any collation of material within a networked environment, it relies on members to share their material with others. Whilst the material made available by INECE is open access, similar training and capacity-building materials held by regional networks are not so readily accessible.

Looking around the world, networks can be found for nearly any area of interest or commodity. Networks exist that cover aspects of health care, academic research, library collections, through to national security, law enforcement and, of direct interest, environmental enforcement networks. Whilst O'Flynn aptly described Australian moves to collaborate as a 'cult of collaboration',[34] the 'cult' is global and not isolated to any one country,

---

[33] International Network for Environmental Compliance and Enforcement (INECE) *Environmental Compliance Training Resource Library*. Available at http://inece.org/resources/ (28 September 2013) (2013b).

[34] O'Flynn (2009) op. cit.

as seen by the broad geographic and commodity coverage of environmental enforcement networks alone.

Kelman, Hong and Turbitt[35] note some of the difficulties that prevent collaborations from working well. These include different cultures, priorities and timing. A majority of the networks considered in this paper are in essence, informal networks. Regardless of their level of formality, Slaughter[36] notes that 'networks allow for informal collaboration'.

Heron[37] claims that a culture of cooperation is much more cost effective than the expense of cultures of conflict. Having established structures within networks may prove difficult, and in the absence of traditional hierarchical structures, there are fewer reported ways to manage network participants. With this in mind, Kelman, Hong and Turbitt[38] claim that 'more centralized networks tend to perform better'. Comparative studies of reported achievements against Key Performance Indicators would provide strong guidance on the most appropriate network structure for performance in the environmental enforcement field. Using a common set of Key Performance Indicators for networks would continue from the extensive work presented by Stahl and Klein[39] over the previous International Conferences for Environmental Compliance and Enforcement.

---

[35] Kelman, S, Hong, S and Turbitt, I, *Are There Managerial Practices Associated with Service Delivery Collaboration Success?: Evidence from British Crime and Disorder Reduction Partnerships*, Harvard University, John F. Kennedy School of Government. Faculty Research Working Paper Series (2011). Available at www.ssrn.com/abstract=1785416

[36] Slaughter, AM, 'Networking Government to Government: The Asian Way' (2008) *International Review* (Autumn).

[37] Heron (2000) op. cit., 29.

[38] Kelman, Hong and Turbitt (2011) op. cit.

[39] Stahl, M, 'Using Indicators to Lead Environmental Compliance and Enforcement Programs', in International Network for Environmental Compliance and Enforcement, *INECE, Seventh International Conference on Environmental Compliance and Enforcement (9–15 April 2005), Marrakech, Morocco. Conference Proceedings Volume 2* (2005). Available at http://www.inece.org/conference/7/vol2/66_Stahl.pdf; Klein, W, 'Measurable Targets for Enforcement Performance' in International Network for Environmental Compliance and Enforcement, *INECE Seventh International Conference on Environmental Compliance and Enforcement (9–15 April 2005) Marrakech, Morocco. Conference Proceedings Volume 2* (2005). Available at http://www.inece.org/conference/7/vol2/56_Klein.pdf; Stahl, M, 'Performance Indicators for Environmental Compliance and Enforcement Programs, Part I: The U.S. EPA Experience', in International Network for Environmental Compliance and Enforcement, *INECE, Sixth International Conference on Environmental Compliance and Enforcement, April 15–19, 2002 Proceedings Volume 2* (2002a). Available at http://www.inece.org/conf/proceedings2/27-Performan%20Indicators.pdf; Stahl, M, 'Performance Indicators

The performance of networks relies on having clearly established goals and objectives to enable network members to work collaboratively in delivering the required tasks and programmes. Elements of relationships, trust, leadership, network structure and focus are critical to the network achieving and delivering its objectives.

7. CONCLUSION

Environmental enforcement networks are established to address specific problems and issues. Their mandates set out where their focus should be and the main activities to undertake as part of addressing those established concerns. These networks are largely informal, with a number established and associated with legislation, directives or regional trade agreements.

Participation in such informal networks presents an opportunity to establish relationships between network members, to build a level of connectedness and trust that will open the flow of information. These connections should transcend any commodity, core agency business or specific network focus to enable ongoing exchanges and continued professional contact.

Capacity building and the enhancement of skills and capabilities is a common theme across environmental enforcement networks. A number of central repositories exist for the sharing of training and capacity-building material, yet these appear either to have restricted access or to be limited by lack of content.

BIBLIOGRAPHY

Asian Environmental Compliance and Enforcement Network (AECEN) *Who We Are: About AECEN*. AECEN Website. Available at www.aecen.org/about-aecen (7 September 2013).

Australasian Environmental Law Enforcement and Regulators neTwork (AELERT) *About Us*. AELERT Website. Available at https://aelert.net/about-us/ (28 August 2013).

Boogers, S, 'Networking among Environmental Prosecutors (Workshop G2 Report)', in International Network for Environmental Compliance and

---

for Environmental Compliance and Enforcement Programs, Part II: The U.S. EPA Experience', in International Network for Environmental Compliance and Enforcement, *INECE, Sixth International Conference on Environmental Compliance and Enforcement, April 15–19, 2002 Proceedings Volume 2* (2002b). Available at http://www.inece.org/conf/proceedings2/28-Stahl.Slides.pdf

Enforcement, *INECE, 9th International Conference on Environmental Compliance and Enforcement, Conference Proceedings, 20–24 June 2011, Whistler, British Columbia, Canada* (Washington, 2011). Available at http://inece.org/conference/9/proceedings/19_TrackG.pdf

Bromm, SE, 'North America's Commission for Environmental Cooperation: One Example of a Successful Regional Network', in International Network for Environmental Compliance and Enforcement, *INECE, 9th International Conference on Environmental Compliance and Enforcement, Conference Proceedings, 20–24 June 2011, Whistler, British Columbia, Canada* (Washington, 2011). Available at http://inece.org/conference/9/proceedings/74_Bromm.pdf

Carley, KM, Lee, J-S and Krackhardt, D, 'Destabilizing Networks' (2002) *Connections* 24(3): 79–92.

Commission for Environmental Cooperation (CEC) *About the CEC*. CEC Website. Available at www.cec.org/Page.asp?PageID=1226&SiteNodeID=310&BL_ExpandID=154 (5 September 2013).

Derder, MR and Zyani, B, 'The Network for Environmental Compliance and Enforcement in Morocco (NECEMAR): An INECE Initiative Supported by a Strong Moroccan Political Will', in International Network for Environmental Compliance and Enforcement, *INECE, 9th International Conference on Environmental Compliance and Enforcement, Conference Proceedings, 20–24 June 2011, Whistler, British Columbia, Canada* (Washington, 2011). Available at http://inece.org/conference/9/proceedings/75_DerderZyani.pdf

East African Network for Environmental Compliance & Enforcement (EANECE) *Overview*. EANECE Website. Available at www.eanece.org/overview.php. (5 September 2013).

European Union Network for the Implementation and Enforcement of Environmental Law (IMPEL) *About IMPEL*. IMPEL Website. Available at www.impel.eu/about (27 August 2013).

Heron, WM, 'A Critical Assessment of the Relevance of a Concept of Cooperative Security' (2000) *Australian Defence Force Journal*, No. 140 January/February 2000: 25–30.

Hollingshead, AB, Wittenbaum, GM, Jacobsohn, GC and Fraidin, SN, 'Competitive Members in Cooperative Groups', *Submission to 18th Annual Conference of the International Association for Conflict Management (IACM 2005)*: Seville, Spain. Available at http://ssrn.com/abstract=732643

International Network for Environmental Compliance and Enforcement (Executive Planning Committee Co-Chairs), 'Conference Outcomes: Whistler Statement. Executive Planning Committee Co-Chairs, Final Conference Statement: 9th INECE International Conference on Environmental Compliance and Enforcement', in International Network for Environmental Compliance and Enforcement, *INECE, 9th International Conference on Environmental Compliance and Enforcement, Conference Proceedings, 20–24 June 2011, Whistler, British Columbia, Canada* (Washington, 2011a). Available at http://inece.org/conference/9/proceedings/04_WhistlerStatement.pdf

International Network for Environmental Compliance and Enforcement (INECE) 'Summary Report: Summit of Regional Network Leadership: Creating and Sustaining Regional Environmental Compliance and Enforcement Networks' in International Network for Environmental Compliance and Enforcement, *INECE, 9th International Conference on Environmental Compliance and*

Enforcement, Conference Proceedings, 20–24 June 2011, Whistler, British Columbia, Canada (Washington, 2011b). Available at http://inece.org/conference/9/proceedings/05_SummitRegionalNetworkLeadership.pdf

International Network for Environmental Compliance and Enforcement (INECE), *About: INECE's Goals*. INECE Website. Available at www.inece.org/about (7 August 2013) (2013a).

International Network for Environmental Compliance and Enforcement (INECE), *Environmental Compliance Training Resource Library*. Available at http://inece.org/resources/ (28 September 2013) (2013b).

Kauppi, M and Viotti, P, *The Global Philosophers: World Politics and Western Thought* (1992). New York: Macmillan.

Kelman, S, Hong, S and Turbitt, I, *Are There Managerial Practices Associated with Service Delivery Collaboration Success?: Evidence from British Crime and Disorder Reduction Partnerships*, Harvard University, John F. Kennedy School of Government, Faculty Research Working Paper Series (2011). Available at www.ssrn.com/abstract=1785416

Klein, W, 'Measurable Targets for Enforcement Performance', in International Network for Environmental Compliance and Enforcement, *INECE, Seventh International Conference on Environmental Compliance and Enforcement (9–15 April 2005), Marrakech, Morocco. Conference Proceedings Volume 2* (2005). Available at http://www.inece.org/conference/7/vol2/56_Klein.pdf

Lehane, J, 'Regional Environmental Compliance and Enforcement Networks (Workshop G4 report)', in International Network for Environmental Compliance and Enforcement, *INECE, 9th International Conference on Environmental Compliance and Enforcement, Conference Proceedings, 20–24 June 2011, Whistler, British Columbia, Canada* (Washington, 2011). Available at http://inece.org/conference/9/proceedings/19_TrackG.pdf

Lehane, J and Pink, G, 'Evolution of a Regional Environmental Enforcement Network: The Australasian Environmental Law Enforcement and Regulators neTwork (AELERT)', in International Network for Environmental Compliance and Enforcement, *INECE, 9th International Conference on Environmental Compliance and Enforcement, Conference Proceedings, 20–24 June 2011, Whistler, British Columbia, Canada* (Washington, 2011). Available at http://inece.org/conference/9/proceedings/76_LehanePink.pdf

Lesser, EL and Storck, J, 'Communities of Practice and Organizational Performance', *IBM Systems Journal* (2001) 40(4): 831–841.

Lomas, J, 'The In-between World of Knowledge Brokering', *British Medical Journal (BMJ)*, 20 January 2007, Vol. 334.

Mackenzie, S, 'Organised Crime and Common Transit Networks', *Trends and Issues in Crime and Criminal Justice*, No. 23 (July 2002). Australian Institute of Criminology, Canberra, Australia.

McCabe, C, 'Panel Speech to Ninth International Conference on Environmental Compliance and Enforcement', noted in Grabiel, D and Heiss, R (2011) *Panel I: The Value of Enforcement Cooperation*, in International Network for Environmental Compliance and Enforcement, *INECE, 9th International Conference on Environmental Compliance and Enforcement, Conference Proceedings, 20–24 June 2011, Whistler, British Columbia, Canada* (Washington, 2011). Available at http://inece.org/conference/9/proceedings/09_panel1.pdf

Network for Environmental Compliance and Enforcement in the Maghreb (NECEMA), *The First Regional Planning Committee meeting of NECEMA:*

20–21 February 2006 (2006). Available through the NECEMA webpages hosted by INECE http://inece.org/mena/rabat/necema_tor.pdf (28 September 2013).

Nicholson, M, 'Networking in Europe: How Networking and Cooperation have Helped Respond to Environmental Compliance and Enforcement Challenges in Impel Member Countries', in International Network for Environmental Compliance and Enforcement, *INECE, 9th International Conference on Environmental Compliance and Enforcement, Conference Proceedings, 20–24 June 2011, Whistler, British Columbia, Canada* (Washington, 2011). Available at http://inece.org/conference/9/proceedings/77_Nicholson.pdf

O'Flynn, J, 'The Cult of Collaboration in Public Policy', *The Australian Journal of Public Administration* (2009) 68(1): 112–116.

O'Leary, G, and Lynott, DJ, 'The Effective Use of an Environmental Enforcement Network in Ireland', in International Network for Environmental Compliance and Enforcement, *INECE, 9th International Conference on Environmental Compliance and Enforcement, Conference Proceedings, 20–24 June 2011, Whistler, British Columbia, Canada* (Washington, 2011). Available at http://inece.org/conference/9/proceedings/78_O'LearyLynott.pdf

Opondo, GK, 'Creating and Sustaining Regional Environmental Compliance and Enforcement Networks: Lessons from the East African Network for Environmental Compliance & Enforcement', in International Network for Environmental Compliance and Enforcement, *INECE, 9th International Conference on Environmental Compliance and Enforcement, Conference Proceedings, 20–24 June 2011, Whistler, British Columbia, Canada* (Washington, 2011). Available at http://inece.org/conference/9/proceedings/79_Opondo.pdf

Pink, G, 'Environmental Enforcement Networks: A Qualitative Analysis' (December 7, 2010) (2010). Available at http://ssrn.com/abstract=1803179 (14 April 2011).

Pink, G, 'Assessing the Utility of Environmental Enforcement Networks: Maximising Benefits to Members', in International Network for Environmental Compliance and Enforcement, *INECE, 9th International Conference on Environmental Compliance and Enforcement, Conference Proceedings, 20–24 June 2011, Whistler, British Columbia, Canada* (Washington, 2011), pp. 797–804.

Pink, G and Lehane, J, 'Environmental Enforcement Networks: Development of a Network Evaluation Matrix', in International Network for Environmental Compliance and Enforcement, *INECE, 9th International Conference on Environmental Compliance and Enforcement, Conference Proceedings, 20–24 June 2011, Whistler, British Columbia, Canada* (Washington, 2011). Available at http://inece.org/conference/9/proceedings/81_PinkLehane.pdf

Secretary-General of the Convention on International Trade in Endangered Species of Wild Fauna and Flora (CITES) *Letter of Understanding* (2010). Available at www.cites.org/eng/news/pr/2010/ICCWC_memo.pdf (28 September 2013).

Slaughter, AM, 'Disaggregated Sovereignty: Towards the Public Accountability of Global Government Networks', in *Government and Opposition Ltd* (2004a). Oxford: Blackwell Publishing, pp. 159–190. First published online, 17 March 2004, DOI: 10.1111/j.1477-7053.2004.00119.x.

Slaughter, AM, 'The Power and Legitimacy of Government Networks', in Alfred Herrhausen Society for International Dialogue, *The Partnership Principle, New Forms of Governance in the 21st Century* (2004b). London: Archetype Publications. Available at http://www.princeton.edu/~slaughtr/Articles/GovtNetworks.pdf (28 September 2013).

Slaughter, AM, 'Networking Government to Government: The Asian Way' (2008) *International Review* (Autumn).

Slaughter, AM and Zaring, D, 'Networking Goes International: An Update' (2006) *Annual Review of the Law and Social Science* (Annu. Rev. Law Soc. Sci.).

Spapens, T, 'Cross-border Police Cooperation in Tackling Environmental Crime', in International Network for Environmental Compliance and Enforcement, *INECE, 9th International Conference on Environmental Compliance and Enforcement, Conference Proceedings, 20–24 June 2011, Whistler, British Columbia, Canada* (Washington, 2011). Available at http://inece.org/conference/9/proceedings/31_Spapens.pdf

Stahl, M, 'Performance Indicators for Environmental Compliance and Enforcement Programs, Part I: The U.S. EPA Experience', in International Network for Environmental Compliance and Enforcement, *INECE, Sixth International Conference on Environmental Compliance and Enforcement, April 15–19, 2002 Proceedings Volume 2* (2002a). Available at http://www.inece.org/conf/proceedings2/27-Performan%20Indicators.pdf

Stahl, M, 'Performance Indicators for Environmental Compliance and Enforcement Programs, Part II: The U.S. EPA Experience', in International Network for Environmental Compliance and Enforcement, *INECE, Sixth International Conference on Environmental Compliance and Enforcement, April 15–19, 2002 Proceedings Volume 2* (2002b). Available at http://www.inece.org/conf/proceedings2/28-Stahl.Slides.pdf

Stahl, M, 'Using Indicators to Lead Environmental Compliance and Enforcement Programs', in International Network for Environmental Compliance and Enforcement, *INECE, Seventh International Conference on Environmental Compliance and Enforcement (9–15 April 2005), Marrakech, Morocco. Conference Proceedings Volume 2* (2005). Available at http://www.inece.org/conference/7/vol2/66_Stahl.pdf

Stas, A, 'The Flemish High Council of Environmental Enforcement – A Coordinated Environmental Enforcement Policy', in International Network for Environmental Compliance and Enforcement, *INECE, 9th International Conference on Environmental Compliance and Enforcement, Conference Proceedings, 20–24 June 2011, Whistler, British Columbia, Canada* (Washington, 2011). Available at http://inece.org/conference/9/proceedings/82_Stas.pdf

United States Environmental Protection Agency and the Netherlands Ministry of Housing, Physical Planning and Environment (Organizers), *International Enforcement Workshop Proceedings* (1990).

Vlaar, PWL, Van Den Bosch, FAJ and Volberda, HW, 'Coping with Problems of Understanding in Interorganizational Relationships: Using Formalization as a Means to Make Sense' (July 24, 2006). *ERIM Report Series Reference No. ERS-2006-034-STR*. Available at http://ssrn.com/abstract=920229

Wenger, E, Trayner, B and de Laat, M, *Promoting and Assessing Value Creation in Communities and Networks: A Conceptual Framework* (2011). Ruud de Moor Centrum, Open Universiteit, Rapport 18. Available at http://wenger-trayner.com/documents/Wenger_Trayner_DeLaat_Value_creation.pdf

Wijbenga, B, Ruessink, H, De Wit, A and Kapitein, P, 'Environmental Policing in the 21st Century – Background, Organisation and Experience in the Netherlands', in International Network for Environmental Compliance and Enforcement, *Proceedings of the 8th International Conference on Environmental Compliance and Enforcement, 5–11 April 2008. International Network for*

Environmental Compliance and Enforcement (INECE). Cape Town, South Africa (2008). London: Cameron May, pp. 323–333.
Wolters, G, 'Foreword', in Zaelke, D, Kaniaru, D and Kružíková, E (eds), *Making Law Work: Environmental Compliance & Sustainable Development*, Volume 1 (2005). London: Cameron May Ltd.

7. Environmental enforcement networks: their 'value proposition' during times of reducing resources and budgets

Grant Pink*

1. INTRODUCTION

Developing and implementing environmental enforcement responses, whether policy, programmatic or legislative, is an increasingly complex task. Complexities arise due to various factors, relating to the nature of environmental issues, which include:

- They have been and are becoming increasingly important to society;[1]
- They require nuanced enforcement responses across an increasing number of topics;[2]

* Adjunct Research Fellow, School of Law, University of New England (UNE), Armidale, NSW, 2351, Australia, email: gpink2@une.edu.au; PhD Candidate, School of Behavioural, Cognitive and Social Sciences, UNE, email: gpink2@myune.edu.au; Director, Regulatory Capability and Performance Section, Department of the Environment, GPO Box 787, Canberra, ACT, 2600, email: grant.pink@environment.gov.au.

Any views or opinions expressed in this paper are those of the author and not those of the University of New England or the Australian Government of Department of the Environment.

[1] See Wijbenga, B, Ruessink, H, De Wit, A and Kapitein, P, 'Environmental Policing in the 21st Century – Background, Organisation and Experience in the Netherlands', in INECE, *8th International Conference on Environmental Compliance and Enforcement, 5–11 April 2008, Cape Town, South Africa, Proceedings* (London: Cameron May Ltd 2008), pp. 323–333 and Bricknell, S, 'Environmental Crime in Australia', *AIC Reports: Research and Public Policy Series 109* (Canberra: Australian Institute of Criminology 2010).

[2] For example, including but not limited to, pollution, trafficking of illegal wildlife and timber, electronic waste, hazardous waste, biodiversity loss and carbon fraud.

- They are like traditional forms of crime in that they are increasingly globalised;[3]
- Their regulators increasingly partner with non-governmental organisations (NGOs)[4], non-regulatory bodies[5] and civil society organisations[6] as a component of their regulatory efforts; and
- They require responses subject to escalating resource constraints.

The issue of resourcing and the matter of budgetary constraints foregrounds the need to maximise existing personnel resources. This is done by retention techniques and, more critically, by capacity building.

In recognition of this issue government agencies are already contributing to and benefiting from capacity building activities facilitated and provided by dedicated environmental enforcement networks.[7] Other enforcement networks (with environmental aspects) also provide

---

[3] See United Nations Office on Drugs and Crime (UNODC) *The Globalization of Crime: A Transnational Organized Crime Threat Assessment* (UNODC: Vienna 2010), p. ii; and Spapens, T, 'Cross-border Police Cooperation in Tackling Environmental Crime', in INECE, *9th International Conference on Environmental Compliance and Enforcement: 24 June 2011, Whistler, British Columbia, Canada: Proceedings* (INECE: Washington 2011); and Wyatt, T, 'A Comparative Analysis of Wildlife Trafficking in Australia, New Zealand, and the United Kingdom', *Transnational Environmental Crime Working Paper 6/2013* (Canberra: Department of International Relations, Australian National University 2013).

[4] White, R, 'NGO Engagement in Environmental Law Enforcement: Critical Reflections', *Australasian Policing: A Journal of Professional Practise and Research* (2012) 4(1), Winter: 7–11.

[5] See International Network for Environmental Compliance and Enforcement (INECE) *Principles of Environmental Compliance and Enforcement Handbook*, April 2009 (Washington: INECE 2009), pp. 66–67; and White, R (ed.), *Environmental Crime: A Reader* (Devon: Willan Publishing, 2009), p. 491.

[6] See Elliott, L, 'Combating Transnational Environmental Crime: "Joined Up" Thinking About Transnational Networks', in K Kangaspunta and IH Marshall (eds), *Eco-Crime and Justice: Essays on Environmental Crime* (Turin: UNICRI, 2009), p. 74.

[7] See Pink, G, 'Environmental Enforcement Networks: A Qualitative Analysis' (2010), http://ssrn.com/abstract=1803179 (accessed 14 April 2011); Pink, G, 'Assessing the Utility of Environmental Enforcement Networks: Maximising Benefits to Members', in INECE, *9th International Conference on Environmental Compliance and Enforcement: 24 June 2011, Whistler, British Columbia, Canada: Proceedings* (INECE: Washington, 2011); and Lehane, J and Pink, G, 'Evolution of a Regional Environmental Enforcement Network: The Australasian Environmental Law Enforcement and Regulators neTwork (AELERT)', in INECE, *9th International Conference on Environmental Compliance and Enforcement: 24 June 2011, Whistler, British Columbia, Canada: Proceedings* (INECE: Washington, 2011).

avenues for capacity building. Several examples of these enforcement networks include: INTERPOL's Environmental Crime Programme,[8] the World Customs Organization (notably *The Green Customs Initiative – Customs Protecting the Environment*),[9] and the United Nations Office of Drugs and Crime (principally where transnational organised crime is suspected).[10]

Networks, and networking activities, are not cost free. In fact, most depend on direct funding (ongoing and non-ongoing), significant amounts of 'in-kind' support, and in some instances sponsorship or partnerships. The concern facing environmental enforcement networks, therefore, is will government agencies be willing and able to continue to fund and support them.

This chapter collected and analysed the viewpoints of senior officials from government environmental regulatory agencies regarding the role played by environmental enforcement networks in developing agency capacity. Moreover, it sought their input and suggestions on how environmental enforcement networks might more effectively assist member agencies, and, finally, asked if there are any areas that are more relevant in times of constrained resources.

2. BACKGROUND

In 2005 the Organisation for Economic Co-operation and Development (OECD) produced a report titled *Funding Environmental Compliance Assurance: Lessons Learned from International Experience*. In it the OECD noted that:

> [t]hroughout the world, authorities responsible for enforcing environmental regulations and promoting compliance with environmental requirements are operating in the context of financial constraints. Such constraints can be a consequence of the general pressures on the state budgets or the changes in

---

[8] See International Criminal Policing Organisation (INTERPOL), *Environmental Crime Programme; Strategic Plan 2011–2013* (Lyon: INTERPOL, 2011), http://www.interpol.int/content/download/12670/87152/version/3/file/StrategicPlan2011–2013.pdf (accessed 15 October 2013).

[9] See World Customs Organization (WCO), The Green Customs Initiative – Customs Protecting the Environment (n.d.), http://www.greencustoms.org/background/ (accessed 8 October 2013).

[10] See United Nations Office on Drugs and Crime (UNODC), *The Globalization of Crime: A Transnational Organized Crime Threat Assessment* (UNODC: Vienna 2010).

> government policies . . . Very often, environmental inspectorates are required to maintain, or even achieve higher performance with fewer resources.[11]

Since this report was released in 2005, and even more so in recent years, governments have continued to work within a resource constrained environment with reducing staff numbers and budgets. Subsequently government regulators have sought to offset and share costs with one another and other stakeholders to achieve efficiencies.

As such, it is anticipated that governments and those agencies engaged in environmental regulation and enforcement will become even more reliant on the assistance and support provided by environmental enforcement networks (EENs or networks). The question that goes directly to the *value proposition* issue is – will regulators and enforcers continue to (or in fact be able to) fund and support EENs to the extent they have previously?

3. SUPPORTING ENVIRONMENTAL ENFORCEMENT NETWORKS

The fact that environmental regulatory agencies (ERAs) have used EENs as a primary vehicle through which to access capacity building opportunities and activities for their staff is well documented.[12] In part, the support for EENs is evidenced by their growth and the fact that government

---

[11] See Organisation for Economic Co-operation and Development (OECD) *Funding Environmental Compliance Assurance: Lessons Learned from International Experience* (Paris: OECD 2005), p. 3.

[12] See Zaelke, D, Kaniaru, D and Kružíková E (eds), *Making Law Work: Environmental Compliance & Sustainable Development, Volume 1* (London: Cameron May Ltd 2005a); Zaelke, D, Kaniaru, D and Kružíková, E (eds), *Making Law Work: Environmental Compliance & Sustainable Development, Volume 2* (London: Cameron May Ltd 2005b); Farmer, A, *Handbook of Environmental Protection and Enforcement: Principles and Practice* (London: Earthscan 2007); Pink, G and Lehane, J, 'Environmental Enforcement Networks and The Network Evaluation Matrix: Their Role in Climate Change Compliance and Enforcement', in *Compliance Strategies to Deliver Climate Benefits* (INECE: online, 2013), http://inece.org/resource/climate-report/ (accessed 7 September 2013); Pink, G and Lehane, J, 'Environmental Enforcement Networks: Their Role in Climate Change Enforcement', in R White, *Climate Change, Crime and Criminology* (New York: Springer-Verlag 2012); Pink, G, 'Environmental Enforcement Networks: A Qualitative Analysis' (2010), http://ssrn.com/abstract=1803179 (accessed on 14 April 2011); and Pink, G, 'Assessing the Utility of Environmental Enforcement Networks: Maximising Benefits to Members', in INECE, *9th International*

agencies are both contributing to and benefiting from capacity building arising out of dedicated EENs and other enforcement networks (with environmental aspects).

EENs, other enforcement networks, and networking activities, are not cost free – all EENs require support. However, the support that they require and the sources of support vary greatly. In most circumstances support is dependent upon, or at least influenced by, the EEN's level of formality and focus.

Generally speaking, support for EENs takes the form of:

- *Direct funding (ongoing and non-ongoing)* – this can be an annual contribution, membership fee, voluntary contribution, or combination thereof;
- *In-kind support* – which can include assistance with project work (lead, support or involvement), printing, housing of secretariat staff (and absorbing some of the associated on-costs of the network's secretariat); and
- *Sponsorship and partnerships* – typically coming from the corporate sector, peak industry bodies, or like-minded institutions where mutually beneficial opportunities exist.

4. RESEARCH QUESTIONS

As outlined above, the concern facing environmental enforcement networks is whether or not government agencies are willing and/or in fact able to continue to fund and support them – and if they are, to what level. It is this question that has provided the catalyst for this research and shaped the subsequent inquiry.

4.1 Research Methodology

A mixed method approach was used as part of an exploratory study to examine how senior officials within ERAs, who were key supporters and funders of EENs, considered the future of EENs as a capacity building vehicle for their agencies. The study was particularly interested in gaining a more comprehensive understanding of how reducing and tightening budgets might impact upon support for and the focus of the activities of EENs.

Conference on Environmental Compliance and Enforcement: 24 June 2011, Whistler, British Columbia, Canada: Proceedings (Washington: INECE 2011).

4.2 Research Participants

The research focused on the perspectives of a small sample of nine senior officials (hereafter 'research participants'). The research participants were identified through purposive sampling.[13] The purposive approach sought to '. . . identify specific groups . . . [who] possess characteristics or live in circumstances relevant to the social phenomenon being studied'.[14] Data were collected directly from the research participants in the form of a short multi-choice and short answer questionnaire.

4.3 Sample Set

The research participants were drawn from Australia, Canada, Ireland, the Netherlands, New Zealand, the United Kingdom and the United States of America.

The research participants were senior officials. They were also primarily administrators and resource allocators and were well placed to advise and speculate on how reduced budgets and fiscal constraints would most likely impact upon EENs.

4.4 Data Collection

Data collection involved asking the research participants to complete an online survey (using the Survey Monkey tool/software).[15] By using the online survey, the research participants remained anonymous. To further protect their anonymity, their responses have been aggregated where possible and where this has not been possible they have simply been attributed to 'a research participant'. They have been coded 'RP' (for Research Participant) and allocated a number from 1 to 9 (reflecting the chronological order in which the survey was time/date stamped by the computer software).

4.5 Survey Questions

Research participants were asked to answer eight questions. Five of which were multiple-choice and quantitative in nature (questions 1, 2, 3, 4 and 6)

---

[13] See Miles, MB and Huberman, AM, *Qualitative Data Analysis: An Expanded Source Book* (2nd edn, Thousand Oaks, CA: Sage Publications 1994).

[14] Mays, N and Pope, C, 'Rigour and Qualitative Research', *British Medical Journal* (1995), vol. 311, p. 109.

[15] See https://www.surveymonkey.com/

and three short answer questions (questions 5, 7 and 8), with the latter seeking more qualitative information. A copy of the questions is located at Appendix 7.1.

4.6 Data Collation

The data relating to the quantitative questions (except for question two) were converted into percentages (due to rounding not all samples equate to 100%) to enable the findings to be more easily visualised. On the other hand, the data relating to the qualitative questions were subjected to iterative thematic review and key word searches in an attempt to determine whether or not themes and common issues were present.

5. RESEARCH RESULTS

A summary of the responses to the eight questions are outlined below.

Question 1 – Value of Networks

When asked what value networks had brought to their agencies, research participants unanimously considered that value had been added by networks. When broken down further, 56% (n = 5) rated it as marginal, 22% (n = 2) rated it as demonstrable and 22% (n = 2) rated it as significant.

Question 2 – Supporting Networks

When asked how their agencies supported networks, research participants indicated that their agencies did so in numerous ways. The most frequent responses reflected that they were supported regularly/routinely and through making financial contributions and by providing 'in kind' support.

Question 3 – Role of Networks in Building Agency Capacity

When asked what level networks had played in building agency capacity, 89% (n = 8) of research participants considered networks had played a role in building agency capacity. When broken down further, 44% (n = 4) rated it as being minor, 22% (n = 2) rated it as major, 22% (n = 2) rated it as moderate, with the remainder 11% (n = 1) suggesting they had not played a role at all.

Question 4 – Areas Where Most Benefit from Networks had been Realised

Research participants were asked to rank from one to six (from most to least) what areas/topics networks had assisted in the building of agency capacity. Staff training/developing expertise was the most popular choice (with an average response of 1.67), next and somewhat clustered were inspections, licensing/permitting (authorising activities), and monitoring and auditing (with average responses of 3.33, 3.44 and 3.44, respectively). Administering legislation and prosecutions/litigation were the least popular of the choices (returning average response rates of 4.11 and 4.44 respectively).

Question 5 – The Single Most Important Capacity Building Role Performed/Facilitated by Networks

The written responses provided by the research participants for this question were diverse. Despite their diversity it was possible for them to be grouped or clustered under the following key three themes: collaboration, value and focus. These themes are now considered in turn:

- **Collaboration**

  Building confidence in existing skills and experience based upon an appreciation of shared problems and situations . . . and sometimes operators. (RP2)
  Shared learning and ensuring consistency. (RP4)

- **Value**

  Common training for field officers . . . benchmarking . . . and collaboration around common enforcement challenges. (RP 3)
  There is a real opportunity to save resources – by seeing what has already been done and importing it for use in your agency (with some contextualisation). (RP9)

- **Focus**

  Specialized training around one technical area . . . (RP6)

Question 6 – Impact of Reducing or Tightening Resources on Networks

When asked what impact reducing budgets or tightening resource constraints would have on their agency's ability to support networks, 11% (n = 1) of research participants expected a minor increase in the level of support that their agency would direct to networks. Whereas, 22% (n = 2) of research participants considered it would make no change to the level of support. Of those research participants that did expect a reduction in their agency's level of support, they expected the reduction to be minor (11% or n = 1), moderate (33% or n = 3) and major (22% or n = 2).

Question 7 – What Might Networks Do Differently

The written responses provided by the research participants for this question were again diverse. Despite their diversity it was possible for them to be grouped or clustered under four themes, with priorities being added to the three identified in question five. These themes are now considered in turn:

- **Collaboration**

  . . . there seems to be a de facto competition for attention from the various IGOs [international governmental organisations], NGOs [non-governmental organisations] and compliance networks. These compete for scarce resources and do not appear coordinated. (RP6)

- **Value**

  If an agency could report back in [respect of] time and costs the saving made from importing and contextualising a product rather than building it from scratch – it would be a compelling driver for senior executive, Secretary or CEO support for the network. (RP9)
  Promote at senior levels the achievements of the network . . . in particular the benefits derived by the agency. (RP8)
  Better use of resources to provide capacity building, such as through opening internal training sessions to partner agency staff within the network (thus reducing costs of having to pay for external facilitators or training that may not be relevant). . . . building the 'esprit de corps' within the network. (RP1)

- **Focus**

  Focus on value and maintain effort to ensure this invaluable facility [of networks] continues to be used and available. It's very low cost and very high value. (RP2)

- **Priorities**

  Prioritise engagement to ensure that the network is resulting in tangible benefits to the agencies involved. Ensure that network activities flow through to reduced duplication of effort . . . (RP7)

Question 8 – Any Final Comments on Capacity Building within Networks

Seven written responses were received. The responses, generally, reinforced the observations and comments reflected in the previous questions.

Of note several research participants made comments around value and contribution. On value, highlighting the need to 'quantify the value of "savings" that agencies can make through cooperation' (RP9), and that the 'challenge for all networks is . . . more broadly to build a willingness amongst its members to contribute equally to the network's activities and initiatives' (RP8).

One research participant provided a mechanism for building willingness and therefore greater participation by introducing the concept of performance indicators for networks, suggesting that:

> . . . Environmental Compliance and Enforcement Networks require robust performance indicators to ensure that their role is actually having a demonstrable benefit to the agencies involved. . . . On the ground business improvement should be a key focus. Without this it will be difficult for agencies to continue to support network activities. (RP7)

6. FINDINGS OF ANALYSIS

This study has found that governments treat participation in networks as any other form of potential investment. Governments are bound to assess the value and return of the investment through the standard processes making it necessary for networks to develop some form of due diligence to satisfy the needs of their membership.

The research participants, who were primarily administrators and resource allocators, considered that networks could improve in the areas of collaboration, value, focus and priorities. These issues are considered briefly in turn:

- **Collaboration**: One research participant made reference to networks competing with one another for scarce resources and then not coordinating the efforts of networks as effectively as they might. This research participant went on to suggest that '[t]o improve would require a clarification of roles . . . and better coordination of objectives' (RP6). On this point, Clifford and Edwards suggest that '[f]or environmental crime enforcement to improve, control agents at all levels of government must agree to put aside traditional [differences and] animosities and embrace the challenge of joint research and practice'.[16]

The issue of collaboration and its challenges has been well documented. White, for example, details how numerous law enforcement agencies, networks and organisations around the world have joined together to tackle the transportation of hazardous waste. He suggests that various operational alliances such as these show how '. . . [e]nvironmental crimes frequently demand a high level of collaboration with non-police agencies'.[17]

- **Value**: EENs have emerged as a key forum for building capacity and sharing information among environmental regulators. To continue to do this, as well as to ensure future contributions, there remains an ongoing need for networks to demonstrate what, where and how they add value for members.[18] This leads to the importance of the 'value proposition' – more simply translated to: 'what are the benefits of being involved in a network and in overall terms what does it cost'.

  The 'value' created by and through EENs can be both tangible and intangible. Gemmell and Circelli[19] provide several examples of tangible benefits arising from the activities of three Regional EENs, specifically the Australasian Environmental Law Enforcement and Regulators neTwork (AELERT), the Network of Heads of European Environment Protection Agencies (NHEEPA) and the European Union Network for the Implementation and Enforcement of Environmental Law (IMPEL).

  It was suggested by one research participant that it is necessary to '[p]romote at senior levels the achievements of the network for its members and in particular the benefits derived by the agency' (RP8). One way that this might be progressed is through what Wenger, Trayner and de Laat refer to as 'framing narratives', for they suggest

[16] See Clifford, M and Edwards, T, *Environmental Crime* (2nd edn, Burlington MA: Jones & Bartlett Learning 2012), p. 366.

[17] See White, R, *Crimes Against Nature: Environmental Criminology and Ecological Justice* (Devon: Willan Publishing, 2008), p. 202; and White, R, 'Environmental Law Enforcement: The Importance of Global Networks and Collaborative Practices', *Australasian Policing: A Journal of Professional Practise and Research* (2011), 3(1), Winter: 16–22.

[18] See Chapter 5 in this volume, 'Evaluating and Assessing Environmental Enforcement Networks: Through Use of the Network Evaluation Matrix'.

[19] See Chapter 8 in this volume, 'Environmental Regulation and Enforcement Networks Operating in Tandem: a Very Effective Vehicle for Driving Efficiencies and Facilitating Knowledge Exchange and Transfer'.

that: 'networks have stories – how they started, what has happened since, what participants are trying to achieve. It is in the context of the narrative that one can appreciate what learning is taking place (or not) and what value is created (or not)'.[20] Continuing, they detail the importance of audience and perspective, with audience referring to the recipient of the value and perspective having both short- and long-term aspects.[21]

- **Focus**: A clear sentiment evident through the responses of the research participants is that networks should be more focused; more specifically suggesting that networks should: 'Have a single strategy . . . be clear that operations and tactics are important but the strategic oversight needs to be in play' (RP4), 'Keep focus on new opportunities that can deliver more value to members . . .' (RP3) and 'Focus on value and maintain effort to ensure this invaluable facility [of networks] continues to be used and available' (RP2).

  The obvious question here is what networks should focus on. And, arising from that, what is the process for making these decisions and equally importantly resourcing them? A parallel consideration can be seen from the comments of a key informant from the earlier research where it was suggested that: '. . . managers are more reluctant to release staff [to network activities] because they've got so many other pressures on their time . . . [especially] when funding is being cut and resources are being reduced'.[22]
- **Priorities**: Given that their involvement in networks includes representing government interest in investing in networks, it is unsurprising to find that the research participants (as senior officials) were clear that networks should give greater attention to the setting and monitoring of its priorities.

  From an individual agency perspective, one research participant suggested that it is important to '[p]rioritise engagement to ensure that the network is resulting in tangible benefits to the agencies involved. Ensur[ing] that network activities flow through to reduced duplication of effort . . .' (RP7). This observation is consistent with

---

[20] Wenger, E, Trayner, B and de Laat, M, *Promoting and Assessing Value Creation in Communities and Networks: A Conceptual Framework* (Ruud de Moor Centrum, Open Universiteit, Rapport 18, 2011), http://www.open.ou.nl/rslmlt/Wenger_Trayner_DeLaat_Value_creation.pdf (accessed 21 February 2014), p. 15.

[21] Ibid.

[22] Pink, G, 'Environmental Enforcement Networks: A Qualitative Analysis' (2010), http://ssrn.com/abstract=1803179 (accessed 14 April 2011), p. 29.

one made in earlier research.[23] It was noted that network projects were impacted because network participants have their own core agency functions and priorities, further noting that these priorities can (at times) be in conflict with what they or their agency have volunteered to do with or on behalf of the network.[24] So it is clear that in terms of network priorities they should be clear, agreed and transparent.[25]

7. CONCLUSION

A small sample of nine senior officials from national environmental regulatory agencies considered that reduced budgets and tightening fiscal constraints would have an impact upon the ability of agencies to support environmental enforcement networks into the future. The anticipated impacts varied from minor to major.

Generally speaking, the comments/suggestions of the research participants were able to be grouped into four main themes or areas. They suggested environmental enforcement networks should improve or at least pay greater attention to issues such as priorities, focus, collaboration and value.

On the issue of value – which is inexorably linked to the 'value proposition' – extremes in viewpoints were evident in this study. At one end of the spectrum, some consider 'networks are an expensive option' (RP5), whereas at the other end they are considered to be '. . . very low cost and very high value' (RP2).

These extremes highlight that whilst networks operate at a collective level, when it comes to assessing the 'value proposition' of involvement it remains an individual consideration – as such 'value' seems to be very much dependent on the viewpoint of the assessing agency. The variability in any assessment of networks is then further compounded by the lack of a standardised set of metrics against which the value of networks can be generally and specifically assessed. On this aspect,

---

23 Pink, G, 'Environmental Enforcement Networks: A Qualitative Analysis' (2010), http://ssrn.com/abstract=1803179 (accessed 14 April 2011).

24 Ibid., p. 29.

25 See International Network for Environmental Compliance and Enforcement (INECE), 'Manual for Creating and Sustaining Regional Environmental Compliance and Enforcement Networks' (2012), http://inece.org/resource/network_manual/ (accessed 5 June 2012), Chapter 4: 'Regional Network Manual: Project Selection'.

Wenger, Trayner and de Laat suggest that 'value' has its own spectrum, spanning immediate value, potential value, applied value, realised value and reframing value.[26] In response to an identified need for networks to have performance indicators, these value categories may prove suitable in forming the foundation of just such metrics for environmental enforcement networks.

This study sought to establish whether or not environmental regulatory agencies considered environmental enforcement networks to be a worthwhile investment. The respondents all stated they found value in the networks in which they were a part. They also supported networks generally as environmental law enforcement tools. Whether agencies continued to support networks was the result of an ongoing assessment between the costs of membership versus perceived and actual benefit. Environmental regulatory agencies, as supporters and funders of networks, are asking that the benefits move from general to specific, intangible to tangible and abstract to more concrete. Thus what can be seen is that the assessment is very much dependent on the way networks promote to governments the benefits and value they provide.

BIBLIOGRAPHY

Bricknell, S, 'Environmental Crime in Australia', *AIC Reports: Research and Public Policy Series 109* (Canberra: Australian Institute of Criminology 2010).

Clifford, M and Edwards, T, *Environmental Crime* (2nd edn, Burlington MA: Jones & Bartlett Learning 2012).

Elliott, L, 'Combating Transnational Environmental Crime: "Joined Up" Thinking About Transnational Networks', in K Kangaspunta and IH Marshall (eds), *Eco-Crime and Justice: Essays on Environmental Crime* (Turin: UNICRI 2009), 55–77.

Farmer, A, *Handbook of Environmental Protection and Enforcement: Principles and Practice* (London: Earthscan 2007).

Gemmell, JC (Campbell) and Circelli, T, 'Environmental Regulation and Enforcement Networks Operating in Tandem: a Very Effective Vehicle for Driving Efficiencies and Facilitating Knowledge Exchange and Transfer', Conference Paper. *Environmental Enforcement Networks: Concepts, Implementation and Effectiveness* (Brussels: Flemish High Council on Environmental Enforcement 2013).

[26] See Wenger, E, Trayner, B and de Laat, M, *Promoting and Assessing Value Creation in Communities and Networks: A Conceptual Framework* (Ruud de Moor Centrum, Open Universiteit, Rapport 18, 2011), http://www.open.ou.nl/rslmlt/Wenger_Trayner_DeLaat_Value_creation.pdf (accessed 21 February 2014), pp. 19–23.

Implementation and Enforcement of Environmental Law (IMPEL), Conference on *Implementation and Enforcement of Environmental Legislation: Working Together to Improve and Innovate 1–4 October 2013*. Conference Programme (2013), http://environmentconference.mepa.org.mt/downloads/EnvironmentConference2013_Programme.pdf (accessed 6 November 2011).

International Criminal Policing Organisation (INTERPOL), *Environmental Crime Programme; Strategic Plan 2011–2013* (Lyon: INTERPOL 2011), http://www.interpol.int/content/download/12670/87152/version/3/file/StrategicPlan2011–2013.pdf (accessed 15 October 2013).

International Network for Environmental Compliance and Enforcement (INECE), *Principles of Environmental Compliance and Enforcement Handbook*, April 2009 (Washington: INECE 2009).

International Network for Environmental Compliance and Enforcement (INECE), *Manual for Creating and Sustaining Regional Environmental Compliance and Enforcement Networks* (2012), http://inece.org/resource/network_manual/ (accessed 5 June 2012).

Lehane, J and Pink, G, 'Evolution of a Regional Environmental Enforcement Network: The Australasian Environmental Law Enforcement and Regulators neTwork (AELERT)', in INECE, *9th International Conference on Environmental Compliance and Enforcement: 24 June 2011, Whistler, British Columbia, Canada: Proceedings* (INECE: Washington 2011).

Mays, N and Pope, C, 'Rigour and Qualitative Research', *British Medical Journal* (1995) vol. 311, 109–112.

Miles, MB and Huberman, AM, *Qualitative Data Analysis: An Expanded Source Book* (2nd edn, Thousand Oaks, CA: Sage Publications 1994).

Organisation for Economic Co-operation and Development (OECD), *Funding Environmental Compliance Assurance: Lessons Learned from International Experience* (Paris: OECD 2005).

Pink, G, 'Environmental Enforcement Networks: A Qualitative Analysis' (2010), http://ssrn.com/abstract=1803179 (accessed 14 April 2011).

Pink, G, 'Assessing the Utility of Environmental Enforcement Networks: Maximising Benefits to Members', in INECE, *9th International Conference on Environmental Compliance and Enforcement: 24 June 2011, Whistler, British Columbia, Canada: Proceedings* (Washington: INECE 2011).

Pink, G and Lehane, J, 'Environmental Enforcement Networks and The Network Evaluation Matrix: Their Role in Climate Change Compliance and Enforcement', in *Compliance Strategies to Deliver Climate Benefits* (INECE: online 2013), http://inece.org/resource/climate-report/ (accessed 7 September 2013).

Pink, G and Lehane, J, 'Environmental Enforcement Networks: Their Role in Climate Change Enforcement', in R White, *Climate Change, Crime and Criminology* (New York: Springer-Verlag 2012).

Pink, G and Lehane, J, 'Evaluation and Assessing Environmental Enforcement Networks: Through Use of the Network Evaluation Matrix', Conference Paper. *Environmental Enforcement Networks: Concepts, Implementation and Effectiveness* (Brussels: Flemish High Council on Environmental Enforcement 2013).

Spapens, T, 'Cross-border Police Cooperation in Tackling Environmental Crime', in INECE, *9th International Conference on Environmental Compliance and Enforcement: 24 June 2011, Whistler, British Columbia, Canada: Proceedings* (INECE: Washington 2011).

United Nations Office on Drugs and Crime (UNODC), *The Globalization of Crime: A Transnational Organized Crime Threat Assessment* (UNODC: Vienna 2010).

Wenger, E, Trayner, B and de Laat, M, *Promoting and Assessing Value Creation in Communities and Networks: A Conceptual Framework* (Ruud de Moor Centrum, Open Universiteit, Rapport 18 2011), http://www.open.ou.nl/rslmlt/Wenger_Trayner_DeLaat_Value_creation.pdf (accessed 21 February 2014).

White, R, *Crimes Against Nature: Environmental Criminology and Ecological Justice* (Devon: Willan Publishing 2008).

White, R (ed.), *Environmental Crime: A Reader* (Devon: Willan Publishing 2009).

White, R, 'Environmental Law Enforcement: The Importance of Global Networks and Collaborative Practices', *Australasian Policing: A Journal of Professional Practise and Research* (2011) 3(1), Winter: 16–22.

White, R, 'NGO Engagement in Environmental Law Enforcement: Critical Reflections', *Australasian Policing: A Journal of Professional Practise and Research* (2012) 4(1), Winter: 7–11.

Wijbenga, B, Ruessink, H, De Wit, A and Kapitein, P, 'Environmental Policing in the 21st Century – Background, Organisation and Experience in the Netherlands', in INECE, *8th International Conference on Environmental Compliance and Enforcement, 5–11 April 2008, Cape Town, South Africa, Proceedings* (London: Cameron May Ltd 2008), 323–333.

World Customs Organization (WCO) The Green Customs Initiative – Customs Protecting the Environment (n.d.), http://www.greencustoms.org/background/ (accessed 8 October 2013).

Wyatt, T, 'A Comparative Analysis of Wildlife Trafficking in Australia, New Zealand, and the United Kingdom', *Transnational Environmental Crime Working Paper 6/2013* (Canberra: Department of International Relations, Australian National University 2013).

Zaelke, D, Kaniaru, D and Kružíková, E (eds), *Making Law Work: Environmental Compliance & Sustainable Development, Volume 1* (London: Cameron May Ltd 2005a).

Zaelke, D, Kaniaru, D and Kružíková, E (eds), *Making Law Work: Environmental Compliance & Sustainable Development, Volume 2* (London: Cameron May Ltd 2005b).

APPENDIX 7.1 SURVEY QUESTIONS

Q1

Which term best describes the value that Environmental Compliance and Enforcement Networks have brought to your Environmental Regulatory Agency? (*Instructions – select one response only*)

- No noticeable value
- Marginal value
- Demonstrable value
- Significant value

Q2

What term best describes how your Environmental Regulatory Agency supports Environmental Compliance and Enforcement Networks? (*Instructions – select multiple answers if appropriate*)

- It does not support them
- It supports them on an ad hoc basis
- It supports them regularly/routinely
- It supports them by providing 'in kind' support (e.g. staff on committees & undertaking projects/initiatives)
- It supports them through financial contributions (whether mandatory or voluntary)
- It supports them by making financial contributions and by providing 'in kind' support

Q3

It has been suggested that Environmental Compliance and Enforcement Networks assist Environmental Regulatory Agencies to build or increase capacity. Which of the statements most accurately reflects your experiences and observations? (*Instruction – select one response only*)

- Environmental Enforcement Networks do not play any role in building capacity within Environmental Regulatory Agencies
- Environmental Enforcement Networks play a minor role in building capacity within Environmental Regulatory Agencies
- Environmental Enforcement Networks play a moderate role in building capacity within Environmental Regulatory Agencies

- Environmental Enforcement Networks play a major role in building capacity within Environmental Regulatory Agencies

Q4

It is widely recognised that Environmental Compliance and Enforcement Networks assist Environmental Regulatory Agencies to build capacity across a variety of areas. Of the areas listed below, please indicate, from your involvement with Networks, where your agency has benefited most in terms of its ability to build or acquire capacity? Noting 1 would be the area/topics where most capacity has been acquired – through to 6 which would be the area/topics where the least capacity has been acquired. (*Instructions – please type inside the respective boxes the numbers 1 to 6 as per your ratings*)

- administering legislation
- licensing/permitting (authorising activities)
- monitoring and auditing
- inspections
- prosecutions/litigation
- staff training/developing expertise

Q5

What do you consider to be the single most important capacity building role performed/facilitated by Environmental Compliance and Enforcement Networks? (*Instructions – free text*)

Q6

What impact will tightening resource constraints have on your agency's ability to support Environmental Compliance and Enforcement Networks? (*Instructions – select most appropriate response*)

- minor reduction in our level of support
- moderate reduction in our level of support
- major reduction in our level of support
- no change to the level of support
- minor increase in our level of support
- moderate increase in our level of support
- major increase in our level of support

Q7

In the context of resource constraints, what if anything would you ask Environmental Compliance and Enforcement Networks to do differently? (*Instructions – free text*)

Q8

Is there anything else you would like to mention about capacity building within Environmental Regulatory Agencies? (*Instructions – free text*)

8. Environmental regulation and enforcement networks operating in tandem: a very effective vehicle for driving efficiencies and facilitating knowledge exchange and transfer

Campbell Gemmell* and Tony Circelli†

1. INTRODUCTION

Environmental regulation and enforcement are often associated with the phrase that it is an activity 'that is more art than science'. This concept is supported by the extensive work undertaken by Professor Malcolm Sparrow[1] on regulation. In Sparrow's terms, environmental regulation is a field of practice which requires 'regulatory craftsmanship' by practitioners and managers alike. The toolkit also requires serious consideration. The metaphoric toolkit and craftsmanship amount in practice, at a high level, to the application of 'the tools of government',[2] and more prosaically to effective and skilful training and experience in assessing environmental problems, ensuring the scientific assessments underpinning regulation are sound, managing the harm potentially arising from environmental pressures, licensing the facility or operator or operation appropriately to limit releases to atmosphere, waters, land and waste or recovery facilities and managing compliance and regulatory relationships thereafter in an effective and efficient manner.[3]

* Professor of Environmental Regulation and Policy, University of Glasgow and Consulting Partner, Canopus Scotland.

† CEO South Australian EPA; Vice Chair AELERT.

[1] Sparrow, MK, *The Regulatory Craft: Controlling Risks, Solving Problems, and Managing Compliance* (2000) and Sparrow, MK, *The Character of Harms: Operational Challenges in Control* (2008).

[2] Freiberg, A, *The Tools of Regulation* (2010).

[3] Gemmell, JC and Scott, EM, 'Environmental Regulation, Sustainability and

Experience in different jurisdictions suggests that there is a great deal of shared challenge and effective networking, and knowledge exchange carries a real premium. When it comes to working together across jurisdictions, environmental regulators have, in the last 20 years, actively engaged and benefited as a result of 'networking' through a variety of different types of environmental networks, including enforcement networks.[4] The networks of officers of European EPAs (European Union Network for the Implementation and Enforcement of Environmental Law – IMPEL) and their heads – chairs, chief executives and/or delegated directors (Network of Heads of European Environmental Protection Agencies – NHEEPA) – have provided significant value to both governance and decision-making processes in the European Union (EU) as well as at national and regional jurisdictional levels.[5]

This chapter details and reflects on the experiences and observations of the authors in terms of the activities, actions, goals and products of environmental enforcement networks. In particular, it will outline circumstances where knowledge transfer and exchanges occurred at individual, team and organisational levels. It will also consider how networks are well positioned to develop important policy positions on environmental regulation as well as using their wide-reaching communication platforms to profile and promote such policies and their effective implementation.

Risk', in *Sustainability Accounting, Management and Policy Journal* (2013) 4(2): 120–144.

[4] Farmer, A, *Handbook of Environmental Protection and Enforcement: Principles and Practice* (2007); INECE, 'Enforcement Cooperation: Strengthening Environmental Governance', in *Proceedings of the 9th International Conference* (2011); Pink, G, 'Assessing the Utility of Environmental Enforcement Networks: Maximising Benefits to Members', in *Proceedings of the 9th International Conference on Environmental Compliance and Enforcement, 20–24 June 2011*; and Lehane, J and Pink, G, 'Evolution of a Regional Environmental Enforcement Network: The Australasian Environmental Law Enforcement and Regulators neTwork (AELERT)', in *Proceedings of the 9th International Conference on Environmental Compliance and Enforcement, 20–24 June 2011*.

[5] Gemmell, JC and Scott, EM, 'Environmental Regulation, Sustainability and Risk', in *Sustainability Accounting, Management and Policy Journal* (2013) 4(2): 120–144; and EPANet/EEA, *The EPA Network – Sharing Experiences across Europe* (2013).

2. NETWORKS OF RELEVANCE TO ENFORCEMENT AND REGULATION

There are a number of active regulatory networks: International Network for Environmental Compliance and Enforcement (INECE), European Union Network for the Implementation and Enforcement of Environmental Law (IMPEL), Network of Heads of European Environment Protection Agencies (NHEEPA/EPANet), Australasian Environmental Law Enforcement and Regulators neTwork (AELERT Network), and European Network of Prosecutors for the Environment (ENPE).

INECE is prominent globally, NHEEPA, IMPEL and the more recent ENPE at the EU level, and AELERT in Australasia. Finally, the United Nations Environment Programme (UNEP) and INTERPOL have also developed a real profile in this area.

In this chapter, however, the focus will be on AELERT and on the two longer-standing European networks, IMPEL and NHEEPA, and particularly their complementary roles. These latter two bodies, each environmental regulatory networks in their own right, with varying elements of focus on enforcement, have been chosen as a primary case study to highlight how networks encourage and enable collaboration, to identify and address shared challenges and opportunities, producing the 'right' environment for 'sharing and engagement' to occur.

3. WHAT THEN DOES A GOOD NETWORK NEED?

A good network needs and demonstrates a combination of some or all of the following:

1. To help drive smart policy and close policy loops based upon robust implementation experience, assisting decision and policy makers;
2. To offer knowledge exchange, agency capacity building, and performance improvement through benchmarking of policy and implementation, innovation and technical dissemination and training;
3. To work together (within the network and with those outside) to identify and focus effort on shared regulatory challenges, and facilitate understanding and application of better regulatory practice;
4. To enable learning and knowledge transfer through peer processes and outcome review;

5. To facilitate procurement benefits (e.g. policy, information technology, training and development) associated with jurisdictions using more consistent practices and building greater scale/critical mass; and
6. To enable stronger peer relationships to form and thrive, that assist in delivering additional reforms and initiatives through bilateral and multilateral partnerships between regulators.

A blend of two central elements is required to achieve success:

1. Authority, based upon experienced senior leaders in the regulatory space coming together motivated to identify and solve complex problems and challenges, through sharing expertise and experience developed from delivering and influencing policy and focused on its practical implementation; and
2. Practical, technical policy and regulatory practice knowledge and expertise.

It is about politically savvy authority being combined with sound technical and policy knowledge. Brought together appropriately this blend can help achieve wide-ranging benefits.

4. THE BENEFITS IN PRACTICE

Regulatory networks demonstrate a broad range of benefits aimed at the specific needs of their particular membership base. The AELERT Network, which was created to focus on operational level collaboration for environmental regulations, details three key objectives:[6]

1. Improving operational effectiveness;
2. Enhancing regulatory compliance capacity; and
3. Promoting consistency of approach to operational regulatory reform.

Some specific case study examples of benefits achieved in these areas are detailed below.

[6] 'AELERT Strategic Plan 2009–2013' (https://aelert.net/wp-content/uploads/2013/11/AELERT-Strategic-Plan-2009–13-FINAL-VERSION.doc).

4.1 Improving Operational Effectiveness – Better Regulation

What does good regulatory practice look like? This is a question asked by many regulators and political masters as well as by regulated parties or those subject to the impacts of the regulated. An Environmental Protection Agency (EPA) will reasonably be expected to do its best to achieve conformance with the mission established in its founding legislation. Networking facilitates comparison and shared learning that give context to the performance and approach of the individual EPA and allow 'stretch' and improvement to be embraced.

Networks also use their broad membership to consider and develop policy statements to the mutual benefit of the represented communities. The benefits of networks include fostering a common policy message that can be developed, shared and discussed with regulatory staff and indeed affected stakeholders, providing greater policy or technical credibility and influence as it represents and uses regulatory expertise from a broader collective, and avoiding duplication, mixed messages and unique approaches to what is often a common issue or regulatory challenge. Examples include the following.

4.1.1 Developing policy positions – the Prague Statement

In response to a commonly perceived view from industry and business sectors that regulation impedes economic development, NHEEPA used its collective knowledge and resources to develop what is now known as the *Prague Statement on Better Regulation*.[7] Through evidence gathered, the Statement demonstrates that a modern approach to regulation can indeed reduce the costs to industry and business, drive innovation, create new markets, and sustain jobs and competitive advantage, alongside the protection of valuable natural resources. The Statement concludes that rather than impeding competitiveness and economic development, good environmental regulation can be beneficial by driving innovation and reducing risk through anticipating new technologies, in providing access to the market, and in reducing waste and costs.

The Statement continues to be an important policy statement used by regulators to encourage a more innovative, competitive and sustainable business culture (often by working with industry bodies to demonstrate and reward better practice), as well as in explaining and encouraging more rational debate on the economic and social value of well-practised

---

[7] NHEEPA, The Contribution of Good Environmental Regulation to Competitiveness, aka 'The Prague Statement', 2005.

environmental regulation with government policy makers and industry stakeholder bodies. Importantly, through the high standing of the NHEEPA network and its ability to distribute, promote and profile the Statement, as well as promotion by other high profile networks (e.g. INECE), the Statement is widely used by many environmental regulators.

4.1.2 Development of a better regulatory practice statement

AELERT member officers, from across Australia and New Zealand, gathered to exchange information on a range of common challenges in the areas of risk-based approaches, compliance planning and stakeholder engagement. As well as improving engagement and cross fertilisation of ideas between regulators, the forum considered and built an agreed statement of the elements associated with better regulatory practice.

The Better Regulatory Practice Statement[8] is used as a key positioning statement for the AELERT Network, and offers key characteristics of 'better practice' that jurisdictions can consider in relation to benchmarking their own compliance and enforcement frameworks/services. It also allows jurisdictions to engage with their staff and stakeholder groups to identify key areas of reform. Noteworthy was an element acknowledged in the Statement of the need to 'collaborate with sister regulators and act as part of a whole'.

4.1.3 Performance measurement and benchmarking

Environmental regulators often must look to peer regulators in other jurisdictions (regionally, nationally and internationally) in order to benchmark their services and effectiveness. This is also a growing government and public expectation as seen in one recent example where peer-based benchmarking has been enshrined in law for a state-based EPA.[9] Further, the concept of performance measurement for regulators is not straightforward. How do regulators know they are working on the right issues or problems? And how do regulators know that they are making a difference?

Strong performance assessment leads to an objective understanding of whether regulators are achieving their strategic and operational agenda;

---

8 https://aelert.net/statement-of-better-practice-in-environmental-regulation/

9 New South Wales, s.16 of the Protection of the Environment Administration Act 1991, where the Environment Protection Authority Board is required to provide the Minister with an annual statement that contains or addresses a number of matters including '. . . an assessment of the success of the Authority in reducing risks to human health and in preventing the degradation of the environment and whether the level of environment protection achieved by the Authority is satisfactory in comparison with other Australian jurisdictions'.

ensures a greater focus on, and accountability for, results; and enables informed organisational learning to occur.[10] Importantly, it allows the organisation to understand which programmes and processes to maintain, which to change and those that should cease.

Networks enable the very few specialist resources available from individual jurisdictions in this field to share progress, challenges and close policy gaps. AELERT has commenced a programme to benchmark performance management frameworks for environmental regulatory functions, and will use this information to pursue an agreed, or at minimum a more consistent, approach that all regulators can use. Pursuing a common framework will also allow the network and others to benchmark individual jurisdictions, and identify successful components of performance frameworks that can be shared.

4.1.4 Mechanism for fostering multilateral collaboration

The benchmark framework by the AELERT Network has also generated interest for an international multilateral initiative to develop a best practice performance framework for environmental compliance and enforcement functions. The project, *Measuring Environmental Compliance: Designing Analytically Sound and Policy-Relevant Indicators*, involves a collaborative effort across Victorian EPA, South Australian EPA, Environment Agency England and Wales, Scottish EPA (SEPA) and the Irish EPA, with central coordination and project management through the Organisation for Economic Co-operation and Development (OECD).

The project uses collective financial and in-kind resources of the participating regulators. By utilising home based and peer international networks, this project has a strong basis and governance to ensure it can be delivered, and enables outcomes to be shared, peer reviewed and discussed more broadly across the networks. It also provides both implementation authority and brings to bear the right technical and regulatory practice (specialist) expertise. The reform is beneficial from both a technical perspective to ensure an effective, relevant and best practice performance framework, and also provides broader benefits such as: (a) having a group of modern regulators who acknowledge the policy challenge; (b) demonstrating a clear commitment to government and stakeholders to improve accountability and outcomes from regulators; and (c) preparedness to benchmark with peers to develop 'best practice' environmental compliance service outcomes.

---

[10] INECE, *Performance Management Guidance for Compliance and Enforcement Practitioners* (2008).

4.1.5 Building and sharing contemporary regulatory practice

Networks are also well positioned to utilise their membership base and communication channels to share individual member reforms. A recent case in point is provided in the South Australian EPA, where a review occurred around the use and application of a 'harms based, problem focused' approach.[11] The reform was developed as part of a number of organisational change initiatives and focused on how it can complement existing regulatory processes and risk-based approaches.

The initiative[12] describes how particular known harms to the South Australian environment will be identified; how a disciplined intelligence and project management approach will be deployed to best understand the problem and to determine the measures that will demonstrate it has/has not been fixed; and the governance arrangements established to determine resourcing and planning decisions, to ensure the necessary organisation capability and systems are developed, and to review the initiative and outcomes achieved.

A similar initiative is being adopted concurrently by the EPA Victoria, and hence collaboration is being employed to share approaches and learnings. Given the current interest and resources being employed in some Australian jurisdictions around the concept, the AELERT Network is being used to broadly share the reform, and invite discussion and comment with all members.

4.2 Improving Operational Effectiveness – Operations

Networks are well positioned to build capability in dealing with new and evasive environmental problems. Pink[13] concludes that 'networks provide individuals, teams, and agencies with access to a vast array of environmental compliance and enforcement expertise'. IMPEL has also done this by sharing technical approaches and developing a working operators' manual. A few AELERT examples are provided.

---

[11] Sparrow, MK, *The Regulatory Craft: Controlling Risks, Solving Problems, and Managing Compliance* (2000) and Sparrow, MK, *The Character of Harms: Operational Challenges in Control* (2008).

[12] EPA (South Australia), *Becoming a Harms-Based Regulator – Developing a Problem-Solving Culture* (2013), http://www.epa.sa.gov.au/xstd_files/Licensing/Report/change_harms.pdf

[13] Pink, G, 'Assessing the Utility of Environmental Enforcement Networks: Maximising Benefits to Members', in *Proceedings of the 9th International Conference on Environmental Compliance and Enforcement, 20–24 June 2011*.

4.2.1 AELERT National Waste Operations Group (NWOG)

A common regulatory challenge in the waste management area is to deter and prevent the illegal dumping of waste. The NWOG[14] is led by the Victorian and South Australian EPAs and brings together state and territory waste regulators for the 'purpose of examining the movement, treatment and disposal of waste from a national perspective'.[15]

Networks allow for teams operating in separate jurisdictions to share: (a) approaches used to identify illegal waste operators and share intelligence methods; (b) research into behavioural aspects of the problem, using this information to design better regulatory interventions to deter poor behaviour and promote/encourage good waste management practices; and (c) intelligence of criminal networks that extend across jurisdictional boundaries.

Although the initial focus of the group is to target illegal waste operations, NWOG allows peers to build capacity and scale that would not otherwise be available to a single jurisdiction, establishing a centre of specialist expertise. The group has the flexibility to consider a range of regulatory interests – to consider the effectiveness or otherwise of regulatory strategies used by states and territories; to coordinate operational programmes for movements of waste between states and territories; and to share intelligence of non-compliant operators with interests across jurisdictions. The AELERT Secretariat provides administrative operational support to the group, and facilitates learning by sharing the project outputs, including through its online and social media communication channels.

4.2.2 Operation Cetus

Networks can effectively bring together regulatory practitioners to deal with common and cross-jurisdictional harms. The AELERT Operations Cluster[16] is an example of a Regulators Network facilitating joint cross-jurisdictional enforcement operations. A particular focus for the Cluster was a joint national operation on compliance and enforcement challenges involving (increasing) human interaction that potentially compromise both individual whales and public safety.

Operation Cetus was conducted over two phases, timed in accordance

---

[14] Established as an operational group under the AELERT Operations Cluster.

[15] Taken from the National Waste Operations Group terms of reference.

[16] Consists of jurisdictional representatives from environment agencies for each Australian state and territory as well as the Australian Commonwealth Government and the New Zealand Government.

with whale migration in the participant's local area – the first in 2011[17] and a follow-up campaign in 2012.[18] In the first phase, the coordinated effort of the jurisdictions amassed a total of 123 separate but coordinated compliance and enforcement activities. The activities included vessel-based patrols, communication with individual recreational boat owners, and covert surveillance operations on commercial whale-watching vessels.

The collaborative operational effort provided a number of benefits[19] including:

1. Extending the capability of patrols to deal with incidents as they were occurring;
2. Building working relationships between the Commonwealth and state agencies, providing more effective compliance of activity occurring across Commonwealth and state controlled waters;
3. Extending the ability to draw a greater media presence, with anecdotal information that created interest and greater awareness from the general public; and
4. Providing a collective set of recommendations (from the regulator's network perspective) relating to necessary changes to regulatory requirements/offences, and guidance/information/training for commercial whale-watching operations.

The programme, coordinated and given authority through the AELERT Network, demonstrated that a national capability can be achieved with respect to cetaceans interaction compliance monitoring, and enhancing cooperation between participating jurisdictions.

4.2.3 Site contamination – policy and operational collaboration

Alongside the AELERT Network, the national Standing Council on Environment and Water (SCEW) also brings together specialist expertise in certain disciplines. As part of the review of the *National Environment Protection (Assessment of Site Contamination) Measure*, key policy/technical professionals from jurisdictions were tasked to review and develop a nationally consistent approach to the assessment of legacy pollution and waste. The Measure is implemented in each jurisdiction to provide the framework for effective environmental management practices

---

[17] End of May to mid-November 2011.

[18] End of May to end of October 2012.

[19] AELERT, *Operation Cetus – Phase II, May–October 2012, Final Report* (2013).

by the community. Significant in-kind and financial contribution was provided by all participants over a number of years.

To ensure implementation of the Measure occurs in a timely and consistent manner, the SCEW participants have sought that the working group remains together as a specialist standing committee. This again brings together, and provides the implementation authority with, a highly specialist group to collaborate and provide service to the entire national collective. It is also provides a mechanism to share practice in a highly contentious and challenging policy space, and develop nationally agreed best practice approaches for issues such as identification of contaminated sites, risk prioritisation approaches, public risk communication, information dissemination and stakeholder engagement.

4.3 Enhance Regulatory Compliance Capacity – Knowledge and Capacity Building

The most recognised and valued output of AELERT from regulatory based operational and field staff is its role in building regulatory capacity and capability at the grassroots level. Two common network functions are discussed here: provision of training and development programmes for environmental regulators, and coordinating and hosting regular network conferences. Clusters around capacity building are common to most practice-based environmental networks (including AELERT, IMPEL and INECE networks).

4.3.1 Modern and relevant Training and Development (T&D) programme

The AELERT Network has used its collective membership to review available T&D programmes for the specialised skills necessary for modern regulatory practitioners. A *Better Regulators Course* has been developed using the leadership of two network members (New South Wales EPA and Brisbane City Council) who have led on this area for a number of years. Through the AELERT Network, this T&D course is delivered on a cost-recovery basis to other network members, and is able to be quickly tailored to reflect any individual strategic development focus and/or to account for particular jurisdictional environmental statutes. The network allows for this programme to remain in the close control of the regulators that need it, and provide additional scope and scale to ensure it remains viable over time.

The collaboration means the T&D programme can continue to evolve to ensure it reflects the contemporary skills required to deal with more complex and evasive environmental challenges, and its ability to be quickly and inexpensively deployed across member jurisdictions. The

T&D programme utilises the collective experience of its membership base and provides important development opportunities for the experienced operators to share their knowledge with others and to gain recognition of their skills.

4.3.2 Engagement and contemporary knowledge sharing – regulators' conferences

Networks play a critical role in leading, coordinating and generating excitement for annual or biennial regulators' conferences. The events allow an opportunity for member agencies to showcase best practice, engage and connect with peers across the diverse network base, and allow for eminent regulatory practitioners and/or environmental leaders to both challenge regulators and inspire them. In challenging financial times, there is often much greater staff demand to attend such conferences than available capacity for agencies. In response, new technologies and innovations are being employed (e.g. webinar methods) to extend the proceedings of conferences to many more practitioners. However, it is the face-to-face engagement, often after hearing a challenging speaker, where participants find most value.

Networks are critical in setting the scene to allow for these exchanges of information, and in providing opportunities to consider new approaches and stimulate ideas for innovation and reform. This offers innovative, cost-effective capability development for network members, as well as providing recognition to leading regulatory practitioners.

4.4 Consistent Practice – Challenges and Opportunities

Examples provided in this chapter show a common and essential objective (at political, organisational and network level) to pursue consistent and best practice regulatory frameworks/outcomes. Consistent practice objectives exist at both policy and operational levels. At the operational level, often the varying legal and regulatory framework of the jurisdictions can be a challenge to collaboration and consistency, that is, operational standards are often developed in collaboration. However their status and method of implementation will vary because of the different legal systems in each jurisdiction. In some defined areas, high-level statutory systems are in place that allow for consistent outcomes to be achieved.[20]

---

[20] National Environment Protection (Assessment of Site Contamination) Measure; Ambient Air Quality National Environment Protection Measure; and others.

Irrespective of the statutory requirements in place at the local, provincial or national level, networks offer a means to build consistent standards and operational practice that over time bring individual regulatory practice towards a more common approach.

In the absence of any unifying statutory framework for regulatory requirements, networks allow members to develop libraries of 'regulatory policy toolkits', such that research, analysis and benchmarking can occur more freely. This promotes better informed policy decisions as individual jurisdictions review their regulatory frameworks over time and facilitates 'good execution'.[21]

There are now many examples of more consistent environmental protection legislation in Australia, with South Australia, Tasmania and Queensland using a similar environmental protection framework, and in some situations, where all states and territories have over time adopted similar legal definitions in complex regulatory areas (such as is defining what is waste).

In addition, there is evidence that collaboration between jurisdictions allows individual members to have an agreed and more consistent approach over time, and engenders a greater willingness to share intellectual property. The New South Wales EPA for example has a mature system for waste tracking as part of its regulatory functions. The South Australian EPA had a manual, paper-based waste tracking system which, with the agreement and support of New South Wales EPA, has now been fully converted to an equivalent (consistent) system using the New South Wales model. This has brought consistent practice in two states, which has been warmly received and supported by waste operators who work across both jurisdictions. The reform has also benefited from a relatively timely implementation timeframe, with little IT risk given it has been tested and assured by New South Wales EPA. This collaboration has resulted in a significantly lower implementation cost, certain outcomes, and consistent practice for operations. In turn, New South Wales has benefited from the bilateral cooperation, utilising aspects of South Australian's risk-based licensing structure in reforming their licensing system, which again brings greater consistency of approach, and the ability for both jurisdictions to share ongoing reforms given the similarity of their regulatory systems.

Other studies (for example, Pink)[22] also conclude that '. . . networks

---

[21] Freiberg, A, *The Tools of Regulation* (2010).

[22] Pink, G, 'Assessing the Utility of Environmental Enforcement Networks: Maximising Benefits to Members', in *Proceedings of the 9th International Conference on Environmental Compliance and Enforcement, 20–24 June 2011.*

have the ability to coalesce environmental compliance and enforcement expertise, which enables agencies to engage in bilateral or multilateral projects and initiatives'. Networks build and sustain strong peer relationships that are utilised in a variety of ways to build capacity, and deliver better and cost-effective outcomes.

5. CONCLUSIONS

This chapter provides only a very few specific examples of the outputs and benefits that environmental regulation and enforcement networks deliver. Effective enforcement and environmental regulation are assisted by a different type of sharing and engagement – facilitated through properly structured and utilised environmental enforcement networks. Networks deliver and demonstrate clear and tangible benefits to the collective membership base. Further, the formal authority provided by senior leaders in participating in the network also provides authority for officers from across their organisations to work with their inter-jurisdictional peers, to share ideas, challenges, even frustrations, in order to innovate, learn and to create better practice outcomes.

Networks also offer a cost-effective and collective approach to progress more consistent outcomes, including offering an expert base to develop and profile important policy positions, and to develop and recommend legislative reforms. They can enable participating members to work towards a common practice over time, through understanding what has worked and what has not.

This chapter also recognises that the strong connections and then relationships are developed through networks to allow peer regulatory organisations to establish effective bilateral and multilateral arrangements, where they can identify and work together on common strategic and operational reforms. Such reforms are often then shared back through the broader communications and engagement channels that networks provide.

These are times where resources are increasingly scarce, and the problems faced increasingly complex and evasive. Effective and respected environmental regulation and enforcement networks are considered a cost-effective mechanism to assist agencies to be best positioned, skilled and motivated, and have access to the best and most effective tools, to deliver the best possible outcomes for the environment and society.

ACKNOWLEDGEMENTS

Thanks are due to colleagues across the networks, especially John Merritt, Nic Maher, John Seager and Will Fawcett.

BIBLIOGRAPHY

AELERT (2013), *Operation Cetus – Phase II, May–October 2012, Final Report.*

EPA (South Australia), *Becoming a Harms-Based Regulator – Developing a Problem-Solving Culture* (2013), http://www.epa.sa.gov.au/xstd_files/Licensing/Report/change_harms.pdf

EPANet/EEA (2013), *The EPA Network – Sharing Experiences across Europe*, EPA Network – 2013, http://epanet.ew.eea.europa.eu/fol249409/epa-brochure-final-web.pdf/download

Farmer, A (2007), *Handbook of Environmental Protection and Enforcement: Principles and Practice*. London: Earthscan.

Freiberg, A (2010), *The Tools of Regulation*. NSW: Federation Press.

Gemmell, JC and Scott, EM (2012), 'Guest Editorial', *Risk Management* 14(1), doi:10.1057/rm.2011.20.

Gemmell, JC and Scott, EM (2013), 'Environmental Regulation, Sustainability and Risk', *Sustainability Accounting, Management and Policy Journal*, 4(2): 120–144.

IMPEL (2003), *Management Reference Book for Environmental Inspectorates, Report No 12*, Brussels: IMPEL.

INECE (2008), *Performance Management Guidance for Compliance and Enforcement Practitioners*, Draft 2nd edition.

INECE (2011), 'Enforcement Cooperation: Strengthening Environmental Governance', *Proceedings of the 9th International Conference*, Whistler, Canada.

Lehane, J and Pink, G (2011), 'Evolution of a Regional Environmental Enforcement Network: The Australasian Environmental Law Enforcement and Regulators neTwork (AELERT)', *Proceedings of the 9th International Conference on Environmental Compliance and Enforcement, 20–24 June 2011*. International Network for Environmental Compliance and Enforcement (INECE), British Columbia, Canada, http://inece.org/conference/9/papers/Lehane-Pink_AELERT_Australia_Final.pdf

NHEEPA (2005), The Contribution of Good Environmental Regulation to Competitiveness, aka 'The Prague Statement'.

Pink, G (2011), 'Assessing the Utility of Environmental Enforcement Networks: Maximising Benefits to Members', *Proceedings of the 9th International Conference on Environmental Compliance and Enforcement, 20–24 June 2011*. International Network for Environmental Compliance and Enforcement (INECE), British Columbia, Canada, http://inece.org/conference/9/papers/Pink_EENs_Australia_Final.pdf

Sparrow, MK (2000), *The Regulatory Craft: Controlling Risks, Solving Problems, and Managing Compliance*. Washington DC: The Brookings Institution.

Sparrow, MK (2008), *The Character of Harms: Operational Challenges in Control*. Cambridge: Cambridge University Press.

9. Countering transnational organized wildlife crime: regional and sub-regional initiatives, global responses and the need for more effective coordination

Edward van Asch*

1. INTRODUCTION

The international character of transnational organized crime makes it difficult to understand and effectively deal with such crimes at the national level only: since crime is global, purely national responses are inadequate.[1] Responses must therefore be based on international or bilateral

* Edward van Asch is a PhD candidate at the University of Sheffield (UK). His research aims to examine the effectiveness of international cooperation to counter transnational organized crime with an emphasis on the illegal wildlife trade in Southeast Asia. He was previously based in Thailand and worked for the United Nations Office on Drugs and Crime (UNODC), the United Nations Environment Program (UNEP) and TRAFFIC Southeast Asia, and was involved in key regional initiatives and projects to increase cooperation and strengthen the capacity of government and law enforcement to counter illegal trade. More recently he worked at the Secretariat of the Convention on International Trade in Endangered Species of Wild Fauna and Flora (CITES) to support the development and coordination of the International Consortium on Combating Wildlife Crime (ICCWC). He holds a Master's Degree in International Criminology from the University of Sheffield and a degree in International Relations with French from the University of Sussex.

The opinions expressed in this chapter are those of the author and do not necessarily reflect the views or position of any organization or his current or previous employers.

[1] See generally Frank G Madsen, *Transnational Organized Crime* (Routledge 2009); United Nations Office on Drugs and Crime (UNODC), *The Globalization of Crime: A Transnational Organized Crime Threat Assessment* (UNODC Vienna 2010), ii; Grant Pink, 'Law Enforcement Responses to Transnational Environmental Crime: Choices, Challenges, and Culture' (Australian National

cooperation as countries cannot effectively deal with transnational organized crime unilaterally. A proportion of such cooperation is created by what Bowling[2] refers to as new forms of cooperation in the form of initiatives at the regional, sub-regional or global level. Such initiatives have emerged to assist countries to combat transnational crime by encouraging them to work together at the international, regional or sub-regional levels. This is particularly the case when the commodity that is illegally traded are protected species.

High demand for protected species has created a lucrative black market that is exploited by unscrupulous traders and fiercely competitive organized networks. One of the main reasons for this is that the illegal wildlife trade generates very large profits with little risk of prosecution. There is evidence to suggest that, while organized groups are not necessarily always involved in the illegal wildlife trade, organized criminal groups displaying different levels of organization are becoming increasingly involved.[3] This is particularly the case when highly lucrative goods such as rhino horns or elephant ivory are involved.

This chapter will examine the development of several types of initiatives in Asia and will be based on emerging ideas from the preliminary research conducted by the author in support of his doctoral research on the effectiveness of international cooperation to combat transnational organized crime, with a focus on the illegal wildlife trade.

As noted above, a premise for the chapter is the assumption that countries should not act unilaterally to counter transnational organized crime and that cooperation amongst countries, often facilitated by a number of international, regional and sub-regional initiatives, is essential

---

University Transnational Environmental Crime (TEC) Project Working Paper 4/2013), 2.

[2] See generally Ben Bowling, *Policing the Caribbean: Transnational Security Cooperation in Practice* (Oxford University Press, Clarendon Studies in Criminology 2010).

[3] The illegal wildlife trade in Southeast Asia is best understood in categories, each with its own specific markets, smuggling methods and trafficking routes, ranging from individual collectors and small traders to highly organized wildlife networks and organized crime groups, with connections all over the world. Most of the illegal wildlife trade is believed to be done by competing networks displaying different levels of organization depending on the volume and value of their trade. In many cases, however, they are as organized as criminal syndicates dealing in drugs, arms or other illicit commodities. See generally Edward van Asch, 'The Illegal Wildlife Trade and Transnational Organized Crime', in Pietro Saitta, Joanna Shapland and Antoinette Verhage (eds), *Getting By or Getting Rich? The Formal, Informal and Criminal Economy in a Globalised World* (Eleven International Publishing, 2013), 147–160.

to effectively counter transnational organized wildlife crime. Specifically, the paper will highlight the need for enforcement actions to be performed along the entire law enforcement chain – from the crime scene, to the initial seizure and investigation, to arrests, culminating in successful prosecutions and convictions. This is, ultimately, what can contribute to effective law enforcement to combat transnational wildlife crime and one of the key roles that can and should be played by sub-regional, regional and global initiatives.

2. THE ILLEGAL WILDLIFE TRADE, A SERIOUS TRANSNATIONAL ORGANIZED CRIME

The harvesting of natural resources is basic to every day human life.[4] Concern over the growing amounts of trade in wild animals and plants and on the need to control it has led to increased cooperation between states and to the development of national and international laws and agreements to regulate the legal trade as well as to combat its illicit equivalent.

The Convention on International Trade in Endangered Species of Wild Fauna and Flora (CITES), which celebrated its 40th anniversary in 2013, is the main international agreement directed towards the protection and control of the international trade in wildlife.[5] It provides varying degrees of protection to close to 35,000 species for which international trade is regulated under the Convention. Such species are included in the CITES Appendices and have varying degrees of protection depending in which Appendix CITES Parties have agreed to list the specific species. The overall objective of CITES is to regulate the trade in wild species of plants and animals to ensure their trade does not pose a threat to their survival in the wild.[6] Contrary to what some may think, CITES is not a general

---

[4] United Nations Office on Drugs and Crime (UNODC), *Transnational Organized Crime in East Asia and the Pacific: A Threat Assessment* (UNODC 2013), 77.

[5] CITES is the main convention dealing with the international wildlife trade and will remain the focus of this paper. There are, however, a number of additional conventions with a focus on biodiversity and wildlife such as the Convention on Biological Diversity (CBD), the Convention on Migratory Species of Wild Animals (CMS) and the Ramsar Convention on Wetlands. See Michael Bowman, Peter Davies and Catherine Redgwell, *Lyster's International Wildlife Law* (2nd edition, Cambridge University Press 2010), 651.

[6] Three per cent of all the species protected by CITES are not allowed to be traded internationally for commercial purposes except in exceptional

wildlife treaty. It only deals with the over-exploitation of CITES-listed species as a result of unsustainable international trade, or, the issue that remains the focus of this paper, unlawful or illegal trade, which is just one of the multiple threats to wildlife.[7]

At the recent 16th meeting of the Conference of the Parties to CITES (CoP16) held in Bangkok, Thailand in March 2013, the seriousness of wildlife crime was discussed and decisions adopted by CITES Parties highlighted the need to counter wildlife crime at the national, sub-regional, regional and global levels. This was not the first time the seriousness of the problem was stressed, but it provided a background for countries around the globe to rally behind what the CITES Secretary-General referred to as a 'watershed moment' for combating wildlife crime.[8]

This 'watershed moment' was the culmination of a number of commitments and declarations made by members of the international community, through a series of pledges, resolutions and decisions or agreed documents on the need to take urgent action to combat the illegal wildlife trade. These included, amongst others, several Resolutions from the United Nations Commission on Crime Prevention and Criminal Justice (or CCPCJ, known also as the UN Crime Commission), the UN General Assembly and the UN Economic and Social Council (ECOSOC) in 2011, 2012 and 2013, respectively, the outcome document 'The Future We Want' of the UN Conference on Sustainable Development in Rio de Janeiro in 2012 (known as Rio+20), the Asia-Pacific Economic Cooperation (APEC) Leaders' Declaration 2012, and statements at a G8 Summit in June 2013,

---

circumstances. The remaining 97% can be traded under strict controls and through a system of permits that requires approval from the CITES Management Authorities of each country involved in the trade. See generally Convention on International Trade in Endangered Species of Wild Fauna and Flora (CITES), http://www.cites.org/ (accessed September 2013).

[7] See Peter H Sand, *Transnational Environmental Law: Lessons in Global Change* (International Environmental Law and Policy Series, Kluwer Law International 1999), 168; Ben Boer, Ross Ramsay and Donald R Rothwell, *International Environmental Law in the Asia Pacific* (International Environmental Law Series, Kluwer Law International 1998), 105; Edward van Asch, 'The Illegal Wildlife Trade and Transnational Organized Crime', in Pietro Saitta, Joanna Shapland and Antoinette Verhage (eds), *Getting By or Getting Rich? The Formal, Informal and Criminal Economy in a Globalised World* (Eleven International Publishing, 2013), 151.

[8] See John E Scanlon, 'CITES CoP16, Bangkok 2013: A "Watershed Moment" for Combating Wildlife Crime' (International Institute for Sustainable Development, guest article #17 2013), http://biodiversity-l.iisd.org/guest-articles/cites-cop16-bangkok-2013-a-%E2%80%98watershed-moment%E2%80%99-for-combating-wildlife-crime/ (accessed September 2013).

as well as a 'call to action' by former Secretary Clinton and a presidential statement by President Obama in July 2013.

It may be useful to first establish some basic definitions of what is considered as 'wildlife' and what constitutes wildlife 'crime', particularly an 'international crime', which is what is referred to when speaking of transnational organized wildlife crime. The term transnational organized crime will also be defined.

Wildlife crime is 'no different from many other forms of illegal activities'.[9] It shares many of the characteristics of other transnational crimes. However, to a significant degree, wildlife crime has yet to be viewed, and accordingly responded to, as 'mainstream' crime.[10] By wildlife we refer to all fauna (e.g. animals, including birds and fish) and flora (e.g. plants, but also timber and forest products). The term wildlife will be used throughout the chapter mainly to refer to protected species for which their international trade is regulated by CITES and protected by national legislation. 'Crime' will be referred to as 'acts committed contrary to national laws and regulations'. This would include:

> illicit exploitation of natural resources, such as the poaching of an elephant, uprooting of a rare orchid, unauthorized logging of trees, or unlicensed netting of sturgeons[;] . . . subsequent acts, such as the processing of fauna and flora into products, their transportation, offer for sale, sale, possession, etc[; and] . . . the concealment and laundering of the financial benefits made out of these crimes.[11]

Wildlife crimes will occur in the country of origin, in transiting countries, and/or in the country of destination. Any international movement of CITES-listed species without the appropriate documentations and permits also involves a violation of the CITES Convention.

For the purposes of this chapter, transnational organized crime will be defined as referred to by Article 2 of the UN Convention against

---

[9] See generally International Consortium on Combating Wildlife Crime (ICCWC), http://www.cites.org/eng/prog/iccwc.php (accessed September 2013).

[10] See generally International Consortium on Combating Wildlife Crime (ICCWC), http://www.cites.org/eng/prog/iccwc.php (accessed September 2013); see also John M Sellar, 'Focusing on Wildlife Crime' (FBI Law Enforcement Bulletin, 2013) http://leb.fbi.gov/2013/july/focusing-on-wildlife-crime-part-1 and http://leb.fbi.gov/2013/july/focusing-on-wildlife-crime-part-2 (accessed September 2013).

[11] See John M Sellar, 'Focusing on Wildlife Crime' (FBI Law Enforcement Bulletin, 2013) http://leb.fbi.gov/2013/july/focusing-on-wildlife-crime-part-1 and http://leb.fbi.gov/2013/july/focusing-on-wildlife-crime-part-2 (accessed September 2013).

Transnational Organized Crime (UNTOC), which refers to organized criminal groups as 'a structured group of three or more persons, existing for a period of time and acting in concert with the aim of committing one or more serious crimes or offenses established . . ., in order to obtain, directly or indirectly, a financial or other material benefit'.[12] Pires and Moreto's definition, somewhat similarly, refers to anything from three or more loosely organized individuals to large and highly organized criminal networks and/or criminal organizations that are involved in some instances of the trade or control the illegal wildlife trade chain.[13]

2.1 Commitment to Curb the Illegal Wildlife Trade

As noted above, there have been a number of declarations and resolutions focused on the need to take urgent action to combat the illegal wildlife trade. Some examples over the past few years are given below.

CITES Parties adopted Resolution Conf. 11.3 (Rev. CoP16) on compliance and enforcement, which reflects the request from CITES Member States (currently 178)[14] to support a more coordinated approach to combating wildlife crime. The Resolution encourages closer communication, collaboration and cooperation between the Convention's institutions, national enforcement agencies, and existing intergovernmental bodies that have a mandate from their Member States to engage in or support wildlife law enforcement.[15]

In 2010, the INTERPOL General Assembly unanimously adopted a Resolution noting the seriousness of environmental crime and calling upon its Member Countries to assist INTERPOL in providing appropriate

---

[12] United Nations Office on Drugs and Crime (UNODC), *The Globalization of Crime: A Transnational Organized Crime Threat Assessment* (UNODC Vienna 2010), 1; see also Grant Pink, 'Law Enforcement Responses to Transnational Environmental Crime: Choices, Challenges, and Culture' (Australian National University Transnational Environmental Crime (TEC) Project Working Paper 4/2013), 9.

[13] Stephen F Pires and William D Moreto, 'Preventing Wildlife Crimes: Solutions That Can Overcome the "Tragedy of the Commons"', *European Journal on Criminal Policy and Research*, 17(2): 101–123 (2011), 117.

[14] CITES has 178 Member Countries as of September 2013. For more information, see Convention on International Trade in Endangered Species of Wild Fauna and Flora (CITES), http://www.cites.org/ (accessed September 2013).

[15] For further details see CITES Resolution Conf. 11.3 (Rev. CoP16), http://www.cites.org/eng/res/11/E-Res-11-03R16.pdf (accessed September 2013).

responses to address the problem of the illegal wildlife trade,[16] among other issues.

The UN Commission on Crime Prevention and Criminal Justice (CCPCJ, known also as the UN Crime Commission) adopted a Resolution on 'Crime prevention and criminal justice responses against illicit trafficking in endangered species of wild fauna and flora' during its meeting in April 2011 in Vienna. The Resolution expresses concern about the involvement of organized criminal groups in the trafficking of endangered species and recognizes the work being conducted at international level by the International Consortium on Combating Wildlife Crime (ICCWC).

The UN Conference on Sustainable Development, held in Rio de Janeiro, Brazil, in June 2012, through paragraph 203 of its outcome document, 'The Future We Want', recognized and emphasized the importance of effective international cooperation among international organizations in combating illicit trafficking in wildlife.[17]

In September 2012, the Asia-Pacific Economic Cooperation (APEC) Leaders Declaration 2012 noted the concern of APEC leaders over the increasing trafficking in protected species and made a commitment to take action to combat the illegal wildlife trade and to take 'meaningful steps' to counter the illegal wildlife trade.[18]

At an event on wildlife trafficking and conservation in November 2012, Hillary Clinton, the US Secretary of State at the time, encouraged

---

[16] See INTERPOL General Assembly Resolution (AG-2010-RAP-08), http://www.cites.org/eng/news/press/2010/20101108_Interpol_resolution.pdf (accessed September 2013).

[17] See United Nations, Report of the United Nations Conference on Sustainable Development (A/CONF.216/16), http://www.uncsd2012.org/content/documents/814UNCSD%20REPORT%20final%20revs.pdf (accessed September 2013).

[18] '[We] are concerned by the escalating illicit trafficking in endangered and protected wildlife, including marine resources, and associated products, which has economic, social, security, and environmental consequences in our economies. We commit to strengthen our efforts to combat illegal trade in wildlife, timber, and associated products, to implement measures to ensure sustainable marine and forest ecosystems management, and to facilitate sustainable, open, and fair trade of non-timber forest products. We will take meaningful steps to promote sustainable management and conservation of wildlife populations while addressing both the illegal supply and demand for endangered and protected wildlife, through capacity building, cooperation, increased enforcement, and other mechanisms.' See Asia-Pacific Economic Cooperation (APEC) Leaders' Declaration (2012) http://www.apec.org/Meeting-Papers/Leaders-Declarations/2012/2012_aelm.aspx (accessed September 2013). See also CITES press release (2012) http://www.cites.org/eng/news/pr/2012/20120912_APEC_declaration.php (accessed September 2013).

countries to continue to combat the illegal wildlife trade. The 'Call for Action' included increased diplomatic efforts, global outreach, strengthened and increased enforcement, and a concerted global response, as the magnitude of the threat requires a commensurate response at all levels – national, regional and global.[19]

In November 2012, the Third Committee of the UN General Assembly adopted a resolution on 'Strengthening the United Nations' crime prevention and criminal justice programme, in particular its technical cooperation capacity'. The resolution expresses concern at the negative effects of transnational organized crime and the serious challenges and threats posed by illicit trade, including the trafficking in endangered and protected species of wild fauna and flora. It emphasizes the need to combat transnational crimes by strengthening international cooperation, capacity-building, criminal justice responses and law enforcement efforts. It also highlights the need to develop comprehensive policies to combat transnational organized crime and corruption.[20]

At a G8 Summit in the United Kingdom in June 2013, G8 Leaders recognized the need to combat the illegal wildlife trade as part of broader efforts to counter criminal trafficking and strengthen border security. In the final communiqué of the meeting, the Leaders agreed to 'take action to tackle the illegal trafficking of protected or endangered species'[21] and highlighted the importance of combating the illegal wildlife trade and to treat it as seriously as other transnational organized crimes such as drug and human trafficking and corruption.

During the 16th meeting of the Conference of the Parties (CoP16) to CITES in March 2013, a large number of resolutions and decisions were

---

[19] Former Secretary Clinton highlighted that 'over the past few years wildlife trafficking has become more organized, more lucrative, more widespread, and more dangerous than ever before . . . it is also a national security issue, a public health issue, and an economic security issue'. For more information see US Department of State releases: US Department of State media release on a Call to Action: http://www.state.gov/r/pa/prs/ps/2012/11/200355.htm (accessed September 2013). See also Secretary Clinton's Remarks at the event: http://www.state.gov/secretary/20092013clinton/rm/2012/11/200294.htm.

[20] For more information, see United Nations General Assembly Resolution (A/C.3/67/L.15/Rev.1) http://www.un.org/ga/search/view_doc.asp?symbol=A/C.3/67/L.15/Rev.1 (accessed September 2013).

[21] See paragraph 70 of the Lough Erne G8 Leaders' Communique (2013), 7 https://www.gov.uk/government/uploads/system/uploads/attachment_data/file/207771/Lough_Erne_2013_G8_Leaders_Communique.pdf (accessed September 2013); see also CITES press release (2013) http://www.cites.org/eng/news/sundry/2013/20130621_g8.php (accessed September 2013).

adopted and revised recognizing the illegal wildlife trade as a serious transnational crime. CoP16 also saw 'unprecedented levels of international cooperation in addressing the threats posed to wildlife, to people and to livelihoods through poaching and smuggling'. CITES' Secretary-General highlighted the success of the conference in addressing a number of issues, including: 'ensuring high-level political engagement; enhancing international cooperation; coordinating enforcement support at global, regional and national levels; deploying a wider-range of operational techniques and enhancing enforcement effectiveness; enacting CITES-implementing legislation; attracting further financing, and reducing demand for illicit goods'.[22]

During a ministerial roundtable hosted by ICCWC alongside CITES CoP16, ministers and high-level government representatives reaffirmed their 'strong commitment . . . to combat transnational organized wildlife and forest crime' and acknowledged the 'escalating levels of poaching and illegal trade, and the increasing involvement of organized crime groups'.[23]

In July 2013, an Executive Order on Combating Wildlife Trafficking was issued by President of the United States Barack Obama. The Executive Order addresses the domestic and international response to wildlife trafficking of the United States of America and highlights the need to treat wildlife crime as a seriously as other transnational crimes such as drugs and arms. It also highlights that illegal wildlife trade operations have expanded 'beyond small-scale, opportunistic actions to coordinated slaughter commissioned by armed and organized criminal syndicates'.[24]

---

[22] See John E Scanlon, 'CITES CoP16, Bangkok 2013: A "Watershed Moment" for Combating Wildlife Crime' (International Institute for Sustainable Development, guest article #17 2013) http://biodiversity-l.iisd.org/guest-articles/cites-cop16-bangkok-2013-a-%E2%80%98watershed-moment%E2%80%99-for-combating-wildlife-crime/ (accessed September 2013).

[23] The report of the roundtable also highlights the broad-reaching impacts of the illegal wildlife trade on species, regional security, national economies, people and their livelihoods. During the meeting, many countries reaffirmed their strong commitment to fight 'the organized crime groups that are behind transnational organized wildlife and forest crime'. See CITES Secretariat, *CITES CoP16 Inf. 54: Chair's Summary of ICCWC Roundtable on Combating Transnational Organized Wildlife and Forest Crime for Ministers and High-Level Representatives* (CITES CoP16 Inf. 54 2013), 3, http://www.cites.org/eng/cop/16/inf/E-CoP16i-54.pdf (accessed September 2013). For further details, see CITES press release (2013) http://www.cites.org/eng/news/pr/2013/20130305_ministerial.php (accessed September 2013).

[24] For further details, see CITES press releases (2013) http://www.cites.org/eng/news/sundry/2013/whitehouse_factsheet.pdf and http://www.cites.org/eng/news/pr/2013/20130702_us_eo.php (accessed September 2013).

In addition, the UN Crime Commission recommended a resolution on 'Crime prevention and criminal justice responses to illicit trafficking in protected species of wild fauna and flora', which recognizes wildlife crime as a serious transnational organized crime and 'strongly encourages member States to take appropriate measures to prevent and combat illicit trafficking in wild fauna and flora, including the adoption of the necessary legislation for the prevention, investigation and prosecution of such trafficking'.[25] The resolution was adopted in July 2013 by the ECOSOC, which serves as the central United Nations forum for discussing international economic and social issues.

As stated by Scanlon 'wildlife crime has become a serious threat to the security, political stability, economy, natural resources and cultural heritage of many countries, and . . . the extent of the response required is beyond the sole remit of environment or wildlife law enforcement agencies, or of one country or region alone'.[26] These above demonstrate that the international community increasingly recognizes wildlife crime as a serious transnational organized crime that requires a 'determined and coordinated response'.[27]

It needs to be noted that the above does not include a number of other statements and declarations and expressions of intent by countries, donors and international, intergovernmental and non-governmental organizations to combat the illegal wildlife trade at the regional level, such as the 2009 Manifesto on Combating Wildlife Crime in Asia,[28] the 2009 Kathmandu Recommendations,[29] the 2010 Hua Hin Declaration on

---

[25] See draft Resolution IV, pp. 42–46 in E/2013/30, http://www.unodc.org/documents/organized-crime/UNODC_CCPCJ_EG.1_2014/Draft_Resolution_II_E.pdf. See also CITES press release (2013) http://www.cites.org/eng/news/sundry/2013/20130502_ccpcj_resolution.php (accessed September 2013).

[26] See John E Scanlon, 'CITES CoP16, Bangkok 2013: A "Watershed Moment" for Combating Wildlife Crime' (International Institute for Sustainable Development, guest article #17 2013), http://biodiversity-l.iisd.org/guest-articles/cites-cop16-bangkok-2013-a-%E2%80%98watershed-moment%E2%80%99-for-combating-wildlife-crime/ (accessed September 2013).

[27] See CITES Secretariat, *CITES CoP16 Inf. 54: Chair's Summary of ICCWC Roundtable on Combating Transnational Organized Wildlife and Forest Crime for Ministers and High-Level Representatives* (CITES CoP16 Inf. 54 2013), 3, http://www.cites.org/eng/cop/16/inf/E-CoP16i-54.pdf (accessed September 2013).

[28] See Manifesto on Combating Wildlife Crime in Asia (ASEAN-WEN, 9 January 2013), http://asean-wen.org/index.php/regional-agreements-protocols/file/7-manifesto-on-combating-wildlife-crime-in-asia-pattaya-workshop-april-2009 (accessed September 2013).

[29] See Kathmandu Recommendations (ASEAN-WEN, 9 January 2013), http://asean-wen.org/index.php/regional-agreements-protocols/file/5-global-tiger-workshop-kathmandu-recommendations (accessed September 2013).

Tiger Conservation,[30] or the Ministerial Statement on ASEAN and the International Year of Forests in 2011[31] in Asia.

It is clear, therefore, that international bodies and national governments have agreed on the need to treat wildlife crimes as serious crimes, that enforcement efforts should be coordinated at national, regional and global levels and that countries need to work together across the trade chain (e.g. among source, transit and destination countries). The above also highlights the need to use available techniques and methods that are used to combat other transnational organized crimes such as drugs trafficking in the fight against the illegal wildlife trade.

2.2 A Transnational Organized Crime

Protected species are used for food or as exotic pets, display materials and/or household decorative objects. Wildlife is also consumed or used in traditional medicine and 'is driven by age-old beliefs, cultural values and traditions and, more recently, to cure hangover'.[32] Demand for protected species is motivated by a number of reasons, usually related to wealth,

---

[30] See Hua Hin Declaration on Tiger Conservation (ASEAN-WEN, 9 January 2013), http://asean-wen.org/index.php/regional-agreements-protocols/file/6-asia-ministerial-meeting-hua-hin-declaration-on-tiger-conservation (accessed September 2013).

[31] See Ministerial Statement (ASEAN-WEN, 9 January 2013), http://asean-wen.org/index.php/regional-agreements-protocols/file/3-asean-ministerial-statement-on-asean-and-international-year-of-forests-2011 (accessed September 2013).

[32] See generally TRAFFIC, *What's Driving the Wildlife Trade? A Review of Expert Opinion on Economic and Social Drivers of the Wildlife Trade and Trade Control Efforts in Cambodia, Indonesia, Lao PDR and Vietnam* (East Asia and Pacific Region Sustainable Development Discussion Papers, East Asia and Pacific Region Sustainable Development Department, World Bank, 2008); Gavin Hayman and Duncan Brack, *International Environmental Crime: The Nature and Control of Environmental Black Markets* (Workshop Report, Royal Institute of International Affairs, Sustainable Development Program 2002); Donald R Liddick, *Crimes against Nature: Illegal Industries and the Global Environment* (Praeguer 2011); Tom Milliken and Jo Shaw, *The South Africa–Viet Nam Rhino Horn Trade Nexus: A Deadly Combination of Institutional Lapses, Corrupt Wildlife Industry Professionals and Asian Crime Syndicates* (TRAFFIC South Africa, 2012); Edward van Asch, 'The Illegal Wildlife Trade and Transnational Organized Crime', in Pietro Saitta, Joanna Shapland and Antoinette Verhage (eds), *Getting By or Getting Rich? The Formal, Informal and Criminal Economy in a Globalised World* (Eleven International Publishing, 2013), 147–162; see United Nations Office on Drugs and Crime (UNODC), *Transnational Organized Crime in East Asia and the Pacific: A Threat Assessment* (UNODC 2013), ch. 7.

power, influence and status, particularly when the wildlife goods are considered non-essential or luxury items.[33]

This is specially the case in countries or communities where emerging economic affluence and disposable income has created a rise in demand for protected wildlife and a lucrative black market for unscrupulous traders and fiercely competitive organized networks to exploit as it generates very large profits with little risk of prosecution.[34]

Wildlife crime, however, affects all countries and impacts developed and developing countries alike.[35] There are different types of trade depending on the volume, value and commodity (i.e. species) illegally traded, and each will generally have its own specific smuggling methods, trafficking routes and markets.[36] Such categories will range from 'individual collectors

---

[33] See generally Edward van Asch, 'The Illegal Wildlife Trade and Transnational Organized Crime' in Pietro Saitta, Joanna Shapland and Antoinette Verhage (eds), *Getting By or Getting Rich? The Formal, Informal and Criminal Economy in a Globalised World* (Eleven International Publishing, 2013), 147–162.

[34] 'The illegal wildlife trade in Southeast Asia is best understood in categories, each with its own specific markets, smuggling methods and trafficking routes ranging from individual collectors and small traders to highly organized wildlife networks and organized crime groups with connections all over the world. . . . Most of the illegal wildlife trade is believed to be done by competing networks displaying different levels of organization depending on the volume and value of their trade'. In many cases, however, they are as organized as criminal syndicates dealing in drugs, arms, or other illicit commodities. See Edward van Asch, 'The Illegal Wildlife Trade and Transnational Organized Crime', in Pietro Saitta, Joanna Shapland and Antoinette Verhage (eds), *Getting By or Getting Rich? The Formal, Informal and Criminal Economy in a Globalised World* (Eleven International Publishing, 2013), 147 (see generally 147–162). See also Mark Shaw and Tuesday Reitano, 'The Evolution of Organized Crime in Africa: Towards a New Response' (Institute for Security Studies, Paper 244 2013), 15.

[35] See CITES Secretariat, *CITES CoP16 Inf. 54: Chair's Summary of ICCWC Roundtable on Combating Transnational Organized Wildlife and Forest Crime for Ministers and High-Level Representatives* (CITES CoP16 Inf. 54 2013), 3, http://www.cites.org/eng/cop/16/inf/E-CoP16i-54.pdf (accessed September 2013).

[36] See generally TRAFFIC, *What's Driving the Wildlife Trade? A Review of Expert Opinion on Economic and Social Drivers of the Wildlife Trade and Trade Control Efforts in Cambodia, Indonesia, Lao PDR and Vietnam* (East Asia and Pacific Region Sustainable Development Discussion Papers, East Asia and Pacific Region Sustainable Development Department, World Bank, 2008); Edward van Asch, 'The Illegal Wildlife Trade and Transnational Organized Crime', in Pietro Saitta, Joanna Shapland and Antoinette Verhage (eds), *Getting by or Getting Rich? The Formal, Informal and Criminal Economy in a Globalised World* (Eleven International Publishing, 2013), 154–155; United Nations Office on Drugs and

dealing in small quantities of specific species to organized networks that will deal in larger shipments and quantities'.[37]

As explained by the author elsewhere, '[s]ome of the illegal wildlife trade is opportunistic. Most of it, however, involves networks of people'.[38] A large proportion of the illegal wildlife trade is believed to be done by competing networks displaying different levels of organization depending on the volume and value of their trade. In many cases, however, they are as organized as criminal groups dealing in drugs, arms or other illicit commodities.[39] While this does not suggest that all illegal trade in wildlife is organized by criminal networks, evidence does suggest, as noted above, an increase in the involvement of organized criminal groups. This was echoed by participants of a ministerial meeting in March 2013 that 'acknowledged the serious nature of transnational organized wildlife and forest crime, and . . . made reference to the disturbing escalation in the levels of poaching and illegal trade, and the increasing involvement of organized crime groups'.[40]

The nature and structure of the illegal trade can be extremely complex, as the relationships between all parties involved continues to change and evolve in response to the availability – or unavailability – of wildlife. As is also the case with other illicit trade in a number of commodities '[f]or each illicit good, the actors involved in sourcing, transporting, protecting and vending . . . will be different'.[41] The trade chains for the illegal wildlife

---

Crime (UNODC), *Transnational Organized Crime in East Asia and the Pacific: A Threat Assessment* (UNODC 2013), 77.

[37] Edward van Asch, 'The Illegal Wildlife Trade and Transnational Organized Crime', in Pietro Saitta, Joanna Shapland and Antoinette Verhage (eds), *Getting By or Getting Rich? The Formal, Informal and Criminal Economy in a Globalised World* (Eleven International Publishing, 2013), 147–162.

[38] Edward van Asch, 'The Illegal Wildlife Trade and Transnational Organized Crime' in Pietro Saitta, Joanna Shapland and Antoinette Verhage (eds), *Getting by or Getting Rich? The Formal, Informal and Criminal Economy in a Globalised World* (Eleven International Publishing, 2013), pp. 155–158. See also Donald R Liddick, *Crimes against Nature; Illegal Industries and the Global Environment* (Praeguer 2011), 48.

[39] Edward van Asch, 'The Illegal Wildlife Trade and Transnational Organized Crime', in Pietro Saitta, Joanna Shapland and Antoinette Verhage (eds), *Getting By or Getting Rich? The Formal, Informal and Criminal Economy in a Globalised World* (Eleven International Publishing, 2013), 155–158.

[40] See CITES Secretariat, *CITES CoP16 Inf. 54: Chair's Summary of ICCWC Roundtable on Combating Transnational Organized Wildlife and Forest Crime for Ministers and High-Level Representatives* (CITES CoP16 Inf. 54 2013), 3, http://www.cites.org/eng/cop/16/inf/E-CoP16i-54.pdf (accessed September 2013).

[41] Mark Shaw and Tuesday Reitano, 'The Evolution of Organized Crime in Africa: Towards a New Response' (Institute for Security Studies, Paper 244 2013), 22.

trade are usually well established, are managed by the same groups of people and have permanent market locations. Trade chains are 'extremely mobile and dynamic and their composition and location shifts over time in response to availability and demand, with flexible distribution lines that are highly creative'.[42] Smuggling methods and routes will shift and adapt to avoid detection and traders will exploit weak wildlife law enforcement and a general lack of knowledge and capacity to identify wildlife.[43]

The networks tend to be highly organized, particularly when dealing with high value commodities. The illegal trades in ivory and rhino horn are some of the most highly organized, and appear to be linked to large organized crime groups, and in some instances, as noted above, to rebel militia and armed groups.[44] Sellar highlighted the common characteristics and arrangements of organized criminal networks, which include: capacity for detailed planning, access to significant financial support and the capability to successfully coordinate, organize and manage international shipments. In addition, organized groups are often able to create fake permits and certificates. Such criminal groups are lured into the illegal wildlife trade by the lucrative profits that can be made and, like their counterparts in other criminal activities, may be heavily armed and violent.[45]

In a recent article, Sellar highlights that:

> Organized crime groups use sophisticated techniques and routes to smuggle their illegal goods . . . Specially designed routes exploit ports by employing limited screening facilities and using several transit and transhipment points to conceal the true country of origin.

---

[42] TRAFFIC, *What's Driving the Wildlife Trade? A Review of Expert Opinion on Economic and Social Drivers of the Wildlife Trade and Trade Control Efforts in Cambodia, Indonesia, Lao PDR and Vietnam* (East Asia and Pacific Region Sustainable Development Discussion Papers, East Asia and Pacific Region Sustainable Development Department, World Bank, 2008), 26.

[43] Edward van Asch, 'The Illegal Wildlife Trade and Transnational Organized Crime', in Pietro Saitta, Joanna Shapland and Antoinette Verhage (eds), *Getting By or Getting Rich? The Formal, Informal and Criminal Economy in a Globalised World* (Eleven International Publishing, 2013), 154–155.

[44] See United Nations, 'Report of the Secretary-General on the Activities of the United Nations Regional Office for Central Africa and on the Lord's Resistance Army-affected Areas' (S/2013/297, 2013) http://www.un.org/en/ga/search/view_doc.asp?symbol=S/2013/297 (accessed September 2013); see also CITES press release (2012) http://www.cites.org/eng/news/pr/2012/20121222_UNSC_elephant_LRA.php

[45] John M Sellar, 'International Illicit Trafficking in Wildlife' (The Police Chief, V74 N6 2007).

> . . . Further, much of the wildlife contraband smuggled around the world is consigned to companies and addresses that either do not exist or serve purely for the period of transport. Front companies with elaborate false credentials conceal the illicit origin of animals, plants, and products. Senior and midlevel organized crime figures also minimize risk by recruiting couriers to transport illegally harvested contraband within countries or across international borders. Many different types of couriers prove effective.[46]

Examples of the degrees of organization involved in the illegal wildlife trade range from highly organized criminal operations to opportunistic selling of wildlife because 'they [local villagers/farmers] come in contact with a particular species, they will probably know where to sell it or "someone" that will know "someone" who will be interested to buy it'.[47]

While the illegal wildlife trade 'is not believed to be led by organized criminal syndicates that one would associate with the 'mafia'',[48] evidence suggests that organized groups, equally equipped, but generally unknown to the broad public, continue to operate with impunity. The illegal trade in ivory and rhino horn between Africa and Asia involves 'highly organized and resourceful criminal groups with strong links to source and demand countries'[49] and appears to be the most organized type of illegal wildlife trade, with highly organized and resourceful groups that use increasingly

---

46 John M Sellar, 'Focusing on Wildlife Crime' (FBI Law Enforcement Bulletin, 2013) http://leb.fbi.gov/2013/july/focusing-on-wildlife-crime-part-1 and http://leb.fbi.gov/2013/july/focusing-on-wildlife-crime-part-2 (accessed September 2013).

47 Edward van Asch, 'The Illegal Wildlife Trade and Transnational Organized Crime', in Pietro Saitta, Joanna Shapland and Antoinette Verhage (eds), *Getting By or Getting Rich? The Formal, Informal and Criminal Economy in a Globalised World* (Eleven International Publishing, 2013), 158.

48 Edward van Asch, 'The Illegal Wildlife Trade and Transnational Organized Crime', in Pietro Saitta, Joanna Shapland and Antoinette Verhage (eds), *Getting By or Getting Rich? The Formal, Informal and Criminal Economy in a Globalised World* (Eleven International Publishing, 2013), 156; See also John M Sellar, 'Focusing on Wildlife Crime' (FBI Law Enforcement Bulletin, 2013) http://leb.fbi.gov/2013/july/focusing-on-wildlife-crime-part-1 and http://leb.fbi.gov/2013/july/focusing-on-wildlife-crime-part-2 (accessed September 2013); Gavin Hayman and Duncan Brack, *International Environmental Crime: The Nature and Control of Environmental Black Markets* (Workshop Report, Royal Institute of International Affairs, Sustainable Development Program 2002), 7.

49 Edward van Asch, 'The Illegal Wildlife Trade and Transnational Organized Crime', in Pietro Saitta, Joanna Shapland and Antoinette Verhage (eds), *Getting By or Getting Rich? The Formal, Informal and Criminal Economy in a Globalised World* (Eleven International Publishing, 2013), 157.

sophisticated methods to poach and smuggle wildlife.[50] Other examples of highly organized networks include a 'notorious reptile trader from Malaysia known internationally as "Anson Wong" and his "family business"'.[51] This is, however, as highlighted by the research conducted to date by the author, 'potentially only one of maybe between six and ten similar networks' that exist in Asia.[52]

---

[50] The demand is thought to be 'fuelled by rumours of rhino horn being a cure for cancer, and being increasingly used in a manner akin to a recreational drug, such as "rhino wine," to improve male sexual performance, and to treat hangovers and other ill-effects of the over-consumption of food, drugs or alcohol' (see CITES press release (2012) http://www.cites.org/eng/news/pr/2012/20120618_rhinos_under_threat_rio.php). United Nations TV (UNTV) and the CITES Secretariat launched in June 2012 a documentary film 'Rhinos Under Threat'. The film shows the involvement of highly organized criminal organizations in the illegal trade in rhino horns from parks in South Africa and Swaziland, to Hanoi in Vietnam. It highlights the increase in trade in recent years and the brutality and impact of the killings on the local communities. The documentary investigates black markets in Hanoi, the demand for rhino horn in Asia and the measures taken by authorities to combat such crimes. See United Nations TV (UNTV) and CITES Secretariat, Documentary: 'Rhinos Under Threat' (UNTV and CITES Secretariat 2012) http://www.youtube.com/watch?v=t3m7FOXOLbY (accessed September 2013). See also INTERPOL, *23rd Meeting of the INTERPOL Wildlife Crime Working Group* (2012).

[51] See generally Bryan Christy, *The Lizard King: The True Crimes and Passions of The World's Greatest Reptile Smugglers* (Twelve 2008); Bryan Christy, 'The Kingpin: An Exposé of the World's Most Notorious Wildlife Dealer, his Special Government Friend, and his Ambitious New Plan' (National Geographic 2010) http://ngm.nationalgeographic.com/2010/01/asian-wildlife/christy-text/1 (accessed September 2013); Bryan Christy, 'The Serpent King' (Foreign Policy 2010) http://www.foreignpolicy.com/articles/2010/12/28/the_serpent_king (accessed September 2013); Bryan Christy, 'Anson Wong Goes Free' (National Geographic 2012), http://newswatch.nationalgeographic.com/2012/02/28/anson-wong-goes-free/ (accessed September 2013); TRAFFIC, 'International Wildlife Trafficker Sentenced to 6 Months in Malaysia' (TRAFFIC News, November 2010), http://www.traffic.org/home/2010/9/6/international-wildlife-trafficker-sentenced-to-6-months-in-m.html (accessed September 2013); TRAFFIC, 'Wong's Sentence Increased to Five Years' (TRAFFIC News, November 2010), http://www.traffic.org/home/2010/11/4/wongs-sentence-increased-to-five-years.html (accessed September 2013); BBC, 'Malaysia Jails Man who Smuggled 95 Snakes on a Plane' (BBC News Asia-Pacific, September 2010), http://www.bbc.co.uk/news/world-asia-pacific-11203270 (accessed September 2013).

[52] Edward van Asch, 'The Illegal Wildlife Trade and Transnational Organized Crime', in Pietro Saitta, Joanna Shapland and Antoinette Verhage (eds), *Getting By or Getting Rich? The Formal, Informal and Criminal Economy in a Globalised World* (Eleven International Publishing, 2013), 157.

3. COUNTERING THE ILLEGAL WILDLIFE TRADE

A wide range of actions to combat the illegal wildlife trade are underway. Efforts include the strengthening of legislative frameworks, increased enforcement and surveillance, increased coordination across multiple agencies on issues related to wildlife crime, awareness-raising to reduce demand, and a number of training and capacity-building events for wildlife law enforcement officials, police, customs and prosecutors.[53]

This has undoubtedly had a positive impact. Over the past few years, there have been a number of successful seizures and arrests of wildlife traffickers. This can be clearly seen by the recent efforts of, for example, countries identified at the 63rd meeting of the CITES Standing Committee and CoP16 as countries of primary concern for the illegal trade in ivory that were urged to develop national ivory action plans to counter trends in illegal trade. After the development and submission of the plans, there has been a clear increase in successful arrests and prosecutions in those countries.[54]

However, while one would normally expect that the individual that is arrested for trade in or possession of illegal wildlife would be thoroughly investigated to examine if he/she is involved in broader illegal operations, in wildlife law enforcement this is – or was – not historically the case. Individuals caught in possession of wildlife generally only receive a fine – in some cases they are also arrested – and the illegal goods they carried are seized. However, there is a lack of interest (but also capacity in many cases) to conduct in-depth investigations and to make use of special investigative techniques that are commonly used for other transnational crimes such as narcotics. This highlights a key deficiency: it is necessary to investigate the entire crime chain associated with the criminal networks behind the crimes and use all available techniques in the process to ensure criminals are brought to justice.

The key problems faced by wildlife law enforcement officers around the world identified by ICCWC, echoed by participants of the ministerial meeting in March 2013, and throughout interviews conducted by the author, include: inadequate legislation, poor governance and corruption;

---

[53] See CITES Secretariat, *CITES CoP16 Inf. 54: Chair's Summary of ICCWC Roundtable on Combating Transnational Organized Wildlife and Forest Crime for Ministers and High-Level Representatives* (CITES CoP16 Inf. 54 2013), 3, http://www.cites.org/eng/cop/16/inf/E-CoP16i-54.pdf (accessed September 2013).

[54] See for example BBC, 'Kenya Seizes Ivory "Going from Uganda to Malaysia"' (BBC News Africa, July 2013), http://www.bbc.co.uk/news/world-africa-23168558 (accessed September 2013).

lack of financial and human resources resulting in inadequate operational wildlife law enforcement capacity and lack of equipment;[55] limited training opportunities; and difficulty accessing the latest technology and modern enforcement tools related to intelligence-gathering and analysis and forensic science that are essential to respond to sophisticated crime groups. There is also evidence to suggest that organized groups have been able to successfully corrupt government and public officials all along the trade chain[56] and that armed militant or rebel groups are involved or fund their illicit activities, particularly in Africa, with the illegal wildlife trade. As acknowledged by the United Nations Secretary-General, Ban Ki-moon, in a report recently presented to the UN Security Council, the 'illegal ivory trade may currently constitute an important source of funding for armed groups'.[57]

It is important to highlight that special investigative techniques and other useful tools such as anti-money laundering legislation, are often not mobilized for wildlife crime.[58] CoP16 highlighted the need to use special techniques and other available resources such as intelligence driven operations, risk profiling, controlled deliveries, covert operations, forensics and the sharing of forensic evidence and the use of anti-money laundering and asset forfeiture legislation. This last point is particularly important, as

---

55 Wildlife law enforcement officers also often lack parity with their counterparts in Customs and Police services and are ill-prepared to respond to the problem. This is sometimes exacerbated by the lack of cooperation within countries and lack of support from certain police and Customs administrations (for more information, see International Consortium on Combating Wildlife Crime (ICCWC), http://www.cites.org/eng/prog/iccwc.php (accessed September 2013).

56 Edward van Asch, 'The Illegal Wildlife Trade and Transnational Organized Crime', in Pietro Saitta, Joanna Shapland and Antoinette Verhage (eds), *Getting By or Getting Rich? The Formal, Informal and Criminal Economy in a Globalised World* (Eleven International Publishing, 2013), 155–158; Donald R Liddick, *Crimes against Nature; Illegal Industries and the Global Environment* (Praeguer 2011), 48.

57 See United Nations, 'Report of the Secretary-General on the Activities of the United Nations Regional Office for Central Africa and on the Lord's Resistance Army-affected Areas' (S/2013/297, 2013) http://www.un.org/en/ga/search/view_doc.asp?symbol=S/2013/297 (accessed September 2013). See also CITES press release, http://www.cites.org/eng/news/pr/2012/20121222_UNSC_elephant_LRA.php

58 See generally International Consortium on Combating Wildlife Crime (ICCWC), http://www.cites.org/eng/prog/iccwc.php (accessed September 2013). See also CITES Secretariat, *CITES CoP16 Inf. 54: Chair's Summary of ICCWC Roundtable on Combating Transnational Organized Wildlife and Forest Crime for Ministers and High-Level Representatives* (CITES CoP16 Inf. 54 2013), 4, http://www.cites.org/eng/cop/16/inf/E-CoP16i-54.pdf (accessed September 2013).

tackling the financial flows of organized wildlife crime is essential given that controlling financial flows and seizing related assets is vital to successfully tackling organized crime in general and organized wildlife crime in particular.[59] It needs to be noted that the use of special investigative techniques may not be essential to combat opportunistic illegal traders and unorganized and small-scale wildlife crime. These techniques are, however, crucial to finding the masterminds behind large-scale illegal wildlife trade and the organized criminal groups that may be involved. Commonly used to combat illicit trade in drugs and other serious crimes, the tools identified above should also be used to combat the illegal wildlife trade. It is also crucial that follow-up investigations and prosecutions are done, especially targeted at the masterminds behind the illegal trade in wildlife. This is particularly important when larger organized criminal groups are involved.[60]

With special attention to the judicial process, there seems to be a general lack of understanding and interest from the judiciary and prosecutors to tackle the illegal wildlife trade. There are many reasons why there are very few investigations and even less prosecutions and convictions. A key one is that national wildlife laws are weak in a number of countries. A further one is that, in many cases, there is no legislation that criminalizes wildlife crime in place. A recent resolution adopted by ECOSOC encourages countries to treat wildlife crime as a serious transnational organized crime. A serious crime, as defined by Article 2 of the UN Convention against Transnational Organized Crime is 'conduct constituting an offence punishable by a maximum deprivation of liberty of at least 4 years or a more serious penalty'. As Sellar notes, this causes 'considerable problems', as national legislation dealing with wildlife crime in some countries 'does not even constitute a crime, but only an administrative matter where a monetary penalty will be imposed', let alone imprisonment.[61] Research

---

[59] Mark Shaw and Tuesday Reitano, 'The Evolution of Organized Crime in Africa: Towards a New Response' (Institute for Security Studies, Paper 244 2013), 22.

[60] See generally John E Scanlon, 'CITES CoP16, Bangkok 2013: A "Watershed Moment" for Combating Wildlife Crime' (International Institute for Sustainable Development, guest article #17 2013) http://biodiversity-l.iisd.org/guest-articles/cites-cop16-bangkok-2013-a-%E2%80%98watershed-moment%E2%80%99-for-combating-wildlife-crime/ (accessed September 2013); CITES Secretariat, *CITES CoP16 Inf. 54: Chair's Summary of ICCWC Roundtable on Combating Transnational Organized Wildlife and Forest Crime for Ministers and High-Level Representatives* (CITES CoP16 Inf. 54 2013), http://www.cites.org/eng/cop/16/inf/E-CoP16i-54.pdf (accessed September 2013).

[61] John M Sellar, 'Focusing on Wildlife Crime' (FBI Law Enforcement Bulletin, 2013) http://leb.fbi.gov/2013/july/focusing-on-wildlife-crime-part-1 and

in Africa actually indicates that a large number of countries in the region 'have an inadequate legal framework under which to investigate, prosecute and prevent organised criminal activities, money laundering and corruption' and that '[s]ome countries have no such legislation in place at all'.[62] Wildlife crime is therefore not generally treated as a serious crime, as legislation is not currently in place in a number of countries.[63]

This is exacerbated by the lack of knowledge and awareness of the scale of the problem and the perception of the seriousness and organization of wildlife crime amongst the judiciary and a large proportion of the enforcement community: they do not see wildlife crime as a serious transnational organized crime and there is a general lack of concern for these crimes compared to other crimes.[64] As Sellar highlights, 'people generally have not heard news sources focusing on a major Mafia figure incarcerated because of the controlling and smuggling of [wildlife]'.[65] This is exemplified by the lack of known prosecutions of wildlife crime or wildlife criminals. While no statistics are available to the knowledge of the author on the number of arrests versus the number of prosecutions of wildlife criminals or networks,[66] interviews conducted as part of the research clearly highlight this as a problem that is identified. Personal experience and consultations with experts and colleagues also seem to highlight this fact.

3.1 The Need for Cooperation

As noted previously, combating transnational organized wildlife crime is a complex matter that requires a holistic and coordinated response,

---

http://leb.fbi.gov/2013/july/focusing-on-wildlife-crime-part-2 (accessed September 2013).

62 Mark Shaw and Tuesday Reitano, 'The Evolution of Organized Crime in Africa: Towards a New Response' (Institute for Security Studies, Paper 244 2013), 19.

63 This, however, is changing thanks to the increasing focus on the illegal wildlife trade by countries in recent years, as highlighted above.

64 World Bank, *Going, Going, Gone: The Illegal Trade in Wildlife in East and Southeast Asia* (Environment and Social Development Department, East Asia and Pacific Region, World Bank, 2005), 3.

65 John M Sellar, 'Focusing on Wildlife Crime' (FBI Law Enforcement Bulletin, 2013) http://leb.fbi.gov/2013/july/focusing-on-wildlife-crime-part-1 and http://leb.fbi.gov/2013/july/focusing-on-wildlife-crime-part-2 (accessed September 2013).

66 Information is usually scattered and available through a number of press releases and news articles.

similar to that afforded to other transnational organized crimes such as the trafficking of drugs, arms or humans.[67] This section will examine how the different initiatives can be of assistance to countries in the fight against transnational organized wildlife crime, identify the limitations and gaps of both initiatives and networks, and highlight the need for more effective coordination and cooperation amongst countries. We will then examine in the concluding section how ICCWC can play a supporting role and assist countries and other initiatives and networks to combat the illegal wildlife trade. Given that initiatives aim to foster cooperation, we will first examine how beneficial different forms of cooperation are and what are the basic requirements for effective cooperation.

One can logically argue that effective international cooperation is based on good cooperation amongst the different law enforcement officers within each country and with their counterparts in their neighbouring country. Enforcement agencies, however, are known for being reluctant to share information,[68] and do not have a very long history of cooperation with one another. As Sellar often stressed: everyone likes to cooperate, but no one likes to be coordinated. This is exemplified by the illegal wildlife trade where there are (or there should be) a number of agencies involved that are not necessarily used to working together. In fact, research on police cooperation indicates that enforcement agencies are more reluctant to share information within their national boundaries than internationally.[69] This is one important factor to keep in mind when talking broadly about international law enforcement cooperation.

Keeping in mind that no cooperation process is perfect, the questions that remain are: 'What are the underlying characteristics that facilitate cooperation?' and 'What are the gaps that hinder cooperation?' In order to understand and answer such questions, first we have to examine the different types of cooperation.

There are, in general terms, two main forms or types of cooperation: formal and informal cooperation. Such cooperation is facilitated through

---

[67] CITES Secretariat, *CITES CoP16 Inf. 54: Chair's Summary of ICCWC Roundtable on Combating Transnational Organized Wildlife and Forest Crime for Ministers and High-Level Representatives* (CITES CoP16 Inf. 54 2013), 4–5, http://www.cites.org/eng/cop/16/inf/E-CoP16i-54.pdf (accessed September 2013).

[68] See generally Laure Guille, 'Police and Judicial Cooperation in Europe' (unpublished PhD thesis, University of Sheffield 2008).

[69] Laure Guille, 'Police and Judicial Cooperation in Europe' (unpublished PhD thesis, University of Sheffield 2008), 333.

a number of bilateral and multilateral arrangements, the former being the oldest form of cooperation.[70]

Given that cooperation at the ground level is driven by efficiency and trust, personal contacts play a major role and enable cooperation amongst enforcement agencies. Interviews conducted to date suggest that existing formal and informal arrangements are complementary to each other: informal cooperation facilitates actual cooperation, whereas formal methods of cooperation ensure the appropriate procedures are taken to ensure that cooperation can lead to a seizure, arrest or a prosecution, as without these mechanisms the evidence would not be able to be used in court.

Informal methods are, as highlighted by a participant interviewed, arguably 'the very essence of cooperation activities' and are generally preferred to official (and often quite bureaucratic) channels and organizations. Nonetheless, formal and secure methods of sharing information such as, amongst others, the I24/7 of INTERPOL, are crucial to effectively deal with the problem. Such mechanisms, however, are often based on more informal efforts and personal contacts.

Transnational crime demands that governments implement methods that enable international and cross-border cooperation and that establish a legal basis for such cooperation. Efforts to sustain effective cooperation are, however, more generally based on the levels of trust and interpersonal communication and relationships: 'personal and informal contacts and the goodwill of the people involved in the process are key elements in terms of trust and speed'.[71] What is clear is that cooperative mechanisms need to be strengthened and enhanced and the number of investigations and prosecutions of wildlife traffickers needs to increase if countries want to effectively deal with the bigger picture.[72]

The most common factors that have been identified throughout the interviews conducted to date as factors that hinder effective communication and cooperation amongst enforcement officers are trust, cultural

---

[70] Malcom Anderson et al., *Policing the European Union: Theory, Law and Practice* (Oxford Clarendon Press 1995); Mathieu Deflem, *Policing Word Society. Historical Foundations of International Police Cooperation* (Oxford University Press 2002); Didier Bigo, 'The European Internal Security Field: Stakes and Rivalries in a Newly Developing Area of Police Intervention', in Malcom Anderson and Monica den Boer (eds) *Policing Across National Boundaries* (Pinter 1994), 161–173.

[71] Laure Guille, 'Police and Judicial Cooperation in Europe' (unpublished PhD thesis, University of Sheffield 2008), 333.

[72] Philip Bean, *Drugs and Crime* (3rd edition, Willan Publishing 2008), 150.

or language barriers, rotation of staff, lack of political support from the highest levels of government or political friction, lack of funds and equipment, and the lack of capacity of enforcement officers in remote locations or in certain countries where they receive limited training. A further problem is that species identification is a specialized skill, with only a limited amount of experts being able to recognize the differences between species. This is all encompassed in the broader problem as noted initially that there is often a lack of coordination amongst different agencies, departments within the same agencies, and sometimes between colleagues that could, for example, be competing for a promotion.[73]

Guille argues that effective cooperation is only possible when trust is built amongst the law enforcement officers that are supposed to work together and that cultural factors such as language barriers or different cultural and social practices and habits also create what we will call an 'invisible curtain' that should be taken into account. In addition, countries do not always share common languages and cultural practices. This can be detrimental to cooperation if trust is not built amongst the officers of the different countries. Political differences and different political regimes may also hinder effective cooperation if they generate mistrust amongst law enforcement officers. A further point highlighted by Guille is the need for political will and support from the higher levels of government. Most law enforcement officers work in a very structured and hierarchical environment in which they will not (and cannot) proceed with a given task without approval from a senior officer. It needs to be noted that political will and support are not reduced only to commitment to take action, but also refer to the allocation of pertinent resources, equipment and staff.[74]

Preliminary interview data indicate that trust is probably the most important factor in cooperation. The absence of trust (or a known person), will probably result in the information not being shared. This appears to happen in developed and developing countries alike, and, unsurprisingly, the reason for this is rather simple: enforcement officers do not trust what they don't know, even when existing formal arrangements could be used.

---

[73] Laure Guille, 'Police and Judicial Cooperation in Europe' (unpublished PhD thesis, University of Sheffield 2008), 333.

[74] See generally Laure Guille, 'Police and Judicial Cooperation in Europe' (unpublished PhD thesis, University of Sheffield 2008).

4. INCREASED WILDLIFE LAW ENFORCEMENT COOPERATION

As noted above, countering transnational organized wildlife crime requires international cooperation: no country can counter it alone.[75] CITES was conceived in an effort to regulate the international wildlife trade and to safeguard certain species from over-exploitation, and it created the basis for cooperation amongst countries to regulate close to 35,000 species.[76]

The growing need to protect endangered species has led to a 'new and intensified focus on transnational collaboration',[77] and emphasized the need for increased collective actions at the national, sub-regional and regional level. However, a further problem, in addition to the challenges identified in the section above, is that countries are not historically used to working together to combat the illegal wildlife trade and there has therefore been a general lack of cooperation and collaboration amongst countries.

This gap has been filled by what Bowling refers to as 'new structures of cooperation',[78] where a myriad of initiatives and mechanisms have emerged to facilitate and foster cooperation between countries[79] and to assist them to fulfil their commitments under CITES. These new models are a 'great promise for effective international action',[80] and have materialized due to the lack of coordination amongst agencies and the inability of certain countries to fully enforce its legislation: '[a]n inability or less than optimal ability in one country is of great concern when considering an

---

75 James WE Sheptycki, *In Search of Transnational Policing: Towards a Sociology of Global Policing* (Ashgate Publishing, 2002), 113.

76 For further details, see Convention on International Trade in Endangered Species of Wild Fauna and Flora, 'What is CITES?' http://www.cites.org/eng/disc/what.php (accessed September 2013).

77 James N Rosenau, 'Governance in a Globalizing World', in David Held and Anthony McGrew (eds) *The Global Transformations Reader: An Introduction to the Globalization Debate* (Polity Press, 2000), 186.

78 Ben Bowling, *Policing the Caribbean: Transnational Security Cooperation in Practice* (Oxford University Press, Clarendon Studies in Criminology 2010), 5–7.

79 See generally United Nations Office on Drugs and Crime (UNODC), *Border Liaison Offices in Southeast Asia (1999–2009): Ten Years of Fighting Transnational Organized Crime* (UNODC Regional Centre for East Asia and the Pacific 2010); ASEAN-Wildlife Enforcement Network (ASEAN-WEN) http://www.asean-wen.org/ (accessed September 2013).

80 Grant Pink, 'Law Enforcement Responses to Transnational Environmental Crime: Choices, Challenges, and Culture' (Australian National University Transnational Environmental Crime (TEC) Project Working Paper 4/2013), 19.

issue such as law enforcement responses to transnational environmental crime[s]'[81] such as wildlife.

In Asia, they have taken the form of the Border Liaison Office (BLO) Mechanism and the ASEAN Wildlife Enforcement Network (ASEAN-WEN), where a number of international, intergovernmental and non-governmental organizations play a central and active role. These are two examples of mechanisms with the potential to effectively counter transnational crime and the illegal wildlife trade in Southeast Asia, and will remain the focus of this chapter as they are part of the broader research of the author. These, however, are two of a number of initiatives that have appeared in Asia and across the world with the same objective in mind.[82] A further initiative that should be highlighted at the global level is the recently developed International Consortium on Combating Wildlife Crime (ICCWC), which will be briefly introduced in the following section.

4.1 New Structures of Cooperation in Asia

4.1.1 The Border Liaison Office (BLO) mechanism[83]

A BLO is essentially a coordinating office for national law enforcement agencies that encourages and facilitates enhanced cross-border cooperation. Located close to key border crossings or 'hot spots', offices are located on both sides of the border and act as a centralized clearing house for informal information exchange amongst law enforcement officers in border areas, thus facilitating formal exchange of information amongst countries. The aims of the mechanism are: to foster cooperation along and across national borders between different national law enforcement agency units working at the borders; to enable direct and real-time communication and information sharing as well as improved multilateral law enforcement; to strengthen law enforcement efforts at the borders and prevent illicit trafficking; to conduct joint operations against transnational organized crime in the region, building trust and mutual understanding;

---

81 Ibid.

82 See International Consortium on Combating Wildlife Crime (ICCWC), 'Report of the First Global meeting of the Wildlife Enforcement Networks' (2013) http://www.cites.org/common/docs/ICCWC%20Report%20-%20First%20Global%20Meeting%20of%20the%20WENs%20-%20Final.pdf (accessed September 2013).

83 See generally United Nations Office on Drugs and Crime (UNODC), *Border Liaison Offices in Southeast Asia (1999–2009): Ten Years of Fighting Transnational Organized Crime* (UNODC Regional Centre for East Asia and the Pacific 2010).

and to promote the dissemination of changing trends and new developments in cross-border trafficking.

Counterparts meet on a regular basis both formally and informally to exchange intelligence and share information on latest trends and smuggling routes, and workshops are periodically held to disseminate the latest modus operandi of traffickers and the trafficking routes. The mechanism was developed in 1993 between Cambodia, China, Lao PDR, Myanmar, Thailand and Viet Nam, and aimed to enable cross-border cooperation efforts against the illegal narcotics trade. During the period 1999–2010, it contributed to strengthening cross-border cooperation on drug control, and has increased the capacity of government law enforcement, prosecution bodies, relevant institutions and civil society to prevent, investigate and prosecute cases of cross-border crimes. Prior to the establishment of the mechanism, little to no cross-border cooperation existed between neighbouring countries.

The BLO programme is considered a hallmark example of multilateral law enforcement cooperation, and has led to calls from participating states to expand the mandate of the BLO mechanism to other transnational organized crimes (TOC), which was realized in 2010 with the expansion of the mandate to include environmental crimes and the illegal wildlife trade, amongst other crimes, through the development of the UNODC PATROL (Partnership Against Transnational-crime through Regional Organized Law-enforcement) programme.

4.1.2 The Association of Southeast Asian Nations Wildlife Enforcement Network (ASEAN-WEN)[84]

ASEAN-WEN is a wildlife law enforcement network involving relevant law enforcement agencies working to combat the illegal wildlife trade (police, customs and environmental agencies) of all ASEAN countries.[85] It aims to enhance cooperation amongst enforcement agencies and increase the capacity of governments to counter the illegal wildlife trade. Through annual meetings and a comprehensive array of workshops and trainings, ASEAN-WEN increases the capacity of and enhances cooperation amongst law enforcement agencies regionally and globally.

It provides a mechanism by which countries can share information and learn from each other's best practices, promotes the implementation

---

[84] See generally ASEAN-Wildlife Enforcement Network (ASEAN-WEN), http://www.asean-wen.org/ (accessed September 2013).

[85] ASEAN countries are: Brunei, Cambodia, Indonesia, Laos, Malaysia, Myanmar, the Philippines, Singapore, Vietnam and Thailand.

of existing national wildlife laws and international agreements (such as CITES), and has contributed to strengthening national laws. The network operates at both the national level[86] and at the regional level[87] to counter the illegal trade in wildlife and to enhance cooperation. Efforts of the network are coordinated by the Program Coordination Unit (PCU), in close cooperation with all its Member States.

ASEAN-WEN was born as a result of Objective Two of the ASEAN Regional Action Plan on Trade in Wild Fauna and Flora (2005–2010). The development of the network is in response to a call from ASEAN Member States to cooperate on improved CITES implementation, including law enforcement. This was followed by the ASEAN Regional Action Plan on Trade in Wild Fauna and Flora.[88] As part of the agreement to establish the network, ASEAN Member Countries agreed to allocate necessary financial and human resources, and to collaborate in cross-border cooperation and coordination to ensure the effective enforcement of legislation governing conservation, trade and sustainable use of wild fauna and flora. The development and nurturing of the network was made possible thanks to the support of the USAID funded ASEAN-WEN Support Program (2005–2010) and the ARREST Program (ongoing).

4.1.3 The International Consortium on Combating Wildlife Crime (ICCWC)

Recognizing that a well-coordinated law enforcement response is required to effectively combat transnational organized wildlife and forest crime, the CITES Secretariat, INTERPOL, the United Nations Office on Drugs and Crime (UNODC), the World Bank and the World Customs Organization

---

[86] At the national level, each country operates an inter-agency task force or a national WEN. All ASEAN countries except Singapore and Brunei have established a national WEN. It needs to be highlighted that while such countries may not have an official WEN, they all have national mechanisms for international and inter-agency cooperation.

[87] At the regional level, countries cooperate bilaterally and multilaterally by sharing information and conducting joint operations to counter the illegal wildlife trade.

[88] ASEAN-WEN is under declaration no. 24 of the ASEAN Declaration on Environmental Sustainability, signed by the Heads of States and Governments of ASEAN in 2007 and is recognized under the ASEAN Charter's ASEAN Socio Cultural Community (ASCC) Blueprint 2009–2015. In 2011 ASEAN Member States, extended the ASEAN Regional Action Plan on Trade in Wild Fauna and Flora (2005–2010). The new Regional Action Plan (2011–2015) aims to sustain earlier efforts and successes of ASEAN-WEN. See generally ASEAN-Wildlife Enforcement Network (ASEAN-WEN), http://www.asean-wen.org/ (accessed September 2013).

(WCO) joined forces and agreed to work together to support national wildlife law enforcement agencies and the sub-regional and regional networks mandated to combat the illegal wildlife trade. This resulted in the International Consortium on Combating Wildlife Crime (ICCWC).

The mission of ICCWC is to ensure that perpetrators of serious wildlife crimes are brought to justice through a 'formidable and coordinated response'[89] by working for, and with, frontline wildlife law enforcement officers that are mandated to take action against the illegal wildlife trade.

United under ICCWC since the launch of the alliance in November 2010, the five organizations have a 'unique pool of thematically relevant technical and programming expertise, presenting the opportunity for a novel approach to the multi-facetted challenges posed by wildlife crime'.[90] Each organization offers specialized expertise to support national enforcement agencies and sub-regional and regional networks and has extensive experience in developing and delivering comprehensive training and capacity-building programmes for law enforcement officers at the global level.

4.2 The Impact and Role of the Initiatives

The new focus on combating transnational wildlife crime as highlighted at CITES CoP16 and shown by the growing commitment of countries in recent years, has emphasized the need for increased transnational collaboration. One of the results of such effort is the emergence of new structures of cooperation that facilitate and foster cooperation at the sub-regional, regional and global levels, as highlighted in the previous section. We will now examine the impact of the initiatives on the illegal trade and if they result in increased actions at all levels of the enforcement chain, from initial seizure to detailed investigations and, ultimately, prosecutions and convictions.

As explained above, the BLO mechanism is a sub-regional programme developed to assist countries to cooperate and share intelligence along and across borders on cases of illicit trade.[91] ASEAN-WEN is a regional initiative created to encourage countries to cooperate at the national,

---

89 See generally International Consortium on Combating Wildlife Crime (ICCWC), http://www.cites.org/eng/prog/iccwc.php (accessed September 2013).

90 Ibid.

91 The UNODC-led initiative brings together relevant national law enforcement agencies working along and across borders to encourage enhanced cross-border cooperation. It enables officers working close to key 'hot spots' on both sides of the national borders to exchange information.

sub-regional and regional levels to counter the illegal wildlife trade in the region.[92] The focus of the former is on cross-border cooperation (along and across borders), while the focus of the latter is to improve coordination at the national and regional levels.

Stopping illegal trade across borders is essential: in order to counter transnational wildlife crime, it is important to have effective border management. The problem is that, as highlighted throughout the paper, smugglers and illegal wildlife traders are often well equipped and largely resourceful, and enforcement officers face a number of challenges.

The BLO mechanism and related projects have the crucial role of strengthening the capacity of border officers to stop, detect and investigate cases of illegal trade. Since 2010, a number of training events have improved, strengthened and expanded the capacity of law enforcement to prevent and investigate cases of cross-border crimes. In addition, the mechanism has built trust and promoted informal cooperation amongst border officials, which has led to increased cross-border cooperation. This is probably the most crucial aspect of the initiative itself as it increases cooperation and should, ideally, result in increased enforcement and further cooperation, and, in turn, lead to (ideally) more secure borders. It is difficult to provide exact details and quantify whether cooperation has increased and if the borders are more secure as a result of the initiative. Preliminary data from interviews conducted to date, however, suggests an increase in the sharing of information amongst countries, and that countries cooperate frequently. This leads to the assumption that there is increased cross-border cooperation and therefore that the borders are more secure.

While secure borders can contribute to increased seizures or to a change in the trends or routes used by smugglers, they are only one part of the enforcement chain. A concerted effort at the national level and the involvement of all relevant institutions is required. There still appears to be a gap with the judiciary and prosecutors in the different countries, and the mechanism would benefit from stronger connections to other initiatives and efforts, particularly with the judiciary. This is not necessarily because of the initiative itself, but rather because the involvement of justice and prosecutors in wildlife crime, particularly in Asia, remains a challenge.

At the other end of the spectrum, ASEAN-WEN encourages more

---

[92] The Association of Southeast Asian Nations Wildlife Enforcement Network (ASEAN-WEN) is a wildlife law enforcement network involving relevant law enforcement agencies working on the illegal wildlife trade (police, customs and environmental agencies) of all ASEAN countries. It aims to enhance cooperation amongst enforcement agencies and increase the capacity of governments to counter the illegal wildlife trade.

effective enforcement and increased engagement of countries at the national and regional level. The initiative has contributed to the increased commitment in the region to combat the illegal wildlife trade. It has also held an important role in raising the profile of wildlife crime in the policy agenda of countries. While it is not possible to know exactly how much the network has contributed to a notable increase in wildlife seizures across the region, it is clear that it has had an impact and that, as a result, countries are increasing their efforts to counter the illegal wildlife trade. Elements of the capacity-building programme also include awareness raising for judges and prosecutors, which seems to be one of the crucial next steps to draw their attention to the magnitude of the problem.

If one analyses both initiatives, one of the main differences between them is the focus. One focuses on the 'macro level' (i.e. the national and regional level) and the other focuses on the 'micro level' (field level).[93] While both levels are essential, there seems to be a gap between the national and field levels, which Sheptycki, Reiner, Anderson et al. and Guille[94] argue is one of the main challenges to effective cooperation. Guille also notes that, in many cases, broad cooperative agreements are signed without prior consultation at the field level. This poses a potential problem for effective cooperation, as political representatives at the macro level do not necessarily understand the operational requirements and needs at the field level. This does not allow field officers to trust the mechanism nor to use it efficiently[95] and it forces field officers to improvise which leads them to use their own informal mechanisms.[96]

---

93 See generally Laure Guille, 'Policing in Europe: An Ethnographic Approach to Understanding the Nature of Cooperation and the Gap between Policy and Practice', *Journal of Contemporary European Research*, 6(2): 257–271 (2010); John Benyon, 'The Politics of Police Co-operation in the European Union', *International Journal of the Sociology of Law*, 24(4): 353–379 (1996).

94 See James WE Sheptycki, *In Search of Transnational Policing: Towards a Sociology of Global Policing* (Ashgate Publishing, 2002); Robert Reiner 'Policing and the Police', in Mike Maguire, Rod Morgan and Robert Reiner (eds) *The Oxford Handbook of Criminology* (2nd edition, Oxford University Press, 1997), 997–1049; Malcom Anderson et al., *Policing the European Union: Theory, Law and Practice* (Oxford Clarendon Press 1995); Laure Guille, 'Police and Judicial Cooperation in Europe' (unpublished PhD thesis, University of Sheffield 2008), 333, 351–353; Laure Guille, 'Policing in Europe: An Ethnographic Approach to Understanding the Nature of Cooperation and the Gap between Policy and Practice', *Journal of Contemporary European Research*, 6(2): 257–271 (2010).

95 Laure Guille, 'Police and Judicial Cooperation in Europe' (unpublished PhD thesis, University of Sheffield 2008), 351–353.

96 See generally James WE Sheptycki, *In Search of Transnational Policing: Towards a Sociology of Global Policing* (Ashgate Publishing, 2002).

Focusing efforts at the border level and at the national and regional levels are both essential. Emphasis should, however, be placed on closing the gap between the national and the field levels. This could be done by bringing the initiatives closer together and ensuring that the national representatives and focal points of such initiatives are aware that other initiatives exist and that they work more closely together in the future.

The initiatives can also contribute to developing capacity in the region to combat wildlife crime. We have highlighted the need for increased cooperation amongst the networks and the strengths of each initiative. Increased cooperation amongst them would undoubtedly result in increased actions at all levels of the enforcement chain. Increased engagement with judges and prosecutors, however, needs to continue.

A further step that should be taken is ensuring that countries are equipped with the appropriate tools and that they use modern investigative techniques such as those used to counter other transnational crimes, to combat the illegal wildlife trade.[97] This is essential to move beyond seizures and ensure follow-up investigations and prosecutions, especially targeted at the masterminds behind the illegal wildlife trade, when organized groups or larger organized criminal networks are involved. This is one of the roles that ICCWC could play, as it continues to provide support to governments and the national, sub-regional and regional initiatives that have been developed to combat the illegal wildlife trade. A further role of ICCWC should be to facilitate increased coordination and support amongst the different initiatives that exist at the global level,[98] as the consortium provides the ideal platform for effective cooperation among intergovernmental bodies that have a mandate from their Member States to engage in or support wildlife law enforcement. The consortium also plays a leading role in raising political support and engaging all relevant stakeholders, including the judiciary and prosecutors, in the fight against transnational wildlife crime.

---

[97] Modern investigative techniques include, amongst others, intelligence driven operations, risk profiling, controlled deliveries, covert operations, and the use of anti-money laundering and asset forfeiture legislation (see generally International Consortium on Combating Wildlife Crime (ICCWC), http://www.cites.org/eng/prog/iccwc.php (accessed September 2013)).

[98] See generally International Consortium on Combating Wildlife Crime (ICCWC), 'Report of the First Global Meeting of the Wildlife Enforcement Networks' (2013), http://www.cites.org/common/docs/ICCWC%20Report%20-%20First%20Global%20Meeting%20of%20the%20WENs%20-%20Final.pdf (accessed September 2013).

5. CONCLUSION

As noted throughout the paper, a broad range of actors are involved in the illegal wildlife trade, ranging from individual collectors and opportunistic traders to highly organized wildlife networks and organized crime groups that can be as organized as their counterparts dealing in illicit drugs or arms.

While most of the illegal trade in wildlife is believed to be done by competing networks displaying different levels of organization depending on the volume and value of their trade, evidence suggests that sophisticated and highly organized criminal groups are increasingly involved in particular types of highly profitable commodities, such as rhino horn and elephant ivory. As highlighted at the ministerial roundtable held alongside CoP16, '[a]n imposing challenge lies ahead to combat the sophisticated criminal groups that are behind wildlife and forest crime, and to put an end to the alarming impacts that their activities are having on species, people and economies'.[99]

The decisions and resolutions adopted at CoP16 demonstrate a clear recognition of countries to: coordinate enforcement efforts; make better use of special investigative techniques used to combat other transnational crimes in the fight against the illegal wildlife trade; conduct in-depth investigations and ensure follow-up prosecutions; and target the masterminds behind the highly organized criminal groups that are involved in the illegal wildlife trade.[100] A well-coordinated multi-disciplinary enforcement response is therefore necessary and countries need to continue to cooperate to effectively deal with transnational organized wildlife crime. On-going efforts must be aligned, and countries need to continue to work together and cooperate to combat the illegal wildlife trade.[101]

A proportion of such cooperation, as highlighted throughout the paper,

---

[99] See CITES Secretariat, *CITES CoP16 Inf. 54: Chair's Summary of ICCWC Roundtable on Combating Transnational Organized Wildlife and Forest Crime for Ministers and High-Level Representatives* (CITES CoP16 Inf. 54 2013), 5, http://www.cites.org/eng/cop/16/inf/E-CoP16i-54.pdf (accessed September 2013).

[100] See John E Scanlon, 'CITES CoP16, Bangkok 2013: A "Watershed Moment" for Combating Wildlife Crime' (International Institute for Sustainable Development, guest article #17 2013), http://biodiversity-l.iisd.org/guest-articles/cites-cop16-bangkok-2013-a-%E2%80%98watershed-moment%E2%80%99-for-combating-wildlife-crime/ (accessed September 2013).

[101] See CITES Secretariat, *CITES CoP16 Inf. 54: Chair's Summary of ICCWC Roundtable on Combating Transnational Organized Wildlife and Forest Crime for Ministers and High-Level Representatives* (CITES CoP16 Inf. 54 2013), 5, http://www.cites.org/eng/cop/16/inf/E-CoP16i-54.pdf (accessed September 2013).

is created by new forms of cooperation[102] in the form of initiatives at the regional, sub-regional or global level. Such initiatives, as Raustiala suggests, involve network enhancing activities, filling gaps and facilitating negotiations amongst countries.[103] In particular, they assist countries by encouraging them to work together to combat the lucrative black market that has emerged and the highly organized networks behind it.

The initiatives highlighted throughout the paper – the BLO mechanism and ASEAN-WEN – have an important role to play in combating transnational organized wildlife crime. They should, however, link with one another and work more closely together to enhance their respective strengths and benefit from each other. Their efforts should also align with those of ICCWC, as it is in a position to create links and synergies between authorities and networks and can provide the necessary tools, services and technical expertise that are needed to combat the illegal wildlife trade effectively.

An issue to keep in mind is that responding to organized crime in a 'traditional way', i.e. treating it as a criminal justice or security issue requiring strengthened cross-border and domestic law enforcement, border control, and intelligence-gathering capacity,[104] is not the ultimate solution to the effective countering of transnational organized crime in general, and the illegal wildlife trade in particular. As a paper reviewing the evolution of transnational organized crime in Africa, published by the Institute for Security Studies, highlights that:

> It is clear from the story of organised crime's evolution across the continent that fighting this phenomenon can no longer be understood in terms of curbing the illicit trade in counterfeit goods, drugs, weapons and people – if that were not challenge enough. Given the almost continent-wide interdependence of organised crime and corruption at the highest levels, and the degree of social entrenchment and identity it has within communities, addressing organised crime . . . also involve[s] preventing and reversing the criminalisation of governments and providing sustainable economic alternatives for its citizens.[105]

---

[102] Ben Bowling, *Policing the Caribbean: Transnational Security Cooperation in Practice* (Oxford University Press, Clarendon Studies in Criminology 2010), 5–7.

[103] Grant Pink, 'Law Enforcement Responses to Transnational Environmental Crime: Choices, Challenges, and Culture' (Australian National University Transnational Environmental Crime (TEC) Project Working Paper 4/2013), 19.

[104] Mark Shaw and Tuesday Reitano, 'The Evolution of Organized Crime in Africa: Towards a New Response' (Institute for Security Studies, Paper 244 2013), 21.

[105] Mark Shaw and Tuesday Reitano, 'The Evolution of Organized Crime in Africa: Towards a New Response' (Institute for Security Studies, Paper 244 2013), 21.

BIBLIOGRAPHY

ASEAN-Wildlife Enforcement Network (ASEAN-WEN), http://www.asean-wen.org/ (accessed September 2013).

BBC, 'Malaysia Jails Man who Smuggled 95 Snakes on a Plane' (BBC News Asia-Pacific, September 2010), http://www.bbc.co.uk/news/world-asia-pacific-11203270 (accessed September 2013).

BBC, 'Kenya Seizes Ivory "Going from Uganda to Malaysia"' (BBC News Africa, July 2013), http://www.bbc.co.uk/news/world-africa-23168558 (accessed September 2013).

Ben Boer, Ross Ramsay and Donald R Rothwell, *International Environmental Law in the Asia Pacific* (International Environmental Law Series, Kluwer Law International 1998).

Ben Bowling, *Policing the Caribbean: Transnational Security Cooperation in Practice* (Oxford University Press, Clarendon Studies in Criminology 2010).

Bryan Christy, 'Anson Wong Goes Free' (National Geographic 2012), http://newswatch.nationalgeographic.com/2012/02/28/anson-wong-goes-free/ (accessed September 2013).

Bryan Christy, 'The Kingpin: An Exposé of the World's Most Notorious Wildlife Dealer, his Special Government Friend, and his Ambitious New Plan' (National Geographic 2010) http://ngm.nationalgeographic.com/2010/01/asian-wildlife/christy-text/1 (accessed September 2013).

Bryan Christy, 'The Serpent King' (Foreign Policy 2010) http://www.foreignpolicy.com/articles/2010/12/28/the_serpent_king (accessed September 2013).

Bryan Christy, *The Lizard King: The True Crimes and Passions of the World's Greatest Reptile Smugglers* (Twelve 2008).

CITES Secretariat, *CITES CoP16 Inf. 54: Chair's Summary of ICCWC Roundtable on Combating Transnational Organized Wildlife and Forest Crime for Ministers and High-Level Representatives* (CITES CoP16 Inf. 54 2013), http://www.cites.org/eng/cop/16/inf/E-CoP16i-54.pdf (accessed September 2013).

Convention on International Trade in Endangered Species of Wild Fauna and Flora (CITES), http://www.cites.org/ (accessed September 2013).

Didier Bigo, 'The European Internal Security Field: Stakes and Rivalries in a Newly Developing Area of Police Intervention', in Malcom Anderson and Monica den Boer (eds), *Policing Across National Boundaries* (Pinter 1994).

Donald R Liddick, *Crimes against Nature: Illegal Industries and the Global Environment* (Praeguer 2011).

Edward van Asch, 'The Illegal Wildlife Trade and Transnational Organized Crime', in Pietro Saitta, Joanna Shapland and Antoinette Verhage (eds), *Getting By or Getting Rich? The Formal, Informal and Criminal Economy in a Globalised World* (Eleven International Publishing 2013).

Frank G Madsen, *Transnational Organized Crime* (Routledge 2009).

Gavin Hayman and Duncan Brack, *International Environmental Crime: The Nature and Control of Environmental Black Markets* (Workshop Report, Royal Institute of International Affairs, Sustainable Development Program 2002).

Grant Pink, 'Law Enforcement Responses to Transnational Environmental Crime: Choices, Challenges, and Culture' (Australian National University Transnational Environmental Crime (TEC) Project Working Paper 4/2013).

International Consortium on Combating Wildlife Crime (ICCWC), 'Report of

the First Global Meeting of the Wildlife Enforcement Networks' (2013) http://www.cites.org/common/docs/ICCWC%20Report%20-%20First%20Global%20Meeting%20of%20the%20WENs%20-%20Final.pdf (accessed September 2013).
International Consortium on Combatting Wildlife Crime (ICCWC), http://www.cites.org/eng/prog/iccwc.php (accessed September 2013).
INTERPOL, *23rd Meeting of the INTERPOL Wildlife Crime Working Group* (2012).
James N Rosenau, 'Governance in a Globalizing World', in David Held and Anthony McGrew (eds), *The Global Transformations Reader: An Introduction to the Globalization Debate* (Polity Press 2000).
James WE Sheptycki, *In Search of Transnational Policing: Towards a Sociology of Global Policing* (Ashgate Publishing, 2002).
John Benyon, 'The Politics of Police Co-operation in the European Union', *International Journal of the Sociology of Law*, 24(4): 353–379 (1996).
John E Scanlon, 'CITES CoP16, Bangkok 2013: A "Watershed Moment" for Combating Wildlife Crime' (International Institute for Sustainable Development, guest article #17 2013), http://biodiversity-l.iisd.org/guest-articles/cites-cop16-bangkok-2013-a-%E2%80%98watershed-moment%E2%80%99-for-combating-wildlife-crime/ (accessed September 2013).
John M Sellar, 'Focusing on Wildlife Crime' (FBI Law Enforcement Bulletin, 2013) http://leb.fbi.gov/2013/july/focusing-on-wildlife-crime-part-1 and http://leb.fbi.gov/2013/july/focusing-on-wildlife-crime-part-2 (accessed September 2013).
John M Sellar, 'International Illicit Trafficking in Wildlife' (The Police Chief, V74 N6 2007).
Laure Guille, 'Police and Judicial Cooperation in Europe' (unpublished PhD thesis, University of Sheffield 2008).
Laure Guille, 'Policing in Europe: An Ethnographic Approach to Understanding the Nature of Cooperation and the Gap between Policy and Practice', *Journal of Contemporary European Research*, 6(2): 257–271 (2010).
Malcom Anderson et al., *Policing the European Union: Theory, Law and Practice* (Oxford Clarendon Press 1995).
Mark Shaw and Tuesday Reitano, 'The Evolution of Organized Crime in Africa: Towards a New Response' (Institute for Security Studies, Paper 244 2013).
Mathieu Deflem, *Policing World Society: Historical Foundations of International Police Cooperation* (Oxford University Press 2002).
Michael Bowman, Peter Davies and Catherine Redgwell, *Lyster's International Wildlife Law* (2nd edition, Cambridge University Press 2010).
Peter H Sand, *Transnational Environmental Law: Lessons in Global Change* (International Environmental Law and Policy Series, Kluwer Law International 1999).
Philip Bean, *Drugs and Crime* (3rd edition, Willan Publishing 2008).
Robert Reiner, 'Policing and the Police', in Mike Maguire, Rod Morgan and Robert Reiner (eds), *The Oxford Handbook of Criminology* (2nd edition, Oxford University Press 1997).
Stephen F Pires and William D Moreto, 'Preventing Wildlife Crimes: Solutions That Can Overcome the "Tragedy of the Commons"', *European Journal on Criminal Policy and Research*, 17(2): 101–123 (2011).
Tom Milliken and Jo Shaw, *The South Africa–Viet Nam Rhino Horn Trade Nexus: A Deadly Combination of Institutional Lapses, Corrupt Wildlife Industry Professionals and Asian Crime Syndicates* (TRAFFIC South Africa 2012).

TRAFFIC, 'International Wildlife Trafficker Sentenced to 6 Months in Malaysia' (TRAFFIC News, November 2010), http://www.traffic.org/home/2010/9/6/international-wildlife-trafficker-sentenced-to-6-months-in-m.html (accessed September 2013).

TRAFFIC, 'Wong's Sentence Increased to Five Years' (TRAFFIC News, November 2010), http://www.traffic.org/home/2010/11/4/wongs-sentence-increased-to-five-years.html (accessed September 2013).

TRAFFIC, *What's Driving the Wildlife Trade? A Review of Expert Opinion on Economic and Social Drivers of the Wildlife Trade and Trade Control Efforts in Cambodia, Indonesia, Lao PDR and Vietnam* (East Asia and Pacific Region Sustainable Development Discussion Papers, East Asia and Pacific Region Sustainable Development Department, World Bank, 2008).

United Nations, 'Report of the Secretary-General on the Activities of the United Nations Regional Office for Central Africa and on the Lord's Resistance Army-affected Areas' (S/2013/297, 2013), http://www.un.org/en/ga/search/view_doc.asp?symbol=S/2013/297 (accessed September 2013).

United Nations Office on Drugs and Crime (UNODC), *Border Liaison Offices in Southeast Asia (1999–2009): Ten Years of Fighting Transnational Organized Crime* (UNODC Regional Centre for East Asia and the Pacific 2010).

United Nations Office on Drugs and Crime (UNODC), *The Globalization of Crime: A Transnational Organized Crime Threat Assessment* (UNODC Vienna 2010).

United Nations Office on Drugs and Crime (UNODC), *Transnational Organized Crime in East Asia and the Pacific: A Threat Assessment* (UNODC 2013).

United Nations TV (UNTV) and CITES Secretariat, Documentary: 'Rhinos Under Threat' (UNTV and CITES Secretariat 2012), http://www.youtube.com/watch?v=t3m7FOXOLbY (accessed September 2013).

World Bank, *Going, Going, Gone: The Illegal Trade in Wildlife in East and Southeast Asia* (Environment and Social Development Department, East Asia and Pacific Region, World Bank, 2005).

10. Can supervision and enforcement networks make self-regulation work?

Martin de Bree,* Han de Haas† and Paul Meerman‡

1. INTRODUCTION

Risk control is needed to be able to prevent certain activities from harming the environment. However, who is primarily responsible for risk control is subject to discussion. A number of different parties are involved in this discussion, in the first place the company and various inspection organizations. But also stakeholders like nearby residents, environmental pressure groups and labour organizations. If politicians see a particular problem in society which is not expected to be solved spontaneously, regulation is a very popular response. This phenomenon, known as the risk regulation reflex of incident regulation reflex (Wetenschappelijke Raad voor het Regeringsbeleid 2013), is especially strong if an incident occurs. This notion has also been articulated by the British Better Regulation Commission (2006):

> There is a sense that the current public debate around risk places an over reliance on Government to manage all risks, at the cost of eroded personal responsibility. Contradictory pressures on those in the regulation business – they are criticised both for intervening and failing to act – have served to emphasise classic regulation as the default response. It is time to step back, explore these dynamics and think differently about the interaction of risk and regulation. The

* Rotterdam School of Management, Erasmus University, the Netherlands, Managing Director Next Step Management BV, email: mbree@rsm.nl, info@nextstepmanagement.nl

† Researcher, Erasmus University, Rotterdam School of Management, Netherlands, www.rsm.nl

‡ Regional Environmental Protection Agency, Midden- and West-Brabant, Netherlands, email: p.meerman@omwb.nl,www.omwb.nl

> Better Regulation Commission wishes this report to be regarded as a declaration that 'enough is enough' – it is time to turn the tide.

In the Netherlands there is a weekly newsletter about public supervision which registers calls for more or stringent supervision by politicians (Velders 2014).

In the classical command and control model politicians and public officers make rules which are enforced by public supervisors (Alemanno and Spina 2014; Van Dorp and Schipper 2013). However, not all problems can be solved by imposing rules and enforcing compliance.[1] Without a certain degree of self-control and correction which one might reasonably expect from civilians and companies, compliance would be far from feasible. Therefore, self-regulation will – to some degree – exist in the practical world where we have limited resources for external (that is, public) rule-making and law enforcement (De Bree 2006).

There is an ongoing debate about the effectiveness of self-regulation and to what extent self-regulation should be allowed. If the public regulator relies on a certain degree of self-regulation, how should regulators monitor the effectiveness of self-regulation? And in what way can cooperation between regulators help doing that?

In this chapter we discuss these questions. We introduce a model for a network, which might support the integral assessment of the environmental performance of companies based upon which the supervisor can adjust its actions for maximum risk control.

We use the term self-regulation in the limited meaning of compliance management, that is, regulatory compliance assurance of regulated companies by means of management systems.

This chapter builds on earlier work on this topic, *inter alia* projects in the chemical industry, the waste industry, the food industry and the transport industry and on a study completed in 2013 about the possibilities of private compliance assurance of environmental legislation and on an IMPEL[2] project regarding the use of compliance management systems for supervision purposes (IMPEL 2012).

---

[1] It is commonly accepted that a command and control approach to regulation and law enforcement has serious limitations with regard to effectiveness (e.g. see Voermans 2009, Borck and Coglianese 2006 and Gunningham 2011).

[2] IMPEL is the European Union Network for the Implementation and Enforcement of Environmental Law (IMPEL). IMPEL is an international non-profit association of the environmental authorities of the EU Member States, acceding and candidate countries of the European Union and EEA countries.

2. PROBLEM DEFINITION

In our modern society, public supervision faces several challenges. As the Dutch Scientific Council concluded in a recent report (Wetenschappelijke Raad voor het Regeringsbeleid 2013), there is a simultaneous call for both more and less supervision, depending on the occurrence of incidents. Another challenge includes how public supervisors may be able to effectively and efficiently assess the level to which regulated entities assure compliance and how public supervisors can join forces to reach this goal. With regard to these challenges, what options do public supervisors have to improve their effectiveness?

First of all, we take a closer look at the concept of self-regulation. Self-regulation means that social parties to some extent take the responsibility to formulate and/or comply with and/or enforce rules, whether or not within a legal framework (Baarsma 2010).

Stucke (2013) examined the effect of the Guidelines Manual of the US Sentencing Commission. In 1991 the US Sentencing Commission provided companies listed at the New York Stock Exchange and NASDAQ (National Association of Securities Dealers Automated Quotations) with strong financial incentives to implement compliance and ethics programmes. These compliance and ethics programmes can be seen as a compliance management system. They both are arrangements implemented by regulated companies to assure regulatory compliance. But although a company has a compliance and ethics programme, there still is unethical and illegal corporate behaviour. Stucke investigated the influence extrinsic incentives have on the effectiveness of a compliance and ethics programme and thus on the quality of self-regulation. Stucke examined the underlying issues for ineffective compliance management and self-regulation. One of the problems is the assumption that inspectorates can recognize ineffective compliance programmes which do not appear to be valid in the real world. On top of that, it is not easy to find out what the actual role of senior management (the real tone at the top) in compliance matters is, whether or not there is window dressing, copycat compliance or the use of uniform standards which do not really fit the company. To really make self-regulation work and distinguish between effective and ineffective systems, governments should use a set of relevant and suitable criteria to assess the self-regulated companies.

Stucke advocates an intrinsic motivated compliance and ethics pro-

---

Information on the IMPEL Network is available through its website at: www.impel.eu

gramme building on the belief that strong ethical values will cascade down in the organization, leading to more effective compliance and ethics programmes. This notion has been underlined by the research of Schaubroeck et al. (2012) which found that ethical leadership influences the ethical behaviour of the whole organization.

Oded (2012) analyses two dominant schools of thought in law enforcement, namely (a) deterrence-based regulation, and (b) cooperation-based enforcement. He argues that although several scholars have proposed mixed regimes, there are still pitfalls. Therefore Oded advocates differentiating between self-policing corporations from non-self-policing corporations and tailoring monitoring efforts and sanctions to these different kinds of regulatees. Oded advocates that third parties (so-called 'corporate monitoring firms') should assess the quality of the self-policing of regulatees. Although Oded's approach seems promising, one of the problems is that third party assessment of compliance management systems is not always as reliable as one would wish.[3]

We argue that if public regulators were able to identify (potential) successful self-regulators and attune their interference to the actual and potential levels of self-regulation, they might be able to unlock a significant potential to improve regulatory compliance.

To achieve self-regulation, it is helpful if not necessary that involved public supervisors assess the quality of self-regulation the same way. This means that regulators should develop a common understanding of self-regulation to be able to comprehend how it works and what relevant underlying mechanisms are decisive for its effectiveness and which of these are receptive for external influence.

Supervisors in the international field of public environmental supervision tend to have their own analytical framework to determine what they consider as good or bad complying companies. This seems to be true with

---

[3] Recent incidents have raised questions about the usefulness of third party verification of environmental management systems, e.g. in the chemical industry: http://www.nu.nl/binnenland/2873437/iso-keurde-functioneren-odfjell-goed.html and with regard to asbestos removal: http://nos.nl/artikel/623271-het-cowboyimago-in-de-asbest.html. The SNIFFER report (2013) concludes that certifying bodies lack the underpinning knowledge to be able to ensure that processes are appropriate and effective. Also it was concluded that the effectiveness of self-policing processes and procedures was not widely evaluated and that the presence rather than the effectiveness of processes and procedures was checked. De Bree (2013) proposes that public enforcers do not rely on third party assessment of private compliance assurance without assessing the check and act functions of these systems themselves.

only few exceptions. This means that a lot of resources are spent on more or less the same thing: assessing the level of compliance.

3. HOW SUPERVISOR NETWORKS CAN HELP UNLOCK OPPORTUNITIES OF SELF-REGULATION

A specific and important aspect of self-regulation by regulated companies is how they assure compliance within their own organization. This phenomenon is indicated with the term compliance management. The notion is that effective compliance management systems can partly replace public supervision. In other words, the better regulated companies assure regulatory compliance by means of a compliance management system, the less intensive or strict public supervision is (De Bree 2013). This is illustrated in Figure 10.1.

Now, how can public supervisors make use of the potential of private compliance assurance, that is, compliance assurance by regulated companies themselves?

More and more industrial companies, typically companies with high risk for the environment as in the chemical, metallurgical and oil industry, have

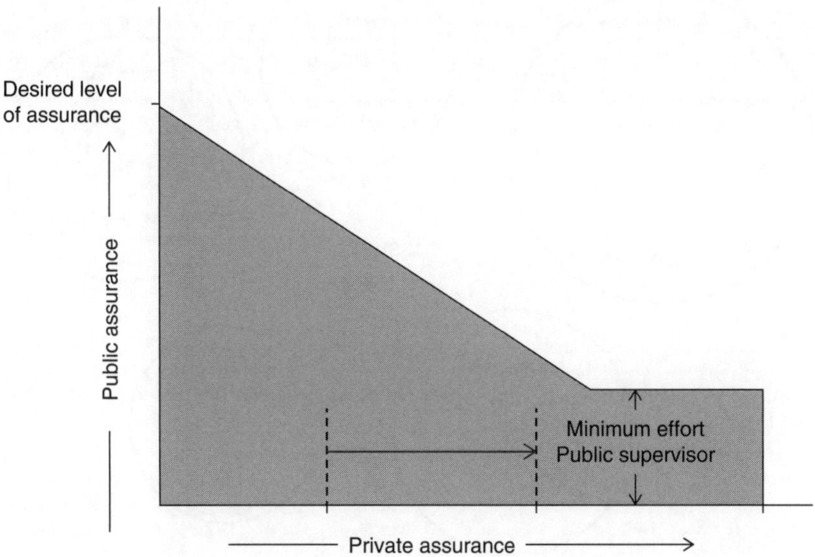

Figure 10.1 Relationship between private compliance assurance and public supervision

multinational oriented organizations. These companies tend to manage their businesses using management systems with an international scope. It is recognized that the fragmented environmental outputs of these companies are to a growing degree controlled by these management systems, most of which are certified or registered following environmental management system standards like ISO 14001 and EMAS (De Vries et al. 2012). We use the term compliance management system for that part of the management system used by a private company which is meant to assure regulatory compliance.

In a recent IMPEL project the requirements for effective private compliance assurance were identified and five aspects were identified for public supervisors who want to base their supervision on compliance management systems, so-called CMS supervision (IMPEL 2012). This IMPEL project will deliver a guidance for CMS supervision in 2015. This guidance can be used by environmental protection agencies in the EU and serve as a common protocol. Figure 10.2 indicates which aspects are important.

These five aspects are:

1. A standard for company compliance management systems (CMS), basically implying a set of requirements for such systems;

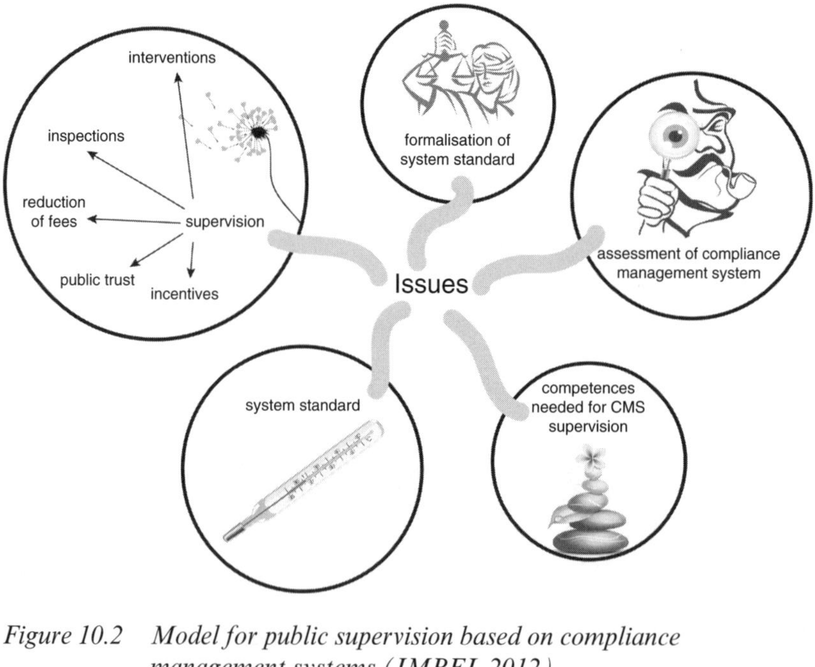

Figure 10.2 Model for public supervision based on compliance management systems (IMPEL 2012)

2. A method for the assessment of compliance management systems using the above mentioned standard. The information delivered by the company should be verified on the basis of sampling, to check whether or not the system actually delivers results. So, this should not be a matter of blind trust, but trust based on a sound analysis of the design, the working and the results of the management system of the regulated company;
3. The standard needs to be formalized in such a way that the public supervisor can use it;
4. For CMS supervision, public supervisors need certain specific competences to be able to assess CMS, both on an individual level (inspector), and on an organizational level (agency);
5. A differentiated supervision strategy; how will companies with effective compliance management systems be treated as opposed to companies without such systems? Will they receive fewer inspections? Are there incentives for CMS? Do they receive a reduction of fees or other interventions?

If this model of five aspects for CMS supervision is made operational, it can serve as a generic (but specific) strategy for public supervision of a certain company or industry.

As long as environmental supervisors (agencies) focus on their own piece of output (soil, waste, air emissions, water discharges, etc.) and monitor compliance, the urge to cooperate might not be that strong. Every field of output has its own expertise, measuring expertise needed and so on.

This fragmentation could also follow geographical boundaries, with environmental agencies in different countries having their own focus on the output within that particular region or country.

But, as Figure 10.3 visualizes, if supervisors shift their analytical attention from compliance to the compliance management system, that is, the processes leading to (non-)compliance, they are all looking at the same system.

We see an example of how a joint focus on management systems induces integration of supervision in the case of Seveso companies. A programme started in the Netherlands in 2008 (named in Dutch 'Eenduidig Toezicht', followed by 'Vernieuwing Toezicht') to create a joint supervision and enforcement policy for Seveso companies by the nine public agencies involved. Supervision in Seveso companies is mainly targeted on the safety control system.

Another interesting development with regard to the question of how a system-based approach may induce the formation of networks is the recent policy by the Dutch Inspectorate for Environment and Infrastructure to

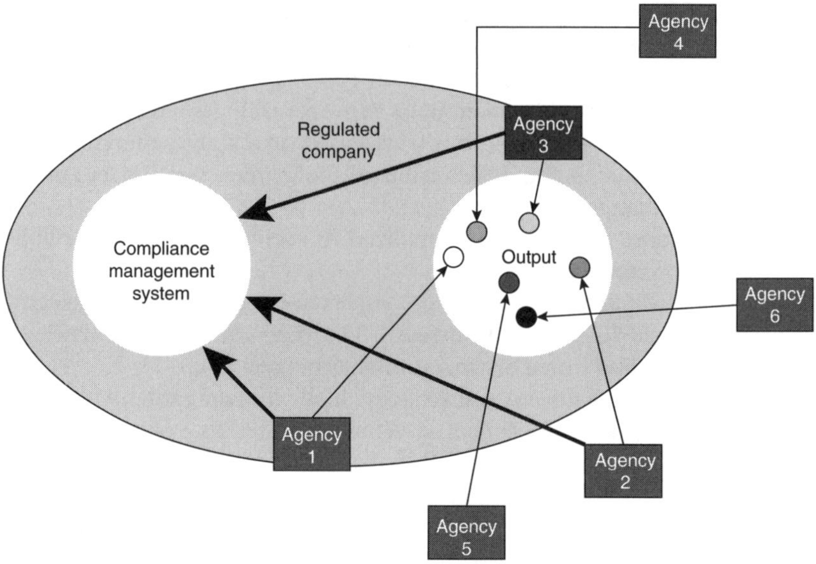

Figure 10.3 Different agencies shift focus from output to a compliance management system

close covenants between regulated companies and the state.[4] The basic idea of this state-level covenant is that if a company has a compliance management system covering a broad range of regulations (for example, environment, transport safety, food safety, labour safety) it may gain a state-level covenant. The covenant prescribes that if the company compliance management system is effective, the company receives less inspections. If the system fails, then the only possible sanction is that the company loses its covenant and, with that, its status apart and falls back into a stricter inspection regime (Inspectie Leefomgeving en Transport 2013).

To be able to do this, the Inspectorate needs to come into an alignment with other inspectorates which are the formal supervisors of the company for a specific area (for example, food quality or labour safety) about how the company's compliance management system is assessed. So here we see an example of how a shared understanding of the concept of compliance

[4] http://www.ilent.nl/over_ilt/het_werk_van_de_ilt/handhaving/toezicht/convenanten/samenwerkingsconvenanten/ and http://www.ilent.nl/actueel/knap_transportgroep_b_v__ondertekent_eerste_rijksbrede_convenant.aspx (March 2014).

management systems may support inspectorates to join forces. This approach is considered a promising new way to reduce the regulatory burden for those companies which have demonstrated not only good intentions, but also effective compliance management.

4. BARRIERS FOR NETWORKS

Self-regulation requires a well aligned network of public regulators to use its capacity efficiently by adjusting its interference to the level of self-regulation and in terms of how they share and interpret information about the supervision of compliance management systems.

Suboptimal networks of public regulators cause problems if self-regulation is anticipated. This is due to the fact that self-regulation requires that public supervisors have a broader and more shared understanding of the processes behind self-regulation. If a regulated company is confronted with supervisors who all have different views on what compliance management systems should look like and how they should work, this approach is probably not very effective. Also, lack of networking may lead to significant inefficiencies in the collection and interpretation of data by supervisors.

Seeing the conceptual advantages of networks (or the disadvantages of the lack of networks) does not mean that networks develop spontaneously. Cooperation in networks between supervisors does not occur by itself. Some difficulties in forming networks are:

- Unwillingness to cooperate;
- Cultural differences;
- Fear for existence or losing influence;
- Differences in language and terminology;
- Belief systems;
- Legal barriers (own formal responsibility); and
- Differences in information systems.

Some of these barriers can be overcome by developing a shared vision on self-regulation. Supervisors should develop a common understanding to be able to understand how self-regulation works and what relevant underlying mechanisms are open for external influence. In the IMPEL study the mentioned model for supervision on compliance management systems has been developed, and this can be used and shared within a network of supervisors, giving the network a substantial ground for existence.

Other barriers have more technical causes, like the lack of a shared information system. In the Netherlands two developments are meant to ease these difficulties.

In the Netherlands, the instrument Inspectionview-companies (later called Inspectionview) was introduced in 2010 after a pilot phase of two years. In 2013 Inspectionview began its implementation phase. Inspectionview is a digital device that enables inspection agencies to share data about inspections and enforcement in certain companies. The main goal of Inspectionview is to improve the exchange of information, working on the information architecture (ICT). The focus is on the exchange of data between the inspection authorities and the access to and analysis of bulk data.

Inspectionview facilitates the cooperation of about five national inspectorates in different fields. Also, regional inspection organizations are using Inspectionview where the companies' concerns with common supervision are addressed. Furthermore, supervisors of the environmental police use the instrument Inspectionview. Information from the Inspectionview can be used to make a selection by the different inspection authorities to choose the companies to inspect (to select the target group). The information from Inspectionview can thus be used for a risk-based approach and effective supervision. Inspectors using Inspectionview (2012) are positive about the features it offers and the results it produces.

High performing companies will experience a lighter burden of inspections while attention is focused on the companies that need it. At the end of 2011, five major national inspectorates shared their data through Inspectionview. At that time, hundreds of inspectors in the Netherlands at all levels of government made use of Inspectionview.

Inspectionview originated from the call of business to decrease the supervisory burdens of all the various inspections done by different inspection authorities. This call has been given a political translation which has been converted to national and regional policy. The development of Inspectionview increases the effectiveness of supervision. Companies that have a good working social and health control system are expected to have a good environmental performance. With a focused check on the environmental aspect to inspect, the supervisor can determine if the company also has a good working environmental control system. By sharing the relevant inspection information between inspectorates supervision can be more focused, resulting in less burden for the company.

As Inspectionview is focused on serving multiple agencies, it facilitates the formation of networks between supervisors.

Another Dutch development in the exchange of information about companies took place with the instrument named Company Dossier.[5] Unlike Inspectionview, Company Dossier is a tool for the company. The digital instrument Company Dossier allows a company to introduce information about his own operations and make it available for regulators and licensing authorities. The entrepreneur determines which entity is given access to its Company Dossier. Company Dossier was developed in 2011 by the business community and the Ministry of Economic Affairs. Within this programme first pilots were executed. Since 2013 the instrument has been considered suitable for use in large groups of branches. Company Dossier offers a tool to an individual company to share the results of self-regulation with the relevant inspection agencies. This is effective because through the Company Dossier multiple inspection agencies can examine the results brought forward as a result of self-regulation by the company.

In preparation for an inspection, an inspector evaluates the results of self-regulation and can prepare a targeted inspection following an audit trail to check specific results. By sharing the information of this inspection with the other inspection agencies using Inspectionview, redundant inspections can be prevented. Each supervisor can perform targeted supervision. In doing so, the company receives attention from the supervisors which is focused on the most relevant issues. Companies with high levels of effective self-regulation receive fewer inspections.

By 2013 it was recognized that by integrating the above described instruments, Inspectionview and Company Dossier, the supervisory burden on businesses can be reduced. Furthermore, it is now recognized that the instruments mutually strengthen each other in helping inspection agencies and the individual supervisor to focus on results. With the combination of Inspectionview and the Company Dossier there is a robust infrastructure of information to be shared between supervisors and between regulated companies and supervisors.

If companies deliver evidence of effective compliance management and self-regulation through Company Dossier, for example, by means of demonstrating the design, operation and results of their compliance management systems, the joined public supervisors can adjust their inspection efforts. Thus the Company Dossier supports the building of trust in regulator–regulatee relationships (IMPEL 2012; Six 2012). It was argued by Killingsworth (2012) that being transparent about organizational values and culture supports a culture within the organization which is favourable for compliance. We emphasize that trust in regulator–regulatee

---

[5] On the website http://www.ondernemingsdossier.nl/company-dossier an English spoken video is available explaining the instrument Company Dossier.

relationships should not be naive trust, that is, not based on promises of effective self-regulation by the regulate alone. We advocate that trust is supported by reality checks enabling the regulator to verify that the self-regulation delivers the desired results.

5. CONCLUSIONS AND RECOMMENDATIONS

Networks of public supervisors offer two important advantages with regard to self-regulation.

1. Networks may facilitate a broader and deeper understanding of the processes which are decisive for effective self-regulation and compliance management within the industry under question. A better understanding among supervisors of the regulated industry can lead to more effective identification and control of public risks.
2. If networks of public supervisors are working well, self-regulation can be stimulated from a consistent general public strategy followed by the network.

Forming effective networks is easier said than done. There are several reasons why networks do not form or operate as effectively as they could. Among these reasons are fear of losing influence or even existence and differences in language and culture. It is important to tackle these issues because suboptimal networks of public regulators may cause problems if self-regulation is aimed for. This is due to the fact that self-regulation requires that public supervisors have a broader and joint understanding of the processes behind self-regulation.

We propose two possible solutions to overcome the barriers to forming effective networks with regard to self-regulation.

First, we argue that networks are more easily formed if network partners have a shared understanding of self-regulation, how self-regulation should be assessed and treated and if supervisors are offered a technical information infrastructure to effectively share relevant information. The model for compliance management system supervision and the guidance to be delivered by the IMPEL project may be a suitable base to create a common understanding of what effective compliance management is, how to assess it and how to react to different levels of compliance management.

Second, we propose an information infrastructure which enables the supervisors and the regulated companies to exchange information about compliance and compliance assurance in order to be able to make all relevant data available for a common understanding of the level of compliance assurance.

As many multinational industrial companies organize their management systems including the parts of those systems aimed at regulatory compliance on international management system standards (for example, ISO 9001), we recommend that supervisors take initiatives to organize supervision on complex industrial companies internationally. A first step might be to start a pilot project for a limited number of industrial companies having such systems, aimed at developing an integrated supervision approach by the different national agencies. In such a project, an international team of supervisors could assess the compliance management systems of the companies, including the results of these systems, using a shared assessment method. The IMPEL model for compliance management system (CMS) supervision and the information infrastructure indicated may serve as supportive tools.

BIBLIOGRAPHY

Alemanno, A. and Spina, A. (2014). Nudging legally: on the checks and balances of behavioral legislation, *International Journal of Constitutional Law* 12(2): 429–456.

Baarsma, B.E.B. (2010). Afwegingskader Bij Het Gebruik Van Zelfregulering sinstrumenten, *Tijdschrift Voor Toezicht* 1.

Better Regulation Commission (2006). Risk, responsibility and regulation – whose risk is it anyway?

Borck, G.C. and Coglianese, C. (2006). Beyond compliance: explaining business participation in voluntary environmental programs, Penn Law School Public Law and Legal Theory Research Paper No. 12–06. Available at http://papers.ssrn.com/sol3/papers.cfm?abstract_id=2000299

De Bree, M.A. (2006). *Waste and Innovation*, Berghauser Pont Publishers, ISBN 90–809618-5-X.

De Bree, M.A. (2013). Private Borging van Regelnaleving in het Omgevingsrecht, RSM Erasmus Universiteit in opdracht van het Ministerie van Infrastructuur en Milieu.

De Vries, H.J., Bayramoglu, D.K. and van der Wiele, A. (2012). Business and environmental impact of ISO 14001, *International Journal of Quality & Reliability Management* 29(4): 425–435.

Gunningham, N. (2011). Enforcing environmental regulation, *Journal of Environmental Law* 23(2): 169–201.

IMPEL (2012). Compliance assurance through company compliance management systems, IMPEL 2011/04, http://impel.eu/projects/compliance-assurance-and-company-compliance-management-systems/

Inspectie Leefomgeving en Transport (2013). ILT Interventiekader.

Inspectie Leefomgeving en Transport (2014). http://www.ilent.nl/over_ilt/het_werk_van_de_ilt/handhaving/toezicht/convenanten/samenwerkingsconvenanten/

Killingsworth, S. (2012). Modelling the message: communicating compliance through organizational values and culture, *Geo. J. Legal Ethics* 25: 961.
Oded, S. (2012). Inducing Corporate Proactive Compliance: Liability Controls & Corporate Monitors, PhD thesis, Erasmus University Rotterdam.
Pret, J. (2012). Ander Toezicht in de Praktijk, *VU Magazine Compliance & Integriteit* 2(3) Jaargang 3.
Schaubroeck, J.M., et al. (2012). Embedding ethical leadership within and across organization levels, *Academy of Management Journal* 55: 1053–1078.
Six, F. (2012). Trust in regulatory relations, *Public Management Review* 1–23.
SNIFFER (2013). *New Opportunities to Improve Environmental Compliance Outcomes Using Certified EMSs*, ER34 Final report.
Stoopendaal, A., De Bree, M.A., Keuter, F. and Robben, P. (2014). Systeem Toezicht in de Nederlandse gezondheidszorg. Een experimentele innovatie van toezicht, *Tijdschrift voor Toezicht* (forthcoming).
Stucke, M.E. (2013). In search of effective ethics & compliance programs. Available at http://papers.ssrn.com/sol3/papers.cfm?abstract_id=2366209.
Van Dorp, R. and Schipper, J. (2013). De Interventie; Hoe los je hardnekkige nalevingsproblemen op? Uitgave Bureau Inspectieraad.
Velders, R. (2014). Newsletter 'Toezicht in het nieuws'.
Voermans, W.J.M. (2009). Zelf wetgever worden, *Regelmaat* (24)5.
Wetenschappelijke Raad voor het Regeringsbeleid (2013). Toezien op Publieke Belangen.

PART III

Thematic networks

11. The Lusaka Agreement Task Force as a mechanism for enforcement against wildlife crime

Emmanuel B. Kasimbazi*

1. INTRODUCTION

It is quite difficult to state the true definition of wildlife crime. Generally, wildlife crime can be defined as any action inconsistent with current legislation which governs the protection of the flora and fauna.[1] Therefore, a wildlife crime is an unauthorized act or omission that violates wildlife or environmental law, subject to criminal prosecution and criminal sanctions and may involve harm or killing of wildlife, the removal from the wild, possession, sale or the exploitation of wildlife incorporating any of

* Dr Emmanuel Kasimbazi is an Associate Professor at the School of Law, Makerere University, Kampala, Uganda as well as a legal consultant and advocate of the High Court of Uganda. He holds an LLM Degree from the University of Calgary, Canada and a PhD Degree from the University of Kwazulu-Natal, Durban, South Africa. He teaches Environmental Law and Policy to both undergraduate and graduate Students and was a Fulbright Scholar at the School of Law, University of Maryland, Baltimore, USA. Dr Kasimbazi is the Chair of the Environmental Law Centre at the School of Makerere University and a member of the IUCN Academy on Environmental Law, and has consulted for many international and national agencies including the World Bank, the African Development Bank, United Nations Environmental Programme (UNEP), United Nations Office for Project Services (UNOPS), Food and Agricultural Organisation (FAO), Nile Basin Initiative, European Union, United Nations Development Programme (UNDP) and various bilateral aid agencies including the German Technical Cooperation (GTZ), the United States Agency for International Development (USAID), the Norwegian Agency for Development Cooperation (NORAD), and the Danish International Development Agency (DANIDA).

[1] Report of the House of Commons Environmental Audit Committee, *Environmental Crime: Wildlife Crime* (Twelfth Report of Session 2003–04), available at http://www.publications.parliament.uk/pa/cm200304/cmselect/cmenvaud/605/60503.htm (accessed 30 October 2013).

the activities above.[2] Related to wildlife crime, is illegal wildlife trafficking which involves taking, trading, exploiting or possessing the world's wild flora and fauna in contravention of local, national and international laws.[3] Generally, illegal wildlife trafficking falls under wildlife crime which the Lusaka Agreement Task Force (LATF) was established to control in Eastern and Southern Africa.

The LATF Secretariat of the Lusaka Agreement was established as a law enforcement institution on Cooperative Enforcement Operations Directed at Illegal Trade in Wild Fauna and Flora.[4] Its jurisdiction covers the Eastern and Southern African territories of the continent of Africa. Through executing its mandate, LATF facilitates regional cooperation and coordinates with international agencies to suppress environmental and wildlife crimes. The work of the Task Force is vital in regulating wildlife crime by enhancing the capacity of local and national law enforcement agencies through training and awareness programs. It is also involved in collecting, collating, analyzing and disseminating information on the illegal trade in wild fauna and flora and investigating cases of a cross-border nature which include wild fauna and flora specimens. It works with international law enforcement agencies such as Interpol, CITES, the World Customs Organization, the Central African Forests Commission, and the Organization for the Conservation of African Wildlife, amongst others, to tackle wildlife crime, and carries out regional joint operations with the relevant national, regional and international organizations.[5] The collaboration with other organizations has made significant improvement in the regulation of wildlife crime in the region.

2. BACKGROUND TO THE REGULATION OF WILDLIFE CRIMES

The regulation of wildlife crimes started in England in the 17th century by implementing laws against illegal hunting and fishing in an effort to

---

[2] Nurse, A, 'Policing Wildife: Perspectives on Criminality in Wildlife Crime' (2011) 11 *The British Society of Criminology*.

[3] Kaaria, BI andMuchiri, NL, 'Enforcement Challenges Across Borders: Detecting and Prosecuting Illegal Wildlife Trafficking' (Paper presented at the 9th International Conference on Environmental Compliance and Enforcement, 20–24 June 2011, Whistler, British Columbia, Canada).

[4] The Lusaka Task Force was established under Article 5 of the Lusaka Agreement.

[5] Kaaria and Muchiri, *supra* note 3.

protect the wildlife and property of landowners and the aristocracy.[6] Further development took place on the international scene during the early 20th century. During this time, international regulations, agreements, and conventions, for instance the Convention for the Protection of Useful Birds to Agriculture of 1902,[7] the Treaty for the Conservation of Fur Seals, 1911,[8] the Convention Concerning the Use of White Lead in Painting, 1921,[9] the Convention for the Regulation of Whaling,[10] the Convention Relating to the Preservation of Flora and Fauna in their Natural State, 1933,[11] and the Convention on Nature, Protection and Wildlife Preservation in the Western Hemisphere, 1940,[12] were signed. These conventions were intended to preserve wildlife resources that were in danger of becoming extinct.

In 1972, the Stockholm Declaration recommended the creation of an environmental agency known as the United Nations Environment Programme (UNEP) which negotiated the adoption of the Convention on the Control of International Trade in Endangered Species of Wild Flora and Fauna of 1973.[13] The International Union for Conservation of Nature (IUCN), which is also known as the World Conservation Union, with the assistance of the World Wide Fund for Nature (WWF) were involved in issues of environmental management, including the maintenance of essential ecological processes and life support systems, the preservation of genetic diversity, and the sustainable use of species and ecosystems. Later, in 1994, in Eastern and Southern Africa, the Lusaka Agreement Task Force was established to fight illegal wildlife activities within the region.

There is controversy on whether or not 'wildlife crime' should be classified as an offence, a crime or a serious crime. According to the

---

[6] Ibid.

[7] The Convention for the Protection of Birds Useful to Agriculture, Mar. 19, 1902, 102 B.F.S.P. 969 (entered into force 11 May 1907).

[8] The 1911 Treaty for the Preservation and Protection of Fur Seals, 104 BFSP 175.

[9] The Convention Concerning the Use of White Lead in Painting (entry into force: 31 August 1923).

[10] The International Convention on the Regulation of Whaling, opened for signature 2 December 1946, 161 UNTS 77 (entered into force 10 November 1948).

[11] The Convention Relative to the Preservation of Fauna and Flora in their Natural State (London Convention), London, opened for signature 8 November 1933 (entered into force 14 January 1936).

[12] The Convention on Nature, Protection and Wildlife Preservation in the Western Hemisphere Washington, 1940 (entered into force on 30 April 1942).

[13] The Convention on International Trade in Endangered Species of Wild Fauna and Flora (CITES) (signed in Washington on 3 March 1973 and entered into force on 1 January 1975).

Association of Chief Police Officers (ACPO),[14] the Police Service has no definition for the term 'wildlife crime' but rather refers to offences falling within specific pieces of legislation as amounting to wildlife crimes. For example in Uganda, none of the laws and regulations concerning conservation and preservation of wildlife resources define or classify wildlife crimes. The classification of wildlife crime is significant on grounds that the police and relevant authorities may investigate an offence on the basis of whether or not it is a 'non-arrestable', 'arrestable', or a 'serious arrestable' offence. Most wildlife crimes may be classified as 'non-arrestable' offences due to the fact that they are seen as minor, trivial and offences which do not attract legal penalties under the existing laws and regulations. Therefore, the Lusaka Agreement is an important instrument for detecting and prosecuting wildlife crimes at the regional level since there is general confusion around many of the terms used in the current national legislation.

3. TYPES OF WILDLIFE CRIMES

Wildlife crimes in the Eastern and Southern Africa region range from illegal logging from the sandalwood forests, whose primary destination is Western Europe; trade in rhino horns, elephant tusks and ivory products, which are sent to black markets across Asia; and poaching and cattle rustling across national borders.[15]

In addition to the above crimes, other criminal activities that are dangerously affecting wildlife in the region include unlawful killing or wounding, robbery involving the taking of protected species from the wild, disturbance of a protected species, cruelty and animal welfare offences, unlicensed and unlawful gambling, damage to property, illegal poisoning and unlawful storage and irrational use of pesticides, theft and handling stolen goods, deception, fraud and forgery, criminal damage of protected sites, and firearms-related offences.[16]

---

[14] The Association of Chief Police Officers (ACPO) brings together the expertise and experience of chief police officers from the United Kingdom, providing a professional forum to share ideas and best practices, coordinate resources and help deliver effective policing which keeps the public safe.

[15] See UNODC, 'Eastern Africa: UNODC to Address Rising Environmental Crime', available at http://www.unodc.org/unodc/en/frontpage/2009/November/eastern-africa_-unodc-to-address-rising-environmental-crime.html (accessed 30 October 2013).

[16] Ibid.

3.1 Causes of Wildlife Crimes

It is globally noticed that the major cause of wildlife crimes is mostly the high profits the offenders get from dealing in illegal wildlife trade. While the general public hardly identifies the causes of wildlife crimes or clarifies the intended impact, the problem of illegal wildlife trafficking in the region is compounded by many factors which hinder local, regional and international enforcement mechanisms for curtailing the problem. The major causes include the following.

3.2 Wildlife Products as Sources of Commodities

The Eastern and Southern Africa region is rich in wild fauna and flora products such as food, vegetables, fruits, medicine, timber, and animal products. All those highly valuable tradable items entice both indigenous and foreign individuals to carry out illegal wildlife trade. The situation is worsened through the gathering, lumbering, collecting and smuggling of wildlife products in bulk and large quantities from various parts of the region to a number of destinations, mostly South Africa, the Asian continent and the rest of the world at large – a significant factor which has contributed to the booming illegal trade in fauna and flora.

3.2.1 Strategic location of the region

The Eastern and Southern Africa region is located almost in the middle of the world, with a long coastline, remote islands, and porous borders which provide easy access to both local and foreign wildlife traders entering and leaving the region. The Indian and Atlantic oceans that surround the region also enable traders to transport illegal wildlife products from the region to various markets globally, a factor which facilitates illegal wildlife activities in the region.

3.2.2 Corruption

Corruption at the local, regional, and international levels also obstructs the prosecution of wildlife crimes, hence hindering the conservation and preservation of fauna and flora. This is done by some officials of the relevant authorities at all levels in the region through colluding with organized wildlife criminals. This evil practice includes the concealment of illegal wildlife products by responsible officials, false declaration through fraudulent entering of incorrect information into customs forms and shipping permit applications and permit fraud through forged, stolen, and recycled documentation. This is done right from the time of the hunting and gathering of the wildlife products to the stage of exportation across borders and overseas.

3.2.3 High market demand

As it is known in economics that, 'the higher the market demand of the goods, the higher the supply of the goods', this also applies to the situation where illegal wildlife activities are very rampant in the struggle to acquire adequate wildlife goods in order to serve the high global market demand. For instance, poaching is driven largely by the high market demand in Asia, making the trade extremely lucrative, where, a kilo of ivory bought at US$20 in Africa can fetch over US$1000 in wealthy markets like Japan.[17] These, along with many other factors have greatly contributed to the current situation of wildlife crime in the region.

4. THE ROLE OF THE LUSAKA AGREEMENT TASK FORCE (LATF) IN PROSECUTING WILDLIFE CRIMES

4.1 Understanding the Role of LATF in the Region

LATF is a law enforcement institution acting as the Secretariat of the Lusaka Agreement on Cooperative Enforcement Operations Directed at Illegal Trade in Wild Fauna and Flora in some parts of sub-Saharan Africa. LATF operates in and across Party States jointly with National Bureaus and other relevant national law enforcement agencies. In this regard, it facilitates cooperative enforcement operations, collects intelligence, investigates cases, participates in arrests and supports the prosecution of wildlife law offenders as obliged under the agreement. The Agreement was adopted in Lusaka, Zambia on 8 September 1994, hence the title 'Lusaka Agreement'; it was first conceptualized during deliberations by the first African Wildlife Law Enforcement Cooperation Conference that was held in Lusaka, Zambia from 9 to 11 December 1992. The Conference was attended by senior officers from Eastern and Southern African countries, who observed that 'regional cooperation' was a suitable way to address the problems affecting the national law enforcement agencies in combating international wildlife smuggling syndicates and other related illegal wildlife activities in the region.

Due to practical and legal challenges that were facing the national

---

[17] Kaaria and Muchiri, *supra* note 3.

institutions mandated to fight wildlife crime, the Conference proposed more effective measures to combat cross-border illegal wildlife trade and activities within the region. One of the key recommendations made was the establishment of a Task Force to complement national enforcement efforts aimed at curtailing illegal trade in wild fauna and flora. Consequently, the Lusaka Agreement was adopted, which facilitated the establishment of the Task Force. The Lusaka Agreement Task Force is currently composed of 13 members of staff, five of whom are Seconded Officers from Party States, inclusive of the Director and Intelligence Officer, while the rest are support staff. It has also established the Governing Council and National Bureaus in all member states. The Annual Budget of the Task Force is mainly financed by the Parties. Besides Party States' contributions, the Task Force also receives grants or donations from cooperating partners and other well-wishers who wish to support specific programs. However, the collected funds from all the existing sources are very little to finance the implementation of LATF's objectives and functions.

Currently, the composition of the Task Force is drawn from seven member countries which have acceded to the Agreement, namely: the Republic of Congo (Brazzaville), Kenya, Uganda, Zambia, the Kingdom of Lesotho, the United Republic of Tanzania, and Liberia. Ethiopia, South Africa, and the Kingdom of Swaziland are signatories to the Agreement. According to Article 12(3) of the Lusaka Agreement, the 'Agreement shall remain open for accession by any African state'. Consequently, all African countries are eligible to join the Lusaka Agreement Task Force for as long as they accept and comply with the obligations under the Agreement. For a country to become a Party, its instruments of ratification, acceptance, approval, or accession must be deposited with the Secretary-General of the United Nations who will notify the Parties accordingly. Although the Lusaka Agreement was closed for signature on 13 March 1995, with seven signatures on board, to date six States (Zambia, Uganda, Tanzania, Kenya, Lesotho, and the Republic of Congo Brazzaville) have ratified or acceded to it, a situation which put Liberia in an unclear position in relation to the Task Force. But this does not deter the Task Force from cooperating and working with countries not privy to the Agreement. In fact, the Task Force occasionally works with non-Party States through their relevant wildlife entities and law enforcement agencies, especially on issues affecting Party States, including capacity building programs, in the combating of illegal wildlife activities and the fostering of wild fauna and flora conservation.

4.2 Institutional Framework of LATF and their Functions

The structure of the Lusaka Agreement comprises of three main organs. The first one is the Governing Council established under Article 7 of the Lusaka Agreement, which is the highest governing body. It consists of the responsible Minister or representative of each Party State who shall attend as the head of the delegation in the Governing Council meetings. The delegation includes high-ranking officials dealing with wildlife law enforcement affairs and officials whose normal duties are connected with the activities of the Task Force. The main function of the Governing Council is to determine the general policies of the Task Force.

The second organ is the National Bureau established under Article 6 of the Agreement. Each Party is required to designate or establish a governmental entity as its National Bureau to facilitate the implementation of the Agreement. The established National Bureaus or designated entities by each Party are expected to work in close liaison with the Task Force. In compliance with this requirement, Uganda, Tanzania, Kenya, and Zambia have established specific National Bureaus for the Agreement. For the purpose of the Agreement, the functions of the National Bureaus include providing to, and receiving from the Task Force information on illegal trade, and coordinating with the Task Force in investigations that involve illegal trade. In practice, the National Bureaus are expected to work hand in hand with the Task Force in undertaking cooperative enforcement measures to combat illegal trade in endangered species.[18] The Task Force is required to facilitate the collection, interpretation and dissemination of information and intelligence. For this purpose a wildlife criminal intelligence database has been established.[19] It also facilitates the cooperative enforcement activities between National Bureaus. This is achieved through coordinating joint operations, designing and planning investigations. In the long term, once the database is fully established and operational, the Task Force will undertake analysis of wildlife crime trends for the purpose of measuring the extent of crime and determining appropriate proactive and reactive measures.[20] The measures may include the profiling of habitual offenders and criminal networks operating at

---

[18] Mrema, EM, 'Lusaka Agreement as a Mechanism for Enforcement of CITES' (Paper presented at the 7th International Conference on Environmental Compliance and Enforcement, 9–15 April 2005, Marrakech, Morocco).

[19] Ibid.

[20] Ibid.

national, sub-regional, and regional levels, with an emphasis on international syndicates.[21]

The third organ is the Task Force which is established under Article 5 of the Agreement. It is composed of a Director, Field Officers who are appointed by the Governing Council, and an Intelligence Officer and such other staff as may be decided by the Governing Council.[22] It also includes at least one Field Officer seconded by each Party and approved by the Governing Council.[23] Each Field Officer is appointed to serve for a term of three years, or such other term as may be determined by the Governing Council.[24]

The Director of the Task Force and other Field Officers retain their national law enforcement authority during their time of service with the Task Force.[25] The Director is the Chief Executive Officer of the Task Force and is accountable to the Governing Council.[26] He or she has the following responsibilities: appointing other support staff as deemed necessary for the functioning of the Task Force; commanding and coordinating the work of the Task Force; preparing budgets annually or as required by the Governing Council; implementing policies and decisions agreed by the Governing Council; providing reports annually and as required by the Governing Council; arranging for and servicing meetings of the Governing Council; and performing such other functions as may be determined by the Governing Council.[27]

The Task Force possesses international legal personality.[28] It has in the territory of each Party the legal capacity required for the performance of its functions under the Agreement. The Task Force in the exercise of its legal personality is represented by the Director.[29]

Article 5(9) of the Lusaka Agreement, mandates the Task Force to perform the following functions:

- To facilitate cooperative activities among the National Bureaus in carrying out investigations pertaining to illegal trade;
- To investigate violations of national laws pertaining to illegal trade, at the request of the National Bureaus or with the consent of the

[21] Ibid.
[22] Lusaka Agreement, Article 5(2) (3).
[23] Ibid.
[24] Ibid.
[25] Ibid.
[26] Ibid., Article 7.
[27] Ibid.
[28] Ibid., Article 8.
[29] Ibid.

Parties concerned, and to present to them evidence gathered during such investigations;
- To collect, process and disseminate information on activities that pertain to illegal trade, including establishing and maintaining databases;
- To provide, upon request of the Parties concerned, available information related to the return to the country of original export, or country of re-export, of confiscated wild fauna and flora; and
- To perform such other functions as may be determined by the Governing Council.

In order to perform the aforementioned functions, the Task Force is obliged, when necessary and appropriate, to use undercover operations as may be agreed upon by the concerned parties. It has been noticed that the Task Force, together with its member states, has the capacity to curtail illegal wildlife activities. However, great efforts are needed for the Task Force to improve the conservation of wildlife in Africa.

The Task Force also facilitates the cooperative enforcement activities between National Bureaus. This is achieved through coordinating joint operations, designing, planning and undertaking investigations. It operates in and across Party States, jointly with National Bureaus and other relevant national law enforcement agencies. In this regard, it facilitates cooperative enforcement operations, collects intelligence, investigates cases, participates in arrests and supports prosecution.

The Task Force is also expected to undertake analyses of wildlife crime trends in order to measure the extent of crime and determine appropriate proactive and reactive measures, such as the blacklisting of habitual offenders and criminal networks.

The competences, knowledge, skills and networking of the Task Force to effectively combat trafficking and illegal trade in wild fauna and flora are enforced by conducting inter-agency workshops in the member states.

4.2.1 The process of prosecuting illegal wildlife crimes

There is no clear set process for prosecuting wildlife crimes by the Lusaka Agreement Task Force under the Agreement. This situation differs from other organizations, such as CITES, which has established a global framework to regulate and control international trade in endangered species of wild animals and plants listed in three appendices. These appendices function under a permit system. Appendix I lists species that are the most endangered among the CITES listed animals and plants.[30] CITES prohibits international trade in specimens of these species except when the purpose of the import is not commercial[31] for instance for scientific research. In these exceptional cases, trade may take place provided it is authorized by the granting of both an import permit and an export permit (or re-export certificate). Article VII of the Convention provides for a number of exemptions to this general prohibition. Appendix II includes those species that may become threatened with extinction if trade is not strictly regulated. It also includes species whose specimens in trade look like those of species listed for conservation reasons.[32] International trade in specimens of Appendix II species may be authorized by the granting of an export permit or re-export certificate. No import permit is necessary for these species under CITES. It is important to note that a permit is needed in some countries that have taken stricter measures than CITES requires. Permits or certificates should only be granted if the relevant authorities are satisfied that certain conditions are met – above all that trade will not be detrimental to the survival of the species in the wild.[33] Appendix III is a list of species included at the request of a party that already regulates trade in the species and that needs the cooperation of other countries to prevent unsustainable or illegal exploitation. International trade in specimens of species listed in this Appendix is allowed only on presentation of the appropriate permits or certificates.[34]

Species may be added to or removed from Appendix I and II, or moved between them, only by the Conference of the Parties, either at its regular meetings or by postal procedures.[35] But species may be added to or removed from Appendix III at any time and by any Party unilaterally (although the Conference of the Parties has recommended that changes be timed to coincide with amendments to Appendices I and II).

The Lusaka Agreement, without a clear prescribed list of species, intends to reduce and ultimately to eliminate illegal trade in wild fauna and flora.[36] This creates a need to lay down the proper procedure for the prosecution of wildlife crimes, with a full list of the endangered species,

---

[30] The Convention on International Trade in Endangered Species of Wild Fauna and Flora (993 UNTS 243 / 27 UST 1087 / 12 ILM 1085 (1973) / [1976] ATS 29), Article II, paragraph 1.

[31] Ibid., Article III.

[32] Ibid., Article II, paragraph 2.

[33] Ibid., Article IV.

[34] Ibid., Article V.

[35] Ibid., Article XV.

[36] Mrema, *supra* note 18.

by the LATF's administration and management with regard to the Agreement. Article 5 of the Lusaka Agreement establishes a Task Force which, in conjunction with the National Bureaus and the Governing Council, is mandated to work and achieve such an objective without compromising State Parties' national sovereignty. According to Article 4 of the Agreement, Parties are duty bound to cooperate and take action to perform the objectives, mainly by investigating and prosecuting cases of illegal trade inside and along the coastline of the region. Further still, Article 4(9) obliges each Party to return any specimen of species of wild fauna and flora confiscated in the course of illegal trade to the country of original export or country of re-export. This is done by determining the country of original export of the specimen(s), and requiring the country of re-export to show evidence that the specimen(s) re-exported were imported by that country in accordance with the provisions of the Convention on International Trade in Endangered Species of Wild Fauna and Flora (CITES) governing importation and re-exportation, and the payment of the costs of returning such specimens of wild fauna and flora. This payment is made by the country receiving the specimen(s), except where there is an agreement by both Parties returning and receiving the specimen(s) to bear costs.

The effective operation of the Task Force as established under the Agreement inevitably entails effective institutional set-up at national level. This ensures a two-way collaborative mechanism to effectively curtail illegal wildlife trade in the region. Consequently, the building of requisite capacities, particularly through the training of personnel of the national entities, who later sensitize the indigenous people and other stakeholders to the dangers of illegal wildlife trade, is paramount for the success of the Task Force's operational activities. Subsequently, the capacity-building efforts of the National Bureaus through the training of national enforcement officers have been emphasized. The training courses on law enforcement are conducted by national experts in different member states to sharpen enforcement officers' skills in combating an ever-increasing illegal trade in wild fauna and flora, and also in being able to effectively implement the Agreement. Countries that have benefited from the training courses include Tanzania, Uganda, Zambia, Ethiopia, and Swaziland. Similar and more advanced courses have been held and continue to be organized both within and outside the countries to further strengthen their ability and capacity to combat environmental crime.

The use of national law enforcement experts from within the signatories to the Agreement to train and coach other relevant individuals clearly indicates the divergence of law enforcement capabilities in the State Parties. While most of the signatories lack technical expertise in law enforcement, intelligence, and investigation capabilities to combat illegal trade in endangered species, a few, like Kenya and South Africa, have the knowledge and expertise required for the task and to facilitate the effective enforcement of the Agreement. To ensure that all participating countries were ready and prepared to work together in undertaking investigation of wildlife crimes where necessary, joint and undercover cross-border operations were instituted when the Task Force was established. Law enforcement officers from Kenya and South Africa offered to assist other countries by conducting training courses for responsible officials on wildlife resources. The Task Force officers have also been exposed to operations and training outside Africa, in countries such as the UK and Israel, among others. All those national enforcement officers who have been trained in these programs under the Agreement continue to be useful in organizing other similar courses. These, with other actions, have enabled the curtailing of the illegal wildlife activities by collaborating with other national, regional and international organizations and institutions to confiscate and control illegal wildlife trade products across the whole world, especially in the Asian continent.

4.2.2 Cases of illegal wildlife trafficking

There are several cases which have been recorded, handled, and prosecuted by LATF in a bid to ultimately eliminate illegal wildlife trafficking within the region. For instance, in June 2009, postal parcels from Arusha, Tanzania, were seized containing 120 live leopard tortoises, between January 2009 and August 2010, 27 live Nile lizards and 20 live frogs were seized in Hong Kong, in October 2010, LATF in a joint operation with the Tanzania National Bureau to the Lusaka Agreement and the National Central Bureau, Interpol – Dar es Salaam, arrested a Chinese national engaged in the illegal trafficking of 1.5 tons of African elephant ivory from Zanzibar-Tanzania to Hong Kong. In another case, elephant ivory weighing 27,114 kilos were seized in Asian countries.[37] LATF also supported Kenya in repatriating over 1.8 tons of contraband ivory.[38] Further, in January 2005, six baby chimpanzees and four guenon monkeys were seized at Jomo Kenyatta International Airport (JKIA), Nairobi, en route to Lagos, Nigeria, without any documents.[39] In January 2006, 228 tortoises were seized at JKIA while in transit to Bangkok, Thailand, from

[37] Kaaria and Muchiri, *supra* note 3.

[38] See Lusaka Agreement Bulletin, available at http://www.lusakaagreement.org/repatriation.html (accessed 30 October 2013).

[39] Kaaria and Muchiri, *supra* note 3.

Entebbe, Uganda, without valid documents.[40] In November 2007, 500 African Grey Parrots with an estimated worth of US$400,000 were intercepted at Douala port in the process of export to Bahrain.[41] The parrots were probably captured illegally in the rainforest of southeast Cameroon. At the international level, between 2005 to 2009, LATF in conjunction with CITES recorded an annual average of more than 317,000 live birds, over 2 million live reptiles, 2.5 million crocodilian skins, 1.5 million lizard skins, 2.1 million snake skins, 73 tons of caviar, 1.1 million coral pieces and nearly 20,000 hunting trophies.[42] In Uganda, 47 poisonous snakes and 147 chameleons that were being smuggled out of the country to the Czech Republic were impounded.[43] In October 2013, the Uganda Wildlife Authority arrested two Chinese and two Guineans in Kampala, with a haul of over 1.9 tons of blood ivory which were to be shipped out of the country, while 116 kilos of ivory were confiscated at the airport in the same month.[44]

Such prosecutions by LATF have escalated the elimination of wildlife crimes in the region.

5. THE IMPACT OF LATF ON PROSECUTING WILDLIFE CRIMES IN THE REGION

The Task Force has to a large extent positively influenced the prosecution of wildlife in sub-Saharan Africa. First, it has fostered warm cooperation between the national, regional, and international wildlife authorities and organizations, such as the East African Community and Southern African region, the Africa Forest Law Enforcement & Governance (AFLEG), and the Conference of Ministers in Charge of Forests of Central Africa (COMIFAC).[45] These organizations have strengthened the forces against illegal trade in wild fauna and flora in the region.

---

[40] Ibid.

[41] Ibid.

[42] Report of the House of Commons, *supra* note 1.

[43] 'UWA Rescues 42 Poisonous Snakes and 147 Chameleons Bound for Czech Republic', available at http://safariadviceuganda.blogspot.com/2012/11/uwa-rescues-42-poisonous-snakes-and-147.html (accessed 30 October 2013).

[44] 'Uganda Impounds Over 2 Tons of Ivory as Two Chinese Arrested in Kampala', retrieved from http://www.eturbonews.com/39200/uganda-impounds-over-2-tons-ivory-two-chinese-arrested-kampala (accessed 1 November 2013).

[45] UNEP, *A Decade of Regional Wildlife Law Enforcement: The Case of The Lusaka Agreement June 2005*, available at http://lusakaagreement.org/wp-content/uploads/2013/12/LATF-Evaluation-Report.pdf

5.1 Challenges Faced by LATF in the Prosecuting Process of Wildlife Crimes

Despite improvement in the enforcement mechanisms of the Task Force to control illegal wildlife trade, the illegal trafficking of wildlife specimens, mainly in elephant ivory and live animals, is escalating. According to Interpol, illegal trade in wild fauna and flora is ranked second after drug trafficking in terms of revenue involved. Illegal wildlife trade is carried out in various ways and involves sophisticated syndicates, hence making it difficult to quantify with precision. Illegal wildlife trade is undoubtedly a booming business in Africa, especially in the Great Lakes region where LATF has jurisdiction. This clearly brings out the challenges affecting the Task Force as regards the control of porous borders which are easy exit points for illegal goods, and so for detecting, prosecuting, and monitoring wildlife crimes in and along the coastline of the all Party States. The major challenges are as follows.

5.1.1 Corruption

This is the most serious problem that has kept wildlife crime prevalent at all levels; such behaviors are a common occurrence in Customs services where officials allow the exportation of illegal products to vast markets around the world. This plays a key role in facilitating the illegal wildlife trade. The known established markets for protected plants, animals, and animal materials in Belgium, China, the Czech Republic, France, Hong Kong, Israel, Japan, Netherlands, Romania, Spain, the United Kingdom, and Vietnam[46] have been abandoned because of the high prices of illegal products in black markets. All officials in the relevant institutions in member states and their associates[47] need to commit themselves to fighting illegal wildlife activities in order to foster conservation of wildlife resources within their respective fields and areas across the region.

5.1.2 Human settlement

The fast growing human population across the region is a dangerous factor as far as wildlife is concerned; almost all activities carried out in the process of establishing human settlements negatively affect the natural environment, where a number of fauna and flora species are destroyed daily and some sold in the vast markets across the world. In Uganda for example, 90,000 hectares of forest land across the country has been cleared

---

[46] Kaaria and Muchiri, *supra* note 3.
[47] Ibid.

for human settlement.[48] The clearing of such a big chunk of land, and the encroachment on land for settlement and human activity in the whole region, clearly depicts the extent to which wildlife species are destroyed and sold. This poses a threat to LATF's activities in wildlife conservation and preservation. To make matters worse, governments of the member states have come up with well-organized human settlement strategies for sustainable development of wildlife, a factor which is positively contributing to the progress of the illegal wildlife activities in Eastern and Southern Africa.

5.1.3 Weak environmental policies and legislation

Wildlife legislation in many member states is not adequate to address illegal wildlife trade in the region. For instance, wildlife crime is not defined by the existing Uganda Wildlife Act.[49] In Lesotho, there is no specific law governing its national authority responsible for wildlife conservation and preservation.[50] With total negligence, irresponsible and illegal practices such as bush meat exploitation are being considered as petty offences and most courts fail to treat the matter as a serious issue. It is worth noting that lack of a common policy and law in the East African Community is affecting the curtailing of wildlife crimes. For example, possession of elephant meat in Kenya results in a small fine, whereas in Tanzania perpetrators may be imprisoned for up to seven years.

5.1.4 Limited coverage

Despite these successes, the Lusaka Agreement faces challenges ahead. With only seven parties (Congo-Brazzaville, Kenya, Liberia, Lesotho, Tanzania, Uganda, Zambia) and three signatories (Ethiopia, South Africa, and Swaziland), the Lusaka Agreement lacks comprehensive coverage on the continent to prevent or address transboundary wildlife crime in the most of the African countries.

5.1.5 Prevailing vast markets

The existence of vast markets for the sale of wildlife trade products stimulates the illegal wildlife activities carried out by criminals in order to satisfy the demanding consumers willing to pay high prices all over the world.

---

48 Musingo, D, 'Encroachers told to leave forest.' New Vision, (Kampala, 23 July 2013), 6.

49 Uganda Wildlife Act Cap 200, Laws of Uganda, 2000.

50 See 'The Wildlife of Lesotho', available at http://www.afrotourist.org/index.php?title=The_Wildlife_of_Lesotho (accessed 30 October 2011).

This need to make money thus means that the masses in the State Parties are not motivated to conserve and preserve wildlife resources.

5.1.6 Inefficiency and ineffective human resources

Illegal wildlife activity is ranked as the second most lucrative illicit trade after drug trafficking. However, the human resources for wildlife conservation and preservation in the region are inadequate and unskilled, while the illegal wildlife trade is a sophisticated business that requires efficient and effective personnel to tackle it. This problem is attributed to the irresponsible and reckless top-decision-makers in the State Parties who are reluctant to make good policies to encourage the training and employment of adequate human personnel to carry out wildlife law enforcement, which would result in the conservation of the fauna and flora.

5.1.7 Poor government financial policy

There is a tendency of many African governments to allocate inadequate financial resources to the implementation of environmental programs, yet there is a great need to finance the customs officials and game rangers in designated wildlife areas under all National Bureaus in order to equip them with firearms and protective equipment and keep them motivated to fight illegal wildlife activities. The governments' reluctance has hindered the development of LATF by hardening its relations with the national authorities of the State Parties, thus hindering wildlife conservation and preservation and maintaining the status quo in the illegal trafficking of wild fauna and flora.

5.1.8 No list of endangered species

Unlike CITES, which has established a global framework to regulate and control international trade in endangered species of wild animals and plants listed in Appendices I, II and III to the Convention which are lists of species afforded different levels or types of protection from overexploitation, the Lusaka Agreement does not provide any list of species, and yet its intention is to reduce and ultimately eliminate illegal trade in wild fauna and flora. This poses a challenge to officers at the border posts determining the products that are specifically controlled by the Agreement.

5.1.9 No strong effective court process for wildlife crimes

The effective process of fighting wildlife crimes requires arresting offenders, gathering evidence, prosecuting the culprits in courts and convicting them. Currently, the process is not strong enough to sanction offenders. As a result, the culprits are acquitted and sometimes given comparatively light sentences or fines which do not act as a deterrent against the commission of similar crimes in the future.

6. COORDINATION OF LATF WITH OTHER ENFORCEMENT NETWORKS IN PROSECUTING WILDLIFE CRIMES

The LATF is obliged under Article 4(2) of the Agreement to cooperate with State Parties to ensure the reduction and ultimately the elimination of illegal trade in wild fauna and flora. The Task Force has taken heed of this mandate by creating strong bonds, partnerships and networking with and among national, regional, and international bodies. LATF has promoted a great networking capability for wildlife crime enforcement in Africa by coordinating with UNEP, the Secretariats of Interpol, CITES, the World Customs Organization, the Central African Forests Commission, the Organization for the Conservation of African Wildlife, US Fish and Wildlife Service, David Shepherd Wildlife Foundation (UK), International Fund for Animal Welfare (IFAW), Forest Bureau CoA (Taiwan), CorpoForestaleDelloStato (Italy), International Network for Environmental Compliance and Enforcement (INECE-USA), Israel Nature and National Parks, Environmental Investigations Agency (EIA), and the Humane Society of the United States & Canada.

It is worth noting that the strong bond between the Task Force and CITES has existed since April 2002 when a Memorandum of Understanding (MOU) was signed. The MOU establishes the principle of warm general cooperation, the willful exchange of information, supportive arrangements, like the exchange of training materials, courses and trainers, and access for the Task Force to the database maintained by the Legislation and Compliance Unit of the CITES Secretariat.[51] A Memorandum of Understanding between the Lusaka Agreement Task Force and the World Customs Organization was approved and has resulted in curtailing wildlife crimes;[52] the partnership between the Congo Agency for Fauna and Protected Areas (CAFPA) and the Kenya Wildlife Service (KWS) is the brainchild of LATF. This collaboration has facilitated meetings between the two agencies which are geared toward the real-

---

[51] UNEP, *supra* note 39.

[52] Decisions of the Bureau of the 8th Governing Council of the Lusaka Agreement, Decision BGC 1/VIII/1, available at http://lusakaagreement.org/wp-content/uploads/2013/10/AllLAGCDecisions.pdf.

ization of the Task Force's goals and objectives.[53] LATF has supported the coordination between the government of Lesotho and Kenya Wildlife Authority (KWS), which has extended the work of the Task Force in Southern Africa.[54] For example, the Director of the Lusaka Agreement Task Force urged all law enforcement agencies in the Lusaka Agreement member states and African countries at large to increase surveillance and monitoring of wildlife trafficking activities, most especially against the illegal trade in elephant ivory, and to enhance law enforcement operations to focus on potential poaching sites and smuggling routes across the continent. This clearly portrays the strong relationship between LATF and the African continent as a whole. This coordination is consistent with the Task Force's motto of 'fostering cooperation among state parties to support conservation of fauna and flora' in fulfillment of its functions under Article 5(9) of the Agreement.

7. LESSONS FROM OTHER REGIONAL WILDLIFE ENFORCEMENT MECHANISMS

The developments in the environment and specifically wildlife sector in other continents are far better than those in Africa; therefore, there is much to learn from other regions neighboring Eastern and Southern Africa and from the world at large. In South-east Asia, UNODC's Director of Operations, Aldo Lale-Demoz, highlighted the existence of the Wildlife and Forest Crime Analytic Toolkit as a technical resource to assist government officials responsible for wildlife and forestry conservation, customs and other relevant agencies in conducting a comprehensive analysis of the strengths and weaknesses of preventive and criminal justice responses related to the protection of fauna and flora.[55] The establishment of anti-poaching brigades in Europe and Asia is also of great value as far as fighting illegal wildlife activities is concerned, and there are challenges for LATF in strengthening its financial position in order to more easily implement its objectives through empowering National Bureaus in the respective member states and signatories and in supporting education programs that will have a powerful influence in addressing illegal and unsustainable wildlife trade through persuading consumers to make informed

---

[53] Lusaka Agreement Bulletin, *supra* note 32.

[54] Ibid.

[55] See 'Wildlife Trafficking: Who Does It? Who Allows it?', available at http://www.scoop.it/t/animal-poaching-who-does-it-who-allows-it (accessed 30 October 2013).

choices. Such education should be extended to the people buying the end product as well as shopkeepers, suppliers, and manufacturers;[56] this is in contrast to the LATF's approach of only sensitizing the responsible officials of public and private institutions and ignoring the final consumers of illegal wildlife products.

8. CONCLUSION AND RECOMMENDATIONS

In a nutshell, the signing of the Lusaka Agreement together with the establishment of the Task Force with its designed institutions and mechanisms to tackle and overcome the problem of illegal wildlife crime is a great blessing as far as wildlife conservation and preservation is concerned in the Eastern and Southern Africa region. The LATF has had a significant influence in the battle against the evil of wildlife crime in the region. It has made some progress towards complying with the rules and objectives of the CITES, enforcing the policies, laws, and regulations of the State Parties and other allied countries. The instituting of the Governing Council and the National Bureaus to carry out the functions and objectives of the Task Force has encouraged State Parties to enact laws and regulations for the conservation of wildlife resources with the efforts of the Interpol, National Police and Customs services to combat wildlife crime. However, the challenges noted above still affect the effectiveness of LATF in controlling wildlife crimes in the Eastern and Southern Africa region. To that effect, the following recommendations are made:

1. *Encourage more African states to join the Task Force*: Out of the over fifty countries on the African continent, only seven are member states to the LATF, whereas three are signatories to the Agreement. The current Task Force is too small and weak to monitor and eliminate illegal trade in wild fauna and flora in the region. For instance, Zambia and Uganda are member states yet their neighbors Zimbabwe and the Democratic Republic of Congo are not, which makes it difficult to eliminate illegal wildlife trade across borders. However much the countries may cooperate, illegal wildlife products may cross borders because what is prohibited in one country may be allowed in another, thus fuelling smuggling. For example, a person can easily smuggle illegal wildlife products from Zambia to Zimbabwe, assuming the former does not categorize the product as illegal. This grants criminals

---

56 Ibid.

enough leeway to enter and exit from the region while carrying out illegal wildlife trafficking. Therefore, a great degree of cooperation is needed among all African states to mobilize and monitor every corner of the continent. More effort should be put into encouraging more African countries to join the Task Force to strengthen the institution in order to reduce and ultimately eliminate illegal trade in wild fauna and flora across the continent and on the surrounding waters.

2. *Promote patriotism among the people of the member states and signatories*: The biggest obstacle to every development in all aspects of the economies on the African continent is corruption at every level. In regard to the wildlife sector, corruption has resulted in increased wildlife trafficking across borders, facilitated by the officials and technocrats of the relevant institutions. Therefore, efforts must be intensified at all levels to fight this vice in the wildlife and environment sectors, and this can only be done through changing the mindset of the people. Thus, LATF must partner with the Ministries of Gender, Labour, and Social Affairs of every member state to making people aware of how to love their respective nations by carrying out activities which are paramount in the development of their economies. Corruption is caused by bad moral values combined with negative attitudes towards development. This, therefore, calls for the inculcation of good morals together with positive thinking and attitudes towards development which encourage positive behavior change in terms of the conservation of wildlife resources. Unless this is done, the making of strong, deterrent and stringent regulations and other mechanisms will not address the problem of illegal trade in fauna and flora and other related crimes in the region.
3. *Harmonize laws to implement the Lusaka Agreement*: The Task Force must follow up the review of the existing laws and make common wildlife laws and regulations for communities like the East Africa Community, and critically assess their enforcement capacities and the needs of the Parties, as requested by the second Governing Council. For instance, Lesotho is in partnership with the Kenya Wildlife Authority, but is yet to designate a National Bureau, and in the meantime the National Environment Secretariat is handling matters pertaining to the Agreement, yet there is supposed to be a public Authority responsible for wildlife management and conservation. There is, therefore, a need for action by the Task Force in order to continue registering success in its work.
4. *Establish a trust fund*: The 'DECISION BGC1/VIII/2' of the 8th Governing Council to establish a trust fund should be implemented consistent with the strategic plan, rules, proposed program of work

and proposals of the Director of the Task Force. Further, the criteria and modalities of the establishment of a trust fund for the Task Force should be developed with the aim of investing any or surplus money in the best interests of increasing the earnings and finances of the Task Force as a beneficiary. If this is done, the implementation of the mandate of LATF will improve in the region.

5. *Encourage and support the planting of trees and the development of wildlife species*: Wild animals live in an environment which is full of trees and bushes, a factor which requires LATF to devote resources to the planting of trees and also to intensify efforts to eliminate the encroachment of natural forests that harbor fauna. Furthermore, the encroachers on forest lands should vacate them to ensure a conducive environment that guarantees the sustainability of wildlife resources. State Parties need to ensure compliance with forestry and other environmental laws for the maintenance of a green environment for its wildlife resources. The mere prevention of wildlife hunting and trafficking is very far from the Task Force's goal of conservation and preservation of fauna and flora. Therefore, at this point, the author strongly recommends that the Task Force spearheads the planting of trees to address the problem of deforestation for better management of wildlife resources in the region.
6. *Establish specialized wildlife crimes courts*: There is a need to establish specialized wildlife courts to handle wildlife crimes. For example the establishment of a Special Criminal Court in Cameroon to handle wildlife crimes is likely to raise the profile of wildlife crime prosecution in the country. This is after the country passed a law in 1994 that has been widely used to prosecute wildlife dealers in the country at lower courts. A clear example is that of the case forwarded to a Special Criminal Court in Yaoundé following the arrests of four suspected ivory dealers in Douala on June 21, 2013 by wildlife officials. The suspects were found in possession of large quantities of raw and carved ivory. Following investigations carried out in the country's capital city Yaoundé by the police, an accomplice of the four suspected traffickers was later arrested. The decision to start legal proceedings concerning a wildlife matter in the Special Criminal Court is unprecedented in a country that has been severely hit in recent times by elephant poachers. Barrister Louis Bernard Tcheugueu, lawyer for the Ministry of Forestry and Wildlife, the government Ministry that brought the matter to court says, 'I feel satisfied that for the first time we see

that state affairs are taken with seriousness'.[57] This implies that the establishment of a specialized criminal court will portray seriousness in prosecuting wildlife crimes.

BIBLIOGRAPHY

Brasher, A and Moyle, A, 'Conservation in the USA: Legislative Milestones' (2004), available at http://marinebio.org/oceans/conservation/moyle/ch9.asp (accessed 30 October 2013).

Decisions of the Bureau of the 8th Governing Council of the Lusaka Agreement, Decision BGC 1/VIII/1, available at http://lusakaagreement.org/wp-content/uploads/2013/10/AllLAGCDecisions.pdf

Kaaria, BI and Muchiri, NL, 'Enforcement Challenges Across Borders: Detecting and Prosecuting Illegal Wildlife Trafficking' (Paper presented at the 9th International Conference on Environmental Compliance and Enforcement, 20–24 June 2011, Whistler, British Columbia, Canada).

Lusaka Agreement Bulletin, available at http://www.lusakaagreement.org/repatriation.html (accessed 30 October 2013).

Mrema, EM, 'Lusaka Agreement as a Mechanism for Enforcement of CITES' (Paper presented at the 7th International Conference on Environmental Compliance and Enforcement, 9–15 April 2005, Marrakech, Morocco).

Musingo, D, 'Encroachers told to leave forest' New Vision, (Kampala 23 July 2013) 6.

Nurse, A, 'Policing Wildlife: Perspectives on Criminality in Wildlife Crime' (2011) 11 *The British Society of Criminology* 38–53.

Report of the House of Commons Environmental Audit Committee, Environmental Crime: Wildlife *Crime* (Twelfth Report of Session 2003–04), available at http://www.publications.parliament.uk/pa/cm200304/cmselect/cmenvaud/605/60503.htm

The 1911 Treaty for the Preservation and Protection of Fur Seals, 104 BFSP 175.

The Convention Concerning the Use of White Lead in Painting (entry into force: 31 August 1923).

The Convention for the Protection of Birds Useful to Agriculture, Mar. 19, 1902, 102 B.F.S.P. 969 (entered into force 11 May 1907).

The Convention on International Trade in Endangered Species of Wild Fauna and Flora (CITES) (signed in Washington on 3 March 1973 and entered into force on 1 January 1975).

The Convention on Nature, Protection and Wildlife Preservation in the Western Hemisphere, Washington, 1940 (entered into force on 30 April 1942).

The Convention Relative to the Preservation of Fauna and Flora in their Natural State (London Convention), London, opened for signature 8 November 1933 (entered into force 14 January 1936).

---

[57] Retrieved from http://irokoheritage.com/2013/07/22/cameroon-special-corruption-court-to-hear-landmark-wildlife-case/ (accessed 5 November 2014).

The International Convention on the Regulation of Whaling, opened for signature 2 December 1946, 161 UNTS 77 (entered into force 10 November 1948).
The Lusaka Agreement on Cooperative Enforcement Operations Directed at Illegal Trade in Wild Fauna and Flora, adopted at Lusaka, Zambia on 8 September 1994.
'The Wildlife of Lesotho', available at http://www.afrotourist.org/index.php?title=The_Wildlife_of_Lesotho (accessed 30 October 2011).
'Uganda Impounds Over 2 Tons of Ivory as two Chinese Arrested in Kampala', available at http://www.eturbonews.com/39200/uganda-impounds-over-2-tons-ivory-two-chinese-arrested-kampala (accessed 1 November 2013).
Uganda Wildlife Act, Cap 200, Laws of Uganda, 2000.
UNEP, *A Decade of Regional Wildlife Law Enforcement: The Case of the Lusaka Agreement June 2005*, available at http://lusakaagreement.org/wp-content/uploads/2013/12/LATF-Evaluation-Report.pdf
UNODC, 'Eastern Africa: UNODC to Address Rising Environmental Crime', available at http://www.unodc.org/unodc/en/frontpage/2009/November/eastern-africa_-unodc-to-address-rising-environmental-crime.html (accessed 30 October 2013).
'UWA Rescues 42 Poisonous Snakes and 147 Chameleons bound for Czech Republic', available at http://safariadviceuganda.blogspot.com/2012/11/uwa-rescues-42-poisonous-snakes-and-147.html (accessed 30 October 2013).
'Wildlife Trafficking: Who Does It? Who Allows It?', available at http://www.scoop.it/t/animal-poaching-who-does-it-who-allows-it (accessed 30 October 2013).

12. Huntington geographic enforcement/compliance initiative: a case study in multi-organisation networking and collaboration

Eugène Lubieniecki

1. DISCUSSION

The Port of Huntington (Port) is the largest inland port in the United States (US), both in terms of total tonnage as well as ton-miles of cargo transported. The Port boundary includes about 200 river miles taking in portions of the Ohio River and the Kanawha and Big Sandy Rivers (Figure 12.1). There is a relatively high concentration of heavy industry and various associated pollution issues within the Port.

The Port is unlike most US ports. No central authority manages the port; it is composed of individually operated port districts and authorities, terminal operators and shippers. The Port is also unique in that operations occur within three different states: West Virginia, Kentucky and Ohio. Additionally, three different EPA Regions (Regions 3, 4 and 5) share environmental jurisdiction over the Port. The US Coast Guard (USCG), US Army Corps of Engineers, and US Fish and Wildlife Service also have federal oversight for environmental protection within the Port. Due to the interconnectedness of operations across the port and the numerous agencies involved in overseeing those operations, a collaborative geographic enforcement initiative was initiated by the EPA Regions 3, 4, 5 and the National Enforcement Investigations Center (NEIC) in 2008 to address priority human health and environmental protection issues.

The Port Project initially involved using available electronic database information to identify several sections of river within the 200-mile-long Port that were thought to have the highest potential for environmental problems (primarily focused on water quality but also including some air quality and hazardous waste indicators). General multimedia reconnaissance inspections were then conducted along the selected river segments

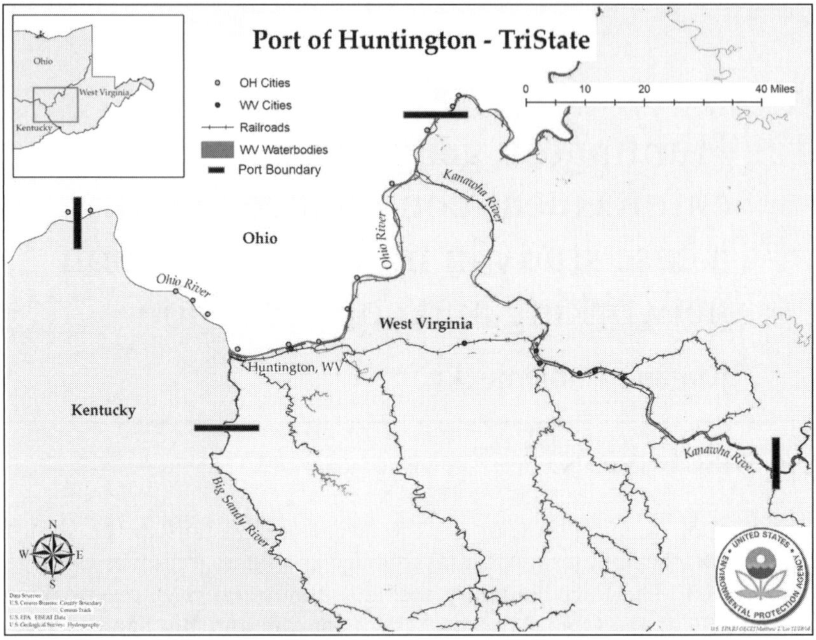

Source: Courtesy of the United States Environmental Protection Agency.

Figure 12.1 Port of Huntington location

to verify database information and gather additional intelligence. From this information priority facilities/industrial sectors were identified for follow-up single or multimedia screening inspections. Based on screening inspection findings, in-depth compliance monitoring investigations were conducted at facilities thought to have the highest potential for environmental issues. Any areas of non-compliance identified during these investigations were to be dealt with as appropriate. The Port Project also included a cooperative compliance assistance programme and a public communications strategy.

This chapter focuses on the enforcement portion of this project and the organisations that provided the major resources for planning and implementation, including EPA Regions 3, 4, 5, the NEIC and the USCG. It discusses the challenges encountered in collaborating across organisations and keys to success regarding multi-organisation cooperation experienced during project planning and implementation.

2. CHALLENGES

Whenever two or more organisations work together there are challenges to overcome. This is not only true for interactions among different organisations, but also interactions with different groups within a single organisation. Some of the major challenges that surfaced during the various stages of the Port Project included:

- *Policies and procedures*: each organisation has policies and procedures that guide its conduct. Some policies are dictated by law (e.g. confidentiality requirements) and are therefore somewhat inflexible, while others may be more easily modified;
- *Structure*: lines of authority, communication and reporting may differ among organisations;
- *Culture*: organisations develop personalities that influence the way members think, act, relate, etc.;
- *Priorities*: different organisations have differing priorities; priorities may be dictated by law, management or both;
- *Resources*: available resources usually differ among organisations;
- *Technology*: computer hardware, software and other technologies may not be compatible among partner organisations;
- *Jargon/semantics/acronyms*: organisations, especially United States federal agencies, tend to develop idiosyncratic terms of art and acronyms. While this specialised vocabulary is well known within its originating organisation, it is often mostly unknown and confusing to those outside of each organisation; and
- *Confidentiality*: because law enforcement often involves the use of confidential information, organisationally imposed limits on the dissemination of such information to other entities both within and without the organisation may cause conflict.

While organisational differences can result in conflict it is important to note that individual personality differences can also result in conflicts and/or determine how well a project team mitigates or compounds potential organisational conflict based on these challenges.

3. TOOLS FOR SUCCESS

The Port Project was in large part successful because key team members recognised and managed the challenges involved with organisation networking and respected organisational differences. Additionally, several of these team members had previous experience working with other organisations and therefore had the insight to deal with organisational differences. These team members also had largely compatible personalities that allowed them to communicate effectively and work together to address the various networking challenges. As discussed below, effective communication became a common thread among the tools that were important to the Port Project's success.

Many of the tools discussed below are strongly interrelated. However, each tool identified is thought to be important enough to justify a separate discussion. Many of these tools were used concurrently and the following discussion is not presented in any priority or sequential order.

3.1 Develop a Core Team

Because proper planning is critical for a successful project outcome, a core project team should be identified to manage and oversee planning. If possible, at least one team member should have previous project planning experience. Each organisation that provides substantial resources to the project should be represented on the core team.

For the Port Project each major organisation involved (EPA Regions 3, 4 and 5, EPA NEIC and the US CG) was represented by two core team members (a primary and a secondary member). These core team members included senior investigators, first line supervisors and managers. The core team often called on other experts from their organisations to assist with discrete aspects of project planning. The core team members became the primary points of contact for each organisation.

In addition to project planning (which included developing a project plan with common project goals and objectives, as discussed later) this team was responsible for identifying and requesting the necessary resources for project implementation, overseeing team personnel during field activities, keeping upper management informed of project activities and progress and continuously assessing and modifying project activities.

This core team also navigated through the various organisational differences and developed many of the tools for success discussed in this chapter.

3.2 Recognise and Respect Differences

One key to dealing with organisational differences is for team members to recognise that differences do exist and that these differences do not make one organisation better than another, just different. Additionally each organisation must recognise and respect the needs of each other organisation and work together, usually through some level of compromise, to help ensure as much as possible that the needs of each organisation are met.

For the Port Project this was important for both internal EPA cooperation as well as cooperation and understanding between EPA entities and the USCG. For instance, the USCG basically follows the concepts and procedures of the Incident Command System for large projects. This system has become the national standard in the US for scene management involving multi-organisational entities and has very formal procedures. Alternatively the various EPA entities involved in the Port Project use various less formal project implementation procedures. Once EPA core team personnel recognised the USCG needs, the Incident Command System was adopted as the general guidance for overall project implementation. Even though this required more formal procedures than normal for EPA personnel, it certainly helped facilitate the cooperation between the EPA and the USCG and likely contributed to the ultimate success of the project. Additionally, as a result of this experience, the EPA is expected to incorporate some of the Incident Command System concepts into their normal project implementation procedures.

3.3 Develop/Implement a Team Communications Strategy

It is well established that effective communication is critical to the success of most projects and that a communication strategy must be developed and implemented. The Port Project core team identified and implemented a number of communication mechanisms to help ensure effective communications between team personnel and the various involved organisations at many levels.

3.3.1 Identify a single point of contact within each organisation

The responsibility of the primary point of contact is to pass information received regarding the project to appropriate personnel within their organisation and pass information from their organisation to other organisational contacts. Because the primary contact is aware of their organisational requirements for internal information flow they are best suited to disseminating that information within their organisation. Establishing a primary point of contact in each organisation helps the organisation meet its requirements for internal information flow and ensures that the organisation is properly informed at all levels. In addition to a primary point of contact for the project the organisation may designate other individuals as project contacts for specific team activities. For instance, the Port Project core team identified a team member from EPA Region 3 (not the primary

Region 3 project contact or a core team member) as the primary contact for the 'team room', as discussed later, because of his expertise in using this tool.

While this is the formal communication system for the project, informal communications between project personnel are encouraged as appropriate for collaboration on individual tasks.

3.3.2 Conduct weekly conference calls

Weekly calls are useful to keep managers and staff updated on project activities and implementation issues. Because the primary organisations involved in the Port Project were located in different geographic areas the core team felt that scheduling weekly calls for the project duration was the most effective way to keep up-to-date with project activities and issues. For each call held an agenda was circulated via e-mail prior to the call. Additionally, any documents/etc. to be discussed during the calls were made available prior to each call. Some of these calls were cancelled when there was no new information to exchange or issues to discuss. However, having a standing conference call scheduled was important to help ensure that the proper personnel were available for discussion if needed.

3.3.3 Create e-mail user group

Creating an e-mail user group is common practice for many organisations that have teams of people working together on a single project. This basically makes information dissemination via e-mail very easy. An e-mail user group was set up for all of the Port Project team members. This was one of the most heavily used communication tools for the Port Project.

3.3.4 Set up a team room

A team room is basically a place where information (photos, reports, documents, etc.) can be posted and shared with other team members. This is a very effective tool to organise and make available electronic information, especially very large files that may not be easily sent via e-mail. Additionally, the information posted in the team room can be identified by posting date and person. Access to the team room is usually controlled by password to help protect the information.

The Port Project team used *Lotus Quickplace* to set up their team room and posted all project information there. Quickplace is a self-service work space expressively designed for team collaboration. (As of 30 April 2010, Quickplace was apparently replaced by *Lotus Quickr*.) A primary contact was identified as the team room manager who was primarily responsible for setting up the team room and dealing with all issues associated with the use of tool. The USCG initially could not access the team room because of computer compatibility issues. However, the team room manager and USCG computer personnel worked together to successfully overcome this challenge. This was critical for effective information sharing and also facilitated joint development of project plans, procedures and sharing of photographs and documents.

3.3.5 Develop briefing materials

Informational presentations are useful to keep staff and management not directly involved in the project informed of project background, activities, goals, issues, resource needs and progress. The Port Project core team developed several computer-based slide presentations. The first presentation was produced to educate management of the Huntington Port issues and to propose a plan to address these issues. This was important in order to obtain initial management support and resource commitments. Following some initial project steps a second presentation was prepared and presented to update management regarding project progress and propose follow-up activities. A third presentation is expected to be developed to present final project outcomes. Each EPA Regional office and the NEIC used the same presentations to ensure a consistent message within the EPA.

3.3.6 Conduct face-to-face meetings

Face-to-face meetings – especially early in the planning process – are important for team members to develop stronger relationships. Because of resource constraints, face-to-face meetings were only held infrequently for the Port Project. An early initial meeting with all major participating organisations represented was held so that core team members could meet and the team could address major strategic planning issues. A discussion of many of the procedures associated with the tools for success addressed here was initiated at this meeting. Other meetings were held to address especially important project issues. Meeting agendas and supporting background information were made available prior to the actual meeting. The Port Project core team rotated the location of these meetings so that travel costs for each organisation were minimised. This also allowed for the maximum number of personnel from each organisation to participate in at least one meeting at some point and meet in person with members of the other organisations without the travel expense.

3.3.7 Confidentiality information/agreements

Different organisations may have different constraints on sharing confidentiality information. Therefore, the networking organisations must agree within the constraints of their organisational requirements on how, when, and what confidential information will be exchanged.

For the Port Project use and exchange of confidential information was discussed during the initial project planning stages. While the EPA entities could more easily exchange this type of information the exchange of confidential information between EPA and the USCG was problematic. The core team agreed that confidential information would not routinely be exchanged and that if a specific need arose it would be dealt with on a case-by-case basis. There was never a need to exchange confidential information during Port Project implementation.

3.4 Develop Mutually Shared Goals

Common goals are critical to ensure that all team members work together efficiently. Differing organisational priorities may inhibit the development of common goals. All project members must both buy in to some mutual primary goals and accept other supplemental goals that address other individual organisational needs. Goals should be completely and honestly discussed, ultimately agreed upon, documented in the project plan and disseminated to all team members.

Because of the complexity of the Port Project the core team initially documented general and some specific project goals in an overarching project plan. More specific goals were developed and documented in individual plans prepared for each major activity of the project (reconnaissance inspections, multimedia screening inspections, in-depth facility-specific single and multimedia investigations, etc.).

As the project progressed some goals were modified. For example, an initial goal of the Port Project reconnaissance inspections was to identify specific environmental and health threats for each school along each stream reach in the project. However, during reconnaissance inspections the implementation team realised that for most schools it would not be possible to identify specific threats because of the relative location of industries and pollution sources to schools. Therefore this goal was dropped from the project plan.

3.5 Identify Specific Roles and Responsibilities

Identifying clear roles and responsibilities is important to help ensure that implementation activities are accomplished and to preclude both duplication of effort and the overstepping of boundaries. Clear roles and responsibilities must be identified for each individual team member as well as for their respective organisations. This includes roles and responsibilities for planning, project implementation, equipment, report preparation and enforcement follow-up. Roles and responsibilities should be documented and provided to all team members to ensure that each team member is aware of his or her responsibility.

To organise the efforts of all participants, the Port Project core team created a spreadsheet which identified each project team member, his or her organisation and the commitment each member and organisation was making for each step of project implementation. Additionally, the spreadsheet identified specific teams, team responsibility and team membership. For example, for a preliminary stage of the project the spreadsheet showed that EPA NEIC committed to providing an infra-red camera (for measuring organic air emissions) and a camera operator for one week to support Land Team A. The spreadsheet also documented that NEIC would prepare a report of camera findings. Another entry in the spreadsheet showed that the USCG was responsible for providing two boats, boat safety equipment and boat operators for River Teams A and B. Assignments should be flexible to allow staffing changes based on field conditions, mid-course corrections, etc.

3.6 Prepare Written Project Plan(s)

A documented project plan helps ensure that all stakeholders are aware of project specifics, including goals, activities necessary to reach those goals, individual roles and responsibilities, time lines, potential safety issues and implementation resources. The project plan should include the following sections:

1. *Background*: a project overview and brief description of the issues the project will address;
2. *Goals and objectives*: a detailed description of goals and objectives with benchmarks for measuring progress;
3. *Major activities and scope of work*: a summary of activities to be performed and specific personnel who will perform each task;
4. *Schedule*: projected dates for implementation of major activities;
5. *Labour budget*: estimated staff time for each task;
6. *Hazard/safety assessment*: identifying potential hazards and appropriate safety requirements (such as monitoring and personnel protective equipment);
7. *Contingencies*: alternatives to implementation plans, staffing and schedule;
8. *Management approval*: approval form for managers to sign documenting organisational commitment to project objectives and to furnish resources; and

9. *Other information*: other important information, such as team contact information.

More than one project plan may be needed for complex projects. For the Port Project the project team created an umbrella project plan that provided an overview of the project, its goals and objectives, major tasks and initial steps. Separate, more specific project plans were prepared for each phase of the project (e.g. reconnaissance inspections, specific facility investigations).

3.7 Develop Project Implementation Procedures

To ensure consistency of information gathering and documentation for a joint project, the project team should agree upon consistent field procedures. This is especially important where evidence may be used for legal enforcement. Project specific procedures can often be developed by melding appropriate aspects of each individual organisation's operation procedures.

For instance, the Port team jointly developed a surveillance checklist to gather and document key target facility information. The checklist incorporated various ideas and procedures from each EPA organisation and the USCG and was designed to address the enforcement needs of all project agencies. This checklist was then successfully used to gather uniform information during the reconnaissance inspections sufficient for future project decision making.

3.8 Obtain Management Support

Support from the individuals who control the resources for each organisation is critical for successful implementation of any project. When multiple organisations share responsibility for a project, each organisation must be assured that the other organisation(s) will uphold its resource commitment(s).

Providing adequate information to managers is critical to ensuring that management understands and agrees with all aspects of the project. The project team must ensure that management is properly informed. Three tools were used to provide this information to management:

1. Visual presentations;
2. Project plan(s); and
3. Management involvement in in-person planning meetings.

Project plans included 'sign-off' forms for management to sign basically documenting their buy-in for the activities in that plan.

3.9 Regularly Assess Project Implementation

Regular implementation review is critical to make sure anticipated outcomes are efficiently reached. Conducting mid-stream assessment allows modifications to current and future planned activities if necessary. For multi-organisational teams this step also helps ensure that implementation is meeting the needs and expectations of each organisation and that each organisation remains actively engaged in the project. Changes to plans should always be documented in the appropriate project plans.

Assessment of Port Project activities prompted many changes to project planning and implementation. Mid-course corrections included reallocation of field personnel and other staffing changes, revisions to data collection tools and data collection plans. While in the field, staff assessed progress daily. Agreed-upon project changes were made almost immediately. This maximised the effective application of resources and ensured the full team worked smoothly towards meeting project goals.

3.10 Conduct Briefings and Debriefings

Project briefings and debriefings are important to keeping implementation on track, accommodating for changing field conditions, ensuring effective use of resources and making sure all stakeholders are aware of project activities.

While field inspections were ongoing, Port Project field staff held morning meetings before each day's activities started. The meetings served two key purposes: (1) to ensure that each team member was aware of and properly prepared for their daily responsibilities; and (2) to ensure that each team member was aware of how these responsibilities related to other team members' activities. Meetings were also held at the end of each day in which team members assessed successes and challenges, progress towards the project plan goals and identified modifications necessary to enhance project implementation. These meetings also helped address organisational needs and furthered the organisational comfort level with project implementation. These discussions resulted in significant project improvements for the Port Project.

3.11 Delineate Organisational Terminology

Every organisation, especially federal agencies, uses terms of art and acronyms. This can complicate communications during inter-agency interactions.

When the EPA and USCG started the Port Project planning process they were not familiar with the terms of art and acronyms (jargon) of the other agency. For example USCG staff used the term 'river right' to identify areas located to the right side of a boat when the boat is traveling downstream. This confused EPA staff until the term was explained. Staff quickly realised that it was important to be sure to explain jargon, both in conversations and in written documents. For the Port Project, an ongoing reference list of acronyms and definitions was maintained in the team room.

3.12 Ensure Complete Project Planning

The importance of thorough project planning to achieve successful project implementation cannot be overstated. 'Proper planning prevents poor performance' is a truism; particularly when complex projects involve staff from many organisations. Not only is up-front project planning crucial for successful project implementation, planning must continue throughout project implementation. Frequent assessment and reassessment are critical to identify necessary midcourse corrections.

Goals for the Port Project evolved throughout project implementation. This required that project plans be modified and documents changed to reflect actual planned activities. Building project plans as living documents helped keep all project personnel informed and working towards common goals, even when these goals are modified. Proper planning throughout the project was very important to the ultimate success of the Port Project.

4. PROJECT OUTCOMES

As a result of the Port Project: (1) various enforcement actions were taken to correct areas of environmental non-compliance resulting in enhanced protection of human health and the environment in the Port of Huntington; and (2) the EPA created a 'lessons learned' document that provides guidance that can be used to help plan and implement large multi-organisation geographic enforcement/compliance initiatives.

The Port Project has enhanced the USCG/EPA working relationship and has advanced the shared goals of an improved environment and protection of human health. The shared success of the Port Project has resulted in the initiation of another joint project in the Chicago, Illinois, area. The keys to success developed for the Port Project were used as a blueprint for the Chicago project. EPA staff and management expect to continue building on their partnership with the USCG as well as with other federal organisations and plan to conduct joint investigations in other areas of the US.

13. The European Union Forum of Judges for the Environment

Luc Lavrysen

1. INTRODUCTION

The activities of the European Union Forum of Judges for the Environment (EUFJE) should be seen against the background of the Judges Programme of the United Nations Environmental Programme (UNEP). Indeed, UNEP and the South African Constitutional Court organised, as a parallel event to the world Summit on Sustainable Development, in Johannesburg from 18 to 20 August 2002, a Global Judges Symposium on the Role of Law and Sustainable Development, after UNEP had organised in the years before several regional Judges Symposia in different parts of the world (Mombasa (1996), Colombo (1997), Manila (1999), Mexico City (2000), Castries (2001), Brisbane (2002)).

The Global Judges Symposium,[1] attended by some 70 Justices from all over the world, including some 30 Chief Justices and representatives from some international courts, was believed to be the largest gathering so far of senior judges to discuss environmental and development issues, and unanimously adopted after two days of intensive dialogue '*The Johannesburg Principles on the Role of Law and Sustainable Development*', that are available in the six UN official languages.

2. THE JOHANNESBURG PRINCIPLES ON THE ROLE OF LAW AND SUSTAINABLE DEVELOPMENT[2]

The judges affirmed in this document, in the first place, their commitment to the pledge made by world leaders in the Millennium Declaration

---

[1] http://www.unep.org/delc/judgesprogramme/GlobalJudgesSymposium/tabid/106158/Default.aspx

adopted by the United Nations General Assembly in September 2000 'to spare no effort to free all of humanity, and above all our children and grandchildren, from the threat of living on a planet irredeemably spoilt by human activities, and whose resources would no longer be sufficient for their needs'. They expressed their firm conviction that the framework of international and national law that has evolved since the United Nations Conference on Human Environment held in Stockholm in 1972 provides a sound basis for addressing the major environmental threats of the day, including armed conflict and attacks on innocent civilians, and should be underpinned by a more determined, concerted and sustained effort to implement and enforce these legal regimes in order to achieve their objectives. They emphasised their commitment to the Universal Declaration of Human Rights and the UN Human Rights Conventions and recognised their close connection with sustainable development and upholding the Rule of Law. The Judges recalled the principles adopted in the Rio Declaration on Environment and Development which lay down the basic principles of sustainable development and affirmed adherence to them. They affirmed that *an independent Judiciary and judicial process is vital for the implementation, development and enforcement of environmental law*, and that members of the Judiciary, as well as those contributing to the judicial process at the national, regional and global levels, are crucial partners for promoting compliance with, and the implementation and enforcement of, international and national environmental law. The rapid evolution of multilateral environmental agreements, national constitutions and statutes concerning the protection of the environment increasingly requires the courts to interpret and apply new legal instruments in keeping with the principles of sustainable development. The fragile state of the global environment requires the Judiciary as the guardian of the Rule of Law, *to boldly and fearlessly implement and enforce applicable international and national laws*, which in the field of environment and sustainable development will assist in alleviating poverty and sustaining an enduring civilisation, as well as ensuring that the present generation will enjoy and improve the quality of life of all peoples, while also ensuring that the inherent rights and interests of succeeding generations are not compromised. The Judiciary has a key role to play in integrating the Human Values set out in the United Nations Millennium Declaration – Freedom, Equality, Solidarity, Tolerance, Respect for Nature and Shared Responsibility – into contemporary global civilisation by translating these

---

[2] http://iospress.metapress.com/content/pd3lahdawm8dkcme/fulltext.pdf

shared values into action through strengthening respect for the Rule of Law both internationally and nationally.

The Judges expressed their conviction that the Judiciary, well informed of the rapidly expanding boundaries of environmental law and aware of its role and responsibilities in promoting the implementation, development and enforcement of laws, regulations and international agreements relating to sustainable development, plays a critical role in the enhancement of the public interest in a healthy and secure environment. They recognised the importance of ensuring that environmental law and the law in the field of sustainable development feature prominently in academic curricula, legal studies and training at all levels, in particular among judges and others engaged in the judicial process. They expressed their conviction that the deficiency in the knowledge, relevant skills and information in regard to environmental law is one of the principal causes that contribute to the lack of effective implementation, development and enforcement of environmental law. They were strongly of the view that there is an urgent need to strengthen the capacity of judges, prosecutors, legislators and all persons who play a critical role at national level in the process of implementation, development and enforcement of environmental law, including multilateral environmental agreements (MEAs), especially through the judicial process. They recognised that the people most affected by environmental degradation are the poor, and that, therefore, there is an urgent need to strengthen the capacity of the poor and their representatives to defend environmental rights, so as to ensure that the weaker sections of society are not prejudiced by environmental degradation and are enabled to enjoy their right to live in a social and physical environment that respects and promotes their dignity.

The Judges were also of the view that the inequality between powerful and weak nations in terms of their relative capacity and opportunity to protect the sustainable development of the shared global environment places a greater responsibility on the former to protect the global environment, and they feel reassured that the implementation and further development of international environmental law aiming at sustainable development, the implementation of agreed international norms and policies, and the strengthening of the capacity of those engaged in promoting the implementation and enforcement of environmental law are cornerstones of the UNEP Programme of Work in the field of Environmental Law.

The following Principles should, according to the final document of the Symposium, guide the Judiciary in promoting the goals of sustainable development through the application of the rule of law and the democratic process: (1) a full commitment to contributing towards the realisation of the goals of sustainable development through the judicial mandate to implement, develop and enforce the law, and to uphold the Rule of Law and the democratic process; (2) to realise the goals of the Millennium Declaration of the United Nations General Assembly which depend upon the implementation of national and international legal regimes that have been established for achieving the goals of sustainable development; (3) in the field of environmental law there is an urgent need for a concerted and sustained programme of work focused on education, training and dissemination of information, including regional and sub-regional judicial colloquia; and (4) that collaboration among members of the Judiciary and others engaged in the judicial process within and across regions is essential to achieve a significant improvement in compliance with, implementation, development and enforcement of, environmental law.

For the realisation of these principles they proposed that the programme of work should include the following:

1. The improvement of the capacity of those involved in the process of promoting, implementing, developing and enforcing environmental law, such as judges, prosecutors, legislators and others, to carry out their functions on a well-informed basis, equipped with the necessary skills, information and material;
2. The improvement in the level of public participation in environmental decision-making, access to justice for the settlement of environmental disputes and the defence and enforcement of environmental rights, as well as public access to relevant information;
3. The strengthening of sub-regional, regional and global collaboration for the mutual benefit of all peoples of the world and exchange of information among national Judiciaries with a view to benefiting from each other's knowledge, experience and expertise;
4. The strengthening of environmental law education in schools and universities, including research and analysis as essential to realising sustainable development;
5. The achievement of sustained improvement in compliance with, and enforcement and development of, environmental law;
6. The strengthening of the capacity of organisations and initiatives, including the media, which seek to enable the public to fully engage on a well-informed basis, in focusing attention on issues relating to environmental protection and sustainable development;
7. An Ad Hoc Committee of Judges consisting of judges representing geographical regions, legal systems and international courts and tribunals, and headed by the Chief Justice of South Africa, should

keep under review and publicise the emerging environmental jurisprudence, providing information thereon;

8. UNEP and its partner agencies, including civil society organisations should provide support to the Ad Hoc Committee of Judges in accomplishing its task;
9. Governments of the developed countries and the donor community, including international financial institutions and foundations, should give priority to financing the implementation of the above principles and the programme of work;
10. The Executive Director of UNEP should continue to provide leadership within the framework of the Montevideo Programme III, in relation to the development and implementation of the programme designed to improve the implementation, development and enforcement of environmental law, including, within the applicable law of liability and compensation for environmental harm under multilateral environmental agreements and national law, military activities and the environment, and the legal aspects of the nexus between poverty and environmental degradation; and
11. This Statement should be presented by the Chief Justice of South Africa to the Secretary-General of the United Nations as a contribution of the Global Judges Symposium to the forthcoming World Summit on Sustainable Development, and for broad dissemination thereof to all Member States of the United Nations.

3. THE FOLLOW-UP

UNEP organised on 30–31 January 2003 in its Headquarter in Nairobi an Ad Hoc Planning Meeting for the Development of a Plan of Work as a follow-up to the Global Judges Symposium relating to the capacity building of judges, prosecutors and other legal stakeholders. The around thirty Chief Justices and Senior Judges who attended the meeting expressed their full support for, and co-operation with, UNEP for the development and implementation of capacity-building programmes directed at the above-mentioned target groups, and undertook to contribute to the programmes for the capacity building of the Judiciary. They urged UNEP to undertake an assessment of the capacity-building needs of developing countries and countries with economies in transition to design and implement programmes responding to their specific needs at national level, utilising existing national and other organisations and institutions for this purpose, and to reinforce where possible, existing training programmes. They encouraged all countries to support these programmes with available resources and to share their experiences in every possible way. They recognised the important role that international organisations, the academic community and regional as well as sub-regional organisations could play in contributing towards the development and implementation of cohesive, concerted and sustained programmes of capacity building in environmental law in developing countries and countries with economies in transition, and called on UNEP and these organisations to co-operate in the design and implementation of the programmes and activities.

Throughout 2003 and 2004 UNEP convened several Regional Chief Justices' Needs-Assessment and Planning Meetings, for the Arab world (Cairo 2004), the Caribbean (Trelawney 2004) and French speaking Africa (Paris 2005). These meetings have drawn up needs-responsive and country-specific national programmes of work for strengthening judicial capacity in the area of environment law and sustainable development.[3]

The UNEP Judges programme[4] included the development of a series of environmental law training materials:

- A UNEP Manual on International Environmental Law;[5]
- A Judicial Handbook on Environmental Law;[6]
- Judicial Training Modules on Environmental Law;[7] and
- Compendia of Summaries of Judgments in environment-related cases from around the world.[8]

From 2008 onwards the UNEP Judges programme came to a sort of standstill due to changes in staff, restrictions in funding and changing priorities.

---

3 K. Kurukulasuriya, 'UNEP's role in strengthening the capacity of judges and other legal stakeholders in the field of Environmental Law', in A. Postiglione (ed.), *The Role of the Judiciary in the Implementation and Enforcement of Environmental Law* (Brussels, Bruylant, 2008), 17–24.

4 http://www.unep.org/delc/judgesprogramme/tabid/78617/Default.aspx

5 http://www.unep.org/delc/Portals/119/publications/UNEP%20Training%20Manual%20on%20International%20Environmental%20Law.pdf

6 http://www.unep.org/delc/Portals/119/publications/Judicial-Handbook-Environmenal-Law.pdf

7 http://www.unep.org/delc/JudicialTrainingModulesEnvironmentalLaw/tabid/102283/Default.aspx

8 http://www.unep.org/delc/Portals/119/UNEPCompendiumSummariesJudgementsEnvironment-relatedCases.pdf

4. WORLD CONGRESS ON JUSTICE, GOVERNANCE AND LAW FOR ENVIRONMENTAL SUSTAINABILITY

UNEP re-launched the programme in the run up to the Rio+20 Conference. After some preparatory meetings, UNEP organised on 17–20 June 2012, the World Congress on Justice, Governance and Law for Environmental Sustainability in Rio de Janeiro/Portobello.[9] One of the purposes of the Congress, which gathered well over 200 participants, including not only Judges, but also Public Prosecutors and Auditors General, was to contribute to the Rio+20 Conference on the role of environmental laws. Another important task was to outline the future actions required by national and international legal stakeholders in order to promote the pursuit of sustainable development in the 21st century founded on the rule of law and effective governance. On 20 June 2012 the Congress adopted the *Rio+20 Declaration on Justice, Governance and Law for Environmental Sustainability*.[10] The Declaration was presented to the President of Rio+20 and to the Heads of State and other high-level representatives at the Rio+20 Conference. The Declaration contains three main elements: Messages to Heads of State and Government, other high-level representatives, and the world community at large; Principles for the Advancement of Justice, Governance and Law for Environmental Sustainability; and Institutional Framework for the Advancement of Justice, Governance and Law for Environmental Sustainability in the 21st Century.

The several messages include that an independent Judiciary and judicial process is vital for the implementation, development and enforcement of environmental law; that environmental law is essential for the protection of natural resources and ecosystems and reflects our best hope for the future of our planet; and that environmental sustainability cannot be achieved without good quality data, monitoring, auditing and accounting for performance. The participants emphasise that environmental and sustainability auditing ensures transparency, access to information, accountability, and efficient use of public finances, while protecting the environment for future generations. In that context they highlight the responsibility of judges, public prosecutors and auditors and stress the need to strengthen existing international governance institutions to protect

---

[9] http://www.unep.org/environmentalgovernance/Portals/8/documents/Events/Advancing_Justice_GovernancenLaw.pdf

[10] http://www.unep.org/rio20/Portals/24180/Rio20_Declaration_on_Justice_Gov_n_Law_4_Env_Sustainability.pdf

the global environment. The principles expressed in the Declaration are summarised to the effect that only through the active engagement of all parts of society, especially national and sub-national institutions and officials responsible for addressing justice, governance and law issues, including judges, prosecutors, auditing institutions and other key functionaries, can meaningful progress be achieved that is sustained and responsive to the needs of the peoples of the world and protective of human rights. The Declaration concludes by defining the purposes of an international institutional network that should be established with UNEP in the lead and with the engagement of other relevant actors. This endeavour should be managed under the guidance of selected members of the professions that participated in the World Congress. A new council of senior legal figures to advance the role of law, justice and good governance in achieving sustainable development, was appointed. The nine-member advisory council includes Chief Justices, senior judges, auditors and legal academics.[11] Led by UNEP, it has to provide strategic guidance to the international community in improving the legal foundations for achieving international environmental goals, and overcoming legal barriers to inclusive sustainable development. The new council aims to meet that request, and is tasked with engaging the legal and auditing community worldwide, supporting the development and implementation of environmental law at all levels, and encouraging the further expansion of environmental jurisprudence. The Council will also provide strategic advice on the provision of information, data and technical assistance to support governments and other bodies. Meanwhile the 1st Asia and Pacific International Colloquium on Environmental Rule of Law,[12] which delivered the Putraya Statement,[13] was organised in December 2013 in Malaysia. Around the same time the Asian Development Bank organised in Manila the Second Asian Judges

---

[11] It includes: Justice Winston Anderson, Judge of the Caribbean Court of Justice; the Rt. Hon. Tun Arifin Zakaria, Chief Justice of Malaysia; Justice Antonio Herman Benjamin, National High Court of Brazil (STJ); Edith Brown Weiss, Francis Cabell Brown, Professor of International Law at Georgetown Law; the Rt. Hon. Lord Carnwath of Notting Hill C.V.O.; Scott Fulton, former General Counsel, US EPA; Justice Ricardo Luis Lorenzetti, Chief Justice of Argentina; Scott Vaughan, Commissioner of the Environment and Sustainable Development, Canada; Justice Philip Waki, Court of Appeals, Kenya.

[12] http://www.unep.org/delc/worldcongress/WorkshopsEvents/ThePutrajaya Statement/tabid/132340/Default.aspx

[13] http://www.unep.org/delc/worldcongress/WorkshopsandEvents/The PutrajayaStatement/tabid/132340/Default.aspx

Symposium on Environment, which led to the creation of the Asian Judges Network on Environment.[14]

5. THE EUROPEAN UNION FORUM OF JUDGES FOR THE ENVIRONMENT[15]

Following up the recommendations made during the Global Judges Symposium of 2002 and the Ad Hoc Planning Meeting in January 2003 in Nairobi, the Judges from Western Europe present at that meeting, considered setting up a regional forum of judges for the environment. The idea was discussed further in London in October 2002, during an IUCN[16] symposium and in Rome in May 2003 during the Symposium on Environmental Law for Judges, organised with the Italian Council of the Judiciary[17] by ICEF, in collaboration with UNEP and IUCN.[18]

On 28 February 2004, the *EU Forum of Judges for the Environment (EUFJE)* was established on the initiative of Guy Canivet, First President of the *Cour de Cassation* (France), Amedeo Postiglione, Judge of the *Corte Suprema di Cassazione* (Italy), Luc Lavrysen, Judge of the Constitutional Court (Belgium) and Lord Justice Robert Carnwath, Judge of the Court of Appeal (England and Wales).[19]

The objective of the Forum is to promote the enforcement of national, European and international environmental law in a perspective of sustainable development. The aim of the Forum is in particular to exchange experiences in the area of training of the judiciary in environmental law, contribute to a better knowledge of environmental law, share experiences with environmental case law and contribute to a more effective enforcement of environmental law. Every judge in the European Union

---

[14] http://ajne2.itkeep.com/about-ajne/

[15] http://www.eufje.org/

[16] See on IUCN's early involvement in networking of the judiciary in environmental matters: N. Robinson, 'The courts confront environmental legal challenges after the Johannesburg Summit', in A. Postiglione (ed.), *The Role of the Judiciary in the Implementation and Enforcement of Environmental Law* (Brussels, Bruylant, 2008), 81–88.

[17] A. Postiglione (ed.), *The Role of the Judiciary in the Implementation and Enforcement of Environmental Law* (Brussels, Bruylant, 2008).

[18] http://www.iucn.org/

[19] G. Canivet, 'Forum of European Judges for the Environment', in A. Postiglione (ed.), *The Role of the Judiciary in the Implementation and Enforcement of Environmental Law* (Brussels, Bruylant, 2008), XIII.

and the European Free Trade Association with a special interest in environmental law can become a member of the Forum. Judges from countries that have applied for membership of the European Union may be admitted as observers. In that capacity, we welcome each year a representative of the Council of State of Turkey, and last year also from Serbia and Ukraine. Representatives of the United Nations Environment Programme (UNEP), the European Commission and the Council of Europe may attend the meetings as observers. The activities of EUFJE are supported by DG Environment of the European Commission.

It was agreed at the inaugural meeting in the European Court of Justice in Luxembourg on 26 April 2004 that the early work of EUFJE was to obtain information about environmental law training facilities offered to members of the judiciary in each of the participating states, as well as particular courts or tribunals which have jurisdiction in respect of environmental cases. On 3 December 2004, EUFJE held its first Annual Conference in the Council of State of the Netherlands, in The Hague.[20] In the following years annual conferences were held in London in 2005 (on waste legislation), in Helsinki in 2006 (on Natura 2000), in Luxembourg in 2007 (on criminal enforcement of environmental law), in Paris in 2008 (on soil pollution), in Stockholm in 2009 (on the Integrated Pollution Prevention and Control Directive), in Brussels in 2010 (on the Application of European Biodiversity Law at national level), in Warsaw in 2011 (on Environmental Protection and Town and Country Planning), in The Hague in 2012 (on the Role of EU Environmental Law in the Courts of the Member States) and in Vienna in 2013 (on Access to Justice in Environmental Matters).

During the Brussels Conference in 2010 the Forum brought together for the first time public prosecutors from the different Member States of the EU. In doing so, the Forum was instrumental in the creation of the European Network of Prosecutors for the Environment (ENPE).[21]

The Forum is also involved in the activities of the Aarhus Convention (UNECE Convention on Access to Information, Public Participation in Decision-making and Access to Justice in Environmental Matters),

---

20 L. Lavrysen, 'The role of national judges in environmental law', *Environmental Law and Policy at the Turn to the 21st Century: Liber Amicorum Betty Gebers – Umweltrecht und -politik an der Wende zum 21. Jahrhundert* (Berlin, Lexxion, 2006), 81–96.

21 http://www.eufje.org/EN/conferences/brussels_2010/program_including_presentations

especially those of the Task Force on Access to Justice.[22] Members of the Forum attended the different meetings of the Task Force and were also involved in the preparation of its capacity-building activities for judges in Kiev,[23] Tirana[24] and Almaty.[25]

6. DEVELOPING DIALOGUE BETWEEN EU NATIONAL JUDGES IN EU ENVIRONMENTAL LAW[26]

Of course, through its activities, the Forum only directly reaches a few judges in each Member State. For that reason the EUFJE welcomes the initiative that was taken by DG Environment of the European Commission. On 9–10 October 2008, a Conference took place in Paris on the role of the national judges in enforcement of EU environmental law. This event stemmed from a joined diagnosis between the European Commission and professional Associations of judges,[27] including the Forum. The Conference confirmed the interest of judges in greater co-operation with EU institutions. It has demonstrated that judges in Europe are asking for more opportunities to exchange views and to benefit from experiences in different EU countries. Based on this diagnosis, the Commission organised a co-operation programme with national judges. Between 2008 and 2012 the Commission contracted the European Institute of Public Administration to develop training modules on various topics of EU environmental law as well as to organise workshops and seminars on the implementation of EU environmental law. Since 2012 the Commission

---

[22] http://www.unece.org/env/pp/ppdm.html

[23] http://www.unece.org/environmental-policy/treaties/public-participation/meetings-and-events/public-participation/2007/high-level-judicial-seminar-on-access-to-justice-in-environmental-matters-for-eastern-europe-and-south-caucasus-region/docs.html

[24] http://www.unece.org/environmental-policy/treaties/public-participation/meetings-and-events/public-participation/public-participation/2008/high-level-judicial-seminar-on-access-to-justice-in-environmental-matters-for-the-south-eastern-european-region/docs.html

[25] http://www.unece.org/centralasianmeeting2012.html

[26] http://ec.europa.eu/environment/legal/law/judges.htm; J.G. Burgues, W. Heermann, Y. Kreins, L. Lavrysen and F. Tiberghien, 'A common heritage: EU environmental law and national judges', *Journal for European Environmental & Planning Law*, 2010, 221–233.

[27] The Association of European Administrative Judges and the Association of Council of States and Supreme Administrative Jurisdictions of the European Union.

has contracted the Academy of European Law to develop further training modules. It should be stressed that the objective was not to develop a programme as if there were no existing national-level training courses intended for judges, or as if this training did not take account of European law. The programme was hosted by national training centres and developed in close co-operation with them by the European Institute for Public Administration. The added-value of an action at Union level is indeed to encourage exchanges between the different Member States and legal traditions, as well as between the national courts and the Commission in order to improve a uniform implementation of Union law. Meanwhile, multiple workshops have been organised and training modules are available on issues such as: EU Law on Environmental Impact Assessment (EIA); EU Law on Nature Protection; EU Waste Legislation; EU Water Legislation; Principles of EU Environmental Law; Protection of Environment through Criminal Law; and Access to Justice in environmental matters and the Role of National Courts and the EU Commission as concerns the implementation of European environmental legislation.[28] Many seminars have already been organised, attended by more than 400 judges and prosecutors from the courts of first instance to the Supreme Courts from 27 Member States.

Finally, the Forum provides input to DG Environment when it is developing proposals for EU legislation with a particular relevance for judges, as in the case of the access to justice proposal,[29] the legal instrument on environmental inspections[30] or when it is evaluating existing legislation such as the environmental liability directive.[31]

7. CONCLUSION

The activities of the EUFJE, together with the Judges Training Programme of the European Commission, and the environmental law related activities of the other European judges associations, have considerably enhanced environmental awareness and knowledge of EU law amongst the Judiciary in the EU. This leads also to increased dialogue between the national Judiciary and the Court of Justice of the European Union via the

28 http://ec.europa.eu/environment/legal/law/training_package.htm
29 http://ec.europa.eu/environment/consultations/access_justice_en.htm
30 http://ec.europa.eu/environment/consultations/inspections_en.htm
31 http://ec.europa.eu/environment/legal/liability/index.htm

references for preliminary rulings in environmental matters.[32] In doing so, the judges of EUFJE hope to have made a small contribution to a better environment for our children.

32 See: J.H. Jans, R. Macrory and A.-M. Moreno Molina (eds), *National Courts and EU Environmental Law* (Groningen, Europa Law Publishing, 2013).

14. The Seaport Environmental Security Network: facilitating international enforcement collaboration to prevent illegal hazardous waste shipments through ports

Danielle Fest Grabiel,* Robert George Heiss,† Meredith Koparova,‡ Deborah Kopsick# and Henk Ruessink◊

1. BEGINNINGS

The Basel Convention on the Control of Transboundary Movements of Hazardous Wastes and Their Disposal, usually known as the Basel Convention, is an international treaty that was designed to reduce the movements of hazardous waste between nations, and specifically to prevent transfer of hazardous waste from developed to less developed countries. The Basel Convention has been widely adopted, with 181 parties to the Basel Convention as of February 2014.

The three main goals of the Basel Convention are: the reduction of hazardous waste generation and the promotion of environmentally sound

* Institute for Governance & Sustainable Development, 2300 Wisconsin Ave, NW, Suite 300B, Washington, DC 20007, dgrabiel@inece.org

† International Compliance Assurance Division, Office of Enforcement and Compliance Assurance, US Environmental Protection Agency, 1200 Pennsylvania Ave MC 2254A, Washington, DC 20460, heiss.robert@epa.gov

‡ INECE Secretariat/Earthspace, 2300 Wisconsin Ave, NW, Suite 300B, Washington, DC 20007, mreeves@earthpace.com

International Compliance Assurance Division, Office of Federal Activities, US Environmental Protection Agency, 1200 Pennsylvania Ave MC 2254A, Washington, DC 20460, kopsick.deborah@epa.gov

◊ Human Environment and Transport Inspectorate, PO Box 1511, 3500 BM Utrecht, the Netherlands, henk.ruessink@ilent.nl

management of hazardous wastes; the restriction of transboundary movements of hazardous wastes; and a regulatory system applying to cases where transboundary movements are permissible.[1]

The regulatory system for transboundary waste stipulates that: (1) a notification procedure is followed to ensure prior informed consent of a state of import and states of transit before an export of waste can take place; (2) all practicable steps are taken to ensure environmentally sound management of waste; (3) the exporting state has a duty to re-import where an export has not complied with the provisions of the Basel Convention.[2] Parties adopt national laws that implement the Basel Convention requirements.

The quantity of illegal movements of hazardous waste is difficult to estimate.[3] Analysis by the European Union Network for Implementation and Enforcement of Environmental Law Transfrontier Shipments of Waste Programme (IMPEL TFS) found approximately 20 percent of inspected shipments had infractions within Europe.[4] A comprehensive study on global environmental crime estimated the profit from the illegal dumping of trash and hazardous waste materials to be $10–12 billion per year.[5] More recently, Europol found that the trafficking of illicit waste in Europe is a high-profit, low-risk activity, where significant work on enforcement capacity is necessary.[6] On electronic waste alone, nearly 50 million metric tons of e-waste[7] are disposed of worldwide

---

[1] Basel Convention Secretariat, Basel Convention at a Glance, http://www.basel.int/Portals/4/Basel%20Convention/docs/convention/bc_glance.pdf (accessed 9 March 2014).

[2] Basel Convention Secretariat, Basel Convention Training Manual on Illegal Traffic for Customs and Enforcement Agencies, http://www.basel.int/TheConvention/Publications/TrainingManuals/tabid/2363/Default.aspx (accessed 9 March 2014).

[3] UNEP, Vital Waste Graphics 3, http://www.grida.no/publications/vg/waste3/ (accessed 9 March 2014).

[4] Isarin, N., 'Inspection & Enforcement of Hazardous Waste & Goods: Fostering International Cross-Border Collaboration by the Inauguration of a Seaport Network', in INECE Secretariat, *Proceedings of the Eighth International Conference on Environmental Compliance and Enforcement* (INECE 2008).

[5] FAS, International Crime Threat Assessment, https://www.fas.org/irp/threat/pub45270chap2.html#6 (accessed 9 March 2014).

[6] Europol, Threat Assessment: Environmental Crime in the EU (2013) https://www.europol.europa.eu/sites/default/files/publications/4aenvironmental_crime_threatassessment_2013_-_public_version.pdf (accessed 9 March 2014).

[7] Electronic waste (or 'e-waste') is electrical and electronic equipment that is no longer suitable for use or that the last owner has discarded (from the Secretariat of the Basel Convention report, *Where are WEEE in Africa*?).

each year.[8] Estimates vary for the quantity of this waste that is shipped illegally to developing countries, but reports from the International Network for Environmental Compliance and Enforcement (INECE),[9] Interpol Environmental Crime Programme,[10] and others[11] have found it to be substantial.

For the implementation of the requirements of the Basel Convention relevant to transboundary movements to be successful, strong cooperation among authorities at the national, regional, and international level is necessary. At the international and regional levels, effective collaboration across borders is critical when ensuring the notification procedure is followed, when undertaking the re-import of a non-compliant shipment, and when investigating actors responsible for an illegal shipment. At the national level, coordination is essential in the operational stage of detecting illegal shipments, as well as in the pre-operational targeting and priority setting and in the enforcement response. In particular, customs agencies are the essential partner of environmental ministries that are seeking to stop illegal exports and illegal imports of hazardous waste at ports.[12]

The opportunities that could result from more effective enforcement cooperation led INECE to develop the Seaport Environmental Security Network (SESN) in 2008. The launch of the network also was driven by

---

8 Guardian, 'Toxic "e-waste" Dumped in Poor Nations, says United Nations' (14 December 2013), http://www.theguardian.com/global-development/2013/dec/14/toxic-ewaste-illegal-dumping-developing-countries (accessed 9 March 2014).

9 INECE, Second International Hazardous Waste Inspection Project: Results and Recommendations (2012), http://inece.org/resource/sesn-report/ (accessed 8 March 2014).

10 Interpol, Press release, 'INTERPOL Operation Targets Illegal Trade of e-waste in Europe, Africa' (25 February 2013), http://www.interpol.int/News-and-media/News/2013/N20130225 (accessed 8 March 2014).

11 ILO, 'The Global Impact of e-waste: Addressing the Challenge' (2012), http://www.ilo.org/wcmsp5/groups/public/---ed_dialogue/---sector/documents/publication/wcms_196105.pdf (accessed 8 March 2014); Huabo Duan, T. Reed Miller, Jeremy Gregory and Randolph Kirchain, 'Quantitative Characterization of Domestic and Transboundary Flows of Used Electronics: Analysis of Generation, Collection, and Export in the United States' (2013), http://step-initiative.org/tl_files/step/_documents/MIT-NCER%20US%20Used%20Electronics%20Flows%20Report%20-%20December%202013.pdf (accessed 8 March 2014).

12 Heiss, B., 'Illegal Exports of Hazardous Waste and Used Electronic Products: Enhancing Collaborative Enforcement with Customs', in INECE Secretariat, *Proceedings of the Ninth International Conference on Environmental Compliance and Enforcement* (INECE 2011).

requests from national authorities, who felt greater coordination, together with coordinated training on targeting and inspecting suspect shipments, could improve the capacity for controlling hazardous waste shipments at seaports.

The term 'enforcement cooperation' is broadly defined in the seaport environmental security context. On the one hand, enforcement cooperation activities are any type of formal or informal information exchange on environmental compliance and enforcement related matters. This type of enforcement cooperation, which is undertaken and facilitated by INECE and the SESN, can help create a level playing field for regulated industries domestically and internationally, resolve and prevent transboundary environmental problems, create efficiencies in the development of tools and programs, and foster the political will needed to strengthen implementation of environmental standards.[13] On the other hand, enforcement cooperation can include enforcement actions undertaken by multiple government authorities working collaboratively in a situation where an illegal shipment is suspected to have occurred. The SESN builds connections between national authorities to support this type of enforcement cooperation, but the actions themselves are the responsibility of the relevant government actors.

A related area is cooperation among police and/or customs authorities at an operational level. This type of coordination can be difficult due to practical problems related to information exchange, sovereignty issues, jurisdiction issues, and complex formal communication structures. However, in cases of cross-border environmental crimes, there is much to be gained from coordination and cooperation among law enforcement authorities and this type of coordination must be encouraged and supported.[14]

SESN developed its international mission and work plans with knowledge gained from the successful operation of the IMPEL TFS project and the input of other experts.

---

[13] INECE Secretariat, 'Whistler Statement', in INECE Secretariat, *Proceedings of the Ninth International Conference on Environmental Compliance and Enforcement* (INECE 2011).

[14] Spapens, T., 'Cross-Border Police Cooperation in Tackling Environmental Crime', in INECE Secretariat, *Proceedings of the Ninth International Conference on Environmental Compliance and Enforcement* (INECE 2011).

2. PRACTICAL ACTIVITIES

Since its establishment, SESN has worked closely with partners in national governments as well as regional and international organizations and enforcement initiatives, including the Secretariat of the Basel Convention, IMPEL TFS, the Asian Network for Prevention of Illegal Transboundary Movement of Hazardous Wastes, United Nations Environment Programme (UNEP), the United Nations Office of Drugs and Crime (UNODC) and the World Customs Organization (WCO). Through these partnerships, SESN has identified how the network can be most effective in implementing its goals of building capacity, raising awareness and facilitating enforcement collaboration on ways to detect and control illegal and dangerous transboundary shipments of environmentally regulated goods through seaports.

As a result of these consultations, SESN created a work program designed to provide hands-on opportunities for enforcement officers to gain practical knowledge and skills in detecting and preventing illegal cross-border movements of waste. These activities included a series of training workshops for frontline enforcement officers and supervisors in West Africa (2008) and Asia (2010 and 2012), the organization of two global enforcement operations (2010 and 2012) focused on hazardous waste shipments through seaports and the development of tools for customs and environment officers working at the frontlines.

From its beginnings, SESN recognized that the law enforcement forces with port interests, especially customs and environmental bodies within a country, as well as police and others, are often not well connected with one another, and that promoting cooperation among these forces is critical to the success of transboundary waste environmental enforcement. In addition to promoting cooperation, SESN focused its efforts on providing educational instruction and facilitating enforcement exercises for the training and diagnostic value they afford. Finally, SESN underlined that key tools, such as intelligence-led enforcement and guidance on practical topics like the take back of wastes, would be of great benefit to participants.

The first INECE SESN International Hazardous Waste Inspection Project at Seaports was a global operational enforcement effort tackling the illegal movements of hazardous waste that took place during the months of June and July 2010. During the simultaneous inspections period, environmental, customs, and other enforcement authorities from Africa, the Americas, Asia, and Europe undertook coordinated environmental inspections at seaports.

The first project provided the means for competent authorities to better evaluate their own capacity for detecting and deterring illegal transboundary movements of hazardous wastes through seaports with the support or tools developed by INECE and international experts. The project was beneficial to participants in identifying gaps in inspection and enforcement programs. The outcomes provide insight into the type of waste, modus operandi and routes that are being used and confirm that cooperation among authorities at the international, regional and domestic levels is essential to an effective enforcement strategy.

A key recommendation from the first inspection project was that SESN should continue to facilitate future inspection projects; the second project was organized in response to this recommendation. Specific recommendations that were adopted and put into practice in the second project included allowing more time for national preparations, providing more capacity building in advance of the detection period, and allowing a longer period for inspections. SESN refined its communications tools and significantly adjusted the reporting forms to emphasize collaboration and to simplify the reporting requirements.

SESN facilitated the second international hazardous waste inspection project at seaports from December 2011 through April 2012. The primary goal of this second inspection project was to build enhanced capacity at seaports for more effective inspections of waste shipments through improved multidisciplinary cooperation among officials from environment and customs ministries and police and port authorities.

Specifically, the objectives of the project were to:

- Promote international good practice for environmental inspections at seaports;
- Facilitate enforcement collaboration among responsible officials within countries (e.g. between environmental and customs officers);
- Facilitate enforcement collaboration between exporting country enforcement officers and importing country enforcement officers; and
- Identify the obstacles to effective enforcement and the capacity-building needs of enforcement officers.

3. INSPECTION PROJECT PLANNING AND IMPLEMENTATION

In support of the second inspection project and other SESN capacity-building priorities, INECE organized two workshops in the Asian region to build capacity and foster networking opportunities. The first workshop, held at Siem Reap, Cambodia, in November 2010, focused on sharing enforcement strategies and developing cooperation tools to detect and prevent the illegal trade in hazardous waste. The Cambodia workshop was held in partnership with the Asian Network for Prevention of Illegal Transboundary Movement of Hazardous Wastes. The second workshop was conducted in Bangkok, Thailand, in January 2012. The Bangkok workshop was organized by INECE with the co-sponsorship of the United Nations Environment Programme Regional Office for Asia and the Pacific (UNEP-ROAP). Customs and environmental officials from 14 countries in the Asian region participated in the two workshops combined. Countries attending the workshop included Australia, Brunei, Cambodia, China, India, Indonesia, Japan, Lao (PDR), Malaysia, Pakistan, the Philippines, Singapore, Thailand, and Vietnam.

The purposes of the Bangkok workshop were to train project participants in conducting hazardous and electronic waste inspections, build enforcement capacity in the region, provide instruction and demonstrations at a port in order to enhance knowledge of participants, and generally to raise awareness about the illegal trade in hazardous waste among enforcement officials in the region. To ensure sustained value for the workshop, SESN emphasized training that participants could provide to others in their respective countries, that is, train-the-trainer opportunities. Each participating country was invited to send pairings of customs and environmental officials in order to encourage inter-agency cooperation as a cornerstone for achieving success. The Bangkok workshop provided an opportunity for INECE to present additional information about the inspection project and the tools and resources that were developed to support it. The workshop included a visit to Laem Chabang port for on-site training.

In addition to the two workshops, SESN developed a series of tools and publications to guide the implementation of the project. These included the project-specific operational guidance document, two reporting forms to facilitate data collection during the project, a web-based collaboration tool, a contact list of officials in participating countries, a guidance document on international communication tools and an operational guidance for the take back of detected illegal shipments of waste.

Countries were encouraged to convene pre-inspection periodic meetings of officials from authorities that would be involved in the project, including customs, environment, and police, and to promote effective cooperating mechanisms. SESN provided an overview of the project that was used during national-level preparations and posted case examples of illegal hazardous waste trade from Asia, Africa, Europe, and North America through the web-based collaboration tool during the project.

Participating countries were invited to submit reporting forms for any inspections conducted during the inspection period, which ran from December 2011 through April 2012. Countries received regular communications from the INECE Secretariat, which provided reminders about the reporting guidelines along with short case examples from participating countries.

3.1 Participation and Inspections

Authorities from ten countries and one special administrative region (SAR) participated in the second inspection project at seaports: Australia, Belgium, Canada, England, Hong Kong, Northern Ireland, Mexico, the Netherlands, Scotland, Singapore, and the United States of America. During the project, 462 inspections, including 591 containers, were reported at 16 ports.

3.2 National and International Enforcement Cooperation

The reporting forms for the inspection project asked participants to consider and report on whether there was any cooperation at the national, international, or institutional levels as part of the inspection of the shipment. Countries reported that cooperation took place at the national level during 95 percent of inspections.

At the national level, some countries reported strong collaboration between responsible authorities. This contributes to efficiencies – for example by enabling 'staff sharing' or leveraging staff from one agency to support the activities of the other – to both agencies' benefit. Cooperation between the environmental inspectorate and customs, which was the most common type of cooperation, was most often for the purposes of targeting and inspection/detection and to a much lesser extent for enforcement action. On the other hand, cooperation between the environmental inspectorate and the competent authority was more frequently for the purpose of an enforcement action and to a lesser extent for targeting and investigation. This was also the case for cooperation with regional authorities. Cooperation with port authorities, which was only reported once, was for preparing containers for inspection.

Relatively few inspections were informed by international cooperation, likely because the majority of participating countries were exporting rather than importing countries. The most common type of cooperation reported was the exchange of intelligence with peer authorities in other countries. Other types of cooperation that were reported were targeting, investigation and cooperation in an international operation.

3.3 Targeting Methods

Intelligence-led targeting, in which information about the highest risks in terms of actors, shipping routes and types of waste is analyzed to determine which containers to inspect, was the most commonly used method of targeting. Belgium primarily used a combination of intelligence-led and regional-national cooperation and targeting, while Australia, Scotland, Singapore, the United Kingdom, and the United States conducted information-led or intelligence-led inspections. At-random inspections, in which inspections are undertaken based on the country's national priorities and/or working methods, was the second most common type of targeting, used by Hong Kong. The Netherlands reported that some of its inspections were based on bilateral targeting and some on random selection.

3.4 Inspection Methods

Participating countries most commonly reported conducting both document inspections and physical inspections of the containers. Only using physical inspections was far less common and inspections conducted by only reviewing the documents or by x-raying the container were infrequently reported.

4. LESSONS LEARNED

During SESN's five years of operation, various lessons were learned:

- *Develop and deliver capacity building on the 'basics'*: SESN recognized the need to continue to build capacity in areas including inspection methods, intelligence-led enforcement, risk profiling, common tactics used by shippers of illegal wastes, targeting techniques and waste take back. Capacity building must be relevant to national circumstances and sustainable. Due to limited financial and human resources, capacity building should focus on moving towards a risk assessment approach, appropriate targeting methodologies and the effective use of intelligence.
- *Incorporate capacity building into national academies*: One strategy for ensuring the sustainability of capacity-building programs is to incorporate these topics into existing institutional structures that support ongoing capacity building, including national customs training academies, existing enforcement capacity development

structures like the UNODC/WCO Container Control Programme and/or into professional development programs for environmental staff.
- *Develop an analytical framework to support national and international cooperation*: Countries need better tools to evaluate the impact of national and international cooperation. These tools include best practices for cooperation, examples of effective institutional structures, guidance on what motivates customs and inspectors to work together, clarity on the role of senior executives in facilitating cooperation, and metrics for measuring and evaluating the degree of cooperation between relevant agencies and results thereof.

Over the past nine years, there have been numerous inspection events conducted by international organizations, each focusing on specific aspects of the inspection process. In some cases, other activities reflected certain differences in approach, such as the scope of the agencies involved or the particular practices that were emphasized. Some promoted immediate law enforcement results rather than the identification and correction of gaps in capacity and/or in cooperation between agencies or the promotion of more advanced targeting techniques, as the SESN project was designed to do.

Common issues relating to capacity, communication and cooperation were identified:

- *Capacity*: lack of sufficient personnel, equipment and knowledge;
- *Communication*: lack of information exchange and coordination on the national and international level; and
- *Cooperation/Coordination*: lack of structural or formal cooperation among agencies that have port responsibilities relating to environmental materials and the need for increased coordination among agencies involved.

The observed similarity in the challenges identified by these projects and confirmed during the SESN international inspection events, underscores the relevance of taking practical actions to implement these suggestions, in collaboration with national authorities and international organizations.

Access to instructional materials and the ability to share these materials can be accomplished, in part, through the institutionalization of educational materials into national training programs. This allows the port inspectors to access the information, while also allowing the information to be customized and updated as required to meet specific national program needs. Additionally, INECE's Environmental Compliance

Training Resource Library shares INECE's capacity-building materials and provides references to relevant capacity-building tools developed by other organizations. This resource library therefore can be used as a 'clearinghouse' of materials that can be used to support officials with responsibilities for environmental controls at seaports seeking to improve their capacity.

Inter-agency cooperation and coordination may be conducted on a formal or informal basis, but there needs to be structure to the arrangement to allow sustainability. Identification of best practices and the outlining of each agency's responsibilities, whether in a formal memorandum of understanding or an informal document, will help meet the need for increased cooperation and coordination. Development of this framework can also help facilitate communications at the national, regional, and international level.

5. FUTURE DIRECTIONS FOR SESN

The activities conducted so far by SESN during its five-year history have tended to corroborate the usefulness of the approaches it initially elected to pursue:

- Promoting cooperation among customs, environmental ministries and other law enforcement agencies to make environmental enforcement at ports more effective;
- Acknowledging the importance of inspection exercises preceded by adequate training, in order to build capacity; and
- Using certain key tools, such as the advanced targeting model of intelligence-led enforcement and guidance on practical topics like the take back of waste.

At the same time, it has become increasingly clear that the particular concerns of SESN in the developing world, including West Africa and parts of Asia, present challenges that require even more in-depth partnering than was the case in the past in order to make further progress. Because illicit activities like smuggling drugs or weapons sometimes intersect with illegal waste traffic at the same port, and the same inspection personnel need to deal with all of them, there are synergies to be gained by combining forces for joint projects with organizations like the UNODC/WCO Container Control Programme. A particular benefit of such a partnership is that the Container Control Program helps establish law enforcement controls at selected ports which can provide the basis for effective environmental enforcement at those same ports. Likewise, partnering with a regional office of UNEP, with its knowledge and local contacts, can enable a network like SESN to strengthen its work through collaboration. This is certainly the case with SESN and its association with UNEP-ROAP and its Regional Enforcement Network (REN). Again, the foundation that exists can facilitate the joint work on inspector training and inspection projects that provide opportunities for the law enforcement agencies of customs, environment, the police, and others to cooperate and improve their capacity.

SESN has been active in developing adaptable instructional materials for workshops in collaboration with the UNODC in West Africa and with the UNEP-ROAP. These materials include facilitated problem-solving exercises designed to engage port inspectors and to hone their skills.

SESN recognizes the critical role of networking with the right partners for particular missions and intends to place future emphasis on pursuing this course. It applauds the work of the Secretariat of the Basel Convention and others in bringing together various networks in order to promote better coordinated enforcement of transboundary hazardous waste control regimes. Under a new network called 'Environmental Network for Optimizing Regulatory Compliance on Illegal Traffic (ENFORCE)', convened by the Basel Convention Secretariat, experts will be able to work together to promote parties' compliance with Basel Convention provisions pertaining to preventing and combating illegal traffic in hazardous wastes and other wastes through the better implementation and enforcement of national law. This will be achieved by bringing together existing resources and enhancing and improving cooperation and coordination between relevant entities with a specific mandate to deliver capacity-building activities and tools on preventing and combating illegal traffic. These initiatives provide an excellent opportunity for networks like SESN to work with existing partners and to identify potential new ones.

6. CONCLUSIONS

A network like SESN that is formed to take on global issues in a complex field like promoting the effective enforcement of the environmental laws with respect to transboundary movements of hazardous and other waste, benefits greatly when an existing parent network like INECE can provide the incubator and nourish the new project with its experience, infrastructure, and connections.

To enhance any new network's prospects for success, there must be effective partnering with international organizations whose memberships and missions are complementary to the objectives of the network. A prime example for SESN is its partnership with WCO. Both symbolically and functionally the alliance between the customs agencies of the world and the environmental enforcers is essential to making progress when facing the challenge of integrating effective hazardous waste enforcement at ports into the much broader portfolio of the work of the customs agencies, in order to foster enhanced cooperation in law enforcement activities.

Regional environmental compliance and enforcement networks and partnerships, as well as national coordination efforts, can further support and augment the activities of global networks like SESN. The new West African Network for Environmental Compliance and Enforcement (WANECE), for example, can be a valuable regional partner in facilitating the effective exchange of information within and among West African countries to control illegal trade in e-waste and hazardous substances and enhance coordination. In addition, the value to SESN of the lessons learned from the extensive operations of the European IMPEL TFS project cannot be overstated.

A disadvantage faced by SESN relative to those networks and organizations that receive continuing financial support through membership fees or annual country commitments is the inability to conduct long-term planning of activities and operations due to uncertain funding levels year to year. This can also complicate partnership engagements with other organizations which do not face this problem and expect longer-term commitments.

Finally, the activities of a network dealing with immediate, specific enforcement challenges like SESN can help to ground and inform an umbrella sponsoring body like INECE and fundamentally influence its whole future direction, with very positive results.

BIBLIOGRAPHY

IMPEL TFS, End of Life Vehicles: 2006–7, http://impel.eu/wp-content/uploads/2010/04/2006-20-End-of-Life-Vehicles-Project-FINAL-REPORT.pdf (accessed 8 March 2014).

IMPEL TFS, Enforcement Actions I: 2006–8, http://impel.eu/projects/enforcement-actions-i (accessed 8 March 2014).

IMPEL TFS, Enforcement Actions II: 2008–11, http://impel.eu/projects/enforcement-actions-ii (accessed 8 March 2014).

IMPEL TFS, Seaport Project I: 2003–4, http://impel.eu/projects/seaport-project-i (accessed 8 March 2014).

IMPEL TFS, Seaport Project II: 2004–6, http://impel.eu/projects/seaport-project-ii (accessed 8 March 2014).

IMPEL TFS, Transfrontier Shipments of Hazardous Waste: 2010–11, http://impel.eu/wp-content/uploads/2012/02/IMPEL-Report.pdf (accessed 8 March 2014).

IMPEL TFS, Verification of Waste Destinations I: 2003–4, http://impel.eu/projects/verification-of-waste-destinations-i (accessed 8 March 2014).
IMPEL TFS, Verification of Waste Destinations II: 2004–6, http://impel.eu/projects/verification-of-waste-destinations-ii (accessed 8 March 2014).
INECE, International Hazardous Waste Inspection Project at Seaports: Results and Recommendations (2010), http://inece.org/seaport/exercise/INECE_SeaportInspectionProjectOutcomes_22dec.pdf (accessed 8 March 2014).
INECE, Negotiating Customs and Environmental Cooperation: Course Materials and Resources (2009), http://inece.org/resource/cooperation-mou/ (accessed 8 March 2014).
INECE, Seaport Environmental Security Network Website, http://inece.org/topics/seaports/ (accessed 8 March 2014).
INECE, Second International Hazardous Waste Inspection Project: Results and Recommendations (2012), http://inece.org/resource/sesn-report/ (accessed 8 March 2014).
Kopsick, Deborah A., Requirements for Effective Seaport Environmental Security: Collective Action at the Ports (2011), http://inece.org/conference/9/proceedings/29_Kopsick.pdf (accessed 8 March 2014).
Robert Heiss et al., International Hazardous Waste Inspection Project at Seaports: Results and Recommendations (*Proceedings of the INECE's 9th International Conference*, 2011), http://inece.org/conference/9/proceedings/25_HeissEtAl.pdf (accessed 8 March 2014).
WCO, Demeter I: 2009 (Executive Summary), http://www.wcoomd.org/~/media/WCO/Public/Global/PDF/Topics/Enforcement%20and%20Compliance/Activities%20and%20Programmes/Environmental%20Crime/Ex_sum_Demeter_EN.ashx?db=web (accessed 8 March 2014).
WCO, Illicit Trade Report 2012, http://www.wcoomd.org/~/media/WCO/Public/Global/PDF/Topics/Enforcement%20and%20Compliance/Activities%20and%20Programmes/Illicit%20Trade%20Report%202012/WCO%20REPORT%202013%20-%20BR.ashx?db=web (accessed 8 March 2014).
WCO, Sky Hole Patching I: 2007, http://www.greencustoms.org/reports/workshop/Sky_hole_patching.pdf (accessed 8 March 2014).
WCO, Sky Hole Patching II: 2010, http://www.greencustoms.org/docs/Sky_Hole_Patching_BKK.pdf (accessed 8 March 2014).

PART IV

Horizontal networks

15. North American working group on environmental enforcement and compliance cooperation: moving from capacity building to operational activities

Deborah Kopsick*and Susan Elizabeth Bromm†

1. ORIGIN OF THE ENFORCEMENT WORKING GROUP

1.1 Formation of the North American Agreement on Environmental Cooperation

The main goal of North American Free Trade Agreement is to facilitate trade among Canada, Mexico and the United States.[1] During the negotiation of the treaty, there were concerns expressed that increased competition would lead to a 'race to the bottom', with pollution-generating companies seeking areas with the lowest wages and the lowest environmental protection requirements. Environmental organizations in the United States launched a campaign to have environmental protection included in the treaty and the North American Free Trade Agreement was only put into force after a trilateral agreement to protect the environment was included.[2]

---

* International Compliance Assurance Division, Office of Federal Activities, U.S. Environmental Protection Agency, 1200 Pennsylvania Ave, N.W. Mail Code 2254A, Washington, DC, USA 20460, kopsick.deborah@epa.gov

† Office of Federal Activities and US Co-chair of the CEC Enforcement Working Group, Office of Enforcement and Compliance Assurance, U.S. Environmental Protection Agency, 1200 Pennsylvania Ave, N.W. Mail Code 2251A, Washington, DC, USA 20460, bromm.susan@epa.gov

1 North American Free Trade Agreement (1992). Available at http://www.worldtradelaw.net/fta/agreements/nafta.pdf

2 Bromm, Susan E. (2011). 'North America's Commission for Environmental Cooperation: One Example of a Successful Regional Network', in J. Gerardu,

Bromm (2011) provides a detailed account of the development and negotiation of the NAFTA and the environmental side agreement.

The North American Agreement on Environmental Cooperation was the solution President William Clinton designated to avoid renegotiation of the treaty. Included among the objectives of this environmental side agreement is the increased cooperation between the three countries to:

- Better conserve, protect and enhance the environment, including wild flora and fauna;
- Develop and improve environmental laws, regulations, procedures, policies and practices; and
- Enhance compliance with and enforcement of environmental laws and regulations.[3]

Multiple articles of the North American Agreement on Environmental Cooperation discuss the need for the three countries to achieve high levels of compliance and enforcement of their own laws and regulations. The agreement also promotes technical cooperation between the countries.[4]

Since enforcement of environmental laws is critical to successful implementation of this agreement, the Council of the Commission for Environmental Cooperation (CEC) is the organization created by the North American Agreement on Environmental Cooperation to ensure this environmental protection occurs.

1.2 Organization of the CEC

The CEC Council is chaired by the Environmental Ministers of Canada, Mexico and the US. The Council meets once a year and works on a consensus basis. The CEC operates under a Five Year Strategic Plan that outlines its objectives, based on the priorities mandated by the three North American environmental ministers.[5]

The Secretariat of the CEC is headed by an Executive Director, and the post is rotated between the participating countries every three to six years.

D. Grabiel, M. Koparova, K. Markowitz and D. Zaelke (eds), *INECE 9th International Conference on Environmental Compliance and Enforcement* (pp. 743–751). Available at http://inece.org/conference/9/papers/Bromm_USEPA_Final.pdf

[3] North American Agreement on Environmental Cooperation (1993). Available at http://www.ustr.gov/sites/default/files/naaec.pdf

[4] Ibid.

[5] CEC Strategic Plan 2010–2015 (2010). Available at http://www.cec.org/Storage/58/10115_Strategic_plan_2011_en.pdf

The three North American countries contribute a total of US$9 million annually to support the CEC Secretariat and its programs.

Also within the CEC is the Joint Public Advisory Committee, consisting of 15 members that provide technical advice to the CEC Council. Each country selects five volunteer citizens to serve on the committee and the Chair position is rotated each year from among the members.

To carry out the technical activities, the CEC has created numerous working groups, addressing specific environmental issue areas. The working group that addresses environmental enforcement is the subject of this paper. This working group is a well-established, formal environmental enforcement network covering North America.

2. EVOLUTION OF THE ENFORCEMENT WORKING GROUP

2.1 Need for Environmental Enforcement Networks

Numerous organizations and authors have recognized the need for and usefulness of environmental networks. Achim Steiner, Executive Director of the United Nations Environment Programme, states this need succinctly when he writes: 'It is said that cooperation occurs only when diverse national interests converge, participating officers have been able to step outside narrow national boundaries, understand each other's issues, and add the extra voluntary effort that is needed to achieve the common goal of protecting our environment'.[6] The World Customs Organization states that 'intelligence cannot be produced without gathering a critical mass of information and data together which must then be evaluated and analyzed before being turned into trends and risk indicators'.[7] In a sense, networks can be viewed as more formal communities of practice, or 'groups of people informally bound together by shared expertise and a

---

[6] United Nations Environment Programme (2007). *Networking Counts: Combating Illegal Trade in Ozone Depleting Substances*, p. 2. Available at http://www.unep.fr/ozonaction/information/mmcfiles/6076-e-networkingcounts.pdf

[7] World Customs Organization (2009). CEN, 'Sharing Information for a More Effective Network'. Available at http://www.wcoomd.org/en/topics/enforcement-and-compliance/instruments-and-tools/~/media/WCO/Public/Global/PDF/Topics/Enforcement%20and%20Compliance/Activities%20and%20Programmes/CEN/CEN_Brochure020709.ashx

passion for a joint enterprise'.[8] Although there is a difference in their level of formality, networks and communities of practice share some key characteristics, such as a desire to develop and share information and a commitment to the goals of achieving more effective operations. A community of environmental law enforcement officials committed to collaborating and sharing best practices and data was needed to protect North America, and the CEC Enforcement Working Group was formed to meet this need.

The International Institute for Sustainable Development uses the term 'networked governance' to refer to 'breaking down institutional silos and creating horizontal channels for knowledge exchange and collaboration that leads to better informed decision making and more effective implementation'.[9] This describes how the Enforcement Working Group trilaterally functions. This networked governance leads to a horizontal decision-making process that makes use of the enhanced communication, cooperation and collaboration constantly under development by the Enforcement Working Group.

2.2 Organization of the Enforcement Working Group

The Enforcement Working Group (EWG) endeavors to enhance environmental law enforcement in Canada, Mexico and the United States through networking, communication and collaboration, achieved through the exchange of information and intelligence. This working group is supported within the established framework of the CEC, which provides functional stability.

The establishment of the Enforcement Working Group in 1996 provided a mechanism for technical cooperation.[10] To facilitate this trilateral cooperation, the Enforcement Working Group is co-chaired by senior enforcement officials from four agencies, including Environment Canada, Mexico's Procuraduría Federal de Proteccion al Ambiente (PROFEPA), the U.S. Environmental Protection Agency and the U.S. Fish and Wildlife

---

[8] Wenger, E. and Snyder, W. (2000). 'Communities of Practice: The Organizational Frontier', *Harvard Business Review*, 78(1) January–February, pp. 139–145. Available at http://hbr.org/2000/01/communities-of-practice-the-organizational-frontier/ar/1

[9] International Institute for Sustainable Development (2014). *Networked Governance: Moving from Vertical to Horizontal Approaches to Decision Making.* Available at http://www.iisd.org/networks/gov

[10] CEC Council Resolution 96–06 (1996). Resolution to Establish the North American Working Group on Environmental Enforcement and Compliance Cooperation. Available at http://www.cec.org/Page.asp?PageID=924&ContentID=1177

Service. The Enforcement Working Group addresses both pollution and wildlife issues. In Canada and Mexico, pollution issues and wildlife issues are enforced by the same agency. In the United States the U.S. Environmental Protection Agency enforces pollution laws and regulations, while U.S. Fish and Wildlife enforces those relating to wildlife. Therefore, both agencies co-chair the Enforcement Working Group.

The co-chairs meet once annually in person and numerous times through teleconferencing or videoconferencing to maintain an open line of communication and to assure project momentum. Ad hoc subgroups may be formed to address specific issue areas.

In accordance with its charter, the activities of the Enforcement Working Group support several areas:

- Strengthening cooperation between the Parties relating to environmental compliance and enforcement;
- Enhancing cooperation to better recognize shared enforcement and compliance challenges;
- Facilitating cooperative enforcement and compliance initiatives;
- Exchanging information and experiences with alternative approaches to enforcement and compliance; and
- Facilitating training opportunities among the three countries.[11]

2.3 Overarching Priorities

In 2009, the environmental ministers from Canada, Mexico and the United States decided on three overarching priorities:

1. Healthy Communities and Ecosystems: protecting, sustaining and restoring the health of people, communities and ecosystems through:
   (a) improved environmental health of vulnerable communities;
   (b) increased resilience of shared ecosystems at risk;
   (c) an enhanced regional approach to sound management of chemicals; and
   (d) strengthened regional environmental and wildlife law enforcement.
2. Climate Change, Low Carbon Economy: working toward aligning domestic standards in relation to climate change and the transitioning to a low carbon economy through:

[11] Ibid.

   (a) improved comparability of emissions data, methodologies and inventories; and
   (b) strengthened engagement of experts and information sharing.
3. Greening the Economy in North America: minimizing environmental impacts of economic growth, while enhancing competitiveness of key industrial sectors, through:
   (a) improving private sector environmental performance.[12]

The majority of the Enforcement Working Group activities fall under the Healthy Communities and Ecosystems priority. Within this priority, the Co-chairs of the Enforcement Working Group decided to focus on five issue areas, including wildlife, ozone depleting substances, hazardous wastes, electronic wastes and noncompliant small engines. These areas were chosen to support the priorities of the North American enforcement agencies so that Enforcement Working Group activities add value to ongoing activities. Proposed activities are outlined in annual Operational Plans,[13] which are reviewed by the Joint Public Advisory Committee and the representatives of the three national environmental ministers. Following revision, if necessary, the Operating Plan is ultimately approved by the three ministers and funded through the CEC Secretariat, with the money obligated by the three countries.

In order to reach consensus on priority areas and specific projects, numerous teleconferences, meetings, and workshops are conducted. The Co-chairs of the three countries meet to identify the top priorities of their respective enforcement programs and they determine which priorities should be addressed trilaterally. In addition, the Enforcement Working Group identified gaps in knowledge regarding the North American environmental law enforcement landscape that might hinder enforcement efforts regarding illegal transboundary shipments of environmentally regulated substances. Using this guidance and information, officials at the working level develop individual projects to address the designated priorities.

2.4 Capacity-building Accomplishments

Initial activities of the Enforcement Working Group focused on establishing relationships among environmental enforcement officials in the three

---

[12] CEC (2010). *Strategic Plan of the Commission for Environmental Cooperation 2010–2015*. Available at: http://www.cec.org/Storage/58/10115_Strategic_plan_2011_en.pdf

[13] CEC (2010). *Operational Plan for 2011–2012*. Available at: http://www.cec.org/Storage/136/16099_Operational_Plan_2011-2012-web-en.pdf

countries, exchanging experiences and building capacity to detect, detain and deter the illegal wildlife and waste trade.

2.4.1 Online training for border inspectors

Accomplishments to date include the development of training programs for enforcement officials and Customs inspectors. Training was provided in both online and face-to-face formats. The first online training was designed for border inspectors who need to determine the legality of transboundary shipments containing ozone depleting substances.[14] The course contains two modules. Module 1 discusses general information on the importance of ozone, sources of ozone depleting substances, international agreements, and the national legislation of the three countries relating to these substances. This module is available to the public on the CEC website. Access to Module 2 is restricted to law enforcement officials and presents specific information on the illegal ozone depleting substance trade. Because it is sometimes difficult to remove numerous officers from their inspection duties at the ports of entry to attend classroom training, the online format was chosen to allow maximum flexibility. The training is available in the three languages of North America – English, Spanish and French. The ozone depleting substances online training is also translated into Mandarin to allow potential Chinese importers to better understand the domestic laws and requirements for these imports.

Using the format of the online ozone depleting substances training course, an online course for border inspectors responsible for investigating hazardous waste shipments was developed and translated into English, Spanish, French and Mandarin. The course represents a trilateral collaboration between environmental, customs and border officials, designed to promote more effective identification and interdiction of illegal hazardous waste shipments.[15] Module 1 describes international and national hazardous waste policy and legislation, as well as the presentation of the characteristics of hazardous wastes and the harm that can be caused due to ineffective control of these wastes. Module 2 instructs customs and border control officials on how to identify and inspect illegal hazardous waste shipments through the use of targeting information on smuggling modi operandi. Access to Module 2 is restricted to law enforcement officials.

---

[14] CEC online ozone depleting substances training. Module 1 available at: http://www.cec.org/ods/main/cec_ods_intro_e.asp. Module 2 is available to law enforcement officials upon request.

[15] CEC online hazardous waste training for environment, customs and border inspectors. Module 1 available at http://www.cec.org/hazwaste/Page.asp?AA_SiteLanguageID=1. Module 2 is available to law enforcement officials upon request.

2.4.2 Wildlife cooperation

The CEC supports activities of the North American Wildlife Enforcement Group (NAWEG), formed in 1995 to encourage information and training exchange and to increase the ability of the three countries to more effectively enforce laws relating to the trade of wildlife.[16] NAWEG is a member of the Enforcement Working Group.

The agencies responsible for the enforcement of wildlife regulations in North America, which includes Environment Canada, U.S. Fish and Wildlife and Profepa, signed a Memorandum of Agreement to facilitate cooperation among their agencies. Realizing the transboundary nature of ecosystems, wildlife habitats and migration corridors, the three countries established a basis for cooperation to help them coordinate activities to address common risks and threats to wildlife. The Memorandum of Understanding also provides requirements for the exchange of information and intelligence as needed to support these activities.

Capacity-building activities include implementation of an accredited multi-module course on wildlife forensics for border inspectors to help them better understand what constitutes penal and administrative offenses related to wildlife shipments.[17] This course has been institutionalized into the Mexican training program for border inspectors. The eight modules provide information on methods and techniques for wildlife identification, management of wildlife, forensic techniques and analysis, geographic information systems and field operations to support legal actions.

2.4.3 Judicial and prosecutorial seminars

A series of three symposia directed at the Mexican judiciary, including judges, prosecutors and law enforcement officers, identified best practices in use in North America, explained environmental law requirements and illustrated successful prosecution techniques.[18]

The first symposium presented information on the judicial systems of Canada, Mexico and the United States, the precautionary principle and the application of domestic decisions and international norms. The second symposium focused on the jurisdiction of the courts, litigation of water quality issues, environmental impact study case studies, valuation of

---

[16] NAWEG website available at http://www3.cec.org/naweg/

[17] CEC (2011). *Report on the Implementation of the First Multimodular Session of the Course in Environmental and Wildlife Criminalistics*. Available at http://www3.cec.org/islandora/en/item/10214-report-first-multimodular-session-course-in-environmental-and-wildlife-en.pdf

[18] CEC (2005–2008). Judicial Training. Available at http://www.cec.org/Page.asp?PageID=861&SiteNodeID=613

environmental damages and judicial review of inspections, investigations and scientific evidence. The third symposium presented information on the development and enforcement of environmental laws, enforcement at the local level, methodologies for use in enforcement cases and procedural challenges.

This information will lead to more successful adjudication of environmental cases by the Mexican judiciary. A desk reference, in Spanish and English, incorporates the information shared during the three seminars, addresses such topics as legal standing to sue, evidentiary requirements, natural resource damages, penalties and judicial review. Besides procedural requirements, the desk reference presents information for prosecutors on the many evidentiary and prosecutorial challenges that exist in developing and adjudicating environmental cases.[19]

2.4.4 Electronic exchange of import/export data

The Hazardous Waste Task Force, an ad hoc group formed under the Enforcement Working Group, designed and implemented a data system that allows the electronic exchange of import and export data among the three countries, a system that had previously been paper-based.[20] The system is not a trilaterally shared data system due to the security requirements of the three countries, but a separate system in each country that uses common data standards to harmonize the data. The information on hazardous waste shipments is exchanged using secure node-to-node technology. This electronic system reduces the potential for data entry errors, improves timeliness of the data exchange and allows for easier data comparison.

2.4.5 INECE networks document

In order to fully understand the characteristics that lead to a successful enforcement network, the Enforcement Working Group supported a workshop on network design, development and maintenance in cooperation with the International Network for Environmental Compliance and Enforcement (INECE). Thirty-one practitioners from ten enforcement networks shared their best practices for network management and

---

19 CEC (2011). *Environmental Legislation in North America: Experiences and Best Practices for its Implementation and Adjudication.* Available in English and Spanish at http://www3.cec.org/islandora/en/item/11119-environmental-legislation-in-north-america

20 CEC (2007). *Tracking Hazardous Waste.* Available at http://www3.cec.org/islandora/en/item/3637-tracking-hazardous-waste-improving-transboundary-tracking-hazardous-waste-in-north-en.pdf

governance. Discussions dealing with challenges such as communication and outreach, funding and capacity building were held.[21]

3. THE MOVE TOWARD OPERATIONS

Recently, the Enforcement Working Group has shifted its emphasis from primarily capacity-building activities to more operational activities, including the strengthening of the three countries' ability to conduct intelligence-led enforcement. For the purposes of discussion in this chapter, intelligence is the knowledge gained through the collection, analysis, dissemination and exploitation of information, and can be strategic, tactical, operational and evidentiary in nature. Intelligence-led enforcement is the approach to law enforcement where this intelligence plays a strategic role in planning, implementing and accessing actions to address illegal activities.

Because the Enforcement Working Group conducts its activities in three different regulatory regimes, it is important to understand the regulatory enforcement landscape. Enforcement efforts need to be coordinated to detect and intercept illegal shipments on shared coastlines and to prevent 'port shopping', where ports of entry with the perceived weakest enforcement capabilities are targeted by illegal waste traders. To fortify North America, in an environmental enforcement sense, the Enforcement Working Group studied the regulatory regimes of the three countries for ozone depleting substances, electronic waste and hazardous waste, and identified existing challenges and opportunities. Possible solutions such as regulatory alignment were identified.

3.1 Intelligence-led Enforcement

Sharing information and intelligence among the three countries is a significant component for the successful investigation and prosecution of the illegal trade in environmentally regulated materials and wildlife. Intelligence-led enforcement can lead to a better understanding of the enforcement landscape, improved information flow, enhanced focus and coordination of investigations. Intelligence-led enforcement uses information that has been analyzed and verified. Along with opportunities, the

---

[21] INECE (2011). *Summit of Regional Network Leadership: Creating and Sustaining Regional Environmental Compliance and Enforcement Networks.* Available at http://inece.org/wp-content/uploads/2013/09/EWG_INECE-Summit-of-Regional-Network-Leadership_final.pdf

exchange of enforcement-sensitive intelligence among countries presents a number of challenges, which are discussed in section 3.1.1.

Also to be considered is the sharing of information with international organizations such as Interpol and World Customs Organization. The Commission for Environmental Cooperation and the World Customs Organization have signed a Letter of Understanding to identify opportunities for coordinated efforts in sharing information and best practices, as well as training and participation in workshops, seminars and meetings.

To build capacity among law enforcement officials to locate and collect information for intelligence-led activities, the Enforcement Working Group held two trilateral training sessions allowing agents and analysts to gain practical skills in internet investigation of potentially illegal activities and entities. These trainings identified sites where illegal trading activities might take place, in addition to sites where information on suspect entities can be obtained.

3.1.1 Challenges to the implementation of intelligence-led enforcement

Before any procedures and protocols for the sharing of intelligence could be developed, it was necessary for the Enforcement Working Group to work through legal, information technology and security issues. Most importantly, the North American Agreement on Environmental Cooperation, which the CEC supports, specifically allows the exchange of data among the three countries and officially sets the requirements for this exchange.[22] Initially, through discussions with legal representatives from the three countries, restrictions on information and intelligence exchange were identified and acknowledged.

Establishing the legality of the exchange of intelligence was the first step. Intelligence analysis capabilities needed to be enhanced and various mechanisms for accomplishing this were explored. The solution proved to be the use of compatible intelligence analysis software that allows the three countries to analyze the intelligence in a similar manner. Each country maintains control of their own data and no data is directly exchanged between the three intelligence analysis platforms. However, output products are similar in format and the information can be added to the receiving country's data system, if appropriate.

How to communicate secure information among the three countries proved to be an obstacle. Numerous mechanisms for exchange of documents were investigated, including encrypted e-mail and password

---

[22] North American Agreement on Environmental Cooperation (1993). Article 21 and 39. Available at http://www.ustr.gov/sites/default/files/naaec.pdf

protected file transfer protocol (FTP) sites. On many occasions, a phone call from the investigator in one country to the investigator in the other country will be sufficient. For very sensitive information, it was decided to explore the use of the Interpol National Central Bureaus, which already operate in the three countries and which provide a level of security all three countries have agreed to.

Information will be submitted to the sending country's Interpol National Central Bureau in the format of a standardized Ecomessage and routed to the appropriate person in the receiving country.[23] Agencies can also use their own designated message format and route the message directly to the receiving country.

With working solutions to these obstacles, the exchange of sensitive information and intelligence can commence. Due to the efforts of the Enforcement Working Group, all three countries now have access to the same intelligence software allowing them to exchange specific outputs in a consistent format, while protecting data residing within their own system.

3.1.2 Results

The results from this exchange of information and intelligence are already being seen. Exchange of information gathered during port checks of ozone depleting substances shipments has led to a better understanding of the modi operandi of illegal smugglers. Through the use of this information, targeted inspections of imports were conducted, resulting in the identification of illegal shipments. This communication between the three countries has also led to the sharing of new technologies and innovations in detection and monitoring which benefits all three countries equally. An example of this is the employment of hand-held refrigerant analyzers at ports of entry to rapidly scan the composition of the gases in cylinders. Without the need to wait for laboratory analysis, a timely decision can be made on detaining suspect shipments. It also allows for the rapid exchange of information on these illegal shipments, so the other two countries can take appropriate action.

Successful enforcement actions in all three countries, although not directly the result of actions by the EWG, were facilitated by the exchange of data and intelligence among the three countries. For example, importers of small engines that do not comply with U.S. and Canadian air emissions regulations have had their products seized by Customs inspectors.[24]

---

[23] Interpol Ecomessage. Available at http://www.interpol.int/Crime-areas/Environmental-crime/Ecomessage

[24] Department of Justice (2012). 'Vehicle and Engine Importers to Pay Civil Penalty to Resolve Clean Air Act Violations: Senior Company Executives Jointly

3.1.3 Some lessons learned

There are some lessons learned from efforts to implement intelligence-led enforcement:

- It has not been possible to implement simultaneous border operations in the three countries as originally planned. This is due to the different amounts of time it takes to go from concept to implementation of field operations in the three countries. The coordination between the environmental agency and the customs agency is critical for success of these operations, and the time it takes to secure this cooperation varies in the three countries.
- There is a need to identify specific data that will be useful for enforcement actions. Obtaining thousands of inspection reports from another country, although forming a wealth of potentially valuable data, could be overwhelming to the available data analysts.
- Depending on national restrictions, certain data cannot be exchanged, for example data with specific personally identifiable information or data related to ongoing enforcement cases, which may take years to adjudicate.

4. FUTURE ACTIVITIES

Future activities of the Enforcement Working Group will include continued enhancement of intelligence-led enforcement in Canada, Mexico and the U.S. This will be accomplished through increased inter-country communication, continued sharing of enforcement-sensitive information and intelligence and analyses of data in a complementary manner.

The Enforcement Working Group will also serve as a platform for the three countries to share information and experience relating to cutting-edge law enforcement issues and techniques such as computer forensics, covert computer operations, use of advanced monitoring, detection and information technology, expanded transparency, and innovative enforcement techniques. The incorporation of technology into enforcement actions can help achieve the most effective use of limited resources and budgets.[25]

Liable for Consent Decree Obligations'. Available at http://www.justice.gov/opa/pr/2012/November/12-enrd-1353.html

25 Giles, Cynthia (2013). 'Next Generation Compliance', *The Environmental Forum*, Sept–Oct, pp. 22–26. Available at http://www2.epa.gov/sites/production/files/2014–09/documents/giles-next-gen-article-forum-eli-sept-oct-2013.pdf

Successful operations, including joint trans-border inspection events, at ports and borders will indicate the value of these exchanges. There continue to be challenges due to the different regulatory regimes of the three countries. However, efforts to harmonize regulations will bring North America closer to collectively deterring illegal trade.

5. NETWORK EVALUATION OF ENFORCEMENT WORKING GROUP

Pink and Lehane (2011) present a framework for evaluating the maturity of environmental enforcement networks. The authors' methodology considers five major themes, namely: members, finances, governance, support and deliverables.[26] Based on criteria within these themes, the Enforcement Working Group is categorized as 'well established' – the most mature level of enforcement network. Reasons for this rating include:

- Stable governance;
- Active enforcement participation from all three countries, including support from the environmental ministers of the three countries;
- Open lines of communication;
- Regular meetings;
- High quality peer reviewed deliverables.

6. CONCLUSIONS

There are a number of factors that explain why the Enforcement Working Group functions as an effective enforcement network for North America:

1. The working group has a stable foundation, being embedded in the Commission for Environmental Cooperation, which is ultimately part of a tri-national treaty, the North American Free Trade Agreement.
2. The working group is funded annually through contributions from the three countries, which ensures the Operational Plan activities can be

[26] Pink, G. and Lehane, J. (2011). 'Environmental Enforcement Networks: Development of a Network Evaluation Matrix', in J. Gerardu, D. Grabiel, M. Koparova, K. Markowitz and D. Zaelke (eds), *INECE 9th International Conference on Environmental Compliance and Enforcement* (pp. 805–821). Available at http://www.inece.org/conference/9/papers/Pink%20Lehane_EENs EvalnMatrix_FINAL.pdf

implemented and completed. Using this funding, the CEC Secretariat provides technical and logistical support to the Enforcement Working Group as needed. This established mechanism allows for the planning of long-term, multi-year projects.

3. The Environmental Ministers from the three countries meet once a year to view the CEC's progress and to guide future activities. This leadership from the highest level within each country's Ministry is invaluable. It ensures that the work of the Group is recognized and allows the activities of the CEC to always be in line with each country's domestic and international priorities.
4. The working group operates under a detailed, formalized, but flexible, Operational Plan and budget, which is finalized through consensus. Specific areas of focus are agreed to by the three countries. These focus areas are selected to add value to the environmental enforcement agencies' programs, both domestically and internationally. With constrained budgets, most enforcement agencies may not have the ability to take on new work. Therefore the Enforcement Working Group provides support to existing programs and priorities and further enhances domestic programs. An example is the development of an electronic hazardous waste import and export information exchange program which meets the national data security needs of all three countries.
5. Regular meetings, workshops, training sessions, videoconferences and frequent teleconferences calls among the Co-chairs and at the working level ensure that the level of coordination and productivity of the Enforcement Working Group remains high. Regularly scheduled trilateral communication and adherence to deadlines ensure projects are completed.
6. The three countries can share law enforcement-sensitive data, as protection from release is already institutionalized in the North America Agreement for Environmental Cooperation, which is part of an international treaty.
7. Coordination with other law enforcement agencies with authority relating to import and export of environmentally regulated substances, such as Customs and Border Control agencies and relevant Justice organizations, contributes to accomplishing the mission of the Enforcement Working Group.
8. The three countries have a relatively similar (though not identical) regulatory regime. There is value to harmonizing regulatory regimes, as it is difficult to conduct coordinated enforcement actions if there are significant differences in the laws and regulatory programs of the three countries. The more similar the regulatory programs, the more effective

coordinated enforcement can be. For example, if all three countries have the same restrictions on the import of certain environmentally regulated commodities (for example, ozone depleting substances), the countries can effectively work together to avoid 'port shopping' – whereby goods travel from port to port seeking entry. If one of the countries has a weaker standard, they are more likely to be an entry port for goods rejected by the other countries.

These factors lead to a level of cooperation and collaboration among the three countries that would not be achievable by a country individually. As a result, the Enforcement Working Group is an effective networking mechanism for stopping illegal transboundary trade of wildlife, environmentally regulated materials and ozone depleting substances in North America.

16. Informal environmental networking: the EPA Network example

William Fawcett*

1. THE NEED FOR INFORMAL COOPERATION

There is a common understanding among the members of the European Network of the Heads of Environment Protection Agencies (EPA Network) on the strong influence of European Union (EU) environmental legislation. EU environmental legislation is transposed and implemented in Member States, and to some extent in candidate countries, European Economic Area states and Switzerland, according to prevailing national legislative frameworks.

National environmental governance structures vary widely across Europe. Therefore, environmental protection agencies can have a wide range of roles and tasks depending on the national context. Effective environmental governance at all levels is crucial in maintaining and improving the European environment. This makes the opportunity to come together in a network and exchange information and experiences all the more important.

The 7th Environment Action Programme (7EAP) from the European Commission, acknowledges the importance of supporting networks of professionals in maximising the benefits of EU legislation.[1] The important role of networks is further described in the EC communication 'Improving the delivery of benefits from EU environment measures: building confidence through better knowledge and responsiveness',[2] which says that knowledge on implementation could be improved by 'working with

---

* Secretary of the EPA Network 2011–2014, http://epanet.ew.eea.europa.eu/; will.fawcett@environment-agency.gov.uk

[1] The Commission proposal for a new general Union Environment Action Programme to 2020 'Living well, within the limits of our planet' 2013. Available at: http://ec.europa.eu/environment/newprg/proposal.htm

[2] Communication on improving the delivery of benefits from EU environment measures: building confidence through better knowledge and responsiveness.

Member States and opening a dialogue with key networks of inspectors, prosecutors and judges in order to identify the crucial categories of information and best means of collecting and collating data'. It also recognises the need for capacity building, noting

> at European level, networks have been created by ombudsmen, environment agencies, inspectors, lawyers working with governments, judges and prosecutors. However, despite a number of initiatives, the potential of cooperation has not been fully realised across all networks. Challenges include ensuring that networks have the necessary secretariat stability to function effectively over extended time-periods and identifying and undertaking projects and initiatives that help network members and facilitate implementation.

Therefore the need for cooperation is appreciated at a European level. The EPA Network is one example of how this can be achieved. Further cooperation between the various European networks and their members will help improve implementation of European legislation as well as the effectiveness of the individual networks.

1.1 Informal Exchange of Information, Views and Good Practice

Networks provide an excellent opportunity for sharing good practice and exchanging information. As the majority of environmental legislation implemented by European countries originates from the European Union, this is one area where cooperation can have tangible benefits. Implementation of this legislation varies across Europe and it is of huge benefit for organisations involved in this to have the opportunity to share their experiences and also to learn from others.

Networks provide the opportunity to work and exchange information at a European level, an opportunity which is not always afforded to national organisations.

Outputs from networks also have the possibility to carry more weight if signed up to by a large number of members. A combined voice of similar organisations will carry more weight than individual members. This is especially true of networks with high level participation, such as the EPA Network.

COM 2012 (95). Available at: http://eur-lex.europa.eu/LexUriServ/LexUriServ.do?uri=COM:2012:0095:FIN:EN:PDF

Table 16.1 Some main features of informal and formal networks

Informal	Formal
Informal governance	Formal governance structure, e.g. a board
Guidelines	Rules and procedures
No fees	Membership fees (in some cases)
Informal information exchange	Structured projects and work programmes

Source: Author.

1.2 Differences between Informal and Formal Networks

There are many types of networks in operation. Some networks are very formal and exist to allow secure exchange of information, for example Interpol. At the other end of the scale there are informal networks that are set up by members to allow the free exchange of information, for example social networks. Some of the main features of informal and formal networks are outlined in Table 16.1.

The benefits of networking are well documented and can include:

- Building relationships/partnerships;
- Information exchange;
- Sharing good practice; and
- Working towards shared goals.

The EPA Network can be considered informal as it was created after the need was identified by its members. There is no board or funding and no strict rules or procedures. This means the Network provides a forum to share good practice and views and speak openly about the real issues faced by members, without the need for maintaining national positions and considering political implications. This is a key benefit for members which was emphasised at a recent meeting of the Berlin plenary in September 2013 where it was described as a 'meeting of environment professionals . . . able to provide professional opinions and not fixed positions'. This informality is the key characteristic of the Network.

There are some additional benefits of informal networking, for example:

- Flexibility to discuss a wide range of topics including emerging issues;
- Flexibility to adapt structures quickly to suit needs;
- Open and honest discussions;

- Building trust among members;
- Participation of members out of interest and not for other reasons, for example obligation or funding; and
- Providing a good platform for strategic wide-ranging discussions and sharing new ideas.

However, there are a number of challenges that all networks face. These might also be felt more keenly by informal networks, for example:

- Uncertainty over practical arrangements, such as secretarial support;
- Varying participation and membership; and
- Lack of resources.

Further challenges for networks are elaborated by Grant Pink,[3] and particularly relevant for informal networks 'is the sense that networks require ongoing commitment and leadership (which frequently falls to an energised few)'. Ensuring all members feel engaged and have a say in network activities is essential.

2. INFORMAL NETWORKING IN PRACTICE: THE EPA NETWORK EXAMPLE

2.1 Overview of the Creation of the Network and Challenges

The EPA Network is an informal grouping bringing together the heads of environment protection agencies and similar bodies across Europe. The Network exchanges views and experiences on issues of common interest to organisations involved in the practical day-to-day implementation of environmental policy, assessing the state of the environment and communication of environmental issues.

The idea of establishing a network of environment protection agencies came about in the summer of 2002. The Scottish Environment Protection Agency (SEPA) and European Environment Agency (EEA) identified a need to create a network where heads of environment agencies across Europe could share experiences. This proposal was supported by the Environment Agency of England & Wales and also Italy and preparation began for the inaugural meeting to be held in Copenhagen in November 2003.

---

[3] Pink, G., 'Environmental Enforcement Networks: A Qualitative Analysis' (2010), available at: http://ssrn.com/abstract=1803179

It was decided at this meeting that the Network should have an informal character and that all European countries could have membership and should decide themselves which relevant agencies should participate. Participation would be self-funded and plenary meetings would take place twice a year. Importantly, it was agreed that the European Commission would be invited to participate in the Network as an observer. This would help connect the implementers with the policymakers.

At an early stage it was agreed that a steering committee (Troika) would be beneficial to give the Network a strategic direction. The EEA agreed to provide secretarial support. It was decided that the Network would consider coordination, information sharing and giving advice to the European Commission on environment policy implementation, and that it would be beneficial to set up so-called interest groups to look in more detail at specific topics outside the plenary meetings.

2.2 Structure and Organisation of the Network

The EPA Network structure has developed over time and remains flexible in order to meet evolving needs. Figure 16.1 shows the current structure of the Network, with the plenary supported by interest groups and by the secretariat and Troika. There are also important links to the European Commission and joint working with other relevant networks.

The Network has one full-time secretary whose job it is to coordinate the Network, arrange the plenary meetings, support the interest groups and maintain the website and communications. The secretary also identifies issues for discussion and liaises with other relevant networks and organisations. Currently the secretary is seconded from one of the member organisations and is based at the EEA in Copenhagen.

The Troika is made up of the hosts of each of the preceding, present and future plenary meetings and provides a strategic steer for the Network. It ensures there is regular communication between the plenary meetings of the Network and can deal with any ongoing issues. Troika meetings are held by teleconference and just before plenary meetings to minimise the costs and time required.

The plenary sets the strategic direction of the Network and is held biannually in one of the member countries. As well as considering and approving the outputs from the interest groups, the plenary discusses issues of strategic importance such as improving implementation of environmental legislation, as well as monitoring and assessing the state of the environment. For example, the plenary agreed a position on priorities for a 7th Environment Action Programme (EAP) and contributed to the review of

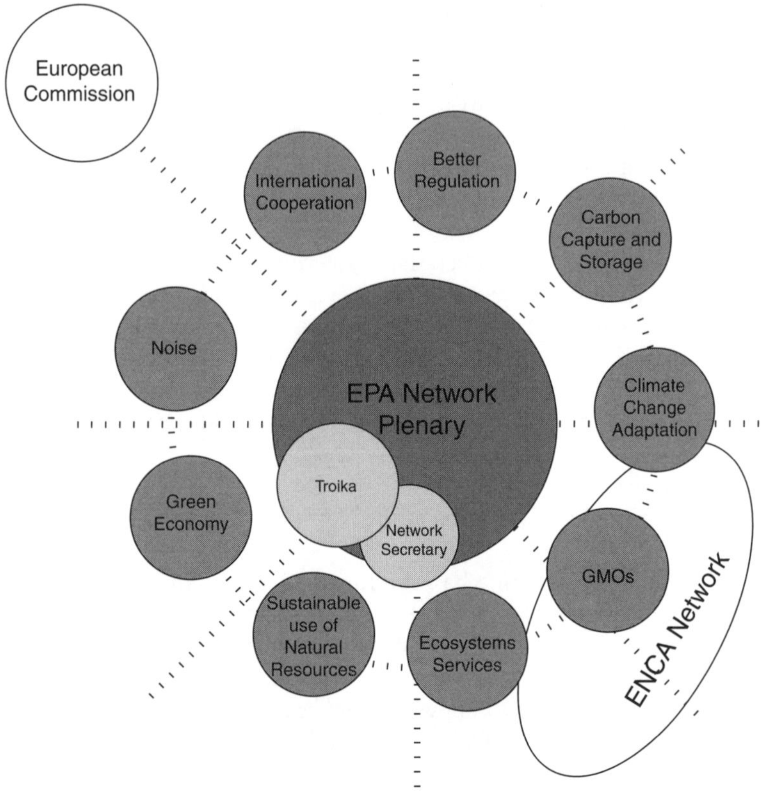

Source: EPA Brochure 07052013.

Figure 16.1 The EPA Network structure

EU water policy as well as considering emerging issues such as ecosystems services and shale gas regulation.

The plenary is where the heads and directors of the EPAs have the chance to meet and discuss issues informally. Around 45 to 55 participants take part in plenary meetings. Participation at a senior level by the European Commission provides enormous benefit, both to discuss recent and upcoming policy developments and to give feedback on challenges and successes.

The EPA Network arranges its work on specific topics through various interest groups. Figure 16.2 shows the current working interest groups (2014).

Any Network member can propose the establishment of an interest group and the work may be carried out over a fixed time frame or be

Source: EPA Brochure 07052013.

Figure 16.2 Interest groups

on-going, as long as there is sufficient interest. Members try to ensure that participation in the Network is a low-cost activity, therefore work is carried out by email and teleconference in addition to face-to-face meetings.

Examples of some interest groups that have completed their work include agriculture, environment and health, contaminated sites and soil protection, performance and evaluation, and quality management.

The tasks of an interest group range from a simple forum for exchanging good practice examples and sharing experiences, to a group trying to promote specific issues and engage with policymakers. Interest groups consider emerging issues and discuss national approaches which help to raise awareness. In 2012, over 150 experts from environmental protection agencies and other relevant organisations, including the European Commission, took part in interest group meetings.

A number of interest groups engage directly with the European Commission and share their knowledge as day-to-day practitioners in implementing environmental measures and assessing the state of the environment. Although the focus is primarily on EU policy, the interest groups also provide an important contribution to work at the global level, such as that carried out by United Nations Environment Programme (UNEP) and Organisation for Economic Co-operation and Development (OECD).

Interest groups report on their activities to the plenary meetings where any outputs from the groups are discussed and approved.

2.3 EPA Network Members

The informality of the EPA Network begins with the voluntary participation in the Network. The heads of agencies identified a need to create a network to share experiences. There is no funding for participation and no membership fee, yet participation at a senior level is increasing, demonstrating the value of participation seen by members.

The Network was designed as an informal one with participating countries free to decide on which agencies from their administrations should participate. The European Commission was also invited to attend.

There are currently 39 organisations participating in the Network. This includes West Balkan agencies that also benefit from the chance to share experiences on environmental issues and implementation of EU legislation.

One important aspect of the EPA Network is the possibility of having a frank and open exchange of views at a high level, amongst the members. This enables discussions on the true nature of issues within the countries. Summaries of discussions are published on the EPA Network website but the detailed exchanges are not recorded. The views expressed in the meetings are therefore those of the people involved and may not necessarily reflect the national political positions. This adds to the informality of the Network.

There are some anomalies in participation in the Network. In the cases of Cyprus and Spain, central environment ministries participate in the absence of an environment agency at national level. However in the case of Spain, the Basque environment agency participates alongside the ministry. Participation by France and Luxembourg has up until now been ad hoc, as suitable agencies have not been identified.

Although the Network was established as a network of environmental protection agencies it has proved to be useful to have involvement of relevant organisations from countries where no national agency exists.

2.4 Cooperation with Other Networks and Organisations

The Network works closely with the European Commission as well as with other networks with complementary roles such as the European Union Network for the Implementation and Enforcement of Environmental Law (IMPEL) and the European Network of Heads of Nature Conservation

Agencies (ENCA). Around half of the EPAs are also involved in IMPEL and some 20 per cent are represented in ENCA. Back-to-back plenary meetings have been held with the ENCA Network and the Interest Groups on genetically modified organisms, Climate Change Adaptation and Ecosystem Services are held jointly between the two networks. Joint meetings have also been held with the IMPEL Network. The two networks also built on work which was done individually initially, to create a joint checklist to assess practicability and enforceability of legislation. This was released in March 2010.[4]

In general, EPAs have quite strong ties to the EEA as around 60 per cent provide members to the EEA Management Board and 85 per cent of them provide the National Focal Point (NFP) to the European Environment Information and Observation Network (Eionet), the partnership network of the EEA and its member and cooperating countries.

The EPA Network and its members are also increasing their engagement with a wider range of stakeholders, for example the judiciary and prosecutors.

3. CONTRIBUTING TO IMPROVING THE ENVIRONMENT

Figure 16.3 illustrates the key stages in the EU policy cycle, beginning with legislation drafted in the EU. This is transposed into national law, and implemented through policies. Inspection, enforcement and monitoring ensure compliance. Then progress is measured and the policies evaluated.

The EPA Network members are involved in contributing to many stages of this cycle. The Network itself plays a role in providing a platform to exchange good practice and also to provide feedback to the policymakers about what works 'on the ground'.

A key difference to other networks is the variety of tasks of members and range of topics discussed. Most networks bring together organisations responsible for a specific topic whereas the EPA Network brings together EPAs. The informality of the network, including its approach to membership, means that all environment agencies are able to join, not just those with a specific focus or institutional setting. EPAs in Europe

[4] IMPEL/EPA Network joint checklist to assess practicability and enforceability of legislation, March 2010. Available at: http://impel.eu/wp-content/uploads/2010/04/IMPEL-and-NEPA-Better-Regulation-Checklist-FINAL.pdf

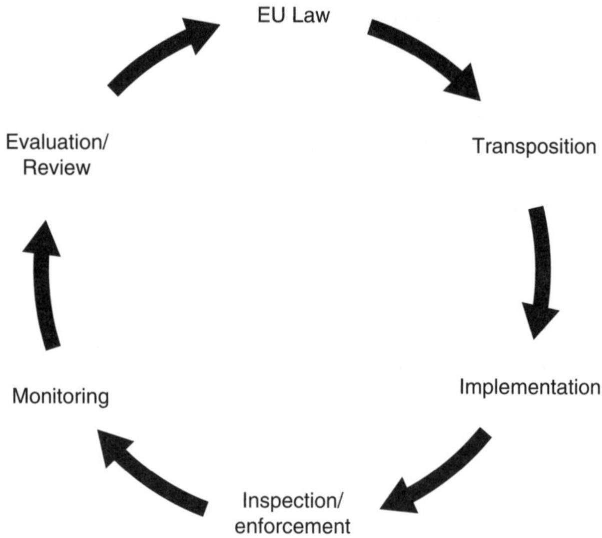

Source: Author.

Figure 16.3 The EU policy cycle

have very different roles, from research and policy advice to monitoring and enforcement. Discussing all these aspects together allows a strategic discussion and contributes to many stages outlined in the policy cycle. Drawn from some internal EPA Network research carried out in 2011, Figure 16.4 shows the range of tasks within the field of environment protection that are carried out by members.

3.1 Successes of the Network

Due to the senior level participation, the Network works well at getting to grips with strategic issues. Some significant outputs of the Network at a strategic level include:

- **7EAP:** The evaluation on the 6EAP and development of the 7EAP were/are key areas of interest to EPA Network members. A range of processes were put in place to provide feedback on the 6EAP and also to provide ideas on priorities for a possible 7EAP. A working group was set up to develop ideas and meetings were held with senior officials in the Commission. The Network contributed to workshops and conferences which were influential in shaping

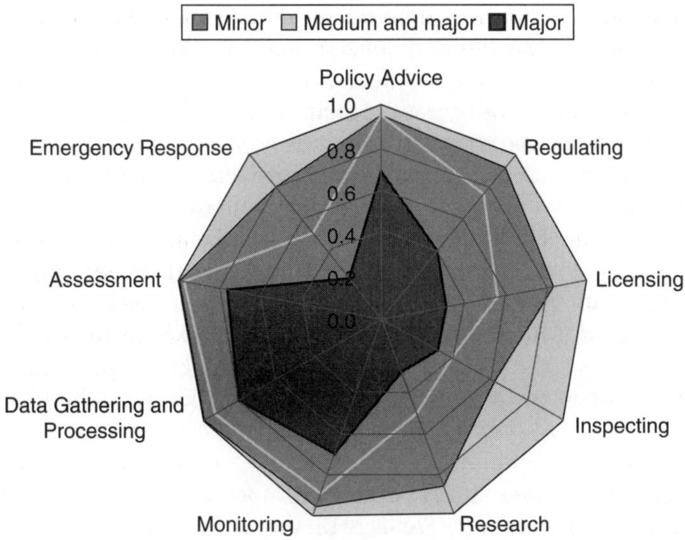

Source: EPA Network internal survey, 2011.

Figure 16.4 Roles in environmental protection

emerging thinking, such as the European Conference 'Towards a genuine 7th Environment Action Programme', organised by the Belgian Presidency.[5]

In 2010 the Network wrote to Commissioners Potočnik and Hedegaard with initial views on why a 7th EAP was important and the main priorities to be included.[6] Following a request for more information and examples from the Commission, the Network developed and agreed a more comprehensive position paper with inputs from organisations across the Network. This was submitted as a response to the final assessment of the 6EAP.[7] This was received very positively by the Commission.

[5] Towards a genuine 7th Environment Action Programme, press release, November 2010. Available at: http://www.eutrio.be/pressrelease/towards-genuine-7th-environmental-action-programme

[6] EPA Network letter on 7EAP – October 2010. Available at: http://epanet.ew.eea.europa.eu/fol249409/letter-to-environment-commissioner-on-7th-environment-action-programme-oct-20/download

[7] Ibid.

When the Commission published its proposal for a 7th EAP, 'Living well within the limits of our planet', in November 2012, it was gratifying to see that the majority of the issues that the Network had highlighted as priorities were included in the proposal.

- **Better regulation reports and checklist:** The Better Regulation Interest Group produced three statements between 2005 and 2008, identifying better regulation practices and setting out a vision for future regulation. The group has had regular contact with the European Commission, for example on the Environment Action Programmes and on examining the implementation of environmental directives. As mentioned, the group developed a checklist with the IMPEL network on the practicability and enforceability of new and existing legislation and IMPEL used this checklist to examine the recast proposal of the Waste Electronics and Electrical Equipment Directive and the Waste Shipments Regulation.[8]
- **IG Work-Noise:** An example at a more technical level is the IG Work-Noise. In 2011 and 2012 the interest group concentrated its work on road traffic noise abatement. Particular focus was directed to the on-going discussion in the EU regarding noise level regulation for cars and trucks. As a result of the discussions, the EPA Network sent letters to the European Commission and the European Parliament committees on Environment, Public Health and Food Safety; Transport and Tourism and Internal Market; and Consumer Protection,[9] asking for tighter noise emission regulations of vehicles in the EU.

3.2 Future Cooperation

There were 26 countries present at the first meeting of the Network in 2003. Since then the number of countries has expanded to 33, comprising 39 organisations in total. Hosts for future plenary meetings have been confirmed for the next two years which shows commitment from members to support the network. This also includes newer members, for example Kosovo. This sets a positive tone for future engagement.

The European Commission has said that they value the work of the EPA Network and this cooperation must continue. Cooperation with

---

[8] IMPEL Project 'Practicability and Enforceability of the WEEE Directive Recast Proposal'. Available at: http://impel.eu/wp-content/uploads/2010/01/assessment_weee_recast.pdf

[9] EPA Network Interest Group on Noise Abatement – Letter to European Parliament – April 2012. Available at: http://epanet.ew.eea.europa.eu/fol249409

other relevant networks could be expanded. It might be useful to map the roles and tasks of the networks and their members that are involved with implementation of European Legislation to help provide a complete picture of environmental governance.

3.3 Challenges with Networking Activities

Despite the successes mentioned above, there are challenges to maintaining effective networks. One key factor is effective secretarial support to drive the network activities, especially in between meetings of the network. Another is obtaining the resources for activities in an increasingly tough financial climate.

It is also difficult to measure the effectiveness and influence of networks. As highlighted in the earlier sections, the benefits of networking activities are widely appreciated but the challenge remains to directly assess or quantify the influence of these informal activities in contributing to a better environment.

4. CONCLUSIONS

The EPA Network can be considered informal as it was created after the need was identified by its members. There is no board or funding and no strict rules or procedures. This means the Network provides a forum to share good practice and views and speak openly about the real issues faced by members.

This type of networking brings with it a number of challenges, for example varying participation and membership and also lack of resources to carry out activities; however, the benefits of networking if organised in this way can be significant. Trust is built between members who can have open and honest discussions, which enable a range of experiences and perspectives to be shared.

Networking not only offers the chance for a large number of organisations to share experiences and good practice but often leads to enhanced bilateral relationships between individual organisations. In a time when EPAs are under increasing financial pressures, the access to expertise and experiences that the EPA Network can provide is invaluable.

17. Developing and sustaining environmental compliance and enforcement networks: lessons learned from the International Network on Environmental Compliance and Enforcement

Jo Gerardu,* Meredith Koparova, Kenneth Markowitz, Durwood Zaelke and Gunnar Baldwin, Jr

1. INTRODUCTION

Over the past four decades, considerable efforts have been made to improve the management of human relationships with the environment.[1] Countries have created environmental agencies, negotiated multilateral agreements and undertaken new initiatives at the local, national, and international levels to protect human health, limit greenhouse gas emissions, conserve biodiversity and wildlife, and manage natural resources. These efforts have involved leaders in governments, parliaments, and the judiciary, in international organisations, businesses, and civil society, and in other sectors of society. Environmental officials have often been at the forefront of efforts to promote the rule of law and good governance through work to advance sustainable development objectives.

These achievements are significant, but global environmental

* Office of the INECE Secretariat, 2300 Wisconsin Ave, NW Suite 300, Washington, D.C., 20007, inece@inece.org

[1] United Nations Environment Programme, *GEO-5: Environment for the Future We Want* http://www.unep.org/geo/geo5.asp (accessed 8 March 2014).

assessments acknowledge growing challenges.[2] There is a continuing loss of biodiversity, climate change, reduction in natural capital and worldwide proliferation of waste. Air and water pollution persist to cause significant health risks, particularly to many people in the developing world. There is a need to further strengthen the stewardship of the Earth and its natural resources, which are the foundation of social and economic development and the heritage of our children and the generations to come.

The GEO-4 Report from the United Nations Environment Programme (UNEP) recognises that these environmental 'issues transcend borders. Protecting the global environment is largely beyond the capacity of individual countries. Only concerted and coordinated international action will be sufficient. The world needs a more coherent system of international environmental governance'.[3] Intra-governmental networks, such as the International Network for Environmental Compliance and Enforcement (INECE) and other regional and topical environmental compliance and enforcement networks, enable cooperation among government regulators, other governmental actors, international and non-governmental organisations, and private actors.

Cooperation on common environmental concerns can help resolve transboundary environmental problems, create efficiencies in the development of tools and programmes, create a level playing field for the regulated industries among countries and ultimately foster the political will needed to reform weak implementation of environmental standards.[4]

Operating as trans-governmental networks focused on environmental compliance and enforcement, INECE and its regional and topical networks provide the forums and mechanisms that enable direct interaction among and between domestic officials, international institutions, and private actors. INECE plays an instrumental role in the compliance and enforcement community by communicating and advancing best practices, fostering mutual learning both vertically and horizontally across

---

[2] UNODC, *The Globalization of Crime: A Transnational Organized Crime Threat Assessment* http://www.unodc.org/documents/data-and-analysis/tocta/TOCTA_Report_2010_low_res.pdf (accessed 8 March 2014).

[3] United Nations Environment Programme, *Global Environment Outlook – GEO4 – Environment for Development* (2007), p. xvi.

[4] INECE, 'Executive Planning Committee Co-Chairs' Final Conference Statement, 9th INECE International Conference on Environmental Compliance and Enforcement' ('Whistler Statement'), in INECE Secretariat, *Proceedings of the 9th International Conference on Environmental Compliance and Enforcement* (INECE 2011).

organisations responsible for enforcement and compliance, and facilitating information exchange.

2. INECE'S HISTORY AS A NETWORK

In many ways, INECE's evolution as a network has reflected the broader global trend towards the 'flat world': the levelling of the playing field for business, the rise of the internet to support knowledge transfer, and the increasing capacity for international communications.[5] Launched in 1989, INECE was an early leader in understanding the value of transgovernmental networks in responding to global challenges by facilitating collaboration and information exchange among officials.[6] At a time when countries were increasingly promulgating new legal requirements to protect human health and the environment and to comply with obligations under multilateral treaties,[7] there was a clear need for flexible mechanisms to quickly disseminate information, harmonise regulations, and respond to common problems from a shared perspective shaped by practical experience.[8]

The seeds of INECE were planted in 1985 with two key activities: a research project on compliance monitoring and enforcement and a bilateral Memorandum of Understanding (MOU) between the United States Environmental Protection Agency (US EPA) and the Netherlands' Ministry of Housing, Spatial Planning and Environment (VROM). First, the Organisation for Economic Co-operation and Development (OECD) commissioned three national case studies from the United States, the Netherlands, and the United Kingdom, on *Improving the Efficiency and Effectiveness of Compliance Monitoring and Enforcement of Environmental Policies*. Ensuing discussions and debates over the final report made it clear that few nations had examined the extent to which environmental policies and requirements were complied with. The report also found that the term 'enforcement' had differing meanings and that there was a clear

---

[5] Thomas Freidman, *The World Is Flat: A Brief History of the Twenty-first Century* (2005).

[6] Anne-Marie Slaughter, *A New World Order* (2004).

[7] Donald Kaniaru, 'The Role of Institutions and Networks in Environmental Enforcement', in INECE Secretariat, *Proceedings of the 6th International Conference on Environmental Compliance and Enforcement* (INECE 2002).

[8] Durwood Zaelke et al., *Making Law Work*, Chapter 12 (2005).

gap in efforts to change behaviour once requirements were established.[9] In that same year, the US EPA and VROM entered into a MOU to promote mutual exchange and transfer of ideas, and environmental enforcement was singled out for exchange. The MOU led to a series of seminars, the outcomes of which were used by the Dutch government to reach consensus on improved structures for environmental enforcement and provided both the Dutch Ministry and US EPA with new strategies for improved programmes.

As follow-up to the seminar series, the first international enforcement workshop was held in 1990 in Utrecht, the Netherlands. Representatives from 13 countries and international organisations attended what was still an extension of the bilateral talks. At the workshop, a strategic framework for compliance and enforcement was used to describe the United States enforcement programme. The US EPA had developed the framework to provide a basis for new compliance and enforcement strategies. It was intended to both reinvigorate enforcement and to better articulate a consistent philosophy and approach to inspire improved enforcement among the 50 states and local government entities. The framework had a positive reception at the workshop and the reaction of those in attendance supported the idea that key concepts seemed to have their roots less in particular cultures than in the nature of human behaviour.

INECE's early work focused on generating international commitment to build the capacity for compliance and enforcement as an essential element of environmental management and on establishing a common set of definitions and a framework for exchange. An international mandate in Agenda 21 of the United Nations Conference on Environment and Development (1992) confirmed consensus on the importance of dedicated programmes for environmental compliance and enforcement to achieve domestic and international environmental goals, sustainable development and free trade.[10]

Chapter 8 of Agenda 21 stated (in part):

> 8.21. Each country should develop integrated strategies to maximize compliance with its laws and regulations relating to sustainable development, with

---

[9] Cheryl Wasserman, 'Improving the Efficiency and Effectiveness of Compliance Monitoring and Enforcement of Environmental Policies, United States: A National Review' (OECD 1984).

[10] Agenda 21, Chapter 8 emphasised that environmental enforcement is an important factor in achieving environmental goals.

assistance from international organizations and other countries as appropriate. The strategies could include:

(a) Enforceable, effective laws, regulations and standards based on sound economic, social and environmental principles and appropriate risk assessment, incorporating sanctions designed to punish violations, obtain redress, and deter future violations;
(b) Mechanisms for promoting compliance;
(c) Institutional capacity for collecting compliance data, regularly reviewing compliance, detecting violations, establishing enforcement priorities, undertaking effective enforcement, and conducting periodic evaluations of the effectiveness of compliance and enforcement programmes;
(d) Mechanisms for appropriate involvement of individuals and groups in the development and enforcement of laws and regulations on environment and development; and
(e) National monitoring of legal follow-up to international instruments.[11]

This mandate made it clear that environmental compliance and enforcement were critical to achieving sustainable development. The mandate also gave international organisations the confidence to move forward and support capacity-building activities – capacity building that could result in better sustainable development and a level playing field.

During its first decade, 1985–1995, the outcomes of the growing partnership also included:

1. Adoption of common definitions, principles and a framework for international exchange;
2. Exchange of experiences of well over 65 country programmes and expert views on over 25 special topics in widely disseminated conference proceedings;
3. International conferences;
4. Exponential growth in networking supported by an accessible databank and years of research reflected in increased participation in international conferences; and
5. Emergence of new institutional arrangements for ongoing regional and international networking and cooperation.

In its second decade, 1995–2005, INECE continued its work to advance environmental compliance and enforcement as the foundation of a stronger and more global rule of law, good environmental governance, and, ultimately, sustainable development (see Figure 17.1).

---

[11] http://sustainabledevelopment.un.org/content/documents/Agenda21.pdf, p. 60.

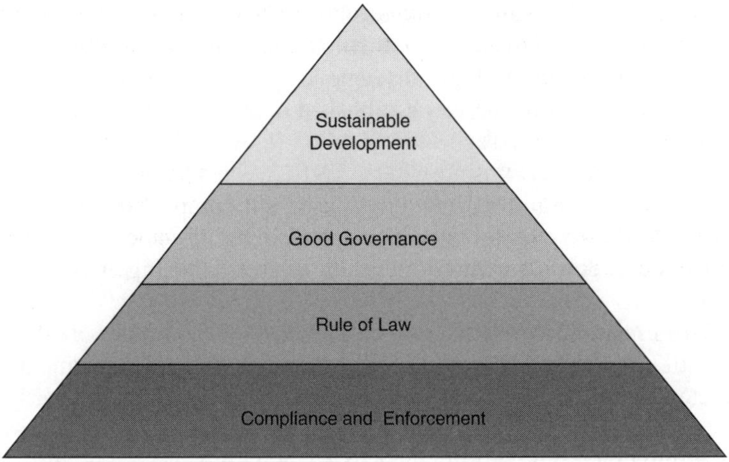

Figure 17.1 INECE's compliance and enforcement pyramid

INECE expanded and improved upon its successful international conference series.[12] These conferences were complemented by interim thematic workshops to educate practitioners, foster enforcement cooperation and promote compliance and enforcement as a key to achieving sustainability objectives. In this period, INECE re-launched its website, including a greater focus on topical work areas and on its broad collection of resources on environmental compliance and enforcement.

In 2005 the leading resource on environmental compliance theory and practice *Making Law Work: Environmental Compliance & Sustainable Development*[13] was published.

A major project of INECE during this time was the development of guidance on performance indicators for environmental compliance and enforcement programmes. This work included the development of a guidance document, a collection of international good practices, and the development of a comprehensive capacity-building programme, and resulted in hundreds of enforcement programme managers around the world trained on this topic.[14]

---

[12] INECE held conferences in Oaxaca, Mexico in 1996; Monterey, California, USA in 1998; San Jose, Costa Rica in 2002; and in Marrakech, Morocco in 2005.

[13] Durwood Zaelke et al. (eds), *Making Law Work: Environmental Compliance & Sustainable Development (Volumes I and II)* (2005).

[14] INECE, *Performance Measurement Guidance for Compliance and Enforcement Practitioners*, 2008 (2nd edition), http://www.inece.org/indicators/guidance.pdf (accessed 8 March 2014).

This decade also saw the expansion of the regional environmental compliance and enforcement networks, with new networks launched in Australia, Africa's Maghreb region, Asia, North America,[15] and Central Europe joining already established networks in Europe and in the Caucasus and Central Asia.

In its years of work since 2005, INECE has emphasised two key themes: (1) understanding how environmental compliance and enforcement programmes create value across all areas of society; and (2) the importance of enforcement cooperation in strengthening environmental governance.

Environmental compliance and enforcement programmes create value across all areas of society: public value through strengthened rule of law, protected ecosystem goods and services, and improved human health; and private value through increased investor confidence, reduced business risks, stimulated innovation, increased competitiveness, and new jobs and markets.[16] This added value is further increased through enforcement cooperation among government officials.

Working under these two themes, INECE continued to advance its goals of raising awareness, building capacity, and developing networks. INECE dramatically improved and expanded its website, better organising the resources section of the site into a searchable 'Environmental Compliance Capacity Building Resource Library' and continues to highlight the best resources on compliance and enforcement for the site's visitors.

As part of its work on building capacity for environmental compliance and enforcement, INECE revised in 2009 the *Principles of Environmental Enforcement Handbook*[17] on the key components of effective compliance and enforcement programmes and has delivered its training programme based on this handbook to officials around the world. (The first edition of this handbook was developed in 1992 by US EPA in consultation with VROM and the Katowice Ecology Department in Poland.)

An important area in this period was INECE's work on climate compliance, which, through a series of workshops beginning in 2004, identified, explored, and made recommendations on the role of compliance in

---

[15] Susan Bromm, 'North America's Commission for Environmental Cooperation: One Example of a Successful Regional Network', in INECE Secretariat, *Proceedings of the 9th International Conference on Environmental Compliance and Enforcement* (INECE 2011).

[16] Network of Heads of European Environment Protection Agencies, *The Contribution of Good Environmental Regulation to Competitiveness* (2005).

[17] INECE, *Principles of Environmental Compliance and Enforcement Handbook* 2009 (2nd edition 2009).

assuring trust and integrity within and among carbon emissions trading platforms. Much of INECE's work focused on the importance of developing both a common set of procedures for monitoring, reporting, and verification, and a standardised language for use in registries.

The enforcement of requirements that result from the environmental impact assessment (EIA) and permitting process has been an increasingly important topic for INECE. Although issues related to EIA have frequently been addressed by presenters and participants at the international conferences organised by INECE, it became a special area of focus for the network in 2012, beginning with the INECE Roundtable Discussion on the Enforcement of EIA Requirements. The outcome document[18] that emerged from this online facilitated discussion, providing a valuable set of expert perspectives into many of the challenges faced by government environmental authorities in assuring compliance with project-specific obligations. In May of 2012, INECE was awarded the Global Environment Award by the International Association for Impact Assessment for its substantial contributions to the practice of environmental assessment. Later in 2012, INECE began a six-month study of mechanisms for funding government EIA-related tasks, with a special focus on Central Africa. The study, conducted on behalf of the Netherlands Commission for Environmental Assessment (NCEA), resulted in two documents, one of which related to systems or funding government EIA tasks in four African countries, and a forthcoming NCEA document covering funding mechanisms and considerations in general.[19]

INECE launched new networks to support environmental compliance practitioners, including the Seaport Environmental Security Network in 2008 and the INECE-IUCN Global Network of Environmental Prosecutors in 2011. INECE also strongly supported the development of regional networks, including in East Africa, East Europe, and the Middle East, and, more recently, in Chile and in West Africa. National compliance and enforcement networks have recently been launched in China and in Jordan.

---

[18] INECE, *A Summary of the INECE Roundtable Discussion on the Enforcement of EIA Requirements* (April 2012), http://inece.org/resource/eia-discussion-summary/ (accessed 8 March 2014).

[19] NCEA, *Les mécanismes de financement de l'action publique en matière d'etudes d'impact environmental* (January 2013), http://api.commissiemer.nl/docs/mer/diversen/ncea_mecanismes-financement-eie2013.pdf (accessed 8 March 2014).

3. LESSONS ON CREATING AND SUSTAINING REGIONAL NETWORKS

Based on INECE's experience in supporting regional networks and the experiences of those networks in developing effective work programmes to raise awareness of the importance of environmental compliance and enforcement, to build capacity, and to leverage experience within each region's own specific cultural contexts, development needs, and environmental objectives, INECE convened the first Summit of Regional Network Leadership in Whistler, Canada in 2011. Thirty-one practitioners from ten networks shared practical experiences and charted future collaboration on substantive issues of mutual concern, including good practices for network management and governance.[20]

When used effectively, regional networks enable government officials and staff at all levels to safeguard the environment on a regional scale, streamlining cross-border enforcement of environmental laws and permitting continuous improvements in capacity based on the cumulative expertise of all participants. But these benefits are not automatic. Networks must be managed effectively based on good practices and driven by commonly shared goals.

Fortunately, geographic areas that have not yet benefitted from regional networks (or need to strengthen existing ones) do not need to proceed by trial and error. A number of highly effective regional networks already offer a wealth of experience, case studies, lessons, and insights that can inform the efforts of new and existing regional networks alike. Although it has been demonstrated that the structure and composition of regional networks may vary, based upon region-specific needs and approaches, there are many common principles and strategies from which reliable guidance can be drawn.

INECE produced an *Online Manual on Creating and Sustaining Regional Enforcement Networks*[21] as a result of an ongoing effort to gather the collective lessons and experiences of successful networks from around the world and to provide useful guidance for network participants and stakeholders to consider. It presents a concise overview of the principal areas of practice that relate to the start and the operation of successful regional networks. This manual demonstrates how cross-border cooperation can

---

20 INECE, *Summit of Regional Network Leadership: Outcomes Report* (2011) http://inece.org/resource/regional_summit_outcomes/ (accessed 8 March 2014).

21 INECE, *Online Manual on Creating and Sustaining Regional Enforcement Networks* (2012) http://inece.org/resource/network_manual/ (accessed 8 March 2014).

be leveraged to acquire significantly greater capabilities than those of domestic government agencies and staff acting alone. The following paragraphs summarise some key recommendations from the *Online Manual on Creating and Sustaining Regional Enforcement Networks*.

The creation of a new regional or national network requires a mission, a strategic planning process, and a commitment from its potential members. Activities needed to establish a network's mission and goals may include identifying and building consensus around a common network agenda; developing a strategic planning process; determining how stakeholders will obtain value from the network; identifying the gap the network is filling, also with a view to ensuring synergies with other networks' activities; and defining the relevant geographical scope of the network. Networks should ensure that the network's structure is appropriate to the objectives of the network. Awareness of the need for and value of the network and strong interest in and commitment from stakeholders are essential.

There are a number of challenges related to the creation of a network, including building a critical mass of members, building trust, recognising different goals and domestic agendas and identifying areas for convergence, low or non-existent budgets, and establishing procedures to protect confidentiality. Additionally, networks can benefit from linking to other networks early to learn from shared knowledge and experiences.

Every network requires a framework to govern how it will operate as an organisation. The framework includes a guiding set of goals and principles, designation of key roles and responsibilities, and a set of rules and procedures that controls how network leaders undertake decision-making and management tasks. Networks should have a well-defined structure, and most networks operate with a secretariat and an ongoing funding commitment by the membership or funding authority.

In drawing up a strategic plan and a work plan, the network needs to select projects and identify possibilities to fund these projects, including prioritisation and management of relationships. Importantly, networks may use performance measures to assess and communicate achievements. Communicating the value and benefits of the network can be invaluable when seeking (financial) support from member organisations or from potential donors.

Networks must engage in a range of outreach and communication activities in order to provide timely, useful information to members and to facilitate cooperation between agencies from different countries. For a network to be effective in helping to advance the work of its members, it must undertake initiatives that encourage stakeholder buy-in and participation. Communications and outreach to target audiences, funders and partners are essential and can be done by providing online information (the primary vehicle for communicating with stakeholders), emails and newsletters, use of social media where appropriate, public forums/workshops, direct peer-to-peer outreach by individual members, webcasts of important meetings, providing translation services where these have sufficient value and integrating liaison-building and networking into communications.

Assessment is the process of evaluating an organisation's performance and progress, relative to its mission and goals. Grant Pink and James Lehane – then of the Australasian Environmental Law Enforcement and Regulators neTwork (AELERT) – developed an assessment tool called the Network Evaluation Matrix which emerged from AELERT's specific experience in self-assessment and which is particularly informative.[22]

4. LOOKING AHEAD

INECE's five year Strategic Plan (2012–2017) provides guidance on future directions for the network. Thematic priorities for INECE identified in the Strategic Plan, and supported by the outcomes of the 2011 International Conference, are: governance and rule of law; air pollution and climate change; illegal trade of waste, and of commodities that may have adverse impacts on the environment; environmental impact assessment and permitting; biodiversity; natural resources, and illegal trade in species; water pollution and management; and enforcement and compliance activities that promote sustainable consumption.

To better support the implementation of its Strategic Plan, INECE modified its governance structure in 2012–2013. The new governance structure consists of a small Executive Committee and a larger Global Council. The Executive Committee of INECE is a decision-making body which is responsible for approving and ensuring the implementation of the INECE Strategic Plan and work programmes in cooperation with the INECE secretariat. The INECE Global Council is a group of environmental compliance and enforcement experts who provide guidance to INECE and advice on the implementation of INECE projects.

Looking ahead to 2014/2015, priorities for INECE will include a

---

22 Grant Pink and James Lehane, 'Environmental Enforcement Networks: Development of a Network Evaluation Matrix' in INECE Secretariat, *Proceedings of the 9th International Conference on Environmental Compliance and Enforcement* (INECE 2009).

number of innovative and practical activities to advance INECE's mission and priorities under its Strategic Plan. One priority will be studying examples of 'next generation environmental compliance'. Technological and informational tools provide new ways to understand how rules are being implemented in real time, while more effective requirement design can help actively facilitate environmental compliance.

A second priority will be further work on promoting compliance with existing and emerging laws that have climate co-benefits, as well as other regulatory tools to support mitigation and adaptation, building on INECE's 2013 report *Compliance Strategies to Deliver Climate Benefits*.[23] A recent study by the global environmental legislators' organisation 'GLOBE' found that 500 climate laws have been passed in the 66 countries covered by the study and that much of the substantive progress on legislative activity on climate change in 2012 took place in emerging economies, including China.[24] Assuring full implementation of these new laws is critical to their success in achieving intended energy security, resource efficiency and cleaner, lower carbon economic growth benefits. INECE is already working with national authorities to design strategies to assure compliance with laws that directly limit climate pollutants through carbon emissions trading programmes as well as laws that govern certain short-lived climate pollutants, including black carbon (soot), tropospheric ozone, and methane, all three air pollutants, along with factory-made hydrofluorocarbons (HFCs) and other fluorinated gases.

INECE will continue its work on seaport environmental security, with a renewed focus on capacity building, coordinated simultaneous environmental inspection work at seaports, and expanding beyond illegal transboundary shipments of hazardous waste to include illegal transboundary shipments of electronic waste and ozone depleting substances.

To advance its work on EIA, in cooperation with the NCEA and the East African Network for Environmental Compliance and Enforcement, INECE is exploring opportunities to embark on a joint study in East Africa that focuses on coherence between EIA and environmental compliance and enforcement functions in the context of actual projects carried out in the region.

INECE will continue to support the growth of environmental compliance and enforcement networks and expects that strong national

---

[23] INECE Secretariat, *Compliance Strategies to Deliver Climate Benefits* (INECE 2013) http://inece.org/resource/climate-report/ (accessed 8 March 2014).

[24] GLOBE, *The GLOBE Climate Legislation Study: A Review of Climate Change Legislation in 66 Countries* (4th edition, 2014), http://www.globeinternational.org/studies/legislation/climate (accessed 8 March 2014).

networks, like those in China, Kenya, Uganda, Tanzania, and Jordan, will increasingly play a role in the success of regional environmental compliance and enforcement networks.

Central to these activities are effective communications to raise awareness, build capacity, and promote cooperation for effective environmental compliance and enforcement. INECE will expand the website, www.inece.org, providing the world's most extensive online library on environmental compliance and enforcement materials. INECE will use social media tools to engage practitioners and new audiences through its website and enhance connections among practitioners.

5. CONCLUSIONS

The 1985 OECD study and the Memorandum of Understanding between the United States and the Netherlands initiated a series of international enforcement meetings held around the world which engaged regulators, inspectors, prosecutors, judges, and other stakeholders in a global discussion about the importance of environmental compliance and enforcement to achieving sustainable development objectives.

The experiences of INECE and the regional and topical environmental compliance and enforcement networks that emerged from this initiative offer lessons learned and good practice for emerging networks, such as those in East Africa, West Africa, and South America, as well as for networks in existence that are interested in assessing their growth, strategic direction, and work programmes.

Grant Pink notes that:

> The literature indicates that networks have been established and utilised in ever increasing amounts over the last twenty-five years. The environmental enforcement field like much of public administration relies heavily on networks especially as the field does not, relatively speaking, have great depth in terms of history, precedent and legal principles. This reflects the rapidly increasing importance of environmental issues within contemporary cultural, political and economic dialogues.[25]

Pink's cited literature dates mostly from 1992 and later, demonstrating the growing involvement of academia in the subject of compliance and

---

[25] Grant Pink, 'Environmental Enforcement Networks: A Qualitative Analysis' (December 7, 2010), http://ssrn.com/abstract=1803179 (accessed 8 March 2014).

enforcement in combination with the growth of enforcement agencies and environmental regulations.

As a pioneer since 1990 in developing informal networks to enable peer-to-peer collaboration and information sharing on environmental compliance and enforcement, INECE has acted to both catalyse and support initiatives to develop similar networks at a regional, national, or topical scale. INECE provides programmatic and strategic support and guidance for network design and development, while also acting as a model for this type of collaboration. INECE has directly and indirectly influenced the development and growth of the approximately twenty-five networks currently in existence that focus on building capacity among government officials to improve environmental compliance and enforcement, and is referred to as 'the network of networks'.

Assuring compliance with national environmental laws and with international treaty obligations is an important strategy in fulfilling our 'moral and ethical responsibility to meaningfully address and to reverse the continuing deterioration of the global environment'.[26] Over the past 24 years, INECE and the regional and topical environmental compliance and enforcement networks have been instrumental in ensuring that environmental laws are meeting their objective to protect human health and the environment, and will continue to act to 'make laws work'.

BIBLIOGRAPHY

An Stas, 'The Flemish High Council of Environmental Enforcement: A Coordinated Environmental Enforcement Policy'. In *Proceedings of the 9th International Conference on Environmental Compliance and Enforcement* (INECE 2011).

Anne-Marie Slaughter, *A New World Order* (Princeton University Press 2004).

Cheryl Wasserman, 'Improving the Efficiency and Effectiveness of Compliance Monitoring and Enforcement of Environmental Policies, United States: A National Review' (OECD October 16, 1984).

Davis Jones, 'Summary of Plenary Session #9: Reports of Regional Meetings and Workshops'. In *INECE 6th International Conference on Environmental Compliance and Enforcement, April 15–19, 2002, San Jose, Costa Rica, Proceedings, Volume 2* (INECE 2002).

Donald Kaniaru, 'The Role of Institutions and Networks in Environmental Enforcement'. In *INECE 6th International Conference on Environmental Compliance and Enforcement, April 15–19 2002, San Jose, Costa Rica, Proceedings, Volume 2* (INECE 2002).

Durwood Zaelke et al. (eds), *Making Law Work: Environmental Compliance*

[26] Ladislav Miko, 'Afterword', in Durwood Zaelke et al. (eds), *Making Law Work: Environmental Compliance & Sustainable Development* (2005).

& Sustainable Development (Cameron May 2005). Especially Chapter 12, 'Transgovernmental Networks'.

Gerard O'Leary and Dara J. Lynott, 'The Effective Use of an Environmental Enforcement Network in Ireland'. In *Proceedings of the 9th International Conference on Environmental Compliance and Enforcement* (INECE 2011).

Gerphas Opondo, 'Creating and Sustaining Regional Environmental Compliance and Enforcement Networks: Lessons from the East African Network for Environmental Compliance & Enforcement'. In *Proceedings of the 9th International Conference on Environmental Compliance and Enforcement* (INECE 2011).

Grant Pink, 'Assessing the Utility of Environmental Enforcement Networks: Maximising Benefits to Members'. In *Proceedings of the 9th International Conference on Environmental Compliance and Enforcement* (INECE 2011).

Grant Pink, 'Building Regulatory Capacity in Environmental Agencies: Through Tailored Training'. In *INECE 8th International Conference on Environmental Compliance and Enforcement: 5–11 April 2008 Cape Town, South Africa, Proceedings* (Cameron May Ltd 2008), 225–233.

Grant Pink, 'Environmental Enforcement Networks: A Qualitative Analysis' (December 7, 2010). Available at http://ssrn.com/abstract=1803179 (accessed 10 July 2011).

Grant Pink and James Lehane, 'Environmental Enforcement Networks: Development of a Network Evaluation Matrix'. In *Proceedings of the 9th International Conference on Environmental Compliance and Enforcement* (INECE 2011).

Grant Pink and James Lehane, 'Environmental Enforcement Networks: Their Role in Climate Change Enforcement'. In R. White (ed.), *Climate Change from a Criminological Perspective* (Springer 2012), 109–133.

INECE, 'Executive Planning Committee Co-Chairs' Final Conference Statement, 9th INECE International Conference on Environmental Compliance and Enforcement' ('Whistler Statement'). In *Proceedings of the 9th International Conference on Environmental Compliance and Enforcement* (INECE 2011).

INECE, *Online Manual on Creating and Sustaining Regional Enforcement Networks* (2012). Available at http://inece.org/resource/network_manual/

INECE, *Summit of Regional Network Leadership: Outcomes Report* (2011). Available at http://inece.org/resource/regional_summit_outcomes/

J.J.A. Gerardu and Durwood Zaelke, 'The Importance of International Environmental Enforcement Networks'. *Environmental Law Network International* (2005).

James Lehane and Grant Pink, 'Evolution of a Regional Environmental Enforcement Network: The Australasian Environmental Law Enforcement and Regulators neTwork (AELERT)'. *Proceedings of the 9th International Conference on Environmental Compliance and Enforcement* (INECE 2011).

K. Michalak and A. Bularga, 'A New Independent States Environmental Compliance and Enforcement Network (NISECEN): An Effective Mechanism to Strengthen Environmental Compliance and Enforcement in Eastern Europe and Central Asia'. In *INECE 6th International Conference on Environmental Compliance and Enforcement, April 15–19, 2002, San Jose, Costa Rica, Proceedings, Volume 2* (INECE 2002).

Kal Raustiala, 'The Architecture of International Cooperation: Transgovernmental

Networks and the Future of International Law'. *Virginia Journal of International Law* (2002), 43.

Michael Nicholson, 'Networking in Europe: How Networking and Cooperation have Helped Respond to Environmental Compliance and Enforcement Challenges in IMPEL Member Countries'. *Proceedings of the 9th International Conference on Environmental Compliance and Enforcement* (INECE 2011).

Mohamed Rida Derder and Brahim Zyani, 'The Network for Environmental Compliance and Enforcement in Morocco (NECEMAR): An INECE Initiative Supported by a Strong Moroccan Political Will'. *Proceedings of the 9th International Conference on Environmental Compliance and Enforcement* (INECE 2011).

S.A. Herman and L.I. Sperling, 'Emerging Networks of Environmental Enforcement and Compliance Cooperation in North America and the Western Hemisphere'. In *INECE 4th International Conference on Environmental Compliance and Enforcement, April 22–26 1996, Chiang Mai, Thailand, Proceedings Volume 1* (INECE 1996).

Susan E. Bromm, 'North America's Commission for Environmental Cooperation: One Example of a Successful Regional Network'. In *Proceedings of the 9th International Conference on Environmental Compliance and Enforcement* (INECE 2011).

Terry Shears, 'European Union Network for the Implementation and Enforcement of Environmental Law (IMPEL)'. *Environmental Law Network International Review* (2005) 2, 8–9.

Thomas Freidman, *The World Is Flat: A Brief History of the Twenty-first Century* (Farrar Straus Giroux 2005).

Thomas Hale and David Held, *Handbook of Transnational Governance: Institutions and Innovations* (Polity Press 2011). See specifically D. Zaelke, K. Markowitz and M.R. Koparova, 'Improving Environmental Compliance and Enforcement through Transgovernmental Networks'.

United Nations Environment Programme, *GEO-5: Environment for the Future We Want* (2012). Available from http://www.unep.org/geo/geo5.asp

United Nations Office on Drugs and Crime, *The Globalization of Crime: A Transnational Organized Crime Threat Assessment* (United Nations publication, Sales No. E.10.IV.6). Available from www.unodc.org/documents/data-and-analysis/tocta/TOCTA_Report_2010_low_res.pdf

18. Environmental inspections and environmental compliance assurance networks in the context of European Union environment policy

Miroslav Angelov and Liam Cashman*

1. INTRODUCTION

Environmental inspections are not an end in themselves but an indispensable means of ensuring compliance with environmental rules. Two other activities serve the same aim: compliance promotion, which involves helping duty-holders to comply, and enforcement, which involves holding non-compliant duty-holders to account. Collectively, these three activities make up 'compliance assurance'.[1] In practice, they are often interconnected, forming a 'compliance assurance chain' that links the work of professionals such as inspectors, prosecutors and judges.

This paper looks at the evolving approach to environmental inspections within the European Union ('Union') as well as the role of networks of professionals ('compliance assurance networks') across the compliance assurance chain.

* Both authors are Officials in the Directorate-General Environment of the European Commission. However, the opinions contained in this chapter are those of the authors and do not represent the formal opinion of the European Commission.

[1] This terminology is frequently used in work by OECD and IMPEL. See for instance, OECD (2009), 'Ensuring Environmental Compliance: Trends and Good Practices'; Mazur, E. (2010), 'Outcome Performance Measures of Environmental Compliance Assurance: Current Practices, Constrains and Ways Forward', OECD Environment Working Papers, No. 18, OECD Publishing; IMPEL (2012), 'Exploring the Use and Effectiveness of Complementary Approaches to Inspection for Ensuring Compliance'; IMPEL (2012), 'Compliance Assurance through Compliance Management Systems'.

2. INSPECTIONS

2.1 Implementation Problems

Over the past decades, an extensive and detailed body of environment law has been developed at Union level. It is estimated that Union legislation is the basis for up to 80 per cent of national environment legislation. However, although Union environment law has led to significant improvements in the state of Europe's environment, its implementation and enforcement remain unsatisfactory.

Implementation and enforcement of Union environment law is primarily the responsibility of the Member States. The main pieces of Union environment legislation largely focus on public goods – clean air, clean water and a healthy biodiversity – that depend on human guardianship to protect them. To a very large extent, this guardianship must be exercised by the competent national authorities.

As indicated in the 7th Environment Action Programme ('the 7th EAP'),[2] despite some successes, the public goods concerned are not in the state they should be in (see box below). This entails costs for society. Based on recent studies, the 7th EAP puts the costs associated with failure to implement environment legislation at broadly EUR 50 billion a year.[3]

To general disappointing progress on air, water and biodiversity must be added a number of specific concerns. For example, Interpol issues regular press releases about the role of organised crime in the waste industry, pointing out that phenomena such as the illegal trade and disposal of electronic waste[4] are increasingly becoming a threat to global environmental health and security.[5] In parallel, and as pointed out in the 2014 Commission's 'Communication on the Union approach against wildlife trafficking' the world is currently facing a significant surge in

---

[2] Decision No 1386/2013/EU of the European Parliament and of the Council of 20 November 2013 on a General Union Environment Action Programme to 2020 'Living Well, Within the Limits of our Planet' – 7th EAP, OJ L 354/171, 28.12.2013 (hereinafter referred to as the '7th EAP').

[3] Ibid, Paragraph 56; COWI 2011, 'The costs of not implementing the environmental acquis'.

[4] Sometimes referred to as e-waste or WEEE (waste electrical and electronic equipment).

[5] For more information about Interpol initiatives on electronic waste see http://www.interpol.int/Crime-areas/Environmental-crime/Projects/Project-Eden and http://www.interpol.int/News-and-media/News/2013/N20131025

Salient points in the 7th EAP related to implementation of EU environment legislation

- The failure to fully implement existing policy is preventing the Union from achieving adequate air and water quality standards;[6]
- A substantial proportion of the Union's population remains exposed to levels of air pollution exceeding WHO recommended standards. Action is especially needed in areas such as in cities, where people, particularly sensitive or vulnerable groups of society, and ecosystems, are exposed to high levels of pollutants;[7]
- Access to water of satisfactory quality remains problematic in a number of rural areas in the Union;[8]
- The adverse consequences of floods and drought for human health and economic activity are being experienced more frequently, partly due to changes to the hydrological cycle and land use;[9]
- Despite the requirement in the Water Framework Directive[10] to protect, enhance and restore all bodies of surface and ground water, and considerable efforts to date, the objective of 'good ecological status' by 2015 is likely to be met only for 53 per cent of surface water bodies in the Union;[11] and
- Only 17 per cent of species and habitats assessed under the Habitats Directive[12] have favourable conservation status.[13]

[6] 7th EAP, Paragraph 47.
[7] Ibid, Paragraph 45.
[8] Ibid, Paragraph 45.
[9] Ibid, Paragraph 45.
[10] Directive 2000/60/EC of the European Parliament and of the Council establishing a framework for Community action in the field of water policy, OJ L 327, 22.12.2000, p. 1.
[11] 7th EAP, Paragraph 19.
[12] Council Directive 92/43/EEC of 21 May 1992 on the conservation of natural habitats and of wild fauna and flora, OJ L 206, 22.7.1992, p. 7.
[13] 7th EAP, Paragraph 6.

illegal cross-border trade in wild fauna and flora.[14] It has become one of the most profitable criminal activities globally. The last-mentioned Communication also points out how limited resources, the lack of specialised units in police and prosecution, and a varying degree of cooperation between wildlife and other enforcement agencies impede effective enforcement.

All of this calls into question how effectively national systems for environmental compliance assurance are working in practice. Several shortcomings can be identified at both Union and Member State levels in terms of legislation and practice.

2.2 Shortcomings at Union Level – A Very Patchy Coverage of Environmental Inspections

Unlike many other European Union policy areas, environment lacks a single comprehensive legal framework on inspections. Many environment instruments contain no inspection provisions and others only minimal ones. Recommendation 2001/331/EC providing for minimum criteria for environmental inspections in the Member States ('RMCEI')[15] has a narrow focus on industrial inspections and is, in any case, non-binding. Moreover, even within its current scope, RMCEI has been identified as in need of improvement in terms of the detail and precision of its content.[16] Only a few instruments contain detailed inspection provisions, the main ones being Directive 2010/75/EU on industrial emissions ('Industrial Emissions Directive')[17] and Directive 2012/18/EU on the control of major-accident hazards involving dangerous substances ('the Seveso III Directive').[18]

---

[14] Commission Communication on the EU Approach against Wildlife Trafficking, COM(2014) 64 final, p. 4.

[15] Recommendation of the European Parliament and of the Council of 4 April 2001 providing for minimum criteria for environmental inspections in the Member States (2001/331/EC), OJ L 118, 27.4.2001, p. 41.

[16] Communication from the Commission to the Council, the European Parliament, the European Economic and Social Committee and the Committee of the Regions on the review of Recommendation 2001/331/EC providing for minimum criteria for environmental inspections in the Member States, COM (2007) 707 final.

[17] Directive 2010/75/EU of the European Parliament and of the Council of 24 November 2010 on industrial emissions (integrated pollution prevention and control), OJ L 334, 17.12.2010, p. 17.

[18] Directive 2012/18/EU of the European Parliament and of the Council of 4 July 2012 on the control of major-accident hazards involving dangerous substances, amending and subsequently repealing Council Directive 96/82/EC, OJ L 197, 24.7.2012, p. 1.

Alongside this legislative patchwork, a voluntary network of national environmental authorities and inspectorates, the European Union Network for Implementation and Enforcement of Environmental Law ('IMPEL'), has developed or highlighted a range of additional good practices, including compliance promotion, use of risk criteria and peer reviews. However, Member States are not equally active in IMPEL and the network has tended to focus mostly on industrial inspections.[19]

Moreover, the Union environment *acquis* covers many matters other than industrial installations. The main legal instruments extend to the following subject areas: water, industrial emissions and major-accident hazards, air quality, waste, chemicals, nature and biodiversity, and environmental impact assessment and information management. These instruments give rise to rules that apply not only to industrial installations but to mobile activities – such as movements of waste and chemicals – and to a very broad range of duty-holders, including the ordinary citizen, SMEs,[20] local authorities, public utilities[21] and farmers.[22] Moreover, some rules relate to international obligations, such as those on wildlife trade, and others involve an interface with other Union policy areas, for example rules on wildlife trade are closely bound up with customs controls.

The typology of rules setting obligations for duty-holders is broad, comprising prohibitions,[23] general binding rules,[24] procedural requirements to be fulfilled before an activity can be undertaken,[25] binding requirements set by permit or similar authorisation,[26] and binding requirements fixed under a contract or agreement.

Furthermore, non-compliance with these rules involves a wide behavioural spectrum.[27] At one end are duty-holders who seek to excel

---

19 For more details about IMPEL see below section 3.3.2.

20 Who *inter alia* needs to respect rules on waste.

21 E.g. in relation to the supply of clean drinking water, the collection and treatment of waste-water or operation of safe waste facilities.

22 E.g. in relation to safe fertilizer use.

23 E.g. against using certain chemicals.

24 E.g. against winter spreading of fertilizers in certain farming areas.

25 E.g. environmental impact assessment requirements.

26 E.g. to operate a waste facility under certain conditions.

27 This draws from a model used by the Scottish Environmental Protection Agency (SEPA) described in its report 'Tackling Environmental Crime. SEPA Enforcement Report 2012–2013', p. 7, available at: http://www.sepa.org.uk/about_us/publications/enforcement_reports.aspx. Recent academic research also stresses the importance of different motivations for compliance or non-compliance and suggests categorisation according to duty-holders' attitudes. See Gunningham, N. (2011), 'Enforcing Environmental Regulation', *Journal of Environmental Law* 23(2), pp. 195–196.

('champions') and comply ('compliant'). At the other are criminals who wilfully break the law. In between are those who may opportunistically offend ('chancers') or are careless or confused about what compliant behaviour entails ('careless', 'confused'). However, this is not fully reflected in the current Union environment legislation and compliance assurance practice on the ground.[28]

Apart from being largely focused on industrial inspections, current environmental inspection provisions fail to take account of the full compliance assurance chain. In addition, they don't cover coordination of inspection activities across different environmental subject areas. Some implementation problems are cross-cutting – for example, illegal land-filling within protected nature sites involves both waste and nature conservation legislation. Without provisions on coordination, inspections may not be guaranteed to cover all relevant problems in the most effective way. The need for robust arrangements for trans-boundary cooperation between Member States, something important in relation to problems such as illegal trade in wildlife and shipments of waste, is also not addressed by the existing Union provisions.

Finally, in contrast to many other policy areas, such as food safety, fisheries, maritime and aviation safety, the existing environmental patchwork lacks provisions on a capacity at Union level to ensure that national inspection systems are broadly consistent, coherent and effective in order to guarantee a uniform application of Union environment law and a level playing field for businesses.

2.3 The Picture at Member State Level

Allowing for wide differences in Member States' systems for ensuring compliance with environment legislation, common patterns of weakness in their functioning are apparent.

Responsibilities for ensuring environmental compliance are spread across a vast array of authorities. Taking the Union as a whole, responsibility for inspections involves all of the following: environmental ministries; centralised multi-purpose environmental protection agencies; specialist environmental agencies, for example for drinking water and

---

[28] The need and added value of targeted responses to different types of non-compliant behaviour has been identified also through work of IMPEL. See for details IMPEL 2008, 'Doing the Right Things II: Step-by-Step Guidance Book for Planning of Environmental Inspections', p. 48; IMPEL 2012, 'Exploring the Use and Effectiveness of Complementary Approaches to Inspection for Ensuring Compliance', pp. 19 and 31.

nature protection; non-environmental ministries; general-purpose law enforcement authorities such as police and customs; specialist environmental prosecutors; and both regional and local authorities.

Empirical research has identified large disparities in Member State administrative structures as well as in how inspections are organised and undertaken across the Union.[29] Responsibilities have often been allocated in an ad hoc manner as different directives required transposition, with no overall design – or limited design – of how best to allocate and deploy limited resources. This is exacerbated by problems of operational capacity, especially where responsibilities are allocated to smaller bodies with inadequate financial resources, few staff or an absence of specialist knowledge.[30] In addition, during the last decade, budgets for inspectorates have in many Member States stagnated or declined, in the face of the financial crisis.[31]

Furthermore, evidence points to insufficient arrangments for coordinating the work of different authorities to make sure that there is optimal division of responsibilities and sharing of best practice and experience.[32] This undermines the effectiveness and efficiency of environmental inspections.

Although there are examples of good practices of strategic and operational identification and planning for the risks of non-compliance,[33] measures for upholding environmental obligations are typically passive

---

[29] See BioIntelligence Service 2011, 'Implementation of EU waste legislation for green growth', pp. 21f.; Milieu 2013, 'Comparative Study of Pressures and Measures in the Major River Basin Management Plans, Task 1c Enforcement Systems', p. 21 and Annex III 'Quantitative information on enforcement activities'; BiPRO/Arcadis 2012, 'Guidance on permitting and inspection of waste management operations', pp. 72f.; Crook, V./TRAFFIC, 2012, *Analysis of EU Member States' CITES Biennial Reports 2009–2010*, p. 18, http://ec.europa.eu/environment/cites/pdf/analysis_2009–2010.pdf

[30] See for details COM(2007) 707 final; BioIntelligence Service 2011, op. cit., p. 22.

[31] COWI/Ecorys 2011, 'Study into Possible Options for Revising Recommendation 2001/331/EC providing for minimum criteria for environmental inspections', pp. 40–45 and 60, http://ec.europa.eu/environment/legal/law/inspections.htm

[32] BioIntelligence Service 2012, 'Stocktaking of the main problems and review of national enforcement mechanisms for tackling illegal killing, trapping and trade of birds in the EU', pp. 65, 73, 93, http://ec.europa.eu/environment/pubs/pdf/BIO_BirdsIllegalKilling.pdf; COM Staff Working Document to Report on REACH Implementation, SWD(2013)25, p. 97.

[33] See for instance about the risk-based inspection programme of the Scottish Environmental Agency and its Dynamic Regulatory Effort Model 'Tackling Environmental Crime. SEPA Enforcement Report 2012–2013', p. 13, and about the UK Environmental Agency's scheme for Operational Risk Appraisal (Opra)

and rarely accompanied by strategic exercises to identify the most serious risks of non-compliance and the optimal ways of mitigating them.

There are often no clear mechanisms within Member States governing how claims of suspected non-compliance from the public should be addressed. Citizens may not know to whom submissions should be made or may fear that their identity will be disclosed to the suspected offender. All this contributes to the lack of confidence in inspection systems.

Public confidence is also undermined by weaknesses in enforcement. Even where inspections detect criminal non-compliance, there is often a very low probability of prosecution.[34] This leads to serious concerns on the part of legitimate businesses about a level playing field.[35]

A common problem referred to in academic literature and other sources is the lack of systematic data collection on inspections and related compliance assurance.[36] This in turn is a contributory factor to another problem, namely the lack of systematic evaluation of the performance of inspection systems and of individual authorities with a view to streamlining and enhancing the effectiveness of their work.

These shortcomings undermine the effectiveness of Union environment law, leave environmental matters lagging behind other Union policies, contribute to implementation failures, reduce resource efficiency and help explain why high numbers of environmental complaints and petitions – 604 complaints in 2011 and 588 in 2012, for instance – call for centralised

---

at: http://www.environment-agency.gov.uk/business/regulation/31827.aspx. See also BiPRO/Arcadis 2012, op. cit., pp. 72f.

[34] See for details and examples, Faure, M. (2010), 'Effective, Proportionate and Dissuasive Penalties in the Implementation of the Environmental Crime and Ship-source Pollution Directives: Questions and Challenges', *European Energy and Environmental Law Review* December, pp. 256–278 (261f.); Faure, M. and Svatikova, K. (2010), 'Enforcement of Environmental Law in the Flemish Region', *European Energy and Environmental Law Review*, 19(2), pp. 60–79.

[35] For instance, a 2014 report by the Environmental Services Association Education Trust (ESAET) highlighted how illegal waste management activities undercut legitimate waste businesses and stressed the need for stronger compliance monitoring and enforcement. See Eunomia Research and Consulting, 'Waste Crime: Tackling Britain's Dirty Secret' (A report commissioned by the Environmental Services Association Education Trust, ESAET), 2014, pp. 24 and 38.

[36] Faure, M. and Svatikova, K. (2012), 'Criminal or Administrative Law to Protect the Environment? Evidence from Western Europe', *Journal of Environmental Law* May, pp. 268 and 274. OECD research also stressed the inadequacy of available enforcement data in many countries to allow assessment of efficiency and effectiveness of enforcement actions, see OECD (2009), 'Ensuring Environmental Compliance: Trends and Good Practices', pp. 42–43.

Commission intervention based on Article 258 of the Treaty on the Functioning of the European Union ('TFEU').[37]

2.4 The Evolving Union Debate on Environmental Inspections

In 2001, recognising the importance of environmental inspections as well as the wide disparity between inspection systems and practices in the Member States, the European Parliament and the Council adopted Recommendation 2001/331/EC providing for minimum criteria for environmental inspections in the Member States ('RMCEI'). Before the adoption of RMCEI there was a lengthy debate between the European Parliament, which wanted a binding directive on inspections, and the Council, which favoured a non-binding recommendation. RMCEI represents a compromise between the positions of the European Parliament and the Council. More specifically, the Commission was asked to review RMCEI on the basis of experience with its implementation and, if necessary, to draft a proposal for a directive.

In 2007, the Commission published a Communication on the review of RMCEI[38] which recognised serious gaps in its implementation. While the Council did not react, the European Parliament, in its 2008 Resolution on the review, stressed that the incomplete and uneven implementation of environment legislation could lead to continuing damage to the environment and to distortions of competition. It supported the transformation of RMCEI into a directive, considered it essential to strengthen IMPEL, and urged the Commission to report on the possibility of establishing a Union-level environmental inspection force.[39] The European Economic and Social Committee recommended improvement of the provisions concerning the planning and carrying out of inspections.[40]

This initial debate on the RMCEI implementation showed that, although non-binding, RMCEI has been influential. Its principal focus is in the area of industrial inspections, and it has helped to build confidence in Union initiatives in this area. Against this background, there have been

---

[37] For more statistics see the European Commission, '29th Annual report on monitoring the application of EU law', p. 55, available at: http://ec.europa.eu/eu_law/docs/docs_infringements/annual_report_30/sg_annual_report_monitoring_eu_law_131023.pdf

[38] COM(2007) 707 final.

[39] European Parliament Resolution of 20 November 2008 on the review of Recommendation 2001/331/EC providing for minimum criteria for environmental inspections in the Member States (2010/C 16 E/15).

[40] European Economic and Social Committee, NAT/383 – CESE 762/2008.

important legislative developments. Binding inspection provisions have been adopted within thematic environment legislation based on RMCEI principles, notably the Industrial Emissions Directive[41] and the Seveso III Directive.[42] However, given that RMCEI focuses mainly on industrial inspections, the adoption of these detailed provisions made it to a certain extent obsolete.

Notwithstanding this legislative progress, there were calls for additional initiatives to strengthen Union environmental inspections. In its 2012 Resolution on 'Our life insurance, our natural capital: an EU biodiversity strategy to 2020', the European Parliament called on the Commission to enhance the implementation of the Birds and Habitats Directives,[43] by strengthening the compliance control mechanisms, including inspections.[44] The Council Conclusions of 11 June 2012 also called for improving inspections regimes on the basis of experience with existing provisions and avoiding unnecessary administrative burdens.[45] The 2012 Commission Communication on 'Improving the Delivery of Benefits from EU Environment Measures: Building Confidence through Better Knowledge and Responsiveness' again raised the subject.[46]

The stakeholder consultation[47] on the proposal for the 7th EAP[48] confirmed support for strengthening inspections.[49] Another subject-specific

---

41 Industrial Emissions Directive 2010/75/EU, Article 23.

42 Seveso III Directive 2012/18/EU, Article 20.

43 Directive 2009/147/EC of the European Parliament and of the Council of 30 November 2009 on the conservation of wild birds, OJ L 20, 26.1.2010, p.7 and Council Directive 92/43/EEC of 21 May 1992 on the conservation of natural habitats and of wild fauna and flora, OJ L 206, 22.7.1992, p. 7.

44 2011/2307 (INI) http://www.europarl.europa.eu/sides/getDoc.do?type=TA&language=EN&reference=P7-TA-2012–146

45 http://www.consilium.europa.eu/uedocs/cms_data/docs/pressdata/en/envir/130788.pdf

46 COM(2012) 95.

47 http://ec.europa.eu/environment/newprg/results.htm

48 COM(2012) 710 final.

49 The Committee of the Regions stressed in its Opinion to the Commission proposal for the 7th EAP that an EU-wide framework for national inspections can reduce unfair competition between EU regions and municipalities due to different or lacking inspection regimes, ensure a level playing field in legal action, and improve trans-frontier cooperation and consistency across the EU. The form and content of inspections should be regulated nationally and developed at local and regional level but on the basis of general principles set by the EU framework, including a streamlined and risk-based, approach. It also stresses the value of a well-defined inspection related role of the Commission. See Opinion of the Committee of the Regions 'Towards a 7th Environment Action Programme: better implementation of EU environ-

online stakeholder consultation took place in the first half of 2013. Its outcome showed that a large majority of stakeholders supported an inspections initiative and agreed with the concepts presented in the consultation document.[50]

Finally, the adopted 7th EAP confirms that enforcing Union environment law and guaranteeing a level playing field in the internal market requires:

> . . . Extending binding criteria for effective Member State inspections and surveillance to the wider body of Union environment law, and further developing inspection support capacity at EU level, drawing on existing structures, backed up by support for networks of professionals, such as IMPEL, and by the reinforcement of peer reviews and best practice sharing, with a view to increasing the efficiency and effectiveness of inspections.[51]

2.5 Follow-up to the 7th EAP: Addressing the Challenges

At the time of writing in 2014, the Commission had not yet tabled any proposal by way of follow-up to the 7th EAP. There is, therefore, no proposal to describe and analyse. With this caveat, the following points seem relevant, taking into account the concepts and approaches supported by the results of the stakeholder consultation carried out in 2013 and the good practices identified across Member States and in the relevant literature.

Academic research and work by the OECD indicate that inspections are likely to be most effective when addressed within a framework that includes other compliance assurance activities, that is, compliance promotion and enforcement.[52] This is because a broad approach better responds to the behavioural spectrum mentioned above.[53] For example, compliance

---

ment law', paragraphs 30–32 (OJ C 17/07, 19.1.2013, pp. 30–36), available at: http://eur-lex.europa.eu/LexUriServ/LexUriServ.do?uri=OJ:C:2013:017:0030:0036:EN:PDF

[50] http://ec.europa.eu/environment/legal/law/pdf/Summary%20Results%20Public%20consultation.pdf

[51] 7th EAP, Paragraph 65.

[52] OECD (2009), op. cit., p. 24; IEEP/Bio Intelligence Service/Ecologic Institute (2013), 'Study on information collection and impact assessment of possible requirements for environmental inspections in the area of EU legislation on water, nature protection and trade in certain environmentally sensitive goods', Final report for the European Commission, DG Environment. Institute for European Environmental Policy, Brussels and London, July, pp. 84 and 93–94.

[53] The Dutch 'Table of Eleven' (see for details: Van Der Schraaf, Angelique A.A. (2005), 'The Compliance Strategy in the Netherlands', in INECE (2005), *Proceedings of the Seventh International Conference on Environmental Compliance*

promotion may be an effective way of improving compliance amongst SMEs that fall into the 'confused' category (because, for instance, they may have limited knowledge and awareness of the rules concerned and how to comply with them). Even viewed from a narrow inspections perspective, therefore, compliance promotion can reduce the compliance gaps and risks that require inspections. And enforcement ensures that inspections bring about useful results so that, for example, detected serious non-compliance is not left empty of consequences.

As for inspections themselves, their main purpose is to verify compliance, detect non-compliance and ensure the evidence basis for appropriate enforcement as well as compliance promotion measures, and thus to enable a proportionate response to different types of non-compliant behaviour. If inspections are to serve the broader environment *acquis*, they need to be suitable for more subject areas than industrial installations. For example, non-compliance can involve clandestine, criminal or unreported activities and highly mobile phenomena such as trafficking in environmentally sensitive goods, for example waste and wildlife. This helps to explain why the 7th EAP refers to 'surveillance' as well as 'inspections'. Inspections typically relate to potential 'unknown *knowns*', that is, unknown non-compliance involving known activities, for example an unknown illegal water discharge from a known and permitted manufacturing activity. In contrast, surveillance encompasses 'unknown *unknowns*', that is, unknown non-compliance involving unknown activities, for example illegal waste disposal by an unknown and unpermitted waste business. A third term, 'investigation' is also useful since non-compliance detected through an inspection or surveillance can present an incomplete picture as regards causation and responsibility. For example, an illegal landfill may be discovered without it being immediately clear who the operator is. A separate umbrella term such as 'compliance monitoring' seems to be appropriate to cover all of these inter-related activities but, for convenience, 'inspections' is treated as the collective short-hand in this chapter. Within such a broad notion of 'inspections' there is clearly room for a wide array of inspection techniques and methodologies.

The diversity of the environment *acquis*, existing Member State administrative arrangements and problems on the ground suggest a need for flexibility in any proposal, with the administrative autonomy of Member

and Enforcement, Marrakech, Morocco, Volume 1, pp. 89f.) is an interesting example of a tool aiming at consideration of multiple behavioural factors to ensure better compliance both through competent authorities' intervention and 'self-enforcement'.

States being respected. At the same time, concerns about a level playing field plead in favour of certain common criteria. One general approach that has emerged amongst several inspectorates is that of risk-based inspections. Risk assessment is a tool that can be used at both strategic and operational levels to target compliance assurance activities. At strategic level, it offers a means of estimating the extent to which non-compliance is likely to occur and its impact, allowing broad priorities to be established. At a more operational level, it offers a means of targeting inspections in the most efficient manner.[54]

At the operational level, too, the dual approach to inspections found in RMCEI still seems relevant. The dual approach envisages both 'routine' and 'non-routine' inspections, the former being organised by means of inspection plans or programmes and the latter being a response to complaints, incidents or other unforeseen circumstances.

This in turn raises a series of governance issues. To what extent should the public be involved? What types of records should be kept of inspection work and related compliance assurance? Should the performance of inspection bodies be evaluated and, if so, on what basis? Should the transparency of inspection and other compliance assurance work be guaranteed and, if so, to what extent?

RMCEI envisaged inspections being carried out in response to complaints. Experience shows that, apart from being a potentially useful source of information, complaints – and how authorities respond to them – are a key indicator of public concerns and public confidence. It is also interesting to note the innovative ways in which the public can now be involved in monitoring activities, for example by means of the citizen observatories supported under the Union research programme, Horizon 2020.[55]

Evaluation – and the capacity of inspection and compliance assurance systems to learn from experience – depends on an ability to examine empirically how compliance assurance works in practice. No less than business, the authorities charged with compliance assurance need to have the right data – that is, records – and the ability to 'mine' them efficiently

---

[54] The Hampton report stresses that 'the use of risk assessment should be embedded throughout the regulatory system, and should inform all aspects of regulators' work such as mandatory data requirements, penalties as well as inspections'. See Hampton, P., 'Reducing administrative burdens: Effective Inspection and Enforcement', UK 2005, HM Treasury, p. 27, available at http://webarchive.nationalarchives.gov.uk/20121212135622/http://www.bis.gov.uk/files/file22988.pdf

[55] See http://ec.europa.eu/avservices/video/player.cfm?ref=I085671

and effectively. At the same time, they need to minimise administrative burdens. Greater use of systems of electronic, geo-referenced records that benefit from the informatics infrastructure created by the INSPIRE Directive,[56] appears to be indispensable for making compliance assurance work more effective and efficient. This will allow the authorities to efficiently correlate, say, state-of-the-environment pollution 'hot spots' with the results of inspections and enforcement and check non-compliance patterns over time.

Transparency can be ensured through publication of compliance assurance and enforcement policies and their outputs and outcomes. The positive role that this can play in building confidence in environmental inspections and compliance assurance is recognised in the academic literature[57] and evident from already established good practices.[58]

Finally, the 7th EAP text mainly focuses on Member State inspections but does allow for a range of actitivites at Union level, including support for networks of professionals. This is something addressed in more detail in the next section.

3. COMPLIANCE ASSURANCE NETWORKS

3.1 Emergence of Environmental Compliance Assurance Networks, their Benefits and the Challenges Presented by their Governance

Recognising the added value of environmental compliance assurance networks, the 7th EAP states:

---

[56] Directive 2007/2/EC of the European Parliament and of the Council of 14 March 2007 establishing an Infrastructure for Spatial Information in the European Community (INSPIRE), OJ L 108, 25.4.2007, p. 1.

[57] For the added value of published enforcement policies see Macrory, R., 'Rethinking Environmental Sanctions', in *The International Comparative Legal Guide to: Environment & Climate Change Law 2011* (published by Global Legal group, in association with Freshfields Bruckhaus Derringer LLP), p. 10; Hampton, Ph., op. cit., p. 57.

[58] For instance, the Flemish High Council of Environmental Enforcement (VHRM) and the Scottish Environmental Protection Agency (SEPA) publish annual environmental enforcement programmes and enforcement reports which are publicly available. See for VHRM at: http://www.vhrm.be/ and for SEPA at: http://www.sepa.org.uk/about_us/publications/enforcement_reports.aspx. The Office of the Spanish Environmental Prosecutor, Fiscalía Coordinadora de Medio Ambiente y Urbanismo, publishes annual reports on its activities, setting out the key issues investigated during the year as well as providing statistics.

> The general standard of environmental governance throughout the Union will be further improved by enhancing cooperation at Union level, as well as at international level, between professionals working on environmental protection, including government lawyers, prosecutors, ombudsmen, judges and inspectors, such as the European Union Network for the Implementation and Enforcement of Environmental Law (IMPEL), and encouraging such professionals to share good practices.[59]

This reflects the evolution of environmental enforcement networks over the last two decades both at national and Union level. With the previously mentioned IMPEL,[60] the EU Forum of Judges for the Environment ('EUFJE'),[61] as well as the more recent European Network of Prosecutors for the Environment ('ENPE')[62] and the EnviCrimeNet[63] as a network mainly consisting of national police officers specialised in combating environmental crime, it seems that the whole environmental compliance assurance chain is covered by relevant Union-level networks.[64] These supra-national networks[65] all reflect an interest on the part of compliance assurance professionals in sharing experience and learning from each other on how best to implement Union environment legislation and apply Union environment law.

The increasing need for cooperation and coordination[66] between different authorities responsible for environmental compliance assurance at national level and the need for specialist knowledge to understand the reasons for non-compliance as well as to find the appropriate mix of measures to address it have also catalysed the emergence of different types of national environmental networks.[67]

---

[59] 7th EAP, Paragraph 63.

[60] http://impel.eu/

[61] http://www.eufje.org/

[62] http://www.basel.int/Default.aspx?tabid=2940

[63] http://envicrimenet.com/

[64] Environmental compliance assurance networks exist also at neighbourhood, e.g. the Environment and Climate Regional Accession Network (ECRAN) – http://www.ecranetwork.org/ and global level, e.g. the International Network for Environmental Compliance and Enforcement (INECE) – http://inece.org/

[65] It should be noted that these networks are largely but not exclusively made up of Member States. Several neighbouring European countries are also involved.

[66] 'Cooperation' could be understood as the arrangements whereby different competent authorities learn from and support each other, and includes but is not limited to the use of networks made up of representatives of different competent authorities. 'Coordination' means the arrangements whereby different competent authorities support each other to avoid unnecessary duplication of work across the compliance assurance chain and ensure overall compliance assurance.

[67] For more details see section 3.2.

As is evident from their declared objectives, networks can, *inter alia*, serve as platforms for sharing specialist knowledge and good practices; for data collection on compliance assurance at different levels; and for undertaking joint inspections and related activities. The following factors underscore their usefulness: the variability of competent authorities and duty-holders; the variability of environmental acts and the discretion of competent authorities in implementing them; the interaction between compliance promotion, inspections and enforcement; and the existence of transboundary problems. By helping to streamline the work of competent authorities, environmental networking at different levels can provide efficiency gains and economic benefits.

The potential and advantages of network cooperation on environmental compliance assurance have been recognised both by the general academic literature[68] and in the work of international organisations. An OECD study, for instance, highlights and analyses important functions of environmental professional networks, such as promoting exchange of information and experiences on environmental compliance assurance, raising professional standards, facilitating training, and channelling participation by national agencies in international environmental compliance and enforcement networks.[69] In relation to combating environmental crime, the Interpol Environmental Crime Program recommends that member countries establish National Environmental Security Task Forces (NESTs), formed from police, customs, environmental agencies, other specialised agencies, prosecutors, non-governmental organisations and intergovernmental partners, and aimed at ensuring a multi-disciplinary approach to cooperation and coordination between relevant authorities,

---

[68] Pink, G., 'Assessing the Utility of Environmental Enforcement Networks: Maximising Benefits to Members', in INECE (2011), *9th International Conference on Environmental Compliance and Enforcement, Conference Proceedings*, pp. 797–804. Some authors argue that the evolution of trans-European administrative networks is a consequence of the continuing marginalisation of purely direct and indirect implementation of EU legislation and the increasing importance of joint action by national, supranational and mixed authorities. See for instance, Chiti, E. (2012), 'The Governance of Compliance', in Cremona, M. (ed.), *Compliance and Enforcement of EU Law*, Oxford University Press, pp. 31–56 (pp. 36f.).

[69] Mazur, E. (2011), 'Environmental Enforcement in Decentralised Governance Systems: Toward a Nationwide Level Playing Field', OECD Environment Working Papers, No. 34, OECD Publishing, p. 32. The study also stresses that networks can serve for benchmarking among different authorities, which in turn is seen as a 'tool that might allow national authorities, the regulated community and the public to know whether there is equality in regulatory and compliance assurance activity', p. 37.

synergies of different professional expertise and collecting information by using intelligence-led approaches to effectively tackle transnational environmental crime.[70]

However, network governance presents challenges. Typical weaknesses of network governance have been extensively analysed in the literature. They include: lower efficiency compared to markets and hierarchical approaches; lack of equity and democratic legitimacy, with members possessing greater links and expertise having an advantageous position compared to other members; a frequent absence of clear structures; and reliable mechanisms for communication and coordination.[71] A recent study has suggested that, to be effective, networks need strong ongoing secretariat capacity, commitment and leadership and representative membership.[72]

3.2 National Environmental Compliance Assurance Networks

In practice, there is a rich variety of national environmental networks. These can be classified according to different criteria:

- *Horizontal/vertical*: Depending on whether the cooperating authorities are at the same or at different administrative level(s), the network can be described as horizontal or vertical.[73] This division can also be applied according to how many links in the compliance assurance chain are covered: thus, an inspector-only or a prosecutor-only network would be horizontal, whereas a network involving both inspectors and prosecutors would be vertical;
- *Ad hoc or thematic/general purpose*;
- *Purely environmental/mixed*; and
- *Formal/informal* depending on whether they have recognised legal status.

[70] A recommended model of NEST formation and structure has been outlined in a National Environmental Security Task Force Manual. See for more details: http://www.interpol.int/Crime-areas/Environmental-crime/Task-forces

[71] See for a more detailed analysis, Meuleman, L. (2011), 'Metagoverning Governance Styles: Broadening the Public Manager's Action Perspective', in Torfing, J. and Triantafillou, P. (eds), *Interactive Policymaking, Metagovernance and Democracy*, ECPR, pp. 95–110 (in particular pp. 97–100).

[72] Pink, G. (2011), op. cit., p. 798.

[73] For more details on horizontal networks, including examples from individual OECD countries, see Mazur, E. (2011), op. cit., pp. 32f.

However, the value of such classifications is largely theoretical. In practice, the functions which the different networks fulfil in their respective national contexts are of greater importance.

The following are some examples of national networks:

- The Network for Ireland's Environmental Compliance and Enforcement ('NIECE') coordinated by the Office of Environmental Enforcement and aimed at harnessing resources and expertise and at ensuring a more consistent approach to the implementation and enforcement of environment legislation;[74]
- The shared service centres of the Dutch municipalities and the horizontal inter-agency cooperation in the Netherlands coordinated by a National Environmental Enforcement Cooperation Secretariat;[75]
- The joint environmental enforcement agencies of municipalities in Sweden;[76]
- The Network of Environmental Inspection (Red de Inspección Ambiental) – REDIA – created in 2008 by the Spanish Autonomous Communities as an instrument for cooperation and exchange of experience between the regional authorities responsible for environmental inspections, with the participation of the national environment ministry;[77]
- The Partnership for Action Against Wildlife Crime (PAW) established in the UK to bring together representatives of all organisations involved in wildlife law enforcement, including nature conservation agencies, police, customs but also non-governmental bodies;[78] and
- The national office located within the Gendarmerie in France, established to coordinate enforcement on environmental and public

[74] Information about the NIECE members and the network's functions is available at: http://www.epa.ie/enforcement/pa/network/

[75] For details see OECD (2009), 'Ensuring Environmental Compliance: Trends and Good Practices', p. 32.

[76] Mazur, E. (2011), op. cit., p. 15.

[77] The main objectives of REDIA are to: promote the exchange of information between the environmental authorities of the Autonomous Communities on environmental inspection; produce guidance documents based on best practices to ensure consistency of coherence of inspection work across the country; channel participation in the work of IMPEL. For more details see COWI/Ecorys (2011), op. cit., pp. 199–200; IEEP/Bio Intelligence Service/Ecologic Institute (2013), op. cit., p. 241.

[78] IEEP/Bio Intelligence Service/Ecologic Institute (2013), op. cit., pp. 374f.

health crime across enforcement agencies, including Customs and the National Hunting and Wildlife Agency.[79]

3.3 Union-level Environmental Compliance Assurance Networks

At Union level, two main categories can be identified. The first covers the general networks of environmental professionals already mentioned.[80] The second consists of specific networks created to support the implementation of individual pieces of EU environment legislation. Examples of the second category are the CITES Enforcement Group established by the CITES Regulation[81] and the Forum for Exchange of Information on Enforcement ('ECHA Forum'[82]) established by the REACH Regulation as a body of the European Chemicals Agency (ECHA).[83] This section focuses on the first category, and in particular on IMPEL as the most developed Union compliance assurance network.

3.3.1 Network coverage of the compliance assurance chain

The past decade has been marked by coverage of the main links in the compliance assurance chain by Union compliance assurance networks. This is a notable development.

The EUFJE was founded in 2004 as an international non-profit association under Belgian law. Its main objective is to contribute to a better

---

[79] Milieu (2006), 'Study on the Enforcement of the EU Wildlife Trade Regulations in the EU-25', Final Report: Overview Paper, p. 12.

[80] Notably those involving environmental inspection authorities (IMPEL), high level managers of national environmental protection agencies (EPA Network), prosecutors (ENPE), police (EnviCrimeNet) and judges (EUFJE).

[81] See Article 14/3 Council Regulation (EC) No 338/97 of 9 December 1996 on the protection of species of wild fauna and flora by regulating trade therein (OJ L 61, 3.3.1997, p. 1).

[82] http://echa.europa.eu/web/guest/about-us/who-we-are/enforcement-forum

[83] The ECHA Forum shall coordinate a network of Member States authorities responsible for enforcement of the REACH Regulation by implementing different tasks, such as spreading good practice and highlighting problems at Union level; proposing, coordinating and evaluating harmonised enforcement projects and joint inspections; developing working methods and tools of use to local inspectors. See Articles 76 and 77 of Regulation (EC) No 1907/2006 of the European Parliament and of the Council of 18 December 2006 concerning the Registration, Evaluation, Authorisation and Restriction of Chemicals (REACH), establishing a European Chemicals Agency, amending Directive 1999/45/EC and repealing Council Regulation (EEC) No 793/93 and Commission Regulation (EC) No 1488/94 as well as Council Directive 76/769/EEC and Commission Directives 91/155/EEC, 93/67/EEC, 93/105/EC and 2000/21/EC.

implementation and enforcement of international, European and national environmental law by sharing experience on judicial training, fostering knowledge of environmental law among judges and ensuring exchange of information and views on environmental case law.[84]

In the context of the crucial role of national judges in applying Union environmental law, trends towards specialisation and the need for knowledge of CJEU case-law, the EUFJE has provided an invaluable platform for exchanges amongst judges dealing with environmental cases. It has also provided the Union institutions with insights into judicial thinking and has promoted an understanding of Union environmental law beyond the Union's boundaries. One of the main activities of the network is the holding of an annual conference, typically devoted to specific subject areas of Union environmental policy or horizontal topics such as access to justice on environmental matters. The methodology used for organising this has included preparation of a questionnaire, country reports and a summary document which analyses the responses to the questionnaire. Documentation is distributed in advance, ensuring that the conference brings high-quality results.[85]

Close cooperation has been established between EUFJE and the Commission. For instance, EUFJE representatives have actively contributed to the establishment and development of the Commission's 'Programme for Cooperation with National Judges and Prosecutors in the Field of EU Environment Law', in particular as members of the Committee steering the programme and as speakers at workshops organised within its framework.[86] In turn, Commission officials regularly participate in the EUFJE annual conference, providing information on identified implementation problems and on ongoing legislative initiatives.

The EUFJE actively cooperates with other networks and has provided an impetus for the creation of ENPE.

ENPE was established in 2012, based on the model of the EUFJE.

---

[84] See Article 3 EUFJE by-laws, available at: http://www.eufje.org/EN/presentation/bylaws?PHPSESSID=p7a1uer2dbccn0embp34r0vov3

[85] More detailed information on the topics, participants and outcomes of the EUFJE annual conferences is available at: http://www.eufje.org/EN/conferences.

[86] In 2008, the Commission launched a special programme for cooperation with national judges and prosecutors in the field of EU environment law. It includes the development of various training modules and organisation of a series of workshops aiming at raising awareness of EU environment law and policy, assisting the national judges in applying them in practice, and providing a forum for exchange of knowledge and experience, in particular on environment case law. For more detailed information see: http://ec.europa.eu/environment/legal/law/judges.htm.

Members of ENPE can be national prosecution authorities, and, in exceptional situations, also individuals. According to its statute, the main purpose of ENPE is to promote the enforcement of environmental criminal law by supporting the operative work of prosecutors. ENPE seeks in particular to: facilitate the exchange of information and experience of the enforcement and prosecution of environmental crime between members; facilitate collection of data about environmental crime and enforcement action taken in relation to environmental crime across the Union; identify and develop good practice for successful prosecutions and produce guidance, tools, common standards and approaches to the prosecution of environmental offences; and share training programmes in relation to environmental criminal law.[87]

Although it is a very recent network, ENPE has quickly become operational and has undertaken several activities, including establishing cooperative relations with the Commission and other environmental enforcement networks, such as INECE and IMPEL[88] and the South-American environmental prosecutors network established in 2008. In cooperation with Eurojust, ENPE co-organised a strategic meeting in November 2013 in The Hague on ways of enhancing coordination of environmental crime prosecutions across the Union.[89] ENPE representatives have already participated in many expert events organised by the Commission and have contributed to the Commission's 'Programme for Cooperation with National Judges and Prosecutors in the Field of EU Environment Law', in particular to the development of its training module on environmental crime.

The EnviCrimeNet was established in 2011 upon the adoption of a respective Council Resolution calling for the creation of an informal network for countering environmental crime.[90] EnviCrimeNet is intended to be an informal network mainly of police authorities dealing with environmental crime but is open to representatives of other professional groups involved in enforcement of environmental law. The network aims

---

87 Article 3 ENPE Statute (available at: http://www.environmentalprosecutors.eu/statutes.html).

88 According to information provided by the ENPE Presidency, ENPE has an agreement with IMPEL to benefit from its secretarial support until ENPE's own secretariat is set up and regular funding for the network's activities is ensured.

89 A report on the outcomes of this conference is available at: http://www.eurojust.europa.eu/press/News/News/Pages/2013/Eurojust-and-ENPE-host-environmental-crime-meeting-.aspx

90 Council Resolution 10291/11 ENFOPOL 152 ENV 368; see Press Release of the 3096th Council Meeting, Justice and Home Affairs 11008/11, Luxembourg, 9 and 10 June 2011.

at: ensuring that Member States become aware of the fight against environmental crime at the strategic level; identifying trends in criminal activities and establishing tactical analyses of particular forms of environmental crime; exchanging good practices on risk assessments and intervention strategies; and improving the exchange of non-operational information and the gathering of criminal intelligence. Europol provides secretarial services to the network and manages its website.

3.3.2 Example of IMPEL

As one of the oldest and most influential networks and because of its particular role in preparing the way for RMCEI as well as in the development of guidance and exchange of good practices on inspections, IMPEL deserves a special mention.

Currently, its membership is drawn from all Member States and is made up of environmental authorities and environmental inspectorates at central or regional level. It also embraces candidate and potential candidate countries as well as EFTA countries.

IMPEL was set up in 1992 as an informal network of Member State regulatory and inspection authorities concerned with the implementation and enforcement of environment law. In its development, it has gone through different stages and since 2008 has the legal status of an association under Belgian law.[91] According to its statute, the core objective of IMPEL is to contribute to effective implementation and enforcement of Union environmental law, mainly through the exchange of information, sharing of best practice and awareness raising.[92] IMPEL has the following structural elements: a general assembly, board, clusters/expert teams and secretariat.[93] The funding sources consist of LIFE+ funding (maximum 70 per cent of the overall network's budget), membership fees and the voluntary contributions of members.[94]

---

[91] For more details about the history of IMPEL see Hedemann-Robinson, M. (2006), *Enforcement of European Union Environmental Law: Legal Issues and Challenges*, Routledge-Cavendish, pp. 459f.; http://impel.eu/about/history/

[92] http://impel.eu/about/

[93] For more detailed information about IMPEL and the structure and functions of the different bodies see Nicholson, M., 'Networking in Europe: How Networking and Cooperation Have Helped Respond to Environmental Compliance and Enforcement Challenges in Impel Member Countries', in INECE (2011) *9th International Conference on Environmental Compliance and Enforcement, Conference Proceedings*, pp. 779–789, pp. 780f.

[94] See for details: BioIntelligence Service/Ecologic/IEEP (2013), 'Study on possible options for strengthening the EU level role in environmental inspections and strengthening the Commission's capacity to undertake effective investigations

Since the establishment of IMPEL, there has been cooperation between the network and the Commission. This became closer around 1996/1997, following the Commission Communication on implementing the EC environment law of 1996,[95] and for some years the IMPEL secretariat was hosted in the Commission's environmental directorate-general. A Memorandum of Understanding setting out the principal arrangements of future cooperation between IMPEL and the Commission was signed in September 2009. There are regular meetings between the IMPEL Board and high level Commission representatives as well as meetings at a more operational level in order to ensure that identified implementation priorities are openly communicated and considered. Commission officials participate in IMPEL projects as well as in the network's general assembly.

IMPEL has been active in identifying and promoting best practices, including those that recognise how inspections fit within a wider compliance assurance context. IMPEL develops methodologies and issues guidance on inspections, organises workshops and helps in the carrying out, on an ad hoc basis, of joint enforcement actions. It has also established the IMPEL Review Initiative as an instrument focusing on review and evaluation of national environmental inspection systems[96] – otherwise known as 'peer reviews'. The explicit references to IMPEL and peer reviews in the 7th EAP show that its work is valued by the Council and Parliament.[97]

IMPEL has played a particularly important role in the development and adoption of the RMCEI. It has developed useful guidance on its implementation, especially in relation to inspection planning. Its cluster 'Transfrontier Shipment of Waste' not only developed methodologies and

---

of alleged breaches in EU environment law', pp. 116–117; http://ec.europa.eu/environment/legal/law/pdf/Environmental%20Inspections.pdf

[95] For analysis of the cooperation and the relationship between IMPEL and the Commission see Hedemann-Robinson, op. cit., pp. 455f.; BioIntelligence Service (2013), 'Evaluating the IMPEL network and its work', pp. 29f.; Martens, M., (2005), 'Double-hatted Agencies on the European Scene? A Case Study of the IMPEL Network', ARENA Working Paper 12/2005, University of Oslo (https://www.sv.uio.no/arena/english/research/publications/arena-publications/workingpapers/working-papers2005/wp05_12.pdf).

[96] The IMPEL peer reviews provide a useful form of external evaluation but are limited in both the extent of what is reviewed and the number of reviews undertaken. See for details: Bio Intelligence Service/Ecologic/IEEP (2013), pp. 111f. Further detailed information on individual projects under the IMPEL Review Initiative is available at: http://impel.eu/categories/43/search_type/and/order/default/

[97] 7th EAP, Paragraph 65.

practical inspection manuals but also facilitated exchange programmes for inspectors and organised joint inspections on waste shipments.[98]

However, the work of IMPEL cannot make up for the narrow scope of current Union provisions on environmental inspections or for shortcomings on the ground. Cooperation within the network is on a voluntary basis. While this has its advantages, it cannot guarantee that identified good practices are followed across the Union. IMPEL has focused mainly on classic inspections of industrial installations and waste shipment inspections: it has not had comparable exchanges of good practices nor developed comparable inspections' guidance in relation to other environmentally sensitive matters such as diffuse water pollution and illegal wildlife activities. However, upon encouragement by the Commission, IMPEL has already shown an openness to expanding its work in the subject-areas of diffuse water pollution and nature conservation.[99] It remains to be seen how the challenges linked to this will be addressed.

IMPEL undertakes its activities primarily within a project structure. The project reports are published and actively disseminated and their findings have positive effects on inspection practice on the ground. However, according to a recent study launched by IMPEL to evaluate its work, there is a great imbalance in membership participation in projects and 'four IMPEL members – the Netherlands, the UK, Germany and France – have been the lead countries in 60% of the projects since 1997'.[100] The study also indicates that the less active IMPEL members 'also do not participate in Cluster meeting groups where many important discussions are held, including setting priorities and developing proposals'.[101] It further explains the possible reasons for this problem, viz. lack of resources, differences in Member States' priorities, lack of support from a high level of government, language barriers. It relativises its scale by stressing that flexibility, also in terms of different levels of participation, could be seen as an advantage.[102] However, in order to avoid any questioning of the representativeness and objectivity of IMPEL's work, it would seem important to foster a more active participation by all members.

In the wake of the above-mentioned evaluation study, IMPEL has taken early steps to implement the recommendations. In particular, it is striving to further improve its communication policy and project implementation

98 More detailed information is available at: http://impel.eu/cluster-2/

99 Bio Intelligence Service (2013), 'Evaluating the IMPEL network and its work', pp. 29–31.

100 Ibid. p. 18.

101 Ibid, p. 41.

102 Ibid, pp. 44f.

strategy. For instance, in April 2014, IMPEL announced the launch of its first e-Newsletter, to be published every two months. It also started preparing abstracts for all of its projects in order to better present their outcomes to the wider public.[103]

IMPEL has been criticised in the academic literature as being 'predicated on the avoidance of the imposition of compulsory standards in areas of implementation and enforcement, either by way of legislative requirements or by way of external impartial audit'.[104] However, statements that 'the influence of IMPEL has also been to dispel any serious strategic thought within the Commission to establish a set of general, legally binding minimum requirements under EC legislation that national authorities must adhere to when inspecting installations'[105] and that 'the incremental, informal and intergovernmentalist approach of the IMPEL model has not resulted in any notable legal enhancement of Member State systems supervising the implementation of EC environmental legislation'[106] appear not to be fully justified. IMPEL provides invaluable input to the development of methodologies and practical tools for proper targeting and planning of inspections. The practical usefulness of the majority of IMPEL projects is highly appreciated by stakeholders.[107] In particular, in new Member States as well as in candidate and potential candidate countries, the network has significantly contributed to the development of structures for environmental inspections. IMPEL also provides the necessary platform for permanent structured exchange of knowledge and good practices between its members. Experience shows that the network cooperates in a constructive way with the Commission and other stakeholders, including through ensuring direct participation in IMPEL projects and network events and is open for dialogue on priorities and strategic issues.

3.4 Future Challenges for Network Cooperation

While recognising the added value of cooperation through networks, the 2012 Commission Communication on 'Improving the Delivery of Benefits from EU Environment Measures: Building Confidence through Better Knowledge and Responsiveness' observed that 'the potential of

---

[103] http://impel.eu/news/impel-launches-first-e-newsletter/

[104] Hedemann-Robinson, op. cit., p. 463.

[105] Ibid.

[106] Ibid, p. 476.

[107] Bio Intelligence Service (2013), 'Evaluating the IMPEL network and its work', p. 26; Nicholson, M., op. cit., pp. 782f.

cooperation has not been fully realised across all networks' and identified challenges such as the need to ensure that networks have a stable structure to function effectively and to target their work at members' needs and better implementation.[108] As for the future, the Communication considered that improvements could be achieved by focusing on the distinct roles and strengths of networks, avoiding duplication, and looking at trans-network cooperation.[109]

The Commission has established cooperation with all the previously mentioned Union-level networks, including the establishment of contact points to ensure permanent cooperation at operational level, regular meetings at high level, and the participation of Commission officials in network projects and events and of network representatives in workshops and conferences organised by the Commission as well as in financial support for some networks.

It will have to be further explored whether other cooperation mechanisms would be effective to ensure enhanced trans-network cooperation and to avoid duplication of work and waste of resources. Stable network structures, including secretariat stability, and sufficient budgets seem to be a necessary pre-condition.

Enhanced cooperation through networks can create synergies and contribute to the proper and equal implementation and enforcement of Union environment legislation as well as a level playing field for businesses. Further possible input to be expected from networks relates not only to exchange of knowledge and good practices on environmental inspections and enforcement but also to provision of information on complementary approaches to ensure compliance, advice on how to close the information gap on compliance assurance at national and Union level and more effective coordination on transboundary problems. Intensified networking would share information and best practices in relation both to specific themes (for example, a cross-cutting guidance on inter-agency cooperation and coordination) or on specific areas of law (for example, best practice on investigation of wildlife crime).

4. CONCLUSIONS

At the present juncture, the European Union lacks a coherent binding framework on environmental inspections, a shortcoming that is recognised

---

[108] COM(2012) 95, p. 9.
[109] Ibid, p. 10.

in the 7th EAP. The ground has been partially prepared to address this shortcoming, not only in the 7th EAP itself, but in public consultation and other activities carried out by the European Commission as well. It remains to be seen whether this will bear fruit in the form of a binding instrument during the currency of the 7th EAP, which runs to 2020.

As the 7th EAP recognises, there is a close connection between environmental inspections and network cooperation. Environmental inspections have already benefited from the network cooperation provided by IMPEL, notably through the latter's development of guidance and its conduct of peer reviews. Inspections represent a vital link within the compliance assurance chain and network cooperation helps to make it a robust one. Network cooperation also helps ensure the robustness of the other links, thereby strengthening the entire chain. This helps to explain why the Union institutions recognise the role of compliance assurance networks. Certainly, there is ample scope for them to contribute to improving the implementation of Union environment law over the coming years.

19. Success and failure factors in developing effective environmental enforcement networks: the case of the East African Network for Environmental Compliance and Enforcement

Gerphas Opondo*

1. HISTORY OF THE EAST AFRICAN NETWORK FOR ENVIRONMENTAL COMPLIANCE & ENFORCEMENT

EANECE[1] is an informal regional initiative whose mission is to promote the rule of law, good environmental governance and sustainable development through the efficient and effective implementation and enforcement of environmental laws. The goals of the network are:

1. To strengthen the capacity of environmental regulators in East Africa for effective implementation and enforcement of environmental requirements;
2. To raise awareness of environmental requirements and the benefits of compliance; and
3. To build and strengthen in-country and cross-border relationships between environmental regulators in East Africa for improved cooperation on national and transboundary environmental issues.

* East African Network for Environmental Compliance & Enforcement, NEMA Hqs, Popo Road, South C, Nairobi, Kenya, eanece@eanece.org; gerry-opondo@yahoo.co.uk

[1] More details about the East African Network for Environmental Compliance & Enforcement can be accessed online at http://www.eanece.org/

The network membership consists of environmental regulators in the East African nations of Burundi, Kenya, Rwanda, Tanzania and Uganda. Currently EANECE has a membership of over fifty governmental agencies in the said five East African nations. Whereas the network membership is restricted to governmental regulatory agencies it continuously collaborates with other entities, including the private sector, academia and civil society organisations, on prioritising environmental compliance and enforcement issues.

The development of EANECE can be traced to the 8th International Conference on Environmental Compliance and Enforcement (2008).[2] During this conference, a regional conference for about 85 compliance and enforcement officials and experts from the Sub-Saharan Africa region, along with international experts, was organised. Participants of this regional conference considered the benefits of a regional environmental compliance and enforcement network as one of the tools necessary for strengthening environmental enforcement capacity in the Sub-Saharan Africa region. The formation of an informal regional network as a forum for information sharing and exchange of ideas was strongly supported. The Sub-Saharan African Network for Environmental Compliance and Enforcement was established during the conference with the objective of enhancing environmental compliance and enforcement in the region by sharing information and experience. Participants agreed to divide the network into four sub-regions, each with a sub-regional focal point, namely: Eastern Africa with Kenya as the focal point; Southern Africa with South Africa as the focal point; Central Africa with Cameroon as the focal point and West Africa with Ghana as the focal point.[3]

One of the overall outcomes of the 8th International Conference on Environmental Compliance and Enforcement was the commitment to support opportunities for regional networking in Africa. In their final Conference Statement, the INECE co-chairs and Executive Planning Committee encouraged the development and growth of environmental compliance and enforcement networks in the Sub-Saharan region of Africa.[4]

---

[2] This conference was held in Cape Town, South Africa on 5–11 April 2008 under the auspices of the International Network for Environmental Compliance and Enforcement (INECE).

[3] Gerardu, J., Jones, D., Reeves, M., Whitehouse, T. and Zaelke, T. (eds) *Summary of the INECE Regional Conference for Sub-Saharan Africa*. Proceedings of the 8th International Conference on Environmental Compliance and Enforcement, 2008, INECE.

[4] Gerardu, J., Jones, D., Reeves, M., Whitehouse, T. and Zaelke, T. (eds) *Conference Outcomes: Cape Town Statement*. Proceedings of the 8th International

The establishment of the Sub-Saharan African Network for Environmental Compliance and Enforcement was greeted with a lot of enthusiasm and optimism. It provided an opportune forum for the region to share information and ideas about tackling its ever-increasing environmental challenges. However, the immediate challenges faced by the Sub-Saharan Network were: lack of clear organisational and leadership structures; unclear communication channels; and resource constraints. Owing to these challenges, the Sub-Saharan Network and its sub-regional affiliates did not live long beyond the conference.[5] By 2009 the idea had more or less completely fizzled out.

Despite the failure of the Sub-Saharan African Network for Environmental Compliance and Enforcement to take off, the idea of developing regional environmental enforcement networks for Africa lived on. In 2010, through the efforts of a few individuals at Kenya's National Environment Management Authority (NEMA), the idea to set up a regional compliance and enforcement network for East Africa was revived. With the financial support of the Danish Embassy in Nairobi, a national environmental regulators' conference was held in Nairobi on 31 March 2010, not only to mobilise support for the establishment of a national environmental enforcement network for Kenya but also to support the establishment of an East African network. Participants at the conference resolved to establish the Kenya Network for Environmental Compliance and Enforcement. In addition they strongly supported the establishment of an East African network. The idea was that the Kenyan network would eventually become a chapter of the East African network, and that the other East African nations would also establish national chapters at the opportune time.[6]

Soon after the establishment of the Kenyan network, efforts to mobilise support across the East African region for the proposed East African Network for Environmental Compliance and Enforcement stepped up a gear. The response across the region was overwhelming. With the support of partners including the Danish Embassy in Nairobi, INECE, the United

---

Conference on Environmental Compliance and Enforcement, 2008, INECE.

[5] Opondo, G., in Gerardu J., et al. (eds), *Creating and Sustaining Regional Environmental Compliance & Enforcement Networks: Lessons from the East African Network for Environmental Compliance & Enforcement*, Proceedings of the 9th INECE International Conference on Environmental Compliance & Enforcement, 2011.

[6] EANECE, Proceedings of the Conference for the Launch of the Kenya Chapter of the Proposed East African Network for Environmental Compliance and Enforcement, 2010.

States Environmental Protection Agency and UNEP, a regional conference was held in Nairobi in May 2010 where delegates from Burundi, Kenya, Rwanda, Tanzania and Uganda, along with environmental compliance and enforcement experts from the international community resolved to establish the East African Network for Environmental Compliance and Enforcement.[7] A charter establishing the informal network was signed by the representatives of the five East African countries. As of November 2013, EANECE had established national chapters in Kenya, Tanzania and Uganda and had plans to establish two more national chapters in Burundi and Rwanda.

2. SUCCESS FACTORS IN THE DEVELOPMENT OF THE EAST AFRICAN NETWORK FOR ENVIRONMENTAL COMPLIANCE & ENFORCEMENT

In the case of EANECE, the following factors are attributable to the success so far registered in its steady growth and development.

- Clear governance structures and separation of roles;
- Effective strategic and action planning;
- Adding value through regular activities;
- Strategic partnerships;
- Effective communication; and
- Working 'informally'.

These success factors are explained in detail below.

2.1 Clear Governance Structures and Separation of Roles

Good governance is critical to the success of any compliance and enforcement network. It is necessary for the network, whether formal or informal, to clearly spell out its governance structure in its charter, constitution or terms of reference. The charter, constitution or terms of reference should outline the mission, vision, goal and objectives of the network, as well as establish the responsible institutions within the network, spelling out clear roles and responsibilities for each institution. A clear separation of roles

---

[7] EANECE, Proceedings of the Launching Conference of the East African Network for Environmental Compliance and Enforcement, 2010.

ensures efficiency in resource utilisation and productivity, and minimises incidences of conflict between the various institutions of the network. However, in spite of the fact that the roles are clearly marked, the institutions of the network must still work in unison and complement each other whenever the situation demands it. Finally, for the institutions to work efficiently there must be a dedicated team with a clear leader. Simply put, networks are merely the people who run them.

At the time of its establishment the members of EANECE agreed upon and signed a charter that spells out the members' aspirations. In addition the charter outlines the network's governance structure with clear roles and reporting and oversight mechanisms for each institution:

1. *National focal points*. The national focal points serve as the primary institutions for working with in-country stakeholders, the secretariat and other partners. These are senior officials appointed by the national environmental regulatory agencies in the member countries and are responsible for all network activities within their country. They are permanent employees of their agency and carry out network activities as part of their day-to-day work without any additional financial burden to the secretariat.
2. *Executive committee*. The executive committee consists of the representatives of member countries, nominated by the national networks, the national focal points and the secretariat. The committee provides overall guidance to help realise the network's mission and objectives. In this respect, it sets the goals, policies, activities, annual work programmes and financial plans of the network, including resource mobilisation. The committee is headed by a chairperson elected by the members on a three-year rotational basis. The executive committee meets at least once a year.
3. *Secretariat*. The secretariat is headed by a regional coordinator who is responsible for the day-to-day running of the network including designing and implementing work programmes in consultation with the executive committee and the national focal points. The coordinator also doubles up as the secretary to the executive committee. Currently the coordinator works alone in the secretariat. However there are plans to expand the staff of the secretariat should the network's resources allow it.

2.2 Effective Strategic and Action Planning

Effective strategic planning articulates not only where an organisation is going and the actions needed to make progress, but also how it will know if it is successful. A strategic plan is therefore an essential tool that sets the priorities, focuses energy and resources, strengthens operations and ensures that all the members of the organisation are working towards a common goal. The strategic plan establishes an agreement within the organisation around intended outcomes and helps to adjust the organisation's direction in response to a changing environment.

Once the strategic plan is in place, an action plan is needed to deliver it. Action plans are a key component of successful project management and are helpful in summarising how specific objectives will be achieved and by when. In the action plan the key objectives, usually derived from the strategic plan, are broken down into detailed tasks. The action plan has two purposes: it ensures that all areas of required action have been taken into account; and it breaks the achievement process down into manageable parts.

Soon after its launch in May 2010 EANECE started to develop a strategic plan and action plan. It was a consultative process across all the member countries and organisations. All the members were called upon to contribute to the network's priority projects and activities in the period 2010–2013. A three-year strategic and action plan covering the period October 2010–September 2013 was adopted during the first meeting of the network's executive committee. The priority areas identified in the strategic and action plan were:

1. *Developing and strengthening national environmental compliance and enforcement networks*. This was seen as essential for the effectiveness, visibility and vibrancy of the regional network. The secretariat worked with the respective national environmental protection agencies to build new and strengthen existing national networks. As at the end of the first strategic and action plan period three out of five national networks had been established. The remaining two have been carried forward to the next planning period of October 2013–September 2016.
2. *Capacity building for environmental compliance and enforcement*. Inadequate institutional capacity to monitor and enforce environmental requirements is a common challenge across the entire East African region. The secretariat continues to work with the network members and partners to improve institutional capacities to design and implement effective compliance and enforcement programmes necessary for effective environmental protection in East Africa. The strategic support of INECE and UNEP has been crucial in the achievement of the capacity-building pillar for East Africa.
3. *Raising awareness concerning the importance of environmental compliance and enforcement*. EANECE endeavours to influence behaviour

change within the regulated community through enhanced awareness of environmental requirements and the benefits of compliance with such requirements. In Kenya, for example, the national network has partnered with the Cleaner Production Centre to sensitise manufacturing industries to environmental requirements and how to achieve compliance while saving costs by simply adopting cleaner production practices. This initiative has received great acceptance among the regulated community because of the immediate reductions in production costs, coupled with better environmental compliance ratings for participating companies.

Despite the fact that EANECE has recorded great progress with several tangible results while implementing the strategic and action plan, at the end of the first planning period in September 2013 about 60 per cent of the proposed activities remained unaccomplished. This was mainly due to financial resource constraints. The network's new strategic and action plan covering the period October 2014–September 2016 is now in place. Whereas the overall priorities stated above have been maintained, there is increased focus and emphasis on the following areas:

1. *Improving urban air quality*. Air pollution, especially in urban areas, not only contributes to global warming but also increases incidences of respiratory diseases such as asthma and bronchitis. EANECE works with relevant entities to build legal and institutional capacity towards improving air quality, particularly in East Africa's fast growing urban areas.
2. *Improving the effectiveness of environmental impact assessment (EIA) systems*. EIA is a legal tool that aims to contribute to accountable decision-making, environmental protection and sustainable development. However, the goal achievement of EIA is significantly influenced by the performance of environmental compliance and enforcement (ECE) and in situations where environmental compliance and enforcement are weak, EIA hardly contributes to environmental protection or sustainable development. Therefore, EANECE is working on a programme that aims to improve the effectiveness of EIA systems by creating an interface between EIA and ECE.
3. *Protecting the ozone layer*. Over the years several illegal shipments of ozone-depleting substances have been intercepted by customs and environmental protection officials at East Africa's entry ports courtesy of increased cooperation under the EANECE. The network has prioritised the promotion of national and regional strategies for

effective implementation of the Montreal Protocol on Substances that Deplete the Ozone Layer.[8]

2.3 Adding Value through Innovative Projects and Regular Activities

For any network to make an impact within and outside its membership it must be vibrant and visible through innovative projects and regular activities. Networks must come up with a range of useful projects and activities that keep members constantly engaged. Such projects and activities must demonstrate the value of participating in the network and must be beneficial to the day-to-day work of the network membership. The network projects and activities must be designed in such a way that they do not appear to be parallel to the regular work of the members. Rather, the projects and activities must complement the day-to-day business of the network membership, and where possible help the members to perform their mandates more efficiently.

EANECE works through its national networks to ensure effectiveness, visibility and vibrancy throughout the region. The national networks serve as forums for strengthening relationships between government agencies involved in environmental regulation in the respective member countries. As a result of the enhanced inter-agency and cross-border relationships, the network has recorded tremendous progress in its projects and activities during the past few years of its existence, including the following:

- Joint enforcement action involving diverse agencies such as environmental protection agencies, police and customs, resulting in successful operations under the Montreal Protocol, the Convention on International Trade in Endangered Species of Wild Fauna and Flora, and the Basel Convention on the Control of Transboundary Movements of Hazardous Wastes and their Disposal.[9]
- Capacity-building activities including enforcement training for more than 120 government officials in five countries, and exchange programmes/twinning arrangements and peer placements within the network membership as well as in more developed jurisdictions such as the United Kingdom.

---

[8] Ozone Secretariat (2000) The Montreal Protocol on Substances that Deplete the Ozone Layer, *United Nations Environment Programme, Nairobi, Kenya.*

[9] Basel Convention Secretariat (1992) Basel Convention on the Control of Transboundary Movements of Hazardous Wastes and their Disposal. *United Nations Environment Programme, Chatelaine, Switzerland.*

- Developing tools for enforcement. The network has developed a harmonised environmental inspection and investigation manual for East Africa, a tool that helps enforcement officers to carry out their day-to-day work in a consistent and transparent manner.
- Conferences and workshops. These serve as forums for information exchange and sharing of ideas. The network organises regular workshops on topical compliance and enforcement issues, and holds its regional summit biennially.

2.4 Strategic Partnerships

Partnerships enable parties to cooperate in order to advance their mutual interests. Different organisations including national, regional and topic-specific compliance and enforcement networks as well as formal environmental protection bodies can learn a lot from the work and experiences of each other. Rather than reinvent the wheel it is possible to duplicate a basic method or strategy that has already previously been created, tested and optimised by others. This way, organisations are able to save time and resources, and can concentrate more on implementation rather than on investigation.

More often than not, a number of strategies in environmental compliance and enforcement have already been tried and tested by other organisations or in other jurisdictions. Thus, creating and developing cross-network and cross-agency partnerships accelerates replication of strategies and helps in optimising the often scarce resources. National, regional and topic-specific networks provide a good medium for building and nurturing such partnerships. EANECE has and continues to reach out to relevant local and international agencies in order to develop mutually beneficial partnerships.

One of the major partnerships that EANECE has recently entered into focuses on developing a programme to strengthen compliance and enforcement in EIA. The strategic partners in the programme are the Netherlands Commission for Environmental Assessment (NCEA) and INECE. The programme seeks to tap into NCEA's long experience with EIA in low- and middle-income countries where environmental compliance and enforcement are weak, and INECE's expertise and long experience in capacity building for environmental compliance and enforcement. The expected results of the programme include:

- Guidance material for EIA and environmental compliance and enforcement, including good practice case studies, templates and checklists;

- Concrete proposals for improving environmental compliance and enforcement in EIA; and
- Strengthened capacity to implement, enforce and assure compliance with EIA requirements and improved knowledge base of the individuals through professional exchange between experts.

2.5 Effective Communication

Sustained communication with network members is important because it motivates people to perform their roles. Different information in different situations and settings demands different kinds of communication channels. Enforcement networks must therefore understand how to tailor messages for maximum results. EANECE uses diverse communication channels to connect (with) its members. The secretariat maintains momentum for progress on key objectives through continuous communication with members and stakeholders on a range of issues that include reporting on the progress of network activities, successes and challenges. The main communication channels of the network include:

- Website (http://www.eanece.org);
- E-Newsletter (issued on quarterly basis);
- E-mails;
- Direct peer-to-peer outreach by individual members; and
- Workshops and round-table events.

In addition, the network is exploring effective ways to use social media such as LinkedIn, Twitter and Facebook to reach out to a wider audience within and beyond its membership.

2.6 Working 'Informally'

Whereas the government agencies and officials participating in EANECE may be formal, getting them to operate and work informally whenever the need arises helps in achieving greater results. When government officials interact, cooperate and work with their peers directly without a formal agreement or other bureaucratic procedures, they are able to build personal relationships and friendships which are crucial in getting the work done. Because many officials from the participating organisations know each other at a personal level, it is easier for them to share information and mobilise resources for joint initiatives at very short notice. More often than not a phone call will be sufficient, unlike in the past when officials had to write formal letters to their peers in different organisations. This mode of operation has been quite helpful in quickening intelligence and information sharing as well as in effecting many joint enforcement actions within East Africa. This has often resulted in efficient and timely enforcement action.

3. FAILURE FACTORS IN THE DEVELOPMENT OF THE EAST AFRICAN NETWORK FOR ENVIRONMENTAL COMPLIANCE & ENFORCEMENT

The successes registered by EANECE have not been without challenges. The first strategic and action plan of October 2010–September 2013 was not fully implemented. The current strategic and action plan of October 2013–September 2016 is already facing implementation challenges as well. These challenges indicate potential failure factors for the development of the network, including the following:

- Inadequate budgets and unsupported financial sustainability strategies; and
- Changing national priorities and political differences.

3.1 Inadequate Budgets and Unsupported Financial Sustainability Strategies

Whereas environmental protection is a primary responsibility of the government, many developing countries do not make sufficient budgetary allocations to meet this goal. In East Africa the annual budget allocation for the environmental protection agencies in Burundi, Kenya, Rwanda, Tanzania and Uganda collectively is approximately US$30 million. This figure is not sufficient to run administrative costs as well as effective environmental protection programmes. For EANECE, whose membership is comprised primarily of government agencies, the insufficient national budget allocation for environmental protection affects the resources that the member agencies may commit to the network activities. In addition to the low national budget allocations, many environmental protection agencies in East Africa heavily rely on development support from foreign donor agencies. Whereas donor agency involvement is meant to play a complementary role, more often than not there are no mechanisms in place to ensure sustainability of the donor-supported initiatives once the donors pull out.

Since its take-off, EANECE has mainly relied on foreign donor funding to sustain the secretariat and carry out network activities. The key partners in this regard have been the Danish Embassy in Nairobi, the United States Environmental Protection Agency, the Institute for Governance and Sustainable Development and INECE. The current financial support to the secretariat runs out in December 2013 with no immediate fall-back position.

Some of the financial sustainability strategies that the network membership has agreed upon in the past include: member institutions mainstreaming network activities into their strategic plans; annual work programmes and budgets; and members paying an agreed annual subscription fee towards supporting the secretariat. Unfortunately, none of the members of the network have met any of the agreed obligations. After December 2013 the Secretariat will be run on a voluntary basis by the newly established Environmental Compliance Institute, a Kenyan based non-governmental organisation whose mission is to promote sustainable societies in Africa by advancing good environmental governance and the rule of law.

The failure by the network membership to put in place a permanent secretariat financed by the members, coupled with its inability to allocate funds for the network's projects and activities is a major failure factor that may greatly impact the future survival of the network.

3.2 Changing National Priorities and Political Differences

Besides the informal compliance and enforcement network, all the participating nations in EANECE are members of the treaty-based East African Community, a regional inter-governmental organisation comprising the Republics of Burundi, Kenya, Rwanda, the United Republic of Tanzania, and the Republic of Uganda, that was revived in 1999 and aims at forming a customs union, a common market, a monetary union and finally a political federation by December 2015.

For the better part of 2013 through to 2014, relations between some of the East African Community member states have been lukewarm. Analysts see a larger economic and diplomatic shift and changes in national priorities behind the differences that have sometimes played out openly. Whereas the government agencies participating in the network engage at an informal level, political support from key decision-makers within government is key to the success of the network. The political differences within the formal East African Community have not yet become pronounced within informal settings such as EANECE. However, it is plausible that if political differences between the member states escalate further it may affect future political commitment to the network with the potential of impacting negatively on the future growth of EANECE.

4. CONCLUSION

In its few years of existence the East African Network for Environmental Compliance and Enforcement has grown steadily despite numerous challenges. Today the network is a good model of how local and regional cooperation can achieve environmental benefits at national and international levels. In an environment where local technical capacity, finances and human resources are often lacking, the network has complemented the work of regulatory agencies in assuring compliance with national environmental laws through collaborative initiatives and the cooperative efforts of various regional and international players in the regulatory regime. At the same time, compliance with international environmental obligations has been enhanced. The network continues to mature and grow systematically, and is expected to emerge from its current challenges to play an even greater role in environmental management in East Africa in coming years.

PART V

Vertical networks

20. Regional environmental enforcement networks in the United States

LeRoy Paddock*

1. INTRODUCTION

States in the United States and four adjoining Canadian Provinces[1] have participated in regional environmental enforcement associations for over twenty-five years. The Regional Associations have focused on training, information exchange and networking. The experience of these networks may provide useful lessons learned for other regions that are considering creating similar regional networks to support environmental enforcement.

The Associations were founded primarily to help states deal with environmental crimes but have evolved to focus more on administrative and civil judicial enforcement, as the emphasis in many states on criminal enforcement, and perhaps the need for criminal enforcement in the illegal disposal of hazardous waste context, diminished in the late 1990s and 2000s. The Associations remain an important source of in-person training, information exchange and networking but have been challenged by loss of funding from the U.S. Environmental Protection Agency as EPA shifted its focus to distance-learning approaches, by the inability to maintain high-level engagement in some member states, by staffing limitations, and by travel restrictions in some states that make centralized

* Working with the National Association of Attorneys General in 1985 and 1986, LeRoy Paddock helped organize the Midwest Environmental Enforcement Association and the Western States Project. He was an active member of the Midwest Association for several years. He interviewed all of the current Regional Association Directors and one former Director in preparing this chapter. The interview notes are on file with the author. All of the Directors have reviewed a draft of this chapter.

[1] Quebec was a member of the Northeast Environmental Enforcement Project until recently. Ontario is a member of the Midwest Environmental Enforcement Association. Alberta and Saskatchewan are part of the Western States Project.

in-person training more difficult. Still, the Associations are providing in-person training to over 1,600 agency personnel each year, continuing their efforts to build relationships among regulators, investigators and attorneys across state lines and into Canada, and serving as a hub for information exchange. This chapter addresses the history and operation of the Regional Associations and concludes with lessons learned from the experience of the Regional Associations in the United States.

2. ORIGINS OF THE REGIONAL ENFORCEMENT ORGANIZATION

Awareness of the scale of improper disposal of hazardous wastes had increased dramatically by the 1970s,[2] leading to the passage in 1976 of the Resource Conservation and Recovery Act,[3] regulating the management of both solid and hazardous waste, and in 1980 of the Resource Conservation and Recovery Act Amendments (RCRA), which added felony criminal penalties for illegal transportation, storage, treatment or disposal of hazardous waste.[4] A felony in the United States is a crime punishable by imprisonment for one year or more. While many environmental violations had been subject to minor criminal penalties, often referred to as misdemeanor crimes that have a maximum jail term of one year, in the past, the fact that hazardous waste violations were now categorized as serious crimes made prosecution more likely and increased the deterrent value of criminal prosecution. The first RCRA regulations, 'Hazardous Waste and Consolidated Permit Regulations', were published in the Federal Register on May 19, 1980.[5]

The United States Department of Justice's history of environmental crimes enforcement notes that:

> On the pollution side, two important developments in the early 1980s altered the circumstances that had limited growth of the [criminal enforcement] program during the preceding decade. First, the Resource Conservation and Recovery Act Amendments of 1980 introduced felonies into the nation's primary hazardous waste regulation statute. The effect of adding felonies to environmental

---

[2] The Northeast Hazardous Waste Project, New Jersey Division of Criminal Justice, *Understanding Hazardous Waste Crime: A Multistate Examination of Offense and Offender Characteristics in the Northeast*, 5 (June 1986) (on file with the author).

[3] 42 USC §§ 6901–6992k (2012).

[4] 42 USC § 6928(d) (2012).

[5] See 45 Federal Register 33066 (May 19, 1980).

> statutes was to focus more attention and more resources – including those of the Federal Bureau of Investigation – on enforcement. Second, in 1982 the Environmental Protection Agency and the Department of Justice established units that were dedicated to investigating and prosecuting environmental crimes. Thus, criminal enforcement as part of environmental enforcement generally was better able to compete with other programs for resources.[6]

Regional enforcement associations in the United States trace their history to 1980 when the Attorneys General from 11 northeastern states met to respond to the need for more interstate cooperation to deal with illegal disposal of hazardous waste.[7] The states found that '[i]llegal hazardous waste management activities pose a major threat to the public health and environment'.[8] The states recognized that 'the problems posed by improper hazardous waste management were far too numerous, transient, and diverse to ever be dealt with adequately on the state level alone'.[9] Instead, a regional approach was seen as a necessity.[10] The states observed that at least occasionally illegal waste activity in the region involved organized criminal syndicates.[11] The northeast states launched the Northeast Hazardous Waste Project to help address these issues. The Project, now renamed the Northeast Environmental Enforcement Project (NEEP), was funded by the member states and the United States Department of Justice (DOJ) during the first three years. After that time, the Project was funded by the U.S. EPA and its National Enforcement Investigations Center which provided the 'essential line of communication and cooperation between the federal and state government'.[12]

Using the experience gained in working with the Northeast Project, U.S. DOJ supported the creation of the three other Regional Environmental Enforcement Associations in the United States – the Midwest Environmental Enforcement Association, the Western States Project, and the Southern Environmental Enforcement Network. In 1985, the National Association of Attorneys General working with the Department of Justice,

---

[6] See http://www.justice.gov/enrd/5472.htm, last visited September 29, 2013.

[7] The founding states were Connecticut, Delaware, Maine, Maryland, Massachusetts, New Hampshire, New Jersey, New York, Pennsylvania, Rhode Island, and Vermont.

[8] The Northeast Hazardous Waste Project, New Jersey Division of Criminal Justice, *Understanding Hazardous Waste Crime: A Multistate Examination of Offense and Offender Characteristics in the Northeast*, iii (June 1986) (on file with the author).

[9] Ibid.

[10] Ibid.

[11] Ibid. at 2.

[12] Ibid.

Environment and Natural Resources Division, and the environmental crimes program at the United States Environmental Protection Agency, then housed at the National Enforcement Investigations Center (NEIC) in Denver, Colorado, began meeting with state officials in the Midwestern and western parts of the United States to discuss the possibility of organizing regional enforcement associations. By 1986 states in both regions agreed that creation of associations analogous to the Northeast Project would be beneficial in supporting their enforcement work, especially related to environmental criminal enforcement that, for most states other than California, was a relatively new activity. The Southern States Environmental Enforcement Network followed shortly thereafter, with the Associations being founded in 1989. Most states belong to one of the Regional Associations. The only exceptions are Iowa, Montana, North and South Dakota and Wyoming.

The Midwest Environmental Enforcement Association (MEEA), the Western States Project (WSP) and the Southern Environmental Enforcement Network (SEEN), like the Northeast Project, were organized with the idea of including regulators, criminal investigators, and lawyers among their membership. This allowed the Associations to do cross-training in some cases and to also enhance communications among the key organizations involved in the environmental enforcement process. This focus on engaging regulators, investigators and lawyers remains an important feature of the regional networks today.

While states make up the bulk of the membership in the Regional Associations, four Canadian Provinces have been active in the work of the Associations (Alberta and Saskatchewan in the WSP, Ontario in MEEA, and until recently, Quebec in NEEP). In addition, several federal agencies have worked closely with the Associations, most notably the EPA Environmental Crimes Program and their Regional Agents-in-Charge, the Federal Bureau of Investigations, the Naval Criminal Investigative Service (NCIS), and other federal agencies. A number of local governments have also worked with the Regional Associations, and a significant number of local government personnel, primarily investigators, have received training through the Associations. In addition, the Regional Associations have worked closely with the Federal Law Enforcement Training Center in Georgia to provide hands-on criminal investigation training.

3. EVOLUTION OF THE REGIONAL ASSOCIATIONS' TRAINING FOCUS

From the time of their founding until the mid-1990s the Associations focused primarily on criminal enforcement for at least two reasons. First, criminal environmental enforcement was a new field for most states. Historically, states had relied on civil enforcement actions to deal with environmental issues, but as the illegal disposal of hazardous waste became a more prominent concern, many of the states passed new laws in the 1980s and early 1990s, adding felony criminal penalties for the most serious environmental violations, especially those involving clear public health risks such as the illegal disposal of hazardous waste. Most criminal enforcement programs set up under these new laws were small and therefore state-by-state training would have been time-consuming and expensive. It therefore made sense to create a source for regional training and information exchange to support these new state criminal enforcement programs. The second reason for focusing on criminal enforcement was that the financial support for the programs came from U.S. EPA's criminal enforcement program.

This situation changed in the early 2000s for several reasons. First, the EPA funding moved from the criminal enforcement program to the National Enforcement Training Institute whose training mission included both civil and criminal enforcement training. In addition, the number of hazardous waste criminal violations significantly decreased in the late 1990s as the Resource Conservation and Recovery Act regulations for management and transportation of hazardous waste began to be implemented. In addition, high profile criminal enforcement actions involving illegal transport and disposal of waste began to deter this kind of criminal activity. While criminal issues remained both in the context of hazardous waste and other environmental statutes, the emphasis on environmental criminal enforcement decreased in several states. Finally, most of the enforcement conducted by states is civil enforcement, and, especially as state budgets became tighter during the recession in the United States, the resources available within states to conduct civil enforcement training diminished, increasing the importance of regional civil training programs.[13] As a result, the Regional Associations now do significantly more civil than criminal enforcement training. Still, criminal enforcement training and information exchange remain an important part of the Regional Associations' work.

---

[13] Northeast Environmental Enforcement Project, *Settlement Package*, 3 (undated, on file with the author).

4. MANAGEMENT AND STAFFING

The Mission of NEEP is typical of the Associations. This is to 'protect the environment by providing members with professional development through quality enforcement training and the opportunity to collaborate on current environmental issues'.[14] MEEA describes its purpose and goal as providing and coordinating training, information and resource support to its Member agencies for the enforcement of the statutes, rules, and regulations relating to the protection of the environment. In furtherance of its goal, MEEA has pursued the following objectives:

1. Establishing and supporting effective lines of communication among all agencies that have a role or an interest in environmental protection and enforcement;
2. Identifying regulators, investigators, and attorneys in Member agencies who will participate in MEEA to share their expertise;
3. Promoting training in detection, investigation, and prosecution of violations of environmental protection statutes, rules, and regulations;
4. Establishing and administering a program to collect, store, and disseminate environmental enforcement information through a computer system available to Member agencies;
5. Developing and maintaining interaction with other similarly constituted groups; and
6. Supporting the development of environmental enforcement legislation.[15]

The Associations are managed by Boards of Directors with representatives from each participating state. The Chair of the Board is selected from among Board members for a two-year term.[16] The Associations' Executive Directors emphasized the importance of the members seeing the Associations as 'their' organizations, helping to ensure the states remain invested in the work of the Associations. At the time the organizations were founded, the state representatives tended to be drawn from senior agency enforcement management ranks allowing the Associations to have a significant 'presence' in the participating states. However, as personnel have changed over time, state representatives in some Regional Associations have come from lower echelons in the agencies. This has

[14] Northeast Environmental Enforcement Project, *FY2009/2010 Report*, 6 (undated, on file with the author).

[15] MEEA *By-Laws 2* (on file with the author).

[16] Ibid. at 11.

lessened the visibility of the Associations in some states, making it harder to retain state financial support and identify candidates for training, as well as lowering the awareness of the value of the Associations among senior managers. This is not an issue in all regions. Some regions have managed to attract and retain senior, influential enforcement managers as representatives to the Association. Maintaining involvement of senior state officials is seen by the Executive Directors as a key to carrying out their education and information dissemination function and in maintaining funding for the organizations.

The Regional Associations function through a small full-time staff. MEEA and SEEN currently employ only an Executive Director. NEEP and WSP have two staff members. The staff member(s) plan and coordinate the training activities, organize the membership conferences, assist with information exchange and deal with the budget and administration of the organizations. Budgets vary by region. The WSP 2013 annual budget was approximately $425,000. The four Associations contribute funds to support a person who manages the R@IN information system discussed below.

5. AREAS OF WORK

The Regional Associations focus on three areas: training which can either be discipline-specific or cross-disciplinary, periodic membership conferences to conduct business and to disseminate information through presentations and panels, and information exchange both informally and through the R@IN information network. Each of these functions is designed to facilitate networking among the participating organizations.

5.1 Training

The arc of training courses provided by the MEEA is a useful example of how training programs have evolved over the more than twenty-five years that the Regional Associations have been in place. Since 1991 MEEA has trained almost 8,000 people in three categories – regulators who are state and occasionally local environmental agency staff who typically conduct civil inspections, investigators who are state or local criminal enforcement personnel, and lawyers who may do either civil or criminal enforcement work. Table 20.1 sets out the percentage of personnel trained in each of these three categories in the five-year period 1992–1996, the five-year period 2009–2013, and the overall numbers for the past across 23 years.

The numbers demonstrate a dramatic change in focus from training

Table 20.1 MEEA training statistics

Period	Regulators	Investigators	Attorneys	Total
1992–1996	766–43%	808–46%	181–11%	1,755
2009–2013	2,000–88%	132–6%	136–6%	2,268
1988–2013	4,762–60%	2,367–27%	901–13%	8,030

Source: Midwest Environmental Enforcement Association, *Personnel trained by MEEA as of June 30, 2013* (on file with the author).

about an equal number of regulators and investigators in the early years of the Project to primarily training regulators in the last five years. This data is consistent with the interviews with all four Executive Directors who have said that once EPA shifted the funding and reporting for the Associations from its Criminal Division to the National Enforcement Training Institute, EPA encouraged the Associations to develop more civil enforcement training. A list of the current training courses being offered by NEEP is attached as Appendix 20.1 and the 2012 training courses offered by WSP is attached as Appendix 20.2.

The number of persons trained by the Regional Associations has remained fairly steady over the last several years, averaging between 400 and 600 students each year for each of the Associations. Some recent courses in the Northeast have attracted large audiences, including a 'verbal judo' course in Maryland that attracted 200 attendees and an advanced attorney training program attended by 90 attorneys.

However, the Associations have had to change their training model because of travel restrictions in several states that resulted from the economic downturn in the United States. Rather than bringing in a small number of students from each state in a Region to a centralized training location, as was typical before the mid-2000s, the Associations have increasingly conducted training programs in individual states, with a focus on training a larger audience from the host state. Appendix 20.3 shows this growing trend of providing training programs designed for a specific state and delivered in the state in order to deal with travel restrictions and to reach a larger cohort of the state agency staff.[17]

The Regional Association staff member(s) plan the conferences and manage the logistics related to conferences, but the training is done for the most part by volunteer instructors from participating states. These

[17] Personnel from member states in one Region are allowed to attend specialized training courses in other Regions.

instructors are typically very experienced regulators, inspectors, and lawyers. The Associations have had little trouble attracting volunteer trainers.

The Associations typically offer training scholarships to a limited number of personnel from each member state. These training scholarships are funded primarily through member dues. This structure is designed to encourage participation in training programs by all member states. Still, even with scholarships available, states have not always participated because of travel restrictions or insufficient support for the training programs by state agency senior managers.

The Regional Associations have experimented with some distance learning but express a strong preference for in-person training. The Directors indicated that one of the fundamental purposes of the organizations is to establish personal relationships both among various organizations within a single state (regulators, inspectors, and attorneys), and among personnel from other states in the region. They believe these personal relationships are an important part of building a regional enforcement network since, once personal connections are established, people are much more likely to contact that person in the future if they need to exchange information or ideas. The in-person training programs, as well at the Associations' periodic membership conferences, provide the opportunity to build these relationships.

The Associations during their first decade or more of operation worked closely with the Federal Law Enforcement Training Center (FLETC)[18] in Glynco, Georgia to provide a hands-on, two week-long Advanced Environmental Crimes Training course for state and local regulators, investigators, and attorneys. The course was offered through the FLETC State and Local Enforcement Training program that provides low or no cost enforcement training for state and local government enforcement personnel.[19] The FLETC environmental crimes training has not been available for the last several years. However, as a result of a major criminal settlement negotiated by the U.S. Department of Justice, $3.5 million has been made available to revive the FLETC environmental crimes training program. The new course was held in January and March 2014, attracting 24 investigators and 23 inspectors for the two sessions. The Regional Associations nominate personnel to participate in the training program. NEEP has run smaller-scale, week-long, hands-on basic environmental crimes training programs housed in Fort Monmouth, New Jersey and Middlesex County, New Jersey for several years.

---

18 See http://www.fletc.gov/, accessed March 14, 2014.

19 See http://www.fletc.gov/osl, accessed March 14, 2014.

5.2 Periodic Membership Conferences

The Associations have typically held membership conferences twice each year, although funding has required some of the Associations to move to a single meeting each year. The membership conferences include shorter training sessions on 'hot topics', as well as important opportunities for networking and exchanging information on enforcement practices and cases. These conferences also serve as business meetings for the Association members.

5.3 Information Exchange

The Associations facilitate information exchange in several ways. These include communications on enforcement issues between state personnel and the Association staff, both formal and informal, at regional conferences, information exchange opportunities, again both formal and informal, at training programs, and through an information exchange website known as R@IN, the Regional Associations Information Network. R@IN serves all four of the Associations.

R@IN is a password protected website that is an enforcement Resource Center including information on cases, contacts, training materials, and multimedia resources. It also includes a calendar of events, news stories, and a discussion forum.

The case section of R@IN is perhaps its most unique feature. A person authorized to have access to R@IN can search for cases that have been entered into the system based on the name of the defendant, the name of the case, the jurisdiction, the location, media type, case type, or the case contact. This allows enforcement personnel, for example, to determine if a potential defendant has been charged with a violation in another jurisdiction or to identify all 'water' cases involving 'criminal' charges filed by a 'local' government agency. Unfortunately, the case aspect of the R@IN system has been less successful because of the very limited number of cases that are entered into the system.

Currently, there are 2,647 active users on the R@IN mailing list. Users reside in all states except North and South Dakota. There are also registered R@IN users from Puerto Rico and the US Virgin Islands. Registered users come from the Canadian Provinces of Alberta, British Columbia, Nova Scotia, Ontario, Quebec, and Saskatchewan. During fiscal year 2013, 868 press releases were reported through the website and e-news. For the most part, these releases report enforcement cases. They are featured for one week and then maintained in the News Archives (a searchable database).[20] The manager of the R@IN system provides a weekly update on enforcement activities to all of the members of R@IN.

6. FUNDING

Funding has been a consistent issue for the Regional Associations over the last several years. For many years member dues and grants from the U.S. EPA supported most of the Associations' work. EPA funding has ended and the economic downturn has resulted in the loss of some dues revenues from some states or a reduction in dues payments in other cases. Grant funding has not proven to be a significant source of revenue perhaps because, as a couple of the Executive Directors have suggested, foundations are reluctant to fund what they see as 'government' training. To fill the gap, the Associations have increasingly relied on state and federal 'Supplemental Environmental Project' (SEP) funding. SEPs are payments made in lieu of a portion of a fine that would normally be assessed in an enforcement case.

6.1 EPA Funding

For many years U.S. EPA through a 'cooperative agreement' provided $250,000 each year to each of the four Regional Associations. Cooperative agreements are legal instruments that establish a relationship between a federal agency and a state or local government, tribal government, or other recipient.[21] Cooperative agreements that involve government-to-government funding do not require competing bidding. This provided predictable, stable funding that allowed the Associations to hire staff and develop a consistent training and information exchange program.

Because of the large amount of funding being awarded to a wide range of

---

[20] During fiscal year 2013 the R@IN experienced the following level of use: 7,733 visits; 4,340 unique visits; 51% new visitors; 49% returning visitors; 29,222 pages viewed; 3.78 pages viewed/visits; 4.05 minutes spent/visit. E-mail from R@IN administrator RoseAnn Wishner to LeRoy Paddock dated September 27, 2013.

[21] The laws, regulations, and guidance for administering cooperative agreements are the Federal Grant and Cooperative Agreement Act of 1977 (*31 U.S.C. §§6301 et seq.*); Office of Management and Budget (OMB) guidance for implementation of the Federal Grant and Cooperative Agreement Act of 1977 (*43 Federal Register 36860 dated August 18, 1978*); OMB Circulars (*see Appendix B for a list of applicable OMB Circulars*); Title 43, Code of Federal Regulations, Part 12; the Departmental Manual, Parts 505 and 507; and Director's Order 20.

organizations by EPA in 'assistance' agreements, these grants came under increasing scrutiny in the 2000s. Ultimately, EPA issued an order[22] in 2005 requiring many types of assistance agreements to be competed including the agreements for the type of work being done by the Associations. The Associations were the only bidders for the first round of the competition, which by this time was limited to $300,000 per year for all of the Associations for three years. However, the latest competition for fiscal years 2013–2015 did attract additional bidders. The bid specifications called for proposals that included traditional classroom training, but noted:

> EPA is particularly interested in receiving applications that address the delivery of training by electronic means or E-Learning. The American Society for Training and Development defines E-learning as a broad set of applications, which include web-based learning, computer-based learning, virtual classrooms, and digital courses. E-Learning can be 'on demand' and should be accessible using standard desktop computer technology. E-Learning overcomes timing, attendance, and travel difficulties faced by the states.[23]

The application from the Regional Associations focused on in-person training consistent with their long-standing approach to training. The evaluations from the Associations' training course, in particular, had pointed out the importance of in-person training for networking. EPA, however, awarded the training funds to Sam Houston State University in Texas, which has a history of providing law enforcement E-Learning. Training modules were still under development by the University and had not yet been offered to state enforcement officials at the time the research for this chapter was conducted.

6.2 Membership Dues

The Associations have charged membership dues to help support the organization from the beginning. For example, SEEN had charged dues of $10,000 per state, but as states faced increased budgetary pressures in the late 2000s, SEEN went over to a sliding dues scale that ranges from $2,500 to $10,000, with differing services for those who pay lower dues. In addition, SEEN allows states to substitute SEP payments that go to SEEN for dues. Association dues and policies about dues payments in hardship

---

[22] See http://www.epa.gov/ogd/competition/5700_5a1_final_order.pdf, accessed March 14, 2014.

[23] See U.S. EPA, *FY2012 State Environmental Enforcement Training (SEET) Grant Solicitation Notice* 3 (on file with the author).

situations vary from Association to Association depending upon the decisions of each Association's Board of Directors. Dues remain an important part of the revenue stream for the Associations but make up less than half of their funding needs.

6.3 Enforcement Settlements

The Regional Associations have increasingly relied on Supplemental Enforcement Projects negotiated as part of enforcement settlements to fund their work. The NEEP describes SEP funding as 'vital' to their existence.[24] Since 1988 the Federal government in the United States has allowed funding from Federal enforcement settlements, under certain conditions, to be used for 'environmentally beneficial projects which a defendant/respondent agrees to undertake in settlement of an enforcement action, but which the defendant/respondent is not otherwise legally required to perform'.[25] 'Environmentally beneficial' means a SEP 'must improve, protect, or reduce risks to public health, or the environment at large. While in some cases a SEP may provide the alleged violator with certain benefits, there must be no doubt that the project primarily benefits the public health or the environment'.[26] SEPs are entered into as an aspect of prosecutorial discretion and therefore the question of whether and what type of SEP may be appropriate is a case-by-case decision made by the prosecutor.[27] SEPs typically offset part, but not all, of the monetary penalty that would otherwise be assessed in an enforcement case. For example, in Massachusetts SEPs must still result in at least 25 percent of the original penalty being assessed as a penalty.[28]

The EPA SEP policy sets out five criteria that should be used in

---

[24] Northeast Environmental Enforcement Project, *Annual Report*, 21 (2009/2010).

[25] U.S. Environmental Protection Agency, *Supplemental Environmental Projects Policy*, 4 (May 1, 1998), available at http://www2.epa.gov/enforcement/policy-issuance-final-supplemental-environmental-projects, accessed March 14, 2014.

[26] Ibid.

[27] Ibid. at 5.

[28] See Commonwealth of Massachusetts, Department of Environmental Protection, *Policy on Supplemental Environmental Projects* 6 (February 21, 2007), available at http://www.google.com/url?sa=t&rct=j&q=&esrc=s&frm=1&source=web&cd=1&ved=0CCsQFjAA&url=http%3A%2F%2Fwww.mass.gov%2Fdep%2Fservice%2Fseppol07.doc&ei=FaZIUrr6NJH64AOJiYC4Ag&usg=AFQjCNEQdeAq8XWPpUTM76Zg1fFffDm3sw&bvm=bv.53217764,d.dmg, accessed March 14, 2014.

determining whether a SEP is appropriate in any particular case. Three of the most important criteria are:

1. Whether a proposed SEP is inconsistent with any provision of the underlying statute;
2. Whether the SEP advances one of the objectives of the environmental statutes that are the basis of the enforcement action, including whether the project is designed to:
   (a) reduce the likelihood that similar violations will occur;
   (b) reduce the adverse impact to which the violation contributed; or
   (c) reduce the risk to public health or the environment potentially affected by the violation; and
3. The settlement defines the type and scope of the project to be performed.[29]

In addition to the Federal government, almost all states now utilize SEPs. A 2007 survey found that 28 states and the District of Columbia had formal SEP laws or policies, and that 13 states informally negotiated SEPs in enforcement settlements. Only two states – North and South Carolina – had formally rejected the use of SEPs.[30]

The Associations have worked through their state liaisons to encourage member states to include funding for the Regional Association in enforcement settlements in appropriate circumstances. To facilitate this effort, NEEP developed a 'Settlement Package' that is distributed to those involved in enforcement actions to raise awareness of the work of the Association and how designation of the Association as a SEP recipient can be accomplished.[31] Each Association provides similar information and each has established a tax-exempt, non-profit entity to accept and administer SEP funds.[32] SEP funding, of course, does not provide a consistent and reliable revenue stream since it depends upon whether a prosecutor is aware of the Regional Association's work, the appropriateness in

29 Ibid. at 5–6.

30 The Public Law Research Institute, *Supplemental Environmental Projects: A Fifty State Survey with Model Practices*, 14 (2007), available at http://gov.uchastings.edu/public-law/docs/plri/ABAHastingsSEPreport.pdf, accessed March 14, 2014. There has been some criticism of SEPs. See David A. Dana, *The Uncertain Merits of Environmental Enforcement Reform: The Case of Supplemental Environmental Projects*, 1998 Wis. L. Rev. 1181 (1998).

31 Northeast Environmental Enforcement Project, *Settlement Package* (undated, on file with author).

32 See http://www.nj.gov/lps/dcj/neep/pdf/future.pdf, accessed March 14, 2014.

any particular case of directing some or all of the SEP to the Regional Associations to support enforcement training, and the frequency and scale of SEP settlements.

The Associations have recently benefitted from a very large federal SEP that will be critical in bridging the gap in operational funding that resulted from the loss of EPA funding. The settlement with Wal-Mart Stores, Inc.[33] for illegal discharge of household and pool cleaning liquids into a sewer system included a total agreed-upon criminal penalty of $60,000,000, of which $20,000,000 was set aside for Supplemental Environmental Projects. $1,500,000 of the SEP went directly to the four Associations with its use unrestricted. Another $3,500,000 was provided to the National Fish & Wildlife Association for the specific purpose of conducting three to six sessions of an environmental crimes course each year until the funding is depleted. The course is to be 'developed and administered' by the Regional Associations. All of the Associations now benefit from SEP settlements.

7. LESSONS LEARNED

7.1 Regional Networks Can Provide Important Networking and Training Opportunities

The Regional Associations have been a valuable asset for state enforcement programs. They provide regional networking opportunities that are not otherwise easily available. This facilitates both the learning process and the law enforcement process itself by exchanging information across state lines. They are also able to provide training that may be difficult to fund in states with budgetary limitations. Demand for training remains strong, perhaps due in part to an approach that now emphasizes in-state training for basic courses that can attract larger audiences. The Associations have also been able to provide very specialized training such as the FLETC environmental crimes training that would not attract a large enough audience in a single state. They are also in a position to quickly respond to new problems and develop training in one region that is open to personnel from any of the four Associations. Although there has been a slight loss of membership in a couple of the Regions, overall membership remains strong. Finally, the Environmental Council of the States

---

[33] See *U.S. v. Wal-Mart Stores, Inc.*, case numbers 13-CR-334 and 13-CR-00333 (May 28, 2013), available at http://www.courthousenews.com/2013/05/29/WalMartPlea.pdf, accessed March 14, 2014.

(ECOS) (the national association for state environmental commissioners) recognized in a 2009 resolution the 'value and importance of the Regional Associations to the States' environmental regulatory and enforcement programs'. See Appendix 20.4.

7.2 Successful Regional Associations Require Consistent Support and Engagement from Senior Enforcement Personnel

Consistent, high-level engagement in and support of regional associations appears to be essentially based on the experience of the U.S. Regional Associations for at least three reasons. First, one of the significant sources of funding for associations is likely to be its own members. High-level engagement and support makes access to agency dues funding more likely. It may also increase the chances that SEP funding will be allocated to the work of the Regional Association. Second, high-level engagement and support increases the likelihood that the work of the regional associations will support important priorities of member organizations. This linkage between member organization priorities and the work of the association is important in assuring that the member organization regularly participates in information exchange and training opportunities, including encouraging its members to serve as instructors for training programs. Finally, high-level engagement and support may increase the likelihood that information about the work of the regional network and opportunities to participate in network training or other activities will be widely disseminated in the member organization. Some of the U.S. Regional Associations have found that in states without high-level engagement there is little communication about the work of the Associations.

7.3 Full-time Staffing is Important to the Success of Regional Associations

The level of training and information exchange provided by the Regional Associations requires a full-time staff and likely more than one full-time staff person to deliver a high quality program and to maintain an effective information exchange.

7.4 In-person Training is a Key to Enhancing Networking

Distance learning can be a very efficient way of reaching a wide audience at low per participant cost. For training that does not require hands-on learning or that does not require participants to work or learn in a team setting, distance learning may be the best approach to training, especially with limited budgets. However, distance learning has its limitations. One of the important limitations is that distance learning does not support networking opportunities, an important value in the context of environmental enforcement. It also does not provide for easy interchange of ideas that may result in new approaches to enforcement.

The Regional Associations have preferred in-person training because of the networking opportunities it creates and the idea-generation possibilities that can best occur when people meet each other, both in the formal classroom setting and in informal discussions that occur in connection with training programs. EPA prefers distance learning because it can reach a large audience in multiple states at comparatively low cost. The ultimate answer to the question of what is the most effective and efficient form of training likely is that both approaches are needed. Distance learning can be used to provide training to a large audience across a wide geographic area. However, in-person training opportunities are needed for some forms of advanced training that require a hands-on setting such as the crime scene investigation training and where working in teams is an important part of the training experience. One constant for the Regional Associations since they were founded was the idea that some training programs should be designed to engage regulators, investigators, and attorneys to help each discipline better understand how to work with and support the other disciplines. Finally, at least some in-person training is key to building the networks that can help facilitate enforcement activities over time. Networking can build the contacts that allow enforcement officials to test out ideas with colleagues in other jurisdictions, as well as the networks that are helpful in dealing with violations that cross national or regional boundaries.

7.5 Regional Associations Need Consistent Sources of Funding

The Regional Associations for many years received $250,000 per year from the U.S. EPA. This funding, along with relatively stable funding from state membership dues allowed the Associations to plan for a base level of programing each year. Without the EPA funding and with less reliable dues income in at least some of the Associations, it has been more difficult to plan for future training and networking events. Inconsistent funding threatens the long-term viability of at least some of the Regional Associations. The funding from the Wal-Mart SEP has essentially replaced the lost EPA funding but only for about a two-year period. SEPs are a far less predictable source of funding since the funding and the level of funding depends upon states or the Federal government deciding to direct some or all of a SEP to the Regional Associations on a case-by-case basis. Further, SEPs may not be a viable funding mechanism for regional networks elsewhere in the world.

7.6 A Regional Information Exchange System such as R@IN can be Useful but Requires Consistent Input from Participating Organizations

A system like R@IN appears to be helpful in providing information on enforcement that may be difficult to find elsewhere and as a way of diffusing information on enforcement cases. The part of R@IN that allows states to enter information on cases and other states to access that information based on a number of different search fields, appears limited because too few cases are entered into the system. Voluntary case databases are hard to maintain without very dedicated personnel in each state who are committed to keeping the case information up to date.

8. CONCLUSION

The Regional Associations in the United States have, over the past 25 years, provided a useful model that can be drawn upon in designing regional enforcement networks elsewhere. In a resolution adopted in 2012, the Environmental Council of the States (ECOS), the national association of state environmental commissioners, recognized 'the value and importance of the Regional Associations to the States' environmental regulatory and enforcement programs'. The Associations provide regional networking opportunities that are not otherwise easily available as well as training that may be difficult to fund in states with budgetary limitations. However, consistent, high-level engagement in and support of regional associations by their members is essential to their success, as is full-time staffing of the associations.

Further, even though distance learning can be a very efficient way of reaching a wide audience at low per participant cost, distance learning has its limitations. One of the important limitations is that distance learning does not support networking opportunities, an important value in the context of environmental enforcement. It also does not provide for easy interchange of ideas that may result in new approaches to enforcement. Regional associations need to find an appropriate balance between in-person and distance learning that preserves the networking and information exchange opportunities provided by in-person meetings.

Regional associations can also serve as a useful focal point for electronic information exchange. A system like R@IN created by the U.S. Regional

Associations appears to be helpful in providing information on enforcement that may be difficult to find elsewhere.

Finally, and perhaps most importantly, regional associations need a consistent source of funding. During the period of almost 20 years when the U.S. Environmental Protection Agency provided base funding to the Regional Associations they were able to provide predictable training and networking opportunities that states could rely on. Today the Associations have to rely more on member dues that have in some regions decreased, and far less predictable enforcement settlements to support the Associations. While the Associations have been able to survive under these circumstances, their ability to deliver needed training and networking opportunities has been significantly diminished, especially for two of the Regional Associations.

APPENDIX 20.1 CURRENT NORTHEAST ENVIRONMENTAL ENFORCEMENT PROJECT TRAINING COURSES

CURRENT TRAINING COURSES

MULTI-MEDIA COURSE FOR REGULATORS

This three-day course is designed for state and local regulatory personnel from Air, Water and Waste programs with more than 3-years' experience. This course is intended to provide an awareness of the different media programs and the options that exist to address violations of those laws found during an environmental inspection.

ENVIRONMENTAL PROSECUTORS TRAINING COURSE

This two-day course is designed for state and local prosecutors. The course progresses through each phase of an environmental prosecution from charging strategies through jury instruction. Faculty will discuss latest decisions and current issues throughout each phase of the course. The course prepares students for trial through review of techniques, strategies, and trial examples.

BASIC INVESTIGATIVE TRAINING COURSE FOR INVESTIGATORS AND INSPECTORS

This three and one-half day course is designed for investigators and regulatory personnel with less than 3-years of experience in the environmental field. The course is intended to present basic skills in developing environmental cases. It also provides an awareness of and cross-training among multiple disciplines. This training is the prerequisite for NEEP's Environmental Scene Investigations Course and FLETC's Advanced Environmental Crimes Training Course.

ENVIRONMENTAL SCENE INVESTIGATIONS

This three-day course consists of both classroom lectures and a series of hands-on practical exercises simulating what is typically encountered by enforcement personnel investigating an environmental incident/case. Each team runs through several environmental incident scenarios which will address the following issues: Box Trailer with drums leaking hazardous materials/medical waste, Tank Trailer discharging material, Abandoned Drums in field, Chemical Warehouse/Hazardous Waste Hits (various simulated clan meth lab processes) and the Use of the Internet in Investigations.

MULTI-MEDIA ENVIRONMENTAL SAMPLING TRAINING

This two and one-half day course for regulatory personnel and investigators consists of both classroom lectures and a series of hands-on practical exercises simulating what is typically encountered by personnel investigating an environmental incident/case. Classroom lectures will include: Objectives of Sampling, Pre-Sampling Phase, Documentation and Chain-of-Custody, Lab Issues, Post Sampling Issues, Digital Media and Post Sampling Legal Issues. In addition, the teams will run through four environmental scenarios which will address the following issues: Solid Media Sampling, Tanker & Drum Sampling, Water Sampling and Sanitary Sewer Sampling.

CIVIL ATTORNEYS TRAINING COURSE

This two-day training course is highly interactive and will progress through each phase of a civil proceeding. Topics include drafting the complaint, motions/depositions, evidence gathering, parallel proceedings, dealing with regulatory agencies and citizen groups, direct case strategy and issues, defense strategies and issues, and negotiations of multi-defendant cases.

REFRESHER COURSE FOR COMPLIANCE/ENFORCEMENT INSPECTORS

This two-day course is designed for regulatory personnel from all media programs and includes such topics as inspection planning & preparation, use of the internet/sources of information, inspection authority & enforcement process, multi-media awareness, interviewing techniques, and inspection report and courtroom testimony.

NEGOTIATION SKILLS WORKSHOP

This two-day course can be tailored toward attorneys, case managers, or field personnel within your agency. The course teaches Basic Principles and Skills, Communication Styles, Planning for Structure and Process, Strategies and Tactics, as well as state-specific policies and procedures. The course includes a one-half day simulation in which all students participate. The simulation is based upon an actual environmental negotiation. This is an in-state course and is available upon request.

PRESENTATION AND TRAINING SKILLS: PRACTICAL TIPS THAT WORK

This one and one-half day program is a modification of the NEEP Train the Trainer program that was designed and delivered in the past exclusively to NEEP faculty members. We have broadened our original Train the Trainer program to meet the needs of anyone who does training, public speaking or meeting facilitation. The program is highly interactive and gives participants hands-on experience in using a wide variety of practical tips, tactics, and *how-to's* for improving presentations. The course includes instruction on how to handle a difficult audience, opening and closing with impact, creating dynamic visuals, involving participants, and how to recognize differences in learning and teaching styles. We will also show you how to deal with anxiety, shorten your preparation time, and organize your material. We have successfully used these innovative presentation techniques in seminars and workshops in many governmental agencies throughout the country.

IN-STATE TRAINING COURSES

These one- or two-day training courses can be tailored toward attorneys, investigators, or regulatory personnel within your state. The state-specific courses are developed based on the agencies' current training needs. Some examples of recent in-state training courses include: Sharpening Management Skills, Listening Skills Workshop, Meth Lab Awareness, Communication Skills, and an overview of new policies and procedures within the state.

[*Source:* Northeast Environmental Enforcement Project Fiscal Years 2011/2012 Report, at page 6, available at http://www.regionalassociations.org/Common/Files/NEEP-FY2011–2012%20Report.pdf]

APPENDIX 20.2 WESTERN STATES PROJECT 2012 TRAINING PROGRAMS

Western States Project 2012 Training Programs

1. Communications Skills for Regulatory Inspectors (Diamond Bar, California – 57)

2. Introduction to Environmental Enforcement (Ontario, California – 82)
3. Introduction to Environmental Sampling and Planning (Boise, Idaho – 45)
4. Environmental Enforcement Seminar for Lawyers (Columbus, Ohio, event organized by NEEP – 7)
5. Communications Skills for Regulatory Inspectors (San Diego, California – 57)
6. Saskatchewan Environmental Awareness Training (Saskatoon, Saskatchewan – 74)
7. Environmental Scene Investigations Training (Sayreville, New Jersey, organized by NEEP – 4)
8. Introduction to Criminal Environmental Investigations (Reno, Nevada – 52)
9. New Mexico Environmental Enforcement Training (Santa Fe, New Mexico – 90)

[*Source:* the Western States Project, on file with the author.]

APPENDIX 20.3 NEEP TRAINING STATISTICS

August 31–September 2, 2010	Advanced Env. Crimes Training; Ft. Monmouth, NJ	50
October 26–28, 2010	72nd Membership Meeting; Annapolis, MD	45
March 1–3, 2011	Strategic Planning Meeting; Baltimore, MD	9
April 12–14, 2011	Committee Meetings/In-Service; Burlington, VT	20
May 17–19, 2011	Inspector's Refresher Training Course; Boston, MA	120
June 1–2, 2011	Inspector's Refresher Training Course; Harrisburg, PA	100
June 15–16, 2011	Inspector's Refresher Training Course; Portland, ME	52
August 30–September 1, 2011	Multi-Media Sampling Training; Middlesex, NJ	50
October 17–20, 2011	73rd Membership Meeting; Buffalo, NY	45

APPENDIX 20.3 CONTINUED

November 15–17, 2011	Inspector's In-State Training; Columbus, OH	32
November 30–Dec. 1, 2011	Inspector's In-State Training; New Castle, DE	73
February 28–29, 2012	Verbal Judo/Meth Lab Training; Trenton, NJ	317
March 28–29, 2012	Inspector's In-State Training; Washington, DC	85
April 24–26, 2012	74th Membership Meeting; Newport, RI	42
May 15–17, 2012	Attorney's Training Course; Columbus, OH	61
TOTAL		**1101**

[*Source:* Northeast Environmental Enforcement Project, Fiscal Years 2011/2012 Report, at page 7, available at http://www.regionalassociations.org/Common/Files/NEEP-FY2011-2012%20Report.pdf]

APPENDIX 20.4 ENVIRONMENTAL COUNCIL OF THE STATES RESOLUTION

Environmental Council of the States Resolution

ECOS

Resolution Number 09–1
Approved March 22, 2009
Alexandria, Virginia

Renewed March 21, 2012
Austin, Texas

As certified by
R. Steven Brown
Executive Director

CONCERNING ENVIRONMENTAL ENFORCEMENT TRAINING FOR STATE AND LOCAL ENVIRONMENTAL REGULATORS

WHEREAS, the Environmental Council of States (ECOS) recognizes that one essential component of meeting environmental protection objectives is environmental compliance and enforcement; and

WHEREAS, ECOS recognizes that training is critical to effective environmental compliance and enforcement efforts; and

WHEREAS, the four Regional Environmental Enforcement Associations (Midwest Environmental Enforcement Association, Northeast Environmental Enforcement Project, Southern Environmental Enforcement Network, and Western States Project, hereinafter, Regional Associations) are widely recognized as major providers of environmental compliance and enforcement training to state and local personnel; and

WHEREAS, the Regional Associations support integrated administrative, civil and criminal enforcement programs; and

WHEREAS, the Regional Associations are major providers of training to State and local regulatory compliance and enforcement personnel through their strategic training partnerships with the National Enforcement Training Institute (NETI) of the U.S. Environmental Protection Agency (U.S. EPA); and

WHEREAS, U.S. EPA's funding of NETI has declined while State and local training needs have increased; and

WHEREAS, State and local program funding for environmental compliance and enforcement training is also subject to increasing constraints.

NOW, THEREFORE, BE IT RESOLVED THAT THE ENVIRONMENTAL COUNCIL OF THE STATES:

Recognizes the value and importance of the Regional Associations to the States' environmental regulatory and enforcement programs and supports strategic training partnerships with U.S. EPA/NETI;

Encourages U.S. EPA, the Department of Justice or other federal entities to provide NETI and the Regional Associations with the funding level necessary to enable them to most effectively address the compliance and enforcement training needs of State and local environmental personnel, provided that this funding does not come at the expense of other state environmental programs;

Recognizes the value and importance of having state representation in U.S. EPA/NETI's determination of necessary training courses, curriculum and delivery; and

Supports the use of criminal and civil supplemental sentencing penalties as a source of funding for the Regional Associations.

[*Source:* Resolution 09–1, March 21, 2012, available at http://www.ecos.org/section/policy/resolution]

21. Ghana's efforts at environmental enforcement networks: legal and institutional structures

Bernadette Araba Adjei* and Larsey Mensah†

1. INTRODUCTION

The significance of environmental compliance and enforcement is seen through the promotion of institutional networking. At the global level, the International Network for Environmental Compliance and Enforcement (INECE) has become well established as its work is viewed as a complex, and a promotion, of networks. One of the main achievements of the 9th INECE meeting, held in 2011 in Whistler, British Colombia, Canada, was the formation of the West African Network for Environmental Compliance and Enforcement (WANECE), which was a response to the 2008 INECE call for the formation of such regional networks.[1]

The concept note for the building of WANECE states that 'WANECE shall build on the work of various West African countries and multiple organizations, including the United Nations Basel Convention Secretariat; . . . and such initiatives as Solving the E-waste Problem (STEP) and the Partnership for Computing Equipment (PACE)'. Its objective then is to 'complement the existing national, sub-regional, regional and global efforts and initiatives, to build the capacity of West African environment officials to secure compliance with, and enforcement of, their environmental laws as a way of protecting the health and environment within their countries, and reducing impacts on the global environment'.[2]

* Email: bernadette.adjei@gmail.com
† Email: larseym@yahoo.com

[1] *Proceedings of the 9th International Conference on Environment, Compliance and Enforcement*, Whistler BC, Canada, June 2011, p. 6.

[2] Concept Paper for the Establishment of the West African Network for Environmental Compliance Enforcement (Mensah 2012, unpublished), pp. 1 and 2.

The work of WANECE is in its preliminary stages and with the focus on institutional collaboration in enforcement compliance is fundamental to environmental protection. Indeed, it provides a platform for harnessing in a cooperative manner, the efforts of various enforcement institutions to achieve results, which may otherwise not be possible if each institution is working independently. This is particularly the case in developing countries, where human and material resources are also in short supply and, therefore, provides the justification for the creation of institutional networks to effectively work at ensuring compliance and enforcement of environmental laws and regulations.

2. THE GHANAIAN CONTEXT

Prior to attempts to create the WANECE, Ghana had initiated efforts at collaborating and networking especially in ports and harbours operations. As elaborated in the proceedings of the 9th INECE Conference of 2011, examples of networking efforts nationally and bilaterally were underway to set up a Committee on Waste Shipment prevention. The committee was envisaged as a technical group made up of the Environmental Protection Agency (EPA), the police, and private sector and NGO actors. There is also the National Nuclear Committee (NNC) which is an inter-agency task force that cooperates in the field of disaster management, security and combating illegal trade in nuclear materials. The NNC inter-agency body has chalked up some successes, notably the detection of shipments of radioactive materials into Ghana from Nigeria.[3] In the area of international cooperation and networking, Ghana in 2009 signed an agreement with the Netherlands that provides for collaboration in inspector exchanges, training programmes and information sharing. The INECE Seaport Environmental Security Network, of which Ghana is a member, is also another example of Ghana's international networking to protect the environment.[4]

Locally the efforts to establish networks solely on environmental protection has been a slow process, although Ghanaian public institutions that work in the environmental management sector or whose work impacts the physical environment have made efforts to put in place a

[3] Presentation by Ms Diana Branful, Assistant Commissioner of the Excise and Preventive Service, Ghana Customs and reported in the *Proceedings of the 9th International Conference on Environment, Compliance and Enforcement*, Whistler BC, Canada, June 2011, p. 22.

[4] Ibid., p. 23.

Compliance and Enforcement Network to harness the efforts of all these institutions.

Currently there are two formal kinds of environmental enforcement networks that are operating in Ghana in the natural resources management regime. The first is the Environmental Compliance and Enforcement Network (ECEN) established under the auspices of the Environmental Protection Agency of Ghana in 2001. The ECEN comprises state institutions in the environmental protection and enforcement sectors and works under a committee structure. The second is the National Security Committee on Lands and Natural Resources (NSCLNR), which is a permanent committee established in 2009 as a network of state institutions in environment to work on compliance and enforcement on matters relating to land, water, forests and mining.

This chapter will focus on these two institutional networks, that is, the ECEN and NSCLNR; examine their strengths and weaknesses, benefits, successes and failure factors. The chapter will further offer suggestions to strengthen efforts for effective collaboration in the environmental enforcement.

3. THE ENVIRONMENTAL COMPLIANCE AND ENFORCEMENT NETWORK (ECEN) OF GHANA

A key driver for the formation of the ECEN by the EPA was the 1992 Constitution of Ghana. Chapter 6 (The Directive Principles of State Policy), Article 36 (9) of the constitution states that 'the State shall take appropriate measures needed to protect and safeguard the national environment for posterity; and shall seek co-operation with other states and bodies for purposes of protecting the wider international environment for mankind'. Thus the constitution has created the platform for setting up networking enforcement cooperation.

In 2001, the EPA made attempts to convene a premier Compliance Enforcement Network meeting to create the platform for cooperation between mainly state institutions such as the Minerals Commission, the police and the district assemblies (local government structures) and to promote enforcement of and compliance with environmental laws and regulations. The key objective for this network was to bring together environmental regulatory and state enforcement agencies to cooperate and find a common ground for effective enforcement and compliance. The network meeting discussed a range of issues, including reclamation bonds for mining entities,[5] the work of the sub-committees, the prosecution of offenders, fines under the Fines (Penalty Units) Act 572 (2000), and strategies to ensure compliance and enforcement. However, the meeting failed to produce a clear framework and guidelines for the future work of the ECEN, which seemed to be solely EPA driven and which was exclusively funding the activities of the network. Notably, an institutional arrangement of a secretariat dedicated to running the ECEN was not put in place, and for the next couple of years the ECEN did not undertake any activities.

As the work of the ECEN lulled, the EPA made efforts to establish bilateral networks for compliance enforcement and started with the Ghana Police Service. In February 2003, the EPA organized a workshop to train police officers. The objective of this workshop was to seek greater collaboration of the police by training them further in the laws and regulations on the environment and areas of collaboration. The workshop dwelt more on the current policy direction of the EPA, familiarization with environmental laws and regulations, and identification of most environmental crimes and how best the police can handle them. This was intended to enhance general understanding in environmental management, and the role of compliance and enforcement.[6] The last session of the workshop, which was the high point, dealt in-depth with EPA–Police collaboration and produced the following interventions through which collaboration could be achieved:[7]

- Setting up of a task force;
- Seminars;
- Police should be represented on the Regional Environmental Network;
- Including police in the EPA training scheme so that some policemen can be sent for training on environmental issues;
- Train police inspectors on Environmental Management; and
- Provide an Environmental desk at the police service.

The roles of the parties and the next steps for collaboration in this bilateral enforcement network were set out for action. A key action agreed on was

---

[5] Issues of mining offences that cause grave environmental degradation has been a pressing issue for compliance networking as it was clear that no one state institution alone can deal with the issue.

[6] Report of the EPA Workshop on Effective Collaboration: A Tool for a Better Environmental Stewardship, 18–19 February, 2003, Bunso, Ghana, p. 2.

[7] Ibid., p. 6.

the use and strengthening of existing task forces like the wildlife network between the EPA and the Forestry Commission. Thus the platform was well positioned for collaboration.

Interestingly, the recommendations for action were the conduit for challenges as lack of resources both material and human led to a virtual freeze in the work of the general ECEN for a period of six years. The six-year hiatus ended in 2009 when the EPA sought to rekindle the work of the Enforcement Compliance Network, drawing on the mandate of the EPA under section 2(j) of the Environmental Protection Act, 1994 (Act 490) which provides that the Agency should: 'act in liaison and cooperate with government agencies such as the District Assemblies, and other bodies and institutions to control pollution and generally to protect the environment'.

The EPA thus triggered the renewal of the ECEN involving local government bodies such as the District, Municipal and Metropolitan Assemblies, the Police Service, the Minerals Commission, the National Petroleum Authority, the Energy Commission, the Factories Inspectorate, Town and Country Planning, the then Ghana Standards Board (now Authority), the Food and Drugs Authority, the Customs Authority (now the Customs division of the Ghana Revenue Authority), the Tourist Board, the National Fire Service, the Attorney General and the Ministry of Justice. Obviously missing were the other natural resources commissions, which are the Forestry, Fisheries, Water Resources, and the Lands Commissions. Also absent was representation from civil society and traditional authorities.

In April 2010 the EPA instituted a training programme for prosecutors to work on behalf of the ECEN to prosecute perpetrators of environmental crimes with the aim of equipping them for the work of the ECEN. However, other ECEN members were not involved or did not participate in this training. The latest effort to rekindle once again the work of the ECEN was a meeting at Accra in May 2010. The main focus was to advance the work of the ECEN by the formation of ECEN subcommittees on awareness creation, legal, industry, mining, and oil and gas. The work of these sub-committees focused on collaboration in their main operational areas and participation was crosscutting. For example, the police and the EPA were on all the sub-committees. It was agreed that the governmental ministries would serve on the ECEN and their sector institutions on the ECEN sub-committees. The obvious challenge was the issue of cohesion and information flow as some governmental ministries and agencies do not have clear channels of communication. What might perhaps have been an oversight was the failure to involve NGOs and CBOs in this network, taking into account their importance as actors in environmental protection and also in this case advocacy in enforcement compliance.

Thus good plans to set up an interagency committee to tackle certain aspects of compliance enforcement were laid and clear institutional structures were put in place for cooperation. However, since 2010 the ECEN has not met or undertaken any work.

4. CHALLENGES TO THE ECEN

One of the main challenges of the ECEN has been the lack of planning, implementation and coordination, or a functioning secretariat dedicated to running this network. Exploring other funding alternatives and instituting financial sharing of responsibilities for funding and logistics among partners would be required in order to bring other partners more fully into the networking system for effective compliance enforcement networking.

The networking effort has been EPA driven and the issues of turf wars and the inclusion of all members in planning and laying out the next steps and establishing the work ethics of the ECEN have been absent.

In the EPA, the ECEN has not been owned by the institution as a whole but has been the sole effort of an over-burdened and understaffed legal department. It seems to have been considered in an ad hoc manner – clearly a big challenge to institutional cohesion. Furthermore, there has been a lack of proper documentation of the ECEN process. Information on it is scattered and a lot of information resides in individuals' memory.

The failure to include NGOs and traditional rulers[8] in the ECEN, as stated earlier, was especially a recipe for future challenges. This is because traditional rulers and families own land and also a number of NGOs and CSOs (Civil Society Organizations)[9] work in the environment sector and play influential roles in seeking to protect community rights.

---

[8] It is important to involve traditional rulers in this process because they are the custodians of some of the land in Ghana, which they assign and devolve to various parties by both state laws and customary law. Customary Law is recognized as part of the laws of Ghana under the 1992 Ghana Republican Constitution Article 11. It is thus crucial that in tackling challenges brought forth by the use of land in a manner not compatible with environmental management practices, traditional rulers are involved, and especially so in enforcement networking.

[9] Non-governmental Organizations and Civil Society Organizations such as CONIWAS (Coalition of NGOs in the Water and Sanitation Sector) and WACAM (Wassa Association Against Mining – working in the mining rich Western Region of Ghana) are very active in Ghana in the environmental sector.

Again the network did not come out with clear guidelines and structures to guide its work.

5. NATIONAL SECURITY COMMITTEE ON LANDS AND NATURAL RESOURCES (NSCLNR)

The National Security Committee on Lands and Natural Resources – a permanent committee established in 2009 – is a network of state institutions in environment and the security forces. Its work has been to address environmental issues through enforcement, compliance and conflict resolution. The committee has a membership drawn from the natural resources commissions on lands, forestry, water resources and minerals, as well as the general environment. The Chamber of Mines is also a member. There is representation from the security agencies such as the Ghana Army, Ghana Police, Bureau of National Investigations, the National Security Council and the Immigration Service.

Some of the successes of this National Security Committee have been to settle land disputes that had turned violent in Accra, the capital city, and to assist the Water Resources Commission in 2011 in tackling high-risk encroachers and illegal aquaculture operators in the Ghana Water Company (a Water Resources Commission licence holder) water supply dam at Weija.

In 2012 the country was plagued with a dramatic increase in illegal mining, especially by foreign nationals. The president of Ghana inaugurated an Inter-Ministerial Working Group under the chairmanship of the Ministry of Lands and Natural Resources to find permanent solutions to the issue of environmental degradation through illegal mining activities. The Working Group structured the assignment into the short, medium and long terms, with specific sub-committees tasked to each time frame. This was very similar to the approach of the ECEN.

The *short term* was for immediate and urgent measures to halt all illegal mining activities nationwide. This task was assigned to the NSCLNR, given its previous compliance networking record.

The *medium term* focus was on the legal and socioeconomic measures. The Working Group brought together in a network the natural resources regulators, that is, the Minerals, Forestry, Water Resources and the EPA, as well as the Chamber of Mines, the umbrella association of mining companies. This committee was charged with reviewing flaws and regulations on natural resources and with determining the loop holes, if any, that existed in them and making proposals for strengthening such regulations and laws. The committee concluded that the legal and institutional framework for mining and environment was adequate. However, strict enforcement was recognized as key and it was recommended that the Attorney General's Department be represented to facilitate the process of strengthening the regulatory framework. In relation to the socioeconomic measures, the aim was to explore and propose alternative livelihoods for persons in illegal mining to prevent them from the indiscriminate rape of the environment, and here the Ministry of Local Government and Rural Development was to play a key role.

A third subcommittee was formed and charged with the *long term* aims of tackling the reclamation of destroyed mine sites. The Chamber of Mines, EPA, WRC (Water Resources Commission), Ministry of Lands and Natural Resources, and the Ministry of Environment, Science, Technology and Innovation constituted the third subcommittee and was given the task of proposing measures to achieve this aim. The EPA already had some guidelines on reclamation stemming from their reclamation bonds and was asked to take the lead in this direction.

The need to create the inter-ministerial working group was premised on the fact that there has been a high incidence of illegal mining involving both Ghanaians and foreigners, which had resulted in massive degradation of the environment. The country under its minerals and mining laws grants licences to indigenous people to mine for minerals.[10] However, some local people contract foreigners, mainly the Chinese, to use earth-moving equipment to do the mining on their behalf. This was because the rudimentary methods used by the local people made mining a tedious process and they realized that a concession that may be mined in about a year using traditional methods could be mined in a month by these sub-contractors.

Among the illegal foreign operators, the Chinese were in the majority and the heavy equipment was mostly owned and operated by them. Their mining methods were rapid and devastating, and no reclamation was carried out in the mined out areas. The local law enforcement agencies did not seem to have the capacity to handle the problem and hence the decision of government to intervene.

The NSCLNR was mandated to handle the short-term measure, make recommendations and enforce actions including:

- Seizure of all equipment used to mine illegally if the miners refuse to comply with directives to acquire licences and be regulated;
- The arrest and prosecution of all people, Ghanaians and non-Ghanaians involved in illegal mining;

---

[10] Minerals and Mining Act 2006, (Act 703) ss 83.

- The deportation of foreigners involved in this illegal activity;
- The revocation of the licences of Ghanaians who have sub-let their concession to non-Ghanaian illegal miners;
- The revocation of the licences of Ghanaians who have engaged the services of non-Ghanaians in mining contrary to the minerals and mining law; and
- Recommendations on sustaining the compliance and enforcement exercise.[11]

The nature of the operation was to be confidential, as previous efforts to curb these activities had been undermined and compromised with the leakage of information to offenders, which led to very little success in effecting arrests, especially by the police. The parts of the country that were most plagued – the Ashanti, Eastern, Central and Western Regions – were the initial points for action. The various District Security Committees and Regional Coordinating Councils[12] were fully involved and helped the NSCLNR in its swoops on illegal mining sites by assisting in providing accurate information and needed logistics at the local level.

The mode of operation of the NSCLNR task force was to include on the team personnel from the relevant state institutions, whether forestry, minerals or water, together with the security forces to effectively locate and apprehend the perpetrators of illegal mining crimes. The swoops were carried out simultaneously in various identified points. Ghanaian nationals arrested were handed over to the police, while foreigners were handed over to the immigration service who contacted the appropriate embassy to determine the status of such persons. Those without valid work permits were to be deported, while those who had breached their permits were to be dealt with within the law. These operations led to the arrest and repatriation of over two hundred Chinese people. Subsequently some Chinese opted for voluntary repatriation.

The NSCLNR proposed the sale of the seized equipment used in the illegal mining to defray the costs of reclamation and repatriation. However, the difficulty was that there were no clear regulatory provisions for such an action.

The National Security Committee was to a very large extent successful in its work. However, the performance of its duties was mainly focused on strict enforcement, and attempts to educate and assist in compliance were largely absent. To promote effective enforcement compliance, however,

---

[11] Minerals and Mining Act 2006 (Act 703), ss 14, 83.

[12] These are local government bodies in Ghana.

the National Security could collaborate with State institutions (mandated as such) to effectively educate the people involved in the breaches of environmental laws and assist such institutions in carrying out their mandates adequately.

6. CHALLENGES OF THE NSCLNR

The heavy reliance on force means that although the illegal activities have been reduced, they are likely to re-occur, especially if perpetrators believe they can do so by operating on the blind side of the law. As such this should be deemed not as a short-term measure, but rather as a long-term nationally driven programme of networking and enforcement.

A stronger involvement of local communities that could do the follow-up work should complement the actions of the NSCLNR. This would ensure greater success and generate interest in the issue of alternate livelihoods – long-term measure on which not much action has been taken.

7. CONCLUSIONS

Efforts at networking and collaboration in compliance enforcement have been going on in Ghana, albeit in a chequered manner. The lack of strong institutional structures, proper documentation and transparent systems of communication and collaboration, with institutions owning the process of improvement, has meant that progress has been slow.

The main challenges for these networking efforts in Ghana have been ineffective coordination, inadequate financing, lack of strong institutional commitment, and inadequate personnel and logistics to drive the efforts. The ECEN especially has been strapped of funds to hold meetings and to undertake activities, and thus its work has not moved beyond a handful of meetings and proposals.

The NSCLNR and its task force have the support and backing of the present government and most of their initial work has been successful to an extent. However, the sustainability of their work is speculative, as a clear institutional success plan for its work beyond presidential approval cannot be guaranteed. Therefore, if not clearly institutionalized by way of legislation, the lack of attention by subsequent governments may create problems, as the work of this committee and its task force is expensive.

Apart from its institutionalization, these compliance enforcement networks require cooperation from the citizenry. Thus, stepping up public education and compliance assistance initiatives and also the involvement of local government and even traditional authority in the work of these networks, will go a long way in the efforts to attain relative success in compliance enforcement networking.

The clear presence of political will to commit to and assist state institutions in the work of enforcement compliance will dramatically improve the work of networking for enforcement compliance.

It is therefore important that lessons learned from the challenges enumerated and suggestions made be taken up and used to effectively plan and strategize for enforcement compliance networking in Ghana.

BIBLIOGRAPHY

Larsey Mensah, Concept Paper for the Establishment of the West African Network for Environmental Compliance Enforcement, 2012 (unpublished).

Proceedings of the 9th International Conference on Environment, Compliance and Enforcement, Whistler BC, Canada, June 2011.

Report of the EPA Workshop on Effective Collaboration: A Tool for a Better Environmental Stewardship, 18–19 February 2003.

Legislation

Environmental Protection Act 1994 (Act 490).
Fines (Penalty Units) Act 572 (2000).
Ghana Republican Constitution 1992.
Minerals and Mining Act 2006 (Act 703).

22. Effective networking, formal versus substantial compliance, conflicting powers: strengths and weaknesses of environmental criminal provisions enforcement networks in Italy

Grazia Maria Vagliasindi*

1. INTRODUCTION

1.1 The National 'Networks' for the Enforcement of Environmental Criminal Provisions in the Italian Scientific Literature

The Italian scientific literature dealing with environmental criminal law does not seem to have attributed specific attention to the issue of environmental enforcement networks from a theoretical perspective.

Theoretical studies have been carried out in Italy on some relevant enforcement institutions whose structure is inspired by an idea of coordination not dissimilar in its substance to the cooperation idea underpinning the concept of network.[1] The effectiveness of criminal law (including environmental criminal law) and its judicial enforcement is a deeply analysed

* Researcher in Criminal Law at the University of Catania, Department of Law, Via Gallo 24, 95124, Catania, Italy, email: gvagliasindi@lex.unict.it; Scientific responsible for University of Catania FP7 Project EFFACE – European Union Action to Fight Environmental Crime (www.efface.eu). The research leading to these results has received funding from the European Union FP7 under grant agreement No. 320276. The text reflects only the author's views and the EU is not liable for any use that may be made of the information contained therein.

[1] See for instance Giuseppe Amato, 'Il potere di monitoraggio attribuito al Procuratore nazionale antimafia: contenuto e limiti' (1998) Cassazione penale 2781; Antonio D'Amato, 'L'impulso del procuratore nazionale antimafia nel procedimento di prevenzione' (2010) Critica penale 27; Giuliano Turone, *Le indagini collegate nel nuovo codice di procedura penale: la disciplina del coordinamento tra uffici diversi del pubblico ministero aggiornata alla più recente normativa antimafia*

topic and a well followed scientific approach.[2] Theoretical-practical studies have been undertaken on the need for investigative and judicial environmental enforcement networks in an international perspective.[3]

Despite this general approach, the research leading to this chapter did not show the existence, within the Italian juridical scientific literature, of conceptual studies on national enforcement networks with specific regard to environmental criminal provisions.

In fact Italian juridical scientific literature on environmental criminal law[4] mainly focuses on the analysis and evaluation of environmental criminal provisions, according to the fundamental principles of criminal law (e.g. the possibility of criminally punishing the damage to the environment in light of the rules on causality or the opportunity to criminalise a certain conduct in light of the *extrema ratio* principle). Effectiveness issues are often taken into consideration in a legal perspective; as such, they generally still concern the criminal provisions characteristics, either isolated (e.g. the possibility of subordinating probation upon conviction for certain environmental crimes to the restoration of the previous state of the environment) or as part of the overall legal system (e.g. the criminal sanction type and level, the applicable statute of limitation and the length

---

(Milano: Giuffrè, 1992); Silvio Sau, *Le indagini collegate: il coordinamento investigativo degli uffici del pubblico ministero* (Padova: Cedam, 2003).

2 See for instance, Carlo Enrico Paliero, *Il principio di effettività nel diritto penale* (Napoli: Editoriale Scientifica, 2011). For an example of the importance attributed to the judicial enforcement in all areas of criminal law (including environmental crime), see the many attentive contributions in the Journal Diritto penale contemporaneo, available (both printed and online versions) at http://www.penalecontemporaneo.it; with specific regard to environmental criminal law, see Amedeo Postiglione, *Controllo dei rifiuti pericolosi in Italia e in Europa: raccolta e analisi delle sanzioni amministrative e penali effettivamente applicate* (Padova: Centro Studi L'uomo e l'ambiente, 1986); Amedeo Postiglione (ed.), *Seconda Giornata per l'ambiente della Corte suprema di cassazione: Prevenzione, controllo, attuazione delle norme, informazione, formazione, partecipazione, accesso: ruolo della magistratura, del mondo scientifico, delle P.A., delle forze di polizia, della società civile, delle imprese* (Proceedings of the Conference held in Rome on 6 October 1999, Napoli: ESI, 2001); Amedeo Postiglione (ed.), *The Role of the Judiciary in the Implementation and Enforcement of Environmental Law* (Proceedings of the Conference held in Rome on 9–10 May 2003, Bruxelles: Bruylant, 2008); Luca Ramacci, *Reati ambientali e indagini di polizia giudiziaria* (Rimini: Maggioli, 2013).

3 See for instance, Amedeo Postiglione, *Global Environmental Governance: The Need for an International Environmental Agency and an International Court of the Environment* (Bruxelles: Bruylant, 2010).

4 It has to be underlined that not much of the Italian juridical scientific literature on the topic of environmental crime is available in English.

of the trial, and their effects on the effective imposition of the sanction). When empirical or specific law and economics assessments are carried out, they generally focus on the characteristics of the authors of environmental crimes (e.g. individuals v. collective entities), or on the relevance of the involved environmental/criminal law principles (e.g. precautionary principle v. offensiveness principle), or on the cost and impact of environmental crime (e.g. in relation to the protection of other relevant interests, like competition).

1.2 The National 'Networks' for the Enforcement of Environmental Criminal Provisions in the Italian Normative and Social System

Although somehow 'neglected' from a purely conceptual and theoretical point of view, the research showed that networking for the enforcement of environmental criminal provisions is, on the contrary, far from being neglected by the Italian normative and social system.

Since the 1980s, the increasing awareness of the importance of environmental protection, together with the awareness of the links between environmental crime and organised crime[5] (lately known as 'Ecomafia'),[6] gave rise in Italy to several environmental enforcement institutions and authorities, as well as to environmental non-governmental organisations.

These institutions and organisations, when individually considered, might not fulfil *tout court* the concept of network as it is defined in some scientific contexts;[7] nevertheless, the above-mentioned institutions,

---

[5] On the topic, see the Report 'Organised Environmental Crime in the EU Member States', available at http://ec.europa.eu/environment/legal/crime/pdf/organised_member_states.pdf (accessed 10 October 2013).

[6] For a scientific article in English on the Ecomafia phenomenon in Italy, with some reference to Italy in a comparative perspective, see Altin Shegani and Evis Xhaxha, 'The Albanian Criminal Law and Environmental Crime – Ecomafia' (28 March 2013) available at http://www.penalecontemporaneo.it (accessed 10 October 2013); from a multidisciplinary perspective, see Elena Past, '"Trash is Gold": Documenting the Ecomafia and Campania's Waste Crisis' (2013) Interdisciplinary Studies in Literature and Environment 1.

[7] See for instance, in the context of political science, the concept of policy network used by Tanja Börzel, 'Organizing Babylon: On the Different Conceptions of Policy Networks' (1998) 76 Public Administration 253, who considers a network as a set of relationships which are interdependent and non-hierarchical, linking actors who share common interests and exchange resources to pursue these interests, acknowledging cooperation as the best way to achieve common goals. With specific regard to environmental enforcement networks, see Grant William Pink, *Environmental Enforcement Networks: A Qualitative Analysis* (Charles Stuart University, 2010), who underlines that the goal of environmental enforcement

authorities and organisations seem to represent, for their abstract structure and/or concrete operational modes, relevant examples of a network-based approach to environmental compliance and enforcement.

Also in light of their actual mutual linkages (see particularly sections 2.3.1 and 2.3.2), they give rise *de facto* to environmental enforcement networks at the political-governmental public level, at the civil society level and at a mixed governmental-civil society level.

For these reasons and within these limits, in this chapter when referring to the above-mentioned institutions, authorities and organisations, the word networks will be hereinafter used.

1.3 Environmental Enforcement in Italy between Effective Networking and Lack of Cooperation

This chapter aims to describe those networks that appear to be more relevant in terms of potential compliance and enforcement benefits.

Only a part of these enforcement networks is specifically related to the environmental field, and, therefore, it specifically concerns the enforcement of environmental criminal provisions.

Other networks, although very relevant for the enforcement of key environmental criminal provisions, were originally created to combat the general phenomenon of organised crime, which recently also included within its ambit organised environmental crime; as such, their role and factual relevance for environmental enforcement is just a portion of a wider, more comprehensive and possibly major aim.

It seems important to keep in mind this distinction when evaluating the structure, relevance and effectiveness of the networks that are going to be described, as their specific links to environmental protection targets sensibly vary in strength and depth.

Together with examples of networking, this chapter describes a case where many different public authorities and actors were called on to intervene for (among other things) environmental criminal provisions enforcement. The hypothesis is that in this case the lack of informal networking for the enforcement of environmental provisions (including the criminal ones) has contributed to causing negative effects on the effectiveness of environmental protection, as well as on other related interests. The

---

networks is to facilitate cooperation and promote the effective implementation and enforcement of environmental law by sharing information and experiences between their members, building relationships and contacts across jurisdictions, raising awareness, improving environmental compliance and developing best practice and procedures.

hypothesis is also that this lack of networking might be at least partially related to a somehow 'formalistic' way of approaching the concept of environmental compliance, which might also contribute to explaining the previously mentioned lack of interest in a conceptual analysis of environmental criminal provisions enforcement networks within the Italian juridical scientific literature.

2. ENVIRONMENTAL CRIMINAL PROVISIONS ENFORCEMENT NETWORKS IN ITALY

In Italy several networks for the enforcement of environmental criminal provisions exist, at the political-governmental public level as well as at the civil society and mixed public-civil society levels.

Environmental enforcement networks are a potential key tool for the effectiveness of environmental protection, both in a global and national dimension, the two dimensions often being interconnected.[8] As is well known, the mere existence of a network doesn't imply that such a network is effective, and therefore that it produces an added value in terms of compliance and enforcement;[9] at the same time, the issue concerning the criteria for assessing the effectiveness of a network is very controversial.[10]

Although these profiles are not going to be specifically analysed in the context of this chapter, the networks we are about to describe seem to represent, for their structure and tasks, valid models of environmental criminal provisions enforcement networks.

---

8 On the relevance of cooperation between the different national authorities and enforcement agencies as well as between the authorities and agencies of different countries and governance levels see Donald Kaniaru, 'The Role of Institutions and Networks in Environmental Enforcement' (Proceedings of Sixth International Conference on Environmental Compliance and Enforcement, 2002) available at http://www.inece.org/conf/proceedings2/10-Role%20of%20Institutions.pdf (accessed 10 October 2013). See also Andrew Farmer, *Handbook of Environmental Protection and Enforcement: Principles and Practice* (London: Earthscan, 2007), 249.

9 See for instance, Garry Robins, Lorraine Bates and Philippa Pattison, 'Network Governance and Environmental Management: Conflict and Cooperation' (2011) 89 Public Administration 1293.

10 See again Garry Robins, Lorraine Bates and Philippa Pattison, 'Network Governance and Environmental Management: Conflict and Cooperation' (2011) 89 Public Administration 1293,1294 and literature therein. See also Grant William Pink, *Environmental Enforcement Networks: A Qualitative Analysis* (Charles Stuart University, 2010).

2.1 At the Public Level: A Network for the Prevention and Repression of all Environmental Crimes

2.1.1 Overview of relevant actors

At the public level, it is first of all worth analysing the *Comando dei Carabinieri per la Tutela dell'Ambiente* (originally called *Nucleo Operativo Ecologico dei Carabinieri*).[11]

The *Comando dei Carabinieri per la Tutela dell'Ambiente* (hereinafter: the *Comando*) was constituted in 1986[12] and it therefore represents the first European police force specifically aimed at the enforcement of environmental legislation.[13]

The *Comando* is a branch of the *Carabinieri* police force specialised in the investigation of environmental crimes.

The *Comando* is functionally dependent on the Ministry for the Environment. Its duties encompass control, prevention and repression of environmental violations, including the investigation of serious and transnational environmental crimes; information management and environmental security monitoring and forecast assessments; coordination and planning of control activities; and the definition of the strategic lines on which the action against environmental crime will be based and further developed.

As for the details of the network structure, the *Comando* is articulated in a central structure in Rome – composed of a *Comando* office, a *Reparto Operativo* (operative branch) and a Data Processing Centre – and in a periphery structure, composed of 29 nationwide offices. These 29 local offices depend upon three environmental protection groups, having an area-based competence (North, Centre and South of Italy, respectively located in Treviso, Rome and Naples).

As it concerns the central structure, the *Reparto Operativo* is composed of personnel specialised in environmental legislation and culture, and it therefore represents the specialised sector of the *Comando*.

The *Reparto Operativo* has a nationwide competence; it coordinates the local offices' activities and it undertakes the most complex investigations.

---

11 The current denomination was established by the Law 23 March 2001, No. 93.

12 By Article 8 of the Law 8 July 1986, No. 349; this Law instituted the Ministry for the Environment.

13 This information, as all the following information on the *Comando Carabinieri per la tutela dell'ambiente* provided in this paragraph, has been found at http://www.carabinieri.it/Internet/Cittadino/Informazioni/Tutela/Ambiente/ (accessed 10 October 2013); the translation is made by the author and it is not to be considered official.

The *Reparto Operativo* oversees several sections. The *Central Operative Section* mainly has investigative tasks on articulated investigations involving wide and serious environmental crimes, ultimately of international relevance. The *Radioactive Substances Pollution Section* focuses on the fight against illegal trafficking of radioactive waste and materials, and it is provided with mobile laboratories for radioactive substance detection. The *Air Pollution, Accidents, Risk, Industrial Plants and Water-Waste-Land Section* controls those industrial plants for which specific anti-accident regulations are in force. The *Analysis Section* is responsible for the management of information flow, for monitoring and forecasting assessments of environmental security (also with regard to the need to optimise the allocation of available resources; the Analysis Section therefore also includes a *Strategic Analysis Office for Environmental Security*, created in 2004, which is structured for the direct support of the strategic choices of the Ministry for the Environment), for the planning and coordination of control activities and for the definition of the strategic lines upon which the action against environmental crime will be based and further developed.

The *Reparto Operativo* carries out judicial police functions on environmental matters, excluding the technical-scientific profiles of the investigations. For the latter, the *Reparto* makes use of the deputed public organisms, and particularly of the Environmental Agencies System – the *Istituto Superiore per la Protezione e la Ricerca Ambientale* (ISPRA, formerly called *Agenzia per la protezione dell'Ambiente e del Territorio*, APAT) at national level and the *Agenzie Regionali per la Protezione dell'Ambiente* (ARPAs) located in each of the Italian Regions – of the National Health System and of the *Carabinieri* Scientific Investigations Group (*Raggruppamento Carabinieri Investigazioni Scientifiche*, Ra.C.I.S.).

The *Reparto* activity areas are soil, water, air and noise pollution; the safeguarding of natural heritage; the use of hazardous substances and industrial activities presenting the risk of relevant accidents; the use of radioactive materials and other radioactive sources; protection from electric, magnetic and electromagnetic exposures; and alarms related to the uncontrolled diffusion of genetically modified organisms.

The *Reparto Operativo* responds to intervention requests mainly from the Ministry for the Environment, the Judiciary and the common *Carabinieri*, as well as from individuals or associated citizens.

In light of its specific competences, the *Comando*, and particularly its *Reparto Operativo* is the specialist interlocutor for police forces at Europol (as per the directives enacted in January 1992 by the General Council for the Fight against Organised Crime; on this organism, see section 2.2.2 below) and Interpol level, in a logic of collaboration and coordination, according to which, environmental security is located in a supranational context.

Together with its very relevant judicial police activities against environmental crimes, the activity concerning environmental information carried out within the Analysis Section of the *Reparto* appears to be very significant from the perspective of an increase of environmental enforcement created by the means of networking.

The environmental information activity is undertaken through a net link with the ISPRA; this activity tends to become wider, since specific agreements with the ARPAs and with some of the Italian Regions have been developed.

The core connecting point of the information activity is the *Sala Situazione*, located in the central office in Rome. Here, a data base receives, organises, elaborates and distributes the information concerning the environmental control activities which are carried out by the competent organisms in the Italian Regions and at national level. In particular, the outcomes of all the environmental controls performed by the 29 nationwide offices of the *Comando* are included in the data base. For each controlled objective, the environmental information system creates a chart with all the data concerning the controlled physical or legal entity, the coordinates of the objective as individuated by the GPS, the outcomes of the control, the violation eventually detected and the photographs of the objective. In the *Sala Situazione* is also located a Crisis Hall (*Sala Crisi*) for the management of the most serious calamities; it is connected by videoconference with the Ministry for the Environment and the ISPRA.

2.1.2 Benefits of the network

The *Comando*'s structure, tasks and achievements demonstrate that it is a relevant model of effective networking on environmental enforcement matters.

Its benefits seem clear in terms of increased effectiveness in the detection and investigation of environmental crimes from a national and transnational perspective: these crimes, for their ontological nature, most often involve different areas of the State or several countries (e.g. the unauthorised dumping of wastewater causing pollution to a cross-State or cross-border watercourse, the illegal shipment of waste, the illegal trade in protected or endangered species) and they therefore require a coordinated action on control, detection and investigation.

Moreover, it has to be underlined that the *Comando* operates together with administrative enforcement authorities (the national and regional environmental agencies) and that it acts on the basis of inputs arising from public administrative and criminal provision enforcement authorities (the

Ministry for the Environment and the Judiciary) as well as from the civil society (the citizens and the associations denouncing a suspected environmental violation).

This network system therefore creates a coordinated approach between administrative and judicial environmental enforcement authorities as well as between all the involved public authorities and the civil society, in its individual or associated forms. Such a coordinated approach concerns (although with different intensity) both the investigative and the environmental information activities, and it clearly results in a benefit in terms of environmental compliance and enforcement, which could not be produced without a similar networking approach.

2.2 At the Public Level: Networks for Investigation and Prosecution of Organised Crime, Including Organised Environmental Crime

Other relevant examples of effective public formal networks on environmental criminal matters are provided for in the legislation on organised crime.

As was stated above, these networks were originally created to combat the general phenomenon of organised crime, which recently also included within its ambit organised environmental crime, the so-called 'Ecomafia'.

2.2.1 Organised environmental crime in Italy: an empirical and normative overview

To understand the importance of the organised environmental crime phenomenon with reference to Italy, we should consider that in 2012, the number of clans involved in the various branches of 'Ecomafia' was 302 (six more than in 2011) and that their turnover estimated for 2012 reached 16.7 billion euros (an increase of 0.1% compared to 2011).[14]

One of the most relevant sectors of the 'Ecomafia' phenomenon is the illegal trafficking of waste.

To fight this illegal activity, in 2001 the Italian legislator introduced the felony of 'Organised activities for the illegal trafficking of waste' (*Attività organizzate per il traffico illecito di rifiuti*), originally provided by Article 53-*bis* of Legislative Decree 5 February 1997, No. 22, and currently provided by Article 260 of Legislative Decree 3 April 2006, No. 152.

Art. 260 of Leg. Dec. No. 152/2006 establishes that:

---

[14] Data provided by Osservatorio Ambiente e Legalità (ed.), *Rapporto Ecomafia 2013* (Milano: Edizioni Ambiente, 2013).

> Whoever, in order to achieve an unfair profit, with more operations and through the establishment of means and continuing organised activities, sells, receives, transports, exports, imports, or otherwise improperly handles large quantities of waste shall be punished with imprisonment from one to six years. If the waste is highly radioactive, the punishment of imprisonment of three to eight years is enforced. The sentence would serve the accessory penalties provided for in articles 28, 30, 32 *bis*, 32 *ter* of the criminal code.[15]

This felony – which is the most serious and probably the only effective provision in the Italian environmental criminal legislation (on this point, see section 3) – cannot be considered an anti-organised crime provision in a strict sense, as the author of the crime can be 'Whoever' and not, as it would be in the case of a strictly anti-organised crime provision, two (more often three) or more people in association.

Nevertheless, this provision has many affinities with the pure anti-organised crime provisions, both from a structural and criminological point of view, and it was introduced in 2001 precisely with the goal of fighting the increasing involvement of organised crime in the illegal trafficking of waste.

2.2.2 Organised environmental crime and 'anti-mafia' networks

Due to increased awareness of the substantial organised crime nature of the felony of 'Organised activities for the illegal trafficking of waste', this crime was recently included in the list of crimes of serious social alarm whose investigation and prosecution is restricted to a 'network' of anti-mafia prosecutors, instituted in 1991:[16] the *Direzione Nazionale Antimafia* directed by the *Procuratore Nazionale Antimafia* at national level, and the *Direzioni Distrettuali Antimafia* at the local level.

The *Direzione Nazionale Antimafia* is an organ of the Prosecutor's Office of the Italian Supreme Court (the *Corte di Cassazione*) and its task is to coordinate the investigations on organised crime. It is composed of 20 prosecutors, expert in organised crime, and it is directed by the *Procuratore Nazionale Antimafia* who coordinates the activities of the 26 *Direzioni Distrettuali Antimafia* and has surveillance, control and avocation powers. As it concerns the coordination tasks, the *Procuratore Nazionale Antimafia* can't give binding directives to the local *Direzioni Distrettuali Antimafia*, but he can recall at the national level the investigations carried out by the

---

[15] The translation is made by the author and it is not meant to be official.

[16] The *Direzione Nazionale Antimafia*, directed by the *Procuratore Nazionale Antimafia*, and the *Direzioni Distrettuali Antimafia* were instituted by the Law Decree 20 November 1991, No. 327, converted into Law 20 February 1992, No. 8.

local *Direzione Distrettuali Antimafia* when the latter has proved to be inert or lacking due coordination with the other local *Direzioni Distrettuali Antimafia*.

As it concerns the phenomenon of organised environmental crime, Law 13 August 2010, No. 136 – establishing an extraordinary plan against organised crime and delegating the Government to enact a new Code of provisions against organised crime – included Article 260 of Leg. Dec. No. 152/2006 among those crimes considered to evoke special social alarm, listed in Article 51, section 3-*bis* of the Criminal Procedure Code.

According to Article 51, section 3-*bis*, of the Criminal Procedure Code, criminal investigation and prosecution of the listed crimes (now including organised activity for the illegal trafficking of waste) is attributed to the *Direzione Distrettuali Antimafia*, the specific anti-mafia office created in the Prosecutor's Office of each of the 26 Court of Appeal Districts. Article 371-*bis* of the Criminal Procedure Code gives the *Procuratore Nazionale Antimafia* competence in the coordination of, and input over the activities of, district anti-mafia prosecutors, as well as in related data and information collection.

Therefore, the formal network for the investigation and prosecution of organised crime now includes the environmental crime of 'Organised activities for the illegal trafficking of waste'.

It is probably still too early to evaluate the environmental compliance and enforcement benefits of the network for the investigation and prosecution of organised crime, as it is only recently that the crime of 'Organised activities for the illegal trafficking of waste' has been included within the network's competences.

Nevertheless, the coordinated system of criminal investigation and prosecution should produce relevant benefits in terms of enforcement of the above-mentioned environmental criminal provision, as the latter has an ontological and structural trans-territory (when not transnational) nature which requires networking activity for its effective detection and prosecution.

From the same perspective can be seen the *Direzione Investigativa Antimafia (D.I.A.)*, an office of the Department of Public Security of the Ministry for Internal Affairs, instituted in 1991.[17] The previously mentioned *Direzione Nazionale Antimafia*, with its coordinator the *Procuratore*

---

[17] The *D.I.A.* was instituted by the Law 30 December 1991, No. 410, which converted into Law the Law Decree 29 October 1991, No. 345. On *D.I.A.*, see Francesco Iannielli and Michele Rocchegiani, *La direzione investigativa antimafia* (Milano: Giuffrè, 1995).

Nazionale Antimafia, and the local *Direzioni Distrettuali Antimafia* make use for their investigations of the *D.I.A.* structure.

As for the latter, the *D.I.A.* is composed of a central structure located in Rome, articulated in three sections (Preventive Investigations, Judicial Investigations and International Relations for Investigative Purposes) with seven offices, and of a periphery structure, articulated in 12 operative centres and eight operative sections, with a total of around 1,300 dedicated personnel.

The task of the *D.I.A.* is to ensure the coordination of preventive investigative activities regarding organised crime, in its national and international dimension; on a semester basis, the Minister for Internal Affairs reports on the outcomes of the *D.I.A.* to Parliament.

Police forces dealing with environmental control (*Corpo Forestale dello Stato*) have recently been included among those police forces through which *D.I.A.* carries out its coordination tasks, as the crime of 'Organised activities for the illegal trafficking of waste' is now included within the *D.I.A.* activities and tasks (see Article 108, section 8, Legislative Decree 6 September 2011, No. 159, 'Code of provisions against organised crime and of preventive measures', as amended by Legislative Decree 15 November 2012, No. 218).[18]

Finally, it is worth recalling the General Council for the Fight Against Organised Crime (*Consiglio generale per la lotta alla criminalità organizzata*), composed of the Minister for Internal Affairs, the heads of each police force, the Directors of internal and external information services and the Director of *D.I.A.* (Article 107, Leg. Dec. No. 159/2011). The General Council issues directives and guidelines on all organised crime prevention and investigation activities and verifies the related achievements.

2.3 At the Civil Society Level and at a Mixed Public–Civil Society Level

2.3.1 Overview of relevant actors

As it concerns the civil society level, it is worth mentioning the networking activities carried out within the non-profit environmental organisation *Legambiente*, and particularly within its National Environment and Legality Observatory (*Osservatorio nazionale ambiente e legalità*).

---

[18] For an overview of the Code of provisions against organised crime and of preventive measures – the so-called *Codice antimafia* – see for example Francesco Menditto, 'Le luci e le (molte) ombre del cd. Codice antimafia' (2012) Cassazione penale 792; it has to be recalled that Legislative Decree 6 September 2011, No. 159 and Legislative Decree 15 November 2012, No. 218, were both enacted on the grounds of the delegation provided by the previously recalled Law No. 136/2010.

Legambiente was constituted in 1980 and it is an organisation working with the so-called 'scientific environmentalism' method.[19]

Within *Legambiente*, the National Environment and Legality Observatory (*Osservatorio nazionale ambiente e legalità*, hereinafter: the Observatory) carries out research, analysis and denunciation activities on the Ecomafia phenomenon. The Observatory plays a bridging role for information and the activities of police forces, judges, competent public authorities (*Direzione Investigativa Antimafia*, *Direzione Nazionale Antimafia*, Minister for Internal Affairs, Europol, Eurojust, etc.), environmentalist associations and anti-organised crime associations, lawyers and common citizens committed to the fight against environmental crimes, particularly when these crimes are perpetrated in an organised manner or otherwise connected to organised crime.

Since 1997, the Observatory annually coordinates and publishes '*Ecomafia*', a Report providing relevant data and information on organised environmental crime, including in terms of its transboundary and global dimensions. In particular, the Report analyses actual trends and the impact of violations of criminal environmental law when committed in a multi-individual or in a purely organised manner.

The scope of the Report includes the illegal dumping of hazardous waste, the illegal trafficking of waste, the smuggling of proscribed hazardous materials, and the illegal exploitation and trafficking of protected wildlife and other natural resources.

The Report is the result of a network activity, and particularly of a collaboration between the Environment and Legality Observatory of *Legambiente*, on one side, and police forces (*Arma dei Carabinieri*, *Corpo Forestale dello Stato e delle Regioni a statuto speciale*, *Capitanerie di porto*, *Guardia di Finanza*, *Polizia di Stato*, *Direzione investigativa antimafia*), a research institute (*Cresme*), judges engaged in the fight against environmental criminality and lawyers, on the other.

2.3.2 Benefits of the network

The above-described network has delivered effective compliance and enforcement benefits with regard to environmental criminal provisions, including those related to organised environmental crime.[20]

---

[19] This information and the following information on *Legambiente* and its activities, including those of the *Osservatorio nazionale ambiente e legalità*, is available at www.legambiente.it (accessed 10 October 2013); the translation is made by the author and it is not to be considered official.

[20] It has to be underlined that the Report also gives relevant data and information on the activities of the networks described in sections 2.1 and 2.2; these data

In fact, the *Ecomafia* report in itself has to be considered as a benefit in terms of compliance and enforcement, as it greatly contributes to informing the civil society regarding a phenomenon which seriously harms the environment as well as many other relevant legal interests protected by the means of criminal law, such as public order and the public economy.

From this perspective, the network's activity greatly contributes to raising the awareness of citizens regarding the importance of environmental compliance, and it seems therefore to contribute to enhancing the deterrence function that environmental criminal provisions, as all criminal provisions, are primarily called on to undertake.

At the same time, the information collected and elaborated in the Report might be useful for the assessment by the legislator of the characteristics, dimensions and offensiveness of the criminal phenomenon, as well as for the assessment of the deterrence effect and overall effectiveness of the existing environmental criminal provisions in fighting it. The information can also be useful in terms of eventually formulating and introducing new and better-tailored criminal law provisions. In fact, it is well known that environmental information should be considered as a fundamental tool in all processes related to sustainable development: environmental data and information are one of the key elements in identifying and developing effective and legitimate policy solutions,[21] and this is also the case in the field of criminal law.

3. FORMAL V. SUBSTANTIAL COMPLIANCE

Despite these positive examples of formal and informal networking, it has to be underlined that Italy still experiences considerable problems in adjusting to the underlying logic and the precise requirements of EU environmental policies.[22]

---

and information give clear indications in the sense of environmental criminal provisions enforcement benefits arising from the network's activities.

[21] See Bernardo De Bernardinis, 'Intervento' in Amedeo Postiglione (ed.), *Proceedings of the International Conference on Global Environmental Governance of 20–21 May 2010* (Rome: Ispra, 2011), 55; see also, although in a partially different perspective, Andrew Farmer, *Handbook of Environmental Protection and Enforcement: Principles and Practice* (London: Earthscan, 2007), 179.

[22] On the issue, from different perspectives, see for example, Charalampos Koutalakis, 'Environmental Compliance in Italy and Greece: The Role of Non-State Actors' (2004) 13 Environmental Politics 754; Geoffrey Pridham, 'Environmental Policies and Problems of European Legislation in Southern Europe' (1996) 1 South European Society and Politics 47.

In particular, among some of the interested Authorities a certain tendency still exists to interpret environmental compliance as the mere formal compliance by the national legislator with the European Union environmental legislation, and therefore as simply the introduction of an extremely high number of normative tools, with a partial lack of a comprehensive and coordinated approach to their overall coherence as well as to enforcement and their chances of effectiveness.

The case of the transposition of the directives 2008/99/EC on environmental crime and 2009/123/EC on ship-source pollution and the introduction of penalties for infringements[23] is illustrative in this sense.

In fact, the obligations of criminal protection established by the directives would have implied an in-depth reform of the Italian legislation on environmental crimes. Nevertheless, the missed consideration upon formulating the Delegation Law 4 June 2010, No. 96, of the specific needs of transposition related to the directives and the consequent limits put in place on the delegated legislator, who was forced to act within the narrow confines of the criminal sanctions for misdemeanours ('*contravvenzioni*'), made it so that the legislation on environmental crimes in Italy remained basically unchanged.[24]

Environmental crimes in Italy are still almost always regarded as misdemeanours ('*contravvenzioni*').[25] Consequently they attract penalties that are, all things considered, ineffective in terms of protecting the

---

23 On the directives and their implementation, see Michael Faure, 'The Implementation of the Environmental Crime Directives in Europe' (Proceedings of the International Conference on Environmental Compliance and Enforcement, 2011) 360 available at http://inece.org/conference/9/proceedings/41_Faure.pdf (accessed 10 October 2013).

24 See Grazia Maria Vagliasindi, 'The European Harmonisation in the Sector of Protection of the Environment through Criminal Law: The Results Achieved and Further Needs for Intervention' (2012) New Journal of European Criminal Law 320.

25 Few rare felonies ('*delitti*') exist, the most relevant one being the crime of 'Organised activity for the illegal trafficking of waste' provided for in Art. 260, Leg. Dec. No. 152/2006; courts also increasingly make use of the general criminal provisions referred to in Articles 434 and 449 of the Criminal Code (respectively, 'Collapse of buildings or other disasters' and 'Crimes of negligent damage'), contesting the Code for 'environmental disaster'. It has to be noted that several bill drafts aimed to introduce environmental felonies ('*delitti*') in the Criminal Code and the related liability of collective entities, but, for the most part, these attempts were swept away by the early termination of the Legislatures. In February 2014 the Chamber of the Deputies approved a draft bill aiming to include four new environmental felonies in the Criminal Code; to become effective, the draft bill needs the approval of the other wing of the Parliament (the Senate).

environment from particularly offensive conduct. It should be noted that this characteristic of Italian environmental crimes (i.e. being '*contravvenzioni*') has a number of additional drawbacks – for example, a short prescriptive period, the possibility of suspended sentences, extinction of the offence by cash settlement ('*oblazione comune*' or '*oblazione speciale*' according to cases) – and these have a negative impact on the effective application of the criminal sanction. In addition, investigative obstacles are created, such as the inability to make use of wire-tapping and the impossibility of applying *in personam* precautionary measures.

Therefore, following the transposition of the directives, Italian environmental criminal law, although formally complying with the criminalisation obligations arising from the directives, substantially betrays these obligations by maintaining one of the main causes of the ineffectiveness of environmental criminal provisions.

Similarly, it should be recalled that, although for a long time and advocated by many,[26] the (administrative) liability of legal persons and collective entities for environmental crimes committed to their benefit was introduced in Italy by Legislative Decree 7 July 2011, No. 121, only because of the necessity of complying with directives 2008/99/EC and 2009/123/EC.[27] However, relevant environmental offences, such as those related to the lack of or the non-compliance with the *Autorizzazione integrata ambientale* (the IPPC permit), were not included in the list of environmental crimes which legal persons (collective entities) can be held responsible for; the consequence is that when a company operates without the required IPPC permit, the company as such will not be held responsible for the related criminal offences.

This somehow 'formalistic' approach might be explained by the legitimate need of the legislator to take into account the economic consequences of the environmental regulatory system. Nevertheless, it seems to negatively influence the relevance of environmental enforcement networking benefits as a conceptual issue, which on the contrary should be taken into account, along with other issues, when enacting and

---

26 See for example, Domenico Pulitanò, 'La responsabilità "da reato" degli enti nell'ordinamento italiano' (2003) Cassazione penale, No. 6 (special supplement), 7; Licia Siracusa, *La tutela penale dell'ambiente* (Milano: Giuffrè, 2007).

27 For an overview of rules on liability of collective entities for environmental crimes in the Italian legal system following Leg. Dec. No. 121/2011, see Grazia Maria Vagliasindi, 'Liability of Legal Persons and Collective Entities for Environmental Crimes in Italian Law' (2012) Eucrim 131; Grazia Maria Vagliasindi, *Attività d'impresa e criminalità ambientale. La responsabilità degli enti collettivi* (Catania: Torre, 2012).

enforcing environmental provisions. Such a conclusion would indirectly contribute to explaining the previously mentioned lack of interest in a mainly substantial-orientated issue like the conceptual analysis of environmental criminal provisions enforcement networks within the Italian juridical scientific literature. From this perspective, this situation would produce a 'vicious circle', as the lack of conceptual analysis on compliance and enforcement networks deprives the interested authorities of the fundamental input in terms of a solid conceptual ground for further interventions that in this field might be provided by the outcome of scientific research.

Moreover, this approach might produce negative effects on the social perception of environmental crime.[28] This diminishes the potential benefits produced by the existing Italian informal network, which aims at informing the civil society on the dimension of a relevant environmental criminal phenomenon such as organised environmental crime and on the related prevention, control and repressive actions undertaken by the competent authorities, often through a network (see sections 2.3.1 and 2.3.2). From this perspective, this 'formalistic' approach might therefore be counted among the indirect causes of the persistent lack of compliance with important environmental legislation whose violations are criminally punished; this seems particularly relevant with regard to corporations, whose environmental actions and choices are nowadays significantly influenced by the consumers' and citizens' opinions and perceptions of the corporations' attitude towards the environment.

[28] In general, on how different legal instruments affect people's moral intuitions and willingness to engage in social enforcement in the field of environmental law, see Yuval Feldman and Oren Perez, 'How Law Changes the Environmental Mind: An Experimental Study of the Effect of Legal Norms on Moral Perceptions and Civic Enforcement' (2009) 36 Journal of Law and Society 501. See also Charalampos Koutalakis, 'Environmental Compliance in Italy and Greece: The Role of Non-State Actors' (2004) 13 Environmental Politics 754; the author challenges the conventional assumption that the poor record of compliance of Italy, Greece and Spain with EU environmental legislation is often attributed to an alleged weakness of civil societal activism in environmental matters, underlining that recent literature offers evidence of high levels of grassroots environmental mobilisations.

4. ENVIRONMENTAL MISCOMPLIANCE BY CORPORATIONS CAUSING ENVIRONMENTAL, HEALTH AND ECONOMIC HARM: THE MISSING 'NETWORK' AND CONFLICTING POWERS

The tension between a formal 'compliance' concept, such as the one exemplified in the previous section, and a substantial compliance concept, such as the one seen in the intense control and investigative and enforcement activities against environmental crimes carried out by police forces, prosecutors and judges, might create serious 'networking' challenges. A more detailed discussion of a case can illustrate the point.

4.1 The Ilva Case

The case in this sense appears paradigmatic (still under judgment), concerning an Italian industrial company – Ilva S.p.a., exporting its products throughout Europe and beyond – and particularly its industrial plant in Taranto.

Apparently the company didn't comply (among other things) with environmental regulations (mainly the IPPC provisions), causing serious environmental pollution (mainly through the emissions of polluting substances into the air) which seems to have provoked serious damage to human and animal health, as well as consequential damage to other economic activities in the area.[29]

---

[29] On 26 September 2013, a press release announced that the European Commission is taking action against Italy in an effort to reduce the environmental impact of the Ilva steel plant in Taranto; while the Commission sees recent commitments made by the Italian authorities to address the situation as a positive sign, it is nevertheless asking Italy to respect its obligations under the IPPC Directive and the Environmental Liability Directive; more information is available at http://europa.eu/rapid/press-release_IP-13–866_en.htm (accessed 10 October 2013). On the various problematic issues raised by the Ilva case, see Gianfranco Amendola, 'La magistratura e il caso Ilva. Prime riflessioni' (2012) Questione Giustizia, No. 5, 9; Angelo Merlin, 'Caso Ilva. Inquinamento e salute: alcuni profili di rischio' (2012) Ambiente & Sicurezza, No. 20, 44; Marina Zalin and Luciano Butti, 'Caso Ilva. Idoneità e legittimità delle nuove disposizioni dopo la conversione del D.L.' (2013) Ambiente & Sicurezza, No. 2, 80; Francesco Viganò, 'In questo numero' (2013) Diritto penale contemporaneo, No. 1, 1; Roberto Bin, 'L'Ilva e il soldato Baldini' (2013) Diritto penale contemporaneo, No. 1, 5; Alessandro Morelli, 'Il decreto Ilva: un drammatico bilanciamento tra principi costituzionali' (2013) Diritto penale contemporaneo, No. 1, 7; Angioletta Sperti, 'Alcune riflessioni sui profili costituzionali del decreto Ilva' (2013) Diritto penale contemporaneo, No. 1, 12; Giuseppe Arconzo, 'Note critiche sul "decreto legge ad Ilvam", tra legislazione

This resulted in the managers and directors being arrested and charged with several crimes: not only environmental ones, but also crimes related to health and safety in the workplace as well as for the crime set out under Article 434 of the Criminal Code (the so-called 'unnamed disaster', in this case defined as an 'environmental disaster').

It also resulted in the precautionary seizure of several productive areas of the industrial plant, which was issued pursuant to Article 321 of the Criminal Procedure Code by the judge for the preliminary inquiry.

The seizure order caused a serious economic threat to the company and to the hundreds of its employees, as the seizure judicial decree had excluded the possibility of using the concerned areas of the plant pending the precautionary seizure, therefore precluding the possibility of continuing productive activity; it has to be recalled that a second precautionary seizure was issued by the judge of the preliminary inquiry, this time concerning materials in stock as they were considered the product of the crimes.

In order to face the economic consequences of the seizure and the strong protests of the employees,[30] a Law Decree was then enacted by the Government, and later converted into Law by the Parliament,[31] introducing both general and *ad hoc* provisions in order to allow the industrial plant to continue operations, despite the judiciary decision to seize the plant and to stop production.

---

provvedimentale, riserva di funzione giurisdizionale e dovere di repressione e prevenzione dei reati' (2013) Diritto penale contemporaneo, No. 1, 16; Domenico Pulitanò, 'Fra giustizia penale e gestione amministrativa: riflessioni a margine del caso ILVA' (2013) Diritto penale contemporaneo, No. 1, 44; Fabio Di Cristina, 'Gli stabilimenti di interesse strategico nazionale e i poteri del Governo' (2013) Giornale di diritto amministrativo 369; Marco Cuniberti, 'Il D.L. sull'Ilva, tra conflitti di attribuzione e dubbi di legittimità costituzionale' (2013) Ambiente & Sviluppo 205; Franco Giampietro, 'Ilva: dalla sentenza della Sovrana Corte n. 85/2013 al D.L. n. 61/2013' (2013) Ambiente & Sviluppo 705; Ugo Salanitro, 'Il decreto Ilva tra tutela della salute e salvaguardia dell'occupazione: riflessioni a margine della sentenza della Corte costituzionale' (2013) Corriere giuridico 1041; Marisa Meli, 'Ambiente, salute, lavoro: il caso Ilva' (2013) Nuove leggi civili commentate 1017; Grazia Maria Vagliasindi, 'Enti collettivi e reati ambientali tra responsabilità "penale" e responsabilità sociale' in Bruno Montanari (ed.), *La costruzione dell'identità europea. Sicurezza collettiva, libertà individuali e modelli di regolazione sociale* (vol. I, Torino: Giappichelli, 2012), 367.

[30] On these protests, see Nazareno Dinoi, 'Ilva, scattano sequestro e arresti, 8mila operai occupano le vie di Taranto' *Corriere del Mezzogiorno* (26 July 2012) available at http://corrieredelmezzogiorno.corriere.it (accessed 10 October 2013).

[31] Law Decree 3 December 2012, No. 207, converted (with amendments) into Law 24 December 2012, No. 231.

Law Decree 3 December 2012, n. 207, as converted into Law 24 December 2012, No. 231, establishes in general that, when a situation of economic crisis occurs within a company of national strategic relevance with more than two hundred employees (and therefore there being a compelling need to safeguard occupation and production),[32] the Minister for the Environment, while revising the IPPC permit, may authorise the industrial plants to continue their economic activities for 36 months, despite the precautionary seizure order eventually imposed by a judge. The Law Decree specifically establishes that the Ilva industrial plant must be considered of strategic national relevance, it puts Ilva back in possession of the seized goods and it authorises the prosecution of its production activities.

These provisions seemed to substantially nullify the effects of the judicial precautionary seizures.

As a consequence of the enactment and conversion into Law of the previously mentioned Law Decree, a conflict of powers challenge was raised by the proceeding prosecutor against the Government and Parliament; moreover, the involved Court for the re-examination of precautionary measures and the judge for the preliminary inquiry challenged the constitutional legitimacy of the Law Decree, as converted into Law.

The Constitutional Court, called on to decide on both issues, did not admit the challenge of conflict of powers[33] or the constitutional legitimacy one;[34] the latter was also declared partly ungrounded. The Constitutional Court decisions considered, among other profiles, the economic protection aims pursued by the Government and Parliament.

After the Constitutional Court decisions, the same judge for the preliminary inquiry ordered the precautionary seizure (finalised to the confiscation order of an equivalent value) of 8 billion euros (the amount corresponding to the estimated proceeds of the crimes attributed to the managers and directors of Ilva) belonging to a holding corporation of the Ilva company; at the time of the seizure the company was managed by the same persons who had managed Ilva at the time of the commission of the facts contested in the Ilva case.

This seizure order was issued pursuant to Legislative Decree 8 June 2001,

---

32 See Ugo Salanitro, 'Il decreto Ilva tra tutela della salute e salvaguardia dell'occupazione: riflessioni a margine della sentenza della Corte costituzionale' (2013) Corriere giuridico 1041.

33 Corte Costituzionale, ord. 13 February 2013, No. 16; Corte Costituzionale, ord. 13 February 2013, No. 17; the decisions are available at www.penalecontemporaneo.it (14 February 2003) (accessed 10 October 2013).

34 Corte Costituzionale, 9 May 2013, No. 85, available at www.penalecontem poraneo.it (9 May 2013) (accessed 10 October 2013).

n. 231, on liability of collective entities for the crimes committed to their benefit, in the specific case of the charge of criminal association in order to commit an 'environmental disaster'. In particular, the order was issued pursuant Art. 24-*ter* of Leg. Dec. No. 231/2001, which includes the crime of unlawful association for committing felonies ('*Associazione per delinquere*') provided by Art. 416 of the Criminal Code among the crimes from which the liability of collective entities can arise when committed for their benefit, read in connection with the above-mentioned Art. 434 of the Criminal Code, providing for the felony of collapse of buildings or other disasters as well as with the felonies of removing or omitting precautions against accidents on workplaces and poisoning water or alimentary substances respectively provided by Articles 437 and 439 of the Criminal Code.

It must be recalled that Articles 434, 437 and 439 of the Criminal Code are not expressly included among the listed crimes for which collective entities can be held responsible; according to the judge for the preliminary inquiry, as well as the Court for the re-examination of precautionary measures who confirmed the order, these provisions could nevertheless have assumed indirect relevance as goal-felonies of the criminal association.

These considerations depose in the sense that the seizure order seems aimed at substantially overcoming the provisions *ad Ilvam* and the related decisions of the Constitutional Court through a reading of the involved provisions, which, also in light of the judicial and normative framework of the Ilva case described so far, seems to force the spirit, if not the letter, of the same provisions.

The Supreme Court annulled the precautionary seizure order issued pursuant Leg. Dec. 231/2001, on the grounds (among other reasons) that the crimes provided by Articles 434, 437 and 439 of the Criminal Code are not included in the list of crimes for which collective entities can be held responsible. The Supreme Court also rejected in the case at stake the possibility for Articles 434, 437 and 439 of the Criminal Code to assume indirect relevance as goal-felonies regarding the crime of unlawful association for committing felonies (with the latter included in the list of crimes attributable to the collective entities), as this reading would violate the principle of legality.[35]

4.2 Lessons from the Ilva Case

As is clear, many relevant actors and institutions were and continue to be involved in this case: the legislator, the government enforcement

---

[35] Corte di Cassazione, 20 December 2013, No. 3635, available at www.penalecontemporaneo.it (11 February 2014), accessed 7 March 2014.

institutions, the judiciary, the company and its employees, the civil society (including media) and other stakeholders.

The case involves the enforcement of many relevant legal provisions, in a framework where the enforcement of environmental legislation is strictly linked to the enforcement of other relevant specific provisions (such as those on safety in workplaces) as well as of general substantial and procedural criminal provisions. The case also involved the constitutional rules on distribution of power and, moreover, the same fundamental concept of separation of powers and the role of the judiciary in the area of criminal law.[36]

Moreover, the case shows the need to adequately take into consideration the links between environmental protection and economic-occupational interests when enacting and enforcing (among other things) environmental provisions, as both activities imply a deep reflection on the balance between environmental protection, health protection and work safety protection, as well as a study on the balance between the above-mentioned factors and economic activities and competition.

Clearly, dealing with such a complex, multilevel and articulated case would require a high level of cooperation and informal networking among all the interested parties.

Looking at the facts, some significant gaps in networking have occurred, reaching the level of a conflict of powers challenge, probably as a consequence of (among other issues) the above-mentioned different approaches to the issue of environmental compliance.

These gaps in networking contributed to generating relevant consequences: the increased time needed to solve the conflict; the emergency (and indeed not thought through enough) introduction of provisions which potentially apply to future similar critical situations; the adoption of judicial decisions which, with the aims of overcoming the legislative intervention and the Constitutional Court decisions, might be interpreted as partially forcing if not the letter at least the rationale of some normative provisions, as well as violating some fundamental principles of punitive law. All these elements do not seem to produce positive effects on the ultimate goal of the protection of the environment and of the other related interests, as well as, in a more general perspective, on the fundamental principles of criminal law and on the same concept of separation of powers.

---

[36] On the latter profiles, see for instance Domenico Pulitanò, 'Fra giustizia penale e gestione amministrativa: riflessioni a margine del caso ILVA' (2013) Diritto penale contemporaneo, No. 1, 44; Francesco Viganò, 'In questo numero' (2013) Diritto penale contemporaneo, No. 1, 1.

5. CONCLUDING REMARKS

The analysis conducted so far demonstrates that, despite a certain indifference towards environmental criminal provisions enforcement networks from a conceptual and theoretical perspective, in Italy there do exist relevant examples of effectiveness in networking (formal and informal, at the public level, at the civil society level and at a mixed public-civil society level) for the enforcement of environmental criminal provisions.

Also, the conceptual importance and practical benefits of networks in the specific field of the fight against organised environmental crime was demonstrated.

The structure, tasks and achievement of these networks depose in the sense that the latter are potentially effective models of environmental enforcement networks.

Nevertheless, these positive examples still coexist with some relevant gaps to be filled when it comes to substantial compliance, as well as to cooperation between powers and authorities which are involved in environmental enforcement. These profiles might contribute to creating challenges to environmental compliance and enforcement, therefore negatively affecting the environmental protection goals achievement and related relevant economic interests and resulting in a substantial breach of the same fundamental principle of sustainable development as well as of the relevant fundamental principles of criminal law.

This conclusion calls for the need to foster informal networking between public authorities as well as between public authorities and corporations and stakeholders for environmental compliance and enforcement.

Moreover, the need to adequately take into consideration the links between environmental protection and economic-occupational interests should not be neglected in the future development of environmental legislation and the related formal and informal compliance and enforcement networks.

This seems necessary to make further progress in ensuring a more effective application of environmental legislation, also through a network culture which can contribute to reaching a greater consistency of approach in the implementation, application and enforcement of environmental legislation.

23. Domestic environmental enforcement networks: the practice of China

Xinyuan Lu,* Hu Qin† and Jun Yang‡

1. RECONSIDERATION OF CHINA'S ENVIRONMENTAL ENFORCEMENT

China traces its history of environmental protection back to 1973, when the first national conference on environmental protection was held. In less than one decade after the conference, China pronounced its first statute on environmental law.[1] And following that, several environmental and resources laws were successively passed. As a measure to ensure the implementation of these environmental statutes, environmental enforcement is therefore listed as a formal responsibility of environmental authorities. But the capacity of enforcement agencies remained very weak in their first two decades, *inter alia* due to insufficient awareness of environmental protection at the level of local governments.

At early stages of environmental protection, the pollution levy was embraced as an instrument to change the emitters' behaviours and to collect money to support local investment in pollution abatement and control projects and to finance the operation of environmental protection

* Subcommittee of Environmental Enforcement of the Chinese Society for Environmental Sciences, Jin Mao Tower, No.18 Xizhimen Wai Street, Beijing, China, email: lxy@12369.gov.cn

† Environmental Defense Fund China Program, Yonghe Plaza, No. 28 Andingmen Wai Street, Beijing, China, email: qinhu@cet.net.cn

‡ Environmental Defense Fund China Program, Yonghe Plaza, No. 28 Andingmen Wai Street, Beijing, China, email: yangjun@cet.net.cn

[1] On September 13, 1979, the 11th Session of the Standing Committee of National People's Congress approved the *Environmental Protection Law (trial version)* of the People's Republic of China, which was the first basic law on environmental protection in China.

agencies.[2] The pollution levy was a very important assurance for local environmental protection as no other instrument was as powerful in making money so quickly. Therefore, at that time the enforcement agencies focused their daily work mainly on a prompt and complete collection of the pollution levy. This early responsibility is still administered by the local enforcement agencies today.

Not all of the local governments were willing to establish their own enforcement agencies. With more and more violations occurring, the National Environmental Protection Bureau (NEPB) of the central government was aware of the importance of professional enforcement teams in ensuring compliance across the country. In a large country like China, it was not easy to execute one initiative at the same time in each province, especially when no experiences or mature scheme was available. In light of this situation, the NEPB chose to begin with a pilot on a smaller scale in 1986 and then extended this to 22 provinces in 1992, including 57 cities and 100 counties. The pilot did work in pushing local governments to establish their own enforcement agencies and enabling the NEPB to accumulate experience in managing national environmental enforcement. On the basis of the pilot, the Department of Personnel of the State Council in 1995 issued a rule to recognize the existence of environmental enforcement and categorized enforcement officers as quasi-public servants to be managed. The rule conferred legitimacy on environmental enforcement.

The establishment of environmental enforcement agencies was the first step on a long road in the fight against environmental violations. The second step was to build up the capacity of these new enforcement agencies. The State Environmental Protection Agency (SEPA), the successor of the NEPB, therefore launched a further initiative to establish organizational standards in enforcement agencies and developed enforcement rules that regulated the behaviour of enforcement officers. In 1999, the SEPA issued a comprehensive rule detailing the nature of the enforcement agency, organizational standards, responsibilities, staff management and inspection norms.[3] The rule served as a guideline for the capacity building of local enforcement agencies. The basic landscape of the environmental enforcement system was characterized by four layers of agencies – national, provincial, municipal and county level – and was framed accord-

---

[2] In Article 18 of *Environmental Protection Law (trial version)*: 'The discharge exceeding the national standard will be charged based on the quantity and density of the pollutants'.

[3] The rule is '*Notice on Instructions on Further Advancing Environmental Monitoring*' issued by SEPA, available at http://www.zhb.gov.cn/gkml/zj/wj/200910/t20091022_171928.htm (China).

ingly. In line with the rule, the total number of enforcement officers went up incrementally and amounted to more than sixty thousand in 2012.[4]

The rapid growth of enforcement officers was not in concert with the increasingly severe pollution levels, driven by the unprecedented economic development in the first decade of the new century. China experienced a steady and rapid growth since its reform and opening up. From 1978 to 2012, China's annual economic growth rate averaged 9.9 per cent and its GDP share in the world rose from 4.4 per cent to 10 per cent, which made it the world's second largest economy. However, this marvellous economic achievement comes at a high price, namely through consuming nearly 60 per cent of the world's cement, 49 per cent of its steel and 20.3 per cent of its energy.[5] Moreover, economic growth causes heavy pollution to China. China has now become one of the largest emitters of CO_2, SO_2, NOx and greenhouse gases. To cut off emissions, companies are required to invest more and more in pollutants abatement. The heavier burdens imposed by the requirement breeds the incentives for rational emitters to benefit from ruling out such investment. Enforcement agencies have to make more effort and spend more resources than ever before to ensure compliance.

In response to the situation, SEPA renewed the standards of capacity building for environmental enforcement agencies in 2006.[6] The new round of initiatives aimed to equip enforcement with cutting-edge enforcement technologies to increase inspection efficiency and the effectiveness of deterrence. These tools included inspection vehicles to increase mobility and inspection frequency and on-site instant detection instruments to capture violations. Emission data management attracted more attention at this stage. Companies were required to install a Continuous Emission Monitoring System (CEMS) to help enforcement agencies to obtain real-time emission data without on-site inspection. As a continuation of equipment-centred capacity building, mobile enforcement was rolled

---

4 Ministry of Environmental Protection, National Communique of Environmental Statistics (2012), available at http://zls.mep.gov.cn/hjtj/qghjtjgb/201311/t20131104_262805.htm

5 See Liu Jianqiang, *Annual Report on Environmental Development of China* (first published 2013).

6 In 1999, the MEP (formerly SEPA) started to carry out enforcement capacity standardization in order to promote enforcement capacity. In the technical document *Notice of the Opinions on Strengthening Environmental Enforcement*, the MEP set up three levels of standards to measure the capacity of enforcement agencies, consisting of two categories: institutional capacity (numbers of staff) and equipment (vehicles, monitoring instruments and office equipment). Since the standards were released, MEP updated them twice, in 2006 and 2011.

out in the 12th Five Year Plan (FYP) (2011–2015).[7] Central government granted seed funding to the local enforcement agencies to adopt mobile technologies, through which their work efficiency and ability to manage data were expected to be enhanced.

Inputs, whether human resources or equipment, for a long time were the priorities of capacity building in environmental enforcement. This approach was justified as the capacity of enforcement agencies was always lagging behind enforcement demands. With enforcement agencies becoming mature, capacity building needed a new approach. The 12th FYP was seeing such new efforts made by the Ministry of Environmental Protection (MEP) (the successor of SEPA). In July of 2012, the MEP issued the *Notice to Strengthen the Effectiveness and Efficiency of Environmental Enforcement and Implementation Pilot of Performance Evaluation.* This marked the end of the input-oriented capacity building and a results-oriented approach was explored.

When strengthening local environmental enforcement, central government is also consistently building up its own capacity to manage enforcement. In 2003 the Bureau of Environmental Supervision was established as an office of the SEPA to oversee the local governments. Among its responsibilities were the supervision of local government to take account of environmental enforcement and the development of enforcement and compliance policies. Later the supervision of local government was strengthened with the establishment of SEPA's six regional offices, which put local government under close scrutiny.[8]

The evolution of environmental enforcement clearly reveals a linear responsive strategy of the government to environmental violations. Local governments are required to accept accountability and establish the enforcement capacity to curb violations, while central government is making efforts to supervise them. This kind of strategy overstressed the importance of inputs and capacity building of enforcement to deter increasing violations. However, the fact that violations have never been eliminated, with the continuous inputs, frustrates the strategy. Furthermore, devising some definite criteria to judge the amount of resources and people

---

[7] The Five Year Plan (FYP) is developed by the central government to arrange key national construction projects, manage the distribution of productive forces and individual sectors' contributions to the national economy, map the direction of future development, and set targets. In 1953, the central government implemented its first FYP. A total of 12 five year plans have been made and implemented to date.

[8] See Bureau of Environmental Supervision of Ministry of Environmental Protection, Environmental Inspection (3th edn) (2009), p. 3.

required to respond to violations is problematic. No matter how strong enforcement agencies are, they cannot solidly address tricky issues like transboundary violations, overlapping functions of different agencies, the high professional skills and expertise needed in some areas and the information asymmetry between emission sources, the public and enforcement agencies.

The weakness of traditional hierarchic organization and rule-based enforcement is being recognized by China. It has been decided to explore new ways of working. The establishment of regional offices of the MEP and performance evaluation is among these efforts. Regional offices are means to solve the transboundary issues. Performance evaluation shows the MEP's tendency to shift rule-based enforcement to result-based capacity building after decades of emphasis on inputs and its attempts to solve information asymmetry by collecting and sharing performance information. These efforts are taking effect to a very limited extent because they are mainly targeted at improving effectiveness from the perspective of those within the bureaucracy. Ways of strengthening enforcement from the perspective of those within enforcement agencies should be reconsidered.

Thinking outside of the bureaucracy is of significance in improving the effectiveness of environmental enforcement in China. Environmental enforcement agencies could play a critical, but definitely not the sole role in cracking down on violations. Multiple stakeholders and authorities are related to the effectiveness of enforcement. Their engagements are indispensable in building a good governance system of environmental enforcement. The benefits of multiple players' involvement are explicit in that this process enables the participants to construct consensus, share knowledge and information, and then, in turn, contribute to developing effective strategies of enforcement, increasing awareness of compliance, innovating in terms of enforcement instruments and encouraging compliance. In recognition of these benefits, what needs to be done is to identify the key stakeholders or players and find ways to get them engaged. Networking is regarded as such a way to approach engagement.

2. KEY PLAYERS OF ENVIRONMENTAL ENFORCEMENT IN CHINA

Networking is based on the identification of key players. The occurrence of multiple players derives from the massive socio-economic change that has happened in the past 30 years. The changes lead the market to play a more basic role in allocating resources and also to create a civil society that is growing up and becoming mature.[9] These players on the market and in civil society have diversified interests in environmental enforcement and compliance. They are challenging the unique position of the bureaucracy to enforce laws. In the new context, the key players of environmental enforcement include the government, the civil society, the general public, business and the judiciary.

2.1 Governments

For a long time, government has been playing a primary role in environmental enforcement and is also expected to be a critical player in the future. In the name of the concept of government, many players are included, consisting largely of the following (apart from enforcement agencies already described above):

- *Governments at both local and central levels.* These governments create administrative laws and promulgate regulations, decrees and policies of environmental enforcement. The power of the enforcement agencies is permitted and mandated by governments. The budgets and staff of enforcement agencies are also controlled by local governments. The close relationship between governments and their enforcement agencies is blamed for the prevalence of local protectionism. To encourage economic growth, local governments always turn a blind eye to violators and prevent a just enforcement. The local levels of government comprise four layers: province, city, county and township.
- *Environmental protection authorities at different levels of governments.* Environmental authorities are bureaucratic organizations that are mandated by local governments to execute the power of environmental management, including enforcement power. Enforcement agencies are affiliated directly to these authorities although they seem like independent organizations on the surface.
- *Other administrative authorities.* These administrative agencies execute powers mandated by environmental and resource conservation statutes, such as with respect to water, ocean, land and mineral resources.

---

[9] The Third Plenary Session of the 18th Communist Party of China (CPC) Central Committee issued *The Decision on Major Issues Concerning Comprehensively Deepening Reforms*, committed to establishing a service government and enabling the market to play a crucial role in the process of resource allocation.

- *Other administrative enforcement agencies.* These agencies are not specialized in environmental enforcement but they have some administrative enforcement responsibilities in particular fields, for example, the police are responsible for noise in open recreational sites.

2.2 Civil Society and NGOs

NGOs have obviously no formal administrative powers, but they are influential in providing environmental services that are related to enforcement and compliance, such as providing legal assistance for pollution victims and disseminating pollution information to attract attention to pollution sources. Water and air are the most common fields that witness NGOs' engagement in environmental law enforcement. One remarkable example is the Institute of Public and Environmental Affairs (IPE). It establishes and maintains the two pollution databases, the China Water Pollution Map and the China Air Pollution Map. The two databases mark emitters breaking laws on maps to inform the public when they purchase the goods produced by the emitters.[10] The Center for Legal Assistance to Pollution Victims (CLAPV) of the China University of Political Science and Law (CUPL), set up more than a decade ago, is another instance. It provides free legal assistance to pollution victims to claim for compensation in respect of property damage and personal injury.

2.3 The General Public and Media

Given the lack of environmental knowledge and the weak awareness of environmental rights, the general public used to show no concern about environmental pollution. Moreover, victims of environmental pollution and those possessing high environmental awareness, had little access to information on the subject. Channels to disclose violations and to participate in the process of inspection were often missing. Now governments and enforcement agencies are providing more information to the public and intend to involve them in the process of enforcement so that public involvement can help them channel an increasing number of complaints and monitor violators that may not be covered by inspections due to budget and staff constraints.

Public media have always been powerful players in the fight against violators because of the greater expertise of its journalists. In addition to the traditional media, such as newspapers, TV and radios, the boom of social

---

[10] See www.ipe.org.cn, the website of IPE.

media based on the internet, such as Weibo (Micro blog) and WeChat in China, is forging an ever stronger link between the public enthusiasm for environmental issues and the media. At the end of June 2013, the number of internet users in China reached 591 million with an internet penetration rate of 44.1 per cent, ranking China as the largest country of internet users in the world.[11] The popularity of smart phones and other terminal equipment and easier access to the wireless network also caused a boom of the users of the mobile-phone net. Everyone potentially became a journalist using their social media account. Information is proliferating faster and more broadly than during any time in history.

Empowerment of the public not only acts as a deterrent to violators, but also creates enormous pressure on enforcement agencies and government. Environmental deterioration and awakened general public awareness lead to increased environmental movements. Such influential movements include *inter alia* movements against p-Xylene projects happening in Dalian city and Xiamen city and the protests against molybdenum-copper polymetallic utilization project in Shifang, Sichuan Province, and against pollution discharges into the sea in Qidong, Jiangsu Province.[12]

2.4 Business

While business is a major source of pollutants, it creates measures to eliminate pollution and monitor violations. The environmental protection industry is growing fast in China. It produces technologies, equipment, products and services to deal with pollution. With investment in enforcement increasing, more enforcement-related products and services are provided by business, including inspection, monitoring, detection, mobile enforcement equipment and software and enforcement management solutions. The environmental industry is not only responsive to the demands of enforcement, but they also provide proactive solutions to enforcement agencies and promote institutional innovation for environmental enforcement. The role of business is exemplified by the third-party operation of the Continuous Emission Monitoring System (CEMS), through which enforcement agencies expend less time and resources in ensuring the reliability and validity of the CEMS data.

---

[11] See China Internet Network Information Center, *The 32nd Statistical Report on Internet Development in China* (2013).

[12] Some particular cases promoted by the public are available at http://trade.safetyw.com/news/show-2084.html (China), http://news.xinhuanet.com/yuqing/2013–10/23/c_125585811_2.htm (China).

Green supply chains provide a new mechanism for businesses to promote environmental compliance. The purchasers at the end of the supply chain take advantage of their procurement influence to leverage the environmental compliance of suppliers, thus accepting an extended social and environmental responsibility which includes suppliers' environmental performance. Initially, ensuring a green supply chain was a practice which was prevalent in transnational companies with a strong sense of environmental protection and who forced their Chinese suppliers to comply with supply chain initiatives. Now more and more local Chinese companies also join with transnational companies in developing green supply chains in order to manage their environmental performance from a holistic perspective.

2.5 The Judiciary

Chinese statutes also award a great deal of power to the judiciary to enforce environmental laws, including civil and criminal enforcement. However, for a long time, the judiciary did not play its expected role because the statutes were too general and vague to specify the thresholds applicable to judicial enforcement. Enforcement agencies did not establish cooperation mechanisms with the judiciary and didn't know how to refer cases to prosecutors and courts. In June 2013, the People's Supreme Courts and the People's Supreme Procuratorate of China jointly promulgated a judicial interpretation to specify the conditions and thresholds of the application of criminal cases.[13] In the wake of the interpretation, the courts actively sought to establish procedures of case referral, and more environmental cases compared to previous years were brought to courts in 2013.[14] The judiciary is therefore now playing a robust part in cracking down on environmental violations.

3. ENVIRONMENTAL ENFORCEMENT NETWORKS

The involvement of multiple players in the process of enforcement is an irreversible trend. The sole solution to the trend is to transfer

---

[13] On June 19, the People's Supreme Courts and the People's Supreme Procuratorate jointly issued the *Judicial Interpretation for Laws on Criminal Cases Related to Environmental Pollution*, available at http://www.mps.gov.cn/n16/n1996048/n1996090/n1996180/3820573.html

[14] From an interview with environmental enforcement officers.

rule-based and responsive enforcement to governance-oriented enforcement.[15] Governance means a continuing process through which conflicting or diverse interests may be accommodated and cooperative action may be taken.[16] Governance is a process that happens in a networking system where participants share their points of view and information, developing common-sense approaches and beliefs, hammering out and implementing feasible solutions and reducing monitoring costs.

Networks as a way to connect different areas have been created in the environmental enforcement field for a long time. Based on the positions of participants and their functions, enforcement networks fall into three streams: non-core networks, solo-core networks and multi-core networks.[17]

3.1 Non-core Networks

A non-core network is event-based, featuring a simple and temporary connection between members. Every member of the network has the ability to initiate a connection with the other participants and no one acts as a dominant core in the process. Information communication between members is bi-directional. The purpose of the networking is to respond to an event, or to solve a specific violation problem. Once the problem is solved, the network usually comes to an end automatically or fades out. Members of the network are purely enforcement agencies.

A non-core network fits into the situation where disputes of (water, air, land) pollution and pollution incidents occur in transboundary areas that could not be dealt with by one enforcement agency due to jurisdictional segmentation. In China, a number of regions or provinces have established

---

[15] The bureaucracy theory established by Woodrow Wilson (see Wilson, W., 'The Study of Administration' (1887) Political Science Quarterly 2, no. 2, pp. 197–222) works very well in the early stages of reform and opening-up policies. With the development of society, the disadvantage of sole solution governance increasingly emerges. Many research articles reflect that, see Tian Qianshan, 'The Social Administration: From Sole Solution Governance to Multi-core Governance ' (2011) Journal of Guangxi Institute of Socialism (5), pp. 73–77.

[16] Yan Jian, *Democracy is a Good Thing: Dialogue with Professor Yu Keping* (first published 2006).

[17] The three streams of enforcement networks are based on polycentric governance, for which the main representative is Elinor Ostrom (Ostrom, E., *Governing the Commons: The Evolution of Institutions for Collective Action* (1990, Cambridge University Press); Ostrom, E., *Understanding Institutional Diversity* (2005, Princeton University Press)). And China also has many studies on this, see Huang Defa, *The Institutional Choice of Governmental Governance Paradigm* (2005).

such kinds of network to share information and work together to discover pollution sources. This kind of network is seen mainly in a water basin or an air pollution control area, such as concerning the Tai Lake and in the Beijing-Tianjin-Hebei air pollution area.

3.2 Solo-core Networks

A solo-core network is capacity-driven, featuring regular communication mechanisms to ensure capacity of monitoring and response to emergency issues. It is not targeted at a specific problem, but at capacity building to solve a category of problems. Usually enforcement agencies or environmental authorities are the founders of the network. These founders play a core role in the network and are the central nodes to collect and disseminate information. The other members of the network rarely communicate directly with each other. Members of the network are diverse, including, other than enforcement agencies, the general public, other government agencies, the courts and businesses.

The solo-core network is very common and is established especially when the enforcement agencies are aware of the tight connection between enforcement and other relevant governmental agencies. An instance of the network is the annual *Campaign against Illegal Corporate Emissions to Ensure Public Health* that was launched in 2003 in which ministries and agencies from central government and their counterpart departments in local governments participated. At the central level, the members include the Ministry of Environmental Protection, the National Development and Reform Committee, the Ministry of Industrialization and Information, the Ministry of Justice, the Ministry of Housing and Urban-Rural Development, the State Administration of Industry and Commerce and the State Administration of Work Safety. This campaign is now becoming a network of governmental agencies prepared to act against major violators.

The public will always be a part of a solo-core enforcement network. The environmental hotline 12369,[18] one of the outreaches that enforcement agencies provide to the public and companies, is a bridge between different players to erect a solo-core network. Beginning in 2001, the hotline has been opened at all levels of enforcement agencies to accept public complaints and provide assistance for the public and companies too. In recent years some enforcement agencies have been employing

[18] Available at http://219.143.244.187:8888/Hotline/, the website of 12369 (China).

social media to disseminate environmental information and interact with the public in addition to using the hotline.[19]

Courts are taking a leading role in setting up networks with enforcement agencies. The networking resulted in the establishment of environmental courts. By the end of 2012, 77 environmental courts had been set up nationwide for the purpose of dealing with an increasing number of environmental civil and criminal cases. The courts at various levels concluded 7,780 environmental pollution cases from 2008 through to June 2012.[20]

3.3 Multi-core Networks

A multi-core network is communication-driven, aiming to build a repository of common sense and mutual understanding based on communication. No network member is a permanent and dominant core, but everyone is able to serve as the core of the network to meet some particular end. The dissemination of information among network members is multidirectional. The philosophy of a multi-core network differs from the other two networks in that it believes that enforcement problems, and solutions to the problems, cannot be defined and worked out by one or two members, but via communications between different stakeholders. Effective solutions require that a common understanding be created based on effective communication. Membership of a multi-core network is very broad, including governmental agencies, business, NGOs, the general public, universities, academia and international organizations.

A multi-core network regards the network as a process of integration, in which multiple players with different interests present their views and knowledge freely and fully. The process will create new knowledge of the situation, and a mental and cognitive model is established by the participants to solve the problems in a specific situation. Therefore, a multi-core network is more likely to spur creative thinking and find innovative ways to address problems.

Environmental problems in China, including enforcement and compliance issues, are becoming more and more complicated in the context of rapid and radical socio-economic changes. Cases such as excessive levels of lead in people's blood, the protests against p-Xylene projects, ground-

[19] Some of the local environmental protection agencies, such as Shandong Province, Chongqing Municipality have established an official micro-blog to increase communication with the public.

[20] Li Hong, '77 Environmental Courts Set Up to Promote Ecological Civilization' (Chinese Court Net, 27 December 2012), http://www.chinacourt.org/article/detail/2012/12/id/807807.shtml

water contamination and smog and haze pollution reveal that neither reliance only on enforcement agencies nor cooperation between governmental agencies can by themselves solve the problems.[21] China's government is realizing this and trying to get other players involved. However, the efforts are not proving as effective as expected because these involvements tend to be in the nature of a solo-core network in which governments take the dominant role and try to constrain the interactions between stakeholders at a lower level. In that situation, the possibility of stakeholders building common knowledge and understandings among themselves to avoid the occurrence of similar problems in the future remains small.

The Subcommittee of Environmental Enforcement (SEE) of the Chinese Society for Environmental Sciences (CSES) features a multi-core network. It intends to open the doors to experts in environmental management, environmental enforcement, environmental economics, environmental law and ecological protection, as well as to personnel from enterprises and academia, and NGOs related to environmental enforcement. Established in September 2012, the SEE aims at drawing on the power of networking to improve the environmental enforcement and supervision system. In only one year 152 environmental agencies, 114 enterprises, three universities and one social organization have joined the network. Following this rapid growth, this chapter will now look more closely at the functions of the SEE.

4. CASE STUDY OF A MULTI-CORE NETWORK: THE SUBCOMMITTEE OF ENVIRONMENTAL ENFORCEMENT

The SEE has been in existence for only two years and it is too early to assess its effectiveness in boosting China's environmental enforcement and compliance. This case study intends to describe how the SEE seeks to create an effective enforcement network.

---

[21] The case of excessive lead in blood is available at http://news.youth.cn/cj/201105/t20110520_1590571_1.htm; the case of p-Xylene is available at http://tag.163.com/news/122/122287/1.html; the case of groundwater contamination is available at http://finance.sina.com.cn/china/20130220/233514598613.shtml.

4.1 Elements for Effective Networking

4.1.1 Creation of a clear profile

The SEE has, since its inception, been committed to improving China's environmental enforcement by integrating the wisdom and strength of governmental agencies, business, academic institutions and NGOs. This commitment is strictly followed in setting up its governance system. The Vice Board Chairpersons are nominated to represent different players. Among the nine Vice Chairmen, two are from government agencies, four from enterprises, one from an academic institution, and two from NGOs.

4.1.2 Enrolment of membership

Soon after its establishment, the SEE invested many efforts in building its capacity in enlisting and maintaining membership as it recognized membership as the foundation of an effective network. Although the SEE's target is a network with multiple players, it adopts a multiple-stage strategy in developing members. The enrolment of members begins with enforcement agencies and enterprises. The rationale in choosing enforcement agencies is that enforcement agencies are the key players at present and the fact that they have joined is supposed to encourage other members. Enterprises are selected because they are the largest group of active players.

For the convenience of members' registration and correspondence, the SEE established contact points in each province with the assistance of the Bureau of Environmental Supervision of the MEP, its strategic partner. Several contact point conferences were held to convey the ideas of the network to potential members and communicate the SEE's membership policies. In one year, the SEE succeeded in enlisting nearly 300 members.

4.1.3 Establishment of communication

Face-to-face communication is a critical element of such a multi-core network. The SEE decided to hold at least one event to create opportunities for the members and related players to exchange their ideas and to get to know each other. In June 2013, the first session of the National Enforcement and Compliance Forum was held in Suzhou City, Jiangsu Province, with more than 300 participants from business, governments and academia. Best practices of compliance and enforcement were introduced at the forum and discussed in terms of their viability to be duplicated in other regions. The forum also helped to establish an informal connection between the participants, through which they could interact with each other to solve their common problems.

4.1.4 Identification of priorities

In accordance with the strategy of membership enrolment, the SEE sets research and training as the priority work areas. Research projects aim to provide answers to problems that enforcement agencies face while training to increase the capability of enterprises' compliance.

The SEE's researches in 2013 focused on greenhouse gases (GHGs) enforcement and enforcement standardization in collaboration with academia, consultancies and enforcement agencies. Greenhouse gas control was set up as a compulsory reduction target for local governments in the 12th FYP. Carbon training as a flexible way to achieve the reduction target is being piloted in seven regions. Traditionally, enforcement has mainly been focused on conventional pollutants. How to enforce GHGs remains a cutting-edge question for the enforcement agencies.

Higher penalties for the violation behaviour of enterprises are always pursued by enforcement agencies. The deterrent effect of penalties is sometimes overstressed, while incentives and guidance for corporate environmental compliance behaviour are ignored. The SEE would like to fill this gap by organizing training sessions for corporate members to provide them with legal and technical knowledge to assist them in compliance. More than 1,000 managers in the enterprises who are responsible for environmental affairs were trained by the SEE in 2013.

4.1.5 Exchange with other networks

As the first and the sole domestic enforcement network, the SEE has no experience to follow. Advanced international experiences in this regard will massively broaden the SEE's international vision. The SEE believes that linking itself to regional or international enforcement work will help it to understand how such a network can be operated effectively and, moreover, to learn from other network members in dealing with the same enforcement problems that China is confronted with.

4.2 Challenges For a Multi-core Network in China

Although enforcement networks are expected to play a vital role in mobilizing resources, providing technical assistance and improving governance of enforcement, domestic networks in China are facing many challenges in terms of governance structure, financial support, staffing and internal management. These challenges are embedded in the socio-economic and political-economic context. Being constrained by laws and regulations and by the lack of financial supports, enforcement networks have to depend heavily on their leaders' social resources or relationships to raise money and enrol members. On the other hand, networks have to depend on governmental resources, as the government in China controls most of the resources. How to handle the relationship with the government while maintaining the characteristics of a social organization remains an issue.[22]

Maintenance of membership is very important in constructing a successful network. Members provide financial and social supports for networks, with expectations on the network to solve the problems they are concerned with. To fulfil members' expectations should be one of the key capabilities of networks. However, in China enforcement networks are facing the same challenges as other NGOs in building such capabilities, namely a lack of resources to recruit full-time employees. Most of the networks' workloads are usually undertaken by volunteers or temporarily undertaken by their members. This will be an obstacle for the enforcement networks in terms of running a long-term capacity-building project to serve their members' expectations.

The capability to integrate interests in conflict is yet to be well developed. The unique role of enforcement networks is to build consensus and balance the competitive interests of different members. Motives for breaking laws and regulations are always diverse. For most of the enterprises, pursuing the benefits from violations is the key reasons behind these violations, and they often knowingly break the laws. That means it is difficult to persuade such enterprises to dialogue with other network members. On the other hand, the victims of pollution are always individuals and do not have a powerful organization to represent them in the dialogue. The enforcement networks have to examine the different interests and identify the key players as the first step to removing these obstacles to establish effective networks.

5. CONCLUSIONS

While China continues to strengthen the capacity of its enforcement agencies, it has recognized the insufficiency of a sole reliance on enforcement agencies to promote compliance. Networking with other players has been widely adopted by local and central enforcement agencies. However, the enforcement-agency-centred network has distinct problems that undermine the effectiveness of the network. For example, it can promote the capacity to punish violators but fails to build a repository of common

---

[22] See Lu Mingyuan 'The Official and Non-official Dual Property of NGO' (2004) Academic Monthly (06); Wang Ming, 'The Society Function and Category of NGO' (2006) Academic Monthly (09).

knowledge and common sense among different players to increase the compliance rate. Multi-core networks have advantages over non-core and solo-core networks in this regard.

The SEE is pioneering ways to establish a multi-core enforcement network in China. In response to the unique challenges for the development of networks, the SEE developed its localized strategy suitable to Chinese situations, which has proved effective, at least up to now. To implement the strategy, domestic resources are leveraged and the SEE wants to learn from others to speed up its development by joining regional and international networks. However, to what extent the multi-core enforcement network will promote environmental compliance in China still needs time to be seen.

24. Environmental enforcement networking efforts in Chile: lessons learnt and challenges ahead

Juan Carlos Monckeberg,* Kay Bergamini† and Cristian Pérez‡

1. INTRODUCTION

1.1 Historical Background

In 1994 the Chilean State enacted the Law N° 19.300 on the General Basis of the Environment. Among other things, this Law created the National Commission of the Environment (CONAMA), a state agency with a co-ordinator status on environmental matters.

The institutional environmental structure proposed in the Law N° 19.300 was built on the model of the 'proposal of Basic Environmental Law and Promotion of Sustainable Development' of 1993, elaborated for Latin America by the United Nations Environment Programme (UNEP), which formulated both criteria and basic norms oriented to regulate environmental management of the State and citizens' actions; with the aim of attaining sustainable development objectives of the countries (Olivares 2010).

However, such a model did not include the idea of having a Minister – but rather a President of the Commission – and also did not incorporate the concept of environmental crime within the penal legislation (Olivares 2010).

* Superintendent, Superintendence of the Environment, Government of Chile, Miraflores 178, Piso 7 Santiago, Chile. Email: jmonckeberg@sma.gob.cl

† Chief, Enforcement Division, Superintendence of the Environment, Government of Chile, Miraflores 178, Piso 7 Santiago, Chile. Email: kbergamini@sma.gob.cl

‡ Biodiversity & International Relations Officer, Enforcement Division, Superintendence of the Environment, Government of Chile, Miraflores 178, Piso 7 Santiago. Email: cristian.perez@sma.gob.cl

According to Cordero (1996), 'when establishing the environmental structure in an inter-sectorial commission; the Law N° 19.300 moved away from its organizational scope, incorporating normative concepts unconnected to the regular way of doing things in Chile, coincident with the project of Framework Law for Central America'.

The structure of the model was based on maintaining environmental enforcement competences in existent ministries as well as in sectorial governmental agencies. Due to the application of such a model, the CONAMA faced the scenario of having different enforcement methodologies and no power over the different state agencies involved in environmental enforcement activities. This situation, added to the dispersal of environmental regulations on diverse legal instruments, overlapping functions of state agencies and the lack of information procedures between the state agencies, were all factors that hindered enforcement of and compliance with environmental law in Chile.

Those deficiencies were factors that justified the review of the whole model and its subsequent reform; which was also reinforced by diverse reports and evaluations both at the national and international levels. Of paramount importance was the release of the report 'Environmental Performance Reviews' (OECD 2005), carried out by the Organisation for Economic Co-operation and Development. In that report, focused on the environmental situation in Chile, developed in the framework of the country's intention to be part of the OECD, was highlighted that 'an *environmental enforcement policy* based on co-ordination of various sectorial enforcement bodies is not the most effective institutional arrangement to assure compliance'.

In practical terms the main difficulties identified were related to: (a) environmental capacities located at sectorial agencies, without a 'purely environmental view'; (b) the duplicity of functions with the consequent increase in public costs; (c) low fines (ca. US$40,000); (d) the absence of both programs and methodologies for proper enforcement activities; and (e) incentives placed on sanctions rather than on environmental compliance.

Thus, as a result of the review a specific recommendation was made for the Chilean State to implement: 'strengthening compliance and enforcement capacities, including institutional reforms; such as the creation of an agency for environmental inspection' (OECD/ECLAC 2005).

1.2 Modification of the Legal Regime

That was the context for the enactment of the Law N° 20.417 of 2010 that reformed the environmental institutional structure in Chile,

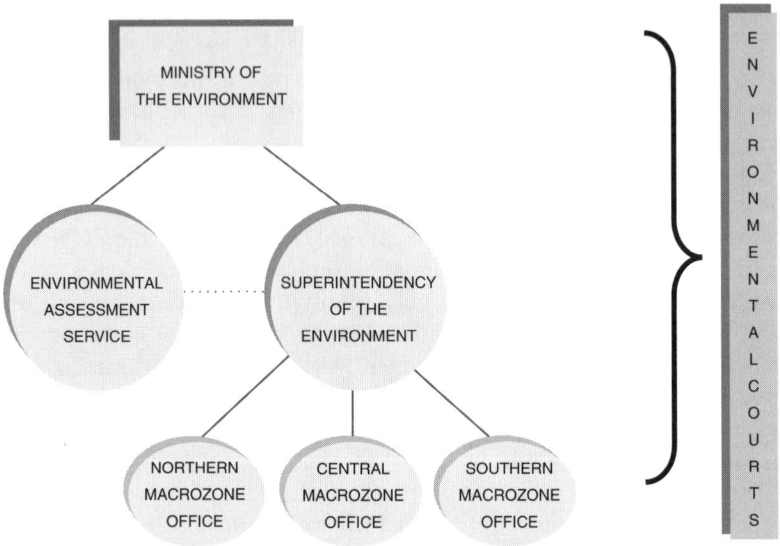

Figure 24.1 Structure of the new model of environmental institutions from an enforcement and compliance point of view

creating the Ministry of the Environment; the Service of Environmental Assessment (SEA); and the Superintendence of the Environment (SMA), in order to correct most of the operational problems detected (see Figure 24.1).

The Ministry of the Environment is the agency in charge of generating public policies on environmental matters and it co-ordinates other agencies under its umbrella. The SEA assesses projects and activities issuing – in cases where it is pertinent – the licenses required to operate. The Superintendence of the Environment is the agency in charge of enforcing fulfilment with the provisions contained in those licenses – as well as with other instruments of environmental management – in order to ensure compliance with environmental law and regulations. Finally, the Environmental Courts review cases when the decisions made by the SMA and other environmental organizations are questioned by the regulated community or by other stakeholders.

The creation of the Superintendence of the Environment responds to the need of having a single authority that could unify criteria, procedures and incentives for compliance with environmental regulations through enforcement activities and other procedures. The SMA is a decentralized public agency – with legal status and its own budget – under the control and oversight of the executive through the Ministry of the Environment.

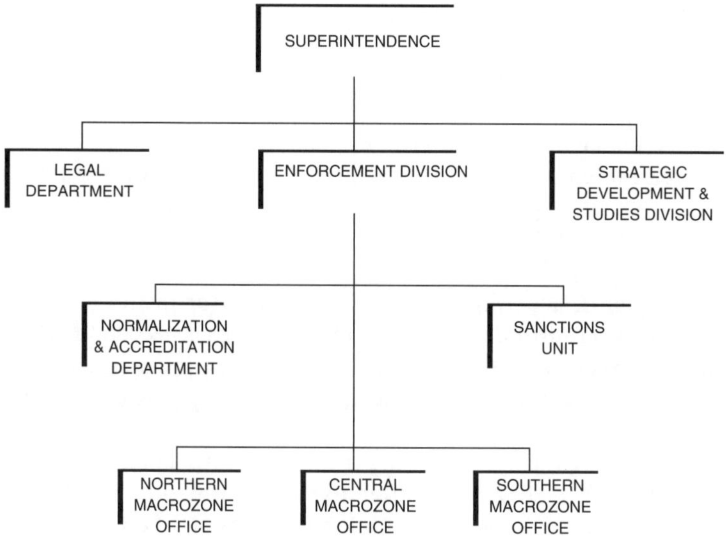

Figure 24.2 SMA technical organization chart

Its mission is to lead and promote strategic compliance with instruments of environmental management under its scrutiny through enforcement activities, providing assistance to compliance, dissuasive sanctions, and making environmental information available to the community (see Figure 24.2).

On December 28, 2012, the SMA assumed functional control, and since that day it has been in charge of the enforcement of all instruments of environmental management contained in Chile's environmental law.

Its main achievements during this short term include the following: (1) the creation and implementation of guidelines for enforcement activities, homologating criteria in the State's agencies that also acknowledge the rights of the regulated community; (2) the establishment of both Programs and Sub-Programs of Enforcement, which allow planning the State's enforcement activities, having a strategic approach to those projects and activities that are generating bigger environmental impacts; and (3) being recognized as a state agency with strong and wide capacities on environmental enforcement matters that are reinforced by very skilled professionals and state of the art technologies.

2. NETWORKING EFFORTS

2.1 Background Information

Simply having environmental laws in place is not enough to address the ever-increasing environmental challenges. Governments must find ways to ensure that the regulated community meets the requirement put forth in the environmental laws and their implementing regulations (Opondo 2011).

In that regard, according to Kaniaru (2002), for institutional frameworks to work, co-ordination with different groups is needed, including at the national level with other enforcement agencies, private sector bodies, and NGOs, among other stakeholders, as well as engaging in international cooperation.

Acknowledging the above, during the implementing period (September 2010 to December 2012); and after its entry into force (28 December 2012), several vertical and horizontal[1] environmental networking activities have been carried out – both domestically and at the international level – by the Superintendence of the Environment. These activities include: working with other national governmental agencies that have environmental competence; working with the regulated community; working with other stakeholders (i.e. the Council of Civil Society); supplying training for its staff on specific environmental matters; working with enforcement agencies from other countries; and promoting the creation of the South American Network of Enforcement and Compliance, among others.

2.2 Vertical Networking Efforts

2.2.1 Working with governmental agencies with competence on environmental enforcement and compliance

These efforts materialized in diverse ways, including having more than 150 meetings with the national governmental agencies with competence on environmental enforcement and compliance, through five workshops and the signature of 20 Memorandums of Understanding (MOU) of dif-

[1] For the purpose of this chapter, 'vertical networking efforts' are understood as those activities carried out by the SMA either under the binding obligations contained at the current environmental legal framework and/or within the country's boundaries; and 'horizontal networking efforts' are those non-binding activities carried out in order to cooperate with other agencies or institutions and/or outside the country's boundaries.

ferent kinds. These MOUs are mostly related to: which activities will be carried out directly by the SMA or will be delegated to other agencies with environmental competence; the use of both human and financial resources in order to carry out those activities; and the association of indicators of success to those activities. This last function is necessary because the MOUs are subject to the public's scrutiny through the annual performance account made by the Superintendent.

To date the number of environmental inspections carried out by the SMA – only for environmental licenses[2] – are 336, with ca. 37 environmental inspections carried out each month. Along the same lines, to date other governmental agencies that have either conducted directly or participated in more environmental inspections are the Ministry of Health (MINSAL), the Service for Agricultural and Husbandry (SAG), and the Service of Geology and Mining (SERNAGEOMIN), as is shown in Figure 24.3.

Otherwise, to date the number of sanction processes is 43; of which 35 stem from environmental inspections done by the SMA or other governmental agencies with competence on environmental enforcement and compliance, showing the importance of the co-ordinated work.

2.2.2 Working with the regulated community

Through methods including workshops, meetings, seminars, information posted on its website, and the signature of three Memorandums of Understanding, the Superintendence has educated the regulated community about its current regulations and procedures. Most of the topics are mainly related to the new system of enforcement in Chile, the use and application of instruments and technical methodologies, and sanctions procedures.

2.2.3 Working with the Civil Society

Council of Civil Society Under its umbrella the SMA hosts this Council which is composed of representatives of the regulated community, the Academy, Non-Governmental Organizations, Workers Associations and the Superintendence itself, as shown in Figure 24.4.

Some of the topics covered during its monthly sessions are: the

---

[2] To date, Chile has five instruments of environmental management which are: (a) Environmental Qualification Resolution (Environmental License, also called RCA); (b) Norm of Environmental Emission Limits; (c) Norm of Environmental Quality Limits; (d) Plan for Environmental Decontamination or Prevention; and (e) Species Management Plan.

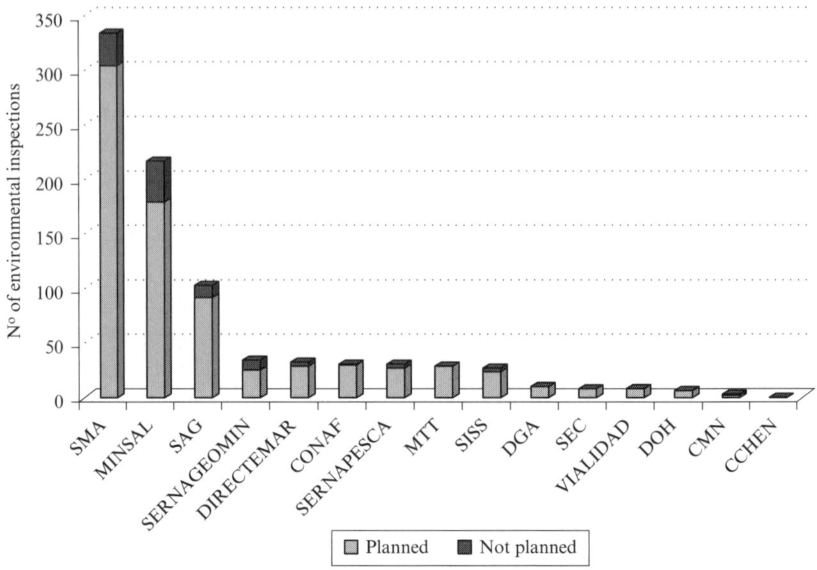

Notes: [a] Acronyms: SMA (Superintendence of the Environment); MINSAL (Health Ministry); SAG (Agricultural and Husbandry Service), SERNAGEOMIN (Geologic and Mining Service); DIRECTEMAR (Maritime Territories Directorate); CONAF (National Forestry Corporation); SERNAPESCA (National Fisheries Service); MTT (Transport and Telecommunications Ministry); SISS (Superintendence of Sanitary Services); DGA (General Water Directorate); SEC (Superintendence of Electricity and Fuels); VIALIDAD (Vial Directorate); DOH (Directorate of Hydraulic Work); CMN (National Monuments Council); CCHEN (Chilean Commission of Nuclear Energy). [b] Planned activities are those activities incorporated in the SMA Annual Programme of Environmental Enforcement Activities. Not planned are those activities arising from denunciations.

Figure 24.3 Number of inspections by all governmental agencies[a] with competence on environmental enforcement and compliance and origin[b] (January 2013–September 2013)

structure of the new system of environmental enforcement; human and technical resources associated with enforcement activities; the relationship between SMA and other agencies with environmental competences; and the role of civil society under this new enforcement system, among other issues.

Denunciations/complaints To date (early October 2013) 1,090 denunciations/complaints have been received by the Superintendence. Topics involved are mostly related to noise, water pollution, annoying odours, among other issues (see Figure 24.5). In practical terms denunciations could be understood also as a finely tuned feedback mechanism,

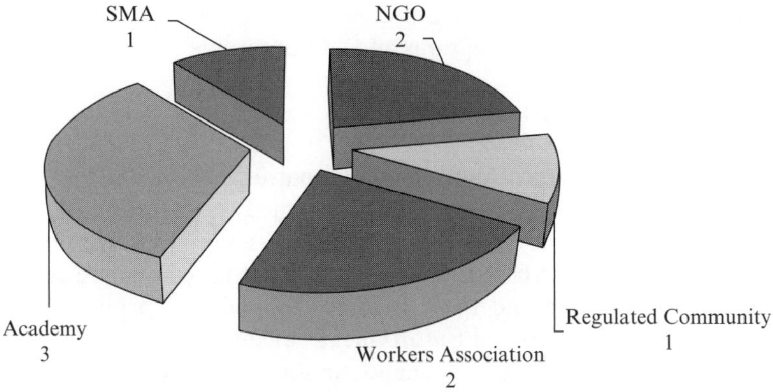

Figure 24.4 Composition of the Civil Society Council

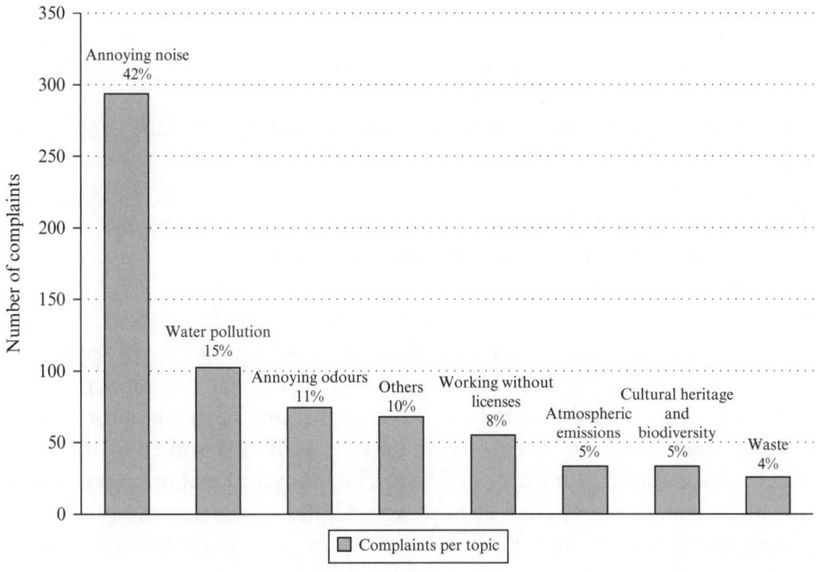

Figure 24.5 Number and topics of denunciations/complaints (January 2013–June 2013)

coming directly from the communities, that at some point should be matched with both SMA programs and sub-programs.

2.3 Horizontal Networking Efforts

2.3.1 Working with agencies from other countries

Horizontal networking efforts have included cooperation activities with agencies from different countries, such as the US Environmental Protection Agency (USEPA); the Centre d'expertise en analyse environnementale du Québec and the Canadian Council of Normalization of Canada; The Evaluation and Enforcement Organism (OEFA) from Peru; and training organizations in Thailand, South Korea and Spain.

Topics covered include capacity-building activities of SMA staff on enforcement methodologies and practices; the creation and application of tools using Geographic Information Systems (GIS) and the adaptation of a Sanction proceeding model to be used in Chile, and other activities with the USEPA; a visit to the Centre d'expertise en analyse environnementale du Québec and the Canadian Council of Normalization of Canada to learn first-hand about normalization and certification procedures as well as about mechanisms of validating environmental laboratories in order to implement a similar model in Chile; giving a course on environmental practices and procedures to professionals of the OEFA in Peru; and several training courses on environmental matters for its staff around the world.

2.3.2 Creation of a Regional Network (South American Network of Environmental Enforcement and Compliance)

The SMA is also leading the process of creating the South American Network of Environmental Enforcement and Compliance, with the collaboration of the USEPA, which expects to attract the membership of several countries of the region. As part of that process, during September 2013, the SMA hosted the first preparatory meeting with the participation of representatives of the OEFA from Peru, the USEPA and environmental experts from the US Embassy in Chile. The inaugural meeting was carried out on November 4–6, 2013 in Santiago, Chile. It was attended by Chile, Colombia, Ecuador and Peru as well as by intergovernmental bodies such as the Economic Commission for Latin America and the Caribbean (ECLAC), the International Network for Environmental Compliance and Enforcement (INECE) and the Organization of American States (OAS), and by USEPA officers, representatives from the US Embassies in Chile and Peru, and an officer from the Canadian Embassy in Chile, among others.

The main objectives behind the creation of the South American Network include the ideas of strengthening enforcement capacities in the countries through capacity-building efforts; sharing expertise on practices, proceedings, methodologies and tools for enforcement activities; advancing towards the elaboration of enforcement guidelines on transboundary projects; and developing indicators and other regional methodologies for regional enforcement, among several other initiatives.

3. LESSONS LEARNT AND CHALLENGES AHEAD

During this implementing period several practical lessons have been learnt. Likewise, various challenges have been identified. In practical terms they are briefly presented here as Vertical Networking Efforts and Horizontal Networking Efforts.

3.1 Vertical Networking Efforts

Although the SMA has approximately 100 officers located around the country, its power has been amplified with the engagement of and collaboration with other national agencies that have environmental competence and expertise on specific matters. Thus, using a strategic approach, its impact has been maximized, which can be seen in the outcomes of its first year of practical enforcement working activities in Chile. In the future, a more articulated collaboration with those agencies – under its technical steering role – through the incorporation and application of new practices and methodologies developed by the SMA, should result in better environmental enforcement activities.

Regarding another aspect, as the former environmental enforcement model applied in Chile involved less stringent and more confusing practices, then there was an undervalued perception of the environmental regulations. Therefore, with the new model in place, a cultural change is expected from the regulated community in order to comply with environmental regulations. This can be helped by the SMA in different ways, including under the SMA's promotion of compliance role.

Since its entry into total functioning, the SMA has been very engaged with the civil society through the functioning of the Council of Civil Society, as well as with the reception of denunciations/complaints. In this regard it is expected that more understanding of the SMA's role, practices and procedures by the civil society in Chile will result in more articulated denunciations submitted for its consideration, which in turn will maximize SMA resources.

Appropriate implementation of the three steps above is of paramount importance since they imply that the credibility of the work of the SMA, as well as of the new environmental system as a whole, will be reinforced.

3.2 Horizontal Networking Efforts

Cooperation with agencies from other countries and with other international organizations is not a binding obligation but rather based on a *bona fide* spirit, with the main objective of learning from other colleagues' knowledge and sharing experiences regarding both enforcement practices and procedures.

Thus, just as it has happened up to now, in the future the SMA will engage in other institutional agreements, in order to maximize its objectives of ensuring compliance with environmental law.

The above could materialize through carrying out specific bilateral activities – such as performing transboundary enforcement activities – or through being part of other networks.

Regarding the latter point, it is understood by the SMA that the creation of the South American Network of Environmental Enforcement and Compliance is only the first step towards improving enforcement of and compliance with environmental laws from a regional point of view. Other steps should be taken in order to build trust and political will between the members. As is reflected by the international experience, the engagement of network members is critical for all activities of the network, both at the operational and project level (Pink and Lehane 2011).

At the practical level, *sine qua non* requisites for networks' success include a well-defined organizational structure, planning and implementing meetings of the Parties, carrying out research activities and conducting training for officers (Bromm 2011).

All of the above could be achieved not by reinventing the wheel but through learning from the examples of the creation of other networks around the world, making regional adaptations as required.

BIBLIOGRAPHY

Bromm, S. (2011). North America's Commission for Environmental Cooperation: One Example of a Successful Regional Network. *Proceedings of 9th International Conference on Environmental Compliance and Enforcement*, 24 June 2011, Whistler, British Columbia, Canada.

Cordero, L. (1996). *Institucionalidad Ambiental en el Derecho Chileno*. Editorial Jurídica ConoSur Ltda, 182 pp.

Kaniaru, D. (2002). The Role of Institutions and Networks in Environmental

Enforcement. *Proceedings of the Sixth International Conference on Environmental Compliance and Enforcement*, April 15–19, 2002. San José Costa Rica, 5 pp.

Olivares, A. (2010). El Nuevo marco institucional Ambiental en Chile. *Revista Catalana de Dret Ambiental*, Vol I, No. 1: 1–23.

Opondo, G. K. (2011). Creating and Sustaining Regional Environmental Compliance and Enforcement Networks: Lessons from the East African Network for Environmental Compliance & Enforcement. *Proceedings of the 9th International Conference on Environmental Compliance and Enforcement*, 24 June 2011, Whistler, British Columbia, Canada.

Organisation for Economic Cooperation and Development – OECD/Economic Commission for Latin America and the Caribbean – ECLAC (2005). OECD 'Environmental Performance Reviews', Chile.

Pink, G. and Lehane, J. (2011). Environmental Enforcement Networks: Development of a Network Evaluation Matrix. *Proceedings of the 9th International Conference on Environmental Compliance and Enforcement*, 24 June 2011, Whistler, British Columbia, Canada.

25. Enforcement of environmental legislation by the Belgian police

Frans Geysels

1. INTRODUCTION

Many contributions to this volume propose a more efficient and effective approach to tackling environmental crime. Adapted structures, structural collaboration, targeted information gathering, a project-based approach, multidisciplinary investigating and an international vision are each methods that have been shown as effective in the fight against environmental crime. All these methods have proven their worth separately but when they are used simultaneously there is a mutual reinforcement of their effectiveness.

2. ADAPTED STRUCTURES

To illustrate this issue, the approach and organisation of the Belgian integrated police serves here as an example.

A central service within the federal judicial police handles the phenomena linked to serious environmental crime[1] which can be divided into four areas:

1. The trafficking of waste;
2. The trafficking of biodiversity;
3. The trafficking in radioactive materials;
4. The trafficking of fireworks.

This department, with competence for serious environmental crime, deals amongst other issues with:

[1] Serious environmental crime is defined as follows: organised and recurring; fraudulent and intended to make considerable profits; supra-local/international and very harmful to the environment and/or public health.

- Making strategic analyses to conceptualise the criminal phenomena;
- Giving advice and ensuring co-ordination in interventions and investigations;
- Developing expert databases;
- Providing specific expertise and support for the police services;
- Ensuring information control and exploitation;
- Developing an 'Environmental Network';
- Providing specific training for members of the 'Environmental Network';
- Promoting an integrated police method to tackle the phenomena;
- Initiating and executing proactive investigations; and
- Concluding 'skeleton agreements' (police-environmental authorities).

Another important task of the central service is improving the field officers' ability to tackle the phenomena on three levels: knowledge, ability and motivation. Since environmental legislation is very diverse, complex and is not always the 'specialty' of just one service or authority, it is often unclear to the non-specialised police officer in the field how to act appropriately. Often, there are doubts as to which investigation techniques and/or strategies are the most suitable, which in turn discourages any attempt to act on infringements related to environmental crime.

Within the Belgian police, an environmental network was established (on a voluntary basis) in order to meet the proclaimed needs. Ideally this network consists of: representatives of all police field units (local, motorway, waterway and railway police) who act as a mouthpiece for their departments, a co-ordinator (environmental co-ordinator) on the judicial district level and an investigation unit on the level of the district judicial police services. Police on local, district and federal levels all have liaisons with competent environmental authorities and the public prosecutor. A specific platform was also created on the district level to create the opportunity for all members to meet regularly and discuss approach and enforcement policy. The central service also has privileged contacts with the College of Attorney-Generals.

This structured network allows communicating information 'top-down' or 'bottom-up', the transfer of specific information to the right person and the organisation of specific training. At this time, it includes 186 out of the 195 local police forces, as well as all the services of the federal police, which brings the total of registered network members to 700.

The entire structure of the Belgian Federal Police can be sketched as shown in Figure 25.1.

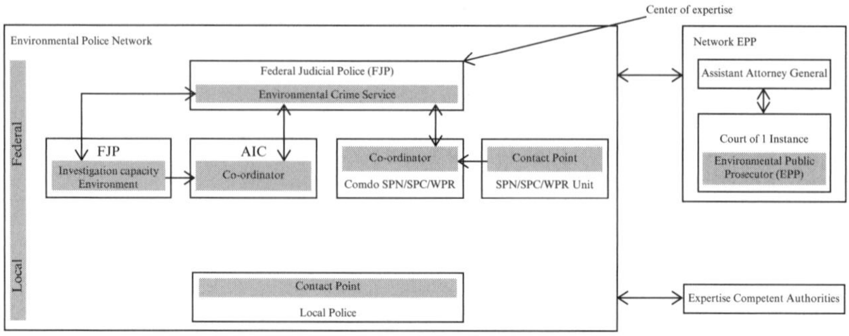

Figure 25.1 The Belgian environmental network for the police

3. STRUCTURED CO-OPERATION

In addition to the regular police – who have a general competence – environmental legislation often provides for the creation of specific environmental enforcement agencies that have a particular and restricted competence. This makes enforcement complex and calls for transparent agreements regarding co-operation and the division of labour. In Belgium, the situation is even more complex since environment-related matters now (largely) belong to the competence of the regions. The police prefer to establish protocol agreements with the environmental agencies. These agreements *inter alia* pertain to:

- Mutual support in the field;
- Training sessions; and
- Information exchange.

The division of labour between police and environmental agencies is based on their specific strengths (see Figure 25.2). Environmental agencies focus rather on checks in situ (company sites) and direct their attention mostly on the conditions set by the respective permits and administrative obligations. Reports are treated internally or, in very exceptional cases, sent to the prosecutor's office. Police services, on the other hand, have a general competence and can direct their attention to all kinds of infringements. Often these include 'regular' offences related to environmental crime for which the environmental agencies are not competent. They often act in response to complaints and/or charges. The local police focus mainly on local forms of nuisance (nuisance caused by odours or noise, pollution of water, soil, air, etc.). The judicial police

	Police	**Customs**	**Environmental authorities**
	• General competence in police matters • Competence in the enforcement of environmental legislation • Approachable 24/24 • Recognisable for the public	• General competence in customs matters – Transfrontier (EU) shipment of goods & waste • Taxes – Transport • Limited competence in environmental legislation	• Specific competence in environmental legislation
Expertise in	• Police matters • Privileged contacts with Public Prosecutors	• Custom matters	• Environmental issues

← **Collaboration** →

And finally... the **Public Prosecutor** as the KEYSTONE of penal enforcement

Figure 25.2 Strengths and competences of the main players in the enforcement of environmental law

mainly investigate environmental crimes that are considered heavy and complex cases.

4. TARGETED INFORMATION GATHERING

The more information one has and the better its quality, the more one is able to tackle illegal behaviour in an intelligence-led way. The same logic is applied to environmental crime. On the one hand there is the intention of optimising the existing data systems and adapting them to the specific needs. On the other hand, new sources of information can be put in use. In particular, access to non-police sources is very important when dealing with environmental crime. The competent environmental agencies are, after all, the authorities who manage the administrative information regarding permits, attestations, production and process information, etc.

The Belgian police have linked the checks of waste transport to a particular system of dataflow. Through the use of a distinct, standardised information carrier (ECO-form), it is possible to report infringements in the same manner. This information is processed centrally, which allows timely investigation as well as strategic and tactical analysis. The data exchange with the competent environmental agencies only enriches the quality of the information and informs the agencies about the actual shipments.

When planning waste transport checks, the police usually invite the environmental agencies to join them in the field so that their expertise and administrative authority can be used to detect illegal waste transports and take all necessary measures. This collaboration results in more and better checks to the satisfaction of the police and the relevant agencies. For several years now, we ascertain that in (an average of) 12.5 per cent of the checked waste transports a violation could be established.

Aside from the opportunity the database offers to act punctually on infringements, it also offers the possibility of providing historic information regarding waste transports, enabling and facilitating large-scale investigations. All movements that waste makes must be registered. The paper trail can be cross-checked with the information resulting from the in-the-field check to determine whether all records have been filled out correctly. Based on experience, it can be assumed that often this is not the case. This additional information is consequently important for investigators since it can indicate that a particular company works with 'adapted' records.

The created system offers several significant advantages deemed important enough to give it a European dimension. During the Belgian presidency of the EU (second half of 2010), the project 'AUGIAS' was launched. This project aimed to motivate European police services to check waste transports, preferably in close co-operation with their own nationally competent environmental authorities and/or Customs. Filling out an ECO-form (WTC-form) for each checked waste transport made the data resulting from these checks exchangeable and manageable. In the course of the project, 25 countries showed interest in the development of such a system on a European level at one time or another. An additional merit of the AUGIAS project is that it also reveals the restrictions when it comes to gathering and/or sharing data. On the one hand, there are the frictions between services that prevent information from being exchanged and on the other hand, there are legal restrictions prohibiting the exchange of certain personalised data. Unfortunately, these problems also occur on an international level. However, INTERPOL and EUROPOL do provide an infrastructure for the exchange of police information. INTERPOL has developed an 'ECO-message' to exchange information in a uniform and complete manner for all issues related to international environmental crime.

5. A PROJECT-BASED APPROACH

Experience teaches that a project-based approach to environmental crime offers the best results. Thanks to integrated co-operation with others, the setting of clear goals, together with a division of labour and regular analysis and reporting, it becomes possible to improve and adjust matters on a permanent basis.

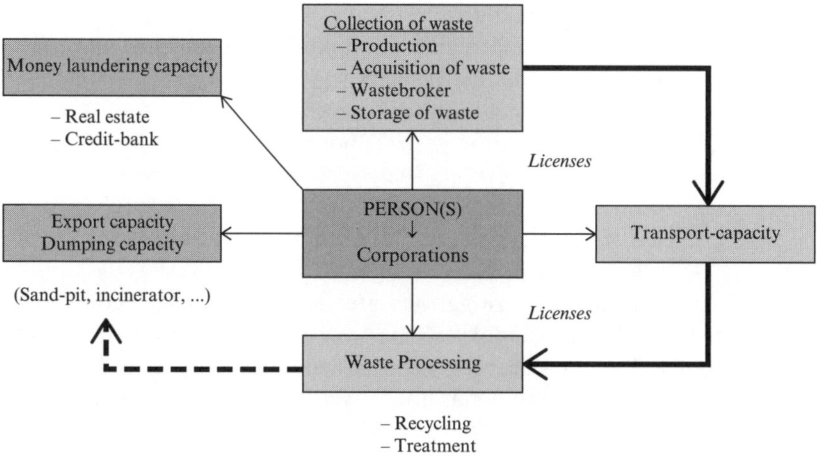

Figure 25.3 Possible composition of a 'risk group' dealing with waste activities

In the centre one can find an individual or a representation in corporations. At first sight the illegal activity may be covered by a legal front of licences (to collect, store, transport and treat waste). Instead of processing the waste properly, however, this waste is dumped, incinerated or exported in an illegal way. The money saved by this act is laundered via money laundering systems. What seems to be legitimate at first sight, may not be all it seems; by looking into the real stream of waste disposal, the complete picture becomes visible.

The goals of the 'Waste' project are:

- To give insight into the actual waste streams in Belgium through specific information gathering by:
  - planned, short controls of waste transports in collaboration with the competent environmental authorities; and
  - regular checks on 'suspicious' waste transports during patrols.
- Detect high-risk groups[2] (see Figure 25.3) and behaviour in the field of waste-disposal through tactical analysis.

---

[2] These so-called 'high-risk groups' may consist of persons and/or companies who try to control the whole waste management cycle (production, transportation and treatment of waste). The companies used to obtain this goal are legal companies who have all the required permits and registrations. Under the cover of this legal facade illegal shipments can be organised, resulting in the illegal disposal of waste in sandpits, incinerators and even third-world countries. Afterwards,

- Handling waste crime by:
  - using traditional police detection and investigation techniques;
  - catching and convicting the perpetrators;
  - confiscating the illegal acquired benefits; and
  - stopping the possible threat to the population and the environment.

6. MULTI-DISCIPLINARY INVESTIGATION

Judicial environmental investigations are usually a police matter. The involvement of environmental agencies as 'experts' is, however, highly recommended. The final decision on whether to integrate environmental agencies in the investigation has to be made by the prosecutor. Since the environmental agencies often provide an unmistakable added value, they are almost always invited to participate in the investigation. This co-operation not only grants the police officers access to the agencies' expertise but also to all relevant administrative data. Their assistance can be invoked for sample taking or for the interpretation of the results of lab analysis. When environmental agencies are involved officially in a police investigation, the legal restrictions on thc sharing of information arc sct aside for the duration of the investigation and within the scope of the same investigation.

7. INTERNATIONAL DIMENSION

Environmental crime often is an international matter that can only be tackled by means of solid international co-operation. This is imperative for all units involved in environmental law enforcement (environmental agencies, police, Customs and prosecutors). Luckily, there already exist some official and unofficial platforms within each of these organisations ('pillars'), as can be seen in Figure 25.4.

This 'Infoflux' scheme only reflects a rough overview of the official platforms that exist and that can be used for the official or unofficial exchange of information between the main enforcement actors.

In our experience, a question yields a better and quicker answer when it is treated within the same 'pillar' (vertical axis). When there is a need to contact an entity in another pillar, the best result is obtained by contact-

---

the illegally acquired benefits are laundered through the usual money laundering channels.

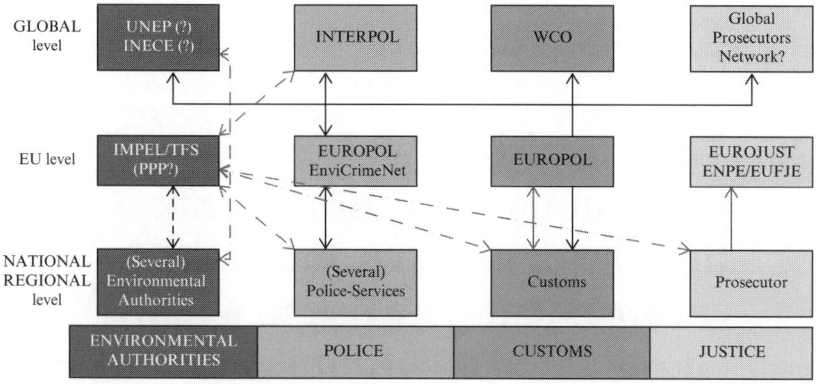

Figure 25.4 Projected Infoflux

ing the national or regional counterpart in another 'pillar' who forwards the message within its own 'pillar'. For instance, when we seek the co-operation of a foreign environmental administration, we ask our own environmental administration to launch the request via an international platform.

8. CONCLUSION

Environmental crime is too important to stop trying to strive for the most efficient and effective approach to tackle it. However, this is only possible when different enforcers co-operate in a constructive manner, using their own and others' strengths to reach their goal: to bring perpetrators to justice, reclaim illegal benefits and restore the environmental damage.

26. The Flemish High Council of Environmental Enforcement: the role of an environmental enforcement network in a new coordinated environmental enforcement landscape within the Flemish region, 2009–2014

Michael Faure and An Stas

1. INTRODUCTION

Belgium is a constitutionally complicated country. In addition to the Belgian federal state, competences are equally allocated to communities and regions. This also has a relevance for environmental law and for environmental law enforcement. Those belong primarily to the competences of the three regions, being the Flemish Region, the Brussels Capital Region, and the Walloon Region. In addition, the federal government still holds a number of competences in the area of the environment, such as the determination of product standards and the transit transportation of waste.[1]

Until 2009, the enforcement of environmental legislation in the Flemish Region was based on criminal provisions in a variety of fragmented (partially sectorial) decrees. Moreover, this enforcement was mainly based on criminal law enforcement. However, since prosecutors often had other priorities and little capacity to enforce environmental legislation, many environmental violations were dismissed.[2] Already in 1995 the Ghent

---

[1] Lavrysen, L., Handboek Milieurecht, 2006, pp. 125–157.

[2] For an empirical analysis showing that prior to 2009 on average more than 65% of environmental violations in the Flemish Region were dismissed, see Faure, M. and Svatikova, K., 'Enforcement of Environmental Law in the Flemish Region', *European Energy and Environmental Law Review*, 2010, vol. 19(2), 60–79.

professor Hubert Bocken and his inter-university commission for the reform of environmental policy had proposed new enforcement provisions in a decree on environmental policy.[3] However, it took until 2007[4] for the Flemish legislature to create the decree of 21 December 2007, as a complement to the decree of 5 April 1995 concerning the general provisions on environmental policy, with the title XVI 'Supervision, enforcement, and safety measures', and entered into force on 1 May 2009.[5] This decree is also known as the 'Environmental Enforcement Decree'.[6]

An important objective of this new regulation was a more effective and harmonised approach to environmental offences.[7] As a reaction to the already mentioned high dismissal rate of environmental violations by the prosecutors, this new decree brought about a revolutionary change and created the possibility of imposing administrative fines.[8] The legislation involved an elaborate mechanism whereby some administrative offences can be handled directly by the administrative fining authority; for other violations (still subject to the criminal law), the public prosecutor in principle has to decide whether to follow a criminal prosecution (or other reactions in the criminal procedure) or to submit the case for

---

[3] Explanatory note, Parliamentary papers of the Flemish Parliament, 2006–2007, no 1249, p. 129.

[4] Faure, M., 'Handhaving van het milieurecht in het Vlaamse Gewest: enkele cijfers'. In: D'Hooge, D., Deketelaere, D. & Draye, A.M. (eds), Liber Amicorum Marc Boes, Brugge, die Keure, 2011, pp. 70–78.

[5] Decree of 21 December 2007 to complement the Decree of 5 April 1995 concerning general provisions on environmental policy with the title XVI 'Toezicht, handhaving en veiligheidsmaatregelen', Bel. Off. Journal, 29 February 2008. For an overview on this title in its original version: Heyman, J., 'Is er een Copernicaanse wending op til in het Vlaams milieuhandhavingsbeleid?', Nullum Crimen, 2008, pp. 303–326. For a discussion of the Environmental Enforcement Decree and the Environmental Enforcement Act, the penultimate edition: Billiet, C.M., De Smedt, P. and Van Landeghem, H., 'Vlaamse milieuhandhaving nieuwe stijl', Tijdschrift voor Milieurecht, 2009, pp. 326–374.

[6] Explanatory note, Parliamentary papers of the Flemish Parliament, 2006–2007, no 1249, p. 3. For an extensive historical overview and explanation of the drafting of the Decree see: Explanatory note, Parliamentary papers of the Flemish Parliament, 2006–2007, no 1249, pp. 3–19. Heyman J. and Deketelaere, K., 'Het Vlaams decreet betreffende milieuhandhaving'. In: Deketelaere, K. (ed.), Jaarboek Milieurecht 2007, Milieurechtstandpunten nr. 22, Bruges, Die Keure, 2008, pp. 221–224.

[7] Geysels, F., Meeus, R., Vanheule, J. and Hoeben, J., Handhavingszakboekje Milieu 2009, p. 6.

[8] Faure, M., Bestuurlijke en strafrechtelijke afdoening van milieustrafzaken in het Vlaamse Gewest. In: Deruyck, F. and Rozie, M. (eds), Het strafrecht bedreven. Liber Amicorum Alain De Nauw, 2011, Brugge, die Keure, p. 263.

administrative fining to the administrative authority. That thus made some form of cooperation between the prosecutors (within the different districts and at the courts of appeal) and the administrative fining authority necessary.

A need for cooperation and networking also existed as far as monitoring and enforcement is concerned. Already, prior to the Environmental Enforcement Decree, a large number of departments of the Flemish Government and actors were involved in the environmental enforcement landscape in the Flemish Region.[9] Following the entry into force of this decree, their numbers merely multiplied. Not only are more departments within the Flemish Government empowered to appoint monitoring agents, at the local level there is even an obligation for the appointment of municipal agents, agents of inter-communal associations, or agents of police districts and provincial agents. Furthermore, both the federal and local police possessed, and currently still possess, competences to enforce the environmental legislative provisions when there is evidence of environmental violations. The mayors and the provincial governors have also been given certain competences for the imposition of administrative measures within the framework of environmental enforcement.[10] Hence, supervision and the competences are spread across a large number of administrative levels and actors.[11] Hence, it may be clear that this also created a need for cooperation and networking.

As was just mentioned, before 2009 sanctioning was mainly imposed on the grounds of a criminal offence under the exclusive competences of the public prosecutors' offices. However, studies have shown that most environmental cases were dismissed by the public prosecutors' offices and no further action was taken with respect to the criminal offence.[12] To counteract this fact the Environmental Enforcement Decree created the possibility of administrative sanctioning, by which the administra-

---

9 Populier, P. (ed.), Heldere handhaving – naar een sterker handhavingsbeleid door betere regelgeving en reglementering, 2010, Politeai, pp. 19–32.

10 Decree of 21 December 2007 to complement the Decree of 5 April 1995 concerning general provisions on environmental policy with the title XVI 'Toezicht, handhaving en veiligheidsmaatregelen', Bel.Gaz., 29 February 2008, article 16.1.2, article 16.2.7, article 16.3.1, article 16.3.24, and article 16.4.6.

11 Stas, A., The Flemish High Council of Environmental Enforcement – a coordinated environmental enforcement policy. In: INECE, 9th International Conference on Environmental Compliance and Enforcement, Proceedings, 2011, p. 823.

12 Faure, M., Handhaving van het milieurecht in het Vlaamse Gewest: enkele cijfers. In: D'Hooge, D., Deketelaere, D. and Draye, A.M. (eds), Liber Amicorum Marc Boes, Brugge, die Keure, 2011, p. 77.

tion within the Flemish Government has the possibility of imposing administrative monetary fines.[13] Hence, both at the level of monitoring and enforcement as well as concerning the sanctioning a large number of stakeholders were created. That is why the Environmental Enforcement Decree was set to create an institutionalised framework for coordination between those stakeholders within the Flemish High Council of Environmental Enforcement (VHRM).[14] Not only did the large number of different stakeholders make it necessary to establish such a network, also the need for cooperation between these actors and the need to make agreements concerning overlapping and complementary competences led to the creation of this formal collaboration.

The VHRM, created in 2009, had a prior and unofficial predecessor established during the 1990s, called the Prosecution Policy Commission. Within this commission the various environmental enforcement actors tried to delineate and implement a coordinated policy via priority memos.[15] The VHRM can be considered as the more formalised and institutionalised successor to the Prosecution Policy Commission, which only possessed an unofficial status.[16] Whereas the Prosecution Policy Commission was primarily focused on reaching agreements between the regional supervisors and the public prosecutors' offices, the VHRM covers a broader spectrum of environmental enforcement actors.[17] Since the VHRM has been created by a legislative act (a so-called decree), it has a formalised and institutionalised status with concrete competences and tasks.[18] One of its

---

[13] Renders, T. and Stas, A., Het Milieuhandhavingsdecreet: een analyse van de Vlaamse Hoge Raad voor de Milieuhandhaving, het systeem van toezichthouders en de bestuurlijke handhaving deel II. In: Tijdschrift Milieu- en Energierecht, 2011–3, pp. 171–172.

[14] Act of the Government of Flanders of 13 February 2009 concerning the appointment of the members of the Flemish High Council of Environmental Enforcement, mentioned in article 16.2.7 of the Decree of 5 April 1995 concerning general provisions on environmental policy, Belg. Off. Journal, 19 March 2009.

[15] Heyman, J. and Deketelaere, K., 'Het Vlaams decreet betreffende milieuhandhaving'. In: Deketelaere, K. (ed.), Jaarboek Milieurecht 2007, Milieurechtstandpunten nr. 22, Bruges, Die Keure, 2008, p. 226.

[16] Billiet, C.M., De Smedt, P. and Van Landeghem, H., 'Vlaamse milieuhandhaving nieuwe stijl', Tijdschrift voor Milieurecht, 2009, p. 331.

[17] Act of the Government of Flanders of 13 February 2009 concerning the appointment of the members of the Flemish High Council of Environmental Enforcement, mentioned in article 16.2.7 of the Decree of 5 April 1995 concerning general provisions on environmental policy, Belg. Off. Journal, 19 March 2009.

[18] Stas, A., 'The Flemish High Council of Environmental Enforcement – a coordinated environmental enforcement policy'. In: INECE, 9th International

main tasks is to propose the priorities for the Environmental Enforcement Policy within the Flemish Region. In the following parts, an overview of the structure of the network, the assigned tasks, and its implementation will be offered.

2. THE ORGANISATION OF THE FLEMISH HIGH COUNCIL OF ENVIRONMENTAL ENFORCEMENT

2.1 Structure and General Tasks

In order to assist the Flemish Government within the context of the general coordination and the substantive content complementation of the environmental enforcement policy, the VHRM was created in 2009.[19] The fact that the VHRM has a solid legal basis is a crucial factor for the working of this particular network. Not only does the VHRM work with a fixed annual budget, it also has a permanent secretariat which is responsible for providing the substantive and administrative support. These two aspects are success factors for the accomplishments of the network. Furthermore, individual membership of the plenary meeting is fixed and obligatory, which has advantages and disadvantages. It is not that particular individuals are forced to be members of the VHRM; rather the decree has indicated the stakeholders which will participate in the VHRM. For that particular agency, participation within the VHRM is hence mandatory. But it is up to the particular agency to decide who will represent that agency within the VHRM. The advantage of this obligation is that particular key players (like, for example, the environmental inspectorate) are hence automatically and continuously represented within the VHRM. A disadvantage, however, could be the fact that the network has not been created voluntarily on a 'bottom-up' basis, but has rather been created by decree, 'top down'.

The VHRM has been given the general task of proposing the principles and the priorities of the environmental enforcement policy in a proactive manner. In order to secure and maintain ongoing consensus on these

---

Conference on Environmental Compliance and Enforcement, Proceedings, 2011, p. 823.

[19] Act of the Government of Flanders of 13 February 2009 concerning the appointment of the members of the Flemish High Council of Environmental Enforcement, mentioned in article 16.2.7 of the Decree of 5 April 1995 concerning general provisions on environmental policy, Belg. Off. Journal, 19 March 2009.

principles and priorities, the VHRM organises in a systematic manner and at regular intervals consultation moments amongst the enforcement actors involved.[20] This consultation takes place during plenary meetings and in working groups. Most of the enforcement actors in the Flemish Region with competence for enforcement of environmental law are represented at the plenary meetings. Nearly all of those stakeholders will also be represented at the meetings of the working groups. This, hence, results in a widespread grassroots-level expertise which is undoubtedly absolutely necessary in order to effectively implement an environmental enforcement policy. Conversely, this broad composition (referring to the fact that all stakeholders in environmental enforcement are represented in the VHRM) does not simplify the decision-making process, especially since the VHRM in principle tries to base decisions on a consensus. There are, moreover, large qualitative differences between the various stakeholders and hence the members of the VHRM. Some stakeholders have more than 20 years' experience with environmental enforcement, while others only received their enforcement competences in May 2009 at the moment the Environmental Enforcement Decree entered into force. A policy-oriented, uniformly accepted synchronisation amongst all of the diverse actors is crucial, yet hardly a simple matter.

2.2 Members

The plenary meeting of the VHRM is composed of official and expert members. There are a large number of different stakeholders represented within the VHRM, both from the monitoring as well as from the enforcement and sanctioning levels. Hence, there are *inter alia* representatives from regional supervisors[21] and enforcement entities, but also representatives of the federal police, local police, the public prosecutors' offices, the cities and municipalities and the provinces. It is important to stress that within the Belgian federal context, some of those stakeholders (like the regional supervisors) belong to the Flemish Region, whereas others (like the public prosecutors, cities, municipalities and provinces) belong to the federal level. In the context of strategic advising, the Social-Economic Council of Flanders and the Environment and Nature Council of Flanders each have a representative member. This broad composition is aimed at

---

[20] Explanatory note, Parliamentary papers of the Flemish Parliament, 2006–2007, no 1249/1, p. 24.

[21] The Administration of the Government of Flanders counts a total of 13 departments, entities, and agencies with the competence to appoint regional supervisors within their personal organisation's remit.

achieving a wide-ranging scope for the VHRM's activities.[22] The members are appointed for five years by the Flemish Government. However, the appointment of the members is renewable. The first composition lasted from May 2009 until May 2014.[23] The second composition started in May 2014.[24] The most important benefit of a changing membership is the fact that it creates room for new ideas and new commitments.

The members of the plenary meeting gather on average once a month and take decisions relating to the assignments and tasks of the VHRM, the tasks of the working groups and the orders executed by the permanent secretariat.

2.3 Working Groups

Whereas the plenary meeting of the VHRM works as a decision-making body, the working groups – together with the permanent secretariat – prepare the decisions of the VHRM. The VHRM can establish working groups to examine particular issues or to study problematic areas. These working groups can be ad hoc or permanent. Their working areas and membership have not been consolidated and can be adapted in keeping with the extent to which the needs of the environmental enforcement actors are evolving. The working groups meet in smaller numbers to investigate the problem and formulate a solution, a proposition or a recommendation that is subsequently presented to the plenary meeting. Not only permanent members of the VHRM are invited to participate in the debates and activities, but also collaborators from other enforcement agencies that do not have a member in the plenary meeting are asked to participate in the working groups. This not only enhances the general expertise and knowledge, but also the consensus on, and the scope of the decisions. It was already mentioned above that a large number of stakeholders are represented at the plenary meeting; the same obviously holds for the working groups too. A great variety of enforcement actors

---

[22] Explanatory note, Parliamentary papers of the Flemish Parliament, 2006–2007, no 1249/1, pp. 24–27.

[23] Act of the Government of Flanders of 13 February 2009 concerning the appointment of the members of the Flemish High Council of Environmental Enforcement, mentioned in article 16.2.7 of the Decree of 5 April 1995 concerning general provisions on environmental policy, Belg. Off. Journal, 19 March 2009.

[24] Act of the Government of Flanders of 4 April 2014 concerning the appointment of the members of the Flemish High Council of Environmental Enforcement for the period 2014–2019, mentioned in article 16.2.7 of the Decree of 5 April 1995 concerning general provisions on environmental policy, Belg. Off. Journal, 28 April 2014.

are working on the problems investigated in these working groups, all of them with their own traditions and visions on the solutions proposed by the groups and wanting to see these integrated in the results. However, the membership of a working group is voluntary, which enhances the engagement and willingness of the members.

3. ASSIGNMENTS AND REALISATIONS

3.1 The Environmental Enforcement Report

One of the most significant tasks – and accomplishments so far – of the VHRM is the annual publication of the Environmental Enforcement Report. The Environmental Enforcement Decree determined a very clear content for the Environmental Enforcement Report. As a minimum requirement, this report needs to contain:

- A general evaluation of the regional environmental enforcement policy conducted during the past calendar year;
- A specific evaluation of the manner in which the separate enforcement instruments were employed in the task;
- An overview of the cases for which, within the fixed time period, no ruling was rendered vis-à-vis the appeals versus the decisions concerning administrative measures, and an evaluation of the decision-making practices of the public prosecutors' offices regarding whether or not to criminally prosecute an observed environmental violation;
- An overview and a comparison of the environmental enforcement policy conducted by the municipalities and the provinces;
- An inventory of the insights gained in the course of the enforcement period, which may be suitable for future use in improving the environmental regulations, policy visions and policy implementation; and
- Recommendations for the further development of the environmental enforcement policy.[25]

The Environmental Enforcement Report is a crucial element in shaping the environmental enforcement policy, as well as supporting and, as

[25] Decree of 21 December 2007 to complement the Decree of 5 April 1995 concerning general provisions on environmental policy with the title XVI 'Toezicht, handhaving en veiligheidsmaatregelen', Bel.Gaz., 29 February 2008, article 16.2.5.

required, updating it. It is all-encompassing and contains all relevant facts and figures about the environmental enforcement policy conducted during the past calendar year. The Environmental Enforcement Report proffers a concrete idea of the manner in which the environmental enforcement policy is being implemented in the field.[26]

The Environmental Enforcement Reports are mainly approached in a quantitative manner. Since the number of environmental enforcement actors that need to be surveyed every year is quite substantial – more than 450 respondents[27] – this quantitative approach is the most practical solution. For instance, questions are asked concerning the number of appointed supervisors and the number of full-time equivalents that these individuals devote to enforcement tasks. In addition, the supervisors are annually asked about the number of controls executed in the last year and the results thereof (advisories, warnings, reports, reports of determination of the observed facts and administrative measures). By asking for this kind of information the VHRM is able to map the current status of the enforcement landscape within the Flemish Region. This is also the case for the sanctioning aspect. The prosecutors' offices in the Flemish Region are asked every year to provide an overview of their registered environmental cases and any follow-up action.[28] The administration within the Flemish Government responsible for the levy of administrative fines, is annually asked to list the kinds of environmental violations found and the number of monetary penalties imposed. Hence, also the sanctioning is analysed in a rather quantitative manner.

One significant effect of the Environmental Enforcement Reports is that the various enforcement actors are – in the framework of the annual survey – encouraged and compelled (some actors have a collaboration obligation) to monitor their own environmental enforcement actions and gather and collect relevant follow-up information. Based on the principle of evidence-based monitoring, targeting the collection of data in itself can already be considered as a great leap forward for the environmental enforcement actors. In the hope of extending the survey and the scope of

[26] Explanatory note, Parliamentary papers of the Flemish Parliament, 2006–2007, no 1249/1, pp. 25–26.

[27] This large number of respondents is related to the fact that with the new decree of 2009, all municipalities in the Flemish Region (308 in total) also have the obligation to appoint a monitoring agent.

[28] Note again that it is remarkable that a Flemish decree can, via the VHRM, ask for the cooperation of public prosecutors, although they formally do not fall directly under the competence of the Flemish Region, but of the Belgian federal authorities.

the Environmental Enforcement Reports in the future, the environmental enforcement actors will be encouraged to monitor even more aspects of their own performances.

The environmental reports not only deliver advantages for the environmental enforcement actors, the reports also form an important reference for the policy-makers. Given the volume of information that is annually gathered and analysed, problem areas in the environmental enforcement policy are being detected and identified. Moreover, the reports already give evidence of the success of the Environmental Enforcement Decree. The Environmental Enforcement Report has turned into a significant instrument to follow up the implementation of the environmental enforcement policy, to evaluate it more thoroughly and to create transparency between the environmental enforcement actors reciprocally and between the environmental enforcement actors and the policy-makers.[29]

Because the Environmental Enforcement Report is published every year, it is possible to compare the evolution of environmental enforcement based on the data gathered in previous reports. So far, the VHRM has published five environmental enforcement reports, covering the period 2009–2013.[30] Since the Environmental Enforcement Decree has already been in force for five years and the Environmental Enforcement Report 2013 is the fifth report of its kind, this report forms an overview report regarding five years' environmental enforcement in the Flanders Region.

The strength of those environmental enforcement reports is that they, on a yearly basis, and based on a good response by the stakeholders involved, provide relevant data, for example on the number of violations, but also the consequences following those violations. Since those data are now available for five years, some trends can be discovered which may show *inter alia* in which areas greater or fewer violations would be detected. Moreover, the reports, for example, also make clear in which districts public prosecutors either prosecute many cases or forward them to the administrative authority for administrative fining, and in which districts prosecutors still dismiss (too) many cases. Collecting this type of

---

[29] As an example of the transparency of data, a reference to the Environmental Enforcement Reports of the Flemish High Council of Environmental Enforcement was made during the workshop 'Towards an Upgraded EU Legal Framework on Environmental Inspections and Surveillance' of the European Commission, Directorate-General Environment (20 September 2013).

[30] The Environmental Enforcement Reports are all translated into English and can be found on the website of the VHRM: http://www.vhrm.be/documenten/milieuhandhavingsrapport

information is hence an important first step towards an evidence-based monitoring and enforcement system. There are, however, undoubtedly also limitations. One problem is underreporting; another issue is that not every authority may interpret the questions in the same manner, which in some cases provides some bias in the data. Another issue is that in this first phase the environmental reports have largely relied upon collection of data and an attempt to interpret those data. However, important data are still lacking. For example, the reports so far could provide information on the number of cases where, for instance, administrative fining, dismissals or criminal prosecution took place. Information on the actual sanctions (for example, the amount of the fine) has not yet been included in the environmental reports. It is, however, the intention to also collect this information in the future. Moreover, an inherent limitation of such a quantitative approach is that merely focusing on numbers will provide some information on the enforcement activity, but not necessarily on the outcome of enforcement actions, for example as far as improvement of environmental quality is concerned. The latter should ultimately of course be the goal of any enforcement action. The numbers alone do obviously not provide detailed information on the quality of the enforcement actions. At this stage, it is also difficult to proceed towards such a qualitative approach. That could be done, for example, through a case method, but the disadvantage of that would be that it would unavoidably create a selection bias. However, given the mere quantitative nature of the reporting, the reports also warn that it would be wrong to draw normative or policy conclusions merely based on the numbers. The numbers are a starting point; the different stakeholders can often provide the story behind the numbers, which can better indicate, for instance, how a particular trend in specific numbers should be interpreted as far as the quality of the enforcement efforts is concerned.

3.2 The Environmental Enforcement Programme

An initial task of the VHRM was the annual publication of an Environmental Enforcement Programme which formulated the priorities for the coming calendar year of the environmental enforcement policy. This programme contained recommendations on environmental enforcement at the provincial and municipal levels, as well as on cooperation with and amongst actors at these policy levels. A restriction of this annual programme was that no directives or instructions could be directed to the environmental enforcement actors, which means no common enforcement plan could be drafted for (a segment of) the enforcement actors.[31] However, the coordinating role of the VHRM was fulfilled by working within the total compass of the combined programmes of the various enforcement entities, to recognise, thus, the overlaps and the lacunae existing within these separate programmes.[32] The VHRM published an annual environmental enforcement programme for 2010 and 2011. A crucial element in this approach was the need for existing and detailed programmes for the various enforcement actors. A purposeful enforcement policy will lead to greater compliance with the regulations than would be the case with random inspections. Given the limited resources at hand and the impossibility of regularly inspecting all systems within the available time span, it may be opportune to work out the enforcement in an organised and specifically formulated manner (for example, by assigning priorities).[33]

After publishing the two enforcement programmes it became clear that not every enforcement actor had its own programme and those who have them don't formulate such programmes in a comparable way. Hence, one of the most important challenges for the VHRM was to convince the various environmental enforcement actors of the need for and the benefits of proper planning. This is not only crucial for the environmental enforcement within the Flemish Region in general – given the significance of programmed supervision – but it also serves to enhance the quality of the enforcement programmes rather than proceeding purely descriptively and collectively. Moreover, the need for multi-annual programming for the VHRM, as well as for the individual environmental enforcement actor – in contrast to annual programming – emerged. It became clear that the priorities in the environmental enforcement actions didn't change annually. A broader time span is necessary to implement an environmental enforcement programme. The policy-makers in the Flemish Region followed the VHRM in the idea that an environmental enforcement programme should be multi-annual and that the different environmental actors should each draft their own multi-annual programme before the VHRM publishes a strategic overarching programme. The Environmental Enforcement Decree was accordingly adapted in 2013 and now states that the VHRM coordinates

---

[31] Explanatory note, Parliamentary papers of the Flemish Parliament, 2006–2007, no 1249/1, p. 25.

[32] Environmental Enforcement Programme 2010, Flemish High Council of Environmental Enforcement, p. 25.

[33] Billiet, C.M. and Rousseau, S., 'Zachte rechtshandhaving in het bestuurlijke handhavingsspoor: de inspectiebeslissing en het voortraject van bestuurlijke sancties. Een rechtseconomische analyse', Tijdschrift voor Milieurecht, 2005, p. 19.

a strategic five-year environmental enforcement programme which contains the enforcement priorities of the enforcement agencies. Therefore, enforcement agencies need to draft individual five-year enforcement programmes. The strategic five-year environmental enforcement programme should include, at least:

- Enforcement priorities of the environmental enforcement actors, coordinated by the VHRM;
- Overarching recommendations of the VHRM with regard to the strategic and operational objectives of regional, provincial and municipal environmental enforcement;
- Strategic and operational objectives with regard to the tasks and activities of the VHRM.

The scope of this strategic environmental enforcement programme is broader than the annual programme. The policy-makers felt it was important that the programme of the VHRM is more than just a collection of programmes of the environmental enforcement actors.

Coordinating a strategic environmental enforcement programme is still quite a challenge. One problem is, as already indicated above, the important difference between the various stakeholders, especially at a level of monitoring and enforcement. One can obviously expect some of the larger regional stakeholders, such as the environmental inspectorate, to draft an environmental enforcement action programme (which they *de facto* already do). However, the question arises whether it is equally useful to ask for such programming from the hundreds of local communities which formally also have enforcement powers, but who in some cases merely have one official who is (and in some cases even only part-time) occupied with enforcement actions. Moreover, the real expertise, for example in knowing where enforcement actions would be needed in a coming period, is of course primarily present within the stakeholders themselves. The VHRM, where all those stakeholders are represented, can at best compare the efforts and plans of the different stakeholders and try to identify gaps or overlaps, for example. However, in that respect, the VHRM also has to take into account that it has no hierarchical competence to direct particular stakeholders regarding what type of enforcement actions to undertake, for example. The drafting of such a strategic environmental enforcement programme hence remains a careful balancing exercise.

The VHRM started the draft of the strategic environmental enforcement programme with the determination of priorities through *inter alia* a consultation of the environmental enforcement actors.[34] The goal is to publish the first five-year environmental programme after the analysis of the individual programmes of the environmental actors, the determinations of the priorities and the set-up of mutual recommendations for implementation, actions and partnerships.

3.3 Protocols

The Environmental Enforcement Decree defines that within the context of the VHRM 'environmental enforcement protocols' can be drafted. These protocols are designed to give further substantive content to the environmental enforcement policy[35] and need to ensure clear agreements about the operating field. The various supervising entities have not only complementary competences and assignments, but sometimes also those that are overlapping.[36] The protocols can contain a territorial demarcation but also a demarcation of content, this is in order that certain determining factors in the activity are controlled. In addition, a protocol is meant to make optimal use of the means and resources at the disposal of the environmental enforcement actors and to ensure harmonisation amongst them.[37]

From a legal point of view an environmental enforcement protocol is not a formal contract; even though such a protocol will be set out in writing, it may be assumed that the involved actors will voluntarily abide by its provisions ('gentlemen's agreements'). Nonetheless, it is not an easy task for the enforcement actors to harmonise the practice of their own competences with other actors with identical competences, nor is it self-evident to other actors that have been appointed as supervisors to implement the assignments entrusted to them. The aim is that such agreements should be broad in scope and should be formed by common consent and

---

[34] Stahl, M., 'Doing what's important: setting priorities for environmental compliance and enforcement programs'. In: Paddock, L., Qun, D., Kotzé, L.J., Markell, D.L., Markowitz, K.J. and Zaelke, D., Compliance and Enforcement in Environmental Law – Toward More Effective Implementation, 2011, Edward Elgar, p.161.

[35] Geysels, F., Meeus, R., Vanheule, J. and Hoeben, J., Handhavingszakboekje Milieu 2009, p.49.

[36] However, it appears from the parliamentary preliminary work that it was actually meant to avoid an overlap of the competences (Explanatory note, Parliamentary papers of the Flemish Parliament, 2006–2007, no 1249/1, p.31). There remain, however, different supervisors competent for certain regulations, e.g., Environmental Permits Decree.

[37] Explanatory note, Parliamentary papers of the Flemish Parliament, 2006–2007, no 1249/1, p.28.

consensus. This requires a great deal of prior research, consultation, and an indisputable willingness for collaboration.

In 2013 the first environmental enforcement protocol, facilitated by the VHRM, was signed by the Flemish Minister for the Environment and the Federal Minister for Justice. This protocol is called the 'Priority note prosecution policy environmental law in the Flemish Region'[38] and forms an agreement between the supervisors and the prosecutors. It determines the priorities with regard to the supervision of certain (types of) environmental crimes and with regard to the criminal prosecution of these crimes. The protocol also contains formal agreements concerning information exchange. The implementation of the protocol will be followed up and evaluated in the Environmental Enforcement Reports.

3.4 Additional Achievements

As a network, the VHRM also has other functions and responsibilities besides the publication of the Environmental Enforcement Report, the publication of the multi-annual environmental enforcement programme, and the facilitation of protocols. During the first five years the VHRM has tried to become a fixed value in supporting and engaging the environmental enforcement actors through *inter alia*:

- *The organisation of consultation and deliberation*: The VHRM forms an institutionalised network that gives the environmental enforcement actors a forum to cooperate and to discuss mutual challenges.
- *The organisation of workshops*: The VHRM has organised a large number of workshops for the members of the VHRM and the members of the working groups, for example concerning the use of databases, enforceability of regulations and the use of enforcement instruments.
- *The organisation of conferences*: The VHRM organises annually a conference in which a specific topic is discussed by academics and practitioners, for example concerning targeted surveillance, local environmental enforcement and environmental enforcement networks.
- *The formulation of policy advice*: The VHRM not only has a role as policy evaluator, but also as 'policy preparer'. The VHRM regularly formulates policy advice for the Flemish Minister for the Environment concerning specific aspects of the environmental enforcement landscape, for example concerning the local environmental enforcement and the environmental enforcement regulation.

---

38 http://www.vhrm.be/english/20130930-priority-note.pdf

- *Connections with other environmental enforcement networks*: The VHRM has made – very rapidly during the time of its existence – connections with other networks such as the International Network for Environmental Compliance and Enforcement (INECE) and the European Union Network for the Implementation and Enforcement of Environmental Law (IMPEL). Participation in international fora can yield useful information. Since various environmental problems cross national boundaries and because of the increasing importance of international environmental policy and European regulations, the usefulness and necessity of international cooperation is beyond dispute. Moreover, these contacts provide a cross-fertilisation of knowledge and experience.
- *The creation of practical tools*: The VHRM developed sample form letters, templates and a glossary in the service of a smoother and more uniform information exchange.

4. AN EVALUATION OF THE NETWORK: SUCCESS FACTORS AND CHALLENGES

The VHRM has been active in the Flemish environmental enforcement landscape for the past five years. As a network, it combines all the environmental enforcement actors active in the Flemish Regions. The VHRM tries to support and engage these actors in working together to make environmental enforcement more effective and more efficient. From its inception the VHRM has benefitted from a few strong features. These particularly relate to its statutory basis (based on a decree) and the fact that it has independent financing and a permanent secretariat. This means that the members can concentrate on executing the tasks of the VHRM and on the networking and do not have to worry about fundraising, for example. These features certainly contribute to the success of the network. The VHRM has used and will use these assets and opportunities for the benefit of environmental enforcement in the Flemish Region. On the other hand, during the past five years it became clear that there are still some challenges to overcome. When assessing the VHRM as an environmental enforcement network – following Pink and Lehane's network evaluation matrix[39] – five major themes can be used as core evaluation criteria:

---

[39] Pink, G. and Lehane, J., 'Environmental enforcement networks: development of a network evaluation matrix'. In: INECE, 9th International Conference on Environmental Compliance and Enforcement, Proceedings, 2011, pp. 805–821.

- *Members*: The VHRM consists of individual members who represent an environmental enforcement agency. The members are appointed by the Flemish Government for a period of five years. As stated before, this obligatory membership has advantages and disadvantages. On the one hand, the core environmental enforcement agencies are, in any case, represented through their appointed membership. Since the VHRM makes decisions by consensus, the decisions are supported by all the environmental enforcement actors. On the other hand, an obligatory membership may cause some members not to feel like a voluntary part of a network, and so see the network as a threat rather than an opportunity. The value of the network for its members varies from member to member and the way that they experience their membership (threat vs. advantage).
- *Finances*: The VHRM can count on a permanent secretariat, which is responsible for the substantive and administrative support, and receives an annual fixed budget. The VHRM does not depend on its members for financial support (this may also explain why some members don't feel related to the network as they don't have a financial responsibility and a sense of reciprocity towards the network). The annual budget gives the VHRM the possibility of organising meetings, workshops and conferences for its members, to set-up projects and to outsource studies.
- *Governance*: The structure and main tasks of the VHRM are determined in the Environmental Enforcement Decree. The VHRM formalised a document with internal regulations which was ratified by the Flemish Government and *inter alia* defines the roles of the chairman, the vice-chairman, the permanent secretary and the members. It also includes written procedures for the course of the meetings. In its Strategic and Operational Programme, the VHRM determined the mission, the vision and the strategic and operational goals of the network. The VHRM maintains an open communication for members and non-members. Most documents are published on the website of the network, such as the environmental reports, protocols, internal regulations, templates, policy guidance, glossary, presentations, etc. The proceedings of the meetings are continuously available for the members to consult. A passive communication concerning the proceedings, which means 'on the basis of an explicit request', is used towards the non-member. The communication with the members is centralised by the permanent secretariat, which is the primary point of contact. The communication procedures are determined in a communication plan.

- *Support*: In the past years the number of interested individuals has increased, but the support the network receives varies from member to member. Some members 'use' the network to their benefit and support the network to gain even more benefits. Other members do not support the network because they consider their membership as a vehicle to counter possible interference from other environmental actors. On the other hand, the VHRM has forged liaisons with other networks, such as INECE and IMPEL, and takes part in activities organised by other networks.
- *Deliverables*: As described above, the VHRM already has some tangible benefits for members, such as the annual environmental enforcement reports and the annual conferences. In the past five years the VHRM has also produced templates and a glossary, organised meetings and workshops, and facilitated the realisation of the first environmental enforcement protocol. Also, the VHRM has made efforts to make itself known to all the environmental enforcement actors within the Flemish Region by organising surveys, offering an internet forum through the use of social media, answering questions from supervisors, giving lectures and presentations, etc.

For some criteria, such as finance, governance and tangible deliverables, the VHRM can be evaluated as a maturing or well-established network within the Flemish environmental enforcement landscape. An annual budget and a permanent secretariat can certainly be considered as success factors. For other criteria, such as membership and support, the VHRM is still emerging or fragile. Concerning the known challenges, the VHRM has to make an effort in the future to overcome these shortcomings.

5. CONCLUDING REMARKS

The VHRM is an interesting network that was created in a very particular institutional environment in the Flemish Region. The VHRM shows some of the complexities of environmental enforcement in a federal state. As a result, the VHRM has members from regional authorities, but equally from authorities that formally fall under the federal level. Moreover, the new Environmental Enforcement Decree of 2009 created an administrative enforcement and fining system in addition to the criminal enforcement. That thus necessitates some collaboration between these two different mechanisms. All those actors and stakeholders from the different enforcement levels are brought together or at least represented within the VHRM. That is at the same time the strength as well as the weakness of this VHRM. The advantage is that it provides a formal (since it is backed by a decree) institutional basis for collaboration and networking between a large variety of actors. Whenever particular issues arise that have to be settled in order to increase the effectiveness of environmental enforcement, the issue can immediately be put on the agenda of either a working group or the plenary meeting. At the same time, this very broad composition of the VHRM also implies that the VHRM has some members with a high degree of specialisation and technical knowledge (focusing, for example, on hazardous waste or the petrochemical industry) whereas others (such as representatives of the local police authorities) will handle environmental complaints in addition to all kind of other complaints of a totally different nature. These totally different backgrounds make collaboration and cooperation an interesting challenge.

The VHRM has functioned now for five years and its most important function probably has been simply to provide a forum for all stakeholders to meet, discuss, and solve issues and tensions. To a large extent, that is precisely what the plenary meetings and working groups are about. In addition, the VHRM has enabled a collection of data published in the environmental enforcement reports. Even though this data collection can undoubtedly still be improved, this is an important step in the process towards an optimal enforcement strategy. If scarce enforcement resources are to be used in an efficient manner, an important first step is that information needs to be collected on simple issues such as violations, remedies and consequences. It is only after a careful evaluation of those data that an evidence-based enforcement policy, targeting monitoring on those sectors where violations are most likely to occur, can be developed. The data collection is therefore obviously not a goal in itself, but a means to improve the quality of the environmental law enforcement.

BIBLIOGRAPHY

Billiet, C.M. and Rousseau, S., Zachte rechtshandhaving in het bestuurlijke handhavingsspoor: de inspectiebeslissing en het voortraject van bestuurlijke sancties. Een rechtseconomische analyse, Tijdschrift voor Milieurecht, 2005, pp. 2–33.

Billiet, C.M., De Smedt, P. and Van Landeghem, H., Het milieuhandhavingsde creet in de praktijk – een jaar nieuwe milieuhandhavingspraktijk onder de loep, 2010, 338 pp.

Billiet, C.M., De Smedt, P. and Van Landeghem, H., Vlaamse milieuhandhaving nieuwe stijl, Tijdschrift voor Milieurecht, 2009, pp. 326–374.

Environmental Enforcement Programme 2009, Flemish High Council of Environmental Enforcement (English version in press).

Environmental Enforcement Programme 2010, Flemish High Council of Environmental Enforcement.

Explanatory note, Parliamentary papers of the Flemish Parliament, 2006–2007, no 1249.

Faure, M., Bestuurlijke en strafrechtelijke afdoening van milieustrafzaken in het Vlaamse Gewest. In: Deruyck, F. and Rozie, M. (eds), Het strafrecht bedreven. Liber Amicorum Alain De Nauw, 2011, Brugge, die Keure, pp. 257–270.

Faure, M., Handhaving van het milieurecht in het Vlaamse Gewest: enkele cijfers. In: D'Hooge, D., Deketelaere, D. and Draye, A.M. (eds), Liber Amicorum Marc Boes, Brugge, die Keure, 2011, pp. 69–86.

Faure, M.G. and Svatikova, K., De handhaving van het milieurecht in het Vlaamse Gewest in de praktijk, Panopticon, 2010, pp. 57–81.

Faure, M. and Svatikova, K., 'Enforcement of Environmental Law in the Flemish Region', *European Energy and Environmental Law Review*, 2010, vol. 19(2), 60–79.

Geysels, F., Meeus, R., Vanheule, J. and Hoeben, J., Handhavingszakboekje Milieu, 2009, 520 pp.

Heyman, J., Is er een Copernicaanse wending op til in het Vlaams milieuhandhavingsbeleid? In: Nullum Crimen 2008, pp. 303–326.

Heyman, J. and Deketelaere, K., Het Vlaams decreet betreffende Milieuhandhaving. In: Deketelaere, K. (ed.), Jaarboek Milieurecht 2007, Milieurechtstandpunten nr. 22, Bruges, Die Keure, 2008, pp. 221–224.

Lavrysen, L., Handboek Milieurecht, 2006, 643 pp.

Pink, G. and Lehane, J., Environmental enforcement networks: development of a network evaluation matrix. In: INECE, 9th International Conference on Environmental Compliance and Enforcement, Proceedings, 2011, pp. 805–821.

Populier, P. (ed.), Heldere handhaving – naar een sterker handhavingsbeleid door betere regelgeving en reglementering, 2010, Politeai, 347 pp.

Renders, T. and Stas, A., Het Milieuhandhavingsdecreet: een analyse van de Vlaamse Hoge Raad voor de Milieuhandhaving, het systeem van toezichthouders en de bestuurlijke handhaving deel II. In: Tijdschrift Milieu- en Energierecht, 2011–3, pp. 160–172.

Stahl, M., Doing what's important: setting priorities for environmental compliance and enforcement programs. In: Paddock, L., Qun, D., Kotzé, L.J., Markell, D.L., Markowitz, K.J. and Zaelke, D., Compliance and Enforcement in Environmental Law – Toward More Effective Implementation, 2011, Edward Elgar, pp. 159–167.

Stas, A., The Flemish High Council of Environmental Enforcement – a coordinated environmental enforcement policy. In: INECE, 9th International Conference on Environmental Compliance and Enforcement, Proceedings, 2011, pp. 822–835.

Stas, A. and Renders, T., Het Milieuhandhavingsdecreet: een analyse van de Vlaamse Hoge Raad voor de Milieuhandhaving, het systeem van toezichthouders en de bestuurlijke handhaving deel I. In: Tijdschrift Milieu- en Energierecht, 2011–2, pp. 93–101.

Concluding and comparative remarks

Michael Faure, An Stas and Peter De Smedt

1. A DIVERSIFIED LANDSCAPE

The 26 chapters in this volume present a wonderful overview of the large variety of environmental enforcement networks that exist on a worldwide basis. The chapters describing and analysing the environmental enforcement networks in this book represent almost all continents. One important and interesting conclusion, therefore, is that apparently in Europe, North and South America, Africa, Australia and Asia, those engaged in the enforcement of environmental law have recognised that creating environmental enforcement networks is of importance. This as such is already an important finding. The mere fact that many different environmental enforcement networks exist shows that those networks apparently respond to a particular demand in practice and that hence enforcers feel that the creation of those networks can add to the effectiveness of enforcement efforts. Of course, between all of the networks that have been described and analysed in this volume, there are to some extent similarities at a general level (in the sense that all networks at an overall level aim at improving environmental enforcement through networking), but the nature and intensity of the different networks can show a lot of variety.

As already the different parts of this volume made clear, there are many differences. One can, for example, distinguish between more general networks (focusing on any type of environmental enforcement) versus thematic networks (focusing, for instance, on specific topics such as wildlife crime[1] or the transboundary shipment of waste).[2] Some networks are rather *ad hoc* and created to solve a particular problem on the spot, whereas other networks have a more structural nature. Many networks are horizontal, including a cooperation between enforcement agencies at the same level, whereas other networks are rather vertical and equally include a collaboration between different hierarchical layers in the enforcement

[1] Described in Chapters 9 and 11.
[2] Described *inter alia* in Chapters 14 and 25.

chain.[3] Moreover, also as far as the regional scope is concerned, a lot of variety could be discovered. Some networks are merely local,[4] whereas other networks are national.[5] Other networks have a rather regional character, for example within a particular nation[6] or combining efforts between different countries.[7] The latter type of networks, bringing together the environmental enforcement efforts of different states in a particular region, makes clear that those networks often are international. The ultimate international network, bringing together all environmental enforcement networks at a worldwide scale is obviously the 'mother of all environmental enforcement networks', the International Network for Environmental Compliance and Enforcement (INECE).[8]

Precisely because the networks described and analysed in this volume show that many different forms and characteristics exist, it is almost impossible to come to general conclusions concerning the functioning of networks that would have validity for all the networks described. Notwithstanding this limitation, it does seem possible to draw a few conclusions based on the rich description and analysis of the various environmental enforcement networks in this volume. That is precisely the goal of these comparative and concluding remarks.

2. THE IMPORTANCE OF NETWORKING RESEARCH

It may perhaps seem strange to some in the first instance to organise an academic conference on a topic which may seem more practically or policy oriented, like networking between environmental enforcement agencies. However, the different studies of Pink[9] show that it is quite possible to

---

[3] An example of the latter is, for example, the Flemish High Council of Environmental Enforcement, described in Chapter 26.

[4] Such as, for example, the network aiming at enforcement collaboration in the Port of Huntington, described in Chapter 12.

[5] See, for example, the efforts towards networking in Ghana described in Chapter 21 and the comparable efforts in Italy described in Chapter 22 as well as in China, described in Chapter 23, and in Chile in Chapter 24.

[6] See, for example, the description of the various regional environmental enforcement networks within the US in Chapter 20.

[7] Such as, for example, the East African Network for Environmental Compliance and Enforcement described in Chapter 19.

[8] Described and analysed in Chapter 17.

[9] His most recent work is *inter alia* to be found in Chapters 1 and 7 and in his joint chapter with Lehane in Chapter 5.

address environmental enforcement networks in an academic manner. The benefits of analysing environmental enforcement networks via an academic conference and a subsequent book are obviously not merely academic. One important feature of this exercise was that the conference preceding this volume provided an opportunity for representatives of environmental enforcement networks from all over the world to come together and exchange experiences on the strengths and weaknesses of their own networks. It is this type of mutual learning which on the one hand can provide academic insights on best practices or good practices as far as environmental enforcement networking is concerned, but at the same time it can equally provide a practitioner's insights on ways to improve the functioning of their own network. These are, therefore, the two goals that this volume hoped to reach: on the one hand trying to analyse the effectiveness of environmental enforcement networking in an academic manner on the basis of particular benchmarks, while on the other hand providing information to practitioners from those networks which may allow them to increase the effectiveness of their networking, and with that hopefully also of environmental enforcement generally.

3. THE NEED FOR NETWORKING

Many of the chapters have addressed the very basic question of why there is a particular need for environmental enforcement networking. Obviously, this is closely related to the subsequent point of what the potential benefits of environmental enforcement networking may be. Many have stressed in the various chapters in this volume that one could make a very basic argument defending the need for networking based on economies of scale. It can be relatively easily explained that networking between environmental enforcement agencies can lead to a cost reduction. The need for such a networking will especially be clear when, for example, research is done in particular countries on best practices. It would make no sense that every country makes those efforts separately, thus reinventing the symbolic wheel.[10] Moreover, even at a less abstract level, networking may be an absolute need in specific cases, for example in transboundary waste or wildlife crime. For those cases, one can even argue that networking is an absolute necessity in order to confront the transboundary nature of those

---

[10] In the words of Pink, Chapter 1, in his concluding thoughts 'a core idea of networking is bringing like-minded people together who share common or similar challenges and attempt to capture and leverage the learnings and benefits'.

types of environmental crime. Without effective networking between agencies, the organised crime organisations, often key players behind the transboundary shipment of waste or wildlife crime, could benefit from the lack of networking between agencies and differences in the approaches of various legal systems. Thus it could easily be argued that networking leads, generally, but especially in specific cases, to economies of scale and therefore to cost saving.

However, many authors in the various chapters have also stressed that reality is often more complex. The cost savings of networking may be apparent in particular concrete cases dealing with transboundary environmental crime. However, even though there may be great benefits in environmental networking also at a more general level, those benefits (equally leading to cost savings), for example resulting from increased capacity building and mutual learning, may be less directly visible. A problem in that respect is that notwithstanding networking's potential for cost saving, networking activities themselves are not cost free.[11] Especially in the current unfortunate times of budget cuts and austerity, there is always a danger of short-termism whereby budget holders could wrongly think that investments in networking only create visible costs in the short-term, whereas the potentially long-term benefits are less visible. There is, hence, especially in times of budget cuts, always a danger that environmental enforcement networks may not be sufficiently supported in the future.[12] Precisely because of that danger, it is quite important to point to the short- and long-term benefits of environmental enforcement networking, since only the generation of those benefits may provide the necessary political justification to finance those networks in the future.

4. THE BENEFITS OF NETWORKING

Obviously, the potential benefits of networking are various, and to a large extent also depend upon the nature of the particular network. On a more general level, mutual learning may be of importance; at a more concrete, case-specific level, bringing perpetrators to justice through mutual cooperation may be the tangible benefit. The benefits of environmental enforcement networking are described in many different ways in the various chapters. Gemmell and Circelli in Chapter 8 stress at a general level the importance of networking in providing knowledge

---

[11] See Pink in Chapter 7.
[12] See the conclusion in Chapter 7 by Pink.

exchange, sharing experiences and training.[13] The importance of providing basic capacity building efforts is also stressed in the chapter on the seaport network dealing with illegal hazardous waste shipments.[14] Gemmell and Circelli also stress that especially when resources are getting scarce, the major benefit of networking is that it can provide a cost-effective mechanism to allow agencies to use the best and most effective tools in order to deliver best outcomes for the environment and for society.[15]

As already mentioned, in some cases the benefits of networking are rather abstract (like mutual learning and capacity building) and may only lead to longer-term benefits. However, many chapters also stress much more concrete and direct short-term benefits, more particularly where grassroots level agencies collaborate in the fight against transboundary crime in specific cases. Therefore, especially the chapters dealing with wildlife crime stress the importance of transboundary enforcement networking as a remedy against the sophisticated criminal groups operating in the illegal wildlife trade.[16] The same argument of course applies to the area of transboundary shipment of waste.[17]

However, there can equally be different benefits of networks. For example, Chapter 22 dealing with various (*inter alia* anti-mafia) networks in Italy indicates the benefits of the *coamando* network in terms of increased effectiveness in the detection and investigation of transnational environmental crime, but also the benefits in increasing the awareness of the citizens on the importance of environmental compliance, thus equally contributing to deterrence of environmental crime.[18] The crucial point is, as already mentioned, that the benefits of the networks may of course equally vary with the types of networks and the types of activities that have been developed by the different networks.

---

13 See the introduction in Chapter 8.

14 See Chapter 14, section 4.

15 See Chapter 8, more particularly the conclusion, section 5, *in fine*.

16 See more particularly Chapter 9 by Van Asch in section 5 (conclusion) and Chapter 11 by Kasimbazi.

17 See Chapters 14 by Grabiel, Heiss, Koparova, Kopsick and Ruessink and 25 by Geysels.

18 See in this respect more particularly the discussion of the anti-mafia networks and the networks combating the so-called Ecomafia in Chapter 22 by Vagliasindi.

5. VARIOUS FORMS AND ACTIVITIES

As already mentioned in the introduction to these comparative and concluding remarks, environmental enforcement networks show a large variety of forms and structures. That necessarily implies that also the activities that those networks develop can largely differ and as a result the benefits generated through these networks may differ as well. Some networks are formal and have even a statutory basis,[19] whereas others have a rather informal character. However, as the example of the European Environmental Protection Agency Network shows, this informal networking should not necessarily be less effective and can equally create benefits, for example in terms of exchanging information, views and good practice, although the informal character of a network undoubtedly creates particular challenges and limits, more particularly as far as the sustainability of the network may be concerned.[20] An important difference between the type of activities that can be employed by particular networks of course concerns the difference between capacity building on the one hand and operational collaboration on the other. Many networks apparently do collaborate as far as capacity building is concerned and many chapters provide examples of networking, training,[21] capacity building[22] or information exchange.[23] The global network INECE, moreover, plays an important role in sustaining the creation of regional networks as well.[24] Interestingly, however, in some cases the collaboration goes beyond the mere training and capacity building and moves towards collaboration at the operational level. This is apparently more particularly the case in the North American working group on environmental enforcement and compliance cooperation, dealing with enforcement cooperation between Canada, Mexico and the United States.[25] Operational cooperation also takes place in the networks discussed earlier dealing with wildlife crime and the transboundary shipment of waste. It may be clear that this type of operational cooperation is especially important in the concrete actions

---

19 Like, for example, the Flemish High Council of Environmental Enforcement, discussed in Chapter 26.

20 See the discussion on informal environmental networking by Fawcett in Chapter 16.

21 See, for example, the practice of the regional enforcement networks in the US described by Paddock in Chapter 20.

22 See Chapter 14 on the Seaport network.

23 Chapter 16 by Fawcett on the European Environmental Protection Agency Network.

24 See Chapter 17 on INECE.

25 Described in Chapter 15 by Kopsick and Bromm.

aimed at combating transboundary environmental crime. Moreover, as the chapter on the Belgian police force shows, this type of operational collaboration often necessitates the creation of multi-disciplinary investigation teams.[26]

6. TESTING NETWORK QUALITY

The fact that so many environmental enforcement networks have been created at a worldwide level may already provide proof of the need for networking and of the fact that apparently stakeholders feel that those networks create important benefits. However, as already repeatedly mentioned, there is wide variety between the different types of networks, both in form as well as in contents. Interestingly, Pink and Lehane can claim the important achievement of having developed instruments to test the quality and maturity of particular environmental enforcement networks. These types of instrument are extremely important since they will allow particular networks to do a critical evaluation of their strength, which obviously also provides the possibility of identifying weak spots and subsequently moving towards improvements. In the first chapter of this volume, Pink already shows the theoretical basis for research on environmental networking, which provides the basis for a further evaluation and testing of the strength of networks. This is further developed in Chapter 5 by Pink and Lehane in which they present the Network Evaluation Matrix (NEM). They apply this matrix to the networks connected to INECE and show how this particular instrument can be used by environmental enforcement networks to enable them to better and more effectively carry out their environmental compliance and enforcement obligations. This point is further developed in Chapter 6 by Lehane where he equally introduces a methodology allowing a critical analysis of environmental enforcement networks. These chapters are of great importance, both academically as well as practically. The evaluation methods developed by Pink and Lehane allow us to critically assess the strengths and weaknesses of particular environmental enforcement networks on the basis of specific predefined benchmarks and parameters. This allows a critical comparison of various networks, but equally the development of best practices and shows the practical value of this type of research. Through this type of academic assessment of the strengths of an environmental enforcement network it can be directly shown (also to policy makers) to what extent a

[26] Chapter 25 by Geysels.

particular network creates (short- or long-term) benefits that would hence justify the investments in and support of the particular network.

7. NETWORKING AS SMART REGULATION

Closely connected to the point just mentioned about the necessity of critically evaluating and measuring the benefits of networks, is the issue that environmental enforcement networks, as many contributors show, can to some extent be considered as a form of so-called 'smart' regulation. The entire idea of smart environmental regulation has been developed by Australian socio-legal scholars, showing how through a smart combination of (more particularly command and control and market-based) instruments, the comparative benefits of particular instruments could be used in an optimal way by looking for so-called 'smart mixes' of instruments.[27] This idea of 'smart regulation' has equally been translated into the need to develop 'smart enforcement', probably best represented in the well-known enforcement pyramid of Ayres and Braithwaite.[28] It was especially Australian socio-legal scholars and criminologists that developed the idea that both regulation and enforcement should be 'responsive', roughly meaning that enforcement efforts should, especially given limited budgets, be used in a 'smart' way, by targeting those efforts especially on those cases where the most benefits of enforcement efforts could be expected. It is therefore no surprise that environmental enforcement networks have to a large extent also flourished in Australia, where the Australasian Environmental Law Enforcement and Regulators neTwork (AELERT) has been very active in improving the effectiveness of environmental enforcement.[29] An important lesson from this literature is that a smart enforcement of environmental crime could be the result of so-called efficient 'targeting'. Given the high costs of criminal prosecution in some jurisdictions, it should not come as a surprise that systems have been developed whereby environmental agencies and prosecutors focus their efforts on specific categories of polluters or violations to achieve better results.[30] This is based on the idea that it may be effective to divide firms

---

[27] See more particularly Neil Gunningham and Peter Grabosky, *Smart Regulation. Designing Environmental Policy* (Oxford: Clarendon Press, 1998).

[28] I. Ayres and J. Braithwaite, *Responsive Regulation: Transcending the Deregulation Debate* (Oxford: Oxford University Press, 1992).

[29] See Chapter 8 by Gemmell and Circelli.

[30] See, for example, Michael M. Stahl, 'Doing What's Important: Setting Priorities for Environmental Compliance and Enforcement Programmes', in

into different classes on the basis of their compliance behaviour and focus enforcement efforts accordingly.[31]

Many contributors in the various chapters to this volume stress that environmental enforcement networking fits into this smart regulation and targeting enforcement efforts agenda.[32] Targeting of environmental enforcement efforts[33] and intelligence-led enforcement methods[34] can all be seen as mechanisms whereby environmental enforcement networks contribute to smart enforcement strategies.

Many contributors, however, also show that there is obviously a clear link between 'smart' regulation and 'smart' enforcement. An effective enforcement is only possible in a better regulation framework.[35] In order to ensure further compliance it is of crucial importance that legislators also pay attention to the quality of environmental regulation.[36] Improving regulation equally necessitates the courage to think about possibilities of self-regulation and compliance management in order to avoid the natural risk regulation reflex of politicians.[37] Moreover, given the fact that an effective compliance is only possible on the basis of a high quality of regulation, it may equally be necessary not only to think about networks of enforcers, but also about networks of regulators. Information exchange and mutual learning between public regulators could equally lead to better regulation and in that way also improve compliance.[38] As far as transboundary environmental crime is concerned (more particularly the transboundary shipment of waste and wildlife crime), harmonisation of regulation may, moreover, be indicated. With regard to the transboundary shipment of waste, this is largely realised through the Basel agreement. CITES aims at doing the same as far as wildlife crime is concerned. However, Kasimbazi

---

LeRoy Paddock et al. (eds), *Compliance and Enforcement in Environmental Law: Towards More Effective Implementation* (Cheltenham: Edward Elgar, 2011), 159ff.

[31] See Jennifer Arlen and Reinier Kraakman, 'Controlling Corporate Misconduct: An Analysis of Corporate Liability Regimes', *New York University Law Review*, 1997, vol. 72, 687ff. and Winston Harrington and Anthony Heyes, 'Theories of Penalties: "Leverage" and "Dealing"', in Anthony Heyes (ed.), *The Law and Economics of the Environment* (Cheltenham: Edward Elgar, 2001), 185ff.

[32] See more particularly Chapter 2 by Gemmell.

[33] For example, stressed in the Seaport initiative with respect to the prevention of illegal hazardous waste shipment; see Chapter 14, section 3.3.

[34] Stressed as methods used in the collaboration between Canada, Mexico and the United States by Kopsick and Bromm in Chapter 15.

[35] See more particularly Chapter 2 by Gemmell, section 3.

[36] This is stressed, for example, by Savaşan in Chapter 4.

[37] So is rightly stressed by De Bree, De Haas and Meerman in Chapter 10.

[38] See De Bree, De Haas and Meerman in Chapter 10, section 5 (conclusions).

stresses that as far as the specific implementing of national laws is concerned, there still is an important need to harmonise laws.[39] Finally, it should equally be stressed that an important stakeholder in the better regulation and better enforcement agenda obviously is the judiciary. It is therefore important and interesting to notice that also the judiciary is moving towards networking with a variety of goals (including mutual learning and information exchange). It is quite important, as stressed in Chapter 13 regarding this final end of the enforcement chain, that attention is paid to the importance of networking in order to also allow the judiciary to play their important role in the environmental law enforcement chain.[40]

8. CHALLENGES

Notwithstanding the fact that many chapters in this volume stress the importance, values and benefits of environmental enforcement networking, there are quite a few who equally mention that networking entails quite a number of challenges. Some of those challenges generally relate to environmental enforcement; other challenges relate more particularly to networking. Pink and Lehane, for example, stress that an important challenge for a network is to create sufficient opportunities for members in order to remain attractive for them.[41] Moreover, as already mentioned, networking is not cost-free.[42] This hence necessitates the need for networks to show their added value given that specific budgets will have to be allocated to networking. An important challenge, not so much for networking itself but more particularly for environmental enforcement, especially in developing countries, is the problem of the independence of enforcement agencies and the danger of corruption which might jeopardise this independence. As Kasimbazi mentions, more particularly in developing countries, this may pose a great problem, for example in the fight against wildlife crime.[43]

Specific challenges were also mentioned in detail in Chapter 12 dealing with the Huntington Port.[44] Among many others factors, different cultures are mentioned as a challenge that should be overcome.[45] Also when

---

39 See Chapter 11 by Kasimbazi.
40 See more particularly Chapter 13 by Lavrysen.
41 See Chapter 5 by Pink and Lehane in section 6 (conclusion).
42 See Pink in Chapter 7 in section 1 (introduction).
43 See Kasimbazi in Chapter 11, section 8 (conclusions and recommendations).
44 See Chapter 12 by Lubieniecki, section 2 (challenges).
45 This is more specifically addressed in further detail in Chapter 3 by Janssen.

different organisations have differing priorities, and if there are problems concerning confidentiality, technology or funding, those may constitute challenges to networking as well.[46] Many contributors mention a lack of resources as a potential challenge, or at least the need to have a constant stream of stable funding which would otherwise jeopardise the sustainability of the network. This is mentioned specifically as a challenge for the informal environmental networking through the European Environmental Protection Agencies, for example.[47] Funding is not only mentioned as an important issue and challenge in developing countries like Ghana[48] and China,[49] but even in a developed country like the US.[50]

Some of the mentioned challenges for successful networking could then also be translated into conditions for a successful environmental enforcement networking or, carefully formulated, best or good practices.

9. CONDITIONS FOR SUCCESSFUL NETWORKING

Many contributors stress, either theoretically at a general level or specifically based on experience, which particular conditions would according to them have to be fulfilled for guaranteed success and the sustainability of environmental enforcement networks. Many of the general elements are mentioned in several chapters. There thus seems to be a high degree of convergence with respect to the question of which conditions would have to be fulfilled for environmental enforcement networks to be successful.

The starting point will always be, as mentioned above, that there may be an important need for networking for the simple reason that it can be a cost-effective means of enforcement and hence a way of 'smart' enforcement. That, however, supposes that the network can also show its added value, which is also necessary because networks are not cost-free. Some networks, like the European Union Network for the Implementation and Enforcement of Environmental Law (IMPEL), have apparently received quite a bit of criticism in the literature,[51] although Angelov and Cashman argue in Chapter 18 that this criticism is not fully justified. The criticism, however, shows that networks, given the fact that they require extra

46 Chapter 12 by Lubieniecki.
47 See Chapter 16 by Fawcett, section 4 (conclusions).
48 See, for example, Chapter 21 by Araba Adjei and Mensah, section 4 (challenges to ECEN).
49 See Chapter 23 by Lu, Qin and Yang, section 4.2.
50 See Chapter 20 by Paddock, section 6.1.
51 More particularly by Hedemann-Robinson.

funding, will always have to show their added value in order to avoid the wrong image of civil servants just meeting and greeting at the expenses of the taxpayer without adding value in terms of the quality of environmental enforcement and compliance.

One important starting point to generate this added value is that networks should either share a common culture or at least recognise and respect differences between the cultures of different organisations.[52] To some extent, attempts have to be undertaken to reconcile possible cultural differences.[53] The importance of culture in networking is also recognised in specific case studies, for example with respect to the Huntington Port.[54]

Lehane presents in Chapter 6 several criteria for successful networking which are also mentioned in many other chapters as well.[55] He notes *inter alia* the already-mentioned point that the network should have an added value to the members, that the network should be effective (in its communication), and that it should have a sustainable source of funding.[56] The point of a sustainable funding is mentioned by many others, for example in Chapter 14 on the Seaport project.[57] An important point for networking is that the benefits, hence the point of creating an added value, should preferably be tangible.[58] Tangible results are of course more easily generated when there is collaboration at the operational level than when the collaboration merely consists of capacity building and mutual learning.

In the analysis of the Huntington Port network, various elements are mentioned as key tools for success, such as the development of a core team, the recognition of and respect for differences and the development and implementation of a clear communication strategy for the team.[59] Similar messages come from the other side of the Atlantic Ocean, more particularly from Africa where it is mentioned that the success of the East African Network for Environmental Compliance and Enforcement (EANECE) was *inter alia* due to strategic partnerships, effective strategic and action planning, clear governance structures and a clear added value.[60] Failure factors hence constitute the mirror image of the indicators for success. Further, in Chapter 19 concerning EANECE, the focus is on

52 This is strongly stressed in Chapter 3 by Janssen.
53 See Chapter 3 by Janssen, section 5 (conclusion: reconciling cultures).
54 Chapter 12 by Lubieniecki, section 2 (challenges).
55 Chapter 6 by Lehane, section 2.3 (critical issues for networks).
56 Ibid.
57 More particularly in Chapter 14, section 6 (conclusions).
58 See Chapter 7 by Pink, section 7 (conclusion).
59 See Chapter 12 by Lubieniecki, section 3 (tools for success).
60 See Chapter 19 by Opondo, section 2 (on success factors).

inter alia inadequate budgets and unsupported financial sustainability as well as on changing national priorities and political differences as important failure factors.

Interestingly, in Chapter 20 dealing with the regional environmental enforcement networks in the US, Paddock indicates the importance of having full-time staff at a network, having a consistent source of funding, but also having in-person contacts. He therefore clearly highlights the limitations of distance learning, which may insufficiently support networking opportunities that one would otherwise have through in-person contacts.[61] Interestingly, the young multicore network in China also indicates particular elements for effective networking, pointing *inter alia* at a clear identification of priorities, at the creation of a clear profile, but also at the establishment of clear communication channels.[62]

It is therefore interesting to notice that notwithstanding the large differences between the various networks described and analysed in this volume,[63] when it comes to identifying conditions for successful environmental enforcement networking, there seems to be a common denominator among the various chapters in the sense that all stress *inter alia* the importance of clear communication channels, the clear identification of added value, sustainable funding, the importance of a core team, and mutual respect for differing cultures as the key elements which may determine the success or failure of a network. It is quite interesting to notice that those elements do not only come from the theoretical literature,[64] but also from the many chapters describing practical experiences with either thematic or horizontal networks. In that sense, the conclusions on the conditions for successful networking as presented here seem to be based on a rather broad foundation.

10. THE FUTURE OF NETWORKING

This book had the ambition of identifying the possibilities and challenges of networking and also trying to identify good and best practices of environmental enforcement networking. However, it may be clear that this book is obviously not the end of the research into the effectiveness

---

[61] See Chapter 20 by Paddock, section 8 (conclusion).

[62] See Chapter 23 by Lu, Qin and Yang, section 4.1 (elements for effective networking).

[63] And also stressed above in sections 1 and 5.

[64] As, for example, developed in the chapters by Pink (1 and 7), by Lehane (6) and by Pink and Lehane (5).

of environmental enforcement networking. There are many interesting points still to develop in future research with respect to the conditions under which effective networking can take place. For example, Pink and Lehane clearly indicate the road ahead for environmental enforcement networks in Chapter 5, while also highlighting the fact that reduced public expenditures tend to require innovative approaches.[65]

Also, many of the specific chapters dealing with either thematic or horizontal networks point at particular challenges for the future. For example, Chapter 15 dealing with the North American working group on environmental enforcement and compliance cooperation mentions many important future activities that will still have to be developed by the enforcement working group.[66] The same is true for INECE itself which, in Chapter 17, was looking ahead at ways to better implement its strategic five-year plan (2012–2017). In addition, Chapter 18, dealing with environmental inspections at EU level, also identified a variety of future challenges for network cooperation.

This book had the ambition of providing some insights on the type of environmental enforcement networks that have been developed, comparing these and providing some insights on the challenges of networks, and the benefits and conditions for successful environmental enforcement networking. The claim of this book is that environmental enforcement networks fulfil an important function in the attempt to come to a 'smart', that is, a cost-effective environmental enforcement. However, in order that such a smart enforcement via effective environmental networking will be accomplished, there are still important challenges ahead, not only in developing, but also in developed countries. Both the increasing importance of transboundary environmental crime (and the increased involvement of organised criminal networks in this domain) as well as reduced public expenditures makes networking in the area of environmental enforcement ever more needed and important. The question of how this can be promoted in an effective manner will hence also in the near future remain high on the academic and policy agenda.

---

65 See Pink and Lehane, Chapter 5, section 2.3 (the future – where next for networks?).

66 See Chapter 15 by Kopsick and Bromm, section 4 (future activities).

Index